American History

A SURVEY

Volume I: To 1877

SEVENTH EDITION

American History

A SURVEY

Volume I: To 1877

Richard N. Current
*Emeritus, University of North Carolina
at Greensboro*

T. Harry Williams
late of Louisiana State University

Frank Freidel
Emeritus, Harvard University

Alan Brinkley
Harvard University

ALFRED A. KNOPF   NEW YORK

THIS IS A BORZOI BOOK
PUBLISHED BY ALFRED A. KNOPF, INC.

Seventh Edition
987654

Library of Congress Cataloging in Publication Data

American history.

   Includes bibliographies and indexes.
   1. United States—History. I. Current, Richard Nelson.
E178.1.A492 1987   973   86-21099
ISBN 0-394-34302-6 (pkb. : v. 1)

Manufactured in the United States of America

Published 1961; reprinted five times
Second edition, 1966; reprinted three times
Third edition, 1971; reprinted four times
Fourth edition, 1975; reprinted four times
Fifth edition, 1979; reprinted three times
Sixth edition, 1983; reprinted six times

Maps and charts by David Lindroth

Cover and text design by Leon Bolognese

Cover photograph: *Tontine Coffee House,* c. 1790, by Frances Guy. Courtesy of The
New-York Historical Society, New York.

Preface

When the first edition of this book appeared in 1959, historians were in general agreement about what was important in the American past. The story of the United States, most believed, was the story of great public events: of politics and government, of war and peace, of great leaders and great events. Much has changed in the years since.

Historical scholarship in America (and, indeed, throughout much of the world) has experienced something close to a revolution during the last two and a half decades. Aspects of the past that received only slight attention in earlier eras have now emerged as central themes in the writing of American history. Scholars today are interested not just in great events and great leaders, but in the experiences of ordinary men and women. They are concerned not just with politics and government, but with less visible changes in the structure of society. Historians in recent years have begun to reveal whole new realms of the American past about which we previously knew relatively little: the historical experiences of blacks, Hispanics, Asians, Indians, and other minorities; the process by which America was settled by successive waves of immigrants and the process by which those immigrants adapted to their new surroundings; the rise and transformation of the city and the wrenching changes in the nature of agrarian society; the evolution of popular culture and popular values; and, perhaps most prominently in recent years, the experiences of American women and the story of the American family.

No single work can hope to tell the full story of any nation. And in the case of the United States, a country of almost unparalleled diversity, in which change has occurred at such a constant and dizzying speed that historical time seems almost to have accelerated, that task is particularly difficult. Nevertheless, this book attempts to present as full a picture as possible of the extraordinary history of the American nation and its people. This new edition, which is the result of the most significant single revision in the long life of this book, tries to ensure that this picture does justice to the many areas of the past that recent scholarship has revealed. It includes, as previous editions have, a thorough discussion of great public events, of politics and government and diplomacy. But it gives at least equal attention to the other, less familiar aspects of the American past. And, above all, it tries to illuminate the way the nation's public history and its social history have interacted with and shaped one another.

Four broad themes in particular shape the contents of this volume. First, we have told the story of the creation of the nation's political institutions and the way they have evolved in response to changing circumstances, changing popular expectations, and the achievements and failures of individual public figures. Second, we have examined the development of America's role in the world, from its position as a weak dependency of the British and Spanish empires to its rise to international preeminence. Third, we have recounted the story of the development of the American economy from its simple agrarian beginnings through its triumphant rise to industrial greatness to its present uncertain condition. And fourth, we have described the way in which the American people have lived: the cultural and social arrangements they have developed for themselves; the impact of social and economic changes on those arrangements; and the efforts of groups divided by class, race, ethnicity, religion, gender, and region to find ways of living together in a single society.

Those familiar with earlier editions of this book will notice many changes in this edition. The most visible, of course, is our new full-color design and our introduction of a wholly new and much larger program of maps, charts, and illustrations. We have added as well a chronology of significant events at the end of each chapter. We have expanded and reorganized the bibliographical essays, both to bring them up to date and to make them easier to use. We have added a new essay on the Vietnam War to our series entitled "Where Historians Disagree," and we have reworked and expanded many of the existing essays in that series.

But the most important changes are those in the narrative itself. What most distinguishes this edition from its predecessors is its more extensive coverage of social, cultural, and economic history—and above all perhaps, our effort to incorporate into the story the results of the recent explosion of scholarship in the field of women's history. We have reviewed and revised virtually every section of the book in light of new evidence and interpretations. We have substantially reorganized several important sections, and we have added several entirely new ones. We have made a significant stylistic revision, to improve the consistency and flow of the narrative.

Several changes will be particularly noticeable to previous users of this book. Chapter 1 has been radically revised to provide more attention to the history of America before Columbus and to explore more fully the interaction among Europeans, Africans, and Indians that dominated the history of sixteenth- and seventeenth-century America. The chapters on the colonial period in general have been substantially recast to take into account the important and rapidly burgeoning new scholarship in that field. There have also been some significant organizational and substantive changes in the chapters dealing with the twentieth century. Chapters 21 and 22 have been thoroughly recast: Chapter 21 now provides an expanded discussion of the social underpinnings of progressive reform and of reform efforts at the state and local level, while Chapter 22 brings together the material on national reform in the progressive era. Chapter 25 consolidates and expands the discussion of the social and cultural impact of the Great Depression. Chapter 26 focuses on the history of the New Deal in its entirety. Chapter 27 offers a comprehensive picture of diplomatic developments in the period from 1921 to 1945, as well as a full discussion of both the domestic and international repercussions of World War II itself. And Chapter 32 presents new material on the Carter and Reagan presidencies and on the social, economic, and cultural events of the 1970s and 1980s. Finally, major new sections on the history of women and the family can be found throughout the book; some of the most important appear in chapters 3, 5, 9, 11, 14, 15, 18, 21, 24–27, 29, and 31. The result of all these changes, we hope, is a book that provides a fuller and richer view of American history, one that illuminates more clearly how the study of history can enhance our understanding of our own world and our own lives.

The editorial and production staffs at Alfred A. Knopf deserve much of the credit for whatever new strengths the present edition brings to this book. David Follmer helped draw up some of the initial plans for this edition, and Chris Rogers presided expertly over the bulk of the revision. David Lindroth is responsible not only for drafting the elegant new maps and charts, but also for conceptualizing many of them. Leon Bolognese contributed a handsome new design for both the cover and the interior. Despite a very tight schedule, Deborah Bull brought both taste and imagination to the task of researching an attractive and effective new set of illustrations. Kathy Bendo and Stacey Alexander saw to the many details of photo permissions and production follow-through with remarkable competence. Evelyn Katrak, as she has done in previous editions, copyedited this enormous manuscript with her usual elegance and professionalism. Our greatest debt is to Elaine Romano, who supervised the preparation of this new edition from start to finish, coordinated the many different aspects of editing and production, repaired uncountable errors and inconsistencies, and made this a much better book than it would otherwise have been—all with unfailing patience, skill, and courtesy.

As always, we appreciate the efforts of the many scholars and teachers who read and commented on the sixth edition of this book and whose suggestions were of incalculable value to us in preparing the seventh. Many of these reviewers have asked not to be identified, and so we have chosen here to thank them all anonymously. We are also grateful to those students and teachers who have used this book over the past several years and who have offered us their unsolicited comments, criticisms, and corrections. We hope they will continue to inform us of their reactions in the future by sending their comments to the authors in care of the College Department, Alfred A. Knopf, Inc., 201 East 50th Street, New York, N.Y. 10022.

ALAN BRINKLEY
Cambridge, Massachusetts
November 1986

Contents

WHERE HISTORIANS DISAGREE

APPENDICES   *A1*

Maps:

Documents and Tables:

INDEX   *I1*

Illustrations

Maps

Charts

American History

A SURVEY

Volume I: To 1877

The New World, to 1775

For thousands of centuries—centuries in which human races were evolving, forming communities, and building the beginnings of national civilizations in Africa, Asia, and Europe—the continents we know as the Americas stood empty of mankind and its works. The human species was not born to the Western Hemisphere. It had to find it. And it did so in two great waves of immigration: the first from Asia, beginning between 25,000 and 40,000 years ago; the second from Europe and Africa, beginning in the sixteenth century. For humans at least, the Americas were indeed what awestruck Europeans of 400 years ago called them: the New World.

The story of this new world is unlike that of any other part of the globe. It is a story of immigrants: of men and women of courage, vision, ambition, greed; of people enchanted by the promise of an unknown land or driven by a desire to escape the hardships of the land they knew. It is a story of thousands, and then millions, who left behind everything that was comfortable, familiar, and predictable to them to seek a future in a world that was strange, sometimes hostile, and always challenging. It is a story of the creation of a civilization where none existed.

It is also the story of how a number of very different peoples found themselves living together in the same land. By the time the first Europeans and Africans arrived to settle in the New World in the sixteenth and seventeenth centuries, there were already flourishing civilizations there that had been developing for many centuries. The early history of European colonization of the Americas was dominated, then, by a sudden and at times violent collision of cultures. That collision had important effects on both European and Indian civilization in the New World.

But it was the European settlement of America, spearheaded first by the Spanish and Portuguese and then by the French, the Dutch, and above all the British—and by the African tribespeople they forcibly transported with them—that largely created the American civilizations we now know. In the areas of Hispanic settlement, those civilizations emerged through a long, slow blending of European culture with that of native societies. In most of North America, however, European settlers made little effort to absorb the existing population. Instead, they generally attempted to isolate themselves from the native cultures, destroyed those cultures when they thought it necessary, and tried to create a society entirely their own.

They did not intend it to be a new civilization. They hoped, rather, to re-create in the New World the societies they had left behind in the Old—improved versions of them, perhaps, but not radically different. Gradually, however, the task proved impossible. In countless ways, large and small, often unnoticed, life in the new land forced the settlers to alter their established customs, patterns, and ideas. Always they found it necessary to adjust to conditions for which their prior experiences had not prepared them. And in the process there emerged an American civilization that, for all its familiar features, differed fundamentally from its European forebears.

The perilous, often heroic, and occasionally foolhardy efforts of these early settlers to create a society for themselves in an alien land, and the long, slow process of adaptation to the New World of their descendants, constitute the story of the first phase of American history. Out of these struggles emerged the institutions, the customs, and the beliefs that would shape much of the nation's future.

The Indian Village of Secoton, by John White, c. 1590   (British Museum)

Chapter 1 # Two Worlds Collide

It is not surprising, perhaps, that most Americans have traditionally considered their history to have begun with the arrival of Europeans in the New World: with the voyages of Columbus in the late fifteenth century, the beginnings of Spanish settlement in the early 1500s, the arrival of the English a century later. The Europeans who "discovered" the Americas and began to people them looked on the continents as a "new world"—unexplored, unexploited, untamed. So successful were they in subduing and dominating the lands they found that their descendants, along with the descendants of other, later immigrant groups, constitute the vast majority of the population of the United States today.

But there is another, much longer American history that stretches back over several millennia before Columbus set foot in the New World, a history about which relatively little is known. It is the history of a substantial population descended from much earlier immigrants and of the elaborate civilizations they created. The Europeans who arrived in America beginning in the sixteenth century did not find an empty land. They found diverse peoples and highly developed cultures. Before they could build their own societies, they had to come to terms with the societies that had preceded them. The coming of the Europeans, in short, was not so much the peopling of a new world as a collision between two cultures that had been developing—along completely different lines— for thousands of years. That collision changed the lives of both the Europeans and the original Americans in fundamental ways.

The Civilizations of America

No one knows precisely when the first human settlers arrived in North America, but it is likely that various tribes of Siberian hunters began crossing the narrow Bering Straits into what is now Alaska at least 30,000 years ago, perhaps much earlier. Year after year, a few at a time, these nomadic peoples entered North America (almost certainly unaware that they were peopling a new continent) and wandered ever deeper into its heart. Ultimately, perhaps as early as 8,000 B.C., the migrations reached the southern tip of South America. By the end of the fifteenth century A.D., when these ancient migrants had their first important contact with Europeans, America was the home of several million men and women. Scholars disagree on the numbers, but the most recent estimates suggest that well over 10 million people lived in South America in 1500 and that at least 2 million lived in North America.

America Before Columbus

The men and women of the Americas had a common Asian ancestry. There were some physical differences from one group to another, but they shared certain basic features (dark skin, straight black hair, high cheekbones) that encouraged Europeans to think of them as a single, undifferentiated people. The natives themselves, however, had no reason to consider themselves part of one race or culture. Spread widely over two enormous continents, different population

5

groups naturally developed in very different ways. The language variations alone were staggering. There were approximately a dozen different linguistic stocks in the Americas, and hundreds of languages and dialects derived from them. In North America, native tribes spoke more than 300 different languages. There were, in addition, substantial variations among tribes in religion, systems of governance, economic life, and cultural outlook. The peoples of America were often as unlike one another as they were unlike the Europeans they eventually encountered.

Although the prehistoric settlers had been largely wandering hunters, most Native Americans eventually established themselves as farmers. As agriculture increased, the nomadic character of many of the early population groups gradually gave way to more sedentary life styles. Tribes established permanent agricultural settlements; and over time, some of them forged ties to one another and developed large and highly sophisticated civilizations.

The most elaborate of these civilizations grew up in South and Central America and in Mexico. In Peru, the Incas created a powerful empire of perhaps 6 million people. They developed a complex political system and a vast network of paved roads that managed to weld together the populations of many tribes under a single ruler. On the Yucatan peninsula of Mexico and in Central America, the Mayas built a sophisticated culture with a written language, a numerical system similar to the Arabic (and superior to the Roman), an accurate calendar, and an advanced agricultural system. They were succeeded as the dominant power in Mexico by the Aztecs, a once-nomadic warrior tribe from the north. In the late thirteenth century, the Aztecs established a precarious rule over much of central and southern Mexico and developed an elaborate administrative structure, a successful educational system, and a form of medical care (including hospitals and nurses) comparable to the most advanced in Europe at that time. The Aztecs also practiced human sacrifice on an unprecedented scale. Their Spanish conquerors discovered the skulls of 100,000 victims in one location when they arrived in 1519. That was one of the reasons why Europeans so often considered the Aztecs "savages," despite their impressive accomplishments.

The peoples of America lacked some of the basic technologies that had contributed to the growth of Asian and European cultures. The Incas, for example, never developed any equivalent for paper or any system of writing. And as late as the sixteenth century, no American society had yet discovered the

wheel. Such absences make all the more impressive the accomplishments of these cultures. Perhaps most striking were their cities. Some were nearly as large as the greatest cities of Europe. Tenochtitlán, the Aztec capital built on the site of the present-day Mexico City, had a population of over 100,000 in 1500 and an impressive complex of majestic public buildings—including temples equal in size to the great pyramids of Egypt. The Mayas (at Mayapan and elsewhere) and the Incas (in such cities as Cuzco and Machu Picchu) produced similarly striking examples of architecture and engineering.

The peoples north of Mexico—in the lands that became the United States and Canada—did not develop political systems as complex as the Incas, Mayas, and Aztecs; nor did they produce comparable cities or technologies. But they were far from the rootless savages that many Europeans later believed them to be. Most of the tribes were engaged in various forms of farming, and in some places they established large agricultural societies. In the Southwest and in parts of the Mississippi Valley, for example, there were complicated irrigation systems and elaborate permanent settlements. On the Pacific coast, the natives established successful fishing communities, farming the surrounding lands to supplement the catch.

Elsewhere, tribes retained something of their older nomadic character. The natives of the basin and the plains were largely wandering hunters, moving their villages periodically in search of better game. In the East, most tribes engaged in farming that would often seem crude to Europeans but that was in many ways well suited to the physical realities of the region; and they tended to settle less permanently than tribes elsewhere. Some cleared land, by setting forest fires or by cutting into trees to kill them, and then planted crops (corn, beans, squash, pumpkins, and others) among the dead or blackened trunks. After a few years, when the land became exhausted (or when the filth from a settlement began to accumulate), they moved on and established themselves elsewhere. In some parts of eastern North America, villages dispersed every winter and families foraged for themselves in the wilderness until warm weather returned and those who had survived this perilous season could begin farming once again. Even in the summer months, many combined agriculture with hunting game and gathering wild fruits and berries. Tasks tended to be divided by sex. Men did the hunting; women did most of the farming, except for clearing the land. (Europeans, when they arrived in North

Tenochtitlán—The Aztec Capital
This is a modern re-creation of the central square of Tenochtitlán, which was dominated by great pyramids comparable in size to those of ancient Egypt. The Aztec pyramids, however, served not as burial monuments but as the sites for human sacrifices on an epic scale. When the Spanish *conquistadore* Hernando Cortés entered Tenochtitlán in 1521, he found a rack in the central square that contained the skulls of about 100,000 sacrificial victims. Mexico City stands today on the site of the Aztec capital. (American Museum of Natural History)

America, were appalled by how hard native women worked at what seemed to the Europeans to be men's tasks. Indian men, they concluded, were lazy; and their disapproval helped reinforce their belief in the superiority of their own culture.)

There were more than two dozen different tribes living east of the Mississippi River by the end of the sixteenth century, many of them loosely linked together by common linguistic roots. The largest of these language groups, the Algonquin tribes, lived along the Atlantic seaboard from Canada to Virginia and included the Narragansetts of New England, the Powhatans of the Chesapeake, and others. Somewhat less numerous, but ultimately more influential, were the Iroquois, who were centered in what is now upstate New York and who formed a wedge between the northern and southern Algonquins. The Iroquois included at least five distinct northern "nations"— Seneca, Cayuga, Onondaga, Oneida, and Mohawk— and had links as well with the Cherokees and the Tuscaroras farther south, in the Carolinas and Georgia. The third largest language group—Muskogean— occupied the southernmost regions of the eastern seaboard and included the Chickasaws, Choctaws, Creeks, and Seminoles.

Linguistic similarities did not, however, necessarily lead to social or cultural ties. The Iroquois did manage at times to hold together the peoples of var-

America in 1600

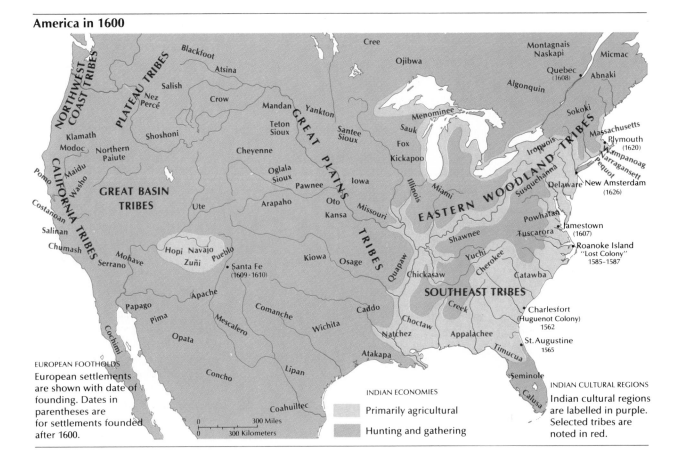

EUROPEAN FOOTHOLDS
European settlements are shown with date of founding. Dates in parentheses are for settlements founded after 1600.

INDIAN ECONOMIES

Primarily agricultural

Hunting and gathering

INDIAN CULTURAL REGIONS
Indian cultural regions are labelled in purple. Selected tribes are noted in red.

Indians of New France

The drawing is by the cartographer Charles Bécard de Granville, who was employed by the French government to make maps of their territories in North America. Granville also produced drawings of the flora and fauna of the region and of the natives he encountered. This depiction of Indian hunters traveling by river dates from approximately 1701. (Gilcrease Institute) ious tribes in an effective confederation; their League of Five Nations (which in the early eighteenth century grew to six) was an important and largely independent power center in North America for well over a century after the arrival of the Europeans. The Iroquois were a crucial factor in the seventeenth-century battle for control of the interior of the continent—a battle that involved the British and the French as well. Other groups, however, were more deeply divided. The various Algonquin tribes, for example, spoke in such different dialects that they could understand one another no better than the English could understand the French or the Spanish; seldom did they create large or durable alliances. And while individual tribes often produced stable and coherent political systems, no group ever emerged in upper North America willing or able to create the large and powerful empires that emerged farther south.

Encounters with Europe

The arrival of Europeans in the fifteenth century began a process of interaction that had profound effects on both the natives and the new immigrants. The impact was greatest on the natives, and in a few respects it was not entirely negative. Horses, which had disappeared from America in the Ice Age, returned aboard Spanish ships beginning in the sixteenth century. The Europeans introduced new crops to America, among them sugar and bananas. White colonists brought with them such livestock as cattle, pigs, and sheep. These imports were usually intended for the use of the Europeans themselves. But Indian tribes in time learned to cultivate the new crops, and the European animals proliferated rapidly and spread widely among tribes that in the past had possessed almost no domesticated beasts. The horse, in particular, became central to the lives of many natives and transformed their societies. Such tribes as the Apache, Comanche, and Sioux in the western plains of North America ultimately built their lives around the horse. They adopted an even more nomadic existence than they had previously known, and they developed new kinds of hunting and warfare.

These modest benefits, however, could not outweigh the much greater costs to the natives of their contact with Europeans. Very quickly, the arrival of white people in the New World produced a catastrophe of epic dimensions for the indigenous populations. Their greatest civilizations met with conquest

and extinction. Their peoples suffered subjugation and death on a massive scale. Much of what happened was a result of the military superiority of the Europeans, which produced a series of decisive conquests. But in the beginning, at least, the most important and the most disastrous effect of the coming of Europeans to America was the arrival with them of devastating diseases.

It would be difficult to exaggerate the consequences of the exposure of Native Americans to such illnesses as influenza, measles, typhus, and above all smallpox—diseases to which Europeans had over time developed at least a partial immunity but to which native Americans were desperately vulnerable. Millions died. Native groups inhabiting some of the large Caribbean islands were virtually extinct within fifty years of their first contact with whites; on Hispaniola—where the Dominican Republic and Haiti are today and where Columbus landed and established a small colony in the 1490s—the native population quickly declined from approximately 1 million to about 500. Some groups fared better than others, of course; most (although not all) of the tribes north of Mexico, whose contact with European settlers came later and was usually less intimate, were spared the worst of the epidemics. But there is reason to believe that in some regions of the Americas as much as 95 percent of the native population died of European diseases within a century. This was a demographic disaster that had no parallel in human history.

For the Europeans, contact with the native population proved far more beneficial. There were costs, to be sure. Syphilis, a disease common in America but previously unknown elsewhere, appeared in Spain shortly after Columbus's return from America (apparently brought back by his sailors, who had contracted it during their sexual encounters with native women in the Caribbean). Within a little more than a decade the disease had spread across the Continent and into Asia. But most of what the Europeans took from the natives was of real and lasting value to them. In both North and South America, the arriving white peoples learned new agricultural techniques from the natives, techniques often far better adapted to the demands of this new land than those they had brought with them from Europe. They discovered new crops, above all maize (corn), which Columbus took back to Europe from his first trip to America and which became an important staple of European as well as American agriculture. Such American foods as squash, pumpkins, beans, sweet potatoes, tomatoes, peppers, and potatoes also found their way into the European diet.

Natives also played an important role in advancing the growth of commerce, particularly in North America. Some aided European explorers and trappers; others traded directly with white merchants. The Iroquois and the Algonquans both played a particularly important (and enduring) role in the growth of the vital North American fur trade. And almost everywhere, Europeans found the natives to be eager customers for manufactured goods: iron pots, blankets, metal-tipped arrows, and eventually guns and rifles. Many natives also developed a taste for another European product—alcohol—with often debilitating and tragic results.

In South America, Central America, and Mexico, the lines between the native and European societies began to blur in time. Many of the Indians there gradually adopted the Spanish language (or in Brazil, Portuguese), the Catholic religion, and other aspects of European social organization. But north of Mexico, there were strict limits to the exchanges between European and indigenous cultures. Christian missionaries flocked to the New World, eager to spread their religion to the "heathen." In most of North America, they found relatively few converts among the natives, who had strong religious convictions of their own. At various times, white settlers attempted to draw native peoples into their schools; but most Indians saw little point to European learning and withdrew. Nor were Europeans often able to recruit Indians successfully as workers. Natives generally worked for the white settlers only under duress—and even then, they usually managed to escape. (The failure to recruit a native work force was one important reason why Europeans in North America decided to resort to the African slave trade in the seventeenth century.)

For all the influence Europeans and Native Americans had on each other, in most of North America they remained members of essentially separate cultures, and they generally attempted to keep a certain distance between them. There were some cases of natives becoming assimilated into white society ("Red Puritans," or "praying Indians," as they were called in New England). Somewhat more frequently, but still not often, whites became absorbed into Indian society, usually through marriage. On the whole, however, each group viewed the other as an alien force; and while the two worlds managed at times to live in peace, there was constant tension and constant potential for conflict.

Europe Looks Westward

Europeans were almost entirely unaware of the existence of the Americas before the fifteenth century. A few early wanderers—Leif Ericson, an eleventh-century Norse seaman, and perhaps others—had glimpsed parts of the New World and had demonstrated that Europeans were capable of crossing the ocean to find it. But even had their discoveries become common knowledge (and they did not), there would have been little incentive for others to follow. For Europe in the Middle Ages (roughly 500–1500 A.D.) was not an adventurous civilization. Divided into innumerable small duchies and kingdoms, its outlook was overwhelmingly provincial. Subsistence agriculture predominated, and commerce was limited; few merchants looked beyond the boundaries of their own regions. Although the Roman Catholic church exercised a measure of spiritual authority over most of the Continent, and although the Holy Roman Empire provided at least a nominal political center, power was for the most part so widely dispersed that no single leader was capable of launching great ventures. Gradually, however, conditions in Europe changed, so that by the late fifteenth century interest in overseas exploration had grown.

Commerce and Nationalism

Two important and related changes provided the first incentive for Europeans to look toward new lands. One was a result of the significant growth in the European population in the fifteenth century. The Black Death, a catastrophic epidemic of the bubonic plague that began in Constantinople in 1347, had decimated Europe, killing (according to some estimates) more than half the people there and debilitating its already limited economy. But a century and a half later, the population had rebounded. With that growth came a rise in land values, a reawakening of commerce, and a general increase in prosperity. Affluent landlords were becoming eager to purchase goods from distant regions; and a new merchant class was emerging to meet their demand. As trade expanded, and as advances in navigation and shipbuilding made long-distance sea travel more feasible, interest in developing new markets, finding new products, and opening new trade routes rapidly increased.

Paralleling the rise of commerce in Europe, and in

The Cognoscenti
This detail from a fifteenth-century Flemish painting depicts a gathering of English navigators and scholars as they discuss the possibilities for transoceanic trade routes. On the table are maps, drawings, and some of the new navigational devices that made possible the great explorations of the era. (National Gallery, London)

part responsible for it, was the rise of new governments that were far more united and powerful than the feeble political entities of the feudal past. In the western areas of Europe in particular, where the authority of the distant pope and the even more distant Holy Roman emperor were necessarily weak, strong new monarchs were emerging and creating centralized nation-states, with national courts, national armies, and perhaps most important, national tax systems. As these ambitious kings and queens consolidated their power and increased their wealth, they became eager to enhance the commercial growth of their nations.

Ever since the early fourteenth century, when Marco Polo and other adventurers had returned from the Orient bearing exotic goods (spices, cloths, dyes) and even more exotic tales, Europeans who dreamed of commercial glory had dreamed above all of trade with the East. For two centuries, that trade had been limited by the difficulties of the long, arduous overland journey to the Asian courts. But in the fourteenth century, as the maritime talents of several western European societies increased, there began to be serious talk of finding a faster, safer sea route to the Orient. Such dreams gradually found a receptive audience in the courts of the new monarchs. By the late fifteenth century, some of them were ready to finance daring voyages of exploration.

The first to do so were the Portuguese. Their maritime preeminence in the fifteenth century was in large part the work of one man, Prince Henry the Navigator, who devoted much of his life to nautical studies and the promotion of exploration. Henry's own principal interest was not in finding a sea route to Asia but in exploring the western coast of Africa—where he dreamed of establishing a Christian empire to aid in his country's wars against the Moors of northern Africa and where he hoped to find new stores of gold. But the explorations he began, while they did not fulfill his own hopes, ultimately led farther than he had dreamed. Some of Henry's mariners went as far south as Cape Verde. After his death in 1460, Portuguese explorers carried on his work and advanced farther still. In 1486, Bartholomeu Diaz rounded the southern tip of the continent (the Cape of Good Hope); and in 1497–1498 Vasco da Gama proceeded all the way to India. In 1500, the next fleet bound for India, under the command of Pedro Cabral, was blown off its southward course and happened upon the coast of Brazil. But by then, another man, in the service of another country, had already encountered the New World.

Christopher Columbus

Christopher Columbus, who was born and reared in Genoa, Italy, obtained most of his early seafaring knowledge and experience in the service of the Portuguese. And as a young man, he became intrigued with the possibility, already under discussion in many seafaring circles, of reaching the Orient by going not east but west. Columbus was an industrious student of geography, and his wide readings convinced him that the Atlantic could provide easier passage to the Orient than either the existing land routes or the arduous sea route around southern Africa. Columbus's optimism rested on several basic misconceptions. He concluded that the world was far smaller than it actually is. And he believed that the Asian continent extended farther eastward than it actually does. He assumed, therefore, that the western ocean was narrow enough to be crossed on a relatively brief voyage. It did not occur to him that anything lay between Europe and the lands of Asia.

Columbus failed to convince the leaders of Portugal of the feasibility of his plan; the Portuguese were more interested in establishing their route to the East around Africa. So Columbus turned from Portugal to Spain. Although the Spaniards were not yet

as advanced a maritime people as the Portuguese, they were at least as energetic and ambitious. And in the fifteenth century they were, like other European nations, busy at the work of establishing a strong nation-state. The marriage of Spain's two most powerful regional rulers, Ferdinand of Aragon and Isabella of Castile, had produced the strongest monarchy in Europe; and like other new monarchies, it would soon grow eager to demonstrate its strength by sponsoring new commercial ventures.

Columbus appealed to Queen Isabella for support—men, money, and ships—for his proposed western voyage. The project would, he promised, extend the sway of Christianity to new lands and, perhaps more important to Isabella, help Spain in its emerging competition with Portugal. For a time, the queen was more interested in consolidating both Christianity and her own power at home; but in 1492 she finally felt secure enough to turn her gaze to foreign ventures. In that year, the Moorish stronghold of Granada fell to the Spanish armies, and the last Muslims were driven from the country; at the same time, the Jews of Spain—the only other significant non-Christian element in the population—were forced to choose between conversion to Christianity or emigration. Confident now of her position within her own nation, Isabella finally agreed to Columbus's request.

Commanding ninety men and three ships—the *Niña,* the *Pinta,* and the *Santa Maria*—Columbus left Spain in August 1492 and sailed west into the Atlantic on what he thought was a straight course for Japan. Ten weeks later, he sighted land and assumed he had reached his target. In fact, he had landed on Watling Island in the Bahamas. When he pushed on and encountered Cuba, he assumed he had reached China. He returned to Spain in triumph, bringing with him several captured natives as evidence of his achievement. (He called the natives "Indians" because they were, he believed, from the East Indies in the Pacific.)

Columbus did not, however, bring back to Spain what he had promised. He had no news of the great khan's court in China; nor did he have any samples of the fabled wealth of the Indies. And so a year later, he tried again, this time with a much larger expedition. As before, he headed into the Caribbean, discovering several other islands and leaving a small and short-lived colony on Hispaniola. On a third voyage, in 1498, he finally reached the mainland and cruised along the northern coast of South America. When he passed the mouth of the Orinoco River (in present-

European Journeys of Exploration and Conquest

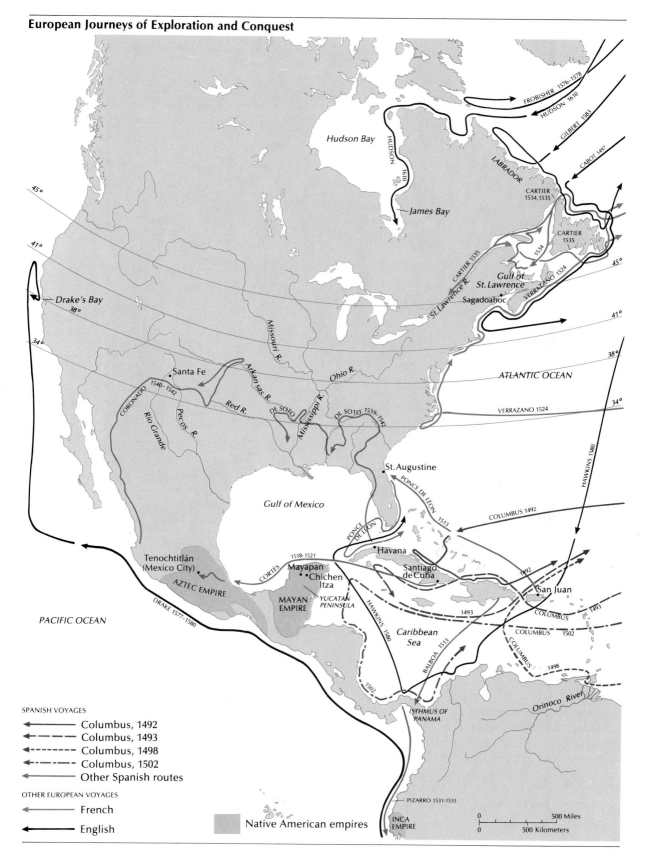

FROBISHER 1576-1578
HUDSON 1610
GILBERT 1583
CABOT 1497

Hudson Bay

HUDSON 1610

James Bay

LABRADOR

CARTIER 1534, 1535

CARTIER 1535

45°

41°

CARTIER 1535

1534

VERRAZANO 1524

Gulf of St. Lawrence

St. Lawrence R.

Drake's Bay
38°

Sagadahoc

45°

34°

41°

Missouri R.

Santa Fe

Arkansas R.

Ohio R.

ATLANTIC OCEAN

38°

CORONADO 1540-1542

Pecos R.

Red R.

DE SOTO

Mississippi R.

DE SOTO 1539-1542

VERRAZANO 1524

34°

Rio Grande

HAWKINS 1560

St. Augustine

PONCE DE LEÓN

Gulf of Mexico

PONCE DE LEÓN 1513

COLUMBUS 1492

Havana

1492

PONCE DE LEÓN

Tenochtitlán
(Mexico City)

1518-1521

CORTÉS

Mayapan
Chichen
Itza

Santiago
de Cuba

San Juan

COLUMBUS 1493

AZTEC EMPIRE

MAYAN
EMPIRE

YUCATAN
PENINSULA

1493

COLUMBUS

DRAKE 1577-1580

PACIFIC OCEAN

HAWKINS 1560

*Caribbean
Sea*

COLUMBUS 1502

COLUMBUS 1498

BALBOA 1513

Orinoco River

1502

ISTHMUS OF
PANAMA

SPANISH VOYAGES

- ← Columbus, 1492
- ←- - Columbus, 1493
- ←···· Columbus, 1498
- ←-·-· Columbus, 1502
- ← Other Spanish routes

PIZARRO 1531-1533

INCA
EMPIRE

0   500 Miles

0   500 Kilometers

OTHER EUROPEAN VOYAGES

- → French
- → English

Native American empires

Columbus's Third Voyage to America, 1498
This drawing, a sixteenth-century re-creation by the Flemish engraver Theodore de Bry, shows Columbus's third expedition to the New World as it encountered natives near the island of Margarita, off the coast of Venezuela. Columbus's men received three pounds of pearls from the natives (the Indian canoes are shown here filled with pearl oysters) in exchange for some pieces of pottery, and then sailed on.   (New York Public Library)

day Venezuela), he concluded for the first time that what he had discovered was not in fact an island off the coast of China, as he had assumed, but a separate continent; such a large freshwater stream could, he realized, emerge only from a large body of land. Still, he remained convinced that Asia was only a short distance away. And although he failed in his efforts to sail around the northwestern coast of South America through to the Indies (he was blocked by the Isthmus of Panama), he returned to Spain believing he had explored at least the fringes of the Far East. He continued to believe that until the day he died.

Columbus's celebrated accomplishments made him a popular hero for a time, but he ended his life in obscurity. Ultimately, he was even denied the honor of giving his name to the land he had discovered. That distinction went instead to a Florentine merchant, Amerigo Vespucci, a passenger on a later Portuguese expedition to the New World who wrote a series of vivid (if largely fictitious) descriptions of the lands he visited. But Christopher Columbus, for all his misconceptions, deserved the fame that ultimately came to him. He had helped dispel the terrors of the unknown ocean. He had demonstrated the existence of the New World. He had opened the way for the explorers of many nations to carry on his work. Just as Columbus had done on his final voyage, they concentrated their efforts at first mainly on the search for a water passage that would lead through the new lands and on to the riches of the Far East. Such a passage did not exist, but the efforts to find it revealed the outlines of both continents and made known the vastness of a territory that Europeans would soon find appealing for different purposes.

Partly as a result of Columbus's initiative, Spain began to devote greater resources and energy to maritime exploration and gradually replaced Portugal as the foremost seafaring nation. The Spaniard Vasco de Balboa pushed his way across the Isthmus of Panama (1513) and became the first European to gaze westward upon the great ocean that separated America from China and the Indies. Seeking access to that ocean, Ferdinand Magellan, a Portuguese in Spanish employ, found the strait that now bears his name at the southern end of South America, struggled through the stormy narrows and into the ocean (so calm by contrast that he christened it the Pacific), then proceeded to the Philippines. There Magellan died in a conflict with the natives, but his expedition went on to complete the first known circumnavigation of the globe (1519-1522). By 1550, Spaniards had explored the coasts of North America as far north as Oregon in the West and Labrador in the East.

The Conquistadores

In time, Spanish explorers in the New World stopped thinking of America simply as an obstacle to their search for a route to the East. They began instead to consider it a possible source of wealth rivaling and even surpassing the original Indies. On the basis of Columbus's discoveries (and with the aid of a papal decree), the Spanish claimed for themselves the whole of the New World, except for a piece of it (today's Brazil) that was reserved for the Portuguese. And by

Cortés in Mexico
In this sixteenth-century drawing, an Indian artist portrayed the great *conquistadore* Hernando Cortés at the head of the army with which he conquered Tenochtitlán, the Aztec capital, in 1521. Cortés is shown here accompanied by an Indian woman, Marina, who served as his interpreter and who reportedly advised him on Mexican affairs. (Bibliothèque Nationale, Paris)

the mid-sixteenth century, they were well on their way to establishing a substantial American empire.

The early Spanish colonists, beginning with those Columbus brought on his second voyage, settled on the islands of the Caribbean, where they tried to enslave the Indians and find gold. They had little luck at either. But then, in 1518, Hernando Cortés, who had been a Spanish government official in Cuba for fourteen years and who had to that point achieved little success, decided to lead a small military expedition (about 600 men) into Mexico after hearing stories of great treasures there. He met strong and resourceful resistance from the Aztecs and their powerful emperor Montezuma; and his first assault on Tenochtitlán, the Aztec capital, failed. But Cortés and his army had, unknowingly, unleashed a far more devastating assault on the Aztecs than a military invasion. They had exposed the natives to smallpox, and an epidemic of that disease decimated the population and made it possible for the Spanish to triumph in their second attempt at conquest. Through his ruthless suppression of the surviving natives, Cortés established a lasting reputation as the most brutal of the *conquistadores* (conquerors).

The news that silver was to be found in Mexico

turned the attention of other Spaniards to the mainland. From the island colonies and from the mother country, a wave of *conquistadores* descended on Mexico in search of fortune—a movement comparable in some ways to the nineteenth-century gold rushes elsewhere in the world but infinitely more vicious. Francisco Pizarro, who conquered Peru (1531–1533) and revealed to the world the wealth of the Incas, opened the way for a similar advance into South America.

The story of the *conquistadores* is one of great military daring and achievement; it is also a story of remarkable brutality and greed. The European invaders were already inadvertently decimating the native population by subjecting them to new diseases. They added to the disaster by quite deliberately destroying many of the most important accomplishments of the native civilizations. They razed cities and dismantled temples and monuments. They destroyed records and documents (one reason why modern scholars have been able to learn so little about the histories of these native societies). The Europeans attempted, in short, to eliminate the underpinnings of the existing civilizations so as to bring the native population under the full political and religious control of Spain. By the 1540s, they had largely succeeded; and in future years, colonization could proceed with much less fear of effective native opposition.

The Spanish Empire

Spanish exploration, conquest, and colonization in America was primarily a work of private enterprise, carried on by individual leaders, with little direct support from the government at home. Those who wished to launch expeditions to the New World had first to get licenses from the crown. By the terms of the licenses, the monarch received a fifth of any wealth found or produced in the new colonies. The organizers of colonies retained a tenth of that wealth. They also received generous estates, other lands to divide among their followers, and the right to make use of native labor. But a license did no more than confer rights; colonizers had to equip and finance their expeditions on their own and assume the full risk of loss or ruin. They might succeed and make a fortune; they might fail—through shipwreck, natural disaster, incompetence, or bad luck—and lose everything, including their lives, as many adventurers did. The New

World did not always attract good or intelligent settlers, but in the beginning it seldom attracted the fainthearted. *coward*

The new colonial population came only in small part from Spain itself and scarcely at all from other countries in Europe. Few Spaniards were either willing or able to emigrate, and other Europeans, with a few exceptions, were excluded from the colonies. Most of the settlers, therefore, came from various outposts of Spanish civilization in the Atlantic—the Azores, the Cape Verde Islands, and elsewhere; but even with these additional sources, the number of European settlers in Spanish America remained relatively small—a fact that helped determine the shape of the society that emerged there.

Colonial officials were expected to take their wives with them to America, but among the ordinary settlers—the great majority—European men outnumbered European women by at least ten to one. Increasingly, therefore, the Spanish immigrants turned to the native population. Almost from the beginning, intermarriage was common in Spanish America, which reveals several things about the colonizers. It reveals, of course, that men living alone in a strange land craved female companionship and the satisfactions of family and that they sought those things in the only places they could. It reveals that in these new and undeveloped colonies, most settlers desperately needed labor—including domestic labor, which their native wives helped provide. And it suggests as well that the Spanish may have had somewhat more flexible ideas about race than the later English colonists would display. The English settlers in North America often faced similar shortages of white women, similar loneliness, a similar need for labor. Seldom, however, did they intermarry with Indian women.

Intermarriage relieved only a small part of the Spaniards' substantial labor shortage. At times, they tried to overcome it by forcing Indians to work for wages. This coercive *forcave* labor system, related but not identical to slavery, survived in many of the mines and on many of the ranches of the South American mainland for centuries. Yet even that was not, in the end, enough to meet the needs of the colonists—particularly once the native population declined (and in some areas virtually vanished) because of disease. As early as 1502, therefore, the European settlers began importing slaves from Africa to work on the plantations of the islands and coastal areas. (The Portuguese had established the African slave trade in Europe a half-century earlier; the introduction of that trade to the New World caused it to flourish and expand greatly.)

The first Spaniards to arrive in the New World, the *conquistadores,* were interested in only one thing: getting rich. More specifically, they were eager to exploit the American stores of gold and silver. And in that, they were fabulously successful. For 300 years, beginning in the sixteenth century, the mines in Spanish America yielded more than ten times as much gold and silver as the rest of the world's mines together. These riches made Spain for a time the wealthiest and most powerful nation on earth.

But after the first wave of conquest, most Spanish settlers in America traveled to the New World for other reasons. And it was they who were of more lasting importance to the future of America. Many went in hopes of creating a profitable agricultural economy in America. And unlike the *conquistadores,* who left little but destruction behind them, they helped establish elements of European civilization in America that permanently altered both the landscape and the social structure. Above all, perhaps, the Spaniards brought with them their religion. Indeed, after the era of the *conquistadores* came to a close in the 1540s, the missionary impulse became one of the principal motives for European emigration to America. Priests or friars accompanied all colonizing ventures. Every settlement became a Christian community. And through the work of zealous missionaries, the gospel of the Catholic church ultimately extended throughout South and Central America.

By the end of the sixteenth century, the Spanish Empire had grown to become one of the largest in the history of the world. It included the islands of the Caribbean and the coastal areas of South America that had been the targets of the first Spanish expeditions. It extended to Mexico and southern North America, where a second wave of European colonizers had established outposts. The Spanish fort established in 1565 at St. Augustine, Florida, became the first permanent European settlement in the present-day United States. Spanish missionaries ventured even farther north in the following years—at times reaching as far as the Chesapeake Bay—although they established no lasting presence in those areas. The Spanish Empire spread southward and westward as well: into the land mass of South America—present-day Chile, Argentina, and Peru—which was the target of a third Spanish military thrust. In 1580, when the Spanish and Portuguese monarchies united (if only temporarily), Brazil came under Spanish jurisdiction as well. From California, Florida, and Mexico to Cape Horn at the tip of South America, Spain's power stood unchallenged.

It was, however, a colonial empire very different from the one that would emerge in North America beginning in the early seventeenth century. Although the Spanish ruled the New World, they did not people it. In the first century of settlement, fewer than a quarter of a million European settlers established themselves in the Spanish colonies. Despite the ravages of disease and war, the vast majority of the population continued to consist of natives. The Spanish, in other words, imposed a small ruling class on a much larger existing population; they did not create a self-contained European society in the New World as the English would attempt to do in the north. The frequent intermarriage in the Spanish colonies produced a population dominated (numerically at least) by *mestizos,* people of mixed race. Europeans and Indians intermarried not only with each other, but also with the Africans imported as slaves; and thus racial distinctions, while not unimportant, became far less rigid and far less central to society in Latin American colonies than they would become in English ones. One result was that slavery in these societies, although often no less brutal than its northern counterpart, was somewhat more flexible and in many areas less lasting than the North American system.

There were also important political differences between the Spanish Empire in America and the later British version. Although the earliest Spanish ventures in the New World had operated largely independent of the throne, by the end of the sixteenth century the monarchy had established an elaborate hierarchical structure by which its authority extended directly into the governance of local communities. Colonists had few opportunities to establish political institutions independent of the crown. The British administration of North America, by contrast, would be far looser and more casual; and European settlers there would quickly develop a political system in which the monarch often played an indirect, even nominal role.

There was, finally, an economic difference. The Spanish were far more successful than the British would be in extracting great surface wealth from their American colonies. But for that very reason, they concentrated relatively less energy on making their colonies profitable agricultural and commercial ven-

Spanish America

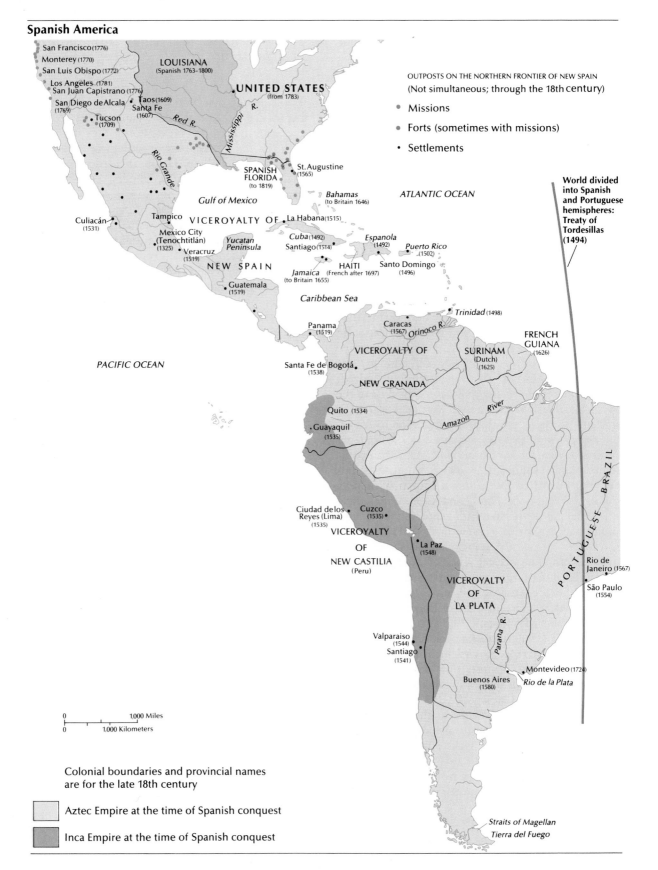

San Francisco (1776)
Monterey (1770)
San Luis Obispo (1772)
Los Angeles (1781)
San Juan Capistrano (1776)
San Diego de Alcala (1769)
Tucson (1709)

LOUISIANA
(Spanish 1763–1800)

UNITED STATES
(from 1783)

Taos (1609)
Santa Fe (1607)

Red R.

Rio Grande

Mississippi R.

OUTPOSTS ON THE NORTHERN FRONTIER OF NEW SPAIN
(Not simultaneous; through the 18th century)

● Missions

● Forts (sometimes with missions)

· Settlements

World divided into Spanish and Portuguese hemispheres: Treaty of Tordesillas (1494)

St. Augustine (1565)

SPANISH FLORIDA
(to 1819)

Bahamas
(to Britain 1646)

ATLANTIC OCEAN

Gulf of Mexico

Culiacán (1531)

Tampico

VICEROYALTY OF

La Habana (1515)

Mexico City (Tenochtitlán) (1325)
Veracruz (1519)

Yucatan Peninsula

Cuba (1492)
Santiago (1514)

Espanola (1492)

Puerto Rico (1502)

NEW SPAIN

HAITI (French after 1697)
Santo Domingo (1496)

Jamaica
(to Britain 1655)

Guatemala (1519)

Caribbean Sea

Trinidad (1498)

Panama (1519)

Caracas (1567)

Orinoco R.

VICEROYALTY OF

SURINAM (Dutch) (1625)

FRENCH GUIANA (1626)

Santa Fe de Bogotá (1538)

NEW GRANADA

Quito (1534)

Guayaquil (1535)

Amazon River

PACIFIC OCEAN

P O R T U G U E S E   B R A Z I L

Ciudad de los Reyes (Lima) (1535)

Cuzco (1535)

VICEROYALTY OF
NEW CASTILIA
(Peru)

La Paz (1548)

Rio de Janeiro (1567)

São Paulo (1554)

VICEROYALTY OF LA PLATA

Valparaiso (1544)
Santiago (1541)

Parana R.

Montevideo (1724)

Buenos Aires (1580)

Rio de la Plata

0   1,000 Miles
0   1,000 Kilometers

Colonial boundaries and provincial names
are for the late 18th century

Aztec Empire at the time of Spanish conquest

Inca Empire at the time of Spanish conquest

Straits of Magellan
Tierra del Fuego

tures. The problem was compounded by the unusually strict and inflexible commercial policies of the Spanish government. To enforce the collection of duties and to provide protection against pirates, the government required all trade with the colonies to be carried on through a single Spanish port and only a few colonial ports, in fleets making but two voyages a year. The system stifled economic development of the New World. The British colonies, on the other hand, faced far fewer restrictions and ultimately produced a large, flexible, and flourishing commercial economy that would sustain prosperity in North America long after depletion of the supplies of gold and silver had begun to debilitate the economies to the south.

The Arrival of the English

England's first documented contact with the New World came only five years after Spain's. In 1497, John Cabot (like Columbus a native of Genoa) sailed to the northeastern coast of North America on an expedition sponsored by King Henry VII. Other Englishmen, continuing Cabot's unsuccessful search for a northwest passage through the New World to the Orient, explored other areas of North America during the sixteenth century. But while England claimed dominion over the lands its explorers surveyed, nearly a century passed before Englishmen made any serious efforts to establish colonies there. Like other European nations, England had to experience an internal transformation before it could begin the work of settling new lands. And that transformation, spurred by a combination of economic and cultural changes, occurred in the course of the sixteenth century.

The Commercial Incentive

Part of the attraction of the New World to the English was its newness, its contrast to their own troubled land. America seemed a place where people could start anew, where a perfect society could be created unencumbered by the flaws and inequities of the Old World. Such dreams began to emerge in England only a few years after Columbus's discovery. They found classic expression in Sir Thomas More's *Utopia* (published in Latin in 1516, translated into English thirty-five years later), which described a mythical and nearly perfect society on an imaginary island supposedly discovered by a companion of Amerigo Vespucci in the waters of the New World.

More's picture of an ideal community was, among other things, a comment on the social and economic condition of the England of his own time. For Tudor England, despite its literary glory (it produced, among much else, the works of Shakespeare) and its adventurous spirit, was in many ways an unhappy nation. The population suffered greatly from the frequent and costly European wars in which England became engaged. They suffered from almost constant religious strife within their own land. But they suffered above all from a harsh economic transformation of their country. The population of England grew steadily in the sixteenth century—from 3 million in 1485 to 4 million in 1603—but the food supply did not increase proportionately. On the contrary, because the worldwide demand for wool was growing rapidly (neither cotton nor silk having yet emerged as a major source of cloth), many landowners were finding it more profitable to convert their land from fields for crops to pastures for sheep. Land tilled at one time by serfs and later by rent-paying tenants was steadily enclosed for sheep runs and taken away from the farmers.

Thousands of evicted tenants roamed the countryside in gangs, begging (and at times robbing), and alarming the more fortunate householders through whose communities they passed. The government passed various laws designed to halt enclosures, relieve the worthy poor, and compel the able-bodied or "sturdy beggars" to work. Such laws had little effect. The enclosure movement continued unabated; relatively few of the dislocated farmers could find reemployment in raising sheep or manufacturing wool; the pressures of surplus population increased.

Amid this growing distress, a rising class of merchant capitalists was prospering from the expansion of foreign trade. At first, England had exported little except raw wool; but the new merchant capitalists helped create a domestic cloth industry that allowed them to begin marketing finished goods. They gathered up raw material, put it out for spinning and weaving in individual households, and sold the cloth both in England and abroad. Initially, most exporters did business entirely as individuals—except for their membership in the Company of Merchant Adventurers, which regulated some of the activities of its members, secured trading privileges for them, and provided protection for their voyages. In time, however, merchants developed more formally collective enterprises. They formed chartered companies, each of which operated on the basis of a charter, acquired from the monarch, giving the company a monopoly for trading in a particular region. Among the first of these were the Muscovy Company (1555), the Levant Company (1581), the Barbary Company (1585), the Guinea Company (1588), and the East India Company (1600). Some were simply regulated associations of individual traders, similar to the Merchant Adventurers, each member doing business separately. Others were joint-stock companies, similar in some respects to modern corporations, with stockholders sharing risks and profits on either single ventures or, as became more common, on a permanent basis. These investors often made fantastic profits from the exchange of English manufactures, especially woolens, for exotic goods; and they felt a powerful urge to continue with the expansion of their trade.

To further this drive, spokesmen for the merchant capitalists developed a set of ideas about the proper relation of government and business—ideas based on the belief that the entire nation benefited from the activities of the overseas traders. The nation as a whole, they argued, would benefit from successful overseas trade in much the same way an individual merchant or firm benefited. Trade surpluses would bring additional gold, silver, and other wealth into the country. This new money would stimulate business, raise prices, and lower interest rates. Hence the government had good reason to promote a favorable balance of trade and assist merchants in expanding their exports. This economic philosophy, restated by Thomas Mun in his book *England's Treasure by Forraign Trade* (1664), came to be known in the eighteenth century as "mercantilism"; it guided the economic policies not only of England but also of Spain, France, and other nation-states.

At first, this mercantilistic program thrived on the basis of England's flourishing wool trade with the European continent, and particularly with the great cloth market in Antwerp. In the 1550s, however, that glutted market collapsed, and English merchants found themselves obliged to look elsewhere for overseas trade. The establishment of colonies seemed to be a ready answer to the problem, as the Oxford clergyman Richard Hakluyt argued in a series of explorers' narratives and in a 1584 essay on "western planting," which established him as the outstanding propagandist for colonization. Colonies would, Hakluyt argued, serve many useful purposes. They would, of course, create new markets for English goods. But they would also help alleviate poverty and unemployment by siphoning off surplus popu-

lation and by creating work at home for the poor who lived there "idly to the annoy of the whole state." Colonial commerce would allow England to acquire from its own colonies products for which the nation had previously been dependent on foreigners—products such as lumber, naval stores, and above all, silver and gold.

The Religious Incentive

In addition to these economic motives for colonization, there were religious ones as well, rooted in the events of the European and English Reformations. The Protestant Reformation began in Germany in 1517 when Martin Luther openly challenged some of the basic practices and beliefs of the Roman Catholic church—until then, the supreme religious authority and also one of the strongest political authorities throughout western Europe. Luther, an Augustinian monk and ordained priest, challenged the Catholic belief that salvation could be achieved through good works or through the church itself. He denied the church's claim that God communicated to the world through the pope and the clergy. The Bible, not the church, was the authentic voice of God, Luther claimed; and salvation was to be found not through "works" or through the formal practice of religion, but through faith alone. Luther's challenge quickly won him a wide popular following among ordinary men and women in northern Europe. He himself insisted that he was not revolting against the church, that his purpose was to reform it from within. But when the pope excommunicated him in 1520, Luther expressed open defiance and began the process that would ultimately lead his followers out of the Catholic church entirely. A schism within European Christianity had begun that was never to be healed.

As the spirit of the Reformation spread rapidly throughout Europe, creating intellectual ferment (and in some places war), other dissidents began offering other alternatives to orthodox Catholicism. The Swiss theologian John Calvin was, after Luther, the most influential reformer and went even further than Luther had in rejecting the Catholic belief that human institutions could affect an individual's prospects for salvation. Calvin introduced the doctrine of predestination. God "elected" some people to be saved and condemned others to damnation; each person's destiny was determined before birth, and no one could change that predetermined fate. But while individuals could not alter their destinies, they could strive to know them. And in this, Calvin established the most powerful element of his religion. Those who accepted his teachings came to believe that the way they led their lives might reveal to them their chances of salvation. A wicked or useless existence would be a sign of damnation; saintliness, diligence, and success could be signs of grace. Calvinism created anxieties among its followers, to be sure; but it also produced a strong incentive to lead virtuous, productive lives. The new creed spread rapidly throughout northern Europe and produced (among other groups) the Huguenots in France and the Puritans in England.

The English Reformation began, however, less as a result of these doctrinal revolts than because of a political dispute between the king and the pope. In 1529, King Henry VIII, angered by the refusal of the pope to grant him a divorce from his Spanish wife (who had failed to bear him the son he desperately wanted), broke England's ties with the Catholic church and established himself as the head of the Christian faith in his country. He made relatively few other changes in English Christianity, however, and after his death the survival of Protestantism remained for a time in doubt, especially when Henry's Catholic daughter Mary ascended the throne. Mary quickly restored England's allegiance to Rome and harshly persecuted those who refused to return to the Catholic fold. Many Protestants were executed (the reason for the queen's enduring nickname, "Bloody Mary"); others fled to the Continent, where they came into contact with many of the most radical ideas of the Reformation. Mary died in 1558, and her half-sister, Elizabeth, became England's sovereign. *Supreme* Elizabeth once again severed the nation's connection with the Catholic church (and along with it, an alliance with Spain that Mary had forged).

The Church of England, as the official religion was now known, satisfied the political objectives of the queen. But it failed to satisfy the religious desires of many English Christians. To large groups of Catholics, it was an affront to their traditional faith; they continued to claim allegiance to the pope. To others, affected by the teachings of the European Reformation, it was a church that had abandoned Rome without abandoning Rome's offensive beliefs and practices. Under Elizabeth, the church began to change theologically and to incorporate some of the tenets of Calvinist faith. But the changes were not far-reaching enough to satisfy the church's critics— particularly the many exiles who had fled the country under Mary and who now returned, bringing their new, more radical religious ideas with them. They

Elizabeth I
The Flemish artist Marcus Gheeraerts the younger moved to England in 1568 (along with his father, also a painter) as a Protestant refugee from his homeland. In approximately 1593 he painted this portrait of the English queen, portraying her as she was seen by many of her contemporaries: a strong, confident ruler presiding over an ambitious, expansionist nation. She stands here on a map of England. (National Portrait Gallery, London)

continued to clamor for reforms that would "purify" the church, and they were known accordingly as "Puritans."

A few Puritans, known as the Separatists, were determined to worship as they pleased in their own, independent congregations, a determination that flew in the face of English law—which outlawed unauthorized religious meetings, required all subjects to attend regular Anglican services, and levied taxes to

ENGLISH MONARCHS, 1485–1625

Henry VII	1485–1509
Henry VIII	1509–1547
Edward VI	1547–1553
Mary I	1553–1558
Elizabeth I	1558–1603
James I	1603–1625

support the established church. But while most Puritans did not wish to leave the church, their demands were by no means modest. They wanted to simplify Anglican forms of worship. They wanted to reduce the power of the bishops, who were appointed by the throne and who were, in many cases, openly corrupt and highly extravagant. And perhaps above all they wanted to reform the local clergy, a group composed in large part of greedy, uneducated men with little interest in (or knowledge of) theology. The Puritans wanted, in short, to see the church give more attention to its spiritual role and less to its temporal ambitions. No less than the Separatists, they grew increasingly frustrated by the refusal of either the political or the ecclesiastical hierarchies to respond to their demands.

Puritan discontent, already festering, grew rapidly after the death of Elizabeth, the last of the Tudors, and the accession of James I, the first of the Stuarts, in 1603. A Scotsman, the new king was widely considered a foreigner. And although a learned man, he was a poor politician—the "wisest fool in Christendom," some called him. Convinced that kings ruled by divine right, James made it clear from the start that he intended to govern as he pleased. He quickly antagonized the Puritans, a group that included most of the rising businessmen, by resorting to illegal and arbitrary taxation, by favoring English Catholics in the granting of charters and other privileges, and by supporting "high church" forms of ceremony. By the early seventeenth century, therefore, a growing number of religious nonconformists were beginning to look for places of refuge outside the kingdom. When combined with the economic and social incentives for colonization, this religious discontent helped turn England's gaze to distant lands.

The English in Ireland

The first experience of the English with colonization came not in the New World but in a land separated from them by only a narrow stretch of sea: Ireland. The English had long laid claim to the island and had for many years maintained small settlements in the area around Dublin. But it was only in the second half of the sixteenth century that serious efforts at large-scale colonization began. Through the 1560s and 1570s, would-be colonists moved through the country, capturing territory and attempting to subdue the native population. And in the process, they developed many of the assumptions that would guide later English colonists in America.

The most important of these assumptions was that the native population of Ireland—approximately 1 million people, loyal to the Catholic church, with their own language and their own culture—was a collection of wild, vicious, and ignorant savages. The Irish lived and worked in ways that to the English seemed crude and wasteful, and they fought back against the intruders with a ferocity that to the English seemed barbaric. Such people could not be tamed, the English concluded. They certainly could not be assimilated into English society. They must, therefore, be suppressed, isolated, and if necessary destroyed.

Whatever barbarities the Irish may have inflicted on the colonizers were more than matched by the English in return. Sir Humphrey Gilbert, who was later to establish the first British colony in the New World (an unsuccessful venture in Newfoundland), served for a time as governor of one Irish district and suppressed rebellions by the natives with extraordinary viciousness. Gilbert was an educated and civilized man; yet he managed to justify, both to himself and to others, various atrocities (such as beheading Irish soldiers killed in battle) by looking on the natives as somehow less than human, not entitled to whatever decencies civilized men and women reserved for their treatment of one another. In dealing with such "savages," any tactics facilitating the transplantation of English culture and society to the new land could be justified. Gilbert himself, Sir Walter Raleigh, Sir Richard Grenville, and others active in Ireland in the mid-sixteenth century derived from their experiences there an outlook they would take with them to America, where similarly vicious efforts to subdue and subjugate the natives ultimately succeeded—as they never did in Ireland.

The Irish experience led the English to another important (and related) assumption about colonization: that English settlements in distant lands must retain a rigid separation from the native population. In Ireland, English colonizers established what they called "plantations," transplantings of English society to a foreign land. Unlike the Spanish in America, the English would not simply rule a subdued native population; they would build a complete society of their own, peopled with emigrants from England itself. The new society would exist within a "pale of settlement," an area physically separated from the natives. That concept, too, they would take with them to the New World.

French and Dutch Rivals

Unlike in Ireland, English settlers in America were to encounter not only natives but also rival Europeans. To the south and southwest were the scattered North American outposts of the Spanish Empire. Despite a peace negotiated with England in 1604, the Spanish continued to look on the English as intruders, and for many years, the English in their settlements along the coast could not feel entirely safe from attack by Spanish ships.

But another and more formidable rival was appearing in the northern parts of the continent in the early sixteenth century: the French. France founded its first permanent settlement in America at Quebec in 1608, less than a year after the English had started their first at Jamestown, but the colony grew in population very slowly. Few French Catholics felt any inclination to leave their homeland, and French Protestants, some of whom might have wished to emigrate, were excluded from the colony. To the English in America, however, the French presented a danger disproportionate to their numbers, largely because of their close ties to the Algonquan Indians.

Unlike the English, who for many years hugged

Cartier in Canada
This early engraving of the French explorer, Jacques Cartier, shows him leading a group of settlers into what is now Canada. Cartier made three voyages of exploration to the New World between 1534 and 1542. On the last he attempted unsuccessfully to establish a permanent European colony along the St. Lawrence River, which he had discovered. Unlike some of the early English colonizing efforts, Cartier's included women as well as men—as this illustration reveals. (Huntington Library)

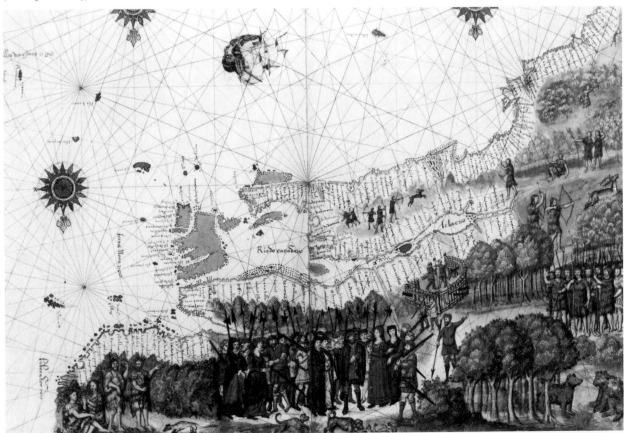

more forward slowly

close to the coastline and traded with the Indians of the interior through intermediaries, the French forged close, direct ties with the Hurons and and other Algonquan tribes deep inside the continent. *Coureurs de bois*—fearless fur traders and trappers—penetrated far into the wilderness; they befriended the Indians, often lived among them, and at times married Indian women.

They also generated important resentments. Through their ties with the Algonquans and through their own tactics, the French were antagonizing the Iroquois, the Algonquans' traditional foes and the most important middlemen in the English fur trade. In 1609, Samuel de Champlain, founder of Quebec and discoverer of Lake Champlain, led an attack on a band of Iroquois, apparently at the instigation of his Algonquan trading partners. The encounter marked the beginning of a historic enmity between the Iroquois and the French, an enmity steadily intensified by the Iroquois resentment of French commercial competition.

Besides the Spanish and the French, the English were soon to find in the New World another European rival, the Dutch. Holland in the early seventeenth century, having won its independence from Spain, was one of the leading trading nations of the world. Its merchant fleet was larger than England's, and its traders were active not only in Europe but in Africa, Asia, and—increasingly—in America. In 1609, an English explorer in the employ of the Dutch, Henry Hudson, sailed up the river that was to be named for him, convinced for a time that he had found the long-sought water route through the continent to the Pacific. He had not found it, of course; but his explorations led to a Dutch claim on territory in America and to the establishment of a permanent Dutch presence in the New World.

For more than a decade after Hudson's voyage, the Dutch maintained an active trade in furs in and around what is now New York. Not long after the first two permanent English colonies took root in Jamestown and Plymouth, the Dutch created a wedge between them when the Dutch West India Company established in 1624 a series of permanent trading posts on the Hudson, Delaware, and Connecticut rivers. The company actively encouraged settlement of the region—not just from Holland itself, but from such other parts of northern Europe as Germany, Sweden, and Finland. It transported whole families to the New World and granted vast feudal estates to "patroons" who would bring still more immigrants to America. The result was the colony of New Netherland and its principal town, New Amsterdam, on Manhattan Is-

land. Its population, diverse as it was, remained relatively small; and the colony was only loosely united, with chronically weak leadership. It would ultimately prove a much less serious rival to English domination of the region than the French.

The First English Settlements

The first permanent English settlement in the New World was established at Jamestown, in Virginia, in 1607. But for nearly thirty years before that, English merchants and adventurers had been engaged in a series of failed efforts to create colonies in the New World. Those failures helped prepare the way for the more lasting ventures to come.

Through much of the sixteenth century, the English had harbored mixed feelings about the New World. They were aware of its existence and intrigued by its possibilities. And like other European peoples, they were—under the leadership of their brilliant and popular ruler, Elizabeth I—developing a strong sense of nationalism that encouraged dreams of expansion into America. At the same time, however, England was leery of Spain, which remained the dominant force in America and, it seemed, the dominant naval power in Europe. Especially after Elizabeth dissolved the Anglo-Spanish alliance that her predecessor, Mary, had created, England remained for a time cowed by the Spanish threat.

All of that changed in the course of the 1570s and 1580s. English "sea dogs" such as Sir Francis Drake won nationwide fame for their successful raids on Spanish merchant ships and began the process of raising confidence about England's ability to challenge Spanish seapower. But far more important was a single event: the attempted invasion of England by the Spanish Armada in 1588. Philip II, the powerful Spanish king who had recently united his nation with Portugal, was determined to subjugate his annoying English rival—to end its challenge to Spanish commercial supremacy and to bring that nation back into the Catholic church. He assembled one of the largest military fleets in the history of warfare to carry his troops across the English Channel and into England itself. But Philip's bold venture turned into a fiasco *complete failure* when the smaller English fleet, taking advantage of its greater maneuverability and the English seafarers' superior knowledge of the waters, dispersed the armada and, in a single stroke, ended Spain's domination of the Atlantic. What inhibitions the English had retained about establishing themselves in the New World were now removed.

The pioneers of English colonization were Sir

Humphrey Gilbert and his half-brother Sir Walter Raleigh—both friends of Queen Elizabeth, both veterans of earlier colonial efforts in Ireland. Even before the defeat of the armada, Gilbert was insisting at court that English bases in America would give still greater opportunities for sapping the power of Spain. In 1578, he obtained from Elizabeth a patent granting him, for six years, the exclusive right "to inhabit and possess at his choice all remote and heathen lands not in the actual possession of any Christian prince."

That same year, Gilbert and Raleigh, with seven ships and nearly 400 men, set out to establish a base in the New World; but storms turned them back before they had crossed the ocean. Gilbert waited five years while he sought to raise enough money to try again. Then, in 1583, he sailed with a second and smaller expedition, reached Newfoundland, and took possession of it in the queen's name. He proceeded southward along the coast, looking for a good place to build a military outpost that might eventually grow into a profitable colony, of which he would be proprietor. Once more a storm defeated him; this time his ship sank, and he was lost at sea.

Raleigh was undeterred. The next year, he secured from Elizabeth a six-year grant similar to Gilbert's and sent a small group of men on an expedition to explore the North American coast. They returned with two captive Indians and with glowing reports of what they had seen. They were particularly enthusiastic about an island the natives called Roanoke and about the area of the mainland just beyond it (in what is now North Carolina). Raleigh, an astute politician, received permission from Elizabeth to name the region "Virginia" in honor of the "virgin queen." He hoped for financial aid in return. Elizabeth offered none. So Raleigh turned to private investors to finance another expedition.

In 1585, Raleigh recruited his cousin, Sir Richard

Roanoke

A drawing by one of the English colonists in the ill-fated Roanoke expedition of 1585 became the basis for this engraving by Theodore DeBry, published in England in 1590. A small European ship carrying settlers approaches the island of Roanoke, at left. The wreckage of several larger vessels farther out to sea and the presence of Indian settlements on the mainland and on Roanoke itself suggest some of the perils the settlers encountered. (New York Public Library)

Grenville, to lead a group of men (most of them from the English plantations in Ireland) to Roanoke to establish a colony. Grenville deposited the settlers on the island, remained long enough to antagonize the natives (by razing an Indian village as retaliation for a minor theft), and returned to England. The following spring, when supplies and reinforcements from England were long overdue, Sir Francis Drake unexpectedly arrived in Roanoke. The colonists boarded his ships and left.

Raleigh tried again in 1587, sending an expedition carrying ninety-one men, seventeen women (two of them pregnant), and nine children—the nucleus, he hoped, of a viable "plantation." The settlers landed on Roanoke and attempted to take up where the first group of colonists had left off. (Shortly after arriving, one of the women gave birth to a daughter, Virginia Dare, the first American-born child of English parents.) Their commander, John White, returned to England after several weeks (leaving members of his own family behind) in search of supplies and additional settlers; he hoped to return in a few months. But the hostilities with Spain intervened, and White did not return to the island for three years. When he did, in 1590, he found the island utterly deserted, with no clues as to the fate of the settlers. Some have argued that the colonists were slaughtered by the Indians, in retaliation for Grenville's (and perhaps their own) hostilities. Others have claimed that they left their settlement and joined native society, ultimately

Wildlife in the New World
Sometime in the 1590s, after he had retired from the seas, John White published these sketches of the wildlife he had encountered during one of his voyages to the New World. They portray a diamondback terrapin, and a swallowtail butterfly. White was one of the original explorers and colonists at Roanoke, but he was away in England when his daughter and granddaughter (Virginia Dare, the first English child born in America) vanished along with the rest of the settlers. (British Museum)

becoming entirely assimilated. But no conclusive answers to the mystery of the "lost colony" have ever been found.

The Roanoke disaster marked the end of Sir Walter

SIGNIFICANT EVENTS

30,000–25,000 B.C. Asians begin migrating to North America across the Bering Straits

1000 A.D. Scandinavian explorers establish temporary settlement in Newfoundland

1420s Portuguese explorers travel down west coast of Africa in search of sea route to Asia

1492 Columbus sails west from Spain in search of Asia, reaches Bahama Islands in the Caribbean

1494 Treaty of Tordesillas divides New World between Spain and Portugal

1497 John Cabot establishes first English claim in North America

1513 Ponce de Leon arrives on Florida mainland Balboa reaches Pacific Ocean by crossing Isthmus of Panama

1517 Martin Luther challenges Catholic church, sparking Protestant Reformation in Europe

1518–1530 Smallpox epidemic ravages Indian societies of Central and South America

1521 Cortés captures Tenochtitlán and conquers Aztec Empire in Mexico

1533 Pizarro captures Cuzco and conquers Incas in Peru

1558 Elizabeth I ascends English throne

1566 English conquest of Ireland begins

1585 "Lost Colony" established on Roanoke Island

1603 James I succeeds Elizabeth I in England

1606 James I establishes Virginia Company, divided between groups at London and Plymouth

Raleigh's involvement in English colonization of the New World. In 1603, when James I succeeded Elizabeth, Raleigh was accused of plotting against the king, stripped of his monopoly, and imprisoned for more than a decade. Finally (after being released for one last ill-fated maritime expedition) he was executed by the king in 1618. No later colonizer would receive grants of land in the New World as vast or undefined as those Raleigh and Gilbert had acquired. But despite the discouraging example of their experiences, the colonizing impulse remained very much alive.

In the first years of the seventeenth century, a group of London merchants to whom Raleigh had assigned his charter rights decided to renew the attempts at colonization in Virginia. A rival group of merchants, from Plymouth and other West Country towns, were also interested in American ventures and were sponsoring voyages of exploration farther north, up to Newfoundland, where West Country fishermen had been going for many years. In 1606, James I issued a new charter, which divided America between the two groups. The London group got the exclusive right to colonize in the south (between the 34th and 41st parallels), and the Plymouth merchants the same right in the north (between the 38th and 45th parallels). These areas overlapped, but neither company was allowed to start a colony within a hundred miles of the other. Each company, as soon as it had begun actual colonization, was to receive a grant of land 100 miles wide and 100 miles deep. The settlers themselves were to retain all the "liberties, franchises, and immunities" that belonged to English citizens at home. Through the efforts of these and other companies the first enduring English colonies would be planted in America.

SUGGESTED READINGS

American Indians   A good introductory account of American Indians, both before and after the arrival of Europeans, is Wilcomb E. Washburn, *The Indian in America* (1975). Other useful studies include Kenneth MacGowan and J. A. Hester, Jr., *Early Man in the New World* (1950); Harold E. Driver, *Indians of North America*, 2nd ed. (1970); and Francisco Guerra, *The Pre-Columbian Mind* (1971). Important studies of interaction between the Indians and the new settlers include Gerald B. Nash, *Red, White, and Black*, rev. ed. (1982); Alfred W. Crosby, Jr., *The Columbian Exchange: Biological and Cultural Consequences of 1492* (1972); Henry Warner Bowden, *American Indians and Christian Missions* (1982); and two works by James Axtell: *The European and the Indian: Essays in the Ethnohistory of Colonial North America* (1981) and *The Invasion Within: The Contest of Cultures in Colonial North America* (1985). See also Francis Jennings, *The Invasion of America: Indians, Colonialism, and the Cant of Conquest* (1975); Neal Salisbury, *Manitou and Providence: Indians, Europeans, and the Making of New England* (1982); and Nathan Wachtel, *The Vision of the Vanquished* (1977).

European Explorations   The European explorations of America are the subject of an unusually rich and sweeping literature. Of special importance is the work of Samuel Eliot Morison, in particular, *Admiral of the Ocean Sea*, 2 vols. (1942), a classic biography of Columbus, and *The European Discovery of America: The Northern Voyages* (1971) and *The Southern Voyages* (1974). See also J. H. Parry, *The Age of Reconnaissance* (1963), and David B. Quinn, *North America from Earliest Discovery to First Settlements* (1977).

Spanish America   Accounts of the Spanish conquests and early Spanish settlements include Charles Gibson, *Spain in America* (1966); James Lockhart, *Spanish Peru, 1532–1560: A Colonial Society* (1968); James Lang, *Conquest and Com-* *merce: Spain and England in the Americas* (1975); and J. H. Elliott, *The Old World and the New, 1492–1650* (1970). The latter two titles include treatment of English colonization as well.

England Looks West   For the European background of colonization, see W. H. McNeill, *The Rise of the West* (1963), and J. H. Parry, *Europe and the New World, 1415–1715* (1949) and *The Age of Reconnaissance* (1963). For England, see Wallace Notestein, *The English People on the Eve of Colonization, 1603–1630* (1954), a good introductory account. Peter Laslett, *The World We Have Lost* (1965), is a pioneering study of the social and demographic forces at work in premodern England, a subject that receives attention as well in Carl Bridenbaugh, *Vexed and Troubled Englishmen, 1590–1642* (1968). Treatments of the religious background of English colonization include Patrick Collinson, *The Elizabethan Puritan Movement* (1967); C. H. George and Katherine George, *The Protestant Mind of the English Reformation* (1961); Michael Walzer, *The Revolution of the Saints* (1965), a challenging and controversial interpretation; and Keith Thomas, *Religion and the Decline of Magic* (1971). David Quinn, *The Elizabethans and the Irish* (1966), and Nicholas Canniny, *The Elizabethan Conquest of Ireland* (1976), reveal some of the links between England's experiences in Ireland and in America. Other important studies of Tudor-Stuart England include Lawrence Stone, *The Crisis of the Aristocracy* (1965), and Mildred Campbell, *The English Yeoman Under Elizabeth and the Early Stuarts* (1942).

First English Colonies   See A. L. Rowse, *Sir Walter Raleigh* (1962), and two works by David B. Quinn: *The Roanoke Voyages, 1584–1590*, 2 vols. (1955), a collection of documents on the Roanoke experiment, and *Raleigh and the British Empire* (1947).

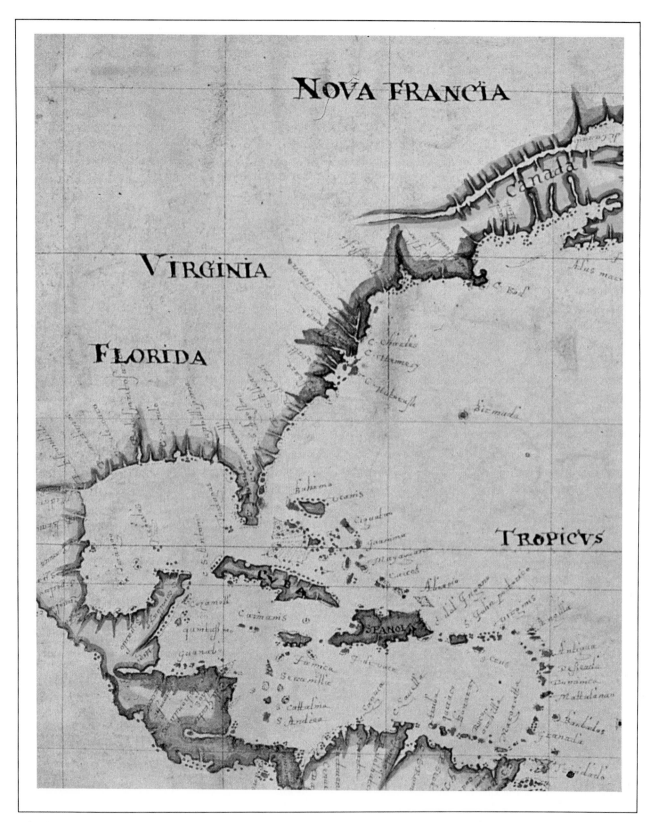

Virginia Company Map of the New World, c. 1607   (New York Public Library)

Chapter 2

The English "Transplantations"

The Roanoke fiasco dampened the colonizing enthusiasm in England—for a time. But the lures of the New World—the presumably vast riches, the abundant land, the religious freedom, the chance to begin anew—those lures were too strong to be suppressed for very long. Propagandizers such as Richard Hakluyt kept the image of America alive in English society; and by the early seventeenth century, the effort to establish permanent colonies in the New World resumed.

The first of these revived efforts were much like the earlier, failed ones. They were largely private ventures, with little planning or direction from the English government. They were small, fragile, and generally unprepared for the hardships they were to face. And although, unlike the Roanoke experiment, they survived, they were at first in many ways no less disastrous.

Three conditions in particular shaped the character of the first English settlements. First, the colonies were business enterprises. The colonists remained directly responsible to the private companies that had financed them, and one of their principal concerns from the beginning was to produce a profit for their corporate sponsors. Second, the English colonies, unlike the Spanish, were designed to be "transplantations" of societies from the Old World to the New. (Hence the term *plantation*, which was used to describe most of the first settlements.) As in Ireland, there were few efforts to blend English society with the society of the natives. The Europeans attempted, as far as they could, to isolate themselves from the Indians and create enclosed societies that would be entirely their own. And third, because the colonies were tied only indirectly to the crown (which chartered the private companies but took little interest in them thereafter), they began from the start to develop their own political and social institutions. However much the settlers may have wished simply to transplant English society to the New World, they were, in fact, developing a distinctive American society.

The Early Chesapeake

Once James I had issued his 1606 charters to the London and Plymouth companies, the principal obstacle to founding new American colonies was, as usual, money. The Plymouth group made an early, unsuccessful attempt to establish a colony at Sagadoahoc, on the coast of Maine; but in the aftermath of that failure, it largely abandoned its colonizing efforts. The London company, by contrast, moved quickly and decisively under the direction of the wealthy merchant Sir Thomas Smith. Only a few months after receiving its charter, the company launched a colonizing expedition headed for Virginia—a party of 144 men aboard three ships, the *Godspeed*, the *Discovery*, and the *Susan Constant*.

The Founding of Jamestown

Only 104 men survived the journey. They reached the American coast in the spring of 1607, sailed into Chesapeake Bay and up a river they called the James, and established their colony on a peninsula extending from the river's northern bank. They named it Jamestown.

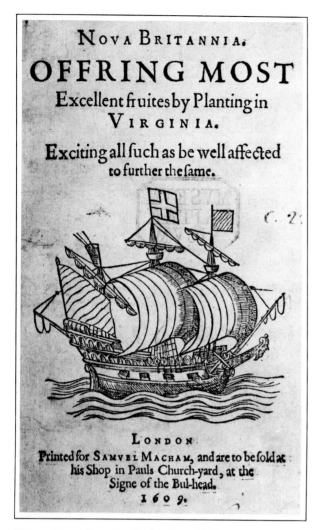

Recruiting for the Colonies, 1609
This title page for a pamphlet by Robert Johnson
describes the attractions of settlement in the New World.
Most accounts of the "excellent fruites" of life in
Virginia were, like this one, written by people who had
never seen America but who shared the excitement that
the colonies inspired among the early seventeenth-
century English.   (New York Public Library)

They chose their site poorly. In an effort to avoid
the mistakes of Roanoke (whose residents were assumed to have been murdered by Indians) and select
an easily defended location, they chose an inland setting that they believed would offer them security.
But the site was low and swampy, intolerably hot
and humid in the summer, and prey to outbreaks of
malaria. It was surrounded by thick woods, which
were difficult to clear for cultivation. And it en-
croached on the territories of powerful local Indians,
a confederation led by the imperial chief Powhatan.

The result could hardly have been more disastrous. For seventeen years, one after another wave of
settlers attempted to make Jamestown a habitable and
profitable colony. Every effort failed. The town became instead a place of misery and death; and the
London Company, which had sponsored it in the
hope of vast profits, saw itself drained of funds and
saddled with endless losses. All that could be said of
Jamestown at the end of this first period of its existence was that it had survived.

The initial colonists, too many of whom were
adventurous gentlemen and too few of whom were
willing laborers, ran into serious difficulties from the
moment they landed. Much like the Indians to the
south, who had succumbed quickly to European diseases when first exposed to them, these English settlers had had no prior exposure to the infections of
the new land and were highly vulnerable to local
diseases. Malaria, in particular, debilitated the colony. Even when it did not kill, it so weakened its
victims that they could do virtually no work. The
promoters in London added to the problems by demanding a quick return on their investment. Energies that would have been better spent growing food
and establishing the foundations of a new society were
diverted to futile searches for gold and only slightly
more successful efforts to pile up lumber, tar, pitch,
and iron for export.

The colony suffered as well from the absence of
women, which made it difficult for the settlers to
establish any semblance of a society. The English
were generally unwilling to intermarry with native
women (who were, in any case, not easily available
to them), and hence Jamestown was at first an entirely male settlement. Without women, settlers could
not establish real households, could not order their
domestic lives, and had difficulty feeling any sense of
a permanent stake in the community.

Greed and rootlessness contributed to the failure
to grow sufficient food; an inadequate diet contributed to the colonists' vulnerability to disease; the ravages of disease made it difficult for the settlers to
recover from their early mistakes. The result was a
community without the means to sustain itself. By
January 1608, when ships appeared with additional
men and supplies, all but 38 of the first 104 colonists
were dead.

Jamestown, now facing extinction, survived the
crisis largely as a result of the efforts of twenty-seven-

year-old Captain John Smith, a famous world traveler. Despite his implausible narratives of hairbreadth escapes from both Turks and Indians, Smith was a sensible and capable man. Leadership in the colony had been divided among the several members of a council, who quarreled continually until the fall of 1608, when Smith as council president asserted his will. He imposed work and order on the community. He also organized raids on neighboring Indian villages to steal food and kidnap natives. During the colony's second winter, fewer than a dozen (in a population of about 200) died. By the summer of 1609, when Smith was deposed from the council and re-

turned to England for the treatment of a serious powder burn, the colony was showing promise of survival.

Reorganization

The London Company (now calling itself the Virginia Company) was in the meantime dreaming of bigger things. In 1609, it obtained a new charter from the king that increased its power over the colony and enlarged its area (to a length of 400 miles north and south and a width extending all the way "from sea to sea, west and northwest"). It raised additional capital by selling stock to "adventurers," who would remain in England but share in future profits. It attracted new settlers by offering additional stock to "planters" who were willing to migrate at their own expense. And it provided free passage to Virginia for poorer people who would agree to serve the company for seven years.

The company envisioned Jamestown as a communal venture. Under its new charter, the company itself would hold title to all land in and control all trade with the colony for seven years. The settlers would contribute their labor to the common enterprise and draw on a company storehouse for subsistence. At the end of the seven years, the profits would be divided among the stockholders. In the spring of 1609, confident that it was poised now to transform Jamestown into a vibrant, successful venture, the company launched a "great fleet" of nine vessels—with about 600 men, women, and children aboard—headed for Virginia.

Disaster followed. One of the Virginia-bound ships was lost at sea in a hurricane. Another ran aground on one of the Bermuda islands and was unable to free itself for months. Many of those who reached Jamestown, still weak from their long and stormy voyage, succumbed to fevers before the cold weather came. That winter of 1609–1610 became known as the "starving time," a period worse than anything before. The local Indians, antagonized by John Smith's raids and other hostile actions by the early English settlers, killed off the game in the woods and kept the colonists barricaded within their palisade. The Europeans lived on what they could find: "dogs, cats, rats, snakes, toadstools, horsehides," and even the "corpses of dead men," as one survivor recalled. When the migrants who had run aground and been stranded on Bermuda finally arrived in Jamestown the following May, they found only about

Captain John Smith

John Smith was famous in England long before he became the leader and (many believe) the savior of the English settlement at Jamestown. According to his own immodest accounts, he had spent much of his youth in eastern Europe fighting in wars against the Turks and was even a slave in Turkey for a time. He returned to England from Virginia in 1609 but made one additional journey to North America five years later. In the years prior to his death in 1631, he wrote numerous books recounting and embellishing on his experiences. (Library of Congress)

60 people (out of 500 residents the previous summer) still alive—and even those were so weakened by the ordeal that they seemed scarcely human. There seemed no point in staying on. The new arrivals took the survivors onto their ship, abandoned the settlement, and sailed downriver for home.

That might have been the end of Jamestown had it not been for a strange twist of fate. As the refugees proceeded down the James toward the Chesapeake, they met an English ship coming up the river—part of a fleet bringing supplies and the colony's first governor, Lord De La Warr. The departing settlers agreed to return to Jamestown. New relief expeditions with hundreds of colonists soon began to arrive, and the effort to turn a profit in Jamestown resumed.

De La Warr and his successors (Sir Thomas Dale and Sir Thomas Gates) imposed a harsh and rigid discipline on the colony. They organized settlers into work gangs; they sentenced offenders to be flogged, hanged, or broken on the wheel. But this communal system of labor did not function effectively for long. Settlers often evaded work, "presuming that howsoever the harvest prospered, the general store must maintain them." Well before the end of the seven-year "communal" period designated by the Virginia Company, Governor Dale concluded that the colony would fare better if the colonists had personal incentives to work. He began to permit the private ownership and cultivation of land. Landowners would repay the company with part-time work and contributions of grain to its storehouses. Under the leadership of these first governors, Virginia was not always a happy place. But it survived and even expanded. New settlements began lining the river above and below Jamestown. This progress was partly because of the order and discipline the governors at times managed to impose. But in greater measure it was because the colonists had discovered at last a marketable crop—tobacco.

Europeans had become aware of tobacco soon after Columbus's first return from the West Indies, where he had seen the Cuban natives smoking small cigars (*tabacos*), which they inserted in the nostril. By the early seventeenth century, tobacco from the Spanish colonies was already widely in use in Europe. Sir Walter Raleigh had popularized the smoking habit, and the demand for tobacco soared despite objections on both hygienic and economic grounds. Some critics denounced it as a poisonous weed, the cause of many diseases. King James I himself led the attack with *A Counterblaste to Tobacco* (1604), in which he urged his people not to imitate "the barbarous and beastly manners of the wild, godless, and slavish Indians, especially in so vile and stinking a custom." Other critics were concerned because England's tobacco purchases meant a drain of English gold to the Spanish importers.

Then in 1612, the Jamestown planter John Rolfe began to experiment in Virginia with tobacco, a coarse strain of which local Indians had been growing for years. The soil and climate were well suited to the crop. Rolfe obtained seeds from the Spanish colonies and began growing tobacco of high quality in Virginia. It found ready buyers in England. Tobacco cultivation quickly spread up and down the James. The character of this tobacco economy—its profitability, its uncertainty, its land and labor demands—transformed Chesapeake society in fundamental ways. (See below, pp. 69–71.)

Of most immediate importance, perhaps, was the pressure tobacco cultivation created for territorial expansion. Tobacco growers needed large areas of farmland to grow their crops; and because tobacco exhausted the soil after only a few years, the demand for new land was incessant. English farmers began establishing plantations deeper and deeper in the interior, isolating themselves from the center of European settlement at Jamestown and encroaching on territory the natives considered their own.

Expansion

Even the discovery of tobacco cultivation was not enough to help the Virginia Company. At the end of the seven-year communal period in 1616, there were still no profits to divide, only land and debts. Nevertheless, the promoters continued to hope that the tobacco trade would allow them finally to turn the corner. In 1618, they launched a last great campaign to attract settlers and make the colony profitable.

The tobacco economy created a heavy demand not only for land but for labor. To entice new laborers to the colony, the company established what they called the "headright" system. Headrights were fifty-acre grants of land, which settlers could acquire in a variety of ways. Those who already lived in the colony received 100 acres apiece. Each new settler received a single headright for himself (or herself). In addition, anyone (new settler or old) who paid for the passage of other immigrants to Virginia would receive an additional headright for each new arrival—an inducement to the prosperous to bring new laborers to America. Hence wealthy settlers often received

Growth of the Chesapeake, 1607–1750

Boundary claimed by Lord Baltimore, 1632

PENNSYLVANIA

Boundary settlement, 1750

Frederick (1648)

Baltimore (1729)

MARYLAND

Providence (Annapolis) (c.1648)

Wilmington (Fort Christina) (1638)

WEST JERSEY

Dover (1717)

LOWER COUNTIES OF DELAWARE

St. Mary's (1634)

Fredericksburg (1671)

VIRGINIA

Fort Royal

Richmond (1645)

Fort Charles

James R.

Fort Henry

Jamestown (1607)

Williamsburg (Middle Plantation) (1633)

Yorktown (1631)

Newport News (1621)

Norfolk (1682)

Fort Christianna

NORTH CAROLINA

Elizabeth City (1634)

Albemarle Sound

Chesapeake Bay

Potomac R.

Rappahannock R.

0 50 Miles
0 50 Kilometers

Virginia Colony
Fairfax Proprietary
To Lord Baltimore, 1632
Granville Proprietary
(1649) Date settlement founded

meeting of an elected legislature, within what was to become in the next century the United States.

A month later, there occurred in Virginia another event that established a less happy but no less momentous precedent. As John Rolfe recorded, "about the latter end of August" a Dutch ship brought in "20 and odd Negroes." The status and fate of these first Africans in the English colonies remains obscure. There is some reason to believe that the colonists did not consider them slaves, that they thought of them as servants to be held for a term of years and then freed, like the white servants with whom the planters were already familiar. For a time, moreover, the use of black labor remained limited. Although Africans continued to trickle steadily into the colony, planters continued to prefer European indentured servants until at least the 1670s, when such servants began to become scarce and expensive. But whether or not anyone realized it at the time, the small group of blacks who arrived in 1619 marked a first step toward the enslavement of Africans within what was to be the American republic.

For several years, as the expansion of the colony proceeded, the European settlers had relatively peaceful relations with the Indians of the region. A truce of a sort had resulted from the capture of the great chief *stop fighting for a while*

headrights for themselves, for members of their families, and for the servants they imported to work for them. Some colonists were able as a result to assemble sizable plantations. In return, they contributed a small quitrent (one shilling a year for each headright) to the company.

The company added other incentives as well. To diversify the colonial economy, it transported ironworkers and other skilled craftsmen to Virginia. It promised the colonists the full rights of Englishmen (as provided in the original charter of 1606), an end to the strict and arbitrary rule of the communal years, and even a share in self-government. On July 30, 1619, in the Jamestown church, delegates from the various communities met as the House of Burgesses to consider, along with the governor and his council, the enactment of laws for the colony. It was the first

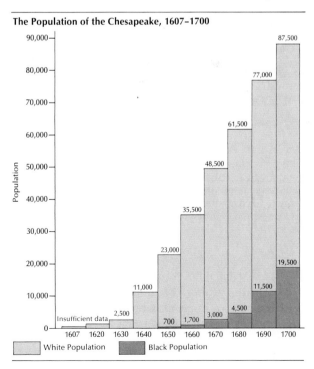

The Population of the Chesapeake, 1607–1700

White Population / Black Population

1607 Insufficient data
1620 2,500
1630 11,000 / 700
1640 23,000 / 1,700
1650 35,500 / 3,000
1660 48,500 / 4,500
1670 61,500 / 11,500
1680 77,000 / 19,500
1690 87,500
1700

An Indian Attack in Virginia
This 1662 illustration of an Indian attack on an English community in Virginia suggests the terror with which whites continued to view the native threat even five decades after the first settlements in the New World. The Europeans are depicted here as virtually helpless while half-naked "savages" slaughter men, women, and children indiscriminately. War canoes, filled with still more Indians, can be seen heading toward shore in the background, a reflection of the whites' awareness that—in the mid-seventeenth century at least—they were still greatly outnumbered.   (New York Public Library)

Powhatan's daughter Pocahontas and her marriage in 1614 to John Rolfe. (Pocahontas accompanied her husband back to England, where, as a Christian convert and a gracious woman, she stirred interest in projects to "civilize" the Indians. She died while abroad.) The death of Powhatan, however, marked

the beginning of the end of the tranquillity. Powhatan's half-brother, Opechancanough, became head of the native confederacy. He recognized, as his brother apparently had not, the dangers of the steady expansion of European settlement into tribal lands. He resented as well the continuing intrusions of English merchants and missionaries into his villages. And so the Indians under Opechancanough began secretly to plan the elimination of the intruders. On a March morning in 1622, tribesmen called on the white settlements as if to offer goods for sale, then suddenly attacked. Not until 347 whites of both sexes and all ages (including John Rolfe) lay dead or dying were the Indian warriors finally forced to retreat.

The surviving English struck back mercilessly at the Indians and ultimately turned back the threat, at least for a time. But the massacre was the final blow to the already staggering Virginia Company in London, which had poured virtually all its funds into its profitless Jamestown venture and now faced imminent bankruptcy. In 1624, James I revoked the company's charter; and the colony at last came under the control of the crown. So it would remain until 1776.

The worst of Virginia's troubles were now over. The colony had weathered a series of disasters and had established itself as a permanent settlement. It had developed a cash crop that promised at least modest profits. It had established a rudimentary representative government. And it could now realistically hope for future growth and prosperity. But these successes had come at a terrible cost. In 1624, the white population of Virginia stood at 1,300. Over the preceding seventeen years, more than 8,500 white settlers had arrived in the colony. More than 80 percent of them—7,200 people—had died.

Maryland and the Calverts

"The most notable feature of the Chesapeake settlements," the historian Wesley Frank Craven wrote, "is the absence of a common purpose and goal except such as was dictated principally by the requirements of their individual interest." That was true not only in Virginia but in the colony that soon grew up alongside it. Maryland was founded under different auspices and for different reasons, but it developed in ways markedly similar to its neightbor to the south.

Like Massachusetts, Maryland emerged in part from the desire of a religious minority in England to establish a refuge from discrimination. In this case, the minority was not dissenting Protestants but Roman Catholics. The new colony was the dream of George Calvert, the first Lord Baltimore, a recent convert to Catholicism and a shrewd businessman. Calvert envisioned establishing a colony both as a great speculative venture in real estate and as a retreat

for English Catholics oppressed by the Anglican establishment at home. He experimented first with a settlement in Newfoundland; but after spending one frigid winter there, he traveled south and decided to relocate his colony in the Chesapeake.

First, however, he had to return to England and win a charter from King Charles I (who succeeded to the throne on the death of his father, James I, in 1625). Winning a charter was a long process, and Calvert died while negotiations were still under way. But in 1632, his son Cecilius, the second Lord Baltimore, finally received a charter and made plans to continue the work his father had begun.

The Maryland charter was remarkable not only for the extent of the territory it granted to Calvert—an area that encompassed parts of Pennsylvania, Delaware, and Virginia, in addition to present-day Maryland—but for the powers it bestowed on him. He and his heirs were to hold their province as "true and absolute lords and proprietaries," and were to acknowledge the ultimate sovereignty of the king only by paying an annual fee to the crown. The Calverts could establish a government however they saw fit, adopt whatever methods they wished for distributing land, and even revive the medieval system of feudal dependency—awarding property to men who would become the vassals of the proprietor.

Since the Virginia Company (which still claimed its land rights in America) objected to the Calvert grant, Lord Baltimore remained at home to defend his interests at court. He appointed his brother Leonard Calvert governor and sent him with another brother to see to the settlement of the family's province. In March of 1634, two ships—the *Ark* and the *Dove*—bearing 200 to 300 passengers entered the Potomac River and turned into one of its eastern tributaries. On a high and dry bluff, these first arrivals laid out the village of St. Mary's (named, diplomatically, for the queen). The neighboring Indians, already threatened by rival tribes in the region, befriended the settlers, sold them land, and provided them with stocks of corn. The early Marylanders knew no massacres, no plagues, no starving time.

The Calverts had spent a large part of the family fortune in the development of their American possessions, and they needed to attract many thousands of settlers if their venture was to pay. As a result, they had to encourage the immigration of Protestants as well as their fellow English Catholics, who were both relatively few in number and generally reluctant to emigrate. The Protestant settlers (mostly Anglicans) outnumbered the Catholics from the start, and the Calverts quickly realized that Catholics would always be a minority in the colony. It seemed prudent to adopt a policy of religious toleration. To appease the non-Catholic majority, Lord Calvert appointed a Protestant as governor in 1648. A year later, he sent from England the draft of an "Act Concerning Religion," which assured freedom of worship to all Christians.

Nevertheless, politics in Maryland remained plagued for years by tensions between the Catholic minority (including the proprietor) and the Protestant majority. Zealous Jesuits and crusading Puritans frightened and antagonized their respective opponents with their efforts to establish the dominance of their own religion. There was frequent violence and, in 1655, a civil war that temporarily unseated the proprietary government and replaced it with one dominated by Protestants. The English in Maryland were spared serious conflict with Indians; but they made up for that by inflicting decades of conflict and instability on themselves.

Despite the latitude provided by their charter, the Calverts established a government in Maryland that soon resembled that of other colonies, and that of England itself. At the insistence of the first settlers, the Calverts agreed in 1635 to the calling of a representative assembly—the House of Delegates—whose proceedings were based on the rules of Parliament. Within fifteen years, the colony had a bicameral legislature, the upper house consisting of the governor and his council.

In other respects, however, the distribution of power in Maryland differed sharply from that in other parts of English America. The proprietor retained absolute authority to distribute land as he wished; and Lord Baltimore initially granted large estates to his relatives and to other English aristocrats, so that a distinct upper class soon established itself in Maryland. By 1640, a severe labor shortage in the colony had forced a modification of the land grant procedure; and Maryland, like Virginia, adopted a headright system—a grant of 100 acres to each male settler, another 100 acres for his wife and each servant, and 50 acres for each of his children. But the great landlords of the colony's earliest years remained powerful even as the population grew larger and more diverse. Like Virginia, Maryland became a center of tobacco cultivation; and as in Virginia, planters worked their land with the aid, first, of indentured servants imported from England and then, beginning late in the seventeenth century, black slaves imported from Africa. But unlike in Virginia, settlement and

trade remained dispersed, centered on scattered large plantations, and few towns of significance emerged.

Turbulent Virginia

By the mid-seventeenth century, the Virginia colony had survived its early disasters and was increasing both its population and the complexity and profitability of its economy. It was also growing more politically contentious, as emerging factions within the state began to compete for the favor of the government.

Virginia had been a royal colony, with its governor appointed by the king, ever since the collapse of the Virginia Company in 1624. One of those royal governors, Sir William Berkeley, dominated the politics of the colony for more than thirty years. He arrived in Virginia in 1642 at the age of thirty-six with an appointment from King Charles I; and with but one interruption he remained in control of the government until the 1670s, at times popular, at times faced with serious challenges.

The colonists responded enthusiastically to Berkeley's policies during the first years of his tenure. The governor helped to open up the interior of Virginia by sending out explorers who crossed the Blue Ridge Mountains. He directed a force that put down the Indians in 1644, when old Chief Opechancanough led them in a bloody attack comparable to the massacre of twenty-two years earlier. Opechancanough was captured and (against Berkeley's orders) was shot and killed. The defeated Indians agreed to a treaty ceding to England all the land between the York and the James rivers east of the mountains, and prohibiting white settlement to the west of them.

This attempt to prevent further encroachment on Indian territory—like many such attempts later in American history—was a failure from the start, largely because of the rapid growth of the Virginia population. Cromwell's victory in 1649 in the English Civil War (see p. 46) and the flight of many of the defeated Cavaliers to the colony added significantly to what was already a substantial increase from other sources. By 1650, Virginia's population of 16,000 was twice what it had been ten years before; by 1660, it had more than doubled again, to 40,000. As the choice lands along the tidewater became scarce, new arrivals and indentured servants completing their terms or escaping from their masters pressed on into the western territories. By 1652, English settlers had established three counties in the territory recently set aside for the Indians. There were frequent clashes between the Indians and the frontiersmen.

When Cromwell seized power in England in 1649, Berkeley had to give up the governorship of Virginia; but King Charles II reappointed him after the Stuart Restoration in 1660. Once back in office, Berkeley, by the force of his personality, and by his success in corrupting the council and the House of Burgesses, made himself practically an autocrat. When the first burgesses were elected in 1619, all men aged seventeen or older were entitled to vote. By 1670, the vote was restricted to landowners and elections were rare. The same burgesses, loyal and subservient to the governor, remained in office year after year. Each county continued to have only two representatives, even though some of the new counties of the interior contained many more people than the old ones of the tidewater area. Thus the more recent settlers on the frontier were underrepresented or not represented at all. A pattern was emerging in Virginia that would repeat itself time and again in other parts of America. New settlements in the west (or the "back country," as it was known) were growing larger and more prosperous, developing interests and political demands of their own. But more established elites near the coast continued to ignore the demands of the back country's citizens for representation and assistance. It was a situation that promised to produce social conflict.

Bacon's Rebellion

And in 1676, it did. Nathaniel Bacon, a young, handsome, ambitious graduate of Cambridge University, arrived in Virginia in 1673. His wealth and family background enabled him to purchase a good farm in the west and to obtain a seat on the governor's council. He established himself, in other words, as a member of the back country gentry—as part of the influential, propertied elite that was emerging in the western region of the state just as other elites had emerged earlier in the east.

The new back country gentry was different in crucial ways from its tidewater counterpart. Isolated geographically from the colonial government, western aristocrats sensed themselves cut off from real political power. As part of a new, still half-formed frontier economy, their position was always precarious, and it became even more so as Virginia began to suffer serious economic difficulties in the 1670s.

The result was a set of frustrations and resentments that came to a head in response to Berkeley's policies for dealing with Indians on the Virginia frontier. Property owners in the back country had long chafed at the governor's attempts to hold steady the line of settlement so as to avoid antagonizing the Indians. It was, they believed, an effort by the eastern aristocracy to protect its dominance by restricting western expansion. (It was also, in part, an effort by Berkeley to protect his own lucrative trade with the Indians.) Gradually, Bacon established himself as the leader of an opposition faction in western Virginia, which—in defiance of Berkeley—attempted to seize additional lands from the natives.

The result was predictable: a bloody confrontation between white settlers and Indians in 1676, in the course of which several hundred whites (including Bacon's overseer) were killed. Bacon and other concerned landholders demanded that the governor send the militia out to pursue and destroy the Indian marauders. Berkeley, however, continued to try to dampen the conflict. He ordered the militia merely to guard the edge of settlement, to engage in no aggressive actions against the Indians. Bacon was outraged; he organized an army of his own and launched a vicious but ultimately unsuccessful pursuit of the Indian challengers. When Berkeley heard of this unauthorized military effort, he dismissed Bacon from the council and proclaimed him and his men to be rebels.

At that point began what became known as Bacon's Rebellion—the largest and most powerful insurrection against established authority in the history of the colonies, one that would not be surpassed until the Revolution. When Berkeley, in an effort to increase his popular support, called for a new election of members of the House of Burgesses, Bacon became a candidate and was overwhelmingly elected. He then marched with his army to Jamestown to demand his seat. And there the young rebel, not yet thirty years old, confronted the governor, who was now seventy. Berkeley's first impulse was to have Bacon arrested and executed; but fearful of the consequences of hanging such a "darling of the people," he pardoned him, promised him a commission to fight the Indians, and restored him to his position on the council. When Bacon, temporarily pacified, departed with his army, the assembly passed a series of reforms, known as Bacon's Laws, to lessen the authority of the governor and transfer greater powers of self-government to the counties.

Convinced now that he had undermined Bacon's popular support, Berkeley withheld the promised commission and renewed the charge that Bacon was a rebel. Once again, Bacon led his army on a march from the frontier to Jamestown—this time gathering wide popular support as he came. Ultimately he forced Berkeley to flee, burned the capital, and—in the midst of widespread social chaos throughout the colony—stood on the verge of taking command of Virginia. Instead, he died of dysentery. Berkeley soon managed to regain control, at which point he saw to the repeal of Bacon's Laws and the execution of thirty-seven of the rebels.

Bacon's Rebellion was significant for several reasons. It revealed the bitterness of the competition among rival elites—and between easterners and westerners in particular—in the still half-formed society of the colonies. But it also exposed something Bacon himself had never intended to unleash: the potential for instability in the large population of free, landless men—most of them former indentured servants—who formed the bulk of Bacon's constituency. The problems of such men were severe and their grievances intense. They were without property and without employment; they were living in areas with few European women and thus were unable to form familial attachments. Instead, they came to constitute a large, floating population. And while Bacon had for a time maintained his popularity among them by exploiting their hatred of Indians, ultimately he found himself, without really meaning to, leading a movement that directed much of its animosity toward the landed gentry (of which Bacon himself was a part). In the years following Bacon's Rebellion, therefore, property owners in both eastern and western Virginia remained uneasy about the potential for revolution among the white lower class. That was one of several reasons for their turning increasingly to the African slave trade to fulfill their need for labor. Enslaved blacks might pose dangers too, but the events of 1676 suggested that the perils of importing a large white working class were even greater.

The Growth of New England

The Plymouth Company, which along with the London (later Virginia) Company had received a royal charter in 1606, never established a permanent settlement in America. It did, however, sponsor explorations of the territory to which it laid claim; and in the process, it gave the region a name. Captain John Smith, after his return from Jamestown, made an exploratory journey for the Plymouth merchants. He wrote an enthusiastic pamphlet about the lands he had seen, calling them "New England."

Plymouth Plantation

The first enduring settlement in New England—the second in English America—resulted from the discontent of a congregation of Puritan Separatists in England. For years, Separatists had been periodically imprisoned and even executed for defying the government and the Church of England; some of them, as a result, began to contemplate leaving England altogether in search of freedom to worship as they wished. It was illegal to leave the realm without the consent of the king; but in 1608 a congregation of Separatists from the hamlet of Scrooby began emigrating quietly, a few at a time, to Leyden, Holland, to begin their lives anew. There they could meet and hold their services without interference. But as aliens, they were not allowed to join the Dutch guilds of craftsmen, and so they had to work long and hard at unskilled and poorly paid jobs. They were particularly troubled by the effects of the tolerant atmosphere of Dutch society, which soon seemed to pose as much of a threat to their dream of a close-knit Christian community as had the repression in England. They watched with alarm as their children began to speak Dutch, marry into Dutch families, and drift away from their families and their church. As a result, some of the Separatists decided to move again, this time across the Atlantic, where they would, they hoped, be able to create the kind of community they wanted without interference and where they could spread "the gospel of the Kingdom of Christ in those remote parts of the world."

Leaders of the Scrooby group obtained permission from the Virginia Company to settle as an independent community with land of their own in Virginia. Although they failed in their efforts to secure a formal guarantee of religious freedom from James I, they received informal assurances that he would "not molest them, provided they carried themselves peaceably." (This was a historic concession by the crown, for it opened English America to settlement not only by the Scrooby group, but by other dissenting Protestants.) The next step was to arrange financing. Several English merchants agreed to advance the necessary funds to the Separatists, on the condition that they agree to a communal plan of settlement like that of Jamestown, with the merchants to share in the profits at the end of seven years.

The migrating Puritans "knew they were pilgrims" even before they left Holland, their leader and historian, William Bradford, later wrote. Their departure for America (from Plymouth, on the English coast) was delayed, and it was not until September 1620 that the *Mayflower,* with thirty-five "saints" (Puritan Separatists) and sixty-seven "strangers" (non-Puritans) aboard, finally put out to sea. By the time they sighted land in November, it was too late in the year to go on. Their original destination was probably the mouth of the Hudson River, in the northeast corner of the London Company's Virginia grant. But they found themselves instead on Cape Cod. After a few explorations of the region, they chose a site for their settlement in an area just north of the cape, an area John Smith had labeled "Plymouth" on his map.

Plymouth lay outside the London Company's territory, and the settlers realized that they would be without a government once ashore. Some of the "strangers" began to display an apparently lawless spirit; one of the "saints" therefore drew up an agreement, the Mayflower Compact, which forty-one of the passengers signed. The compact was like the church covenant by which the Separatists formed congregations, except that it established a civil government and professed allegiance to the king. Then, on December 21, 1620, the Pilgrims stepped ashore at Plymouth Rock.

They settled on cleared land that had been an Indian village until, four years earlier, a smallpox epidemic had swept through the region and depopulated it. The Pilgrims' first winter was a difficult one; half the colonists perished from malnutrition, disease, and exposure. Those who survived, however, managed to keep the colony alive.

The Pilgrims' experience with the Indians was, for a time at least, markedly different from the experiences of the early English settlers farther south. That was in part because the New England natives, decimated by smallpox, were significantly weaker than their southern neighbors. It was also, perhaps, because the Pilgrims were less actively hostile. They discovered important friends—Squanto, Samoset, Massasoit—who showed them how to gather seafood and cultivate corn. Squanto, who had earlier been captured by an English explorer and taken to Europe, spoke English and was of particular help to the new settlers. After the first harvest, the settlers invited the Indians to join them in an October festi-

Growth of New England, 1620–1750

(1639)   Date settlement founded

To Mason and Gorges, 1622

To Massachusetts Bay, 1629

To Plymouth Colony, 1630

To New Haven Colony, (1636)

To Hartford Colony, 1662

To Duke of York, 1664

To Rhode Island, 1663

The New England Population, 1620–1700

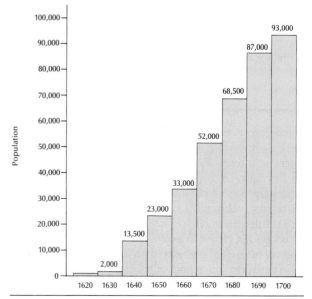

val, the original Thanksgiving. They could not aspire to rich farms on the sandy and marshy soil, but they soon developed a profitable trade in fish and furs. From time to time new colonists arrived from England, and in a decade the population reached the modest total of 300.

The people of "Plymouth Plantation" were entitled to elect their own governor, and they chose the remarkable William Bradford again and again. As early as 1621, Bradford won them title to their land by securing a patent from the Council for New England (the successor to the old Plymouth Company, which had charter rights to the territory). But he never succeeded in his efforts to obtain a royal charter giving the Pilgrims clear rights of self-government. Nevertheless, Bradford governed for many years without any real interference from England. He terminated the communal labor plan, distributed land among the families, and thus, as he explained it, made "all hands very industrious." He and a group of fellow "undertakers" assumed the colony's debt to its original financiers in England and, with earnings from the fur trade, finally paid it off—even though the financiers had not lived up to their agreement to continue sending supplies.

The Pilgrims were always a poor community. As late as the 1640s, they had only one plow among them. They clung, however, to the belief that God had put them in the New World for a reason, that they were serving as an example to the world of a truly Christian community. Governor Bradford wrote in retrospect: "As one small candle may light a thousand, so the light here kindled hath shone to many, yea in some sort to our whole nation." Ultimately, however, their light was overshadowed by the larger and more ambitious Puritan colonies to their north.

The Massachusetts Bay Experiment

Turbulent events in England in the 1620s (combined with the example of the Plymouth colony) generated a strong interest in colonization among other groups of Puritans. A protracted and often bitter struggle was in progress between king and Parliament; and for a time, religious dissenters suffered severely from the results. James I had created serious tensions for years by his effort to assert the divine right of kings and by his harsh, repressive policies toward Puritans. The situation worsened after his death in 1625, when he was succeeded by his son, Charles I. Charles was

even more aggressively autocratic than his father; and his efforts to restore Roman Catholicism to England and to destroy religious nonconformity launched the nation on the road that in the 1640s would lead to civil war. The Puritans were particular targets of Charles's wrath (many of them were imprisoned for their beliefs), and for them the climate of England was becoming intolerable. The king's dissolution of Parliament in 1629 (it was not recalled until 1640) ensured that there would be no political redress.

In the midst of this political and social turmoil, a group of Puritan merchants began organizing a new enterprise designed to take advantage of opportunities in America. At first, their interest was largely an economic one. They obtained a grant of land in New England for most of the area now comprising Massachusetts and New Hampshire; they acquired a charter from the king (who was evidently unaware of their religious inclinations) allowing them to create the Massachusetts Bay Company and to establish a colony in the New World; and they bought equipment and supplies from a defunct fishing and trading company that had attempted (and failed) to establish a profitable enterprise in North America. In 1629, they were ready to dispatch a substantial group of settlers to New England.

Among the members of the Massachusetts Bay Company, however, were a number of Puritans who saw the enterprise as something more than a business venture. They began to consider the possibility of emigrating themselves, of creating in New England a refuge for Puritans. Members of this faction met secretly in Cambridge in the summer of 1629 and agreed to move en masse to America if the other members of the company would transfer control of the enterprise to them. When those investors who preferred to remain in England concurred and sold their stock to the prospective emigrants, no obstacle remained.

The new owners of the company elected as their governor John Winthrop, a gentleman of means, university-educated, with a deep piety and a forceful character. Winthrop had been instrumental in organizing the migration; and he commanded the expedition that sailed for New England in 1630: seventeen ships and 1,000 people, the largest single migration of its kind in the seventeenth century. Winthrop carried with him the charter of the Massachusetts Bay Company, which meant that the colonists would be responsible to no company officials in England, only to themselves.

Unlike the two previous English settlements in America—Jamestown and Plymouth—the Massachu-

The Charter of the Massachusetts Bay Company
This is the first of four pages of a royal charter confirming the establishment of the Massachusetts Bay Company in 1629. Charles I, whose picture appears in the upper left corner, granted the charter. The Puritan leaders of the company took the document with them when they emigrated to America in 1630.   (Massachusetts State Archives)

setts migration immediately produced several new settlements. Although the port of Boston, at the mouth of the Charles River, became the company's headquarters and the colony's capital, colonists moved almost simultaneously into a number of other new towns in eastern Massachusetts: Charlestown, Newtown (later renamed Cambridge), Roxbury, Dorchester, Watertown, Ipswich, Concord, Sudbury, and others.

The Massachusetts Bay Company soon transformed itself into the Massachusetts colonial government. According to the terms of the original company charter, the "freemen" (the eight stockholders) were to meet as a General Court to choose officers and adopt rules for the corporation. But this commercial definition of government, which concentrated authority in what was, in effect, a corporate board of directors, quickly gave way to a more genuinely political system. The definition of "freemen" changed to include all male citizens, not just the stockholders. John Winthrop dominated colonial politics just as he had dominated the original corporation; but after 1634, he and most other officers of the colony had to face election each year. By 1644, the General Court had evolved into a bicameral legislature, with a lower House of Deputies and an upper chamber consisting of the governor and his council.

Unlike the Separatist founders of Plymouth, the Puritan founders of Massachusetts had come to America with no intention of breaking away from the Church of England. They only wanted, they claimed, to rescue the church from what they saw as the evil influence of Rome. Yet if they continued to feel any real attachment to the Anglican establishment, they

Boston Harbor
The founders of Boston (and of the Massachusetts Bay Colony, of which it was the capital) envisioned the town as a peaceful, harmonious, religious community. But they also hoped to create a thriving commercial center that would contribute to their own and the empire's prosperity. This early view of Boston harbor, showing the north battery, built in 1646, suggests the growing commercial orientation of the city even in its early years.   (Library of Congress)

gave little sign of it in their behavior. In every town, the community church had (in the words of the prominent minister John Cotton) "complete liberty to stand alone," without connection to any Anglican hierarchy and without adherence to Anglican ritual. Each congregation chose its own minister and regulated its own affairs. Thus arose in Massachusetts—as well as in Plymouth—what came to be known as the Congregational church.

The Massachusetts Puritans were not grim or joyless, as many observers would later come to believe. But they were serious and pious people. They strove to lead useful, conscientious lives of thrift and hard work, and they honored material success as evidence of God's favor. "We here enjoy God and Jesus Christ," Winthrop wrote to his wife soon after his arrival; "is this not enough?" Like the Pilgrims in Plymouth, he and the other Massachusetts founders believed they were founding a holy commonwealth, a model—a "city upon a hill"—for the corrupt world to see and emulate. But if Massachusetts were to become a beacon to others, it had first to maintain its own purity and "holiness." And to that end, the preachers and the officers of the government worked closely together. Ministers had no formal political power, but they exerted great influence on the church members, who alone could vote or hold office. The government in turn protected the ministers, taxed the people (members and nonmembers alike) to support the church, and enforced the law requiring attendance at services. In this Puritan oligarchy, dissidents had no more freedom of worship than the Puritans themselves had had in England.

Like other new settlements, the Massachusetts Bay colony had early difficulties. During their first winter (1629–1630), nearly 200 died and many others decided to leave. But more rapidly than Jamestown or Plymouth, the colony grew and prospered. The nearby Pilgrims and neighboring Indians helped with food and advice. Incoming settlers, many of them affluent, brought needed tools and other goods, which they exchanged for the cattle, corn, and other produce of the established colonists. The dominance of nuclear families in the colony (a sharp contrast to the early years at Jamestown) helped ensure a feeling of commitment to the community and a sense of order among the settlers. And the strong religious and political hierarchy ensured a measure of social stability.

John Winthrop
Unlike some English emigrants to America, John
Winthrop did not travel to the New World to improve
his economic circumstances. Born to a socially
prominent family, he had studied at Trinity College,
Cambridge, and had become a prosperous lawyer. His
strong Puritan views, and the dismay with which he
viewed the religious climate of early seventeenth-century
England, motivated him to establish a new society in
America. "The eyes of all people are upon us," he said in
his famous sermon, "A Model of Christian Charity,"
which he delivered on the ship *Arabella* shortly before it
arrived in New England. The new colony would be "a
city upon a hill," an example of virtue and godliness to
the rest of the world. (American Antiquarian Society)

Exodus from the Bay Colony

It did not take long for English settlement to begin
moving outward from Massachusetts Bay to various
parts of New England (and to other places in English
America). Eventually, such migrations would occur
as a result of the growing population pressures in the
original settlements. At first, however, it was a response to the unproductiveness of the stony soil
around Boston and the oppressiveness of the Massachusetts government.

Not all the incoming settlers were Puritan
"saints"; and as the population increased, the proportion of those who could vote or hold office declined.
The Puritan authorities considered opposition to their
church as much a threat to the community as heresy
or treason. Independent thinkers—and Puritanism
occasionally bred them—had little choice but to conform or leave. Such thinkers were responsible for
new settlements north and south, in New Hampshire
and Rhode Island. Families seeking richer lands as
well as greater religious and political independence
began new settlements in the west, in Connecticut.

The Connecticut Valley, 100 miles beyond the
settled frontier, contained such fertile lands that English families began moving there in the early 1630s,
despite the presence of native tribes more powerful
than those in eastern Massachusetts and despite the
claims of the Dutch to those lands. The valley appealed in particular to Thomas Hooker, a minister of
Newtown (Cambridge), who defied the Massachusetts government in 1635 and led his congregation
through the wilds to establish the town of Hartford.
Four years later, the people of Hartford and of two
other newly founded upriver towns, Windsor and
Wethersfield, established a colonial government of
their own and adopted a constitution known as the
Fundamental Orders of Connecticut. This created a
government similar to that of Massachusetts Bay but
gave a larger proportion of the people the right to
vote and hold office. Another Connecticut colony,
the project of a Puritan minister and a wealthy merchant from England, grew up around New Haven on
the Connecticut coast. The Fundamental Articles of
New Haven (1639) established a Bible-based government even stricter than that of Massachusetts Bay.
New Haven remained independent until 1662, when
a royal charter officially sanctioned the Hartford colony and awarded it jurisdiction over the New Haven
settlements.

Rhode Island had its origins in the religious dissent of Roger Williams, an engaging but controversial young minister who lived for a time in Salem,
Massachusetts. Even John Winthrop, who considered him a heretic, called Williams a "sweet and amiable" man; and William Bradford described him as "a
man godly and zealous, having many precious parts,
but very unsettled in judgment." Williams was a
confirmed Separatist who argued that the Massachusetts church should abandon even its nominal allegiance to the Church of England. He was friendly
with the neighboring Indians and proclaimed that the
land the colonists were occupying belonged to the

natives and not to the king or to the Massachusetts Bay Company. The colonial government considered Williams a dangerous man and voted to deport him, but he escaped before they could send him back to England. During the bitter winter of 1635–1636, he took refuge with Narragansett tribesmen; and the following spring he bought a tract of land from them and, with a few followers, created the town of Providence on it.

By that time another, greater challenge to the established order had appeared in Massachusetts Bay. Anne Hutchinson, an intelligent and charismatic woman from a substantial Boston family, had come to Massachusetts with her husband in 1634 as part of a community led by the minister John Cotton. Hutchinson shared Cotton's belief that the Holy Spirit dwelled within and guided every true believer. And she went further than Cotton in arguing that the faithful could communicate directly with God (as she claimed she herself had done) and that they could win assurance of grace and salvation—a direct challenge to the doctrine of predestination. Such teachings (known as the antinomian heresy) were a serious threat to the authority of both the church and the government, which insisted that faith was not open to differing personal interpretations. And Hutchinson served as well as an affront to prevailing assumptions about the proper role of women in Puritan society. She was not a retiring, deferential wife and mother, but a powerful religious figure in her own right (as well as an active midwife).

Hutchinson developed a large following among women (and ultimately also among men) in Boston. As her influence grew, and as she began to deliver open attacks on some members of the clergy, the Massachusetts hierarchy mobilized to stop her. Hutchinson's followers were numerous and influential enough to prevent Winthrop's reelection as governor in 1636; but the next year he returned to office and directed the orthodox ministers to charge her with heresy. In 1638, after a trial at which Winthrop himself presided and at which Hutchinson embarrassed her accusers by displaying a remarkable knowledge of theology, she was convicted of sedition and banished as "a woman not fit for our society." With her family and some of her followers, she moved to a point on Narragansett Bay not far from Providence. (Later still, she moved south into New York, where in 1643 she and her family died during an Indian uprising.)

In time, other communities of dissidents arose in Rhode Island. Roger Williams (who, having paid for

the land, considered himself the proprietor of the region) was advocating complete freedom of worship and denying that government had any authority at all over religious practice. In 1644, he obtained a charter from Parliament empowering him to establish a single government for the various settlements around Providence. The new government was based on the Massachusetts pattern, but it did not restrict the vote to church members nor tax the people for church support. A royal charter of 1663 confirmed this arrangement and added a guarantee of "liberty in religious concernments." For a time, Rhode Island was the only colony in which all faiths (including Judaism) could exist without interference.

New Hampshire and Maine were established in 1629 when two English proprietors, Captain John Mason and Sir Ferdinando Gorges, divided a grant they had received from the Council for New England along the Piscataqua River and created two separate settlements. Despite lavish promotional efforts, especially by Gorges, few settlers moved into these northern regions until the religious disruptions in Massachusetts Bay. In 1639, John Wheelwright, a disciple of Anne Hutchinson, led some of his fellow dissenters to Exeter, New Hampshire, and other groups—of both dissenting and orthodox Puritans—soon followed. The Massachusetts Bay Company tried to extend its authority over this entire northern territory; but after a long legal battle in England, New Hampshire became a separate colony in 1679. Maine remained a part of Massachusetts until 1820.

Settlers and Natives

It was inevitable, perhaps, that the expansion of European society in New England would eventually create serious conflicts with the Indians. In part, that was because of the attitudes of the Puritan settlers, who had from the beginning viewed the natives as "pernicious creatures" who should be either "civilized" by conversion to Christianity and European ways or, failing that, displaced or even exterminated. Occasionally, an exceptional colonial leader would advocate tolerance and respect for the Indian: Roger Williams in Rhode Island; or John Eliot, a missionary who translated the Bible into an Indian language. For the most part, however, the English attitude toward the natives was stern, disapproving, and often brutal. And the potential for conflict was greatly increased by the colonists' insatiable appetite for land and their steady encroachments into territory the natives considered their own.

In 1637, hostilities broke out between English settlers in the Connecticut Valley and the Pequot Indians of the region, a conflict that ended disastrously for the natives. White frontiersmen marched against a palisaded Pequot stronghold and set it afire. About 400 Indians died—burned to death in the flaming stockade or killed by the white attackers as they attempted to escape. Those who survived were hunted down, captured, and sold as slaves. The Pequot tribe was almost wiped out—an early step in a process of displacement and extermination of the tribes that would become a distinctive feature of American history for nearly two centuries.

The bloodiest and most prolonged encounter between whites and Indians in the seventeenth century began in 1675: a conflict that whites would remember for generations as King Philip's War. As in Connecticut nearly forty years before, an Indian tribe—in this case the Wampanoags, under the leadership of Metacomet, a chieftain known to the white settlers as King Philip—rose up in retaliation against the encroachments of the English settlers into what they considered their lands and (more immediately) against the efforts by a colonial government to impose English law on the native tribes. (A court in Plymouth had recently tried and hanged several Wampanoags for murdering a member of their own tribe.)

For over a year, the natives inflicted terror on a string of Massachusetts towns, destroying or depopulating twenty of them and causing the deaths of over 1,000 people (including at least one-sixteenth of the white males in the colony). The war greatly weakened both the society and the economy of Massachusetts. As before, however, the whites ultimately prevailed. Massachusetts leaders recruited guides and spies from among the so-called "praying" Indians of the region—natives who had been converted to Christianity by missionaries and who had settled in or near the towns of the whites. These new allies helped arrange an ambush in 1676 in which Metacomet was shot and killed. After that the fragile alliance that Metacomet had managed to forge among the local tribes collapsed, and the Europeans were soon able to crush the uprising. Some Wampanoag leaders were executed; others were sold into slavery in the West Indies. The power of the Wampanoags and their allies was forever destroyed.

Yet these victories by the white colonists did not end the danger to their settlements. This was in part because other Indians in other tribes survived, capable of launching future wars. It was also because the New England settlers faced competition not only

Metacomet

This eighteenth-century engraving by Paul Revere shows the Indian chieftain Metacomet, known to the English as King Philip of Mount Hope (the site of his tribe's principal stronghold). Metacomet, son of Massasoit, became chief of the Wampanoags in 1662 and inherited his tribe's resentment at having been forced from their lands along the Narragansett Bay by European settlers. In 1675, after several years of tension between the Wampanoags and English authorities in Plymouth, he launched the first of many attacks on white settlements in eastern Massachusetts, sparking the prolonged conflict that became known as King Philip's War. (New York Public Library)

from the natives but also from the Dutch and the French, who claimed the territory on which some of the outlying settlements were established. The French, in particular, would pose a constant threat to the English and would later support hostile Indians in their attacks on the New England frontier.

The Restoration Colonies

By the end of the 1630s, then, English settlers had established the beginnings of what would eventually become six of the thirteen original states of the American republic: Virginia, Massachusetts, Maryland, Connecticut, Rhode Island, and New Hampshire. But for nearly thirty years after Lord Baltimore received the charter for Maryland in 1632, the English government launched no additional colonial ventures. It was preoccupied with troubles of its own at home.

The English Civil War

England's problems had begun during the rule of the unpopular James I. James attracted widespread opposition before he died in 1625, but he never came into open conflict with Parliament. His son, Charles I, was not so fortunate. After he dissolved Parliament in 1629 and began ruling as an absolute monarch, he steadily alienated a growing number of his subjects—and the members of the powerful Puritan community above all. Finally, desperately in need of money, Charles called Parliament back into session and asked it to levy new taxes. But he antagonized the members by dismissing them twice in two years; and in 1642, they organized a military force, thus launching the English Civil War.

The conflict between the Cavaliers (the supporters of the king) and the Roundheads (the forces of Parliament, who were largely Puritans) lasted seven years. Finally, in 1649, the Roundheads defeated the king's forces, captured Charles himself, and—in an action that horrified not only much of continental Europe at the time but future generations of Englishmen and women—beheaded the monarch. To replace him, they elevated the stern Roundhead leader Oliver Cromwell to the position of "protector," from which he ruled for the next nine years. When Cromwell died in 1658, the Protectorate fell upon hard times. His son and heir proved unable to maintain his authority; and two years later, King Charles II, son of the beheaded monarch, returned from exile and seized the throne.

One result of the Stuart Restoration was the resumption of colonization in America. Charles II quickly began to reward faithful courtiers with grants of land in the New World; and in the twenty-five years of his reign, he issued charters for four additional colonies: Carolina, New York, New Jersey, and Pennsylvania. The new colonies were all proprietary ventures (modeled on Maryland rather than on Virginia and Massachusetts), thus exposing an important change in the nature of American settlement. No longer did private companies take an interest in launching colonies, realizing at last that there were no quick profits to be had in the New World. In their place were emerging ventures with different aims: not so much quick commercial success as permanent settlements that would provide proprietors with land and power.

The Carolinas

Carolina (a name derived from the Latin form of "Charles," *Carolinus*) was, like Maryland, carved in part from the original Virginia grant. Charles II awarded the territory to a group of eight court favorites, all prominent politicians already active in colonial affairs. In successive charters issued in 1663 and 1665, the eight proprietors received joint title to a vast territory stretching south to the Florida peninsula and west to the Pacific Ocean. Like Lord Baltimore, they received almost kingly powers over their grant.

Also like him, they expected to profit as landlords and land speculators. They reserved tremendous estates for their own development; and they planned to sell or give away the rest in smaller tracts (using a headright system similar to those in Virginia and Maryland) and to collect annual payments as quitrents from the settlers. Although committed Anglicans themselves, they welcomed any settlers they could get, whatever their faith. Indeed, the charter of the colony guaranteed religious freedom to anyone who would worship as a Christian. The proprietors also promised a measure of political freedom: laws were to be made by a representative assembly. With these and other incentives, they hoped to attract settlers from the existing American colonies and thus to avoid the expense of financing expeditions from England.

Their initial efforts to profit from settlement in Carolina failed dismally. Governor Berkeley of Virginia, one of the proprietors, did manage to encourage a number of landless people from his own colony to settle in the area of Carolina just to the south, along Albemarle Sound. But the region was isolated by the Dismal Swamp and had no adequate harbor; and it grew slowly. Further south, there was for a time virtually no growth at all. A few early coloniz-

Charles Town Harbor Before 1739
Fifty years after its founding in the 1680s, Charles Town (later Charleston), South Carolina, was the largest city and the leading commercial center of the Southern colonies. This watercolor depicts the heavy traffic of English ships in and out of the harbor. (Colonial Williamsburg)

ing ventures were quickly abandoned, and most of the original proprietors soon concluded that the Carolina venture could not succeed. One man, however, persisted—Anthony Ashley Cooper, soon to become the earl of Shaftesbury. Cooper convinced his partners that since settlers were not going to flock to Carolina from other parts of North America, the proprietors themselves should finance expeditions to Carolina from England. And in the spring of 1670, the first of these expeditions—a party of 300—set out from England. Only 100 people survived the difficult voyage, but those who did established a settlement in the Port Royal area of the Carolina coast. Ten years later they founded a city at the junction of the Ashley and Cooper rivers, which in 1690 became the colonial capital. They called it Charles Town. (It was later renamed Charleston.)

The earl of Shaftesbury wanted a planned and well-ordered community with a uniform pattern of settlement and a clearly defined social order. With the aid of the English philosopher John Locke, he drew up the Fundamental Constitution for Carolina in 1669, a document that was more a response to their analysis of problems in England than a reflection of realities in America. According to this Constitution, the Carolina territory was to be divided into counties of equal size, with each county divided into equal parcels. The largest number of parcels would be distributed among the proprietors themselves (who were

to be known as "seigneurs"); a local aristocracy (consisting of lesser nobles known as "landgraves" or "caciques") would receive fewer parcels; and ordinary settlers ("leet-men") would receive less land still. At the bottom of this stratified society would be poor whites, who would have no political rights, and black slaves, whose subjection would be complete. "Every freeman of Carolina," the constitution stated, "shall have absolute power and authority over his Negro slaves, of what opinion or religion soever." Proprietors, nobles, and other landholders would have a voice in the colonial parliament in proportion to the size of their landholdings.

In fact, however, Carolina developed along lines quite different from the almost utopian vision of Shaftesbury and Locke. For one thing, the colony was never really united in anything more than name. The northern and southern regions of the colony remained widely separated and were socially and economically distinct from each other. The northern settlers were mainly backwoods farmers, largely isolated from the outside world, scratching out a meager existence at subsistence agriculture. They developed no important aristocracy and for many years imported virtually no black slaves. In the south, fertile lands and the good harbor at Charles Town promoted a far more prosperous economy and a far more stratified, aristocratic society. There too, however, the carefully planned social order of the Fundamental Constitution largely failed to take root. Settlements grew up rapidly along the Ashley and Cooper rivers, and colonists established a flourishing trade in corn, lumber, cattle, pork, and (beginning in the 1690s) rice—which was to become the colony's principal commercial crop. Traders from the interior used Charles Town to market furs, hides, and Indian slaves.

Southern Carolina very early developed close ties to the large (and now overpopulated) European colony on the island of Barbados. For many years, Barbados was Carolina's most important trading partner. And during the first ten years of settlement, most of the new settlers in Carolina were Barbadians, some of whom arrived with large groups of black workers and established themselves quickly as substantial landlords. African slavery had taken root on Barbados earlier than in any of the mainland colonies; and these Caribbean migrants—tough, uncompromising profit seekers—established a similar slave-based plantation society in Carolina. (The proprietors, too, encouraged the importation of blacks; four of them had a financial interest in the African slave trade.)

For several decades, Carolina remained one of the most factious of all the English colonies in America. There were tensions between the small farmers of the Albemarle region in the north and the wealthy planters in the south. And in southern Carolina there were conflicts between the rich Barbadians and the smaller landowners around them. After Lord Shaftesbury's death, the proprietors proved unable to establish order; and in 1719, the colonists seized control of the colony from them. Ten years later, the king divided the region into two royal colonies: North and South Carolina.

New Netherland and New York

In 1664, one year after he issued the Carolina charter, Charles II granted to his brother James, the duke of York, all the territory lying between the Connecticut and Delaware rivers. Unlike other such grants, however, this one faced a major challenge from prior European claims. Some of the territory presumably belonged to the Massachusetts Bay Company by virtue of the sea-to-sea grant it had secured decades before. A far more serious challenge, however, lay in the Dutch claim to the entire area, and in the existence of Dutch settlements at New Amsterdam and other strategic points.

The emerging conflict between the English and the Dutch in America was part of a larger struggle between the two nations in the seventeenth century arising from their commercial rivalry throughout the world. The English had particular reason for resenting the presence of Dutch settlements in the New World, where they served as a wedge between England's own northern and southern colonies and provided smuggling bases for the Dutch. In 1664, troop-carrying vessels of the English navy, under the command of Richard Nicolls, put in at New Amsterdam and extracted a surrender from the arbitrary and unpopular Dutch governor, Peter Stuyvesant, who tried but failed to mobilize resistance to the invasion. Under the Articles of Capitulation, the colony surrendered to the British and received in return assurances that the Dutch settlers would not be displaced. Several years later, in 1673, the Dutch reconquered and briefly held their old provincial capital. But in 1674 they lost it again, this time for good.

The duke of York finally possessed New Netherland (which he renamed New York) both on paper and in fact; and he was free to rule virtually as an absolute monarch. But he recognized the problems inherent in governing a society with so diverse a population. New York contained not only Dutch and English but Scandinavians, Germans, French, and a large number of Africans (imported as slaves by the Dutch West India Company); and there were, of course, several different religious faiths among these groups. James made no effort to impose his own Roman Catholicism on the colony. Like other proprietors before him, he delegated powers to a governor and a council. The Duke's Laws, which the first governor, Roger Nicolls, issued, provided for no representative assemblies. (The English Parliament had overthrown and executed James's father, Charles I, and the duke was unwilling to see a similar breeding ground for revolt established in his American lands.) The laws did, however, establish local governments and guarantee religious toleration.

These concessions failed to satisfy all New Yorkers. Many settlers complained about the inequality of property holding and political power. In addition to confirming the great Dutch "patroonships" already in existence (among them, Rensselaerswyck, a vast 700,000 acre empire near Albany), James granted large estates to some of his own political supporters in order to create a class of influential landowners loyal to him. Power in the colony thus remained widely dispersed—among wealthy English landlords, Dutch patroons (who remained for many years an unassimilated and powerful minority), fur traders, and the

New Amsterdam
Shown here is the "Stadt Huys" (state house) in New Amsterdam, on Manhattan Island. New Netherland, of which New Amsterdam was the capital, was the principal Dutch possession in the New World until it was captured by the English in 1664 and renamed New York. Dutch influence in the colony remained strong long after control passed to England, as this 1679 drawing by the Dutch travelers Josef Dankers and Peter Stuyler suggests. (Long Island Historical Society)

duke's political appointees. Like Carolina, New York would for many years be a highly factious society.

By 1685, when the duke of York ascended the English throne as James II, New York contained about four times as many people (around 30,000) as when he had taken it over some twenty years before. Most of them still lived within the Hudson Valley, close to the river itself, with the largest settlement at its mouth, in the town of New York (formerly New Amsterdam).

Originally, James's claims in America extended south of the Hudson to the Delaware Valley and beyond. But shortly after receiving his charter, he gave a large portion of that land to a pair of political allies, both Carolina proprietors, Sir John Berkeley and Sir George Carteret. Carteret named the territory New Jersey, after the island in the English Channel on which he had been born. The new proprietors soon found themselves embroiled in a series of political disputes with the leadership of New York; and partly as a result, the venture in New Jersey generated few profits for them. In 1674, Berkeley sold his half interest to two enterprising members of the Society of Friends; and the colony was divided into two jurisdictions: East Jersey and West Jersey. The squabbling (and profitlessness) of New Jersey continued, and the Quaker proprietors of West Jersey began to look instead to the more tranquil, and as yet unsettled, lands to their west. In 1702, the two halves of the colony were again joined and became a single royal colony.

In one respect, at least, the European settlements in New Jersey resembled those in New York (from which much of the population had come). There was enormous ethnic and religious diversity, and there were relatively few efforts by the weak colonial government to impose strict control on the divergent groups in the population. But unlike New York, New Jersey developed no important class of large landowners; most of its residents remained small farmers. Nor did New Jersey (which, unlike New York, had no natural harbor) produce any single important city.

The Quaker Colonies

More than any other colony (except perhaps Massachusetts), Pennsylvania was born out of the efforts of dissenting English Protestants to find a home for their own distinctive social order. The Society of Friends originated in mid-seventeenth-century England and grew into an important force as a result of the preachings of George Fox, a Nottingham shoemaker, whose followers came to be known as Quakers from his admonition to them to "tremble at the name of the Lord." The essence of Fox's teachings was the doctrine of the Inner Light, the illumination from God within each soul, which when rightly heeded could guide human beings along the paths of righteousness. Unlike the Puritans, Quakers rejected the concepts of predestination and original sin. All people had divinity within themselves and need only learn to cultivate it; all could attain salvation.

A Quaker Meeting
An anonymous artist painted this view of a Quaker meeting in approximately 1790. Because the Society of Friends (or Quakers) believed that all people were equal in the eyes of God, they appointed no ministers and imposed no structure on their religious services. Members of the congregation stood up to speak at will.   (Museum of Fine Arts, Boston)

Of all the Protestant sectarians of the time, the Quakers were the most anarchistic and the most democratic. They had no church government except for periodic meetings, at which the congregations were represented on a local, regional, and national basis. They had no traditional church buildings, only meetinghouses. They had no paid clergy, and in their worship they spoke up one by one as the spirit moved them. Disregarding traditional social distinctions, they treated women as equals and addressed one another with the terms "thee" and "thou," words commonly used in speaking to servants and social inferiors. They refused to take oaths. And as confirmed pacifists, they would not take part in wars. The Quakers were unpopular enough as a result of these beliefs and practices, and they increased their unpopularity by occasionally breaking up other religious groups at worship. Many were jailed.

As a result, like the Puritans before them, George Fox and his followers looked to America for asylum. A few of them went to New England. But there (except in Rhode Island), they were greeted with fines, whippings, and banishment; three men and a woman who refused to leave were actually put to death. Others migrated to northern Carolina, and there, as the fastest-growing religious community, they soon were influential in colonial politics. But most Quakers desired a colony of their own, and Fox himself visited America in 1671–1672 to look over the land. As the head of a despised sect, however, he could not get the necessary royal grant without the aid of someone influential at the court. Fortunately for his cause, his teachings had struck the hearts of a number of wealthy and prominent men, one of whom in particular made possible a large-scale effort to realize the Quaker dream.

William Penn—whose father was Sir William Penn, an admiral in the Royal Navy and a landlord of valuable Irish estates—received a gentleman's education at his father's expense but could not overcome his mystical inclinations despite his father's discipline. Converted to the doctrine of the Inner Light, the younger Penn took up evangelism and, although always moderate and soft-spoken, was sent repeatedly to prison, where he wrote a powerful tract, *No Cross, No Crown*—the first of what would eventually be several dozen religious books. With George Fox he visited the European continent and found Quakers there who, like Quakers in England, longed to emigrate to the New World.

Penn turned his attention first to New Jersey, half of which (after 1674) belonged to two fellow Quakers and of which Penn himself became a proprietor. But in 1681, he received from the king an even more valuable grant of land. Penn had inherited his father's Irish lands and also his father's claim to a large debt from the king. Charles II, who possessed more land than cash, paid the debt with a grant of territory between New York and Maryland—an area larger than England and Wales combined and one that (unknown to him) contained more value in soil and minerals than any other province of English America. Within this fabulous estate Penn was to have the rights of both landlord and ruler; he was to make token acknowledgement of the feudal suzerainty of the king by the payment of two beaver skins a year. At the king's insistence, the territory was to be named Pennsylvania, after Penn's late father.

Like most other American proprietors, Penn intended to make money from land sales and quitrents and from private property to be worked for him. He promptly sold several large tracts to rich Quaker associates and one tract of 15,000 acres to a group of German immigrants. Through his informative and honest advertising—as in his pamphlet entitled *A Brief Account of the Province of Pennsylvania,* which was translated into several European languages—Penn made Pennsylvania the best-known and most cosmopolitan of all the colonies. Settlers flocked to the province from England and the Continent, joining a substantial group of Swedes and Finns who were already there. But Penn and his descendants were to find almost hopeless the task of collecting quitrents, and the colony never became a great source of profit for them. (Indeed, Penn himself, near the end of his life, was imprisoned in England for debt and died in poverty in 1718.)

Penn, however, was much more than a mere real estate promoter, and he undertook in Pennsylvania what he called a "Holy Experiment." Colonies, he said, were the "seeds of nations," and he proposed to plant in his realm the seeds of brotherly love. He devised a liberal Frame of Government with a representative assembly. He personally sailed to Pennsylvania in 1682 to oversee the laying out, between the Delaware and the Schuylkill rivers, of the city he named Philadelphia ("Brotherly Love"), which with its streets laid out in a grid, like those of Charles Town, helped set the pattern for most later cities in America. Penn believed, as had Roger Williams, that the land belonged to the Indians, and he was careful to see that they were reimbursed for it, as well as to see that they were not debauched by the fur traders' alcohol. Indians honored Penn as a rarity, an honest white man, and during his lifetime the colony had no major conflicts with the natives. More than any other English colony, Pennsylvania prospered from the outset—because of Penn's successful recruitment of emigrants, because of his thoughtful planning, and because of the region's mild climate and fertile soil.

In 1701, shortly before he departed for England for the last time, Penn agreed to a Charter of Liberties for the colony that established a representative assembly (consisting, alone among the English colonies, of only one house) and that greatly limited the authority of the proprietor. The charter also permitted "the lower counties" of the colony to establish their own representative assembly. The three counties did so in 1703 and as a result became, in effect, a separate colony: Delaware. Until the Revolution, however, it continued to have the same governor as Pennsylvania.

The Founding of Georgia

The establishment of the Restoration proprietary colonies expanded English settlement along the length of the Atlantic coast from New England to South Carolina. Although the population of each colony continued to grow, pushing the frontier of settlement steadily westward, for several decades there were no attempts to enlarge the English realm in America farther north or south. Not until 1733 did another new colony emerge: Georgia, the last English colony on the mainland of what would become the United States.

Georgia was unique in its origins. It was founded neither by a corporation (as Massachusetts and Virginia had been) nor by a wealthy proprietor (as in the case of Maryland, the Carolinas, Pennsylvania, and others). Its guiding purpose was neither the pursuit of profit nor the desire for a religious refuge. Instead, Georgia emerged from the work of a group of unpaid trustees. And while its founders were not uninterested in economic success, their primary motives were military and philanthropic. They wanted to erect a military barrier against the Spaniards on the southern border of English America; and they wanted to provide a refuge for the impoverished, a place where English men and women without prospects at home could begin a new life.

The need for a military buffer between South Carolina and the Spanish settlements in Florida was growing urgent in the first years of the eighteenth century. There had been tensions between the English and the Spanish ever since the first settlement at Jamestown; and although in a treaty of 1676 Spain had recognized England's title to lands already occupied by English settlers, conflict between the two colonizing powers continued. In 1686, Spanish forces from Florida attacked and destroyed an outlying

America in 1700

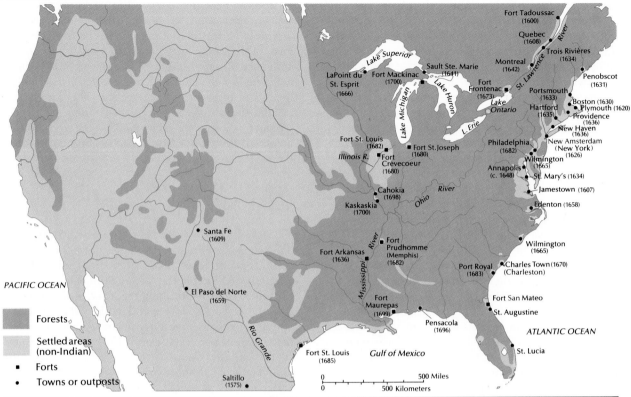

South Carolina settlement south of the treaty line. And when Spain and England resumed their war in Europe in 1701, hostilities erupted in America again. The war ended in 1713, but another European conflict with repercussions for the New World was continually expected.

General James Oglethorpe, a hero of the late war with Spain, was therefore keenly aware of the military advantages of an English colony south of the Carolinas. Yet his interest in settlement rested even more on his philanthropic hopes. As head of a parliamentary committee investigating English prisons, he had grown appalled by the plight of honest debtors rotting in confinement. Such prisoners, and other poor English people in danger of succumbing to a similar fate, could, he believed, become the farmer-soldiers of the new colony in America.

A 1732 charter from King George II transferred the land between the Savannah and Altamaha rivers to the administration of Oglethorpe and his fellow trustees for a period of twenty-one years. In their colonization policies they were to keep in mind the needs of military security. Landholdings were limited in size so as to make settlement compact. Blacks—free or slave—and Roman Catholics were excluded, to forestall the danger of wartime insurrection or collusion with enemy coreligionists. And the Indian trade was strictly regulated, with rum prohibited, to lessen the risk of Indian complications.

Oglethorpe himself led the first expedition, which built a fortified town at the mouth of the Savannah River in 1733 and later constructed additional forts south of the Altamaha. Only a few debtors were released from jail and sent to Georgia, but hundreds of needy tradesmen and artisans from England and Scotland, and religious refugees from Switzerland and Germany, were brought to the new colony at the expense of the trustees, who raised funds from charitable individuals as well as from Parliament. Although other settlers came at their own expense, immigrants were not attracted in large numbers during the early years. Newcomers generally preferred to settle in South Carolina, where there were no laws against big plantations, slaves, and rum. Before the twenty-one years of the trusteeship expired, those restrictions were repealed in Georgia, and after 1750, the new colony developed along lines similar to those of South Carolina.

The establishment of Georgia completed the political division of North America by the English. The thirteen colonies did not constitute a single nation; nor did they often think of themselves as part of a single society. Yet despite the radical variations among them, all shared one important characteristic: They were all subject to the authority of the British crown. Ultimately, that common political bond would force the diverse societies of the colonies into a fateful alliance.

The Development of Empire

The English colonies in America had originated as quite separate projects; and for the most part they grew up independent of one another, with little thought that they belonged—or ought to belong—to a unified imperial system. Yet the growing commercial success of the colonial ventures was by the mid-seventeenth century producing pressure in England for a more rational, uniform structure to the empire. Reorganization, many claimed, would increase the profitability of the colonies and the power of the English government to supervise them. Above all, it would contribute to the success of the mercantile system, which had become the foundation of the English economy.

The Navigation Acts

One of the arguments for colonization in the first place had been that colonies would increase the wealth of the mother country and lessen its dependence on other nations. According to the theory of mercantilism, English prosperity depended on increasing exports to foreigners and decreasing imports from them. Colonies would help by providing a market for England's manufactured goods and a source of supply for raw materials it could not produce at home. To benefit fully from its new possessions, England would have to exclude foreigners (as Spain had done) from its colonial trade.

In theory, the mercantile system offered benefits to the colonies as well by providing them with a ready market for the raw materials they produced and a source for the manufactured goods they did not. But some colonial goods were not suitable for export to England; the mother country itself produced wheat, flour, and fish and had no interest in importing them from America. And colonists often found it more profitable to deal with the Spanish, French, or Dutch even in the goods that England was willing to import. Thus a considerable trade soon developed between the English colonies and non-English markets.

For a time, the English government made no serious efforts to restrict this challenge to the principles of mercantilism; but gradually it began passing laws to regulate colonial trade. During Oliver Cromwell's Protectorate, in 1650 and 1651, Parliament passed laws to keep Dutch ships out of the English colonies. Under Charles II, after the Restoration, the government adopted three Navigation Acts. The first of them, in 1660, closed the colonies to all trade except that carried in English ships. This law also required certain items, among them tobacco, to be exported from the colonies only to England or to an English possession. The second act, in 1663, provided that all goods sent from Europe to the colonies had to pass through England on the way, and that they could be subject to English taxation in the process. And the third act, in 1673, was a response to the widespread evasion of the new export controls by the colonial shippers—who frequently left port claiming to be heading for another English colony but then sailed to a foreign port. The new act imposed duties on the coastal trade among the English colonies, and it provided for the appointment of customs officials to enforce the Navigation Acts. These acts, with later amendments and additions, were to form the legal basis of England's mercantile system in Amerca for a century.

The Dominion of New England

Enforcement of the Navigation Acts required not only the stationing of customs officials in America

ENGLISH MONARCHS, 1603–1702	
James I	1603–1625
Charles I	1625–1649
Charles II	1660–1685
James II	1685–1688
William and Mary	1688–1702

but the establishment of an agency in England to oversee colonial affairs. Except in Virginia—which became a royal colony in 1624, giving the king the right to appoint the governor—all the colonial governments operated largely independently of the crown. They had governors chosen by the proprietors or by the colonists themselves, and representative assemblies that were claiming increasing power for themselves. The king could not, therefore, rely on the colonial governments—least of all on Massachusetts, which behaved much like an independent republic and even usurped the sovereign's prerogative of coining money. Massachusetts merchants were particularly blatant in their violations of the Navigation Acts.

After a royal commission visited the Bay Colony and reported to London the extent of the colony's illegal business, Charles II acted to increase his control of Massachusetts in particular and the American empire in general. In 1675 he formed a special committee, the Lords of Trade (consisting of some of his official advisers on the Privy Council), to make recommendations for imperial reform. And following their advice to increase his control over the colonial governments, he moved in 1679 to deny Massachusetts authority over New Hampshire and chartered a separate, royal colony whose governor he would himself appoint.

The king wanted to make Massachusetts a royal colony as well, but he needed legal grounds to revoke its corporate charter. He soon found them. When the Lords of Trade ordered Massachusetts to enforce the Navigation Acts, the General Court replied that under the terms of the colony's charter Parliament had no power to legislate for the colony. And when the Lords of Trade sent a customs official to Boston to supervise the enforcement of the acts, the General Court not only refused to recognize him but arrested the local agents he appointed. Finally the king began legal proceedings that led, in 1684, to revocation of the charter.

Charles II's brother James II, who succeeded to the throne in 1685, went much further. He created a single Dominion of New England, which combined Massachusetts with the rest of the New England colonies and later with New York and New Jersey as well. He eliminated the existing assemblies within the new dominion, and appointed a single governor, Sir Edmund Andros, to supervise the entire region from Boston. Andros was an able administrator but a stern and tactless man; his rigid enforcement of the Navigation Acts and his brusque dismissal of the col-

onists' claims to the "rights of Englishmen" made him quickly and thoroughly unpopular.

The "Glorious Revolution"

James II was not only losing friends in America; he was making powerful enemies in England by attempting to exercise autocratic control over Parliament and the courts and by appointing his fellow Catholics to high office. By 1688, his popular support had all but vanished; and Parliament was emboldened to invite his Protestant daughter Mary and her husband, William of Orange, ruler of the Netherlands and Protestant champion of Europe, to assume the throne. James II (perhaps remembering what had happened to his father, Charles I) offered no resistance and fled to France. William and Mary became joint sovereigns. By this "Glorious Revolution," as the English called it, the long struggle between king and Parliament was at last largely settled, in Parliament's favor.

The Glorious Revolution had immediate consequences in the colonies. Bostonians, hearing of the challenge to James II in England, moved quickly to overthrow his American viceroy. A mob set out after Andros and other royal officials. Andros escaped but later surrendered and was imprisoned. The Massachusetts leaders hoped to win back their old corporate charter. Their hopes were not realized. While the new sovereigns made no effort to retain the dominion government James II had established, they did combine Massachusetts with Plymouth and establish it as a royal colony in 1691. Under the new charter, they themselves appointed the governor; but they restored the General Court and abolished the religious test for voting and officeholding.

Andros had been governing New York through a lieutenant governor, Captain Francis Nicholson, who enjoyed the support of the wealthy merchants and fur traders of the province—the same groups who had dominated the colony for years. Other less favored colonists—farmers, mechanics, small traders, and shopkeepers—had a long accumulation of grievances against both Nicholson and his allies. When they heard the news of James's fall in England and Andros's arrest in Boston, rebellious militiamen seized the New York City fort, and Lieutenant Governor Nicholson fled to England.

The leadership of the New York rebels fell to Jacob Leisler, a German immigrant and prosperous merchant who had married into a prominent Dutch family but had never won acceptance as one of the

SIGNIFICANT EVENTS

1607   Jamestown founded

1609   Pilgrims flee to Holland from England

1611   Tobacco production established in Virginia

1619   First African workers arrive in Virginia
Virginia House of Burgesses meets for first time

1620   Pilgrims found Plymouth colony

1622   Powhatan Indians attack English colony in Virginia

1624   Dutch establish settlement on Manhattan Island

1630   Puritans establish Massachusetts Bay colony at Boston

1634   First English settlements founded in Maryland

1635   Roger Williams founds settlement in Rhode Island

1636   Connecticut colony founded

1637   Anne Hutchinson expelled from Massachusetts Bay colony
Pequot War fought

1642–1648   English Civil War

1649   Charles I executed

1660   English Restoration: Charles II becomes king
First Navigation Act passed

1663   Carolina colony chartered
Second Navigation Act passed

1664   English capture New Netherland
New Jersey chartered

1675–1676   King Philip's War in New England

1673   Third Navigation Act passed

1676   Bacon's Rebellion in Virginia

1680   New Hampshire chartered

1681   William Penn receives charter for Pennsylvania

1685   James II becomes king

1686   Dominion of New England established

1688   Glorious Revolution in England: William and Mary ascend throne

1689   Glorious Revolution in America: rebellion breaks out against Andros in New England; Leisler leads rebellion in New York

1696   Parliament establishes Board of Trade and Plantations

1702   Queen Anne ascends throne

1713   Treaty of Utrecht concludes Queen Anne's War

1714   George I becomes king, beginning Hanover dynasty

1732   Georgia chartered

colony's ruling class. Leisler proclaimed himself the new head of government in New York; and when dispatches arrived from the king and queen addressed to "Our Lieutenant-Governor and Commander-in-Chief of our Province of New York, or in his absence to such as for the time being take care to keep the peace and administer the laws," he claimed that they were intended for him. For two years, he governed the colony; but in 1691, William and Mary appointed a new governor. Leisler resisted this challenge to his authority; and although he soon yielded, his hesitation allowed his old political enemies to charge him with treason. He and one of his sons-in-law were hanged, drawn, and quartered.

In Maryland, the people at first assumed (erroneously) that the Catholic Lord Baltimore had sided with the Catholic James II and had opposed the accession of William and Mary. So in 1689, an old opponent of the proprietor's government, John Coode, started a new revolt as head of an organization calling itself "An Association in Arms for the Defense of the Protestant Religion, and for Asserting the Right of King William and Queen Mary to the Province of Maryland and All the English Dominions." The insurgents drove out Lord Baltimore's officials and, through an elected convention, chose a committee to run the government. In 1691, William and Mary used this opportunity to deprive the proprietor of his authority and to transform Maryland into a royal colony. (It became a proprietary colony again in 1715, after the fifth Lord Baltimore joined the Anglican church.)

Thus the Glorious Revolution of 1688 in England touched off revolutions, mostly bloodless, in several colonies. Under the new king and queen, the representative assemblies that had been abolished were revived, and the scheme for colonial unification from above was abandoned. What was not abandoned, however, was the English government's commitment to increase its control over its colonial possessions. The new sovereigns made several provinces into royal colonies in which they appointed the governor and over which they had potentially greater direct control than in the past. Still, the events of the 1690s seemed to the colonists to confirm their belief that they had certain rights that England could not violate. That belief would survive to help shape their responses to the transformation of the empire in the eighteenth century.

SUGGESTED READINGS

General Histories   The classic and still the fullest account of the early English colonies in North America is Charles M. Andrews, *The Colonial Period in American History*, 4 vols. (1934–1938). Other general accounts include Clarence L. Ver Steeg, *The Formative Years, 1607–1763* (1964), and John E. Pomfret and F. M. Shumway, *Founding the American Colonies, 1583–1660* (1970).

Jamestown   The history of the early Jamestown settlement can be examined through the writings of its early leaders in *Travels and Works of Captain John Smith*, 2 vols. (1910). Modern studies include Bradford Smith, *Captain John Smith* (1953); Philip L. Barbour, *The Three Worlds of Captain John Smith* (1964); Alden T. Vaughn, *American Genesis* (1975); and Wesley Frank Craven, *The Dissolution of the Virginia Company* (1932).

The Chesapeake   A good introduction to the Chesapeake colonies is Wesley Frank Craven, *The Southern Colonies in the Seventeenth Century* (1949). An important examination of colonial Virginia is Edmund S. Morgan, *American Slavery, American Freedom* (1975). See also W. F. Craven, *White, Red, and Black: The Seventeenth Century Virginian* (1971), and Richard L. Morton, *Colonial Virginia*, 2 vols. (1960). For Bacon's Rebellion, see, in addition to the relevant chapters in Morgan, Wilcomb E. Washburn, *The Governor and the Rebel* (1958), and T. J. Wertenbaker, *Torchbearer of the Revolution* (1940). For Maryland, see David B. Quinn (ed.), *Early Maryland in a Wider World* (1982); Gloria L. Main, *Tobacco Colony: Life in Early Maryland, 1650–1720* (1982); and Lois G. Carr and David W. Jordan, *Maryland's Revolution of Government, 1689–1692* (1974). Thad Tate and David L. Ammerman (eds.), *The Chesapeake in the Seventeenth Century* (1979), is a collection of essays.

Plymouth   Plymouth Plantation, like Jamestown, can be studied through the writings of one of its founders: William Bradford, *Of Plymouth Plantation*, a landmark of American literature published in many editions, among them that of Samuel Eliot Morison (1952). See also George Langdon, *Pilgrim Colony* (1966), and John Demos, *A Little Commonwealth* (1970), an important social history of the settlement.

Massachusetts Bay   The founding of Boston and the Massachusetts Bay colony is examined in Samuel Eliot Morison, *Builders of the Bay Colony* (1930); Darrett Rutman, *Winthrop's Boston* (1965); and R. E. Wall, *Massachusetts Bay: The Crucial Decade, 1640–1650* (1972). On the political life of Massachusetts Bay and on the religious issues that underlay it, see Edmund S. Morgan, *The Puritan Dilemma: The Story of John Winthrop* (1958). Alden T. Vaughn, *New England Frontier: Puritans and Indians* (1965), examines the interaction between colonists and natives. Bernard Bailyn, *The New England Merchants in the Seventeenth Century* (1955), is a valuable study of the importance of commerce in the Puritan world.

New England Puritanism   The classic works remain those of Perry Miller, among them *The New England Mind: The Seventeenth Century* (1939), *The New England Mind: From Colony to Province* (1953), *Orthodoxy in Massachusetts* (1933), and *Errand into the Wilderness* (1956). More recent studies of Puritanism include Edmund S. Morgan, *Visible Saints* (1963) and *The Puritan Family* (1966); Sacvan Bercovitch, *The American Jeremiad* (1978) and *The Puritan Origins of the American Self* (1975); David Hall, *The Faithful Shepherd* (1972); Robert Middlekauff, *The Mathers* (1971); and Larzer Ziff, *Puritanism in America* (1973). Dissenters from Puritan orthodoxy are discussed in Edmund S. Morgan, *Roger Williams: The Church and the State* (1967); Kai Erikson, *Wayward Puritans* (1966), a study of the ideas of Anne Hutchinson that should be supplemented by Emery Battis, *Saints and Sectaries* (1962); and W. K. B. Stoever, *A Faire and Easy Way to Heaven* (1978). J. V. James, *Colonial Rhode Island* (1975), M. J. A. Jones, *Congregational Commonwealth: Connecticut, 1636–1662* (1968), and Paul R. Lucas, *Valley of Discord* (1976), examine two of the colonies created by the exodus from Massachusetts. Douglas Leach, *Flintlock and Tomahawk* (1958), examines King Philip's War.

The Restoration Colonies.   An important study of the English Civil War is Christopher Hill, *The World Turned Upside Down* (1972). The founding of the Restoration colonies receives attention in the general works mentioned above, particularly Andrews. For more specific treatment, see, for the Carolinas, H. T. Merrens, *Colonial North Carolina* (1964); M. E. Sirmans, *Colonial South Carolina* (1966); Clarence L. Ver Steeg, *Origins of a Southern Mosaic* (1975); Robert Weir, *Colonial South Carolina* (1983); Roger Ekirch, *Poor Carolina* (1981); and Peter H. Wood, *Black Majority* (1974), an important examination of relations among whites, blacks, and Indians in early South Carolina. On

New York, see Michael Kammen, *Colonial New York* (1975); Thomas J. Condon, *New York Beginnings* (1968); Van Cleaf Bachman, *Peltries or Plantations* (1969); and George L. Smith, *Religion and Trade in New Netherland* (1973). See also Patricia Bonomi, *A Factious People* (1971), for a valuable account of politics in early New York. On Pennsylvania, see Edwin B. Bronner, *William Penn's Holy Experiment* (1962); Mary Maples Dunn, *William Penn: Politics and Conscience* (1967); and James T. Lemmon, *The Best Poor Man's Country* (1972). J. E. Pomfret is the author of two studies of colonial New Jersey: *The Province of West New Jersey, 1609–1702* (1956) and *The Province of East New Jersey* (1962). For Georgia, consult T. R. Reese, *Colonial Georgia: A Study in British Imperial Policy in the Eighteenth Century* (1963), and K. Coleman, *Colonial Georgia* (1976).

The Development of Empire   The most comprehensive study of the eighteenth-century British imperial system is Lawrence Gipson's remarkable fifteen-volume work, *The British Empire Before the American Revolution* (1936–1970). Important studies of imperial administration of more modest length include two works by Stephen S. Webb, *The Governors-General* (1979), which challenges the traditional assumption that mercantilism was the primary motivating force behind the empire, and *1676: The End of American Independence,* which argues that the American colonies enjoyed virtual independence until the late 1670s, when the crown began to tighten its control. See also Michael Kammen, *Empire and Interest* (1970); Thomas C. Barrow, *Trade and Empire* (1967); I. K. Steele, *The Politics of Colonial Policy* (1968); and James Henretta, *Salutary Neglect* (1972). Michael Hall, *Edward Randolph and the American Colonies* (1960), examines the career of a colonial official. Viola Barnes, *The Dominion of New England* (1923), has long been the standard work on the imperial reorganization. Lawrence Harper, *The English Navigation Laws* (1939), examines problems of enforcement. The best general accounts of the events of 1688–1689 are David S. Lovejoy, *The Glorious Revolution in America* (1972), and J. M. Sosin, *English America and the Revolution of 1688* (1982). Sosin, *English America and the Restoration Monarchy of Charles II: Transatlantic Politics, Commerce, and Kinship* (1980), explores the background to the Glorious Revolution.

Detail from The Fishing Lady, a Sampler Embroidered c. 1750 (Museum of Fine Arts, Boston)

Chapter 3 # Life in Provincial America

As the extent of settlement in North America grew, and as the economies of the colonies began to flourish, several distinctive ways of life emerged. The new American societies differed considerably from the society they had all attempted, to one degree or another, to re-create in the New World: the society of England. They differed as well from one another.

There were three obvious reasons for the divergence between the culture of the colonies and that of the homeland. First, English society had not been transplanted whole to the New World; American settlers tended to be drawn from particular, and not entirely typical, segments of English society: the discontented, the adventurous, the visionary. Second, the immigrants found in the New World an environment so different—both physically and socially—from the one they had left that many elements of English society were never to take root in America. Third, some of the early colonists—and many more as time went on—were not English at all. Beginning with the Dutch settlements in New York, the area that would become the United States became a magnet for immigrants from many lands: Scotland, Ireland, the European continent. And beginning with the first importation of slaves into Virginia, English North America became the destination for thousands of forcibly transplanted Africans. English culture continued to predominate, but American society took its eventual shape from a wide range of influences.

Just as the colonies were becoming increasingly different from England, so were they different from one another. Not until the mid-eighteenth century did the colonists begin to call themselves "Ameri-cans"—and for good reason, because the pattern of society in some areas of North America seemed to resemble that of others scarcely at all. The civilization of Puritan New England differed markedly from that of the mid-Atlantic colonies; it differed even more from the plantation economies of the South. And although Americans would ultimately discover that they had enough in common to join together to form a single nation, these regional differences continued to affect their society well beyond the colonial period.

The Colonial Population

It was many years after the beginning of European colonization before the European settlers in North America came to outnumber the native population they found there. But after the uncertain beginnings at Jamestown and Plymouth, the European population grew rapidly and substantially—through continued immigration and through natural increase—until by the late seventeenth century, whites and their black servants became the dominant population group along the Atlantic coast.

The Early Population

A few of the early settlers were members of the English upper classes: usually the younger sons of the lesser gentry, men who stood to inherit no land at home and aspired to establish estates for themselves

This Indenture MADE the _Thirteenth_ Day of _May_
in the Year of our Lord one thousand, seven hundred and _eighty four_ BETWEEN
Alex.r Beard of Broughsham in the County of Antrim Taylor
by Consent of his Father of the one Part, and _John Duhey of Cullybackey_
in the said County——Gentleman—— of the other Part,
WITNESSETH, that the said _Alexander Beard_ doth hereby covenant, promise
and grant, to and with the said _John Duhey——his-——_Executors,
Administrators and Assigns, from the Day of the Date hereof until the first and next
Arrival at _Philadelphia——_in America, and after for and during the Term
of _three——_Years to serve in such Service and Employment as the said
_John Duhey——_or _his_ Assigns shall there employ _him_ according to the
Custom of the Country in the like Kind. In Consideration whereof the said _John_
Duhey doth hereby covenant and grant to and with the said _Alexr_
Beard to pay for _his_ Passage, and to find allow _him_ Meat, Drink, Apparel
and Lodging, with other Necessaries, during the said Term; and at the End of the said
Term to pay unto _him_ the usual Allowance, according to the Custom of the Country
in the like Kind. IN WITNESS whereof the Parties above-mentioned to these
Indentures have interchangeably put their Hands and Seals, the Day and Year first
above written.

Signed, Sealed, and Delivered,
in the Presence of

Peter Dillon   _Alexr Beard_

John Weir   _John Duhey_

A Certificate of Indenture

This contract, dated May 13, 1784, was made relatively late in the history of indentured servitude in America, but the printed form suggests the degree to which the system had long ago become standardized. Originally, such contracts were written in two identical parts on a single sheet, which was then torn in two. The documents thus were left with indented (or "indentured") edges—hence the term by which the contracts, and the system as a whole, became known.

in America. For the most part, however, the early colonial population was decidedly unaristocratic. It included some members of the emerging English middle class—businessmen who migrated to America for religious or commercial reasons or (like John Winthrop) both. But the dominant element was free English laborers. Some came to the New World independently. The religious dissenters who formed the bulk of the population of early New England, for example, were mostly men and women of modest means who arranged their own passage, brought their families with them, and established themselves from the start on their own land.

Others—especially in the Southern and later in the mid-Atlantic colonies—came as indentured servants. At least three-fourths of the immigrants to the Chesapeake in the seventeenth century arrived in that capacity. The system of temporary servitude in the New World developed out of existing practices in England. Young men and women bound themselves to a master for a fixed term of servitude (usually four to five years). In return they received passage to America, food, and shelter. Upon completion of their terms of service, male indentures (the vast majority) could expect to receive such benefits as clothing, tools, and occasionally land; in reality, however, many left service without anything approaching adequate preparation or resources to begin earning a living on their own. There was also a substantial minority of women indentures; most worked as domestic servants and were expected to marry when their terms of servitude expired.

Most indentured servants came to the colonies voluntarily, but some did not. Beginning as early as 1617, the English government occasionally dumped shiploads of convicts in America to be sold into servitude, although some criminals, according to Captain John Smith, "did chuse to be hanged ere they would go thither, and were." The government also transported prisoners taken in battles with the Scots and the Irish in the 1650s, as well as other groups deemed undesirable: orphans, vagrants, paupers, and those who were "lewd and dangerous." Still other involuntary immigrants were neither dangerous nor indigent but simply victims of kidnapping, or "impressment."

It was not difficult to understand why the system of indentured servitude proved so appealing to those in a position to employ servants in colonial America. It provided a means of coping with the severe labor shortage in the wilderness; and in the Chesapeake country the headright system (by which masters received additional land grants for every servant they imported) offered another incentive. For the servants themselves, the attractions were not always so clear. Those who came voluntarily often did so to escape troubles in England; others came in the hope of establishing themselves on land or in trades of their own when their terms of service expired. Yet the reality often differed sharply from the hope.

By the late seventeenth century, when indentured servants had become one of the largest elements of the population, serious problems were beginning to develop. Some former indentures managed to establish themselves quite successfully as farmers, tradespeople, or artisans. Others, however, found themselves without land, without employment, without families, and without prospects; and there grew up in some areas a large floating population of young single men—such as those who formed the backbone of Bacon's Rebellion—who traveled restlessly from place to place in search of work or land. These "herds of roving bachelors," as they have been called, became a particular source of social turbulence in the Chesapeake; but other regions had similar problems at times.

Even those free laborers who found employment or land for themselves and settled down with families often did not stay put for very long. The phenomenon of families simply pulling up stakes and moving to another, more promising location every several years was one of the most prominent characteristics of the colonial population.

Indentured servitude remained an important source of population well into the eighteenth century; but beginning in the 1670s, the flow began to decline substantially. A decrease in the English birth rate and an improvement in economic conditions there reduced the pressures on many English men and women who might otherwise have considered emigrating. After 1700, those who did travel to America as indentured servants generally avoided the Southern colonies, where working conditions were arduous and prospects for advancement slim, and settled in the mid-Atlantic colonies—especially Pennsylvania and New York—where they could anticipate better opportunities. That was one reason for the increasing centrality of black slavery in the Southern agricultural economy.

Birth and Death

At first, new arrivals in most colonies—whatever their background or status—could anticipate great hardship: inadequate food, frequent epidemics, and—in an appallingly large number of cases—early death. Gradually, however, conditions of settlement improved enough to allow the population to begin to expand. By the end of the seventeenth century, the European population in the English colonies of North America had grown to over a quarter of a million.

Although immigration remained for a time the greatest source of population increase, the most important long-range factor in the growth of the colo-

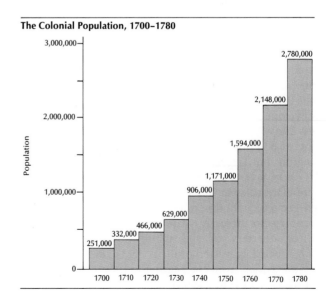

The Colonial Population, 1700–1780

nial population was its ability to reproduce itself. Marked improvement began in New England and the mid-Atlantic colonies in the second half of the seventeenth century, and after the 1650s natural increase became the most important source of population growth there. The New England population more than quadrupled through reproduction alone in the second half of the seventeenth century. This dramatic performance was less a result of unusual fertility (families in England and in the other colonies were probably equally fertile) than of extraordinary longevity. Indeed, the life spans of the early New Englanders were nearly equal to those of people in the twentieth century. In the first generation of American-born colonists, according to one study, men who survived infancy lived to an average age of seventy-one, and women to seventy. The next generation's life expectancy declined somewhat—to sixty-five for men who survived infancy—but remained at least ten years higher than in England and approximately twenty years higher than in the American South. Scholars disagree on the reasons for this remarkable longevity, but some of the factors that undoubtedly contributed to it include the cool climate and the relatively disease-free environment it produced, clean water (a stark contrast to England in these years), and the absence of large population centers that might breed epidemics.

Conditions improved much more slowly in the South. The mortality rates in the Chesapeake region did not begin to match those in the North until nearly a hundred years later. Throughout the seventeenth century, the average life expectancy for men in the region was just over forty years, and for women slightly less. Fully half of all children died before the age of twenty; those who survived often lost one or both of their parents before reaching maturity. The continuing ravages of disease (particularly malaria) and the prevalence of salt-contaminated water kept the death rate high in the South; only after the settlers developed immunity to the local diseases (a slow process known as "seasoning") did life expectancy greatly increase. Population growth was substantial in the region, but largely as a result of immigration.

Whenever they occurred, natural increases in the population were in large part a result of a steady improvement in the sex ratio through the seventeenth century. In the early years of settlement, more than three quarters of the white population of the Chesapeake consisted of men. And even in New England, which from the beginning had attracted more families (and thus more women) than the Southern

colonies, 60 percent of the inhabitants were male in 1650. Gradually, however, more women began to arrive in the colonies. Not until well into the eighteenth century did the ratio begin to match that in England (where women were a majority); but by the late seventeenth century, the proportion of males to females in all the colonies was becoming more balanced.

Women and Families

The importance of reproduction in the labor-scarce society of colonial America had significant effects on both the status and the life cycles of women. The high ratio of men to women meant that few women remained unmarried for long. The average European

A Boston Woman and Her Baby, c. 1674
This oil portrait by an unknown Boston artist is of Mrs. Elizabeth Freake and her daughter Mary. The lives of most New England women in the seventeenth century were largely consumed by childbearing and child rearing, although women also performed other important functions in the home-centered economies of the time. (Worcester Art Museum)

woman in America married for the first time at twenty or twenty-one years of age, considerably earlier than in England; in some areas of the Chesapeake, the average bride was three to four years younger. Widows generally remarried quickly.

In the Chesapeake, the most important factor in shaping the structure of families and the role of women remained, until at least the mid-eighteenth century, the extraordinarily high mortality rate. Under those circumstances, the traditional patriarchal family structure of England—by which husbands and fathers exercised firm, even dictatorial control over the lives of their wives and children—was difficult to maintain. Because so few families remained intact for long, rigid patterns of familial authority were constantly undermined. Sexual mores were also more flexible than in England or other parts of America. Premarital sexual relationships were frequent, and over a third of Chesapeake marriages occurred with the bride already pregnant.

Women in the Chesapeake could anticipate a life consumed with childbearing. The average wife experienced pregnancies every two years. Those who lived long enough bore an average of eight children apiece (up to five of whom typically died in infancy or early childhood); childbirth was one of the most frequent causes of female death. Few women survived to see all their children grow to maturity.

In New England, where many more immigrants arrived as part of a nuclear family and where death rates declined far more quickly, family structure was more stable and more traditional. Because the ratio of men to women was less unbalanced, most men could expect to marry. But women remained in the minority; and as in the Chesapeake, they married young, began producing children early, and continued to do so well into their thirties. Unlike in the South, however, their children were more likely to survive (the average family raised six to eight children to maturity); and their families were more likely to remain intact. Patriarchal customs prevailed, and women were less seldom cast in roles independent of their husbands.

Women may have been subordinate to their husbands, but they were at least as important to the New England agricultural economy as the men. Not only did they bear and raise children who at a relatively young age became part of the work force, but they themselves were continuously engaged in tasks vital to the functioning of the farm—gardening, raising poultry, tending cattle, spinning, and weaving, as well as cooking, cleaning, and washing.

Among other things, longevity meant that, unlike in the Chesapeake (where three-fourths of all children lost at least one parent before reaching the age of twenty-one), New England parents lived to see their children and even their grandchildren grow to maturity. The lives of most New England women were nearly as consumed by childbearing and child rearing as those of women in the Chesapeake. Even women who lived into their sixties spent the vast majority of their mature years with young children in the home.

The longevity in New England also meant that parents continued to influence their children's lives far longer than did parents in the South. They were less likely than parents in England actually to arrange marriages for their children; but few sons and daughters could choose a spouse entirely independent of their parents' wishes. Men tended to rely on their fathers for land to cultivate—generally a prerequisite for beginning a family of their own. Women needed a dowry from their parents if they were to hope to attract a desirable husband. Stricter parental supervision of children meant, too, that fewer women became pregnant before marriage than in the South (although even in Puritan New England, the premarital pregnancy rate was not insubstantial—as much as 20 percent in some communities).

The Beginnings of Slavery

The growth of the black population of early America occurred along lines very unlike those of the white population. Africans came to the New World to provide a labor supply for a white population too small to sustain its economy on its own and unable to recruit a native work force sufficient for its needs. They came under circumstances radically different from those of white immigrants. And their lives after arrival developed along very separate paths as well.

The demand for black servants to supplement the always scarce Southern labor supply existed almost from the first moments of settlement. The supply of African laborers, however, remained relatively restricted during much of the seventeenth century because of the nature of the slave trade. That trade had begun in the sixteenth century, when Portuguese ships began visiting the west coast of Africa. There they captured native men and women and shipped them across the Atlantic to the new colonies in South America. The commerce grew more extensive, more sophisticated, and more horrible in the seventeenth

WHY HISTORIANS DISAGREE

"Facts" Versus Interpretations

Unlike some other fields of scholarship, history is not an exact science. We can establish with some certainty many of the basic "facts" of history—that the United States declared its independence in 1776, for example; or that the North won the Civil War; or that the first atomic bomb was detonated in 1945. But wide disagreement remains, and will always remain, about the *significance* of such facts. There are as many different ways of viewing a historical event as there are historians viewing it. In reading any work of history, therefore, it is important to ask not only what facts the author is presenting but how he or she is choosing and interpreting those facts.

Historians disagree with one another for many reasons. People of different backgrounds, for example, often bring different attitudes to their exploration of issues. A black historian might look at the American Revolution in terms of its significance for the members of his or her race and thus draw conclusions about it that would differ from those of a white historian. A Southerner might view Reconstruction in terms different from a Northerner. Social, religious, racial, ethnic, and sexual differences among historians all contribute to the shaping of distinctive points of view.

Historians might disagree, too, as a result of the methods they use to explore their subjects. One scholar might choose to examine slavery by using psychological techniques; another might reach different conclusions by employing quantitative methods and making use of a computer. Because history is an unusually integrative discipline—that is, because it employs methods and ideas from many different fields of knowledge, ranging from science to the humanities, from economics to literary criticism—the historian has available an enormous range of techniques, each of which might produce its own distinctive results.

One of the greatest sources of disagreement among historians is personal ideology—a scholar's assumptions about the past, the present, politics, society. Historians who accept the teachings of Karl Marx and others that economics and social classes lie at the root of all historical processes will emphasize such matters in their examination of the past. Others might stress ideas, or the influence of particular individuals, or the workings of institutions and bureaucracies. A critic of capitalism, for example, might argue that American foreign policy after World War II was a reflection of economic imperialism. A critic of communism would be more likely to argue that the United States was merely responding to Soviet expansionism.

Perhaps most important, historical interpretations differ from one another according to the time in which they are written. It may not be true, as many have said, that "every generation writes its own history." But it is certainly true that no historian can entirely escape the influence of his or her own time. Hence, for example, historians writing in the relatively calm 1950s often emphasized very different issues and took very different approaches from those who wrote in the turbulent 1960s, particularly on such issues as race and foreign policy. A scholar writing in a time of general satisfaction with the nation's social and political system is likely to view the past very differently from one writing in a time of discontent. Historians in each generation, in other words, emphasize those features of the past that seem most relevant to contemporary concerns.

All of this is not to say that present concerns dictate, or should dictate, historical views. Nor is it to say that all interpretations are equally valid. On some questions, historians do reach general agreement; some interpretations prove in time to be without merit, while others become widely accepted. What is most often the case, however, is that each interpretation brings something of value to our understanding of the past. The history of the world, like the life of an individual, has so many facets, such vast complexities, so much that is unknowable, that there will always be room for new approaches to understanding it. Like the blind man examining the elephant, in the fable, the historian can get hold of and describe only one part of the past at a time. The cumulative efforts of countless scholars examining different aspects of history contribute to a view of the past that grows fuller with every generation. But the challenge and the excitement of history lie in the knowledge that that view can never be complete.

Africans Bound for America
Shown here are the below-deck slave quarters of a Spanish vessel en route to the West Indies. A British warship captured the slaver, and a young English naval officer (Lt. Francis Meynell) made this watercolor sketch on the spot. The Africans seen in this picture appear relatively comfortable compared to conditions on other slave ships, in which prisoners were often chained and packed together so tightly that they had no room to stand or even sit.
(National Maritime Museum, London)

century; and before it ended in the nineteenth century, it was responsible for the forced immigration of as many as 11 million Africans to North and South America and the Caribbean. (Until the late eighteenth century, the number of African immigrants to the Americas was higher than that of Europeans.) Flourishing slave marts grew up on the African coast, where native chieftains made large supplies of blacks available by capturing enemy tribespeople in battle and bringing them—tied together in long lines, or "coffles"—out of the forests and to the ports. Then, after some haggling on the docks between the European traders and the African suppliers, the terrified victims were packed into the dark, filthy holds of the ships for the horrors of the "middle passage"—the journey to America. For weeks, occasionally months, the black prisoners were kept chained in the bowels

of the slave ships, unable to stand, hardly able to breathe, supplied with minimal food and water. Women were often victims of rape and other sexual abuse. Those who died en route—and there were many—were simply thrown overboard. Slave traders accepted such deaths as an inevitable result of the system. They tried to cram as many Africans as possible into their ships to ensure that enough would survive to yield a profit at journey's end. Upon arrival in the New World, slaves were auctioned off to white landowners and transported—frightened and bewildered—to their new homes.

The first black laborers arrived in English North America before 1620; and as English seamen began to establish themselves'in the slave trade, the flow of Africans to the colonies gradually increased. But North America was always a much less important market for African slaves than other parts of the New World, especially the islands of the Caribbean and Brazil; fewer than 5 percent of the blacks imported to the Americas arrived in the English colonies. In the beginning, those blacks who did arrive in what became the United States came not from Africa, but from the West Indies. Not until the 1670s did traders start importing them directly from Africa to North America. Even then, however, the flow remained small for a time, mainly because a single group—the Royal African Company of England—maintained a monopoly on the trade and managed as a result to keep prices high and supplies low.

A turning point in the history of the black population in North America was 1697, the year that the Royal African Company's monopoly was finally broken. With the trade now opened to English and colonial merchants on a competitive basis, prices fell and the number of blacks arriving greatly increased. By the end of the century, about 25,000 slaves lived in America (approximately 10 percent of the population). But because blacks were so heavily concentrated in a few Southern colonies, they were already beginning to outnumber whites in some areas. The unbalanced sex ratio among African immigrants (there were perhaps twice as many men as women in most areas) retarded the natural increase of the black population. But in the Chesapeake, at least, the slave population by the mid-eighteenth century was increasing at a higher rate through reproduction than through continued importations from Africa. In South Carolina, by contrast, the arduous conditions of rice cultivation ensured that the black population would not be able to do more than barely sustain itself through natural increase until much later.

By 1760, the number of blacks in the colonies had increased tenfold since the turn of the century—to approximately a quarter of a million. A relatively small number (16,000 in 1763) lived in New England; there were slightly more in the middle colonies (29,000). The vast majority, however, continued to live in the South. By then, the flow of free white laborers to that region had all but stopped, and blacks had become permanently established as the basis of the Southern work force.

It was not entirely clear at first that the status of black laborers in America would be fundamentally different from that of white indentured servants. In the rugged conditions of the seventeenth-century South, it was often difficult for whites and blacks to maintain strictly separate roles. In some areas—South Carolina, for example, where the number of black arrivals swelled more quickly than anywhere else—whites and blacks lived and worked together for a time on terms of relative equality. Some blacks were treated much like white hired servants; and some were freed after a fixed term of servitude. A few blacks themselves became landowners, and some apparently owned slaves of their own.

Gradually, however, relations between the races evolved in such a way that by the early eighteenth century a rigid distinction had become established between blacks and whites. (See "Where Historians Disagree," page 67.) White servants were necessarily freed after a term of servitude, their masters being required by contract to release them. But there was no such legal necessity to free black workers, and the assumption slowly spread that blacks would remain in service permanently. Another incentive for freezing the status of blacks was that the children of slaves provided white landowners with a self-perpetuating labor force. White assumptions about the inferiority of the black race contributed further to the growing rigidity of the system; most whites considered blacks a lesser breed, capable of little more than manual labor. Indeed, many whites convinced themselves that they were actually helping the Africans by "civilizing" and Christianizing them; conversion to Christianity did not, however, entitle slaves to freedom.

Whites were willing to tolerate a certain ambiguity in the system when the number of blacks remained small; but by the early eighteenth century, once the slave trade increased and the black population began to grow, they moved quickly to clarify the status of Africans. The result was the evolution of a system of permanent servitude, a system made legal in the early eighteenth century when colonial assemblies began to pass "slave codes" limiting the rights of blacks and ensuring almost absolute authority for white masters. One factor, and one factor only, determined whether a person was subject to the slave codes: color. And while in the colonial societies of Spanish America, people of mixed race were granted a different (and higher) status than pure Africans, English America recognized no such distinctions. Any African ancestry was enough to classify a person as black.

New Immigration

Perhaps the most distinctive and enduring feature of the American population was its polyglot character, its bringing together of peoples of many different races, ethnic groups, and nationalities. The forced importation of Africans was one important contribution to this multicultural peopling of the new land,

WHERE HISTORIANS DISAGREE

The Origins of Slavery

How did the institution of slavery establish itself in the New World? How did white people come to believe that Africans should be kept in bondage? Historians have offered a number of different interpretations.

The debate had its origins in an important 1950 article by Oscar and Mary Handlin ("Origins of the Southern Labor System," *William and Mary Quarterly*). They pointed out that in the seventeenth century many residents of the American colonies (and of England) lived in varying degrees of "unfreedom," that there was nothing unusual or new about a dependent labor force. What was new was the transformation of black servitude in America into a permanent system, based on race, with the condition of slavery passed from one generation to the next. The Handlins identified this transition from "servant" to "slave" more as a legal process by which colonial legislatures sought to increase the available labor force than as a response to racial prejudice. The leaders of the Chesapeake hoped to attract white laborers to the New World; to do so, they had to make clear the distinction between voluntary and involuntary servitude. Hence the institutionalization of slavery: It was an effort to persuade whites that their status would be higher than that of blacks.

Winthrop Jordan, in *White over Black* (1968), offered a different view of how slavery developed in America. Jordan emphasized that Europeans had long viewed people of color—and particularly black Africans—as inferior beings preeminently fit to serve whites. Slavery did not evolve slowly from a system of relative racial equality. Blacks and whites were viewed and treated differently from the beginning; and the institution that finally emerged was a natural reflection of the deep-seated racism that the white settlers had brought with them. David Brion Davis, similarly, argued in *The Problem of Slavery in Western Culture* (1966) and later works that American slavery emerged not so much from the legal or economic conditions of the colonies as from a deeply embedded set of cultural assumptions. Davis placed less emphasis than Jordan on racism; he argued, instead, that the notion of slavery was an integral part of Western culture and that African servitude in America was not profoundly different from other forms of slavery in other societies.

Several historians in the 1970s returned to an emphasis on the particular conditions within the American colonies that helped produce the slave system. But unlike the Handlins, they saw the legal process by which slavery emerged as secondary to other issues. Peter Wood, in *Black Majority* (1974), emphasized the economic benefits that the black labor force provided whites in colonial South Carolina. In the early years of settlement (the "frontier period") in South Carolina, blacks and whites often worked together. Black workers were relatively few in number, and differentiations in status were relatively vague. After the 1690s, however, whites discovered that African workers were better suited than Europeans to do the arduous work of rice cultivation, which was now coming to dominate the economy of the colony. Importation of black workers rapidly increased; and by the early eighteenth century, whites were becoming uneasy about the presence of a black majority in the colony. The hardening of the slave system, through legislation and in practice, reflected white fears of black resistance or even revolt.

Edmund S. Morgan, in *American Slavery, American Freedom* (1975), also argued that the labor system in the South was at first relatively flexible and later grew more rigid. In an examination of colonial Virginia, Morgan suggested that the early colonists did not at first intend to create a permanent system of human bondage. By the late seventeenth century, however, the flourishing tobacco economy had created a growing need for cheap labor. The existence of a large, dependent white labor force, which was difficult to recruit and even more difficult to control, was unappealing to the colonists. African workers could be recruited and controlled more easily. The creation of a rigid slave system in the eighteenth century was, therefore, less a result of historic racism than a response to economic and social needs. Racism emerged largely as a result of slavery; it was not the cause of slavery. (Morgan went on to argue that the later development of democratic ideas in Virginia was made possible by the existence of slavery. A dependent white labor force would have made the idea of political equality difficult to sustain; but by making the dependent workers into slaves, outside the political world of whites, it was possible to believe that all white citizens were politically equal.)

but equally important was the arrival of substantial non-English groups from Europe. By the early eighteenth century, the flow of immigrants from England itself began to decline substantially—a result not only of the improvement of economic conditions there but of new restrictions on emigration imposed by a government alarmed at the continuing exodus, which threatened to depopulate whole regions of the country. White immigration continued, however, as large numbers of French, Germans, Swiss, Irish, Scots, and Scandinavians contributed to the patchwork of the American population.

The earliest, although not the most numerous, of these immigrants were the French Calvinists, or Huguenots. The Edict of Nantes of 1598 had granted them liberties and privileges that enabled them to constitute practically a state within the state in Roman Catholic France. In 1685, however, the edict was revoked; and soon thereafter, singly and in groups, the Huguenots began seizing opportunities to leave the country. About 300,000 left France in the following decades, and a small proportion of them traveled to the English colonies in North America.

Many German Protestants suffered similarly from the arbitrary religious policies of their rulers; and all Germans, Catholics as well as Protestants, suffered from the devastating wars between their principalities and King Louis XIV of France (the "Sun King"). The Rhineland of southwestern Germany, the area known as the Palatinate, experienced particular hardships. Its proximity to France exposed its people to slaughter and its farms to ruin at the hands of invaders. And the unusually cold winter of 1708–1709 provided a final blow to the precarious economy of the region. More than 12,000 Palatinate Germans sought refuge in England, and approximately 3,000 of them soon found their way to America. They arrived in New York and tried at first to make homes in the Mohawk Valley, only to be ousted by the powerful landlords of the region. Some of the Palatines moved farther up the Mohawk, out of reach of the patroons; but most made their way to Pennsylvania, where they received a warm welcome. After that, the Quaker colony became the usual destination of Germans, who sailed for America in growing numbers. (Among them were Moravians and Mennonites with religious views similar to those of the Quakers.) Many German Protestants went to North Carolina as well, especially after the founding of New Bern in 1710 by a company of 600 German-speaking Swiss.

The most numerous of the newcomers were the so-called Scotch-Irish—Scotch Presbyterians who had settled in northern Ireland (in the county of Ulster) in the early seventeenth century. The Ulster colonists had prospered for a time despite the handicap of barren soil and the need for constant struggle to suppress the Catholic natives. But in the first years of the eighteenth century, the English government prohibited the export to England of the woolens and other products that had become the basis of the Ulster economy; at the same time, the government virtually outlawed the practice of Presbyterianism and insisted on conformity with the Anglican church. After 1710, moreover, the long-term leases of many Scotch-Irish expired; English landlords doubled and even tripled the rents. Thousands of tenants left for America in successive waves.

Often coldly received at the colonial ports, most of the Scotch-Irish pushed out to the edge of the American wilderness. There they occupied land with scant regard for ownership, believing that "it was against the laws of God and nature that so much land should be idle while so many Christians wanted it to labor on and to raise bread." There they were also ruthless in their displacement and suppression of the Indians, just as they had been with the Irish.

Immigrants from Scotland itself and from southern Ireland added other elements to the colonial population. Scottish Highlanders, some of them Roman Catholics who had been defeated in rebellions in 1715 and 1745, settled in several colonies, North Carolina above all. Presbyterian Lowlanders, faced in Scotland with high rents in the country and unemployment in the towns, left for America in large numbers shortly before the American Revolution. The Irish migrated in trickles over a long period, and by the time of the Revolution they were almost as numerous as the Scots, although less conspicuous. Many of them had by then abandoned their Roman Catholic religion and with it much of their ethnic identity.

The continuing immigration and the improving natural increase contributed to the rapid population growth of the colonies in the eighteenth century. In 1700, the colonial population totaled less than 250,000; by 1775, it was over 2 million—a nearly tenfold increase. Throughout the colonial period, the population nearly doubled every twenty-five years.

The Colonial Economy

Although colonial Americans engaged almost from the beginning in a wide range of economic pursuits, it was farming that dominated all areas of settlement throughout the seventeenth and eighteenth centuries.

Dominant Immigrant Groups in Colonial America, c. 1760

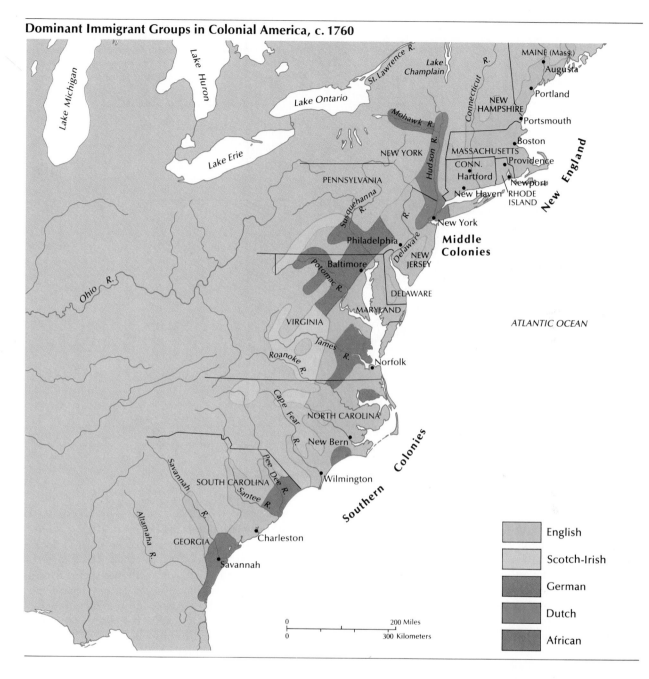

Beyond that basic similarity, however, the economies of the different regions varied markedly from one another; and even within colonies, different areas grew in different ways.

The Southern Economy

In the Chesapeake region, where tobacco early established itself as the basis of the economy, a strong demand for the crop in Europe enabled some planters to grow enormously wealthy and at times allowed the region as a whole to prosper. But throughout the seventeenth and eighteenth centuries, tobacco growers experienced the same problem that would afflict American farmers repeatedly for centuries: periodic overproduction. Production of tobacco frequently exceeded demand. The result was a boom-and-bust cycle in the Chesapeake economy. A series of severe

Selling Tobacco
This late seventeenth-century label was used in the sale of American tobacco in England. The drawing depicts Virginia as a land of bright sunshine, energetic slaves, and prosperous, pipe-smoking planters. (American Heritage)

declines in the price of the crop, beginning in 1640, followed by varying degrees of recovery, became the pattern.

Most of the Chesapeake planters believed that the way to protect themselves from the instability of the market was to grow more tobacco. That, of course, only made the problem worse; but it also helped change the nature of the Chesapeake economy as a whole. Those planters who could afford to do so expanded their landholdings, enlarged their fields, and acquired additional laborers. After 1700, tobacco plantations employing several dozen slaves or more were common.

South Carolina and Georgia were unsuitable for the growing of tobacco, and they relied instead on rice production. The low-lying coastline with its many tidal rivers made it possible to establish, through the construction of dams and dikes, rice paddies that could be flooded and then drained. Rice cultivation was arduous work—performed standing knee deep in the mud of malarial swamps, under a blazing sun, surrounded by insects—a task so difficult and unhealthy that white laborers generally refused to perform it. Hence the far greater dependence of planters in South Carolina and Georgia on slaves than their Northern counterparts. Yet it was not only because blacks could be compelled to perform these difficult tasks that whites found them so valuable. It was also because they were much better at the work than whites. They showed from the beginning a greater resistance than whites to malaria and other local diseases (although the impact of disease on black workers was by no means inconsiderable). And they proved more adept—perhaps because many had come from similar climates in Africa—at performing the basic agricultural tasks required.

In the early 1740s, another staple crop contributed to the South Carolina economy: indigo. Eliza Lucas, a young Antiguan woman who managed her family's American plantations, experimented with cultivating the West Indian plant (which was the source of a blue dye in great demand in Europe) in America and discovered that it could grow on the high ground of South Carolina, which was unsuitable for rice planting. It was harvested during the season when the rice was still growing. Indigo became an important complement to rice and a much-sought import in England.

Because of their early dependence on large-scale cash crops, the Southern colonies developed less of a commercial or industrial economy than the colonies to the north. The trading in tobacco and rice was handled largely by merchants based in London and, later, in the Northern colonies. Few cities of more than modest size developed in the South; no substantial local merchant communities emerged. A pattern was established that would characterize the Southern economy, and differentiate it from that of other regions, for more than two centuries.

The Northern Economy

The economies of the Northern colonies—the settlements stretching from Pennsylvania into Maine—were more varied than those of the South. In the North, as in the South, agriculture continued to dominate, but it was agriculture of a far more diverse kind. In addition to farming, there gradually emerged an important commercial sector of the economy.

One reason that agriculture did not remain the exclusive economic pursuit of the North was that conditions for farming were far less favorable than in the South. In most of New England, in particular, colder weather and rocky soil made it almost impossible for colonists to develop a successful commercial farming system. Instead, most settlers cultivated relatively small areas of land, growing food, raising animals, and in general attempting to make themselves self-sufficient. Modest cash crops—scrawny livestock, apples, and corn—enabled New Englanders to trade for those things they could not grow or make for themselves.

Conditions for agriculture were far better in southern New England and the middle colonies, where the soil was fertile and the weather slightly more temperate. Farmers in New York, Pennsylvania, and the Connecticut River valley cultivated staple crops for sale both at home and abroad. The region was the chief supplier of wheat to much of New

England and to parts of the South. Some areas of the region were, for various reasons, less productive than others. In New York, for example, the concentration of land ownership and the maintenance of great estates (some of them thousands and even hundreds of thousands of acres large) discouraged production. Few people were willing to work as tenants on large estates when they could get farms of their own in other colonies. In Pennsylvania, by contrast, German immigrants succeeded in greatly increasing production by applying the methods of intensive cultivation they had practiced in Europe. The sex ratio in the German communities was relatively balanced, and women commonly worked alongside the men in the fields—a practice that other immigrant groups on occasion found appalling.

From time to time, entrepreneurs in New England and the middle colonies (particularly New Jersey and Pennsylvania) attempted to augment their agricultural economy with industrial enterprises. Beginning with a failed effort to establish an ironworks in Saugus, Massachusetts (near Boston), in the mid-seventeenth century, colonists embarked on innumerable industrial ventures. Many such ventures failed, but the colonists did manage to establish a wide range of industrial activities on a modest scale. At the simplest level, almost every colonist engaged in a certain amount of industry at home. Women, in particular, were active in spinning, weaving, making soap and candles, and other tasks basic to the life of the family. Men engaged in carpentry. Occasionally these home industries provided families with goods they could barter or sell. Beyond these private efforts, craftsmen and artisans established themselves in colonial towns as cobblers, blacksmiths, riflemakers, cabinetmakers, silversmiths, printers, and so forth. In some areas, entrepreneurs harnessed the water power of the many streams and rivers to run small mills—some for grinding grain, others for processing cloth, still others for milling lumber. And in several places, large-scale shipbuilding operations began to flourish.

The largest industrial enterprise anywhere in English North America was that of the German ironmaster Peter Hasenclever, in northern New Jersey. Founded in 1764 with British capital, it employed several hundred laborers, many of them imported from ironworks located in Germany. There were other, smaller ironmaking enterprises in every Northern colony (with particular concentrations in Massachusetts, New Jersey, and Pennsylvania); and there were ironworks as well in several of the Southern colonies.

But these and other growing industries did not become the basis for the kind of explosive industrial growth that Great Britain experienced in the late eighteenth century. That was in part because of such restrictions as those imposed by the Iron Act of 1750—a measure passed by Parliament restricting colonists from engaging metal processing (and stifling the development of a steel industry in America). Similar prohibitions applied to the manufacture of woolens (the Woolen Act of 1699) and hats (the Hat Act of 1732), although Americans often disregarded such legislation. The real obstacles to industrialization, however, were more basic: an inadequate labor supply, an inadequate domestic market, and an inadequate infrastructure of transportation facilities, energy supplies, and other necessities. Americans would not overcome such obstacles until the mid-nineteenth century.

More important to the economy of the Northern colonies than manufacturing were the so-called extractive industries: those that exploited the natural resources of the continent. A flourishing fur trade grew up during the first decades of settlement; but by the mid-seventeenth century the supply of fur-bearing animals had been nearly exhausted, and the trade all but ceased. For the next century and more, the colonists relied instead on lumbering—which took advantage of the vast forests of the New World; mining—which exploited iron and other mineral reserves throughout the colonies; and fishing—particularly in the waters off the New England coast. These extractive industries provided what manufacturing and agriculture often failed to give the colonists: commodities that could be exported to England in exchange for manufactured goods. And they helped, therefore, to produce the most distinctive feature of the Northern economy—a thriving commercial class.

The Rise of Commerce

The inability of any one colony, or any one region, to attain genuine economic self-sufficiency made the development of some level of commerce inevitable. The form that commerce took, however, reflected not only economic necessity but a wide array of complicated legal restrictions and the financial peculiarities of the seventeenth- and eighteenth-century world.

Perhaps the most remarkable feature of colonial commerce in the seventeenth century was that it was able to survive at all. American merchants faced such bewildering and intimidating obstacles, and lacked so many of the basic institutions of trade, that they managed to stay afloat only with difficulty. There was, first, no commonly accepted medium of exchange. The colonies had almost no specie (gold or silver coins). They experimented at times with different forms of paper currency—tobacco certificates, for example, which were secured by tobacco stored in warehouses; or land certificates, secured by property. Such paper was not, however, acceptable as payment for any goods from abroad; and it was, in any case, ultimately outlawed by Parliament. For many years, colonial merchants had to rely on a haphazard system of barter or on crude money substitutes such as beaver skins.

A second obstacle was the near impossibility of rationalizing trade. In the fragmented, jerry-built commercial world of colonial America, no merchants could be certain that the goods on which their commerce relied would be produced in sufficient quantity; nor could they be certain of finding adequate markets for them. Few channels of information existed to inform traders of what they could expect in foreign ports; and vessels sometimes stayed at sea for several years, journeying from one market to another, trading one commodity for another, attempting to find some way to turn a profit. Engaged in this chaotic commerce, moreover, were an enormous number of small, fiercely competitive companies, which made the problem of rationalizing the system even more acute.

Despite these and other problems, commerce in the colonies not only survived but grew. There was an elaborate coastal trade, through which the colonies did business with one another and with the West Indies, largely in such goods as rum, agricultural products, and fish. The mainland colonies received sugar, molasses, and at times slaves from the Caribbean markets in return. There was as well an expanding international trade, which linked the North American colonies in an intricate network of commerce with England, continental Europe, and the western coast of Africa. This commerce has often been described, somewhat inaccurately, as the "triangular trade," suggesting a neat process by which merchants carried rum and other goods from New England to Africa, exchanged their merchandise for slaves whom they then transported to the West Indies (hence the term "middle passage" for the dread journey—it was the second of the three legs of the voyage), and then exchanged the slaves for sugar and molasses, which they shipped back to New England

Overseas Trade During the Colonial Period

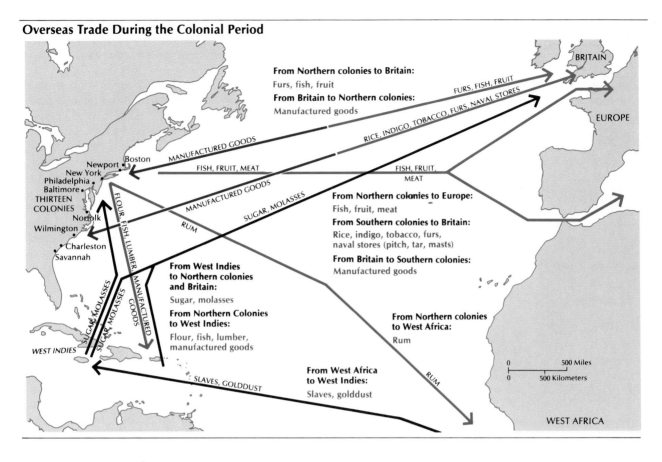

From Northern colonies to Britain:
Furs, fish, fruit

From Britain to Northern colonies:
Manufactured goods

From Northern colonies to Europe:
Fish, fruit, meat

From Southern colonies to Britain:
Rice, indigo, tobacco, furs,
naval stores (pitch, tar, masts)

From Britain to Southern colonies:
Manufactured goods

From West Indies
to Northern colonies
and Britain:
Sugar, molasses

From Northern Colonies
to West Indies:
Flour, fish, lumber,
manufactured goods

From Northern colonies
to West Africa:
Rum

From West Africa
to West Indies:
Slaves, golddust

to be distilled into rum. In fact, the system was almost never so simple. The "triangular" trade in rum, slaves, and sugar was in fact a maze of highly diverse trade routes: between the Northern and Southern colonies, America and England, America and Africa, the West Indies and Europe, and more.

Out of this confusing and highly risky trade there emerged a group of adventurous entrepreneurs who by the mid-eighteenth century were beginning to constitute a distinct merchant class. Concentrated in the port cities of the North (Boston, New York, Philadelphia, and other, smaller trading centers), they enjoyed protection from foreign competition within the English colonies, since the British Navigation Acts had excluded all non-British ships from the colonial carrying trade. And they had access to a market in England for such colonial products as furs, timber, and American-built ships. But that did not satisfy all their commercial needs. Many colonial products— fish, flour, wheat, and meat, all of which England

could produce for itself—required markets altogether outside the British Empire. Ignoring laws restricting colonial trade to England and its possessions, many merchants developed markets in the French, Spanish, and Dutch West Indies, where prices were often higher than in the British colonies. The profits from this commerce enabled the colonies to import the manufactured goods they needed from Europe.

In the course of the eighteenth century, the colonial commercial system began to stabilize. In some cities, the more successful merchants expanded their operations so greatly that they were able to dominate some sectors of trade and curb some of the destabilizing effects of competition. Merchants managed, as well, to make extensive contacts in the English commercial world, securing their position in certain areas of transatlantic trade. But the commercial sector of the American economy remained open to newcomers, largely because it—and the society on which it was based—was expanding so rapidly.

A New England Merchant
An unknown artist produced this oil portrait of the
Massachusetts merchant Moses Marcy in the
mid-eighteenth century. Marcy is portrayed here with
the accouterments of the prosperous trader: elegant garb,
a stately home, and a large seagoing vessel. On the table,
along with his clay pipe and punchbowl, lies a fat
volume that may represent his account book. (Old
Sturbridge Village, Massachusetts)

Patterns of Society

It was not only in the composition of its population
and the structure of its economy that the society of
the colonies differed from that of England. It was
also in the nature of its most basic social institutions.

Although there were clear class distinctions in the
colonies, the sharply defined and deeply entrenched
class system of England failed to reproduce itself in
America. In England, where land was scarce and the
population large, the relatively small proportion of
the people who owned land had enormous power
over the great majority who did not; the imbalance
between land and population became a foundation of
the English economy and the cornerstone of its class
system. In America, of course, precisely the inverse
was true. Land was abundant; people were scarce.
Aristocracies emerged there, to be sure; but they
tended to rely less on land ownership than on control
of a substantial work force, and they were generally
less secure and less powerful than their English counterparts. Far more than in England, there were opportunities in America for social mobility—both up
and down.

There emerged, too, new forms of community
whose structure reflected less the British model than
the realities of the American wilderness. These forms
varied greatly from one region to another, but several basic—and distinctly American—types emerged.

The Plantation

The plantation system of the American South illustrated clearly both the differences between the colonial and English class systems and the way in which
colonial communities evolved in response to local
conditions. The first plantations emerged in the early
settlements of Virginia and Maryland, in response to
the establishment of tobacco as the economic basis of
the Chesapeake. Some planters hoped to re-create in
America the entrenched, landholding aristocracy of
England; and in a few cases—notably in the great
Maryland estates granted by Lord Baltimore to his
relatives and friends—a semblance of such an aristocracy did emerge. The Maryland plantation of Charles
Carroll of Carrollton, reputedly the wealthiest man
in the colonies, covered 40,000 acres and contained
285 slaves. And there were other plantations—in
Maryland, Virginia, and the tobacco-growing regions
of North Carolina—that eventually attained similar
size.

On the whole, however, colonial plantations were
rough and relatively small estates. In the early days in
Virginia, they were little more than crude clearings
on the frontier, where landowners and indentured
servants worked side by side in conditions so horrible
that death was an everyday occurrence. Even in later
years, when the death rate declined and the landholdings became more established, plantation work forces
seldom exceeded thirty people. Most landowners
lived in rough cabins or simple houses, with their
servants or slaves nearby. Relatively few lived in
anything resembling aristocratic splendor.

Total Population in the Southern and Middle Colonies, c. 1775

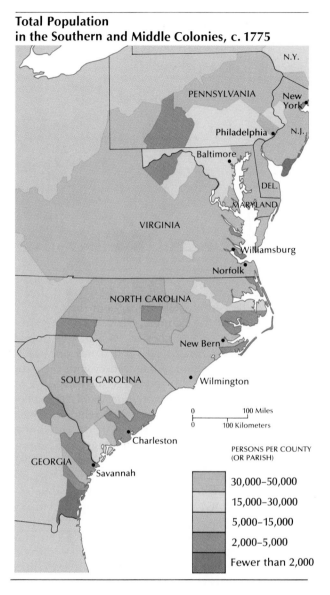

PERSONS PER COUNTY (OR PARISH)

- 30,000–50,000
- 15,000–30,000
- 5,000–15,000
- 2,000–5,000
- Fewer than 2,000

Black Population: Proportion of Total Population, c. 1775

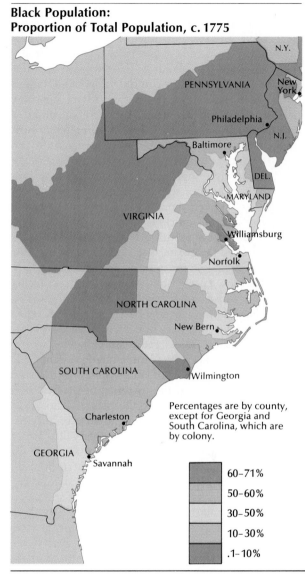

Percentages are by county, except for Georgia and South Carolina, which are by colony.

- 60–71%
- 50–60%
- 30–50%
- 10–30%
- .1–10%

The economy of the plantation, like all agricultural economies, was a precarious one. In good years, successful growers could earn great profits, expand their operations, and move closer to becoming true landed aristocrats. But without control over their markets, even the largest planters were constantly at risk. When prices for their crops fell—as tobacco prices did, for example, in the 1660s—they faced the prospect of ruin. The plantation economy created many new wealthy landowners, but it also destroyed many—another obstacle to the creation of an entrenched aristocracy similar to that in England.

Because plantations were often far from cities and

towns—which were, in any case, relatively few in the South—they tended to become self-contained communities. Residents lived in close proximity to one another in a cluster of buildings that included the "great house" of the planter himself (a house that was usually, although not always, far from great), the service buildings, the barns, and the cabins of the slaves. Wealthier planters often created something approaching a full town on their plantations, with a school (for white children only), a chapel, and a large population. Smaller planters lived more modestly, but still in a relatively self-sufficient world.

On the larger plantations, the presence of a substantial slave work force altered not only the economic but the family lives of the planter class. Plantation mistresses, unlike the wives of small farmers, could rely on servants to perform ordinary household chores and could thus devote more time to their husbands and children than women in other parts of colonial society. But they also had to endure the frequent sexual liaisons between their husbands or sons and black women of the slave community. Southern women generally learned to pretend not to notice these relationships, but they were almost certainly a source of anxiety and resentment.

Although the English class system did not reproduce itself, Southern society was highly stratified in its own way. Even though the fortunes of planters could rise and fall quickly, at any given time there were always a few particularly wealthy landowners, who exercised far greater social and economic influence than their less prosperous neighbors. Within a particular area, a great landowner not only controlled the lives of those who worked his own plantation but the livelihood of independent farmers working small plots, who depended on him to market their crops and supply them with credit. Some whites rented their farms from wealthy planters. Independent farmers, working small plots of land with few or no slaves to help them, formed the majority of the Southern agrarian population; it was the planters, however, who dominated the Southern agrarian economy.

The black slaves, of course, lived very differently. On the smaller farms with only a handful of slaves, it was not always possible for a rigid separation to develop between whites and blacks. But over three-fourths of all blacks lived on plantations of at least ten slaves; nearly half lived in communities of fifty slaves or more. And in these larger establishments, they began to develop a society and culture of their own—influenced by their white masters, to be sure, but also partly independent of them.

Although whites seldom encouraged formal marriages among slaves, usually hoping only that they would produce children rapidly, blacks themselves developed a strong and elaborate family structure. Slaves attempted to construct nuclear families, and they managed at times to build stable households, even to work together growing their own food in gardens provided by their masters. But such efforts were in constant jeopardy; any family member could be sold at any time to another planter, even to one in another colony. As a result, blacks placed special emphasis on extended kinship networks and created surrogate "relatives" who were entirely unrelated to their own families.

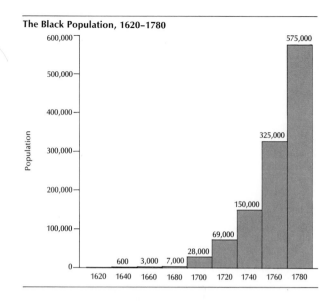

The Black Population, 1620–1780

Blacks also developed languages of their own. In South Carolina, for example, the early slaves communicated with one another in "Gullah"—a hybrid of English and African tongues that not only reinforced the blacks' sense of connection with their ancestry but enabled them to engage in conversations their white masters could not understand. There began to emerge too a distinctive slave religion, which blended Christianity with African folklore and which became a central element in the emergence of an independent black culture.

Nevertheless, black society was subject to constant intrusions from and interaction with white society. Black house servants, for example, at times lived in what was, by black standards, great luxury; but they were also isolated from their own community and under constant surveillance from whites. Black women were frequently subjected to the sexual advances of owners and overseers and gave birth to mulatto children, who were seldom recognized by their white fathers but were generally accepted as members of the slave community. On some plantations, black workers were treated with kindness and even affection by their masters and mistresses, and at times displayed genuine devotion in return. On others, they encountered physical brutality and occasionally even sadism, against which they were virtually powerless.

There were occasional acts of individual resistance by slaves against masters, and on at least two occasions during the colonial period there were actual slave rebellions. In the most important such revolt, the so-called Stono Rebellion in South Carolina in

1739, about 100 blacks rose up, seized weapons, killed several whites, and attempted to escape south to Florida. The uprising was quickly crushed and the majority of participants executed. The most frequent form of resistance was simply running away, but that provided no real solution either. There was nowhere to go.

Most slaves, male and female, worked as field hands (with the women shouldering the additional family burdens of cooking and child rearing). But on the larger plantations, which aspired to genuine self-sufficiency, some slaves learned trades and crafts: blacksmithing, carpentry, shoemaking, spinning, weaving, sewing, midwifery, and others. These skilled craftsmen and craftswomen were at times hired out to other planters. Some set up their own establishments in towns or cities and shared their profits with their owners. On occasion, they were able to buy their freedom. There was a small but significant free black population living in Southern cities by the time of the Revolution.

As an economic unit, the Southern plantation was both efficient and productive and helped the agricultural output of the region to expand greatly in the course of the colonial period. As a social unit, it achieved stability at the cost of human freedom.

The Puritan Community

A very different form of community emerged in Puritan New England, but one that was also distinctively American. Since much of the Northeast was settled by large groups of immigrants arriving together (entire Puritan congregations often moving to the New World en masse), the characteristic social unit in New England was not the isolated farm but the town. Each new settlement drew up a "covenant" among its members, binding all residents together in a religious and social commitment to unity and harmony. The structure of the towns generally reflected the spirit of the covenant. Colonists laid out a village, with houses and a meetinghouse arranged around a central pasture, or "common." They also

The New England Town: Sudbury, Massachusetts, 17th Century

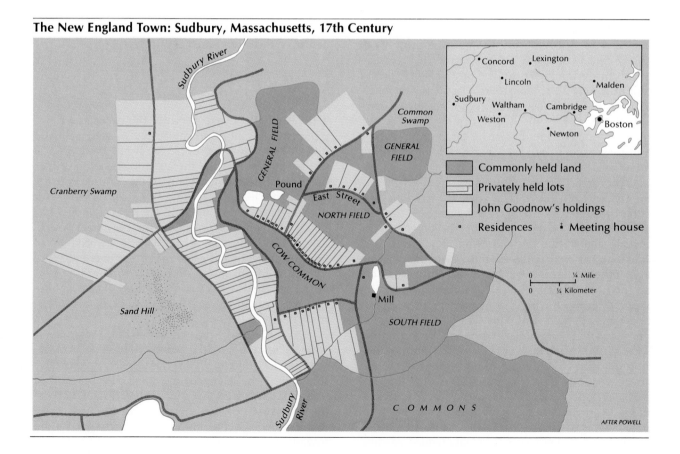

divided up the outlying fields and woodlands of the town among the residents; the size and location of a family's field depended on the family's numbers, wealth, and social station. But wherever their lands might lie, families generally lived with their neighbors close by, reinforcing the strong sense of community.

Once established, a town was generally able to run its own affairs, with little interference from the colonial government. Residents held a yearly "town meeting" to decide important questions and to choose a group of "selectmen," who governed until the next meeting. As a rule, all adult males were permitted to participate in the meeting. But important social distinctions remained, the most crucial of which was membership in the church. Only those residents who could give evidence of grace, of being among the elect (the "visible saints") assured of salvation, were admitted to full membership, although other residents of the town were required to attend church services.

Central to the Puritan community was the family. And the dominant figure in most families was the husband and father, who exercised nearly dictatorial power over his wife and children. The English system of primogeniture—the passing of all property to the firstborn son—was not re-created in New England. Instead, a father divided up the lands allotted to him among all his sons. His control of this inheritance was one of the most effective means of exercising power over the family. Often a son would reach his late twenties before his father would allow him to move into his own household and work his own land.

The early Puritan community, in short, was a tightly knit organism. The town as a whole was bound together by the initial covenant, by the centralized layout of the village, by the power of the church, and by the town meeting. The family was held together by a rigid patriarchal structure that limited opportunities for younger members to strike out on their own. Yet as the years passed and the communities grew, this rigid communal structure came under increasing strain. This was partly because of the increasing commercialization of New England society, which introduced new forces and new tensions into the communities of the region. But it was also a result of other important pressures that had been developing within even purely agricultural communities: pressures that were a result primarily of population growth.

As towns grew larger, residents tended to cultivate lands farther and farther from the community center and, by necessity, to live at increasing distances from the church. Often, groups of outlying residents would eventually apply for permission to build a church of their own, the first step toward creation of a wholly new town. Such applications were frequently the occasion for bitter quarrels between the original townspeople and those who proposed to break away.

The practice of distributing land through the patriarchal family structure contributed further tensions to the Puritan community. In the first generations, fathers generally controlled enough land to satisfy the needs of all their sons. By the third generation, however, when such lands were being subdivided for the third time, there was often too little to go around, particularly in communities surrounded by other towns, with no room to expand outward. Sons began to chafe at their inability to escape from the control of their fathers and at the lack of prospects for independent estates. The result was that in many communities, groups of younger residents were breaking off and moving elsewhere—at times far away—to form towns of their own, further challenging and eroding the original patriarchal, communal nature of the community.

The Witchcraft Phenomenon

The result of this gap between the expectation of a united community and the reality of a diverse and divided one was often severe social and psychological strain. At the extreme, these tensions could produce bizarre and disastrous events. One example was the widespread hysteria in the 1680s and 1690s over witchcraft in New England. The most famous outbreak (although by no means the only one) was in Salem, Massachusetts, where the strange behavior of several adolescent girls and the mysterious actions of two West Indian slaves steeped in voodoo lore produced hundreds of accusations of witchcraft. Nineteen residents of Salem were put to death before the trials finally ended in 1692.

On the surface, the witchcraft crisis was an example of wild superstition and social hysteria. A closer examination, however, reveals deeper origins. Research into the background of the phenomenon in Salem has indicated that the witchcraft turmoil there reflected some of the severe social tensions in the town: tensions between those who were gravitating toward the new commercial economy of the town's thriving seaport and those who remained tied to the languishing agricultural economy of the community's western areas. Residents of the outlying areas of the town resented the favored position of their eastern neighbors. Such jealousy could not be openly expressed in a "godly" community; it may have found expression instead in the form of accusations of witchcraft. The accusations were usually made by the relatively isolated and unsuccessful members of the community against people associated with its more prosperous segments.

The accusations were also generally leveled by adolescent girls against older women—suggesting that social anxieties may have been intersecting with anxieties over sexual roles. In the tense social climate of Salem and similar communities, young girls faced frightening uncertainty about their futures, which would, they knew, be determined less by their own actions and desires than by the wishes of their parents and their future husbands. By leveling accusations of witchcraft against older women, these adolescents may have been expressing indirectly their frustrations at the uncertainty and powerlessness of their own lives.

The Puritan vision of community—a vision of a "peaceable kingdom" united in a common purpose—was a heavy burden to bear, particularly when the realities of life tended to transform towns into something very different. Few communities reacted to these tensions as violently as Salem. But social change created uneasiness in towns throughout New England.

Cities

To call the commercial centers that emerged along the Atlantic coast in the eighteenth century "cities" would be to strain today's definition of that word. Even the largest colonial community was scarcely bigger than a modern small town. Yet by the standards of the eighteenth century, cities did indeed exist in America. The two largest ports—Philadelphia and New York—had populations of 28,000 and 25,000 respectively, which made them larger than most English urban centers. Boston (16,000), Charles Town (later Charleston) in South Carolina (12,000), and Newport in Rhode Island (11,000) were also substantial communities by the standards of the day.

Baltimore in 1752
Baltimore remained a small and relatively quiet port even two decades after its founding in 1729. Most Maryland tobacco growers shipped their crops from their own wharves along the river and had little need for a central harbor. (Maryland Historical Society, Baltimore)

Colonial cities served as trading centers for the farmers of their regions and as marts for international trade. Their leaders were generally merchants who had acquired substantial estates. Although in most colonial communities disparities of wealth were generally not very great, in cities they sometimes came to seem enormous. Wealthy merchants and their families moved along crowded streets dressed in fine imported clothes, often riding in fancy carriages, coming in and out of large houses with staffs of servants. Moving beside them were the numerous minor tradesmen, workers, and indigents, dressed simply and living in crowded and often filthy conditions. It would be an exaggeration to claim that sharp class divisions emerged in the cities; but more than in any other area of colonial life (except, of course, in the relationship between masters and slaves), social distinctions were real and visible in urban areas.

There were other distinctive features of urban life as well. Cities were the centers of much of what industry existed in the colonies, such as the distilleries for turning imported molasses into exportable rum. They were the locations of the most advanced schools and sophisticated cultural activities and of shops where imported goods could be bought. In addition, they were communities with social problems that were peculiarly urban: crime, vice, pollution, traffic. Unlike smaller towns, cities were required to establish elaborate corporate governments. They set up constables' offices and fire departments. They developed systems for supporting the urban poor, whose numbers grew steadily and became especially large in times of economic crisis.

Perhaps most important for the political future of the colonies, cities became places where new ideas could circulate and be discussed. Because there were printers, it was possible to have regular newspapers. Books and other publications from abroad introduced new intellectual influences. And the taverns and coffee houses of cities provided forums in which people could gather and debate the issues of the day. It was hardly surprising that when the Revolutionary crisis began to build in the 1760s and 1770s, it manifested itself first in the cities.

The Colonial Mind

Two powerful forces were competing for the American mind in the eighteenth century. One was the traditional intellectual and religious outlook of the sixteenth and seventeenth centuries, with its emphasis on a personal God, intimately involved with the world, keeping watch over individual lives. The other was the new spirit of the Enlightenment, a movement that was sweeping both Europe and America and that stressed the importance of science and human reason. The old views made possible such phenomena as the belief in witchcraft and other superstitions; and they placed great value on a stern moral code in which intellect was less important than faith. The Enlightenment, by contrast, suggested that individuals had substantial control over their own lives and the course of their societies; that the world could be explained and therefore could be structured along rational scientific lines. The intellectual climate of colonial America was shaped by the tension between these two impulses.

The Pattern of Religions

The American colonists brought their religions with them from abroad. But like so many other imported institutions, religion took on a new and distinctive pattern in the New World. In part, this was because of the sheer number of different faiths established in America. With the immigration of diverse sectarians from several countries, the colonies became an ecclesiastical patchwork. Toleration flourished to a degree unmatched in any European nation, not because Americans deliberately sought to produce it, but because conditions virtually required it.

The experience of the Church of England illustrated how difficult the establishment of a common religion would be in the colonies. By law, Anglicanism was established as the official faith in Virginia, Maryland, New York, the Carolinas, and Georgia. In these colonies everyone, regardless of belief or affiliation, was supposed to be taxed for the support of the church. Actually, except in Virginia and Maryland, the Church of England succeeded in maintaining its position as the established church only in certain localities. To strengthen Anglicanism, in America and elsewhere, the Church of England in 1701 set up the Society for the Propagation of the Gospel in Foreign Parts (SPG). Missionaries of the SPG founded a number of new Anglican communions in the colonies, especially in Massachusetts and Connecticut. But Anglicanism never succeeded in becoming the dominant religious force in America that some members of the SPG envisioned.

Even in areas where a single faith had once predominated, the forces of denominationalism soon began to be felt. In New England, for example, Puritans had originally believed themselves all to be part of a single faith: Calvinism. In the course of the eighteenth century, however, there was a growing tendency for different congregations to affiliate with different denominations. Some became Congregationalists; others identified themselves as Presbyterians. In belief, these two groups were essentially the same, but they differed in ecclesiastical organization. Although each Congregationalist church was virtually autonomous, the Presbyterians had a more highly centralized government, with a governing body of presbyters (made up of ministers and lay elders) for the churches of each district. In the early eighteenth century, many of the Puritan churches of Connecticut, and most of those founded in colonies to the south by emigrants from New England, adopted the Presbyterian form of government.

In parts of New York and New Jersey, Dutch settlers had established their own Calvinist denomination—Dutch Reformed—which survived long after the colonies became part of the British Empire. The American Baptists (of whom Roger Williams is considered the first) were also originally Calvinist in their theology. Then, in Rhode Island and in other colonies, a bewildering variety of Baptist sects sprang up. They had in common a belief that infant baptism did not suffice and that rebaptism, usually by total immersion, was necessary when individuals reached maturity. Some Baptists remained Calvinists, believers in predestination; others came to believe in salvation by free will.

Protestants extended toleration to one another more readily than to Roman Catholics. To strict Puritans, the pope seemed no less than the Antichrist. They viewed their Catholic neighbors across the border in New France (Canada) not only as commercial and military rivals but as agents of the devil, bent on frustrating the divine mission of the wilderness Zion in New England. In most of the English colonies, however, Roman Catholics were far too small a minority to occasion serious conflict. They were most numerous in Maryland, and even there they numbered no more than 3,000. Ironically, they suffered their worst persecution in that colony, which had been founded as a refuge for them and had been distinguished by its Toleration Act of 1649. According to Maryland laws passed after 1691 (after the overthrow of the original proprietors), Catholics not only were deprived of political rights but also were forbidden to hold religious services except in private houses.

Jews in provincial America totaled no more than about 2,000 at any time. The largest community lived in New York City. Smaller groups settled in Newport and Charleston, and there were scattered Jewish families in all the colonies. Nowhere could they vote or hold office. Only in Rhode Island could they practice their religion openly.

The Decline of Piety

By the beginning of the eighteenth century, Americans had become deeply troubled by the apparent decline in piety in their society. In part, this was a result of the rise of denominationalism. With so many diverse sects existing side by side, some people were tempted to doubt whether any particular denomination, even their own, possessed a monopoly of truth and grace. More important, however, were other changes in colonial society. The movement of the population westward and the wide scattering of settlement had caused many communities to lose touch with organized religion. The rise of towns and the multiplication of material comforts led to an increasingly secular outlook in densely settled areas. The progress of science and free thought in Europe—and the importation of Enlightenment ideas to America—caused at least some colonists to adopt a rational and skeptical view of the world.

Concerns about declining piety were not new to the eighteenth century. They had surfaced as early as the 1660s in New England, where the Puritan oligarchy found itself faced with a steady deterioration of the power of the church. As the first generation of American Puritans died, the number of church members rapidly declined, for few of the second generation seemed to harbor enough religious passion to demonstrate the "saving grace" that was a prerequisite for membership. The children of "saints" had generally been baptized and had attended church; but in the absence of a true "conversion experience," many had never become full members. When these people began to have children of their own, the clergy was faced with a dilemma. Should the infants of these unconverted churchgoers be baptized? In 1662, a conference of ministers attempted to solve the problem by instituting the Halfway Covenant, which gave people of the third and later generations the right to be baptized but not the right to partake of communion or vote in church affairs.

As time passed, this carefully drawn distinction between full and half members was often forgotten, and in many communities the church came to include as voters and officeholders the families of all who could take part in colonial politics. Qualification for membership in the church, in other words, became largely secular. Orthodox Puritans, however, continued to oppose the transformation that was enveloping the erstwhile land of the saints. Sabbath after Sabbath, ministers preached sermons of despair (known as jeremiads) deploring the signs of waning piety. "Truly so it is," one minister lamented in 1674, "the very heart of New England is changed and exceedingly corrupted with the sins of the times." There was, he said, a growing spirit of profaneness, pride, worldliness, sensuality, gainsaying and rebellion, libertinism, carnality, formality, hypocrisy, "and a spiritual idolatry in the worship of God." Only in relative terms was religious piety actually declining in New England. By the standards of later times (or by the standards of other societies of the seventeenth century), the Puritan faith remained remarkably strong. It did not, however, remain the pervasive force it once had been for maintaining stability and social order.

The Great Awakening

By the early eighteenth century, similar concerns were emerging in other regions and among members of other faiths. Everywhere, it seemed, piety was in decline and opportunities for spiritual regeneration were dwindling. At the same time, social and economic changes were creating new tensions within communities. For many colonists, the anxieties were becoming nearly unbearable. The result was the first great American revival.

It was known as the Great Awakening. Although the first stirrings (or "freshenings") began in some places early in the century, the Great Awakening was truly launched in the 1730s and reached its climax in the 1740s. Then, for a time, a new spirit of religious fervor seemed for thousands of Americans to have reversed the trend away from piety.

That the movement was not purely religious in origin is suggested by the identity of those who responded most frequently to it: residents of areas where social and economic tensions were greatest; women (who constituted the majority of converts) frustrated by their social and familial subjugation; younger sons of the third or fourth generation of settlers—those who stood to inherit the least land and who thus faced the most uncertain futures. The social origins of the revival were evident too in much of its rhetoric, which emphasized the potential for every individual to break away from the constraints of the past and start anew in his or her relationship to God (and, implicitly, to the world).

Wandering exhorters from England did much to stimulate the revivalistic spirit. John and Charles Wesley, the founders of Methodism (which had begun as a reform movement within the Church of England), visited Georgia and other colonies in the 1730s with the intention of revitalizing religion and converting Indians and blacks. George Whitefield, a powerful open-air preacher and for a time an associate of the Wesleys, made several evangelizing tours through the colonies. Everywhere he went Whitefield drew tremendous crowds, and it was said (with some exaggeration) that he could make his hearers weep merely by uttering, in his moving way, the word "Mesopotamia."

But the Wesleys, Whitefield, and other evangelizers from abroad were less important to American revivalism in the long run than the colonial ministers attempting to restore religious fervor in America. Theodore Frelinghuysen, of the Dutch Reformed church, and Gilbert Tennent, a Presbyterian, were important native voices of evangelism. The outstanding preacher of the Great Awakening, however, was the New England Congregationalist Jonathan Edwards—a deeply orthodox Puritan but also one of the most profoundly original theologians in American history. From his pulpit in Northampton, Massachusetts, Edwards attacked the new doctrines of easy salvation for all. He preached anew the traditional Puritan ideas of the absolute sovereignty of God, the depravity of the human race, predestination, the necessity of experiencing a sense of election, and salvation by God's grace alone. His vivid descriptions of hell could bring his listeners to their knees in terror. Day after day, agonized sinners crowded his parsonage to seek his aid; at least one committed suicide in despair at his inability to experience grace.

The Great Awakening spread over the colonies like a religious epidemic. It was most contagious in frontier areas and among the comparatively poor and uneducated. Its particular impact on women was perhaps partly because of their lower rates of literacy. It was strongest of all in the Southern back country. The Awakening created a sharp division in the Presbyterian church between a large and rapidly growing group of revivalistic "New Light" Presbyterians and the traditional "Old Lights." New Methodist and Baptist sects attracted other converts.

George Whitefield
Whitefield succeeded John Wesley as leader of the
Calvinistic Methodists in Oxford; like Wesley, he was a
major force in promoting religious revivalism in both
England and America. He made his first missionary
journey to the New World in 1738 and returned in the
mid-1740s for a celebrated journey through the colonies
that helped spark the Great Awakening.   (National Portrait
Gallery, London)

The Great Awakening not only led to the division
of existing congregations and the founding of new
ones. It also affected areas of society outside the
churches. Some of the revivalists denounced book
learning as a snare and a delusion, a positive hin-
drance to salvation; and in some communities the
result was a retreat from commitments to secular education. But other evangelists saw education as a
means of furthering their own brand of religion and
founded schools for the preparation of New Light
ministers. Perhaps more important, by challenging
the importance of formal church hierarchies and in-

sisting that salvation could come only through individual grace, the revival implicitly challenged
traditional sources of authority and traditional patterns of deference in colonial society. It injected a
vaguely egalitarian spirit into what had traditionally
been a strongly hierarchical and deferential society.

Language and Letters

The divergence of American culture from its English
origins was evident, too, in the development of a
distinctive colonial language and literature. As early
as the mid-seventeenth century, newcomers to the
colonies noticed a gradual Americanization of the
English language. New words originated in borrow-
ings from the Indians (for example, *skunk, squash*),
from the French (*prairie, cuisine*), and from the Dutch
(*boss, cookie*). Americanisms also arose from the combining of words already in the English language (*bull-
frog, snowplow*), from the formation of new adjectives
based on existing nouns (*kinky, chunky*), from the
adoption of unfamiliar uses for familiar words (*branch*,
to mean "stream"), and from the retention of old
English expressions that were being dropped in England. After 1700, English travelers in America began to notice a strangeness in accent as well as
vocabulary, and in 1756 the great lexicographer
Dr. Samuel Johnson mentioned the existence of an
"American dialect." In fact, there were several American dialects and several American accents, reflecting
the distances between and the social diversity among
the various colonies.

Colonial America produced relatively little literature of real artistic importance, certainly nothing to
compare with the literary output of England or Europe in the same years. Benjamin Franklin was one of
the most significant of the colonial writers, although
his work consisted largely of pragmatic, advisory essays—as suggested by such titles as *Advice to a Young
Man on Choosing a Mistress* (1745), *Reflections on
Courtship and Marriage* (1746), *Observations Concerning
the Increase of Mankind* (1755), and *Advice to a Young
Tradesman* (1762). The most prolific colonial literary
figures, however, were theologians such as Jonathan
Edwards.

Education

Most colonists placed a high value on education, despite the difficulties they confronted in gaining access
to it. Families provided schooling for their children
as best they could, generally teaching their children
to read and write at home. In Massachusetts, a 1647

law required every town to support a public school; and while many communities failed to comply, a modest network of educational establishments emerged as a result. Elsewhere, the Quakers and other sects operated church schools. And in some communities, widows or unmarried women conducted "dame schools" by holding private classes in their homes. In cities, master craftsmen set up evening schools for their apprentices; at least 100 such schools appeared between 1723 and 1770.

Only a relatively small number of children received education beyond the primary level; but white male Americans, at least, achieved a high degree of literacy. By the time of the Revolution, well over half of all white men could read and write—a rate substantially higher than in most European countries. The literacy rate for women lagged behind that for men until the nineteenth century; and while opportunities for further education were scarce for males, they were almost nonexistent for females. Nevertheless, colonial girls often received the same home-based education as boys in their early years, and their literacy rate was substantially higher than that of their European counterparts.

Black slaves had virtually no access to education. Occasionally a master or mistress would teach slave children to read and write, but they had few real incentives to do so. Indeed, as the slave system became more firmly entrenched, strong social (and ultimately legal) sanctions developed to discourage any efforts to promote black literacy, lest it encourage slaves to question their stations in life.

Nowhere was the intermingling of the influences of traditional religiosity and the new spirit of the Enlightenment clearer than in the colleges and universities that grew up in colonial America. Of the six colleges in operation by 1763, all but two were founded by religious groups primarily for the training of preachers. Yet in almost all, the influences of the new scientific, rational approach to knowledge could be felt.

Harvard, the first American college, was established in 1636 by the General Court of Massachusetts at the behest of Puritan theologians who wanted to create a training center for ministers. Two years later, in 1638, instruction began in Cambridge. In that same year the college was named for a Charlestown minister, John Harvard, who had died and left his library and half his estate to the college. Decades later, in 1693, William and Mary College (named for the English king and queen) was established in Williamsburg, Virginia, by Anglicans; like Harvard, it

was conceived as an academy to train clergymen. And in 1701, conservative Congregationalists, dissatisfied with the growing religious liberalism of Harvard, founded Yale (named for one of its first benefactors, Elihu Yale) in New Haven, Connecticut. Out of the Great Awakening emerged the College of New Jersey, founded in 1746 and known later as Princeton (after the town in which it was located). One of its first presidents was Jonathan Edwards.

Despite the religious basis of these colleges, students at most of them could derive something of a liberal education from the curricula, which included not only theology but logic, ethics, physics, geometry, astronomy, rhetoric, Latin, Hebrew, and Greek. From the beginning, Harvard was intended not only to provide an educated ministry but also to "advance learning and perpetuate it to posterity." King's College, founded in New York in 1754 and later renamed Columbia, was even more devoted to the spread of secular knowledge. It had no theological faculty and was interdenominational from the start. The Academy and College of Philadelphia, which became the University of Pennsylvania, was from its birth in 1755 a completely secular institution, founded by a group of laymen under the inspiration of Benjamin Franklin. It offered courses in utilitarian subjects—mechanics, chemistry, agriculture, government, commerce, and modern languages—as well as in the liberal arts.

By the mid-eighteenth century, the colonies were (in comparison with most European nations) well supplied with colleges; and from them emerged a group of men steeped in the ideas and principles of the Enlightenment. Some Americans continued to travel to England for a university education, and they brought home with them still more new theories and philosophies. After 1700, however, most colonial leaders received their entire education in America. But the advantages of higher education were not widely shared. Women and blacks were excluded from all colleges and universities. And among white men, only those from relatively affluent families could afford to attend.

The Allure of Science

The clearest indication of the spreading influence of the Enlightenment in America was an increasing interest in scientific knowledge. Most of the early colleges established chairs in the natural sciences and introduced some of the advanced scientific theories of

The Magnetic Dispensary
In this 1790 painting, artist Samuel Collings caricatured the popular enthusiasm that Benjamin Franklin and others had produced for scientific experiments. The men and women shown here are rubbing iron rods with silk cloth to produce static electricity. A popular pastime was to place the charged rods over people's heads to watch their hair stand on end. (Library Company of Philadelphia)

Europe, including Copernican astronomy and Newtonian physics, to their students. But the most vigorous promotion of science in these years occurred outside the colleges, through the private efforts of amateurs and the activities of scientific societies. Leading merchants, planters, and even theologians became corresponding members of the Royal Society of London, the principal English scientific organization. Benjamin Franklin, the most celebrated amateur scientist in America, won international fame through his experiments with electricity (and most notably through his 1752 demonstration, using a kite, that lightning and electricity were the same).

The high value that influential Americans were beginning to place on scientific knowledge was clearly demonstrated by the most daring and controversial scientific experiments of the eighteenth century: inoculation against smallpox. The Puritan theologian Cotton Mather had learned of experiments in England by which people had been deliberately infected with mild cases of smallpox in order to immunize them against the deadly disease. Despite strong opposition from many of his neighbors, he urged inoculation on his fellow Bostonians during an epidemic in the 1720s. The results confirmed the effectiveness of the technique. Other theologians (including Jonathan Edwards) took up the cause, along with many physicians. By the mid-eighteenth century, inoculation had become a common medical procedure in America.

SIGNIFICANT EVENTS

1636 Harvard College founded in Massachusetts

1640 Instability in tobacco markets begins

1647 Massachusetts law requires a public school in every town

1662 Halfway Covenant established in New England

1650 Population of New England begins to grow by natural increase

1670s Flow of indentured servants declines; slave traders begin importing slaves directly from Africa to North America

1685 Edict of Nantes revoked in France; Huguenots begin migrating to North America

1690s Rice production becomes central to South Carolina economy

1691 Official toleration of Catholics ends in Maryland

1692 Witchcraft trials begin in Salem

1693 College of William and Mary founded in Virginia

1697 Royal African Company monopoly of slave trade broken; slave importations begin to increase

1701 Yale College founded in Connecticut

1708–1709 First major migration of Palatinate Germans to North America begins

1710 Major Scotch-Irish migrations to North America begin

1720 Cotton Mather initiates smallpox inoculations in Massachusetts

1734 Great Awakening begins in Massachusetts
John Peter Zenger tried in New York

1739 George Whitefield arrives in North America; Great Awakening intensifies

1739 Stono slave rebellion in South Carolina

1740s Indigo production begins in South Carolina

1746 College of New Jersey founded at Princeton

1764 Major ironworks established in New Jersey

Concepts of Law and Politics

In law and politics, as in other parts of their lives, Americans in the seventeenth and eighteenth centuries believed that they were re-creating in the New World the practices and institutions of the Old. But as in other areas, they managed, without meaning to or even realizing it, to create something very different.

Changes in the law in America resulted in part from the scarcity of English-trained lawyers, who were almost unknown in the colonies until after 1700. Not until a full generation after that did authorities in England try to impose the common law and the statutes of the realm on the provinces. By then, it was already too late. Although the American legal system adopted most of the essential elements of the English system, including such ancient rights as trial by jury, significant differences had already become well established.

Pleading and court procedures were simplified in America, and punishments were made less severe. Instead of the gallows or prison, colonists more com-

monly resorted to the whipping post, the branding iron, the stocks, and (for "gossipy" women) the ducking stool. In a labor-scarce society, it was not in the interests of communities to execute or incarcerate potential workers. Crimes were redefined. In England, a printed attack on a public official, whether true or false, was considered libelous. In the colonies, at the 1734 trial of the New York publisher John Peter Zenger, who was powerfully defended by the Philadelphia lawyer Andrew Hamilton, the courts ruled that criticisms of the government were not libels if factually true—a verdict that brought some progress toward freedom of the press. There was a subtle but decisive transformation in legal philosophy; colonists came to think of law as a reflection of the divine will or the natural order, not as an expression of the power of an earthly sovereign.

Even more significant for the future of the relationship between the colonies and England were important differences that were emerging between the American and British political systems. Because the royal government that was in theory the ultimate authority over the colonies was so far away, Americans created a group of institutions of their own that gave them—in reality, if not in theory—a large measure of self-government. In most colonies, local communities grew accustomed to running their own affairs with minimal interference from higher authorities. Communities also expected to maintain strict control over their delegates to the colonial assemblies; and those assemblies came to exercise many of the powers that Parliament exercised in England (even though in theory Parliament remained the ultimate authority in America). Provincial governors had broad powers on paper, but in fact their influence was sharply limited. They lacked control over appointments and contracts; such influence resided largely in England or with local colonial leaders. Nor could they ever be certain of their tenure in office; because governorships were patronage appointments,

a governor could be removed any time his patron in England lost favor. And in many cases, governors were not even familiar with the colonies they were meant to govern; some were native-born Americans, but most were Englishmen who came to the colonies for the first time to assume their offices. The results of all this were that the focus of politics in the colonies became a local one; the provincial governments became accustomed to acting more or less independently of Parliament; and a set of assumptions and expectations about the rights of the colonists took hold in America that was not shared by policymakers in England. These differences caused few problems prior to the 1760s, because the British did little to exert the authority they believed they possessed. But when, beginning in 1763, the English government began attempting to tighten its control over the American colonies, a historic crisis resulted.

SUGGESTED READINGS

General Histories   General portraits of colonial society in the eighteenth century include James A. Henretta, *The Evolution of American Society, 1700–1815* (1973), and Richard Hofstadter, *America at 1750: A Social Portrait* (1971).

Population and Family   The most important reference for the study of the colonial population is Robert V. Wells, *The Population of the British Colonies in America Before 1776* (1975). A valuable local study, particularly interesting for its information on birth and death, is Philip Greven, *Four Generations* (1970), which examines colonial Andover, Massachusetts. Greven is also the author of an important examination of women and the family in the colonial period: *The Protestant Temperament: Patterns of Child-Rearing, Religious Experience, and the Self in Early America* (1977). See also Edmund S. Morgan, *The Puritan Family* (1966); J. William Frost, *The Quaker Family in Colonial America* (1972); Christopher Jedrey, *The World of John Cleaveland: Family and Community in Eighteenth-Century New England* (1979); Laura Thatcher Ulrich, *Good Wives: Image and Reality in the Lives of Women in Northern New England, 1650–1750* (1982); Roger Thompson, *Women in Stuart England and America* (1974); Lyle Koehler, *A Search for Power: "The Weaker Sex" in Seventeenth-Century New England* (1982); and Daniel Blake Smith, *Inside the Great House: Planter Family Life in Eighteenth Century Chesapeake Society* (1980).

Colonial Slavery   There are a number of significant studies of the origins of American slavery. In particular, see Edmund S. Morgan, *American Slavery, American Freedom* (1975), which studies the institution in Virginia; Peter Wood, *Black Majority* (1974), which examines South Carolina; and Winthrop Jordan, *White over Black* (1968), a sweeping study of American racial attitudes. David Brion Davis, *The Problem of Slavery in Western Culture* (1966),

offers a broader view of the origins of the institution. On the colonial slave trade, see Philip D. Curtin, *The Atlantic Slave Trade* (1969); Daniel Littlefield, *Rice and Slaves: Ethnicity and the Slave Trade in Colonial South Carolina* (1981); and Jay Coughtry, *The Notorious Triangle: Rhode Island and the African Slave Trade, 1799–1807* (1981). Studies of white indentured servitude include Abbot E. Smith, *Colonists in Bondage* (1947), and David W. Galenson, *White Servitude in Colonial America: An Economic Analysis* (1982). Gerald Mullin, *Flight and Rebellion* (1972), and parts of Eugene Genovese, *From Rebellion to Revolution* (1979), examine slave resistance in the colonial period. A significant study of colonial society in terms of race relations is Gary B. Nash, *Red, White, and Black,* rev. ed. (1982). Charles Joyner, *Down by the Riverside: A South Carolina Slave Community* (1984), is a local study of the low country. T. H. Breen and Stephen Innes, *"Myne Own Ground," Race and Freedom on Virginia's Eastern Shore* (1980), is an important interdisciplinary study.

Immigration   The complicated story of immigration to the colonies has not yet been told in a single, comprehensive work, but Bernard Bailyn has published the first two volumes of a sweeping study: *The Peopling of British North America: An Introduction* (1986), and *Voyages to the West: A Passage in the Peopling of America on the Eve of the Revolution* (1986). Pieces of the puzzle can be examined in Albert B. Faust, *The German Element in the United States,* 2 vols. (1909); Ian C. C. Graham, *Colonists from Scotland: Emigration to North America, 1707–1783* (1956); James G. Leyburn, *The Scotch-Irish: A Social History* (1962); Frederic Klees, *The Pennsylvania Dutch* (1950); and R. J. Dickson, *Ulster Immigration to the United States* (1966). And for an overview, consult Marcus L. Hanson, *The Atlantic Migration, 1607–1860* (1940). See James Kettner, *The Development of American Citizenship* (1978), for a study of naturalization.

The Colonial Economy General studies include the Henretta work mentioned above; Alice Hanson Jones, *Wealth of a Nation to Be* (1980), which examines the economic condition of the colonies on the eve of the Revolution; Jackson Turner Main, *The Social Structure of Revolutionary America* (1965), which examines the impact of economic inequality on colonial society; and parts of Stuart Bruchey, *Roots of American Economic Growth, 1607–1861* (1965). An ambitious recent overview is John J. McCusker and Russell R. Menard, *The Economy of British America, 1607-1787* (1985). The Southern plantation economy is examined in Carl Bridenbaugh, *Myths and Realities: Societies of the Colonial South* (1963); Paul G. E. Clemens, *The Atlantic Economy and Colonial Maryland's Eastern Shore: From Tobacco to Grain* (1980); Edmund S. Morgan, *Virginians at Home* (1952); and Lewis C. Gray, *History of Agriculture in the Southern United States to 1860*, 2 vols. (1933). Three works by Jacob M. Price—*France and the Chesapeake*, 2 vols. (1973); *The Tobacco Adventure to Russia* (1961); and *Capital and Credit in the British Overseas Trade: The View from the Chesapeake, 1700-1776* (1980)—are important studies of the tobacco trade. Harry R. Merrens, *Colonial North Carolina in the Eighteenth Century* (1964), and Stephen Innes, *Labor in a New Land: Economy and Society in Seventeenth Century Springfield* (1983), are useful local studies.

The New England Town In addition to the studies of Puritanism cited in the readings for Chapter 2 and the Greven study of Andover listed above, see Kenneth Lockridge, *A New England Town* (1970), a study of Dedham, Massachusetts; Michael Zuckerman, *Peaceable Kingdoms* (1970), which challenges the prevailing modern view of the Puritan community as rife with social tension; Darrett Rutman, *Winthrop's Boston* (1965), which examines changes in the early seventeenth century; and Charles Grant, *Democracy in the Connecticut Frontier Town of Kent* (1961). Paul Boyer and Stephen Nissenbaum, *Salem Possessed* (1974), is an important study of witchcraft in Salem, linking the phenomenon to social tensions in the community. John Putnam Demos, *Entertaining Satan: Witchcraft and the Culture of Early New England* (1982), is an important interdisciplinary investigation of the subject. E. M. Cook, Jr., *The Fathers of Towns* (1976), examines colonial leadership. Sumner Chilton Powell, *Puritan Village* (1963), is one of the first of the "new" social histories of the New England towns, in this case Sudbury, Massachusetts. Richard Bushman, *From Puritan to Yankee* (1967), examines social and economic changes in Connecticut in the eighteenth century. Robert Gross, *The Minutemen and Their World* (1976), is an important study of Concord, Massachusetts, at the time of the Revolution.

Cities and Commerce Two works by Carl Bridenbaugh, *Cities in the Wilderness* (1938) and *Cities in Revolt* (1955), have long been the standard references on colonial urban life. A more recent work by Gary B. Nash, *The Urban Crucible* (1979), adds an important new dimension to the subject. G. B. Warden, *Boston, 1687-1776* (1970), examines the development of one of the first colonial towns into one of the first colonial cities. Stephanie G. Wolf, *Urban Village*

(1976), examines aspects of city life in Germantown, Pennsylvania. The rise of commerce is chronicled in the above-cited studies of cities and also in Stuart Bruchey, *The Colonial Merchant* (1966); J. F. Shepherd and G. M. Walton, *The Economic Rise of Early America* (1979); James B. Hedges, *The Browns of Providence Plantation,* vol. 1 (1952), a study of a colonial merchant family; and Frederick B. Tolles, *Meeting House and Counting House: The Quaker Merchants of Colonial Philadelphia, 1682–1763* (1948). Bernard Bailyn, *The New England Merchants in the Seventeenth Century* (1955), is an important history of early commerce. Arthur Jensen, *The Maritime Commerce of Colonial Philadelphia* (1963), examines colonial trade in Pennsylvania; Randolph S. Klein, *Portrait of an Early American Family* (1975), is a study of a Philadelphia merchant family.

Colonial Religion The studies of Puritanism listed in the readings for Chapter 2 are among the most important works. For a general overview, see Sidney Ahlstrom, *A Religious History of the American People* (1972). W. W. Sweet, *Religion in Colonial America* (1942), is an institutional history of the churches. Carl Bridenbaugh, *Mitre and Sceptre: Transatlantic Faiths, Ideas, Personalities, and Politics, 1689–1775* (1962), examines the interaction between religion and politics. Sidney Mead, *The Lively Experiment: The Shaping of Christianity in America* (1963), is another important general study. Studies of particular denominations include J. T. Ellis, *Catholics in America* (1965); J. R. Marcus, *Early American Jewry* (1951); and Janet Whitman, *John Woolman, American Quaker* (1942). William C. McLoughlin, *New England Dissent, 1630–1833,* 2 vols. (1971), is an important study of the colonial Baptists.

The Great Awakening Among many other works, see Edwin S. Gaustad, *The Great Awakening in New England* (1957); J. M. Bumsted and John E. Van de Wetering, *What Must I Do to Be Saved? The Great Awakening in Colonial America* (1976); and Alan Heimert, *Religion and the American Mind* (1966), which traces the divisions that emerged during the Great Awakening into the Revolutionary era and beyond. Perry Miller, *Jonathan Edwards* (1949), is an important analysis of the ideas of the preeminent American leader of the Awakening; Ola Winslow, *Jonathan Edwards* (1940), and Patricia Tracy, *Jonathan Edwards: Pastor* (1980), are other important biographies. Conrad Wright, *The Beginnings of Unitarianism in America* (1955), traces the subject back to the early eighteenth century. J. W. Davidson, *The Logic of Millennial Thought* (1977), examines an important strand of theology.

Education Lawrence A. Cremin, *American Education: The Colonial Experience, 1607–1783* (1970), the first volume in a comprehensive history of American education, is the basic source. See also Bernard Bailyn, *Education in the Forming of American Society* (1960); James Axtell, *The School upon a Hill: Education and Society in Colonial New England* (1974); and Robert Middlekauff, *Ancients and Axioms* (1963). Samuel Eliot Morison examines the beginnings of America's first university in *The Founding of Harvard College* (1935). Jurgen Herbst, *From Crisis to Crisis* (1982), is a comparative study of Harvard, Yale, and William and Mary. Kenneth Lockridge, *Literacy in Colonial New England* (1974), is a general examination of colonial learning.

Culture and the Enlightenment   Louis B. Wright, *The Cultural Life of the American Colonies* (1957), and Daniel J. Boorstin, *The Americans: The Colonial Experience* (1958), are important overviews. See also Richard Beale Davis, *Intellectual Life in the Colonial South,* 2 vols. (1978); Henry May, *The Enlightenment in America* (1976); and Howard Mumford Jones, *O Strange New World* (1964). Brook Hindle, *The Pursuit of Science in Revolutionary America* (1956), examines the institutions of scientific study. Carl Van Doren, *Benjamin Franklin* (1941), and V. W. Crane, *Benjamin Franklin and a Rising People* (1954), are standard biographies of the Enlightenment's leading American figure; but Franklin's own *Autobiography* is the best source. H. Leventhal, *In the Shadow of Enlightenment* (1976), examines occultism in eighteenth-century America.

Law and Politics   An invaluable study of colonial politics is Bernard Bailyn, *The Origins of American Politics* (1968). Other studies of law and government include Jack P. Greene, *The Quest for Power* (1963), which examines the colonial assemblies; J. R. Pole, *Political Representation in England and the Origins of the American Republic* (1966); Leonard W. Labaree, *Royal Government in America* (1930); and Robert Zemsky, *Merchants, Farmers, and River Gods* (1971), a study of politics in colonial Massachusetts. The intellectual context of colonial politics is discussed in Caroline Robbins, *The Eighteenth-Century Commonwealthman* (1959), and J. G. A. Pocock, *The Machiavellian Moment* (1975). Local studies of the law in particular colonies include Gerald W. Gawalt, *The Promise of Power: The Emergence of the Legal Profession in Massachusetts, 1760–1840* (1979), and A. G. Roeber, *Faithful Magistrates and Republican Lawyers: Creators of Virginia Legal Culture, 1680–1810* (1981).

The Boston Massacre, engraving by Paul Revere, 1770   (American Antiquarian Society)

Chapter 4   The Empire Under Strain

As late as the 1750s, few Americans saw any reason to object to their membership in the British Empire. The imperial system provided them with many benefits: opportunities for trade and commerce, military protection, political stability. And those benefits were accompanied by few costs; for the most part, the English government left the colonies alone. While Britain did attempt to regulate the colonists' external trade, those regulations were usually so laxly administered that they could be easily circumvented. Some Americans predicted that the colonies would ultimately develop to a point where greater autonomy would become inevitable. But few expected such a change to occur soon.

By the mid-1770s, however, the relationship between the American colonies and their British rulers had become so strained, so poisoned, so characterized by suspicion and resentment that the once seemingly unbreakable bonds of empire were on the verge of dissolution. And in the spring of 1775, the first shots were fired in a war that would ultimately win America its independence. How had it happened? And why so quickly?

In one sense, it had not happened quickly at all. Ever since the first days of settlement in North America, the ideas and institutions of the colonies had been diverging from those in England in countless ways. Only because the relationship between America and Britain had been so casual had those differences failed to create serious tensions in the past. In another sense, however, the Revolutionary crisis emerged in response to important and relatively sudden changes in the administration of the empire. Beginning in 1763, the English government embarked on a series of new policies toward its colonies—policies dictated by changing international realities and new political circumstances within England itself—that brought the differences between the two societies into sharp focus. In the beginning, most Americans reacted to the changes with relative restraint. Gradually, however, as crisis followed crisis, a large group of Americans found themselves fundamentally disillusioned with the imperial relationship. By 1775, that relationship was, for all practical purposes, damaged beyond repair.

A Loosening of Ties

After England's Glorious Revolution of 1688 and the collapse of the Dominion of New England, the English government (or the British government after 1707, when Great Britain was created by the union of England and Scotland) made no serious or sustained effort to tighten its control over the colonies for over seventy years. During those years, it is true, an increasing number of colonies were brought under the direct control of the king. New Jersey in 1702, North and South Carolina in 1729, Georgia in 1754—all became royal colonies, bringing the total to eight; in all of them, the king had the power to appoint the governors and other colonial officials. During those years, Parliament also passed new laws supplementing the original Navigation Acts and strengthening the mercantilist program—laws restricting colonial manufactures, prohibiting paper currency, and regulating trade. On the whole, however, the British government remained uncertain and divided about the extent to which it ought to interfere in colonial affairs. The colonies were left, within broad limits, to go their separate ways.

A Tradition of Neglect

In the fifty years after the Glorious Revolution, the British Parliament established a growing supremacy over the king. During the reigns of George I (1714–1727) and George II (1727–1760), both of whom were German-born and unaccustomed to English ways, the prime minister and his fellow cabinet ministers began to become the nation's real executives. They held their positions not by the king's favor but by their ability to control a majority in Parliament.

These parliamentary leaders were less inclined than the seventeenth-century monarchs had been to engage in experiments in imperial organization. They depended heavily on the support of the great merchants and landholders, most of whom feared that any such experiments would require large expenditures, would increase taxes, and would diminish the profit of the colonial trade. The first of the prime ministers, Robert Walpole, deliberately refrained from strict enforcement of the Navigation Acts, believing that relaxed trading restrictions would stimulate commerce.

Meanwhile, the day-to-day administration of colonial affairs remained decentralized and inefficient. There was no colonial office in London. The nearest equivalent was the Board of Trade and Plantations, established in 1696—a mere advisory body that had little role in any actual decisions. Real authority rested in the Privy Council (the central administrative agency for the government as a whole), the admiralty, and the treasury. But those agencies were responsible for administering laws at home as well as overseas; none could concentrate on colonial affairs alone. To complicate matters further, there was considerable overlapping and confusion of authority among the departments.

Few of the London officials, moreover, had ever visited America; few knew very much about conditions there. What information they did gather came in large part from agents sent to England by the colonial assemblies to lobby for American interests; and these agents, naturally, did nothing to encourage interference with colonial affairs. (The best known of

them, Benjamin Franklin, represented not only his native Pennsylvania but also Georgia, New Jersey, and Massachusetts.)

It was not only the incoherence of administrative authority in London and the ministerial policy of salutary neglect that weakened England's hold on the colonies. It was also the character of the royal officials in America—the governors and other officers of the royal colonies and (in all the colonies) the collectors of customs and naval officers. Some of these officeholders were able and intelligent men; most were not. Appointments were generally made as the result of bribery or favoritism, not in response to merit. Many appointees remained in England and, with part of their salaries, hired substitutes to take their places in America. Such deputies were generally poorly paid and faced great temptation to augment their incomes with bribes. Few resisted the temptation. Customs collectors, for example, routinely waived duties on goods when merchants paid them to do so. Even honest and well-paid officials usually found it expedient, if they wanted to get along with their neighbors, to yield to the colonists' resistance to trade restrictions.

Resistance to imperial authority centered in the colonial legislatures. By the 1750s the assemblies had established the right to levy taxes, make appropriations, approve appointments, and pass laws for their respective colonies. Their legislation was subject to veto by the governor or the Privy Council; but they had leverage over the governor through their control of the colonial budget, and they could circumvent the Privy Council by repassing disallowed laws in slightly altered form. The assemblies came to look upon themselves as little parliaments, each practically as sovereign within its colony as Parliament itself was in England. In 1754, the Board of Trade reported to the king, regarding the members of the New York assembly: they "have wrested from Your Majesty's governor the nomination of all offices of government, the custody and direction of the public military stores, the mustering and direction of troops raised for Your Majesty's service, and in short almost every other part of executive government."

Intercolonial Disunity

Despite their frequent resistance to the authority of London, the colonists continued to think of themselves as loyal English subjects. In many respects, in fact, they felt stronger ties to England than they did

An Appeal for Colonial Unity
This sketch, one of the first American editorial cartoons, appeared in Benjamin Franklin's Philadelphia newspaper, the *Pennsylvania Gazette,* on May 9, 1754. It was meant to illustrate the need for intercolonial unity and, in particular, for the adoption of Franklin's Albany Plan.
(Library Company of Philadelphia)

to one another. "Fire and water," an English traveler wrote, "are not more heterogeneous than the different colonies in North America." New Englanders and Virginians viewed each other as something close to foreigners. A Connecticut man denounced the merchants of New York for their "frauds and unfair practices," while a New Yorker condemned Connecticut because of the "low craft and cunning so incident to the people of that country." Only an accident of geography, it seemed, connected these disparate societies to each other.

Yet for all their differences, the colonies could scarcely avoid forging connections with one another. The growth of the colonial population, which produced an almost continuous line of settlement along the seacoast, brought the people of the various colonies into closer and closer contact. So did the gradual construction of roads and the rise of intercolonial trade. The colonial postal service likewise helped increase communication. In 1691, it had operated only from Massachusetts to New York and Pennsylvania. In 1711, it was extended to New Hampshire in the north; in 1732, to Virginia in the south; and ultimately, all the way to Georgia.

Still, the colonists were loath to cooperate even when, in 1754, they faced a common threat from their old rivals, the French, and France's Indian allies.

A conference of colonial leaders—with delegates from Pennsylvania, Maryland, New York, and New England—was meeting in Albany in that year to negotiate a treaty with the Iroquois. The delegates stayed on to talk about forming a colonial federation for defense. Benjamin Franklin proposed, and the delegates tentatively approved, a plan by which Parliament would set up in America "one general government" for all the colonies, each of which would "retain its present constitution" except for certain powers to be granted to the general government—such as the authority to govern all relations with the Indians.

War with the French and Indians was already beginning when this Albany Plan was presented to the colonial assemblies. None approved it. Only the Massachusetts assembly even gave it serious attention. "Everyone cries, a union is necessary," Franklin wrote to the Massachusetts governor, "but when they come to the manner and form of the union, their weak noodles are perfectly distracted." Not until twenty years later, in the midst of another war, did the American colonies begin to think of themselves as a single, united nation.

The Struggle for the Continent

In one sense, the war that raged in North America through the late 1750s and early 1760s was but one part of a larger struggle between England and France for dominance in world trade and naval power. The British victory in that struggle, known in Europe as the Seven Years' War, confirmed England's commercial supremacy and cemented its control of the settled regions of North America.

In another sense, however, the conflict was the final stage in a long struggle among the three principal powers in northeastern North America: the English, the French, and the Iroquois. For more than a century prior to the conflict—known in America as the French and Indian War—these three groups had maintained a precarious balance of power. The events of the 1750s upset that balance, produced a prolonged and open conflict, and established the dominance of the English societies throughout the region.

The French and Indian War had one additional significance to the English colonists in America. By bringing the Americans into closer contact with British authority than ever before, it raised to the surface some of the underlying tensions in the colonial relationship—tensions that would ultimately become crucial to the final break with England.

New France and the Iroquois Nation

The French and the English had coexisted relatively peacefully in North America for nearly a century. But by the 1750s, as both English and French settlements expanded, religious and commercial tensions began to produce new frictions and new conflicts.

The origins of the crisis lay in part in the expansion of the French presence in America in the late seventeenth century—part of Louis XIV's search for national unity and increased world power. The French finance minister, Jean Colbert, persuaded the king that he could best increase the nation's glory by creating a new, four-part empire. France itself would be the center, the source of capital and manufactured goods; its West Indian islands (especially Martinique and Guadeloupe) would be suppliers of sugar and other exotic products; posts along the African coast would support the slave trade; and the settlements in Canada would be a market for exports from France and a granary for provisioning the West Indies. In response to Colbert's proposals, France began to devote new attention to the development of its North American territories.

Colbert had intended Canada to be a compactly settled agricultural province, but ambitious French officials in America (most notably Jean Talon and Count Frontenac) had little patience with the limits Colbert had set. They did nothing to curb, and indeed a great deal to promote, the expansion of French settlement. The lucrative fur trade drew immigrant peasants ever deeper into the wilderness. Missionary zeal drew large numbers of Jesuits into the interior in search of potential converts. The bottomlands of the Mississippi River valley attracted farmers discouraged by the short growing season in Canada.

By the mid-seventeenth century, the French Empire in America comprised a vast territory. Louis Joliet and Father Jacques Marquette, French explorers of the 1670s, journeyed together by canoe from Green Bay on Lake Michigan as far south as the junction of the Arkansas and Mississippi rivers. (They were the first to confirm that the Mississippi flowed into the Gulf of Mexico, not—as most had believed—the Gulf of California.) A year later, René Robert Cavelier, Sieur de La Salle, began the explorations that finally, in 1682, took him to the delta of the Mississippi,

where he took possession of the surrounding country for France and named it Louisiana in the king's honor. Subsequent traders and missionaries wandered to the southwest as far as the Rio Grande, and the explorer Pierre Gaultier de Varennes, Sieur de La Vérendrye, pushed westward in 1743 from Lake Superior to a point within sight of the Rocky Mountains. The French had by then revealed the outlines of, and laid claim to, the whole continental interior.

To secure their hold on this vast territory, they founded a string of widely separated communities, strategically located fortresses, and far-flung missions and trading posts. Fort Louisbourg, on Cape Breton Island, guarded the approach to the Gulf of St. Lawrence. Would-be feudal lords established large estates ("seigneuries") along the banks of the St. Lawrence River; and on a high bluff above the river stood the fortified city of Quebec, the center of the French Empire in America. Montreal to the south and Sault Sainte Marie and Detroit to the west marked the northern boundaries of French settlement. On the lower Mississippi emerged plantations much like those in the Southern colonies of English America, worked by black slaves and owned by "Creoles" (white immigrants of French descent). New Orleans, founded in 1718 to service the French plantation economy, soon was as big as some of the larger cities of the Atlantic seaboard; Biloxi and Mobile to the east completed the string of French settlement.

But the French were not, of course, alone in the continental interior. They encountered there a large and powerful Indian population, and their relations with the natives were crucial to the shaping of their empire. Both the French and the English were aware that the battle for control of North America would be determined in part by which group could best win the allegiance of native tribes—as trading partners and, at times, as military allies. The Indians, for their part, were principally concerned with protecting their independence, and what alignments they formed with the European societies growing up around them were generally marriages of convenience, determined by which group offered the most attractive terms. For the most part, the English—with their more advanced commercial economy—could offer the Indians better and more plentiful goods. But the French offered something that was often more important: tolerance. Unlike the English settlers, who strove constantly to impose their own social norms on the Indians they encountered, the French settlers in the interior often adjusted their own behavior to Indian patterns. French fur traders frequently married Indian women and adopted tribal ways; Jesuit missionaries interacted comfortably with the natives and converted them to Catholicism by the thousands without challenging most of their social customs. By the mid-eighteenth century, therefore, the French had far better and closer relations with most of the Indians of the interior than did the English.

The most powerful native group, however, had a rather different relationship with the French. The Iroquois Confederacy—the five Indian nations (Mohawk, Seneca, Cayuga, Onondaga, and Oneida) that had formed a defensive alliance in the sixteenth century—dominated the Ohio Valley and a large surrounding region. The Iroquois had formed very early an important commercial relationship with the English and Dutch along the eastern seaboard; and in the 1640s, they had fought—and won—a bitter war against the Hurons, their major competitors in that trade. The Hurons had been nearly exterminated, and the few survivors had fled the region.

The Hurons had been the principal trading partners of the French in the early seventeenth century, and their disappearance pushed French traders farther into the interior in search of the furs the natives had once provided. For nearly a century, however, neither the French nor the English raised any serious challenge to Iroquois control of the Ohio Valley. The Iroquois maintained their autonomy in part by avoiding too close a relationship with either group. They traded successfully with both the English and the French and astutely played the two groups off against each other. As a result, they managed to maintain an uneasy balance of power in the Great Lakes region.

Anglo-French Conflicts

As long as England and France remained at peace in Europe, and as long as the precarious balance in the North American interior survived, English and French colonists coexisted without serious difficulty. But after the Glorious Revolution in England, the English throne passed to one of Louis XIV's principal enemies, William III, who had previously been and remained still the *stadholder* (chief magistrate) of the Netherlands and who had long opposed French expansionism. William's successor, Queen Anne (the daughter of James II), ascended the throne in 1702 and carried on the struggle against France and its new ally, Spain. The result was a series of Anglo-French wars that continued intermittently for nearly eighty years.

ENGLISH MONARCHS, 1702–1820	
Anne	1702–1714
George I	1714–1727
George II	1727–1760
George III	1760–1820

The wars had important repercussions in America. King William's War (1689–1697) produced only a few, indecisive clashes between English and French in northern New England. Queen Anne's War, which began in 1701 and continued for nearly twelve years, generated more substantial conflicts: border fighting with the Spaniards in the south as well as with the French and their Indian allies in the north. The Treaty of Utrecht, which brought the conflict to a close in 1713, transferred substantial areas of French territory from the French to the English in North America, including Acadia (Nova Scotia) and Newfoundland.

Two decades later, European rivalries led to still more conflicts in America. Disputes over British trading rights in the Spanish colonies produced a war between England and Spain and led to clashes between the British in Georgia and the Spaniards in Florida. (It was in the context of this conflict that the last English colony in America, Georgia, was founded in 1733; see pp. 51–53.) The Anglo-Spanish conflict soon merged with a much larger European war, in which England and France lined up on opposite sides of a territorial dispute between Frederick the Great of Prussia and Maria Theresa of Austria. (France supported Prussia, in the hope of seizing the Austrian Netherlands; England supported Austria, to keep Holland from the French.) The English colonists in America were soon drawn into the struggle, which they called King George's War; and between 1744 and 1748 they engaged in a series of conflicts with the French. New Englanders captured the French bastion at Louisbourg on Cape Breton Island; but the peace treaty that finally ended the conflict forced them (in bitter disappointment) to abandon it.

In the aftermath of King George's War, relations among the English, French, and Iroquois in North America quickly deteriorated. In a classic blunder, the Iroquois began for the first time to grant trading concessions in the interior to English merchants. In the context of the already tense Anglo-French relationship in America, that decision set in motion a disastrous chain of events. The French, fearful that the English were using the concessions as a first step toward expansion into French lands (which to some extent they were), began in 1749 to construct new fortresses in the Ohio Valley. The English, interpreting the French activity as a threat to their western settlements, protested and began making military preparations and building fortresses of their own. The balance of power that the Iroquois had carefully and successfully maintained for so long rapidly disintegrated; and the five Indian nations had no choice now but to ally themselves with the British and assume an essentially passive role in the conflict that ensued.

For the next five years, skirmishes between the English and the French grew in intensity, until in the summer of 1754, open hostilities broke out between a military force from Virginia (commanded by George Washington) and a French force at Fort Duquesne, on the site of what became Pittsburgh. The Virginians were routed. The clash marked the beginning of the French and Indian War, the climactic event in the long Anglo-French struggle for empire.

The Great War for the Empire

The French and Indian War lasted nearly nine years, and it moved forward in three distinct phases. During the first of these phases, from the Fort Duquesne debacle in 1754 until the expansion of the war to

Europe in 1756, it was primarily a local, North American conflict. The colonists managed the war largely on their own. The British provided modest assistance during this period, but they provided it so ineptly that it had little impact on the struggle. The British fleet failed to prevent the landing of large French reinforcements in Canada; and the newly appointed commander in chief of the British army in America, General Edward Braddock, failed miserably in a major effort in the summer of 1755 to retake the crucial site at the forks of the Ohio River where Washington had lost the battle for Fort Duquesne; a French and Indian ambush a few miles from the fort left Braddock dead and what remained of his forces in disarray. The local colonial forces, meanwhile, were preoccupied with defending themselves against raids on their western settlements by the Indians of the Ohio Valley. Virtually all of them (except the Iroquois) were now allied with the French, having interpreted the defeat of the Virginians at Fort Duquesne as evidence of British weakness. By late 1755, many English settlers along the frontier had withdrawn to the east of the Allegheny Mountains to escape the hostilities.

The second phase of the struggle began in 1756, when the governments of France and England formally opened hostilities and a truly international conflict (the Seven Years' War) began. In Europe, the

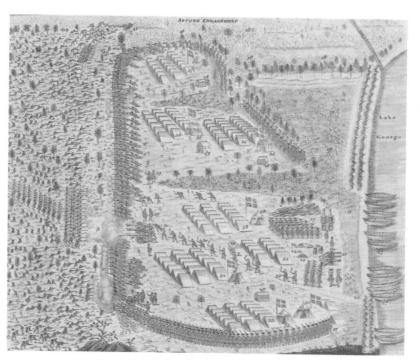

Battle at Lake George, 1755
Here, French and Indian forces attack a British encampment on Lake George in upstate New York during the first phase of the French and Indian War. The British drove off the assault and inflicted heavy losses on the enemy.
(Anne S. K. Brown Military Collection, Brown University)

war was marked by a realignment within the complex system of European alliances. France allied itself with its former enemy, Austria; and England joined France's former ally, Prussia. The fighting now spread to the West Indies, India, and Europe itself. But the principal struggle remained the one in North America, where so far England had suffered nothing but frustration and defeat.

Beginning in 1757, William Pitt, the new English prime minister, began to transform the war effort in America by bringing it for the first time fully under British control. Pitt himself began planning military strategy for the North American conflict, appointing military commanders, and issuing orders to the colonists. Military recruitment had slowed dramatically in America after the defeat of Braddock, and to replenish the army British commanders began forcibly enlisting colonists (a practice known as "impressment"). Officers also began to seize supplies and equipment from local farmers and tradesmen and to compel colonists to offer shelter to British troops—all generally without compensation. The Americans, who had long ago become accustomed to running their own affairs and who had been fighting for over two years without much assistance or direction from the British, resented these new impositions and firmly resisted them—at times, as in a 1757 riot in New York City, violently. By early 1758, the friction between the British authorities and the colonists was threatening to bring the war effort to a halt.

Beginning in 1758, therefore, Pitt initiated the third and final phase of the war by relaxing many of the policies that Americans had found obnoxious. He agreed to reimburse the colonists for all supplies requisitioned by the army. He returned control over recruitment to the colonial assemblies (which resulted in an immediate and dramatic increase in enlistments). And he dispatched large numbers of additional troops to America.

Finally, the tide of battle began to turn in England's favor. The French, who had always been outnumbered by the British colonists and who, after 1756, suffered from a series of poor harvests, were unable to sustain their early military successes. By mid-1758, the British regulars in America (who did the bulk of the actual fighting) and the colonial militias were seizing one French stronghold after another. Two brilliant English generals, Jeffrey Amherst and James Wolfe, captured the fortress at Louisbourg in July 1758; a few months later Fort Duquesne fell without a fight. The next year, after a siege of Quebec, supposedly impregnable atop its towering cliff, the army of General James Wolfe struggled up a hidden ravine under cover of darkness, surprised the larger forces of the Marquis de Montcalm, and defeated them in a battle in which both commanders were slain. The dramatic fall of Quebec on September 13, 1759, marked the beginning of the end of the American phase of the war. A year later, in September 1760, the French army formally surrendered to Amherst in Montreal.

Not all aspects of the struggle were as romantic as Wolfe's assault on Quebec. The British resorted at times to such brutal military expedients as population dispersal. In Nova Scotia, for example, they uprooted several thousand French inhabitants, whom they suspected of disloyalty, and scattered them throughout the English colonies. (Some of these Acadians eventually made their way to Louisiana, where they became the ancestors of the present-day Cajuns.) Elsewhere, English and colonial troops were inflicting worse atrocities on the Indian allies of the French—for example, offering "scalp bounties" to those who could bring back evidence of having killed a native. The French and their Indian allies committed similar atrocities in return, and hundreds of families along the English frontier perished in savage raids on their settlements.

Peace finally came after the accession of George III to the British throne and the resignation of Pitt, who, unlike the new king, wanted to continue hostilities. Pitt's aims were largely realized nevertheless in the Peace of Paris, signed in 1763. Under its terms, the French ceded to Great Britain some of their West Indian islands and most of their colonies in India. The French also transferred Canada and all other French territory east of the Mississippi, except the island of New Orleans, to Great Britain. They ceded New Orleans and their claims west of the Mississippi to Spain, thus surrendering all title to the mainland of North America.

The French and Indian War had profound effects on the British Empire and the American colonies. It greatly expanded England's territorial claims in the New World. At the same time, it greatly enlarged Britain's debt; financing the vast war had been a major drain on the treasury. And it generated substantial resentment toward the Americans among English leaders. They were contemptuous of the colonists for what they considered American military ineptitude during the war; they were angry that the colonists had made so few financial contributions to a struggle waged largely for American benefit; they were particularly bitter that some colonial merchants had been

The Thirteen Colonies in 1763

HUDSON'S BAY COMPANY

Lake Superior

QUEBEC

St. Lawrence R.
Quebec

MAINE
(Mass.)

Montreal

Fort Michilimackinac

Lake Michigan

Lake Huron

LaBaye

Fort
Frontenac

N.H.

Falmouth

Merrimac R.

Lake Ontario
Fort
Stanwix   Mohawk R.
Fort Niagara   Bennington
Albany
NEW YORK
Kingston
Poughkeepsie

Portsmouth
Gloucester
Boston
MASS.
Providence Plymouth
Hartford
CONN.   R.I.
New Haven   Newport
Southampton

B R I T I S H

Fort Detroit

Lake Erie

St. Joseph

Maumee R.

PENNSYLVANIA

Appalachian Mountains

Susquehanna R.

Hudson R.

Delaware R.

New York
Perth Amboy
Trenton
NEW JERSEY
Burlington

Reading
Philadelphia
New
Castle
Dover
DELAWARE

Illinois R.

Fort
Duquesne

Ohio R.

St. Louis

Vincennes

Ohio R.

Wabash R.

Baltimore
Annapolis
Potomac R.
MARYLAND

Shenandoah R.

VIRGINIA

Richmond
James R.
Petersburg
Williamsburg
Norfolk

ATLANTIC   OCEAN

SPANISH
LOUISIANA

R.

Cumberland

Roanoke R.

Edenton

NORTH CAROLINA
Greensville
New Bern
Portsmouth

Tennessee R.

Cape Fear R.

Fayetteville

Mississippi R.

DISPUTED TERRITORY
(Claimed by Spain and Britain)

Camden
Columbia
Augusta
Ashley R.

Santee R.

Wilmington

Kingston

SOUTH
CAROLINA
Cooper R.
Charleston

Savannah R.

GEORGIA

Altamaha R.

Savannah

WEST   FLORIDA

Mobile

Pensacola

EAST FLORIDA

St. Augustine

New Orleans

Gulf of Mexico

NON-INDIAN
SETTLEMENT

Before 1700

1700–1763

Frontier line
in 1763

Proclamation Line
of 1763

★ Provincial capital

0   150 Miles
0   200 Kilometers

selling food and other goods to the French in the West Indies throughout the conflict. All these factors combined to persuade many English leaders that a major reorganization of the empire, giving London increased authority over the colonies, would be necessary in the aftermath of the war.

The war had an equally profound but very different effect on the American colonists. It was an experience that forced them, for the first time, to act in concert against a common foe. The colonies were still far from united, but they had learned certain lessons in cooperation. The friction of 1756–1757 over British requisition and impressment policies, and the 1758 return of authority to the colonial assemblies, established an important precedent in the minds of the colonists; it seemed to confirm the illegitimacy of English interference in local affairs. And for thousands of Americans, those who served in the colonial armed forces, the war served as an important socializing experience. The colonial militias, unlike the British regiments, had generally viewed themselves as a "people's army." The relationship of soldiers to their units was, the soldiers believed, in some measure voluntary; their army was a communal, not a coercive or hierarchical organization. The contrast with the British regulars, whom the colonists widely resented for their arrogance and arbitrary use of power, was striking; and in later years, the memory of that contrast helped to shape the American response to British imperial policies.

In important respects, therefore, the French and Indian War established attitudes and assumptions among both the British and the Americans that would shape their behavior during the crises that led to the American Revolution.

The New Imperialism

With the treaty of 1763, England found itself truly at peace for the first time in more than fifty years. Undistracted by war, the British government could now turn its attention to the organization of its empire. And after the difficult experiences of the previous decade, many English leaders were convinced that the question of imperial organization could no longer be ignored.

In fact, they had virtually no choice; even if policymakers had wished to revert to the old colonial system with its half-hearted enforcement of the mercantilist program, they would have found it virtually impossible to do so. Saddled with enormous debts from the many years of fighting, England was desperately in need of new revenues from its empire. And responsible for vast new lands in the New World, the imperial government could not long avoid expanding its involvement in its colonies.

Burdens of Empire

The experience of the French and Indian War, however, suggested that such increased involvement would not be easy to establish. Not only had the colonists proved so resistant to British control that Pitt had been forced to relax his policies in 1758, but the colonial assemblies had continued after that to respond to British needs slowly and grudgingly. Unwilling to be taxed by Parliament to support the war effort, the colonists were generally reluctant to tax themselves as well. Defiance of imperial trade regulations and other British demands continued, and even increased, through the last years of the war.

The problems of managing the empire were compounded after 1763 by a basic shift in Britain's imperial design. In the past, the English had viewed their colonial empire primarily in terms of trade; they had opposed acquisition of territory for its own sake. But by the mid-eighteenth century, a growing number of English and American leaders (including both William Pitt and Benjamin Franklin) were beginning to argue that land itself was of value to the empire— because of the population it could support, the taxes it could produce, and the sense of imperial splendor it would confer. The debate between the old commercial imperialists and the new territorial ones came to a head at the conclusion of the French and Indian War. The mercantilists wanted England to return Canada to France in exchange for Guadeloupe, the most commercially valuable of the French "sugar islands" in the West Indies. The territorialists, however, prevailed. The acquisition of the French territories in North America was a victory for, among others, Benjamin Franklin, who had long argued that the American people would need these vast spaces to accommodate their rapid and, he believed, limitless growth. But Franklin and his supporters in the colonies were soon to discover that the new acquisitions brought with them unexpected problems.

With the territorial annexations of 1763, the area of the British Empire was suddenly twice as great as it had been, and the problems of governing it were thus made many times more complex. Almost immediately, England faced a series of sharply conflicting pressures as it attempted to devise a policy for governing the new lands. Some argued that the empire should restrain rapid settlement and development of the Western territories. To do otherwise would be to risk further costly conflicts with the Indians and might help encourage France to launch a new attack somewhere in America in an effort to recover some of its lost territories and prestige. And restricting settlement would keep the land available for hunting and trapping. Others wanted to see the new territories opened for immediate development; but they disagreed among themselves about who should control the Western lands. Colonial governments made fervent, and often conflicting, claims of jurisdiction. Others argued that control should remain in England, that the territories should be considered entirely new colonies, unlinked to the existing settlements. There were, in short, a host of problems and pressures that the British could not ignore.

At the same time, the government in London was running out of options in its effort to find a way to deal with its staggering war debt. Landlords and merchants in England itself were objecting strenuously to increases in what they already considered excessively high taxes. The colonies, on the other hand, had contributed virtually nothing, the British believed, to the support of a war fought in large part for their benefit. The necessity of stationing significant numbers of British troops on the Western frontier even after 1763 was adding even more to the cost of defending the American settlements. And the half-hearted response of the colonial assemblies to the war effort had suggested that in its search for revenue, England could not rely on any cooperation from the colonial governments. Only a system of taxation administered by London, the leaders of the empire believed, could effectively meet England's needs.

The Role of George III

At this crucial moment in Anglo-American relations, with the imperial system in desperate need of redefinition, the government of England was thrown into turmoil by the accession to the throne of a new king. George III assumed power in 1760 on the death of his grandfather. And he brought two particularly unfortunate qualities to the office. First, he was determined, unlike his two predecessors, to reassert the authority of the monarchy. Pushed by his ambitious mother, he removed from power the longstanding and relatively stable coalition of Whigs, who had (under Pitt and others) governed the empire for much of the century. In their place, he created a new coalition of his own through patronage and bribes and gained an uneasy control of Parliament. Yet the new ministries that emerged as a result of these changes were inherently unstable, each lasting in office an average of only about two years.

In addition to these dangerous political ambitions, the king had serious intellectual and psychological limitations. He suffered, apparently, from a rare mental disease that produced intermittent bouts of insanity. (Indeed, in the last years of his long reign he was, according to most accounts, a virtual lunatic, confined to the palace and unable to perform any official functions.) Yet even when George III was lucid and rational, which was most of the time in the 1760s and 1770s, he was painfully immature (he had been only twenty-two when he ascended the throne) and insecure—striving constantly to prove his fitness for his position but time and again finding himself ill equipped to handle the challenges he seized for himself. The king's personality, therefore, contributed both to the instability and to the intransigence of the British government during these critical years.

More immediately responsible for the problems that soon emerged with the colonies, however, was George Grenville, whom the king made prime minister in 1763. Grenville, a brother-in-law of William Pitt, did not share Pitt's sympathy with the American point of view. He agreed instead with the prevailing opinion within Britain that the colonists had been too long indulged and that they should be compelled to obey the laws and to pay a part of the cost of defending and administering the empire. He fancied himself something of an efficiency expert, and he was indeed an able administrator. Furthermore, as chancellor of the exchequer and first lord of the treasury, he was well acquainted with matters of public finance. He promptly undertook to impose a system upon what had been a rather unsystematic aggregation of colonial possessions in America.

The Western problem was the most urgent. With the repulse of the French, frontiersmen from the English colonies had begun immediately to move over the mountains and into the upper Ohio Valley. Objecting to this intrusion, an alliance of Indian tribes, under the Ottawa chieftain Pontiac, prepared to fight back. As an emergency measure, the British government issued a proclamation forbidding settlers to advance beyond a line drawn along the mountain divide between the Atlantic and the interior.

Although the original emergency soon subsided,

George III
This portrait by the Scottish artist Allan Ramsay shows the 22-year-old English king in his coronation robes as he ascended the throne in 1760. American patriots during the long revolutionary crisis came to consider George III a vicious and brutal tyrant. In reality, the king was a man of limited ability who tried desperately, stubbornly, and generally unsuccessfully to play a role for which he was fundamentally ill-suited. As early as 1780, he began to suffer intermittently from insanity. After 1810, he was blind and permanently deranged and spent the last decade of his sixty-year reign as an invalid, barred from all official business by the Regency Act of 1811. His son (later King George IV) served as regent in those years. (Colonial Williamsburg Foundation)

the new principle of the Proclamation Line of 1763 remained in force—the principle of controlling the westward movement of population. Earlier, the British government had encouraged the rapid peopling of the frontier for reasons of both defense and trade. But the official attitude had gradually changed—and not only in response to the Indian threat. Officials in London also feared that the interior might draw so many people away from the coast that markets and investments in the original settlements would suffer. And they wanted as well to reserve opportunities for land speculation and fur trading for English rather than colonial entrepreneurs.

Having announced the new policy tentatively in 1763, the English government soon extended and elaborated it. A definite Indian boundary was to be located, and from time to time relocated, in agreement with the various tribes. Western lands were to be opened for occupation only gradually, and settle-

ment was to be carefully supervised to see that it proceeded in a compact and orderly way.

The Grenville ministry soon made a number of other efforts to increase its control of the colonies. Regular British troops, London announced, would now be stationed permanently in the provinces; and under the Mutiny Act of 1765 the colonists were required to assist in provisioning and maintaining the army. Ships of the British navy were assigned to patrol American waters and search for smugglers. The customs service was reorganized and enlarged. Royal officials were ordered to take up their colonial posts in person instead of sending substitutes. Colonial manufacturing was to be restricted, so that it would not compete with the rapidly expanding industry in Great Britain.

The Sugar Act of 1764, designed in part to eliminate the illegal sugar trade between the continental colonies and the French and Spanish West Indies, lowered the duty on molasses and raised the duty on sugar; and it established new vice-admiralty courts in America to try accused smugglers—thus depriving them of the benefit of sympathetic local juries. The Currency Act of 1764 required the colonial assemblies to stop issuing paper money (a widespread practice during the war) and to retire on schedule all the paper money already in circulation. Most momentous of all, the Stamp Act of 1765 imposed a tax on every printed document in the colonies: newspapers, almanacs, pamphlets, deeds, wills, licenses.

The new imperial program was an effort to reapply to the colonies the old principles of mercantilism. And in some ways, it proved highly effective. British officials were soon collecting more than ten

North America in 1763

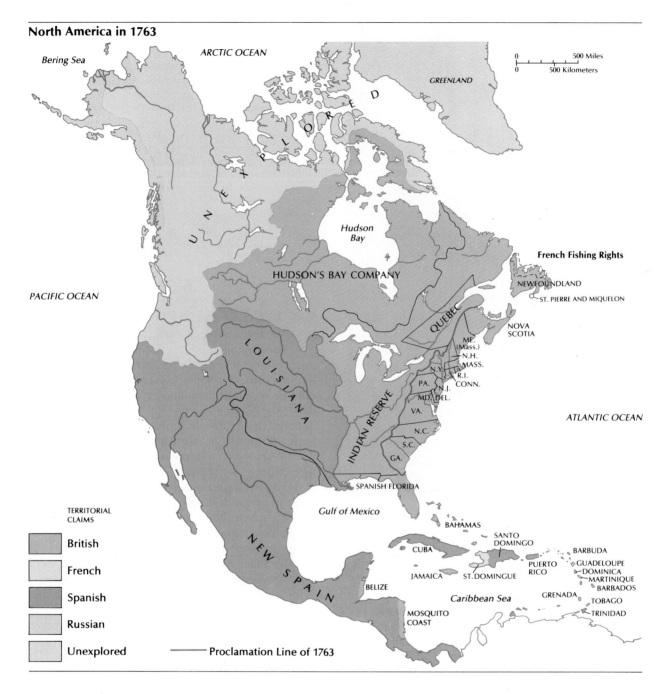

TERRITORIAL CLAIMS	
	British
	French
	Spanish
	Russian
	Unexplored

—— Proclamation Line of 1763

times as much annual revenue in America as before 1763. But the new policies created many more problems than they solved.

The Colonial Response

The colonists may have resented the new imperial regulations, but they faced many obstacles to an effective effort to resist them. For one thing, Americans continued to harbor as many grievances against one another as against the authorities in London. In 1763, for example, a band of Pennsylvania frontiersmen known as the Paxton Boys descended on Philadelphia to demand relief from taxation and money to support their own defense needs; bloodshed was averted only by concessions from the colonial government.

In 1771, a small-scale civil war broke out as a

result of the so-called Regulator movement in North Carolina. The Regulators were farmers of the Carolina upcountry who organized to oppose the high taxes that local sheriffs (appointed by the colonial governor) collected. The western counties were badly underrepresented in the colonial assembly, and the Regulators failed to win redress of their grievances there. Finally they armed themselves and began resisting tax collections by force. To suppress the revolt, Governor William Tryon raised an army of militiamen, mostly from the eastern counties, who defeated a band of 2,000 Regulators in the Battle of Alamance. Nine on each side were killed and many others wounded. Afterward, six Regulators were hanged for treason.

The bloodshed was exceptional, but the bitter conflicts within the colonies were not. After 1763, however, the new policies of the British government began to create common grievances among virtually all colonists that to some degree counterbalanced these internal divisions. For under the Grenville program, as the Americans saw it, all people—in all classes, in all colonies—would suffer.

Northern merchants would suffer from restraints on their commerce, from the closing of the West to land speculation and fur trading, from the closing of opportunities for manufacturing, and from the increased burden of taxation. Southern planters, in debt to English merchants, would now have to pay additional taxes and would be unable to ease their debts by speculating in Western land. Professional men—ministers, lawyers, professors, and others—depended on merchants and planters for their livelihood and thus shared their concerns about the effects of English law. Small farmers, the largest group in the colonies, would suffer from increased taxes and from the abolition of paper money, which had been the source of most of their loans. Workers in towns faced the prospect of narrowing opportunities, particularly because of the restraints on manufacturing and paper money.

The new restrictions came, moreover, at the beginning of a postwar economic depression. The British government, by pouring money into the colonies to finance the fighting, had stimulated a wartime boom; that flow stopped after 1763. Now the authorities in London proposed to aggravate the problem by taking money *out* of the colonies. The imperial policies would, many colonists feared, doom them to permanent economic stagnation and a declining standard of living.

In reality, most Americans soon found ways to live with (or circumvent) the new British policies.

The American economy was not, in fact, being destroyed. But economic anxieties were rising in the colonies nevertheless, and they created a growing sense of unease, particularly in the cities—the places most directly affected by British policies and the places where resistance first arose. The periodic economic slumps that were occurring with greater and greater frequency, the frightening depression of the early 1760s, the growth of a large group within the population who were unemployed or semiemployed, and who were in either case a destabilizing element in the community: all combined to produce a feeling in some colonial cities—and particularly in Boston, the city suffering the worst economic problems—that something was deeply amiss.

Whatever the economic consequences of George III's and Grenville's programs, the political consequences were—in the eyes of the colonists, at least—far worse. Nowhere else in the world did so large a proportion of the people take an active interest in public affairs; and Americans were accustomed (and deeply attached) to a wide latitude in self-government. The keys to self-government, they believed, were the provincial assemblies; and the key to the power of the provincial assemblies was their long-established right to give or withhold appropriations for the costs of government within the colonies. By attempting to circumvent the colonial assemblies, raise extensive revenues directly from the public, and provide salaries directly and unconditionally to royal officials in America, the British government was challenging the basis of colonial political power: control over public finance.

Home rule, therefore, was not something new and different that the colonists were striving to attain. It was something old and familiar that they desired to keep. The movement to resist the new imperial policies, a movement for which many would ultimately fight and die, was thus at the same time democratic and conservative. It was a movement to conserve liberties Americans believed they already possessed.

Stirrings of Revolt

By the mid-1760s, therefore, a hardening of positions had begun in both England and America that would bring the colonies into increasing conflict with the mother country. The victorious war for empire had given the colonists a heightened sense of their own importance and a renewed commitment to protecting their political autonomy. It had given the British a strengthened belief in the need to tighten administration of the empire and a strong desire to use the colonies as a source of revenue. The result was a progression of events that, more rapidly than anyone could have imagined, destroyed the English empire in America.

The Stamp Act Crisis

Prime Minister Grenville could not have devised a better method for antagonizing and unifying the colonies than the Stamp Act if he had tried. The new tax fell on all Americans, of whatever section, colony, or class. And it evoked particular opposition from some of the most powerful and strategically placed members of the population—people with substantial economic and political power, and people with particular influence over public opinion. Merchants and lawyers were obliged to buy stamps for ships' papers and legal documents. Tavern owners, often the political oracles of their neighborhoods, were required to buy stamps for their licenses. Printers—the most influential group in distributing information and ideas in colonial society—had to buy stamps for their newspapers and other publications.

The actual economic burdens of the Stamp Act were, in the end, relatively light. What made the law obnoxious to the colonists was not so much its immediate cost as the precedent it seemed to set. In the past, taxes and duties on colonial trade had always been interpreted as measures to regulate commerce, not raise money. Some Americans had even managed to persuade themselves that the Sugar Act of 1764, which was in fact designed primarily to raise money, was not fundamentally different from the traditional nature of imperial duties. The Stamp Act, however, could be interpreted in only one way. It was a direct attempt by England to raise revenue in the colonies without the consent of the colonial assemblies. If this new tax were allowed to pass without resistance, the door would be open for far more burdensome taxation in the future.

Few colonists believed that they could do anything more than grumble and buy the stamps—until the Virginia House of Burgesses sounded a "trumpet of sedition" that aroused Americans to action almost everywhere. The "trumpet" was sounded by a group of young Virginia aristocrats. They hoped, among other things, to challenge the power of tidewater planters who (in alliance with the royal governor) dominated Virginia politics. Foremost among the malcontents was Patrick Henry, who had already achieved fame through his fiery oratory and his defiance of British authority. Henry made a dramatic speech to the House in May 1765, concluding with a vague prediction that if present policies were not revised, George III, like earlier tyrants, might lose his head. There were shocked cries of "Treason!" and, according to one witness, an immediate apology from Henry (although many years later he was quoted as having made the defiant reply: "If *this* be treason, make the most of it"). Henry introduced a set of resolutions declaring that Americans possessed the same rights as the English, especially the right to be taxed only by their own representatives; that Virginians should pay no taxes except those voted by the Virginia assembly; and that anyone advocating the right of Parliament to tax Virginians should be deemed an enemy of the colony. The House of Burgesses defeated the most extreme of Henry's resolutions, but all of them were printed and circulated as the "Virginia Resolves" (creating an impression in other colonies that the people of Virginia were more militant than they actually were).

In Massachusetts at about the same time, James Otis persuaded his fellow members of the colonial assembly to call an intercolonial congress for concerted action against the new tax. In October 1765, the Stamp Act Congress, as it was called, met in New York with delegates from nine colonies and decided to petition the king and the two houses of Parliament. Their petition conceded that Americans owed to Parliament "all due subordination," but it denied that the colonies could rightfully be taxed except through their own provincial assemblies.

Meanwhile, in several colonial cities mobs began taking the law into their own hands. During the summer of 1765 serious riots broke out up and down the coast, the largest of them in Boston. Men belonging to the newly organized Sons of Liberty terrorized stamp agents and burned the stamps. The agents, themselves Americans, hastily resigned, and the sale of stamps in the continental colonies virtually ceased. In Boston, the mob attacked as well such pro-British "aristocrats" as the lieutenant governor, Thomas Hutchinson (who had privately opposed passage of the Stamp Act but who, as an officer of the crown, felt obliged to support it once it became law). Hutchinson's elegant house was pillaged and virtually destroyed.

The Stamp Act crisis brought the colonies to the

Patrick Henry and the Parson's Cause, 1763
A dispute over ministerial salaries in the 1750s and early 1760s, known as the "Parson's Cause," became the occasion for some of the earliest colonial challenges to British authority. In 1759 the Privy Council in England responded to appeals from Anglican ministers in Virginia and overturned a colonial law regulating (and limiting) their salaries. As a result, ministers were able to sue for back pay. In a 1763 trial in Hanover County, the young Virginia attorney Patrick Henry persuaded a jury to rule against the Rev. James Maury in one such suit on the grounds that the king and his government had exceeded their authority. This painting by George Cooke (c. 1830) portrays Henry addressing the court as a large crowd of onlookers presses at the doors. (Virginia Historical Society)

brink of war with the British government. But the crisis subsided, largely because England backed down. The authorities in London were not deterred by the legislative resolutions, the petitions, or the riots; what changed their attitude was economic pressure. Even before the Stamp Act, many New Englanders had stopped buying English goods to protest the Sugar Act of 1764. Now the colonial boycott spread, and the Sons of Liberty intimidated those colonists who were reluctant to participate in it. The merchants of England, feeling the loss of much of their colonial market, begged Parliament to repeal the Stamp Act, while stories of unemployment, poverty, and discontent arose from English seaports and manufacturing towns.

The Marquis of Rockingham, who succeeded Grenville as prime minister in July 1765, tried to appease both the English merchants and the American colonists; and he finally convinced the king that the Stamp Act should not survive. On March 18, 1766, it was repealed. Rockingham's opponents were strong and vociferous, and they insisted that unless the colonists were compelled to obey the Stamp Act, they would soon cease to obey any laws of Parliament. To satisfy them, Parliament passed on the same day the Declaratory Act, declaring parliamentary authority over the colonies "in all cases whatsoever." In their rejoicing over the repeal, most Americans paid little attention to this sweeping declaration of Parliament's power.

The Townshend Program

The Rockingham government's policy of appeasement was not as well received in England as it was in America. English landlords, a powerful political force, angrily protested that the government had "sacrificed the landed gentlemen to the interests of traders and colonists." They were fearful, in other words, that the retreat of the government from its policy of taxing the colonies would result in renewed taxes on them. The king finally bowed to their pressure and dismissed the Rockingham ministry. To replace it, he called upon the aging but still powerful William Pitt to form a government. Pitt had been a strong critic of the Stamp Act and had a reputation in America as a friend of the colonists (although some Americans had looked askance at his acceptance of a peerage in 1766). Once in office, however, Pitt (now Lord Chatham) was so hobbled by gout and at times so incapacitated by mental illness that the actual leadership of his administration fell to the chancellor of the exchequer, Charles Townshend—a brilliant, flamboyant, and at times reckless politician known to his contemporaries variously as "the Weathercock" and "Champagne Charlie."

Townshend had to deal almost immediately with the litany of imperial problems and colonial grievances left over from the Grenville ministry. With the Stamp Act repealed, the greatest American grievance involved the Mutiny (or Quartering) Act of 1765, which required the colonists to provide quarters and supplies for the British troops in America. The British considered this a reasonable requirement. The troops were stationed in North America to protect the colonists from Indian or French attack and to defend the frontiers; lodging the troops in coastal cities was simply a way to reduce the costs of supplying them. To the colonists, however, the law was another assault on their liberties. They did not so much object to quartering the troops or providing them with supplies; they had been doing that voluntarily ever since the last years of the French and Indian War. They resented that these contributions were now made mandatory, and they considered it another form of taxation without their consent. They responded with defiance. The Massachusetts Assembly refused to vote the mandated supplies to the

troops. The New York Assembly soon did likewise, posing an even greater challenge to imperial authority, since the army headquarters were in New York City.

To enforce the law and to try again to raise revenues in the colonies, Townshend steered two measures through Parliament in 1767. First, the New York Assembly was disbanded until the colonists agreed to obey the Mutiny Act. (By singling out New York, Townshend thought he would avoid Grenville's mistake of arousing all the colonies at once.) Second, new taxes (known as the Townshend Duties) were levied on various goods imported to the colonies from England—lead, paint, paper, and tea. The colonists could not logically object to taxation of this kind, Townshend reasoned, because it met standards they themselves had accepted. Benjamin Franklin, as a colonial agent in London trying to prevent the passage of the Stamp Act, had long ago argued for the distinction between "internal" and "external" taxes and had denounced the stamp duties as internal taxation. Townshend himself had considered the distinction laughable; but he was now imposing duties on clearly external transactions.

Townshend's efforts to satisfy colonial grievances were, however, to no avail. The new duties were no more acceptable to Americans than the stamp tax. Although they were ostensibly external taxes, they would be paid by colonial merchants and, indirectly, by colonial consumers. Their purpose was the same as that of the Stamp Act: to raise revenue from the colonists without their consent. And the suspension of the New York Assembly, far from isolating New York, aroused the resentment of all the colonies. They considered this assault on the rights of one provincial government a precedent for the annihilation of the rights of all of them.

The Massachusetts Assembly took the lead in opposing the new measures by circulating a letter to all the colonial governments urging them to stand up against every tax, external or internal, imposed by Parliament. At first, the circular evoked little response in some of the legislatures (and ran into strong opposition in Pennsylvania's). Then Lord Hillsborough, secretary of state for the colonies, issued a circular letter of his own in which he warned that assemblies endorsing the Massachusetts letter would be dissolved. Massachusetts defiantly reaffirmed its support for the circular. (The vote in the Assembly was 92 to 17, and "ninety-two" became a patriotic rallying cry throughout British America.) The other colonies, including Pennsylvania, promptly rallied to the support of Massachusetts.

Besides persuading Parliament to levy import duties and suspend the New York Assembly, Townshend took steps to enforce commercial regulations in the colonies more effectively than ever. The most fateful of these steps was the establishment of a board of customs commissioners in America. Townshend hoped the new board would stop the rampant corruption in the colonial customs houses; and to some extent his hopes were fulfilled. The new commissioners virtually ended the smuggling in Boston, where they established their headquarters, although smugglers continued to carry on a busy trade in other colonial seaports.

The Boston merchants—accustomed, like all colonial merchants, to loose enforcement of the Navigation Acts and doubly aggrieved now that the new commission was diverting the lucrative smuggling trade elsewhere—were indignant; and they took the lead in organizing another boycott. In 1768, the merchants of Philadelphia and New York joined them in a nonimportation agreement, and later some Southern merchants and planters also agreed to cooperate. The colonists boycotted British goods subject to the Townshend Duties; and throughout the colonies, American homespun and other domestic products became suddenly fashionable, while English luxuries fell from favor.

Late in 1767, Charles Townshend died—before the consequences of his ill-conceived program had become fully apparent. The question of dealing with colonial resistance to the Townshend Duties fell, therefore, to the new prime minister, Lord North. Hoping to break the nonimportation agreement and divide the colonists, Lord North secured the repeal in March 1770 of all the Townshend Duties except the tea tax.

The Boston Massacre

Whatever pacifying effects the repeal of the Townshend Duties might have had was negated by an event in Massachusetts that occurred before news of the repeal reached America. The harassment of the new customs commissioners in Boston had grown so intense that the British government had placed four regiments of regular troops within the city. The presence of the "redcoats" was a constant affront to the colonists' sense of independence and a constant reminder of British oppression. Everywhere they went, Bostonians encountered British soldiers—arrogant, intrusive, sometimes coarse and provocative. There was particular tension between the redcoats and Boston laborers. Many British soldiers, poorly paid and poorly treated by the army, wanted jobs in their off-duty hours; and they thus competed with local workers in an already tight market. Clashes between them were frequent.

On the night of March 5, 1770, a few days after a particularly intense skirmish between workers at a ship-rigging factory and British soldiers who were trying to find work there, a mob of dockworkers, "liberty boys," and others began pelting the sentries at the customs house with rocks and snowballs. Hastily, Captain Thomas Preston of the British regiment lined up several of his men in front of the building to protect it. There was some scuffling; one of the soldiers was knocked down; and in the midst of it all, apparently, several British soldiers fired into the crowd, killing five people (among them a mulatto sailor, Crispus Attucks).

This murky incident, almost certainly the result of panic and confusion, was quickly transformed by local resistance leaders into the "Boston Massacre"—a graphic symbol of British oppression and brutality. The victims became popular martyrs; the event became the subject of such lurid (and inaccurate) accounts as the widely circulated pamphlet *Innocent Blood Crying to God from the Streets of Boston*. A famous engraving by John Hancock portrayed the massacre as a carefully organized, calculated assault on a peaceful crowd. The British soldiers, tried before a jury of Bostonians, were found guilty of no more than manslaughter and were given only a token punishment. Colonial pamphlets and newspapers, however, convinced many Americans that the soldiers were guilty of official murder. Year after year, resistance leaders marked the anniversary of the massacre with demonstrations and speeches.

The leading figure in fomenting public outrage over the Boston Massacre was Samuel Adams, the most effective dissenter in the colonies. Adams (a distant cousin of John Adams, second president of the United States) was born in 1722 and was thus somewhat older than other leaders of colonial protest. As a member of an earlier generation with strong ties to New England's Puritan past, he was particularly inclined to view public events in stern moral terms. A failure in business, he had occupied several political and governmental positions; but his real importance was as a publicist, a voice unflagging in expressing outrage at British oppression. England, he argued, had become a morass of sin and corruption; only in America did public virtue survive. He spoke frequently at Boston town meetings; and as one unpopular English policy followed another—the

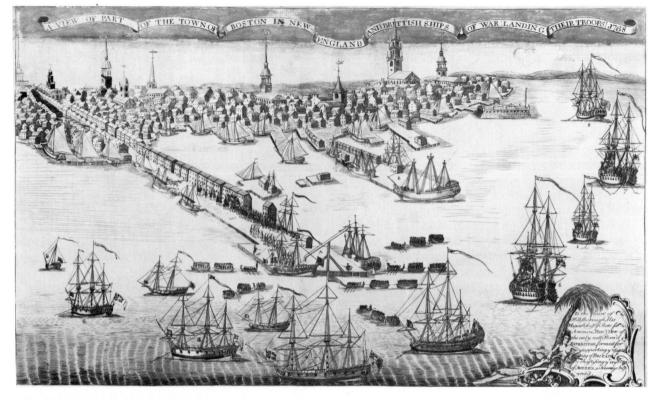

The British in Boston, 1768
British troops arrived in Boston on September 30, 1768, marched into the city, and pitched tents on the Boston common. The soldiers were charged with ensuring the safety of British customs officers, who three months earlier had been driven from the city by local residents and had appealed to England for protection. The presence of the troops became a continuing irritant in relations between the colonists and the British government. This 1770 engraving by Paul Revere shows troops embarking from British naval vessels at Long Wharf and marching "with insolent Parade" up King Street into the city.   (Henry Francis du Pont Winterthur Museum)

Townshend Duties, the placement of customs commissioners in Boston, the stationing of British troops in the city (with its violent results)—his message attracted increasing support. In 1772, he proposed the creation of a "committee of correspondence" in Boston to publicize the grievances against England throughout the colony, and he became its first head. Other colonies followed Massachusetts's lead, and a loose network of political organizations was soon established that kept the spirit of dissent alive through the 1770s.

The Philosophy of Revolt

A superficial calm settled on the colonies for approximately three years after the Boston Massacre. In re-

ality, however, American political life remained restless and troubled. The crises of the 1760s had helped to arouse an ideological excitement in the colonies; the events of the early 1770s had produced instruments for publicizing colonial grievances; and gradually a political outlook took hold in America that would ultimately serve to justify revolt.

"The Revolution was effected before the war commenced," one of the greatest of the Revolutionary leaders, John Adams, afterward remarked. "The Revolution was in the minds and hearts of the people." Adams exaggerated. Few Americans were willing to consider complete independence from England until after the war had begun; and even those few (among them Samuel Adams) generally refrained from admitting that independence was their goal. But John Adams was certainly correct in arguing that well before the fighting began in 1775, a profound ideological shift had occurred in the way many Americans viewed the British government and their own.

The ideas that would support the Revolution emerged from many sources. Some were indigenous to America, drawn from religious (particularly Puritan) sources or from the political experiences of the colonies. But these native ideas were enriched and enlarged by the importation of powerful arguments from abroad. Of most importance, perhaps, were the "radical" ideas of those in Great Britain who stood in opposition to their government. Some were Scots, who viewed the English government as tyrannical. Others were embittered "country Whigs," who considered the existing system corrupt and oppressive. Drawing from some of the great philosophical minds of earlier generations—most notably John Locke—these English dissidents framed a powerful argument against their government; and while that argument had only limited appeal in England, it found a ready audience in the troubled colonies.

Central to this emerging ideology was a new concept of what government should be. Because humans were inherently corrupt and selfish, government was necessary to protect individuals from the evil in one another. But because any government was run by corruptible people, it needed safeguards against abuses of power.

In the eyes of most Englishmen and most Americans, the English constitution was the best system ever devised to meet these necessities. By distributing power among the three elements of society—the monarch, the aristocracy, and the common people—the English political system ensured that no individual or group could exercise authority unchecked by another. Yet by the mid-seventeenth century, dissenters in both England and America were becoming deeply concerned that this noble constitution was being eroded. The king and his ministers were exercising such corrupt and autocratic authority, they believed, that the elements of power were no longer in balance. The independence of the various elements of government was being undermined; a single center of power was emerging; and the system was thus threatening to become a dangerous tyranny.

Except among such disenchanted groups as the Scots and the "country Whigs," such arguments found little sympathy in England—largely because of the way in which most English people viewed their constitution. They revered it, but they considered it a flexible, constantly changing entity—an assortment of laws and customs that had evolved through many

centuries and that remained elastic and vague. The English constitution was not a written document; nor was it a fixed set of unchangeable rules. It was a general sense of the "way things are done." Americans, by contrast, drew from their experience with colonial charters, in which the shape and powers of government were permanently inscribed on paper; and they had difficulty accepting the idea of a flexible, changing set of basic principles. Many argued that the English constitution should itself be written down, to prevent fallible politicians from tampering with its essence.

Part of that essence, Americans believed, was their right to be taxed only with their own consent. When Townshend levied his "external" duties, the Philadelphia lawyer John Dickinson published a widely circulated pamphlet, *Letters of a Pennsylvania Farmer,* which argued that even external taxation was legal only when designed to regulate trade and not to raise a revenue. Gradually, most Americans ceased to accept even that distinction, and they finally took an unqualified stand: "No taxation without representation." Whatever the nature of a tax—whether internal or external, whether designed to raise revenue or to control trade—it could not be levied without the consent of the colonists themselves.

This clamor about "representation" made little sense to the English. Only about 4 percent of the population of Great Britain was entitled to vote for members of Parliament, and some populous boroughs in England had no representatives at all. According to the prevailing English theory, such apparent inequities were of no importance. Members of Parliament did not represent individuals or particular geographical areas. Instead, each member represented the interests of the whole nation and indeed the whole empire, no matter where the member happened to come from. The unenfranchised boroughs of England, the whole of Ireland, and the colonies thousands of miles away—all were thus represented in the Parliament at London, even though they elected no representatives of their own.

This was the theory of "virtual" representation. But Americans, drawing from their experiences with their town meetings and their colonial assemblies, believed in "actual" representation. Every community was entitled to its own representative, elected by the people of that community and directly responsible to them. Since they had none of their own representatives in Parliament, it followed that they were not represented there. But even having representatives in Parliament, many believed, would not re-

John Dickinson
This 1770 portrait by Charles Willson Peale shows the Pennsylvania lawyer and popular opponent of British mercantile policies. Dickinson was more moderate than many colonial agitators; but in his famous *Letters from a Farmer in Pennsylvania to the Inhabitants of the British Colonies,* published in 1768, he suggested that Americans might have to use force in resisting British oppression if conciliation failed. He was later a delegate to the Constitutional Convention of 1787.   (Historical Society of Pennsylvania)

of commonwealths, each with its own legislative body, all tied together by common loyalty to the king (a view that augured the structure of the British Commonwealth in the twentieth century). This concept allowed them to vent their anger not at the empire itself, but at the English Parliament, which was presumptuously exerting authority to which it was not entitled over the colonies. Not until very late did they begin to criticize the king himself. And not until the colonies were ready to declare their independence in 1776 were they ready to repudiate the English constitution.

What may have made the conflict between England and America ultimately insoluble was a fundamental difference of opinion over the nature of sovereignty. By arguing that Parliament had the right to legislate for England and for the empire as a whole, but that only the provincial assemblies could legislate for the individual colonies, Americans were in effect arguing for a division of sovereignty. Parliament would be sovereign in some matters; the assemblies would be sovereign in others. To the British, such an argument was untenable and absurd. Sovereignty, they believed, was by definition unitary. In any system of government there must be a single, ultimate authority. And since the empire was, in their view, a single, undivided unit, there could be only one authority within it: the English government of king and Parliament. Thus it was that the Anglo-American crisis ultimately presented the colonists with a stark choice. In the eyes of the English, there was, in effect, no middle ground between complete subordination and complete independence. Slowly, cautiously, Americans found themselves moving toward independence.

That movement began with resistance, rather than with sentiment for open revolt. Opposition to British policies in the 1760s had not taken the form of repudiation of England but of refusal to obey certain unjust laws. During this stage of the crisis, the colonists justified their actions by citing the teachings of the Bible and the ideas of John Locke. To show that resistance against tyranny was lawful in God's sight, they pointed to such biblical events as the overthrow of a king of Israel who had burdened his people with unjust taxes. To show that resistance had justification in the philosophy of the Enlightenment, they pointed to Locke's *Two Treatises on Civil Government* (1690), in which he had attempted to justify the English revolution of 1688–1689 by which Parliament had won supremacy over the king. Locke argued that humans had originally lived in a state of nature and had en-

solve the problem. For participation in the decisions of Parliament would in effect bind them to those decisions, even though they would be outnumbered and outvoted. More important, American members of Parliament would be so isolated from the people who had elected them that they would not be able to perform as true representatives. Thus most colonists reverted to the argument that they could be fairly represented only in their own colonial assemblies.

According to the emerging American view of the empire, these assemblies played the same role within the colonies—had the same powers, enjoyed the same rights—that Parliament did within England. The empire, the Americans argued, was a sort of federation joyed complete liberty; later, they had agreed to a "compact" and established a government to protect their "natural rights," especially their right to the ownership and enjoyment of private property. But the government was limited by the terms of the compact and by "natural law." It could not, for example, take property without the consent of the owners. Americans took particular note of Locke's statement: "If any one shall claim a power to lay and levy taxes on the people by his own authority, and without such consent of the people, he thereby invades the fundamental law of property, and subverts the end of government."

The biblical and Lockean justifications for resistance included, however, a possible justification for actual rebellion as well. The Bible suggested that people had a right not only to resist but to overthrow unjust rulers. And Locke had argued that if a government should persist in exceeding its rightful powers, the people would be released not only from their obligation to obey particular laws but from their obligation to obey the government at all. They would have the right to dissolve the "compact" and make a new one, to establish another government. The right to resist was, in other words, only the first step. If resistance proved ineffective, if a government proved to be so thoroughly corrupt and tyrannical that it could not be reformed, then citizens were entitled to revolt against it. They had a "right of revolution."

By the early 1770s, the relationship between America and England had become poisoned by resentment and mutual suspicion. Americans had become convinced that a "conspiracy against liberty" existed within the British government. And they had articulated a philosophy that seemed to them to justify whatever measures might be necessary to protect themselves from that conspiracy. Only a small distance remained to be traversed before the colonies would move from resistance to revolution, before they would be ready to break their ties with the empire. That distance was crossed quickly, beginning in 1773, when a new set of British policies shattered forever the imperial relationship.

The Tea Excitement

The apparent calm in America in the first years of the 1770s masked a growing sense of frustration and resentment in response to the continued and increasingly heavy-handed enforcement of the Navigation Acts. The customs commissioners, who remained in America despite the repeal of the Townshend Acts, proved to be clumsy, intrusive, and arrogant officials, who harassed colonial merchants and seamen constantly with petty restrictions (and who also enriched themselves through graft and through illegal seizures of merchandise). The popular anger lying just beneath the surface was visible in occasional acts of rebellion. At one point, colonists seized a British revenue ship on the lower Delaware River. And in 1772, angry residents of Rhode Island boarded the British schooner *Gaspée,* set it afire, and sank it in Narragansett Bay. The British response to the *Gaspée* affair further inflamed American opinion. Instead of putting the accused attackers on trial in colonial courts, the British sent a special commission to America with power to send the defendants back to England for trial. Once again, the British were challenging America's right to exercise independent authority.

What finally revived the revolutionary fervor of the 1760s to its old strength, however, was a new act of Parliament—one that the English government had expected to be relatively uncontroversial. It involved the business of selling tea. In 1773, Britain's East India Company (which possessed an official monopoly on trade with the Far East) was sitting on large stocks of tea that it could not sell in England. It was on the verge of bankruptcy. In an effort to save it, the government passed the Tea Act of 1773, which gave the company the right to export its merchandise directly to the colonies without paying any of the regular taxes that were imposed on the colonial merchants, who had traditionally served as the middlemen in such transactions. With these privileges, the company could undersell American merchants and monopolize the colonial tea trade.

The act proved inflammatory for several reasons. First, it angered influential colonial merchants, who feared being replaced and bankrupted by a powerful monopoly. The East India Company's decision to grant franchises to certain American merchants for the sale of their tea created further resentments among those excluded from this lucrative trade. More important, however, the Tea Act revived American passions about the issue of taxation without representation. The law provided no new tax on tea. But the original Townshend duty on the commodity—the only one of the original duties that had not been repealed—survived. It was the East India Company's exemption from that duty that put the colonial merchants at such a grave disadvantage in competition with them. Lord North assumed that most colonists

Taking the Pledge

This British caricature, published in London in March 1775, ridiculed the American buy-at-home movement. Entitled "A Society of Patriotic Ladies, at Edenton in North Carolina," it shows a group of crass and buffoonish women sitting amid provincial chaos, emptying their tea canisters and signing a pledge that reads: "We the Ladies of Edenton do hereby Solemnly Engage not to Conform to that Pernicious Custom of Drinking Tea, or that we the aforesaid Ladies will not promote the Wear of any Manufacture from England until such time that all Acts which tend to Enslave this our Native Country shall be repealed." (Metropolitan Museum of Art, Bequest of Charles Allen Munn, 1924)

would welcome the new law because it would reduce the price of tea to consumers by removing the middlemen. But resistance leaders in America argued that it was another insidious example of the results of an unconstitutional tax. The colonists responded by boycotting tea, of which many of them—especially women—were extremely fond. They drank instead such substitutes as coffee and chocolate.

Meanwhile, with strong popular support, leaders in various colonies made plans to prevent the East India Company from landing its cargoes in colonial ports. In Philadelphia and New York, determined men kept the tea from leaving the company's ships; and in Charleston, they stored it away in a public warehouse. In Boston, after failing to turn back the three ships in the harbor, local patriots staged a spectacular drama. On the evening of December 16, 1773, three companies of fifty men each, masquerading as

Mohawks, passed through a tremendous crowd of spectators (which served to protect them from official interference), went aboard the three ships, broke open the tea chests, and heaved them into the harbor. As the electrifying news of the Boston "tea party" spread, other seaports followed the example and staged similar acts of resistance of their own.

When the Bostonians refused to pay for the property they had destroyed, George III and Lord North decided on a policy of coercion, to be applied only against Massachusetts—the chief center of resistance. In four acts of 1774, Parliament closed the port of Boston, drastically reduced the powers of self-government in the colony, permitted royal officers to be tried in other colonies or in England when accused of crimes, and provided for the quartering of troops in the colonists' barns and empty houses.

These Coercive Acts—or, as they were more

widely known in America, Intolerable Acts—were followed by the Quebec Act, which was separate from them in origin and quite different in purpose. Its object was to provide a civil government for the French-speaking Roman Catholic inhabitants of Canada and the Illinois country. The law extended the boundaries of Quebec to include the French communities between the Ohio and Mississippi rivers. It also granted political rights to Roman Catholics and recognized the legality of the Roman Catholic church within the enlarged province. In many ways it was a liberal and much-needed piece of legislation. But to many in the thirteen colonies, the Quebec Act was a threat. They were already alarmed by rumors that the Church of England was scheming to appoint a bishop for America who would impose Anglican authority on all the various sects. And since the line between the Church of England and the Church of Rome had always seemed to Americans dangerously thin, the passage of the Quebec Act convinced many of them that a plot was afoot in London to subject Americans to the tyranny of the pope. Those interested in Western lands, moreover, believed that the act would hinder westward expansion.

Lord North might have gotten away with the Coercive Acts or the Quebec Act alone. But the combination of the two was too much for most colonists to bear. By late 1774, from New Hampshire to Georgia, the peoples of the American colonies were ready to take a united stand.

Cooperation and War

Revolutions do not simply happen. They must be organized and led. Beginning in 1765, colonial leaders developed a variety of organizations for converting popular discontent into action—organizations that in time formed the basis for an independent government.

New Sources of Authority

The passage of authority from the royal government to the colonists themselves began on the local level, where the tradition of autonomy was already strong. In colony after colony, local institutions responded to the resistance movement by simply seizing authority on their own. At times, entirely new, extralegal bodies emerged semispontaneously and began to perform some of the functions of government. In Massachusetts in 1768, for example, Samual Adams called a convention of delegates from the towns of the colony to sit in place of the General Court, which the governor had dissolved. The Sons of Liberty, which Adams had helped to organize in Massachusetts and which sprang up elsewhere as well, became another source of power. Its members at times formed disciplined bands of vigilantes, who made certain that all colonists respected the boycotts and other forms of popular resistance. And in most colonies, committees of prominent citizens began meeting to perform additional political functions.

The most famous and most effective of these new groups were the committees of correspondence, which Adams had inaugurated in Massachusetts in 1772. Virginia later established the first intercolonial committees of correspondence, which made possible continuous coopertion among the colonies. And Virginia took the greatest step of all toward united action in 1774 when, after the royal governor dissolved the assembly, a rump session met in the Raleigh Tavern at Williamsburg, declared that the Intolerable Acts menaced the liberties of every colony, and issued a call for a Continental Congress.

Variously elected by the assemblies and by extralegal meetings, delegates from all the thirteen colonies except Georgia were present when, in September 1774, the First Continental Congress convened in Philadelphia's Carpenters' Hall. They made five major decisions. First, in a very close vote, they rejected a plan (proposed by Joseph Galloway of Pennsylvania) for a colonial union under British authority (much like the earlier Albany Plan), with a legislative council made up of representatives from the colonial assemblies and a president-general to be appointed by the king. Second, they endorsed a statement of grievances, whose tortured language reflected the conflicts among the delegates between moderates and extremists. The statement reflected the influence of the moderates by seeming to concede Parliament's right to regulate colonial trade by addressing the king as "Most Gracious Sovereign"; but it included a more extreme demand for the repeal of all oppressive legislation passed since 1763. Third, they approved a series of resolutions from a Suffolk County (Massachusetts) convention recommending, among other things, that military preparations be made for defense against possible attack by the British troops in Boston. Fourth, they agreed to nonimportation, nonexportation, and nonconsumption as means of

The First Battles of the Revolution

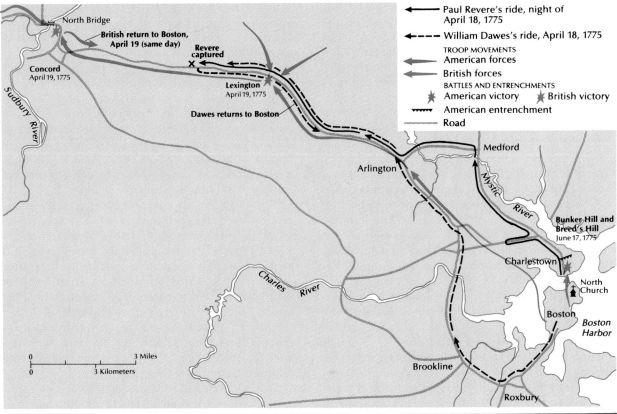

stopping all trade with Great Britain, and they formed a "Continental Association" to see that these agreements were enforced. And fifth, the delegates agreed, on adjournment, to meet again the next spring, thus indicating that they conceived of the Continental Congress as a continuing organization.

Through their representatives in Philadelphia the colonies had, in effect, reaffirmed their autonomous status within the empire and declared economic war to maintain that position. The more optimistic of the Americans supposed that economic warfare alone would win a quick and bloodless victory, but the more pessimistic had their doubts. "I expect no redress, but, on the contrary, increased resentment and double vengeance," John Adams wrote to Patrick Henry; "we must fight." And Henry replied, "By God, I am of your opinion."

During the winter, the Parliament in London debated proposals for conciliating the colonists. Lord Chatham (William Pitt) urged the withdrawal of troops from America, and Edmund Burke called for

the repeal of the Coercive Acts; but their efforts were in vain. Lord North finally won approval early in 1775 for a series of measures known as the Conciliatory Propositions, but that were in fact far less conciliatory than the approaches Burke or Chatham had urged. Parliament now proposed that the colonies, instead of being taxed directly by Parliament, would tax themselves at Parliament's demand. With this offer, Lord North hoped to divide the American moderates, whom he believed represented the views of the majority, from the extremist minority. But his offer was too little and too late. It did not reach America until after the first shots of war had been fired.

Lexington and Concord

For months, the farmers and townspeople of Massachusetts had been gathering arms and ammunition and training as "minutemen," preparing to fight on a

The Battle of Lexington, 1775

Here, British troops under Lieutenant Colonel Francis Smith are rescued in Lexington on April 19,1775 by a relief force from Boston under Lord Percy after being repulsed by Patriot forces at the Old North Bridge in Concord. But the redcoats, openly arrayed along the road, continued to encounter fire from colonial forces hiding around them. One British soldier described the nightmarish retreat from Lexington to Boston: "We were fired on from Houses and behind Trees . . . the Country was . . . full of Hills, Woods, stone Walls . . . which the Rebels did not fail to take advantage of." This is one of several engravings by Amos Doolittle, a Connecticut militiamen who was not present at the battle but who accurately re-created the scene on the basis of accounts by participants. (I. N. Phelps Stokes Collection of American Historical Prints, Prints Division, New York Public Library)

minute's notice. The Continental Congress had approved preparations for a defensive war, and the citizen-soldiers only waited for an aggressive move by the British regulars in Boston.

In Boston, General Thomas Gage, commanding the British garrison, knew of the warlike bustle throughout the countryside but considered his army too small to do anything until reinforcements should arrive. He resisted the advice of less cautious officers, who assured him that the Americans would never dare actually to fight, that they would back down

quickly before any show of British force. Major John Pitcairn, for example, insisted that a single "small action" with the burning of a few towns would "set everything to rights."

When General Gage received orders to arrest the rebel leaders Sam Adams and John Hancock, known to be in the vicinity of Lexington, he still hesitated. But when he heard that the minutemen had stored a large supply of gunpowder in Concord (eighteen miles from Boston) he at last decided to act. On the night of April 18, 1775, he sent a detachment of about

SIGNIFICANT EVENTS

1713	Treaty of Utrecht concludes Queen Anne's War
1718	French found New Orleans
1744–1748	King George's War
1754	Albany Plan for intercolonial cooperation rejected
	Battle of Fort Duquesne begins French and Indian War
1756	Seven Years' War begins in Europe
1757	British policies provoke riots in New York
1758	Pitt returns authority to colonial assemblies
	British capture Fort Duquesne
1759	British forces under Wolfe capture Quebec
1760	George III becomes king
	French army surrenders to Amherst at Montreal
1763	Peace of Paris ends Seven Years' (and French and Indian) War
	Grenville becomes prime minister
	Paxton uprising in Pennsylvania
1764	Sugar Act passed
	Currency Act passed
1765	Stamp Act crisis
	Mutiny Act passed
1766	Stamp Act repealed
	Declaratory Act passed
1767	Townshend Duties imposed
1768	Boston, New York, and Philadelphia merchants make nonimportation agreement
1770	Boston Massacre
	Most Townshend Duties repealed
1771	Regulator movement quelled in North Carolina
1772	Committees of correspondence established in Boston
	Gaspée incident in Rhode Island
1773	Tea Act passed
	Bostonians stage tea party
1774	Intolerable Acts passed
	First Continental Congress meets at Philadelphia
1775	Clashes at Lexington and Concord begin American Revolution

1,000 men out from Boston on the road to Lexington and Concord. He intended to surprise the colonials and seize the illegal supplies without bloodshed.

But patriots in Boston were watching the British movements closely; and during the night two horsemen, William Dawes and Paul Revere, were dispatched to warn the villages and farms. When the redcoats arrived in Lexington the next day, several dozen minutemen awaited them on the town common. Shots were fired and minutemen fell; eight of them were killed and ten more wounded. Advancing to Concord, the British discovered that the Americans had hastily removed most of the powder supply, but they burned what was left of it. All along the road from Concord back to Boston, the British were harassed by the continual gunfire of farmers hiding behind trees, rocks, and stone fences. By the end of the day, the British had lost almost three times as many men as the Americans.

The first shots—the "shots heard round the world," as Americans later called them—had been fired. But who had fired them first? According to one of the minutemen at Lexington, Major Pitcairn had

shouted to the colonists on his arrival, "Disperse, ye rebels!" When this command was ignored, he had given the order to fire. British officers and soldiers told a different story. They claimed that the minutemen had fired first, that only after seeing the flash of American guns had they begun to shoot. Whatever the truth, the rebels succeeded in circulating their account well ahead of the British version, adorning it with horrible tales of British atrocities. The effect was to rally to the rebel cause thousands of colonists, North and South, who previously had had little enthusiasm for it. Now that the English had, as they believed, opened fire on American citizens, the issue was clearly drawn.

It was not immediately clear to the British, and even to many Americans, that the skirmishes at Lexington and Concord were the first battles of a war. Many saw them as simply another example of the tensions that had been afflicting Anglo-American relations for years. But whether they recognized it at the time or not, the British and the Americans had taken a decisive step. The War for Independence had begun.

SUGGESTED READINGS

General Histories   The coming of the American Revolution has spawned a vast literature and a large amount of historical controversy, which continues today. John Shy, *The American Revolution* (1973), is an excellent, although already out-of-date, bibliography. For general studies of the progress toward revolt, see John C. Miller, *Origins of the American Revolution* (1957); Merrill Jensen, *The Founding of a Nation* (1968); Edmund S. Morgan, *The Birth of the Republic* (1956), a concise account; and J. R. Alden, *A History of the American Revolution* (1969). Charles M. Andrews, *The Colonial Background of the American Revolution* (1924, rev. 1931), is a classic account by one of the most important chroniclers of the establishment of the colonies; Lawrence Henry Gipson, *The Coming of the Revolution, 1763–1775* (1954), summarizes the views of the preeminent historian of the British Empire in the eighteenth century. Ian R. Christie and Benjamin W. Labaree, *Empire or Independence, 1760–1776* (1976), and Ian R. Christie, *Crisis of Empire* (1966), are both useful general studies. Robert Middlekauff, *The Glorious Cause: The American Revolution, 1763–1789* (1982), is a recent narrative.

The British Imperial System   Lawrence Henry Gipson, *The British Empire Before the American Revolution,* 15 vols. (1936–1970), is the outstanding study of the nature of the imperial system and the changes in the 1760s. Relations between the colonies and England before the 1760s are discussed in Robert C. Newbold, *The Albany Congress and Plan of Union of 1754* (1955); Richard Pares, *War and Trade in the West Indies, 1739–1763* (1936); and Howard H. Peckham, *The Colonial Wars, 1689–1762* (1963), which includes discussion of the French and Indian War. Alan Rogers, *Empire and Liberty* (1974), is another useful study of the period of the war. The accession of George III and his influence on colonial relations can be examined in Lewis B. Namier, *England in the Age of the American Revolution,* rev. ed. (1961) and *The Structure of Politics at the Accession of George III,* rev. ed. (1961). A differing view, stressing the wider context of English politics, can be found in John Brewer, *Party Ideology and Popular Politics at the Accession of George III* (1976). See also Bernard Donoughue, *British Politics and the American Revolution: The Path to War, 1773–1775* (1965), and John Brooke, *King George III* (1972). Michael Kammen, *A Rope of Sand* (1968), examines the influence of the colonial agents and British politics on the colonies.

The French and the Indians   On the French, the Indians, and the West, see Thomas P. Abernethy, *Western Lands and the American Revolution* (1937), and J. M. Sosin, *Whitehall and the Wilderness* (1961), both of which discuss British policies. John R. Alden, *John Stuart and the Southern Colonial Frontier* (1944), David H. Corkran, *The Cherokee Frontier* (1962), R. S. Cotterill, *The Southern Indians* (1954), and Howard H. Peckham, *Pontiac and the Indian Uprising* (1947), examine the relationship between the white settlers and the native tribes. Fred Anderson, *A People's Army: Massachusetts Soldiers and Society in the Seven Years War* (1984), is an important study of the social impact of that conflict and of the vital role of the Iroquois in colonial New England. See also William Pencak, *War, Politics, and Revolution in Provincial Massachusetts* (1981).

Merchants and the Empire   Some of the economic tensions of the 1760s and 1770s are discussed in Joseph Ernst, *Money and Politics in America, 1755–1775* (1973). Earlier examinations of economic influences on the Revolution include Arthur M. Schlesinger, *The Colonial Merchants and the American Revolution* (1917), which argues that merchants were instrumental in fomenting resistance, and Oliver M. Dickinson, *The Navigation Acts and the American Revolution* (1951), which de-emphasizes economic regulation as a cause. John Shy, *Toward Lexington* (1965), discusses the role of the presence of British troops in the process leading to revolution.

American Resistance   Most of the major events leading to conflict have been the subject of individual studies. David Ammerman, *In the Common Cause* (1974), examines the Coercive Acts and the response to them. Hiller B. Zobel, *The Boston Massacre* (1970), discusses one of the early conflicts. Edmund S. Morgan and Helen M. Morgan, *The Stamp Act Crisis* (1953), is an elegant account of the most important political event of the 1760s. Benjamin W. Labaree, *The Boston Tea Party* (1964), examines one of the last controversies before the outbreak of war. See also John Shy, *Toward Lexington* (1965).

Revolutionary Ideology   The most important study of the ideas and principles that led to the American Revolution is Bernard Bailyn, *The Ideological Origins of the American Revolution* (1967). Ian R. Christie, *Wilkes, Wyvil, and Reform* (1962), and George Rudé, *Wilkes and Liberty* (1962), examine one of the most important British influences on American revolutionary ideology. Isaac Kramnick, *Bolingbroke and His Circle* (1968), examines another of the English ideological influences on Americans. Clinton Rossiter, *Seedtime of the Republic* (1953), traces later American ideas about liberty to the Revolutionary period. Pauline Maier, *From Resistance to Revolution* (1972), shows how political ideas led to the rise of resistance and how colonial leaders influenced the popular crowd. Dirk Hoerder, *Crowd Action in Revolutionary Massachusetts* (1977), is an alternative interpretation stressing class consciousness. Nathan Hatch, *The Sacred Cause of Liberty* (1977), examines religious influences. Richard Merritt, *Symbols of American Community, 1735–1775* (1966), traces the rise of American nationalism. Gary B. Nash, *The Urban Crucible* (1979), examines the role of cities in the coming of the Revolution. Rhys Isaac, *The Transformation of Virginia, 1740–1790* (1982), describes the disintegration of a stable social order in the face of religious revivals and political upheavals prior to and during the Revolution.

Revolutionary Politics   For events in individual colonies, see—among many others—Carl Becker, *The History of Political Parties in the Province of New York* (1909), an influential study arguing that the Revolution involved not only differences between the colonies and England but social tensions within the colonies themselves. Richard D. Brown, *Revolutionary Politics in Massachusetts* (1970), examines the committees of correspondence. David Lovejoy, *Rhode Island Politics and the American Revolution* (1958), emphasizes the unifying influence of opposition to the British. Studies of other colonies include L. R. Gerlach, *Prologue to Independence* (1976), on New Jersey; Theodore Thayer, *Pennsylvania Politics and the Growth of Democracy* (1953); Ronald Hoffman, *A Spirit of Dissension* (1973), on Maryland; R. E. Brown and B. K. Brown, *Virginia, 1705–1786* (1964); and Charles S. Sydnor, *Gentlemen Freeholders* (1952), also on Virginia.

The New Nation, 1775–1820

The shots fired at Lexington and Concord represented only one of many steps along the road to the creation of an independent American nation. The first steps had been taken many years before 1775, when the first European settlements in the New World had begun to develop ideas and institutions different from those of the societies they had left behind. And the steps continued for many years after 1775, as Americans fought first to win their independence and then to build a new government and a new society.

There was a series of vital stages in the progression toward nationhood after the outbreak of hostilities. First was the decision to demand independence. In the spring of 1775, that decision still seemed far away. Many Americans continued to believe that they were fighting simply to protect their proper position within the British Empire. To them, all that would have been necessary to resolve the conflict would have been a retreat by England from its unpopular policies. But as the war continued and expanded in the ensuing months—and as political agitation for a complete break with England grew—sentiment for independence gained favor. Finally, in July 1776, the leaders of the thirteen colonies, meeting in Philadelphia, declared America to be a new, autonomous nation.

P·A·R·T T·W·O

Much remained to be done. To secure their independence, the American people had to fight a long and difficult war against the greatest military power in the world, a war that few objective observers believed they could win. For nearly seven years it continued, with the American cause at first on the verge of collapse. Gradually, however, the new nation gained strength; and finally, in 1781, it secured a decisive military victory over the British. Two years later, a peace treaty confirmed the end of the war and the independence of the American republic. Britain remained a far more formidable power than the United States. But English military power had proved poorly suited to the new kind of war being fought in North America. And the fledgling American forces had displayed a spirit and persistence that few could have anticipated.

The War for Independence resolved the question of whether the new nation would survive. It did not, however, resolve the question of what it would be. In political terms, at least, the answer to that question emerged from an extraordinary process, beginning during the war itself and culminating in 1789 with the creation of a new federal government. There were few precedents in history for this self-conscious effort by Americans to create a political system for themselves, a system based on carefully argued ideas about the role of government and the nature of man. From the deliberations first of the individual states and then of the nation as a whole, came one of the stablest and most enduring political systems in the world.

The framing of the Constitution, however, still did not complete the process of nation building. For the next three decades, the United States engaged in a series of intense and often bitter political conflicts, as competing factions fought with one another to determine the directions the new nation would take. Would the central government be strong or weak? Would the nation's economy be agrarian or industrial? Would the United States play an active role in the world or remain isolated from it? Such questions produced controversies that at times threatened to tear the new nation apart. And when, beginning in 1812, the United States found itself engaged in another war with Great Britain, the survival of the republic appeared precarious indeed.

By 1820, many of these initial controversies had been, if not fully resolved, then at least made manageable. And the threat from overseas had been for the moment dispelled. The American nation was not yet complete. It could be argued that it never would be. But the initial stage of development had come to an end. The United States sensed itself secure in its nationhood and ready for a period of rapid expansion and change—a period that would ultimately produce new crises of its own.

The Battle of Princeton, 1777, by William Mercer   (Historical Society of Pennsylvania)

Chapter 5

The American Revolution

Two struggles occurred simultaneously during the seven years of war that began in April of 1775. One was the military conflict with Great Britain. The second was a political conflict within America. The two struggles had profound effects on each other.

The military conflict was, by the standards of later wars, a relatively modest one. Battle deaths on the American side totaled fewer than 5,000. The technology of warfare was so crude that cannons and rifles were effective only at extraordinarily close range; and fighting of any kind was virtually out of the question in bad weather. Yet the war in America was, by the standards of its own day, an unusually savage conflict, pitting not only army against army, but at times the population at large against a powerful external force. It was this shift of the war from a traditional, conventional struggle to a new kind of conflict—a revolutionary war for liberation—that made it possible for the United States finally to defeat the vastly more powerful British.

At the same time, Americans were wrestling with the great political questions that the conflict necessarily produced: first, whether to demand independence from Britain; then, how to structure the new nation they had proclaimed. Only the first of these questions had been resolved by the time of the British surrender at Yorktown in 1781. But by then the United States had already established itself—both in its own mind and in the mind of much of the rest of the world—as a nation with a special mission, a society dedicated to new, enlightened ideals. Thomas Paine, himself an important figure in shaping the Revolution, reflected the opinion of many when he claimed that the American War for Independence had "contributed more to enlighten the world, and diffuse a spirit of freedom and liberality among mankind, than any human event . . . that ever preceded it."

The States United

Although many Americans had been expecting a military conflict with Britain for months, even years, the actual beginning of hostilities in 1775 found the colonies generally unprepared for the enormous challenges awaiting them. A still-unformed nation, with a population less than a third as large as the 9 million of Great Britain, and with economic and military resources proportionately still smaller, faced the task of mobilizing for war against the world's greatest armed power. And Americans faced that task deeply divided about what they were fighting for.

Defining American War Aims

Three weeks after the battles of Lexington and Concord, when the Second Continental Congress met in the State House in Philadelphia, the delegates (again from every colony except Georgia, which was not represented until the following autumn) agreed to support the war. But they disagreed about its purpose. At one extreme was a group led by the Adams cousins (John and Samuel), Richard Henry Lee of Virginia, and others, who already favored independence; at the other extreme was a group led by such moderates as John Dickinson of Pennsylvania, who hoped for an early reconciliation with Great Britain. Most of the delegates tried to find some middle ground between these positions. Their uncertainty was reflected in the nature of two very different declarations, which they adopted in quick succession. Although they dismissed Lord North's Conciliatory Propositions as insincere, they voted for one last appeal to the king: the so-called Olive Branch Petition. Then, on July 6, 1775, they adopted a Declaration of the Causes and Necessity of Taking Up Arms. It proclaimed that the British government had left the American people with only two alternatives, "unconditional submission to the tyranny of irritated ministers or resistance by force." The Americans had chosen resistance.

Throughout the first year of the war, most Americans believed they were fighting not for independence but for a redress of grievances within the British Empire. During that year, however, many of them began to change their minds, for several reasons. First, the costs of the war—human and financial—were so high that the original war aims began to seem too modest to justify them. Second, what lingering affection they retained for the mother country greatly diminished when the British began trying to recruit Indians, black slaves, and foreign mercenaries (the hated "Hessians") against them. Third, and most important, they felt that they were being forced toward independence when the British government rejected the Olive Branch Petition and instead enacted the Prohibitory Act, which closed the colonies to all overseas trade and made no concessions to American demands except an offer of pardon to repentant rebels. The British enforced the Prohibitory Act with a naval blockade of colonial ports. And Americans were confronted with a choice between submitting meekly to British authority or defying the blockade—which they could not hope to do effectively without creating a sovereign nation.

The publication in January 1776 of an impassioned pamphlet clarified and crystallized these feelings. It was called, simply, *Common Sense*. Its author, unmentioned on the title page, was Thomas Paine, who had emigrated from England to America less than two years before (with letters of introduction from Benjamin Franklin, whom he had met in London). Long a failure in various trades, Paine now proved a brilliant success as a revolutionary propagandist. His pamphlet, reprinted month after month by the thousands, passed from hand to hand, read

COMMON SENSE;

ADDRESSED TO THE

INHABITANTS

O F

A M E R I C A,

On the following interesting

S U B J E C T S.

I. Of the Origin and Design of Government in general, with concise Remarks on the English Constitution.

II. Of Monarchy and Hereditary Succession.

III. Thoughts on the present State of American Affairs.

IV. Of the present Ability of America, with some miscellaneous Reflections.

Man knows no Master save creating HEAVEN,
Or those whom choice and common good ordain.
THOMSON.

PHILADELPHIA;
Printed, and Sold, by R. BELL, in Third-Street.
MDCCLXXVI.

Common Sense

Shown here is the title page of the first edition of Thomas Paine's influential pamphlet, published anonymously in Philadelphia on January 10, 1776. Paine went on to serve in Washington's army during the campaigns in New Jersey and at the same time wrote a series of essays designed to arouse support for the Patriot cause. They were collectively titled *The Crisis;* the first of them contains the phrase "These are the times that try men's souls." In later years Paine took an active part in the French Revolution, on behalf of which he published *The Rights of Man* (1791–1792). He also wrote *The Age of Reason* (1794–1796), which attacked conventional Christian beliefs and promoted his own "deist" philosophy. He returned to America in 1802 and spent the last years before his death in 1809 in poverty and obscurity. (Library of Congress) and reread, debated and discussed, helped change the American outlook toward the war. Paine's purpose was to expose the folly of continuing to believe reconciliation with Britain was possible. He wanted to turn the anger of Americans away from the specific parliamentary measures they were resisting and toward what he considered the root of the problem—the English constitution itself. It was not enough, he argued, for Americans to continue blaming their problems on particular ministers, or even on Parliament. It was the king, and the system that permitted him to rule, that was to blame. Thus it was simple common sense for Americans to break completely with a government that could produce so corrupt a monarch as George III, a government that could inflict such brutality on its own people, a government that could drag Americans into wars in which America had no interest. The island kingdom of England was no more fit to rule the American continent than a satellite was fit to rule the sun. "O! ye that love mankind! ye that dare oppose not only the tyranny but the tyrant, stand forth!" Paine declared.

The Decision for Independence

Common Sense had an enormous influence on American thinking. It sold more than 100,000 copies in only a few months, and to many of its readers it was a revelation. Although sentiment for independence was still far from unanimous, the first months of 1776 saw a rapid growth of support for the idea.

In the midst of all this, the Continental Congress (meeting again in Philadelphia) was moving slowly and tentatively toward a final break with England. It opened American ports to the ships of all nations except Great Britain, entered into communication with foreign powers, and recommended to the various colonies that they establish governments without the authority of the empire, as in fact most already were doing. Congress also appointed a committee to draft a formal declaration of independence. On July 2, 1776, it adopted a resolution: "That these United Colonies are, and, of right, ought to be, free and independent states; that they are absolved from all allegiance to the British crown, and that all political connexion between them and the state of Great Britain is, and ought to be, totally dissolved." Two days later, on July 4, Congress approved the Declaration of Independence itself, which provided the formal justifications for the actions the delegates had in fact taken two days earlier.

The Declaration was largely the work of Thomas Jefferson, a thirty-three-year-old Virginian, although it was slightly revised by Benjamin Franklin and John Adams, his colleagues on the drafting committee. Congress made more drastic changes, striking out passages that condemned the British people and the slave trade. As Adams afterward observed, Jefferson said little in the document that was new. Its virtue lay in the eloquence with which it expressed beliefs already widespread in America.

The document was in two parts. In the first, Jefferson restated the familiar contract theory of John Locke: the theory that governments were formed to protect the rights of life, liberty, and property; Jefferson gave the theory a more idealistic tone by referring instead to the rights of "life, liberty and the pursuit of happiness." In the second part he listed the alleged crimes of the king, who, with the backing of Parliament, had violated his contract with the colonists and thus had forfeited all claim to their loyalty.

The Declaration of Independence exerted an incalculable influence on later history. Its ringing endorsement of the idea that "all men are created equal" helped stimulate humanitarian movements of many kinds in the United States; abroad it helped to inspire the French Revolution's own Declaration of the Rights of Man. More immediately, the Declaration—and its claim of American sovereignty—led to increased foreign aid for the struggling rebels and prepared the way for France's intervention on their side. It steeled American Patriots, as those opposing the British called themselves, to fight on, to reject the idea of a peace that stopped short of winning independence. And at the same time it created deep divisions within American society.

At the news of the Declaration of Independence, crowds in Philadelphia, Boston, and other places gathered to cheer, fire guns and cannons, and ring church bells. But there were many in America who did not rejoice. Some had disapproved of the war from the beginning. Others had been willing to support it only so long as its aims did not conflict with their basic loyalty to the king. Such people were a minority, but a large one; and whether openly or secretly, they remained Loyalists, as they chose to call themselves, or Tories, as they were known to the Whig or Patriot majority.

The Declaration of Independence simply confirmed what circumstances had already ensured: that the American people, at war with Great Britain, would have to devise a means of governing themselves and supporting their military struggle. To meet

Raising the Liberty Pole, 1776
In this nineteenth-century engraving by John C. McRae, Americans celebrate the Declaration of Independence in July 1776 by raising a flagpole decked with Patriot banners. In the background other enthusiasts take down a sign bearing a likeness of George III.   (Library of Congress)

these new demands, new institutions emerged at both the local and the national levels.

The individual colonies now began to call themselves states—a reflection of their belief that each province was now in some respects a separate and sovereign entity. And as states, they had to create new governments to replace the royal governments that independence had repudiated. By 1781, most states had produced written constitutions for themselves that established republican governments; some of these governments survived, with only minor changes, for decades to come.

At the national level, however, the process was more uncertain and less successful. For a time, Americans were uncertain whether they even wanted a real national government; the Continental Congress had never been considered more than a coordinating

mechanism, and virtually everyone considered the individual colonies (now states) the real centers of authority. Yet fighting a war required a certain amount of central direction, and Americans began almost immediately to try to reconcile these two contradictory assumptions.

No sooner had the Congress appointed a committee to draft a declaration of independence than it appointed another to draft a plan of union. And after much debate and many revisions, the Congress adopted the committee's plan in November 1777. The document (which was not formally ratified by the states until 1781) was known as the Articles of Confederation; and it did little more than confirm the weak, decentralized system already in operation. The Continental Congress would survive as the chief coordinating agency of the war effort, but its powers over the individual states would be extraordinarily limited. Indeed, the Articles did not make it entirely clear that the Congress was to be a real government at all. The war was won as much in spite of as because of its efforts. (See pp. 144–148 for a fuller discussion of the structure of the new state and national governments.)

Mobilizing for War

Congress and the states faced overwhelming tasks in raising and organizing armies, providing the necessary supplies and equipment, and paying the costs of war. Supplies of most kinds were scarce at the outset, and shortages persisted to the end. America was a land of hunters and thus contained numerous gunsmiths. But these craftsmen were not able to meet the wartime demand for guns and ammunition; nor were they able to produce heavy arms. Congress in 1777 established a government arsenal at Springfield, Massachusetts. Even so, Americans managed to manufacture only a small fraction of the equipment they used. They supplemented their own manufactures with matériel that fell into their hands on the seizure of British forts, the surrender of British armies, and the capture of supply ships by American privateers. But they got most of their war materials from European nations, particularly from France.

One of the nation's severest problems was finding a way to finance the war. Congress lacked the authority and the states generally lacked the inclination to impose taxes on the public. Hard currency (gold and silver) was scarce in America, as it always had been; and when Congress requisitioned money from the states, none of them contributed more than a small part of its expected share. Congress had only limited success raising money by floating long-term loans at home, since few Americans could afford war bonds and those few usually preferred to invest in more profitable ventures, such as privateering. So it had no choice in the end but to issue paper money. Continental currency came from the printing presses in large and repeated batches. The states added sizable paper-currency issues of their own.

The result, predictably, was inflation. Prices rose to fantastic heights, and the value of paper money fell proportionately. Many American farmers and merchants began to prefer doing business with the British, who could pay for goods in gold or silver coin. (That was one reason why George Washington's troops suffered from severe food shortages at Valley Forge in the winter of 1777-1778; many Philadelphia merchants would not sell to them.) Congress tried in vain to stem the inflationary spiral. It recommended price control regulations, but soon realized the futility of that approach. It tried to retire its paper currency by accepting it for payment of taxes at a fortieth of its face value and declaring it worthless for any other purpose. Ultimately, however, it was able to finance the war effort only by borrowing heavily from other nations.

Only a small proportion of eligible American men were willing to volunteer for the American armies once the first surge of patriotism ebbed after 1775. The states had to resort to persuasion and force, to bounties and the draft. Once recruited, militiamen remained under the control of their respective states. Congress very early recognized the disadvantages of this decentralized system and called for a Continental army with a single commander in chief. George Washington, a forty-three-year-old Virginia planter-aristocrat who had commanded colonial forces during the French and Indian War, possessed more experience than any other American-born officer available. He had also been an early advocate of independence. Above all, he was admired, respected, and trusted by nearly all Patriots. He was the unanimous choice of the delegates, and he took command in June 1775.

Congress had chosen well. Throughout the war, Washington kept faithfully at his task, despite difficulties and discouragements that would have daunted a lesser man. He had to deal with serious problems of morale among soldiers who consistently received short rations and low pay; open mutinies broke out in 1781 among the Pennsylvania and New Jersey troops. During the discouraging winter of Valley Forge, moreover, some congressmen and army officers apparently began conspiring (in the so-called Conway Cabal, named for Thomas Conway, one of its alleged leaders) to replace Washington as commander in chief. And the Continental Congress, Washington's "employers," always seemed too little interested in supplying him with manpower and equipment and too much interested in interfering with his conduct of military operations

Washington was not without shortcomings as a military commander; indeed, he lost more battles than he won. Yet for all his faults and failures, he was indisputably a great war leader. With the aid of foreign military experts such as the Marquis de Lafayette from France and the Baron von Steuben from Prussia, he succeeded in building and holding together a force

Revolutionary Soldiers

Jean Baptiste de Verger, a French officer serving in America during the Revolution, kept a journal of his experiences illustrated with watercolors. Here he portrays four American soldiers carrying different kinds of arms: a black infantryman with a light rifle, a musketman, a rifleman, and an artilleryman.   (Brown University Library)

of fewer than 10,000 men (not counting the militias of the separate states) that ultimately prevailed against the mightiest power in the world. Even more important, perhaps, in a new nation still unsure of either its purposes or its structure, with a central government both weak and contentious, Washington was the indispensable man whose steadiness, courage, and dedication to his cause provided the army—and the people—with a symbol of stability around which they could rally. He was not the most brilliant of the country's early leaders. But in the crucial years of the war, at least, he was the most successful in holding the new nation together.

The War for Independence

On the surface, at least, all the advantages in the military struggle between America and Great Britain appeared to lie with the British. They possessed the greatest navy and the best-equipped army in the world. They had access to the resources of an empire. They had a coherent structure of command. The Americans, by contrast, were struggling to create an army and a government at the same time that they were trying to fight a war.

Yet the United States had advantages that were not at first apparent. Americans were fighting on their own ground, far from the center of British might. They were more committed to the conflict; the British people were only half-heartedly supporting the war. And beginning in 1777, the Americans had the benefit of substantial aid from abroad, after the American war had merged with a world contest in which Great Britain faced the strongest powers of Europe—most notably France—in a struggle for imperial supremacy.

But the American victory was not simply the result of these advantages, or even of the remarkable spirit and resourcefulness of the people and the army. It was a result, too, of a series of egregious blunders and miscalculations by the British in the early stages of the fighting, when England could (and probably should) have won. And it was, finally, a result of the transformation of the war—through three distinct phases—into a new kind of conflict that the British military, for all its strength, could not hope to win.

The First Phase: New England

For the first year of the fighting—from the spring of 1775 to the spring of 1776—the British remained uncertain about whether or not they were actually engaged in a war. Many English authorities continued to believe that what was happening in America was a limited, local conflict and that British forces were simply attempting to quell pockets of rebellion in the contentious area around Boston. Gradually, however, the colonial forces took the offensive and proved to England that the war was not confined to Massachusetts, that the entire territory of the American colonies was becoming a battleground.

After the British withdrawal from Concord and Lexington in April 1775, American forces besieged the army of General Thomas Gage in Boston. The Patriots suffered severe casualties in the Battle of Bunker Hill (actually fought on Breed's Hill) on June 17, 1775, and were ultimately driven from their position there. But they inflicted far greater losses on the enemy (indeed, the heaviest casualties the British were to suffer in the entire war) and thereafter continued to tighten the siege. By the first months of 1776, the British finally concluded that Boston was not the best place from which to wage a continental war. Not only was it in the center of the most fervently anti-British region of the colonies; it was also tactically indefensible—a narrow neck of land, easily isolated and besieged. By late winter, in fact, Patriot forces had surrounded the city and had occupied strategic positions on the heights. And so, on March 17, 1776 (a date still celebrated in Boston as Evacuation Day), the redcoats departed Boston for Halifax with hundreds of Loyalist refugees. Within a year from the firing of the first shots, the enemy had been driven—temporarily—from American soil.

Elsewhere, the war was proceeding fitfully and inconclusively. To the south, at Moore's Creek Bridge in North Carolina, a band of Patriots crushed an uprising of Loyalists on February 27, 1776, and thereby discouraged a British plan to invade the Southern states. The British had based those plans on the expectation of substantial aid from local Tories; they realized now that such aid might not be as effective as they had hoped. To the north, the Americans themselves undertook an invasion of Canada—hoping to remove the British threat and to win the Canadians to their cause. Benedict Arnold, the intrepid commander of a small American force, threatened Quebec in late 1775 and early 1776 after a winter march of incredible hardship. He was joined by Richard Montgomery, who combined his forces with Arnold's and took command of both. Montgomery was killed in the assault on the city; and although a wounded Arnold kept up the siege for a time, the Quebec campaign ended in frustration. A civilian commission sent to Canada by Congress and headed by the seventy-year-old Franklin met with no more success in its efforts to win the allegiance of the northern colonists. Canada was not to become the fourteenth state.

The British evacuation in 1776 was not, therefore, so much a victory for the Americans (although their accomplishments so far had been impressive) as a reflection of changing English assumptions about the war. By the spring of 1776, it had become clear to the British that the conflict was not a local phenomenon in the area around Boston. The American campaigns in Canada, the agitation in the South, and the growing evidence of colonial unity all suggested that England must be prepared to fight a much larger conflict. The departure of the British marked, therefore, a shift in strategy more than an admission of defeat.

The Second Phase: The Mid-Atlantic Region

The next phase of the war, which lasted from 1776 until early 1778, was when the British were in the best position to win. Indeed, had it not been for a series of blunders and misfortunes, they probably would have crushed the rebellion then. For during this period the struggle became, for the most part, a traditional, conventional war. And in that, the Americans were woefully overmatched.

The British regrouped quickly after their retreat from Boston, and they soon managed to put the Americans on the strategic defensive (a position they maintained for the rest of the war). During the summer of 1776, in the weeks immediately following the Declaration of Independence, the waters around the city of New York became filled with the most formidable military force Great Britain had ever sent abroad. Hundreds of men-of-war and troopships and

The Battle of Bunker Hill, 1775
Here, British troops attack Patriot forces outside Boston on June 17, 1775, in the first great battle of the American Revolution. The British ultimately drove the Americans from their positions on Breed's Hill and Bunker Hill, but only after suffering enormous casualties. General Gage, the British commander, reported to his superiors in London after the battle: "These people show a spirit and conduct against us they never showed against the French." This anonymous painting reveals the array of British troops and naval support and also shows the bombardment and burning of Charles Town from artillery in Boston. (National Gallery of Art, Washington)

32,000 disciplined soldiers arrived, under the command of the affable Sir William Howe. Howe felt no particular hostility toward the Americans. He hoped to awe them into submission rather than shoot them; and he believed that most of them, if given a chance, would show that they were loyal to the king. In a parley with commissioners from Congress, he offered them a choice between submission with royal pardon and a battle against overwhelming odds.

To oppose Howe's awesome array, Washington could muster only about 19,000 poorly armed and trained soldiers, including both Continentals and state troops; he had no navy at all. Yet without hesitation,

the Americans rejected Howe's offer and chose continued war—which meant inevitably a succession of defeats. The British pushed the defenders off Long Island, compelled them to abandon Manhattan, and then drove them in slow retreat over the plains of New Jersey, across the Delaware River, and into Pennsylvania.

For eighteenth-century Europeans, warfare was a seasonal activity. The British settled down for the winter with occupation forces at various points in New Jersey and with an outpost of Hessians (German mercenaries) at Trenton on the Delaware. But Washington did not content himself with sitting still. On

The Revolution in the North, 1775–1776

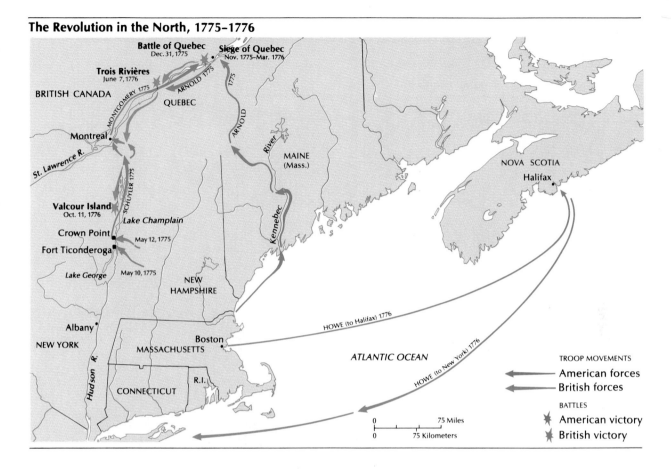

Christmas night 1776, he daringly recrossed the icy river, surprised and scattered the Hessians, and occupied the town. Then he advanced to Princeton and drove a force of redcoats from their base in the college there. But Washington was unable to hold either Princeton or Trenton, and he finally took refuge for the rest of the winter in the hills around Morristown. As the campaign of 1776 came to an end, the Americans could console themselves with the thought that they had won two minor victories, that their main army was still intact, and that the invaders were no nearer than before to the decisive triumph that Howe had so confidently anticipated. The heavy British advantages in men and supplies, however, remained.

For the campaigns of 1777 the British devised a strategy that, if Howe had stuck to it, might have cut the United States in two and prepared the way for final victory by Great Britain. Howe would move from New York up the Hudson to Albany, while another force, in a gigantic pincers movement, would come down from Canada to meet him. One of Howe's ambitious younger officers, the dashing John

Burgoyne, secured command of this northern force and elaborated on the plan by preparing for a two-pronged attack along both the Mohawk and the upper Hudson approaches to Albany.

But after setting this plan in motion, Howe made a major (and many believed inexplicable) blunder and adopted a different plan for himself. He decided to launch an assault on the rebel capital Philadelphia—an assault that would, he hoped, discourage the Patriots, rally the Loyalists, and bring the war to a speedy conclusion. He removed the bulk of his forces from New York by sea, landed at the head of the Chesapeake Bay, brushed Washington aside at the Battle of Brandywine Creek on September 11, and proceeded north to Philadelphia, which he was able to occupy with little resistance. Meanwhile, Washington, after an unsuccessful October 4 attack at Germantown (just outside Philadelphia), went into winter quarters at Valley Forge. The Continental Congress, now dislodged from its capital, reassembled at York, Pennsylvania.

Howe's move to Philadelphia left Burgoyne to

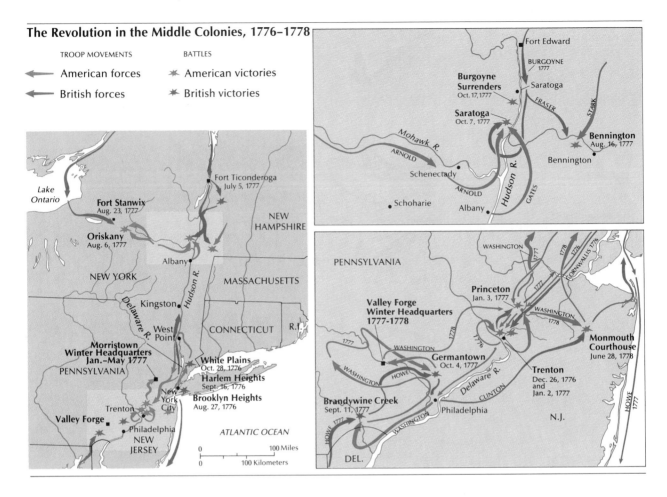

The Revolution in the Middle Colonies, 1776–1778

TROOP MOVEMENTS

← American forces

← British forces

BATTLES

✳ American victories

✳ British victories

carry out his twofold campaign in the north alone. He sent Colonel Barry St. Leger with a fast-moving force up the St. Lawrence River toward Lake Ontario and the headwaters of the Mohawk, while Burgoyne himself advanced directly down the upper Hudson Valley. He got off to a flying start. He seized Fort Ticonderoga easily and with it an enormous store of powder and supplies; that caused such consternation in Congress that the delegates removed General Philip Schuyler from command of American forces in the north and replaced him with Horatio Gates.

By the time Gates took command, Burgoyne had already experienced a sudden reversal of his military fortunes as a result of two staggering defeats. In one of them—at Oriskany, New York, on August 6—a Patriot band of German farmers led by Nicholas Herkimer held off a force of Indians and Tories commanded by St. Leger. That gave Benedict Arnold time to go to the relief of Fort Stanwix and close off the Mohawk Valley to St. Leger's advance. (Oriskany also marked the dissolution of the three-century-old

Iroquois Confederation. The Senecas, Cayugas, and Mohawks—who believed a British victory would help stem white encroachments on their lands—allied themselves with the English; the other two nations either supported the Patriots or remained neutral.) In the other battle—at Bennington, Vermont, on August 16—New England militiamen under the Bunker Hill veteran John Stark severely mauled a detachment that Burgoyne had sent out to seek supplies. Short of materials, with all help cut off, Burgoyne fought several costly engagements and then withdrew to Saratoga, where Gates surrounded him. On October 17, 1777, Burgoyne ordered what was left of his army, nearly 5,000 men, to lay down their arms.

The amazing news from the woods of upstate New York reverberated throughout the United States and Europe. The British surrender at Saratoga was the great turning point in the war—above all, perhaps, because it led directly to an alliance between the United States and France.

The British failure to win the war during this

period, a period in which they had overwhelming advantages, was in large part a result of their own mistakes. And in assessing them, the role of William Howe looms large. Howe's problems were not entirely of his own making. He was hobbled in part by his instructions from his superiors in England: He was told to conciliate the Americans, and he was told, at the same time, to defeat them. His efforts to fulfill that contradictory mandate accounted for many of his problems. But it also seems clear that Howe himself was ill suited to serve as commander in a war of revolution. Time and again, he showed not only serious deficiencies in tactical and strategic judgment, but a lack of aggressive instincts. With the Continental army weakened and in disarray, Howe refrained from moving in for the final attack, although he had several opportunities. Instead, he repeatedly allowed Washington to retreat and regroup; and he permitted the American army to spend a long winter unmolested in Valley Forge, where—weak and hungry—they might have been easy prey for British attack.

Some believed that Howe did not want to win the war, that he was secretly in sympathy with the American cause. His family had close ties to the colonies; and he himself was linked politically to those forces within the British government that opposed the war. Others pointed to personal weaknesses: Howe's apparent alcoholism, his romantic attachments (he spent the winter of 1777–1778 in Philadelphia with his mistress when many were urging him to move elsewhere). But the most important problem, it seems clear, was lack of judgment.

Whatever the reasons, the failure of the British to crush the Continental army in the mid-Atlantic states, combined with the stunning American victory at Saratoga (which was a direct result of Howe's strategic incompetence), transformed the war and ushered it into a new and final phase.

Securing Aid from Abroad

Central to this transformation of the war was American success in winning the indirect assistance of several European nations, and the direct support of France. Even before the Declaration of Independence, Congress drew up a plan for liberal commercial arrangements with other countries and prepared to send representatives to the capitals of Europe to negotiate treaties with the governments there. Such treaties would, of course, require European recognition of the United States as one of the sovereign nations of the world. "Militia diplomats," John Adams called the early American representatives abroad; and unlike the diplomatic regulars of Europe, they knew little of the formal art and etiquette of Old World diplomacy. Since transatlantic communication was slow and uncertain (it took from one to three months to cross the Atlantic), they had to interpret the instructions of Congress very freely and make crucial decisions entirely on their own.

Of all the possible foreign friends of the United States, the most promising and the most powerful was France, which was still smarting from its defeat at the hands of Great Britain in 1763. King Louis XVI of France, who had come to the throne in 1774, had an astute and determined foreign minister in the Count de Vergennes; and Vergennes quickly realized that France had a great deal to gain from the creation of an independent United States. If Britain were to lose that crucial part of its empire, the relative power of France would increase.

From the beginning, therefore, there was interest in an alliance on both the American and French sides; and diplomatic efforts began almost as soon as the first shots in the war were fired. For a time, however, France remained reluctant to provide the United States with what it most wanted: diplomatic recognition. Through a series of covert bargains, facilitated by the creation of a fictional trading firm and the use of secret agents on both sides (among them the famed French dramatist Caron de Beaumarchais), the Americans secured large quantities of much-needed supplies. But they wanted more.

After the Declaration of Independence, Benjamin Franklin himself went to France to lobby for further aid and for diplomatic recognition of the United States. A natural diplomat, the equal if not the superior of the world's best at that time, Franklin became a popular hero among the French—aristocrats and common people alike. (He also became a particular favorite of many Parisian women.) But Vergennes was at first reluctant to accede to Franklin's requests; he wanted some evidence that the Americans had a real chance of winning before he would agree to open French intervention. The news that Vergennes and Franklin were waiting for—the news from Saratoga—arrived in London on December 2 and in Paris on December 4, 1777. In London, the reports of Burgoyne's surrender persuaded Lord North to launch a new peace offensive: an offer of complete home rule within the empire for Americans if they would quit the war. In Paris, Franklin learned of Lord North's intentions from a British spy and made certain that Vergennes heard of them as well. The news worried the foreign minister. He feared the Americans might accept the offer and thus destroy France's opportunity to weaken Britain's imperial power; and he realized that French assistance might help persuade the Americans to continue the struggle. On February 6, 1778, therefore, Vergennes signed a series of agreements with the American diplomats that signaled the formal recognition of the United States as a sovereign nation and laid the groundwork for greatly expanded French assistance to the American war effort.

The entrance of France into the conflict substantially altered the British approach to the war. It was now an international conflict involving England's traditional European rivals. In the course of the next two years, France, Spain, and the Netherlands all drifted into another general war with Great Britain in Europe. France and the Netherlands allied themselves openly with the United States; all three nations contributed indirectly to the ultimate American victory by complicating England's task and directly by offering financial and material assistance. But it was France that served as America's truly indispensable ally. Not only did it furnish the new nation with most of its money and munitions, but it also provided a navy and an expeditionary force that proved invaluable in the final, successful phase of the revolutionary conflict.

The Final Phase: The South

The last phase of the military struggle in America was fundamentally different from either of the first two. The British government had never been fully united behind the war in the first place; after the defeat at Saratoga and the intervention of the French, it imposed new limits on its commitment to the conflict. Instead of a full-scale military struggle against the American army, therefore, the British chose a different strategy. They would attempt to enlist the support of those elements of the American population—a majority, they continued to believe—who were still loyal to the crown; they would, in other words, work to undermine the Revolution from within. Since Loyalist sentiment was considered to be strongest in the Southern colonies, the main focus of the British effort shifted there; and it was thus in the South, for the most part, that the war was fought to its conclusion.

The new strategy was a ludicrous failure. British forces spent three years (from 1778 to 1781) moving through the South, fighting small battles and large,

and attempting to neutralize (or to use the terminology of a later American war, "pacify") the territory through which they traveled. All such efforts ended in frustration. The British badly overestimated the extent of Loyalist sentiment. While it was true that in Georgia and the Carolinas there were numerous Tories, some of them disgruntled members of the Regulator movement, it was also true that Patriot sentiment was far stronger than the British believed. In Virginia, support for independence was as fervent as in Massachusetts. And even in the lower South, Loyalists often feared to offer aid to the British because they realized they might face reprisals from the Patriots around them. There were also severe logistical problems facing the British in the South. Patriot forces could move at will throughout the region, living off the resources of the countryside, blending in with the civilian population and leaving the British unable to distinguish friend from foe. The British, by contrast, suffered all the disadvantages of an army in hostile territory.

It was this phase of the conflict that made the war truly "revolutionary"—not only because it introduced a new kind of warfare, but because it had the effect of mobilizing and politicizing large groups of the population who had previously remained aloof from the struggle. With the war expanding into previously isolated communities, with many civilians forced to involve themselves whether they liked it or not, the political climate of the United States grew more heated than ever. And support for independence, far from being crushed as the British had hoped, greatly increased.

That was the backdrop against which the important military encounters of the last years of the war occurred. In the North, where significant numbers of British troops remained, the fighting settled into a relatively quiet stalemate. Sir Henry Clinton replaced the hapless William Howe in 1778 and moved what had been Howe's army from Philadelphia back to New York. There the British troops stayed for more than a year, with Washington using his army to keep watch around them. The American forces in New York did so little fighting in this period that Washington sent some troops west to strike back against hostile Indians who had been attacking white settlers. During that same winter, George Rogers Clark, with orders from the state of Virginia—not from either Washington or Congress—led a daring expedition over the mountains and captured settlements in the Illinois country from the British and their Indian allies.

During this period of relative calm, the American

The Revolution in the South, 1778–1781

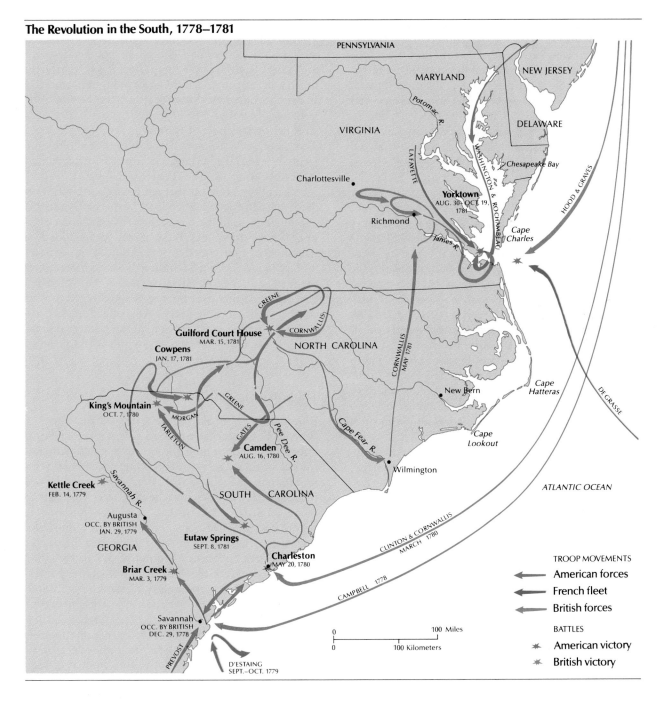

forces—and George Washington in particular—were shocked by the exposure of treason on the part of General Benedict Arnold. Arnold had been one of the early heroes of the war; but now, convinced that the American cause was hopeless, he conspired with British agents to betray the Patriot stronghold at West Point on the Hudson River. In the nick of time, the scheme was exposed and foiled; and Arnold fled to

the safety of the British camp, where he spent the rest of the war.

But the decisive fighting took place in the South. The British did have some significant military successes during this period. On December 29, 1778, they captured Savannah, on the coast of Georgia; and 17 months later, on May 20, 1780, they took the port of Charleston, South Carolina. They even inspired some Loyalists to take up arms and advance with them into the interior. But although the British were able to win conventional battles, they were constantly harassed as they moved through the countryside by Patriot guerrillas led by such resourceful fighters as Thomas Sumter, Andrew Pickens, and Francis Marion, the "Swamp Fox." Penetrating to Camden, South Carolina, Lord Cornwallis (Clinton's choice as British commander in the South) met and crushed a combined force of militiamen and Continentals under Horatio Gates on August 16, 1780. Congress recalled Gates, and Washington gave the Southern command to Nathanael Greene, a former Quaker blacksmith from Rhode Island and probably the ablest of all the American generals of the time next to Washington himself.

Even before Greene arrived in the war theater, the tide of battle already had begun to turn against Cornwallis. At King's Mountain (near the North Carolina–South Carolina border) on October 7, 1780, a band of Patriot riflemen from the backwoods killed, wounded, or captured an entire force of 1,100 New York and South Carolina Tories, upon whom Cornwallis had depended as auxiliaries. Once Greene arrived, he confused and exasperated Cornwallis by dividing the American forces into fast-moving contingents while refraining from a showdown in open battle. One of the contingents inflicted what Cornwallis admitted was "a very unexpected and severe blow" at Cowpens on January 17, 1781. Finally, after receiving reinforcements, Greene combined all his forces and maneuvered to meet the British on ground of his own choosing, at Guilford Court House, North Carolina. After a hard-fought battle there on March 15, 1781, Greene was driven from the field; but Cornwallis had lost so many men that he decided at last to abandon the Carolina campaign.

Cornwallis withdrew to the port town of Wilmington, North Carolina, to receive supplies being sent to him by sea; later he moved north to carry on raids in the interior of Virginia. But Clinton, concerned for the army's safety, ordered him to take up a position on the peninsula between the York and James rivers and wait for water transport to New York or Charleston. So Cornwallis retreated to Yorktown and began to build fortifications there.

At that point, George Washington decided to try to trap Cornwallis at Yorktown. He coordinated his efforts with the Count de Rochambeau, commander of the French expeditionary force in America, and Admiral de Grasse, commander of a French fleet in American waters. Washington and Rochambeau marched a French-American army from New York to join Lafayette in Virginia, while de Grasse sailed with additional troops for the Chesapeake Bay and the York River. These joint operations, perfectly timed and executed, caught Cornwallis between land and sea. After a few shows of resistance, he asked for terms on October 17, 1781 (four years to the day after the capitulation of Burgoyne at Saratoga). Two days later, as a military band played the old tune "The World Turn'd Upside Down," he surrendered his whole army of more than 7,000.

Except for a few skirmishes, the fighting was now over; but the war was not yet won. British forces continued to hold the seaports of Savannah, Charleston, Wilmington, and New York. Before long, a British fleet met and defeated Admiral de Grasse's fleet in the West Indies, ending Washington's hopes for further French naval assistance. For more than a year, then, although there was no significant further combat between British and American forces, it remained possible that the war might resume and the struggle for independence might still be lost.

Winning the Peace

The victory at Yorktown had immediate repercussions in England. Cornwallis's defeat provoked outcries against continuing the war and raised demands for cultivating American friendship as an asset in international politics. Lord North resigned; Lord Shelburne emerged from the political wreckage as prime minister; and British emissaries appeared in France to talk informally with the American diplomats there. Benjamin Franklin outlined for them what he called the "necessary" terms of peace, including independence and the establishment of the Mississippi as the western boundary of the United States. He also added several "desirable" terms, including the cession of Canada.

The three principal American diplomats—Franklin, John Jay, and John Adams—were under instructions to cooperate fully with France in their negotiations with England. But the French soon proved less reliable as diplomatic allies than they had as military supporters. Vergennes insisted that France could not agree to any settlement of the war with England until its ally Spain had achieved its principal war aim: winning back Gibraltar from the British. There was, moreover, no real prospect of that happening soon. And the American diplomats began to fear that their alliance with France might keep them

The Surrender of Cornwallis

The principal British army in America surrendered at Yorktown, Virginia, on October 19, 1781. Although not until 1783, after two years of difficult negotiations, did the British sign a treaty formally recognizing the independence of the United States, Yorktown marked the end of major hostilities. In this 1846 print by Nathaniel Currier, George Washington (on horseback in the foreground) accepts the sword of the British commander, Lord Cornwallis. The Marquis de Lafayette (mounted on a white horse to the right of Washington) looks on. (Library of Congress)

at war indefinitely. Disillusionment with the French increased when Jay learned that Vergennes's private secretary had gone on a secret mission to England; there were rumors that the French and Spanish were planning to bargain away American independence in a larger settlement with the British.

As a result, Franklin, Jay, and Adams soon ceased to keep Vergennes informed of their diplomatic efforts. They proceeded on their own and soon drew up a preliminary treaty with Great Britain. After the preliminary articles were signed on November 30, 1782, Franklin skillfully pacified Vergennes (who had, in any case, been kept informed of the American efforts by his own spies) and avoided an immediate rift in the French-American alliance.

The final treaty was signed September 3, 1783, when both Spain and France agreed to end hostilities. It included a number of provisions that Franklin, Jay, and Adams had opposed, some of which were to lead to serious friction with Great Britain and Spain in the years ahead. And it failed to include most of Franklin's "desirable" terms (including the cession of Canada to the United States). But the treaty did endorse the "necessary" terms Franklin had outlined; and it was, on the whole, remarkably favorable to the United States in granting a clear-cut recognition of independence and a generous, though ambiguous cession of territory—from the southern boundary of Canada to the northern boundary of Florida and from the Atlantic to the Mississippi. With good reason the

American people celebrated as the last of the British occupation forces embarked from New York and General Washington, at the head of his troops, rode triumphantly into the city.

War and Society

Historians have long debated whether the American Revolution was a social as well as a political revolution. Some have argued that the colonists were struggling not only over the question of home rule, but over "who should rule at home." Others claim that domestic social and economic concerns had little to do with the conflict. (See "Where Historians Disagree," pp. 138–139.) Whatever the motivations of Americans, however, there can be little doubt that the War for Independence had important effects on the nature of American society.

Loyalists and Minorities

Any war produces both winners and losers. The losers in the American Revolution included not only the British but American Loyalists. Estimates differ as to how many Americans remained loyal to England during the Revolution, but it is clear that there were

───── WHERE HISTORIANS DISAGREE ─────

The American Revolution

One of the oldest and most enduring controversies among American historians involves the nature of the American Revolution. Two broad schools of interpretation have emerged. One group of scholars has argued, and continues to argue, that the Revolution was primarily a political and intellectual event; that Americans in the 1770s were fighting to defend principles and ideals. Others have maintained, and still maintain, that much of the motivation for the Revolution was social and economic; that Americans were inspired to fight because of economic interests and social aspirations. Although there is a wide range of views and approaches within each of these schools, the question of "ideas" versus "interests" remains the crucial divide in interpretation.

The emphasis on ideology as the cause of the Revolution reflects, to some extent, the view of those who were involved in the event itself. Early histories of the Revolution, written by participants and contemporaries, invariably emphasized the high ideals of the Founding Fathers. That approach continued in an almost unbroken line throughout the nineteenth century, culminating in the work of one of the first great American historians, George Bancroft, who wrote in 1876 that the Revolution "was most radical in its character, yet achieved with such benign tranquillity that even conservatism hesitated to censure." Its aim, he believed, was to "preserve liberty" against the threat of British tyranny.

In the early twentieth century, historians first began seriously to examine the social and economic forces that may have contributed to the Revolu-

tion. Influenced by the reform currents of the progressive era, during which the power of economic interests came under scorching criticism, a number of scholars adopted the ideas of Carl Becker, who wrote in 1909—in a case study of New York—that not one but two questions were involved in the struggle. "The first was the question of home rule; the second was the question, if we may so put it, of who should rule at home." In addition to the fight against the British, in other words, there was also in progress a kind of civil war, a contest for power between radicals and conservatives that led to the "democratization of American politics and society." J. Franklin Jameson, expanding on Becker's views, argued in an influential book—*The American Revolution Considered as a Social Movement* (1926)—that the "stream of revolution, once started, could not be confined within narrow banks, but spread abroad upon the land. . . . Many economic desires, many social aspirations were set free by the political struggle, many aspects of society profoundly altered by the forces thus let loose."

Other "progressive" historians accepted the importance of economics as a cause of the Revolution but differed with Becker and Jameson over the form economic influences took. Arthur M. Schlesinger, for example, argued in an influential 1917 study that it was the colonial merchants who were chiefly responsible for arousing American resistance to the British; and that although they spoke of principles and ideals, their real motives were economic self-interest: freedom from the restrictive policies of British mercantilism. In the end,

many—at least a fifth (and some estimate as much as a third) of the white population. Their motivations were varied. Some were officeholders in the imperial government, who stood to lose their positions as a result of the Revolution. Others were merchants whose trade was closely tied to the imperial system. (Most merchants, however, supported the Revolution.) Still others were people who lived in relative isolation and who thus had not been exposed to the wave of discontent that had turned so many Americans against Britain; they had simply retained their traditional loyalties. There were also cultural and eth-

nic minorities who feared that an independent America would not offer them sufficient protection. And there were those who, expecting the British to win the war, were simply currying favor with the expected victors.

What happened to these men and women during the war is a turbulent and at times tragic story. Hounded by Patriots in their communities, harassed by legislative and judicial actions, the position of many of them became intolerable. Up to 100,000 fled the country during the war. Those who could afford to—for example, the hated Tory governor of Mas-

WHERE HISTORIANS DISAGREE

however, the Revolution could not be controlled by the merchants and became a far more broadly based social movement than they had anticipated or desired.

Economic interpretations of the Revolution prevailed for several decades; but the relatively conservative political climate of the 1950s helped produce new studies that reemphasized the role of ideology. Robert E. Brown, in *Middle-Class Democracy and the American Revolution in Massachusetts* (1955), contended that long before 1776, Massachusetts was "very close to a complete democracy" and that the internal social conflicts that some historians ascribed to the era simply did not exist. Edmund S. Morgan, like Brown, argued in 1956 that most Americans of the Revolutionary era shared the same basic political principles, that the rhetoric of the Revolution could not be dismissed as propaganda—as Schlesinger had claimed—but should be taken seriously as the motivating force behind the movement. The preeminent statement of the importance of ideas in the conflict came from Bernard Bailyn, in *The Ideological Origins of the American Revolution* (1967). After reading hundreds of Revolutionary pamphlets, Bailyn concluded that they "confirmed my rather old-fashioned view that the American Revolution was above all else an ideological, constitutional, political struggle and not primarily a controversy between social groups undertaken to force changes in the organization of the society or the economy."

By the time Bailyn's book was published, however, a new group of historians was already reviving a social and economic approach to the Revolution. Influenced by the New Left of the 1960s, they claimed that domestic tensions between classes contributed in crucial ways to the development of the Revolutionary movement. Historians such as Jesse Lemisch and Dirk Hoerder pointed to the actions of mobs in colonial cities as evidence of the social concerns of resisting Americans. Joseph Ernst reemphasized the significance of economic pressures on colonial merchants and tradesmen. Gary B. Nash, in *The Urban Crucible* (1979), emphasized the role of increasing economic tension and distress in colonial cities in creating a climate in which the Revolutionary movement could flourish. Edward Countryman, in *A People in Revolution* (1981) and *The American Revolution* (1985), also emphasized the social and economic roots of the Revolution. And Rhys Isaac suggested in *The Transformation of Virginia, 1740–1790* (1982) that the religious and cultural changes in colonial life, and the relationship between those changes and class alignments, underlay the new political outlook that led to the Revolution.

Many of the new socioeconomic interpretations of the Revolution argue not that the struggle was a direct expression of the material interests of the participants but that social and economic concerns were important in shaping the ideology of the conflict. "Everyone," Gary Nash has written, "has economic interests; and everyone . . . has an ideology." Only by exploring the relationships between the two, he maintains, can historians hope fully to understand either.

sachusetts, Thomas Hutchinson—fled to England, where many lived in difficult and lonely exile. Others of more modest means moved to Canada, establishing the first English-speaking community in the province of Quebec. Some returned to America after the war and, as the early passions and resentments faded, managed to reenter the life of the nation. Others remained abroad for the rest of their lives.

Most Loyalists were people of average means, but a substantial minority consisted of men and women of wealth. They left behind large estates and vacated important positions of social and economic leadership. Even some who remained in the country saw their property confiscated and their positions forfeited. The result was new opportunities for Patriots to acquire land and influence, a situation that produced important social changes in many communities. It would be an exaggeration, however, to claim that the departure of the Loyalists was responsible for anything approaching a social revolution. The Revolution did not create a general assault on the wealthy and powerful in America. When the war ended, those who had been wealthy at its beginning were, for the most part, still wealthy. Those who had wielded social and political influence (which often accompanied the possession of wealth) continued to wield it. Indeed, the distribution of wealth became more uneven in the aftermath of the war than it had been in the decades preceding it.

The war had a significant effect on other minorities as well, and on certain religious groups in particular. No sect suffered more than the Anglicans, many of whose members were Loyalists and all of whom were widely identified with England. In Virginia and Maryland, where the colonial governments had recognized Anglicanism as the official religion and had imposed a tax for its maintenance, the new Revolutionary regimes disestablished the church and thus eliminated the subsidy. In other states, Anglicans had benefited from aid from England, which also ceased with the outbreak of war. By the time the fighting ended, many Anglican parishes no longer even had clergymen, for there were few recruits to take the places of those who had died or who had left the country as Loyalist refugees. Since there had never been an American bishop or an intercolonial organization of the church, there was little institutional strength from which those Anglicans who remained could rebuild their church; and although Anglicanism survived in America, it was to remain permanently weakened from its losses during the Revolution. Also

weakened were the Quakers in Pennsylvania and elsewhere, who won widespread unpopularity because of their pacifism. Their refusal to support the war destroyed much of the social and political prestige they had enjoyed, and the church was never to recover fully.

While the war was weakening the Anglicans and the Quakers, it was improving the position of the Roman Catholic church. On the advice of Charles Carroll of Carrollton, a Maryland statesman and Catholic lay leader, most American Catholics supported the Patriot cause during the war. The French alliance brought Catholic troops and chaplains to the country, and the gratitude with which most Americans greeted them did much to erode old hostilities toward Catholics, whom Americans had in the past often denounced as agents of the devil. The church did not greatly increase its numbers as a result of the Revolution, but it did strengthen itself considerably as an institution. Shortly after the peace treaty was signed, the Vatican provided the United States with its own Catholic hierarchy. (Until then, the American church had been controlled by the English bishops.) Father John Carroll (also of Maryland) was named head of Catholic missions in America in 1784 and, in 1789, the first American bishop. In 1808 he became archbishop of Baltimore. Hostility toward

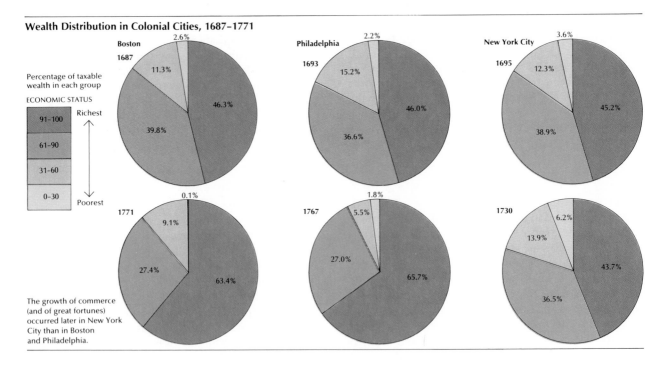

Wealth Distribution in Colonial Cities, 1687–1771

Percentage of taxable wealth in each group

ECONOMIC STATUS

91–100	Richest
61–90	
31–60	
0–30	Poorest

Boston 1687: 2.6%, 11.3%, 39.8%, 46.3%
Philadelphia 1693: 2.2%, 15.2%, 36.6%, 46.0%
New York City 1695: 3.6%, 12.3%, 38.9%, 45.2%

Boston 1771: 0.1%, 9.1%, 27.4%, 63.4%
Philadelphia 1767: 1.8%, 5.5%, 27.0%, 65.7%
New York City 1730: 6.2%, 13.9%, 36.5%, 43.7%

The growth of commerce (and of great fortunes) occurred later in New York City than in Boston and Philadelphia.

Catholics had not disappeared forever from American life, but the church had established a solid footing from which to withstand future assaults.

For the largest of America's minorities—the black population—the war had limited, but nevertheless profound, significance. For some, it meant freedom. Because so much of the fighting occurred in the South during the last years of the war, many slaves came into contact with the British army, which—in the interests of disrupting and weakening the American cause—emancipated thousands of them and took them out of the country. For other blacks, the Revolution meant exposure to the idea, although not the reality, of liberty. In the towns and cities of the South, where large groups of both free and enslaved blacks lived, the ideology of the Revolution had a pronounced effect. Although most blacks could not read, few could avoid exposure to the new and exciting ideas; and in many cases, they attempted to apply those ideas to themselves. The result was a series of incidents in several communities in which blacks engaged in open resistance to white control. In Charleston, South Carolina, Thomas Jeremiah, a free black, was executed after white authorities learned of elaborate plans for a slave uprising. It would be many years before blacks would be in a position to make more than sporadic efforts on behalf of their freedom; but the experience of the Revolution produced distinct stirrings of discontent.

That was one reason why Revolutionary sentiment was more restrained in South Carolina and Georgia than in other colonies. Blacks constituted a majority in South Carolina and almost half the population in Georgia, and whites in both places feared that revolution would foment slave rebellions. The same fears helped prevent English colonists in the Caribbean islands (who were far more greatly outnumbered by black slaves) from joining with the continental Americans in the revolt against Britain.

Abigail Adams
When this portrait was painted in the mid-1780s, Abigail Adams was living in London, where her husband, John Adams, was serving as the first American ambassador. Harboring strong political opinions, she was outspoken on public issues, and critics often charged John Adams with being "under the sovereignty of his wife." But she was generally more a fierce defender of her husband's policies than an active force in shaping them. During much of her married life, she lived apart from her husband, who spent many years traveling on diplomatic assignments. As a result, she became a ceaseless letter writer; her correspondence survives today as one of the most important sources of information about her extraordinary family. (New York State Historical Association, Cooperstown)

Women's Rights and Women's Roles

The Revolutionary emphasis on liberty and the "rights of man" led some American women to question their position in society as well. "By the way," Abigail Adams wrote to her husband John Adams in 1776, "in the new code of laws which I suppose it will be necessary for you to make, I desire you would remember the ladies and be more generous and favorable to them than your ancestors. Do not put such unlimited power into the hands of husbands."

Other women argued similarly for enhancing the status of their sex. Judith Sargent Murray, one of the leading essayists of the late eighteenth century, wrote in 1779 that women's minds were as good as those of men and that girls as well as boys therefore deserved access to education. Murray later served as one of the leading defenders of the works of the English feminist Mary Wollstonecraft, whose *Vindication of the*

Rights of Women was published in America in 1792. After reading it, Murray rejoiced that "the Rights of Women" were beginning to be understood in the United States and that future generations of women would inaugurate "a new era in female history."

But in most respects the new era did not arrive. Some political leaders—among them Benjamin Franklin and Benjamin Rush—voiced support for the education of women and for other feminist reforms. Yale students in the 1780s debated the question, "Whether women ought to be admitted into the magistracy and government of empires and republics." And there was for a time wide discussion of the future role of females in the new republic. But few concrete reforms were enacted into law or translated into practice; and indeed, women lost certain protections and privileges under the new regime that they had enjoyed under the old.

In colonial society, under the doctrines of English common law, an unmarried woman had certain legal rights, but a married woman had had virtually no rights at all. She could own no property and earn no independent wages; everything she owned and everything she earned belonged to her husband. She had no legal authority over her children; the father was, in the eyes of the law, the autocrat of the family. Because she had no property rights, she could not engage in any legal transactions (buying or selling, suing or being sued, writing wills). She could not vote. Nor could she obtain a divorce; that too was a right reserved almost exclusively to men. That was perhaps what Abigail Adams (who herself enjoyed a very happy marriage) meant when she chided her husband not to put "such unlimited power into the hands of the husbands."

The Revolution did little to change any of these legal customs. In some states, it did become easier for a woman to obtain a divorce. And in New Jersey, women obtained the right to vote (although that right was repealed in 1807). Otherwise, there were few advances and some setbacks—including the loss of the right of a widow to regain her dowry from her husband's estate. That change left many widows without any means of support and was one of the reasons for the increased agitation for female education; such women needed a way to support themselves.

The Revolution, in other words, far from challenging the patriarchal structure of American society actually confirmed and strengthened it. Few American women ever doubted that they should continue to occupy a sphere distinct from men or that their place remained in the family. Nevertheless, the Revolutionary experience did contribute to an alteration of women's expectations of their status within the family. In the past, they had often been little better than servants in their husbands' homes; both men and women had generally viewed the wife as a clear subordinate, performing functions in the family of far less importance than those of the husband. But the Revolution encouraged people of both sexes to reevaluate the contribution of women to the family and the society.

Part of this change was a result of the participation of women in the Revolutionary struggle itself. Some women had played an active and influential role in the politics of the Revolution. Mercy Otis Warren of Massachusetts, for example, was one of the leading pre-Revolutionary propagandists and pamphleteers. But more important were the new domestic and economic tasks that women began to perform, by necessity, in the course of the war. Some (Abigail Adams, for example) managed farms and businesses in the absence of their husbands. Others (among them Martha Washington, who spent the winter of 1778–1779 at Valley Forge with her husband) traveled with the Patriot army, helping to keep the soldiers fed and clothed and occasionally themselves engaging in battle. The legendary "Molly Pitcher"—so named because she carried pitchers of water to soldiers on the battlefield—watched her husband fall during one encounter and immediately took his place at a field gun. After the war, most such women returned to their traditional domestic roles. But the wartime experience had raised a challenge to the idea of the wife's complete subordination within the family.

As the republic searched for a cultural identity for itself during and immediately after the Revolution, it also began to place additional value on the role of women as mothers. The new nation was, most Americans liked to believe, producing a new kind of citizen, steeped in the principles of liberty. Mothers had a particularly important task, therefore, in instructing their children in the virtues that the republican citizenry was now expected to possess. Wives were still far from equal partners in marriage, but their ideas and interests were increasingly considered worthy of respect.

The War Economy

Inevitably, the Revolution produced important changes in the structure of the American economy.

After more than a century of dependence on the British imperial system, American trade suddenly found itself on its own. No longer did it have the protection of the great British navy; on the contrary, English ships now attempted to drive American vessels from the seas. No longer did American merchants have access to the markets of the empire; those markets were now hostile ports—including, of course, the most important source of American trade: England itself.

Yet while the Revolution was responsible for much disruption in traditional economic patterns, it served in the long run to strengthen the American economy. Well before the war was over, American ships had learned to evade the British navy with light, fast, easily maneuverable vessels. Indeed, the Yankees began to prey on British commerce with hundreds of privateers. For many a shipowner, privateering proved to be more profitable than ordinary peacetime trade. More important in the long run, the end of imperial restrictions on American shipping opened up enormous new areas of trade to the new nation. Colonial merchants had been violating British regulations for years, but the rules of empire had nevertheless served to inhibit American exploration of many markets. Now, enterprising merchants in New England and elsewhere began to develop new commerce in the Caribbean and South America. By the mid-1780s, American merchants were developing an important new pattern of trade with the Orient; and by the end of that decade, Yankee ships were regularly sailing from the eastern seaboard around Cape Horn to California, there exchanging manufactured goods for hides and furs, and then proceeding across the Pacific to barter for goods in China. There was also a substantial increase in trade among the American states.

When English imports to America were cut off—first by the prewar boycott, then by the war itself—there were desperate efforts throughout the states to stimulate domestic manufacturing of certain necessities. There was no great industrial expansion as a result, but there were several signs of the economic growth that was to come in the next century. Americans began to make their own cloth—"homespun," which became both patriotic and fashionable—to replace the now unobtainable British fabrics. It would be some time before a large domestic textile industry would emerge, but the nation was never again to rely exclusively on foreign sources for its cloth. There was, of course, pressure to build factories for the manufacture of guns and ammunition. And there was a growing awareness that America need not forever be dependent on other nations for manufactured goods. Having broken politically with the British Empire, citizens of the new nation began to dream of breaking economically with it too—of developing a strong economy to rival that of the Old World.

Banner of the Society of Pewterers

Members of the American Society of Pewterers carried this patriotic banner when they marched in a New York City parade in July 1788. Its inscription celebrates the adoption of the new federal Constitution and predicts a future of prosperity and freedom in "Columbia's Land." The banner also suggests the growing importance of American manufacturing, which had received an important boost during the Revolution when British imports became unavailable. (New-York Historical Society)

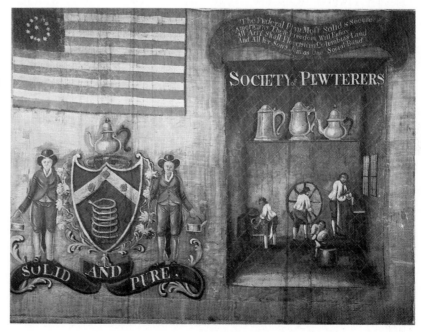

The war stopped short of revolutionizing the American economy. Not until the nineteenth century would that begin to occur. But it did serve to release a wide range of entrepreneurial energies that, despite the temporary dislocations, encouraged growth and diversification.

The Creation of State Governments

At the same time that Americans were struggling to win their independence on the battlefield, they were also struggling to create new institutions of government for themselves, to replace the British system they had repudiated. The construction of these new political institutions occurred in several stages and continued over a period of more than fifteen years. Yet its most crucial phase occurred in the very first years after independence, during the war itself; and it occurred not at the national but at the state level.

The formation of state governments began early in 1776, even before the adoption of the Declaration of Independence. It was the most creative period of American political development; for in it was determined the basic structure of the republic, and in it were resolved many of the early problems of republicanism. At first, the new state constitutions reflected primarily the fear of bloated executive power that had become so pronounced during the 1760s and early 1770s. Gradually, however, Americans began to become equally concerned about the instability of a government too responsive to the popular will. In a second phase of state constitution writing, therefore, they gave renewed attention to the idea of balance in government.

The Assumptions of Republicanism

If Americans agreed on nothing else when they began to build new governments for themselves, they agreed that those governments would be republican. To them, that meant a political system in which all power was derived from the people, rather than from some supreme authority (such as a king) standing above them. The success of any government, therefore, depended on the nature of its citizenry. If the population consisted of sturdy, independent property owners, then the republic could survive. If it con-

sisted of a few powerful aristocrats and a great mass of dependent workers, then it would be in danger. From the beginning, therefore, the ideal of the small freeholder became basic to American political ideology.

Another crucial part of that ideology was the concept of equality. The Declaration of Independence had given voice to that idea in its most ringing phrase: "all men are created equal." It was a belief that stood in direct contrast to the old European assumption of an inherited aristocracy. Every citizen, Americans believed, was born in a position of equality with every other citizen. It would be the innate talents and energies of individuals that would determine their roles in society, not their position at birth. The republican vision did not, in other words, envision a society without social gradations. Some people would inevitably be wealthier and more powerful than others. But all people would have to earn their success. There would be no equality of condition, but there would be full equality of opportunity.

In reality, of course, these assumptions could not always be sustained. The United States was never able to become a nation in which all citizens were independent property holders. From the beginning, there was a sizable dependent labor force—the white members of which were allowed many of the privileges of citizenship, the black members of which were allowed virtually no rights at all. American women remained both politically and economically subordinate, with few opportunities for advancement independent of their husbands. Nor was it possible to ensure full equality of opportunity. American society was more open and more fluid than that of most European nations; but it remained true that wealth and privilege were often passed from one generation to another. The conditions of a person's birth survived as a crucial determinant of success.

Nevertheless, in embracing the assumptions of republicanism, Americans were adopting a powerful, even revolutionary new ideology, one that would enable them to create a form of government never before seen in the world. Their experiment in statecraft became a model for many other countries and made the United States for a time the most admired and studied nation on earth.

The First State Constitutions

Two of the original thirteen states saw no need to produce new constitutions. Connecticut and Rhode

Island already had corporate charters which provided them with governments that were republican in all but name; they simply deleted references to England and the king from their charters and adopted them as constitutions. In the other eleven states, however, it was necessary to create entirely new governments. In doing so, Americans at first devoted their greatest efforts to avoiding what they considered to be the problems of the British system they were repudiating.

The first and perhaps most basic decision was that the constitutions were to be written down. In England, the constitution was not a document but a vague understanding about the way society should be structured. Americans believed that the vagueness of that understanding had allowed the British government to become corrupted. To avoid a similar fate, they insisted that their own government rest on clearly stated and permanently inscribed laws, so that no individual or group could pervert them.

The second decision was that the power of the executive, which Americans believed had grown bloated and threatening in England (and even, at times, in the colonies), must be limited. Only one state went so far as to eliminate the executive altogether: Pennsylvania. But most states inserted provisions sharply limiting the power of the governor over appointments, reducing or eliminating his right to veto bills, and preventing him from dismissing or otherwise interfering with the legislature. Above all, every state forbade the governor or any other executive officer from holding a seat in the legislature, thus ensuring that the two branches of government would remain wholly separate, that the English parliamentary system would not be re-created in America. The constitutions also added provisions protecting the judiciary from executive control, although in most states the courts had not yet emerged as fully autonomous branches of government.

In limiting the executive and expanding the power of the legislature, the new constitutions were moving far in the direction of direct popular rule. They did not, however, move all the way. Only in Georgia and Pennsylvania did the legislature consist of one house. In all the other states, there was an upper and a lower chamber; and in most cases, the upper chamber was designed to represent the "higher orders" of society. In all states, there were property requirements for voters—in some states, only the modest amount that would qualify a person as a taxpayer, in other states somewhat greater requirements. Such requirements tended to have little impact, since prop-

erty ownership was widespread among the white male population. But universal suffrage was not yet an accepted part of American government.

The initial phase of constitution writing proceeded rapidly. Ten of the states completed the process before the end of 1776. Only Georgia, New York, and Massachusetts delayed. Georgia and New York completed the task by the end of the following year, but Massachusetts did not finally adopt its version until 1780. By then, the construction of state governments had moved into a new phase.

Revising State Governments

By the late 1770s, Americans were already growing concerned about what they perceived as the excessive factiousness and instability of their new state governments. Legislatures were the scene of constant squabbling. Governors were unable to exercise sufficient power to provide any real leadership. It was proving extraordinarily difficult to get the new governments to accomplish anything at all. To many observers, the problem began to appear to be one of too much democracy. By placing so much power in the hands of the people (and of their elected representatives in the legislature), the state constitutions were inviting disorder and political turbulence.

As a result, most of the states began to revise their constitutions to cope with these problems. Massachusetts was the first to act on the new concerns. By waiting until 1780 before finally ratifying its first constitution, Massachusetts allowed these changing ideas to shape its government; and the state produced a constitution that was to serve as a model for the efforts of others.

Two changes in particular characterized the Massachusetts and later constitutions. The first was a change in the process of constitution writing itself. In the first phase, the documents had usually been written by state legislatures. As a result, they could easily be amended (or violated) by those same bodies. By 1780, sentiment was growing to find a way to protect the constitutions from the people who had written them, to make it difficult to change the documents once they were approved. The solution was the constitutional convention: a special assembly of the people that would meet only for the purpose of writing the constitution and that would never (except under extraordinary circumstances) meet again. The constitution would, therefore, be the product of the popular will; but once approved, it would be protected from the whims of public opinion and from the political moods of the legislature.

The second change was similarly a reflection of the new concerns about excessive popular power: a significant strengthening of the executive. In Massachusetts, the governor under the 1780 constitution became one of the strongest in any state. He was to be elected directly by the people; he was to have a fixed salary (in other words, he would not be dependent on the good will of the legislature each year for his wages); he would have expanded powers of appointment; and he would be able to veto legislation. Other states soon followed. Those states that had weak or nonexistent upper houses strengthened or created them. Most states increased the powers of the governor; and Pennsylvania, which had had no executive at all at first, now produced a strong one. By the late 1780s, almost every state had either revised its constitution or drawn up an entirely new one to make allowances for the belief in the need for stability.

Opportunity, Toleration, and Slavery

The new state governments—both under the first constitutions and under the later, revised ones—adopted a number of policies that increased opportunities for social and political mobility. In one way or another, they multiplied opportunities for land ownership and thus enlarged the voting population. For example, they eliminated the legal rights of primogeniture (the requirement that a father's estate be passed intact to his first son) and entail (whereby a man kept his estate intact from generation to generation by willing that it never be sold). In fact, neither practice had ever been widespread in America; but in a few places, the new laws did contribute to the erosion of landed aristocracies.

The new states also moved far in the direction of complete religious freedom. Most Americans continued to believe that religion should play some role in government; but they did not wish to give special privileges to any particular denomination. In some states, religious tests survived as a qualification for officeholding. (Atheists, and in a few places Catholics, were barred from office; but since there were few of either in most of the states in question, the requirements were largely meaningless.) More characteristic, however, was the erosion of the privileges that many churches had once enjoyed. New York and the Southern states, in which the Church of England had been tax-supported, soon saw to the complete disestablishment of the church; and the New England states stripped the Congregational church of many of its privileges. Boldest of all was Virginia, which in its Declaration of Rights announced the principle of complete toleration. And in 1786, Virginia enacted a Statute of Religious Liberty, written by Thomas Jefferson, which called for the complete separation of church and state.

More difficult to resolve was the question of slavery. The rhetoric of the Revolution—which emphasized the importance of liberty and the danger of enslavement—could not help but direct attention to America's own institution of bondage. And in some places, it cast the institution into disrepute. In areas where slavery was weak—in New England, where there had never been many slaves, and in Pennsylvania, where the Quakers were outspoken in their opposition to slavery—it was abolished. Pennsylvania passed a general gradual-emancipation act in 1780; and the supreme court of Massachusetts ruled in 1783 that the ownership of slaves was impermissible under the state's bill of rights. Even in the South, there were some pressures to amend the institution (a result, in part, of the activities of the first antislavery society in America, founded in 1775). Every state but South Carolina and Georgia prohibited the further importation of slaves from abroad, and even South Carolina laid a temporary wartime ban on the slave trade. Virginia passed a law encouraging manumission (the freeing of slaves), and other states encountered growing political pressures to change the institution.

In the end, however, most of the pressures came to naught. Slavery survived in all the Southern and border states; and it would continue to survive for nearly a century more. The reasons were many. Racist assumptions about the natural inferiority of blacks persuaded many Americans that there was nothing incompatible in asserting innate human rights while denying those rights to blacks. And economic pressures made it difficult to free slaves. Many Southerners had enormous investments in their black laborers and were unwilling to consider losing them.

An equally important obstacle was that few Southerners—even such men as Washington and Jefferson, who expressed deep moral misgivings about slavery—could envision any alternative to it. If slavery were abolished, what would happen to the blacks? Some argued that they should be sent back to Africa, but that was clearly unrealistic. The black population was too large; and many slaves were now so many generations removed from Africa that they felt but

Bruton Parish Church, Williamsburg
Anglican churches such as this one in the colonial capital of Virginia broke with the Church of England in 1789 and became part of the Protestant Episcopal Church of America. The new ecclesiastical body adopted its own constitution, revised the Book of Common Prayer, and appointed its own bishops. But it made no fundamental change in doctrine or in forms of worship, and the American episcopate remained loosely tied with its English counterpart. This nineteenth-century painting by A. Wordsworth Thompson shows the church as it appeared before the Revolution.
(Metropolitan Museum of Art)

little identification with it and had no wish to return. Few whites believed that blacks could be integrated into American society as equals. Even those most opposed to slavery usually shared the general assumptions about the unfitness of blacks for citizenship. In maintaining slavery, Jefferson once remarked, Americans were holding a "wolf by the ears." However unappealing it was to hold on to, letting go promised to be even worse. Jefferson himself, for all his qualms, never let go. He continued to own slaves until he died; and unlike George Washington, he made no provision for their freedom on his death.

There was, finally, a more subtle obstacle to the elimination of slavery. The economy of the South depended, most Southerners believed, on a large, servile labor force. Yet the ideals of republicanism required a homogeneous population of independent, property-owning citizens. Were slavery to be abolished, the South would find itself with a substantial unpropertied laboring class; and whether that class were black or white, its existence would raise troubling implications for the future of democracy. The social tensions that would inevitably ensue would, Southerners feared, ultimately destroy the stability of society.

Thus, just as in the early years of settlement, so during the Revolution: Americans encountered only vague, philosophical pressures to abolish slavery but powerful social and economic pressures to maintain it. As a result, slavery survived.

The Search for a National Government

Americans were much quicker to agree on the proper shape of their state institutions than they were to decide on the form of their national government. At first, most believed that the central government should remain a relatively weak and unimportant force—indeed, it should remain something less than a government at all. Each state would be virtually a sovereign nation. National institutions would serve only as loose, coordinating mechanisms, with little independent authority. Such beliefs reflected the assumption that a republic operated best in a relatively limited, homogeneous area; that were a republican government to attempt to administer too large and diverse a nation, it would founder. It was in response to such ideas that the Articles of Confederation emerged.

The Confederation

No sooner did the Continental Congress appoint a committee to draft a declaration of independence in 1776 than it appointed another to draft a plan of union. After much debate and many revisions, the Congress adopted the committee's proposal in November 1777 as the Articles of Confederation.

The Articles provided for a national political structure very similar to the one already in operation. Congress was to survive as the central—indeed the only—institution of national authority. But its powers were to be somewhat expanded. It was to have the authority to conduct wars and foreign relations, and to appropriate, borrow, and issue money. But it could not regulate trade, draft troops, or levy taxes directly on the people. For troops and taxes it would have to make requisitions of the states; it would, in effect, have to address formal requests to the state legislatures, which could and often did refuse them. There was to be no separate, single, strong executive (the "president of the United States" was to be merely the presiding officer at the sessions of Congress). Congress itself was to see to the execution of laws through an executive committee of thirteen, made up of one member from each state; through ad hoc and standing committees for specific functions; and through such administrative departments as it might choose to create. There were to be no Confederation courts, except for courts of admiralty; disputes among the states were to be settled by a complicated system of arbitration. States were to retain their individual sovereignty, each of the legislatures electing and paying the salaries of two to seven delegates to Congress, and each delegation, no matter how numerous, having only one vote. At least nine of the states (through their delegations) would have to approve any important measure, such as a treaty, before Congress could pass it; and all thirteen state legislatures would have to approve before the Articles could be ratified or amended.

Ratification was delayed by differences of opinion about the proposed plan. The small states insisted on equal state representation, but the larger states wanted representation to be based on population. More important, the states claiming Western lands wished to keep them, but the rest of the states demanded that all such territory be turned over to the Confederation government. The "landed" states founded their claims largely on colonial charters. The "landless" states, particularly Maryland, maintained that as the fruit of common sacrifices in war the Western lands had become the rightful property of all the states. At last New York gave up its rather hazy claim, and Virginia made a qualified offer to cede its lands to Congress. Then Maryland, the only state still holding out against ratification, approved the Articles of Confederation, and they went into effect in 1781. The Confederation thus came into being in time to conclude the war and make the peace. Until then, during the years of fighting from 1775 to 1781, the Second Continental Congress had served as the agency for directing and coordinating the war effort of the thirteen states.

In later years, it became popular to characterize the performance of the Confederation, which existed from 1781 until 1789, as an almost total failure. Such judgments are not entirely fair. The Confederation did manage to solve some of the problems facing the new nation. It performed particularly creditably in organizing America's territories in the West. Yet the new government was far from a success. Lacking adequate powers to deal with interstate issues, lacking any effective mechanisms that would have permitted it to enforce its will on the states, and lacking sufficient stature in the eyes of the world to be able to negotiate effectively, it suffered a series of damaging setbacks.

Diplomatic Failures

Evidence of the low esteem in which the rest of the world held the Confederation was its difficulty in persuading Great Britain (and to a lesser extent Spain) to live up to the terms of the peace treaty of 1783. That treaty had recognized the independence of the United States and granted the new nation a vast domain—on paper. But Americans found it hard to exercise their full sovereignty in fact.

Even though the treaty had pledged the British to evacuate American soil, British forces continued to occupy a string of frontier posts along the Great Lakes within the United States. The Canadians and the British wanted to maintain points of contact with Indian tribes in the Northwest for the conduct of the fur trade and the continuance of defensive alliances with them. Nor did the British honor their agreement to make restitution to slaveowners whose slaves the British army had confiscated. The British justified these violations of the treaty by pointing to American violations. The United States had not honored its promise to make restitution to the Loyalists; and it had reneged on the agreement to honor debts to English creditors.

There were disputes as well over boundaries. The two countries argued over the northeastern boundary of the new nation. And the peace arrangements led also to a boundary dispute between the United States and Spain. Britain ceded Florida back to Spain in the 1783 settlement (it had acquired Florida in the 1763 treaty) but made no precise definition of the territory's northern boundary. The Spanish and the Americans disagreed sharply over that definition.

The peace with Great Britain failed in other ways to give Americans the benefits they desired and expected. Above all, American shippers and traders wanted commercial arrangements that would give them privileges of trading and shipping on equal terms with British subjects in all parts of the British Empire. American merchants now had new opportunities for exploiting worldwide routes of trade, which before the war had been legally closed to them. But while commerce was expanding in new directions, most American trade continued in the prewar, imperial pattern. To earn the British funds needed to pay for British imports, Americans wanted full access to British markets; England, however, placed sharp postwar restrictions on that access.

In 1784, Congress sent John Adams as minister to London with instructions to get a commercial treaty and speed up the evacuation of the frontier posts; but that effort simply produced more humiliation for the Confederation. Taunted by the query whether he represented one nation or thirteen, Adams made no headway in England. And throughout the 1780s, the British government refused even to return the courtesy of sending a minister to the American capital.

In dealing with the Spanish government, the Confederation demonstrated similar weakness. Spain, unlike England, was willing to discuss its differences with the United States, and in 1785 its representative, Diego de Gardoqui, arrived in New York (where Congress had moved from Philadelphia) to negotiate with the secretary for foreign affairs, John Jay. After months of friendly conversations, Jay and Gardoqui initialed a treaty in 1786. It called for the Spanish government to grant Americans the right to trade with Spain but not with its colonies; it accepted the American interpretation of the Florida boundary; and (in a secret article) it called for a Spanish-American alliance to protect American soil from British encroachments. The United States would guarantee Spanish possessions in America and would agree to "forbear" (although not officially to abandon) its right to navigate the Mississippi for twenty years. But the treaty came to naught. Southern states were incensed at the idea of giving up their access to the Mississippi in exchange for trading privileges that would benefit only Northern merchants. Jay could not win ratification of the treaty by the necessary nine states.

The Needs of the West

The Confederation's principal accomplishment was its successful resolution of some of the explosive controversies involving settlement and development of Western lands. During and after the Revolution, an unprecedented number of American settlers moved into the areas that were the focus of postwar dispute. When the war began, only a few thousand lived west of the Appalachian divide; by 1790 their numbers had increased to 120,000—providing evidence of the tremendous potential for growth and development in the West. But the colonial governments had long ignored these Western settlements. So, for a time, did the Continental Congress, and it now faced a daunting task as it tried to include them in the political structure of the new nation. The settlers needed protection from the Indians into whose lands they were moving, access to outside markets for their surplus crops, and courts with orderly processes of law. At the beginning of the 1780s, they had received none of those things from the European settlements on the eastern seaboard. At times, in fact (as with the Paxton Boys uprising in Pennsylvania in 1763 and the Regulator movement in North Carolina in 1771), there had been overt hostilities between the eastern and western settlements.

For a time, Congress faced the additional difficulty of not having clear-cut jurisdiction over the trans-Appalachian region. For several years after independence, conflicts of authority persisted among Congress, the states, and the frontier settlements themselves. With Virginia's agreement in 1781 to cede its Western territory to Congress, the landed states began to yield their claims to the Confederation. But the process was a slow one, and one state after another found grounds on which to resist or delay its cession. Not until 1802 did the last of the states, Georgia, give up its claim.

Nevertheless, by 1784 the states had ceded enough land to the Confederation to permit Congress to begin making policy for the national domain. The most momentous decision was that settlements in the territory would be transformed ultimately into states with the same rights and privileges as the original thirteen. The Ordinance of 1784, based on a plan advanced by Thomas Jefferson, outlined a process for transition to statehood of the territory between the Ohio River and the Great Lakes. The territory would be divided into ten self-governing districts, each to be represented by a delegate in Congress as soon as its population reached 20,000, and each to be admitted as a state when its population equaled the number of free inhabitants of the smallest existing state.

Having prepared a scheme of territorial government, Congress in the Ordinance of 1785 provided a system for surveying and selling the Western lands—

State Claims to Western Lands and Cessions to National Government, 1782–1802

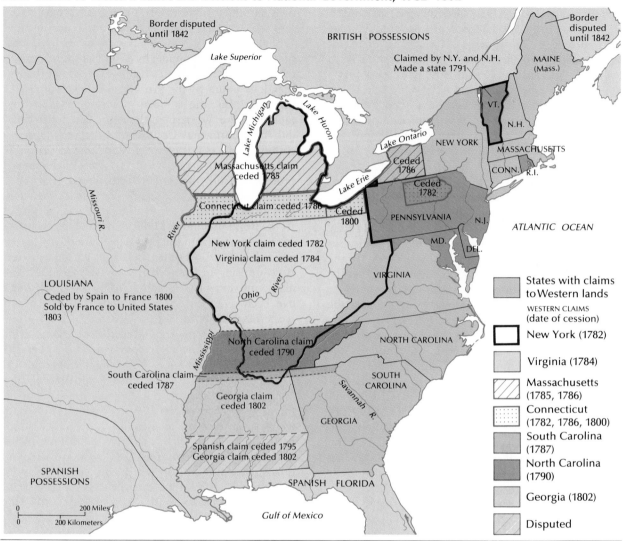

Border disputed until 1842

BRITISH POSSESSIONS

Lake Superior

Claimed by N.Y. and N.H. Made a state 1791

Border disputed until 1842

MAINE (Mass.)

Lake Michigan *Lake Huron*

VT.

N.H.

Lake Ontario

NEW YORK

MASSACHUSETTS

Massachusetts claim ceded 1785

Ceded 1786

CONN. R.I.

Lake Erie

Connecticut claim ceded 1786

Ceded 1782

Ceded 1800

PENNSYLVANIA

N.J.

Missouri R.

River

New York claim ceded 1782

Virginia claim ceded 1784

MD.

DEL.

ATLANTIC OCEAN

LOUISIANA

Ceded by Spain to France 1800 Sold by France to United States 1803

Ohio *River*

VIRGINIA

Mississippi

North Carolina claim ceded 1790

NORTH CAROLINA

South Carolina claim ceded 1787

Savannah R.

SOUTH CAROLINA

Georgia claim ceded 1802

GEORGIA

SPANISH POSSESSIONS

Spanish claim ceded 1795 Georgia claim ceded 1802

SPANISH FLORIDA

0   200 Miles
0   200 Kilometers

Gulf of Mexico

States with claims to Western lands

WESTERN CLAIMS (date of cession)

New York (1782)

Virginia (1784)

Massachusetts (1785, 1786)

Connecticut (1782, 1786, 1800)

South Carolina (1787)

North Carolina (1790)

Georgia (1802)

Disputed

an activity the Confederation was eager to begin, since it was in desperate need of money. The land to the north of the Ohio was to be surveyed and marked off into neat rectangular townships before any of it was sold. Each township was to be six miles square and was to contain thirty-six sections of equal size. (This grid system established a pattern that would dominate Western land policy in America for many decades to come.) In every township, four sections were to be set aside for the U.S. government and one for a public school. The rest of the sections were to be sold at auction for not less than $1 an acre. Since there were 640 acres in a section, the prospective buyer of government land had to have at least $640—a very

large sum by the standards of the day—in ready cash or in United States certificates of indebtedness.

These terms favored the large speculators too much and the ordinary frontiersman too little to suit Jefferson, who believed that the West ought to belong to actual settlers on the ground. But the large speculators desired still further advantages, and Congress, eager to realize returns from its new domain and disappointed by the slow progress of the survey, soon gave in to lobbying groups composed of some of its own members and various former army officers. It disposed of several million unsurveyed acres to the Ohio and Scioto companies (land speculation businesses) by accepting as payment the loan certificates that had been issued during the war to American soldiers. Those certificates were by now almost worthless, and most of the soldiers had long since sold them to speculators at a fraction of their original worth; but Congress agreed to accept them at face value—a tremendous boon for the speculators. Millions of acres besides had been reserved at the time of cession by Virginia and Connecticut to be granted their Revolutionary war veterans as a bounty. Thus even before the government surveys had been well started, most of the choicest land north of the Ohio River was already spoken for (as was all the land south of the Ohio, to which the ordinances of Congress did not apply).

To protect their interests in the Northwest, the directors of the Ohio and Scioto companies demanded a territorial government that would give less power to the inhabitants than Jefferson's Ordinance of 1784 had envisioned; and the companies' skillful lobbyist, Manasseh Cutler, carried their case to Congress. Some of the congressmen themselves disliked Jefferson's idea of creating as many as ten new states north of the Ohio, since these states in time might gain political ascendancy. Soon Congress replaced the original law—which had never gone into actual effect—with the Ordinance of 1787. This famous "Northwest Ordinance" established one Northwest Territory for the time being, provided for its subsequent division into several territories (not fewer than three or more than five), and laid out three stages for the evolution of each territory into a state. In the first stage, officials appointed by Congress would govern the territory; in the second, an elected legislature would share power with them; and in the third, once the population reached 60,000, the people might frame a constitution and apply for statehood. Slavery would be outlawed in all of the new territory.

The Northwest Ordinance and other efforts by Congress did not provide a perfect solution to the problems of Western lands. For one thing, Congress was unable to resolve the virtually insoluble problem of white incursions into Indian lands. Congress negotiated treaties with the Iroquois and others in 1785 and 1786 by which the Indians ceded much of their land to the United States in exchange for relatively worthless trinkets. But when the Indians became aware of how badly they had been misused, they repudiated the treaties and opened hostilities against the Western settlers. The Confederation mobilized its now diminished armed forces to quell the uprising, but with little success—especially when a similar conflict broke out on the Southwestern frontier as a result of similar Indian grievances.

Land Survey: Ordinance of 1785

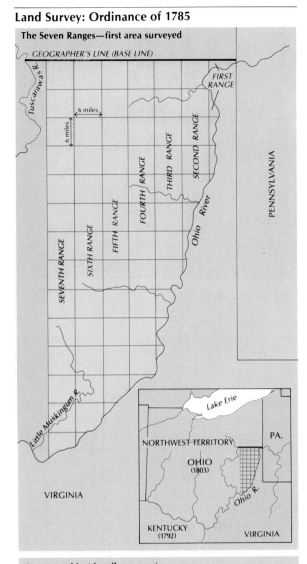

The Seven Ranges—first area surveyed

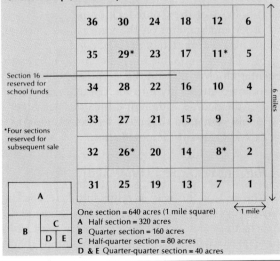

One township (six miles square)

	36	30	24	18	12	6
	35	29*	23	17	11*	5
Section 16 reserved for school funds	34	28	22	16	10	4
	33	27	21	15	9	3
*Four sections reserved for subsequent sale	32	26*	20	14	8*	2
	31	25	19	13	7	1

One section = 640 acres (1 mile square)
A Half section = 320 acres
B Quarter section = 160 acres
C Half-quarter section = 80 acres
D & E Quarter-quarter section = 40 acres

Cincinnati, 1800
Settlement of the lands west of the Appalachians proceeded rapidly in the 1790s after the Ordinance of 1785 and the Northwest Ordinance of 1787 established procedures for distributing public lands in the territories. Ohio grew particularly fast, and the city of Cincinnati gained importance as a port and trading center, linking farmers in southeastern Ohio to the trade along the Mississippi River. (Cincinnati Historical Society)

The Western lands to the south, moreover, experienced little of the orderly development that the Ordinance of 1787 provided for the Northwest Territory. Beginning in the late 1770s, there was rapid settlement in the region that became Kentucky and Tennessee; by the 1780s, the settlers and speculators there were trying to set up governments of their own without guidelines from Congress and then asking for recognition as states. Congress was never able to sort out and resolve the conflicting claims in that region.

Despite all the problems, however, the Western land policies of the Confederation imposed a degree of order and stability on the unorganized territories of the new nation that decades of colonial and British efforts had been unable to create. In 1780, it had not been at all clear that the Western lands could be incorporated effectively into the United States. By the end of the decade, although difficulties persisted, little doubt remained that these territories would continue to be part of the new nation.

Debts, Taxes, and Daniel Shays

At the end of the war, foreign ships crowded into American seaports with cargoes of all kinds, and the American people bought extravagantly with cash or credit—satisfying a desire for foreign goods that had found few outlets during the Revolution. As a result, there was a rapid and substantial flow of hard currency out of the country. Consumer indebtedness to importing merchants increased greatly. And a postwar depression, which lasted from 1784 to 1787, was intensified. The depression increased the perennial American problem of an inadequate money supply, a problem that bore particularly heavily on debtors. It was in dealing with this increasingly serious problem of debts that Congress was perceived as having most seriously failed.

The Confederation itself had an enormous outstanding debt, and few means with which to pay it. It had borrowed money during the war that was now due to be repaid; it owed money to its Revolutionary soldiers; it had substantial debts abroad. Its powers of taxation, in the meantime, were limited. Because it could not impose taxes directly on the people, it had to make requisitions of the states, which the states often refused to meet. On the whole, Congress received only about one-sixth of the money it requisitioned—barely enough to meet the government's ordinary operating expenses. The nation was faced with the prospect of defaulting on its obligations, a possibility that threatened to destroy the fragile new government.

This alarming prospect brought to the fore a group of leaders who would play a crucial role in the shaping of the republic for several decades. Committed nationalists, they were seeking ways to increase the powers of the central government and to permit it to meet its financial obligations. Robert Morris, the head of the Confederation's treasury; Alexander Hamilton, his young protégé; James Madison of Virginia; and others were soon lobbying for a "continental impost"—a 5 percent duty on imported goods, to be levied by Congress and used to fund the debt. The impost would, the nationalists believed, not only preserve the financial integrity of the new nation; it would strengthen the national government by making it principally responsible for the nation's debts.

But their schemes met with substantial opposition. Many Americans feared that the impost plan was the first step toward the creation of a corrupt center of privilege, that it would concentrate too much financial power in the hands of Robert Morris and his allies in Philadelphia. The first effort to secure the impost, in 1781, received the approval of twelve state delegations in Congress; but it required unanimity, and Rhode Island's refusal to agree killed the plan. A second effort in 1783 also failed to win approval. Angry and discouraged, the nationalists largely withdrew from any active involvement in the Confederation. But some of them—most notably Alexander Hamilton—would return to fight virtually the same battles again in the first years of government under the Constitution.

In the absence of any effective action by Congress, the domestic debt problem remained in the hands of the states, which generally relied on increased taxation to deal with their financial difficulties. To the state creditors—that is, the bondholders—this was sound, honest public finance, which protected their legitimate interests. But poor farmers, already burdened by debt and now burdened again by taxes on their lands, considered such policies unfair, even tyrannical. They demanded that the state governments issue paper currency to increase the money supply and make it easier for them to meet their obligations. Resentment ran especially high among farmers in

SIGNIFICANT EVENTS

1775 Second Continental Congress meets
Americans capture Fort Ticonderoga
George Washington appointed to command American forces
Battle of Bunker Hill
Montgomery assault on Quebec fails

1776 Thomas Paine's *Common Sense* published
British troops leave Boston
Declaration of Independence debated and signed (July 2–4)
Howe routs Americans on Long Island
Battle of Trenton
First state constitutions written

1777 Articles of Confederation adopted
Battles of Princeton, Brandywine, and Germantown
Howe occupies Philadelphia
Washington camps at Valley Forge for winter
Burgoyne surrenders to Gates at Saratoga

1778 French-American alliance concluded
British leave Philadelphia
War shifts to the South
British capture Savannah
Clinton replaces Howe

1779 British capture Charleston

1780 Cornwallis defeats Gates at Camden, South Carolina
Patriots defeat Tories at King's Mountain, South Carolina
Massachusetts constitution ratified
Slavery abolished in Pennsylvania

1781 Battles of Cowpens and Guilford Court House
Cornwallis surrenders at Yorktown
Articles of Confederation ratified
Continental impost proposed

1781–1784 States cede Western lands to Confederation

1783 Treaty of Paris with Great Britain recognizes American independence
Slavery abolished in Massachusetts

1784–1785 First ordinances establishing procedures for settling Western lands enacted

1786 Virginia Statute of Religious Liberty passed

1786–1787 Shays's Rebellion in Massachusetts

1787 Northwest Ordinance enacted

New England, who felt that the states were extorting money from them to swell the coffers of wealthy bondholders in Boston and other towns. Debtors who failed to pay their taxes found their mortgages foreclosed and their property seized; sometimes they found themselves in jail.

Throughout the late 1780s, therefore, mobs of distressed farmers rioted periodically in various parts of New England. They caused the most serious trouble in Massachusetts. Malcontents in the Connecticut Valley and the Berkshire Hills, many of them Revolutionary veterans, rallied behind Daniel Shays, himself a former captain in the Continental army. Organizing and drilling his followers, Shays put forth a program of demands that included paper money, tax relief, a moratorium on debts, the removal of the state capital from Boston to the interior, and the abolition of imprisonment for debt. During the summer of 1786, the Shaysites concentrated on the immediate task of preventing the collection of debts, private or public, and went in armed bands from place to place to keep courts from sitting and to prevent sheriffs' sales of confiscated property. In Bos-

ton, members of the legislature, including Samuel Adams, denounced Shays and his men as rebels and traitors.

When winter came, the rebels advanced on Springfield hoping to seize weapons from the arsenal there. An army of state militiamen, financed by a loan from wealthy merchants who feared a new revolution, set out from Boston to confront them. In January 1787, this army met Shays's ragged troops, killed several of them, captured many more, and scattered the rest to the hills in a blinding snowstorm.

As a military enterprise, Shays's Rebellion was a fiasco. But it had important consequences for the future of the United States. In Massachusetts, it resulted in a few immediate gains for the discontented groups. Shays and his lieutenants, at first sentenced to death, were soon pardoned, and some concessions to Shays's earlier demands were granted in the way of tax relief and the postponement of debt payments. Far more significant, however, the rebellion added urgency to a movement already gathering support throughout the new nation—the movement to produce a new, national constitution.

SUGGESTED READINGS

General Histories Robert Middlekauf, *The Glorious Cause: The American Revolution, 1763–1789* (1982), is a narrative overview. Merrill Jensen, *The Founding of a Nation: A History of the American Revolution, 1763–1789* (1968), and Edmund S. Morgan, *The Birth of the Republic, 1763–1789* (1956), are earlier surveys. Michael Kammen, *A Season of Youth: The American Revolution and the Historical Imagination* (1978), explores ways in which later generations of Americans have viewed the Revolution.

The Road to Independence There are several studies of the ideas underlying the Declaration of Independence. Carl Becker, *The Declaration of Independence* (1922), is a classic work emphasizing the influence of John Locke on the Founding Fathers. Morton White, *The Philosophy of the American Revolution* (1978), is a more modern version of that argument. Challenging both is Garry Wills, *Inventing America* (1978), a controversial study emphasizing the influence of Scottish radicals on Jefferson. For studies of Thomas Paine and his influence on the shaping of the American war aims, see Eric Foner, *Tom Paine and Revolutionary America* (1976), a provocative interpretation, and David Hawke, *Paine* (1974), a biography. Other studies of political thought during the Revolution include Peter Shaw, *The Character of John Adams* (1976) and *American Patriots and the Rituals of Revolution* (1981); John R. Howe, Jr., *The*

Changing Political Thought of John Adams (1966); and Edmund S. Morgan, *The Meaning of Independence* (1976).

The War A good introduction to the vast literature on the military history of the Revolution is Willard Wallace, *Appeal to Arms* (1950), or John R. Alden, *The American Revolution* (1964). Piers Mackesy, *The War for America* (1964), and Don Higginbotham, *The American War for Independence* (1971), are fine standard accounts, as is Howard H. Peckham, *The War for Independence* (1958). A fuller account can be found in Christopher Ward, *The War of the Revolution*, 2 vols. (1952). John Shy, *A People Numerous and Armed* (1976), is a brilliant study of the social influences on the military effort; Charles Royster, *A Revolutionary People at War* (1979), discusses political ideas and military behavior. G. W. Allen, *Naval History of the American Revolution*, 2 vols. (1913), remains the standard account. See also Samuel Eliot Morison, *John Paul Jones* (1959). Studies of Washington as commander include T. G. Frothingham, *Washington: Commander in Chief* (1930); the appropriate volumes of Douglas Southall Freeman, *George Washington*, 7 vols. (1948–1957); and James T. Flexner, *George Washington in the American Revolution* (1968). Charles Royster, *Light-Horse Harry Lee and the Legacy of the American Revolution* (1981), examines one of the leading military figures of the war and his subsequent career. E. Wayne Carp, *To Starve the Army* *at Pleasure: Continental Army Administration and American Political Culture, 1775–1783* (1984), explores the impact of American political culture on the performance of the Continental army.

Revolutionary Diplomacy Samuel F. Bemis, *The Diplomacy of the American Revolution* (1935), is a classic work. The peace negotiations are recounted in Richard B. Morris, *The Peacemakers* (1965). Gerald Sourzh describes the influence of America's preeminent diplomat in *Benjamin Franklin and American Foreign Policy,* rev. ed. (1969). See also L. S. Kaplan, *Colonies into Nation: American Diplomacy, 1763–1801* (1972). Clarence L. Ver Steeg, *Robert Morris* (1954), and E. J. Ferguson, *The Power of the Purse* (1961), examine the efforts to finance the Revolution.

The Loyalists Important studies of the Loyalists include Wallace Brown, *The King's Friends* (1965), and Robert M. Calhoon, *The Loyalists in Revolutionary America* (1973). The ideas of the Loyalists are examined in Mary Beth Norton, *The British Americans: The Loyalist Exiles in England 1774–1789* (1972), and William H. Nelson, *The American Tory* (1962). Bernard Bailyn, *The Ordeal of Thomas Hutchinson* (1974), is a sensitive biography of a leading Tory. See also Paul H. Smith, *Loyalists and Redcoats* (1964), and James W. St. G. Walker, *The Black Loyalists* (1976).

Women See Mary Beth Norton, *Liberty's Daughters* (1980); Linda K. Kerber, *Women of the Republic* (1980); and Linda Grant DePauw, *Founding Mothers* (1975). Carl Degler, *At Odds* (1980), and Nancy Woloch, *Women and the American Experience* (1984), are sweeping studies of women and the family in American history, beginning with the colonial era and the Revolution.

Social Effects See J. F. Jameson, *The American Revolution Considered as a Social Movement* (1962), which argues that the war worked to enhance social and economic democracy. Similar views are expressed in Staughton Lynd, *Class Conflict, Slavery and the United States Constitution* (1968), and Merrill Jensen, *The American Revolution Within America* (1974). Richard McCormick, *Experiment in Independence* (1950), a study of New Jersey in the 1780s, argues that there was little class conflict during the Revolutionary period. Jackson Turner Main, *The Social Structure of Revolutionary America* (1965), emphasizes inequality. Jerome J. Nadlehaft, *The Disorders of War: The Revolution in South Carolina* (1981), emphasizes the democratizing effect of the Revolution on politics. Robert Gross, *The Minutemen and Their World* (1976), is a local study of Concord, Massachusetts.

Slavery and the Revolution Some of the most significant literature on the Revolutionary period deals with the anomalous existence of slavery in a society fighting a war for "liberty." David Brion Davis, *The Problem of Slavery in the Age of Revolution* (1975), places the issue of slavery in America in a larger world context and traces attitudes toward the institution into the nineteenth century. Edmund S. Morgan, *American Slavery, American Freedom* (1975), suggests that the existence of slavery allowed white Southerners to avoid some of the troubling implications of their Revolutionary ideology. Arthur Zilversmit, *The First Emancipation* (1967), discusses early antislavery activity; and Benjamin Quarles, *The Negro and the American Revolution* (1961), discusses the impact of the struggle on blacks themselves. Duncan MacLeod, *Slavery, Race, and the American Revolution* (1974), is critical of the way the Founding Fathers handled the issue.

State Governments Gordon S. Wood, *The Creation of the American Republic* (1969), is the single most important modern study. Examinations of political developments in individual states include Stephen E. Patterson, *Political Parties in Revolutionary Massachusetts* (1973), and Irwin Polishook, *Rhode Island and the Union, 1774–1795* (1969). Willi Paul Adams, *The First American Constitutions* (1980), is a broader study, as are three works by Jackson Turner Main: *Political Parties Before the Constitution* (1973), *The Sovereign States, 1775–1783* (1973), and *The Upper House in Revolutionary America, 1763–1788* (1967).

The Articles of Confederation The classic account of national politics under the Articles of Confederation is John Fiske, *The Critical Period of American History, 1783–1789* (1883), a bleak portrait of the first national government. Modern studies of this period include Jack N. Rakove, *The Beginnings of National Politics* (1979), which is critical of the Articles, and Merrill Jensen, *The New Nation* (1950) and *The Articles of Confederation,* rev. ed. (1959), which provide more favorable views. H. James Henderson studies national party politics in *Party Politics in the Continental Congress* (1974). Jack Eblen, *The First and Second United States Empires* (1968), studies the administration of the territories from the 1780s into the twentieth century.

Philadelphia, engraving by William Birch, 1799 (Historical Society of Pennsylvania)

Chapter 6 # The Constitution and the New Republic

By the late 1780s, most Americans had grown deeply dissatisfied with the deficiencies of the Confederation—with its factiousness, its instability, its ineffectuality in the face of such crises as Shays's Rebellion, and above all with its inability to deal with the economic problems that afflicted the new nation. A decade earlier, they had deliberately avoided creating a genuine national government, fearing that it would encroach on the sovereignty of the individual states. Now they were ready to reconsider. Serious discussions began in 1786 about the construction of a new political system; and in 1787, the nation created for itself what the individual states had created for themselves years before: a written constitution and a government consisting of three independent branches.

The American Constitution derived most of its principles from the state documents that had preceded it. But it was also a remarkable achievement in its own right. Out of the contentious atmosphere of a fragile new nation, Americans fashioned a system of government that has survived as one of the stablest and most successful in the world. William Gladstone, the great nineteenth-century British statesman, once called the Constitution the "most wonderful work ever struck off at a given time by the brain and purpose of man." And although Gladstone may have exaggerated, the American people in the years that followed almost universally agreed. Indeed, to them the Constitution took on some of the characteristics of a sacred document, a holy mystery. Its framers were viewed by later generations as men almost godlike in their wisdom. Its provisions, set out in a brief 7,000 words, were considered for years to come to be an unassailable "fundamental law," from which all public policies, all political principles, all solutions of controversies must spring.

Yet the adoption of the Constitution did not complete the creation of the republic. It only defined the terms in which debate over the future of government would continue. Americans may have agreed that the Constitution was a nearly perfect document, but they disagreed—at times fundamentally—on what that document meant. Some believed that the founders had intended the federal government to exercise broad powers beyond those specifically enumerated in the Constitution ("implied powers"). Others argued that the framers had intended to limit federal power to the precise areas specified in the Constitution ("expressed powers"), that all other authority would remain at the state level. Out of this disagreement emerged the first great political battles of the new nation.

Toward a New Government

So unpopular and ineffectual had the Confederation Congress become by the mid-1780s that it began to lead an almost waiflike existence. In 1783, its members timidly withdrew from Philadelphia to escape from the clamor of army veterans demanding their back pay. They took refuge for a while in Princeton, New Jersey, then moved on to Annapolis, and in 1785 settled in New York. Through all of this, the delegates were often conspicuous largely by their ab-

157

sence. Only with great difficulty was a quorum secured to permit ratification of the treaty with Great
Britain ending the Revolutionary War. Eighteen
members, representing only eight states, voted on
the Confederation's most important piece of legislation, the Northwest Ordinance. In the meantime, a
major public debate was beginning over the future of
the Confederation.

Advocates of Centralization

Weak and unpopular though the Confederation was,
it satisfied for a time a great many—probably a majority—of the people. They did not want a strong or
prestigious central government, and they were willing to tolerate the deficiencies of Congress in order to
avoid the even greater problems they believed a more
powerful national state would produce. They had
fought the Revolutionary War to avert the danger of
what they considered remote and tyrannical authority; now they desired to keep political power centered in the states, where it could be carefully and
closely controlled.

Important groups in the population, however,
were beginning to clamor for a national government
capable of dealing with the new nation's many problems—particularly the economic problems that most
directly afflicted them. Some military men, many of
them members of the exclusive and hereditary Society of the Cincinnati (formed by Revolutionary army
officers in 1783), were disgruntled at the refusal of
Congress to fund their pensions. They began aspiring to influence and invigorate the national government; some even envisioned a form of military
dictatorship and flirted briefly (in 1783, in the so-
called Newburgh Conspiracy) with a direct challenge
to Congress, until George Washington intervened and
blocked the potential rebellion.

American manufacturers—the artisans and "mechanics"—wanted to replace the varying state tariffs
with a uniformly high national duty. Merchants and
shippers wanted to replace the thirteen different (and
largely ineffective) state commercial policies with a
single, national one. Land speculators wanted the
"Indian menace" finally removed from their Western
tracts. Creditors wanted to stop the states from issuing paper money. Investors in Confederation securities wanted the Confederation debt made good and
the value of their securities enhanced. Large property
owners in general looked for protection from the
threat of mobs, a threat that seemed particularly

menacing in light of such episodes as Shays's Rebellion.

By 1786, such demands had grown so powerful
that the issue was no longer whether the Confederation should be changed but how drastic the changes
should be. Even the defenders of the existing system
reluctantly came to agree that the government needed
strengthening at its weakest point—its lack of power
to tax. The failure of Congress to approve Robert
Morris's continental impost discouraged those who
believed that such strengthening could occur within
the present system.

The most resourceful of the reformers was the
political genius, New York lawyer, one-time military aide to General Washington, and illegitimate son
of a Scottish merchant in the West Indies—Alexander
Hamilton. From the beginning, Hamilton had been
dissatisfied with the Articles of Confederation. He
now saw little to be gained by piecemeal amendments, and he called for a national convention to
overhaul the entire document. To this end, he took
advantage of a movement for interstate cooperation
that began in 1785 when a group of Marylanders and
Virginians met in Alexandria to settle differences between the two states.

One of the Virginians, James Madison, was as
eager as Hamilton to see a stronger government. He
induced the Virginia legislature to invite all the states
to send delegates to a larger conference on commercial questions. This group met at Annapolis in 1786,
but representatives from only five states appeared.
Nevertheless, the delegates adopted a report drafted
by Hamilton (who was representing New York) recommending that Congress call a convention of special delegates from all the states to gather in
Philadelphia the next year and consider ways to "render the constitution of the Federal government adequate to the exigencies of the union."

At that moment, in 1786, there seemed little possibility that the Philadelphia convention would be
any better attended or would accomplish any more
than the meeting at Annapolis. Supporters of the idea
believed that only by winning the support of George
Washington could they hope to prevail. For a time,
however, Washington showed little interest in joining the cause. Although he was one of the wealthiest
men in the country, he was suffering from a common
planter's malady: a temporary shortage of cash. So he
was reluctant to undertake the trouble and expense of
an extended visit to Philadelphia.

But then, early in 1787, the news of Shays's Rebellion spread throughout the nation, news that

George Washington at Mount Vernon
Washington was in his first term as President in 1790 when an anonymous artist painted this view of his home at Mount Vernon, Virginia. Washington appears in uniform, along with members of his family, on the lawn. After he retired from office in 1797, Washington returned happily to his plantation and spent the two years before his death in 1799 "amusing myself in agricultural and rural pursuits." He also played host to an endless stream of visitors from throughout the country and Europe. (National Gallery of Art, Washington)

seemed to augur other, more dangerous insurrections elsewhere. Thomas Jefferson, then the American minister in Paris, was not alarmed. "I hold," he confided in a letter to James Madison, "that a little rebellion, now and then, is a good thing, and as necessary in the political world as storms in the physical." At Mount Vernon, however, Washington took the news less calmly. "There are combustibles in every State which a spark might set fire to," he exclaimed. "I feel infinitely more than I can express for the disorders which have arisen. Good God!" Some suggested that Washington make himself a military dictator; he refused even to consider the possibility. But after Congress issued its calls for a constitutional convention, he borrowed money for the journey and, in May, left Mount Vernon for Philadelphia.

A Divided Convention

Fifty-five men, representing all the states except Rhode Island, attended one or more sessions of the convention that sat in the Philadelphia State House from May to September 1787. They constituted a remarkable collection of talent, but they were far from the godlike creatures that later generations would at times describe. These "Founding Fathers," as they were to become known, were on the whole relatively young men. Many of them were in their twenties and thirties, and only one (Benjamin Franklin, then eighty-one years old) was genuinely aged. The average age was forty-four. They were men of practical experience in business, plantation management, and politics. And they were well educated by the standards of their time; more than a third were college graduates. Most represented the great property interests of the country and, as such, feared what one of them called the "turbulence and follies" of democracy.

The convention's first decision (after unanimously choosing Washington to preside over its sessions) was to conduct its business in complete secrecy. There would be no official transcript of its deliberations; there would be no reports to the press. (In fact, if James Madison had not kept a private diary chronicling the proceedings, historians would know little about what happened in Philadelphia.) The second decision, of great importance, was that each state delegation would have a single vote (as in the Confederation Congress); but major decisions would not require unanimity, as they did in Congress, just a simple majority.

Almost all the delegates agreed that the United States needed a stronger central government. There were great differences of opinion, however, as to how much stronger the government should be, what specific powers it should have, and what its structure should be. There were differences, in particular, over how power should be divided among the large and small states and over how economic interests in different sections of the country should be protected.

Among the states, Virginia was then much the largest in population—more than twice as large as New York, more than four times as large as New Jersey, more than ten times as large as Delaware. Among the delegations at Philadelphia, the Virginians were also the best prepared for the work of the convention. And among the Virginians, James Madison (thirty-six years old) was the most important intellect. Even before the convention met, he had devised in some detail a plan for a new "national" government. The Virginians controlled the agenda from the moment the convention began.

Edmund Randolph of Virginia opened the deliberations by proposing that "*a national* government ought to be established, consisting of a *supreme* Legislative, Executive, and Judiciary." For all its vagueness, this was a drastic proposal. It called for the creation of a government very different from the existing confederation. It is an indication of how committed the delegates were to fundamental reform that they approved this resolution after only perfunctory debate. That opened the way for Randolph to introduce the details of Madison's plan. The Virginia Plan (as it came to be known) proposed the abandonment of the Articles of Confederation and the creation of a wholly new government; it also proposed giving the

larger influence within that new government to the richer and more populous states. It called for a national legislature consisting of two houses. In the lower house, the states would be represented in proportion to their population; thus the largest state (Virginia) would have about ten times as many representatives as the smallest (Delaware). Members of the upper house were to be elected by the lower house; thus some of the smaller states might at times have no members at all in the upper house.

The proposal aroused immediate opposition among delegates from Delaware, New Jersey, and other small states. But the opponents were at first uncertain how to proceed. For a while, some argued that Congress had called the convention "for the sole and express purpose of revising the Articles of Confederation," and that the states in commissioning their "deputies" had authorized them to do no more than revise the Articles. They challenged the convention's authority to consider such drastic changes. Eventually, however, William Paterson of New Jersey submitted a substantive alternative to the Virginia Plan, a proposal for a "federal" as opposed to a "national" government. The New Jersey Plan envisioned what was in effect simply a revision and strengthening of the Articles. It preserved the existing one-house legislature, in which each state had equal representation; but it gave the legislature expanded powers to tax and to regulate commerce. After a spirited debate, the majority of the delegates voted to table Paterson's proposal.

The Virginia Plan remained the basis for discussion. But its supporters now realized they would have to make concessions to the small states if the convention was ever to reach a general agreement. They soon conceded an important point by agreeing to permit the members of the upper house to be elected by the state legislatures rather than by the lower house of the national legislature. Thus each state would be sure of always having at least one member in the upper house. There remained, however, the question of how many members each state should have.

Questions also remained about the number of representatives each state should have in the lower house. If the number was to depend on population, were slaves to be counted as part of the population? Were slaves, in other words, to be considered persons or property? The delegates from the states with large and apparently permanent slave populations—especially those from South Carolina—wanted to have it both ways. They argued that slaves should be considered persons in determining representation (although they never considered permitting slaves to vote). But they wanted slaves to be considered property if the new government were to levy taxes on each state on the basis of population. Representatives from states where slavery had disappeared or was expected to disappear argued that slaves should be included in calculating taxation but not representation. No one argued seriously for turning the slaves into citizens.

Differences Compromised

The delegates bickered for weeks. By the end of June, as both temperature and tempers rose to uncomfortable heights, the convention seemed in danger of collapsing. Benjamin Franklin, who remained a calm voice of conciliation through the summer, warned that if they failed, the delegates would "become a reproach and by-word down to future ages. And what is worse, mankind may hereafter, from this unfortunate instance, despair of establishing governments by human wisdom, and leave it to chance, war and conquest." Partly because of Franklin's soothing presence, the delegates refused to give up.

Finally, on July 2, the convention agreed to create a "grand committee," with a single delegate from each state (and with Franklin as chairman), to resolve the disagreements. The committee returned with a proposal that became the basis of the "Great Compromise" and that finally resolved the difficult problem of representation. The committee proposed a legislature in which the states would be represented in the lower house on the basis of population, with each slave counted as three-fifths of a free person in determining the basis for both representation and direct taxation. (The three-fifths formula was based on the specious assumption that a slave was three-fifths as productive as a free worker and thus contributed only three-fifths as much wealth to the state.) And the committee proposed that in the upper house, the states should be represented equally with two members apiece. The proposal broke the deadlock. On July 16, 1787, the convention voted to accept it.

In the ensuing weeks, while several committees worked on the details of various parts of the emerging constitution, the convention as a whole agreed to other important compromises on the issue of tariffs and trade regulations and on the most explosive issue of all: slavery. The representatives of the Southern states feared that the power to regulate trade, if granted to the national government, might lead to export duties on their crops, commercial agreements (as in the recent Jay-Gardoqui treaty) that would sacrifice the interests of rice and tobacco growers, and interference with the slave trade. The South Carolinians proposed that a two-thirds vote in the legislature be required not only to approve commercial treaties but also to pass commercial laws. Although the convention rejected that proposal, it made some important concessions to the Southerners. The new legislature would not be permitted to tax exports; it would be forbidden to impose a duty of more than $10 a head on imported slaves; and it would have no authority to stop the slave trade for twenty years. To those delegates who viewed the continued existence of slavery as an affront to the principles of the new nation, this was a large and difficult concession. They agreed to it because they feared that without it the Constitution would fail.

Other differences of opinion the convention was unable to harmonize, and it disposed of them by evasion or omission—leaving important questions alive that would surface again in later years. One such question was whether the new courts or some special agency should be empowered to review and disallow acts of the legislature. The proposal for a "council of revision," a part of the original Virginia Plan, was dropped, and no provision was added to confer the power of judicial review explicitly on the courts. There was no bill of rights, restraining the powers of the national government in the way that bills of rights restrained the state governments. Madison opposed the idea, arguing that specifying rights that were reserved to the people would, in effect, *limit* those rights. Others, however, feared that without such protections the national government might abuse its new authority.

The Constitution of 1787

Many minds contributed to the creation of the American Constitution, and its terms were the result of many compromises. But the man who made the single greatest contribution to the new concept of government embodied in the document was James Madison, the most creative political thinker of his generation. It had been Madison who devised the Virginia Plan, from which the final document ultimately emerged. And it was Madison who did most of the drafting of the Constitution itself. But Madison's most important achievement was in helping to resolve two important philosophical questions

James Madison

Madison (seen here in a portrait by Gilbert Stuart) was often overshadowed by the more charismatic Thomas Jefferson; but he was at least as important a figure as his fellow Virginian in developing the political ideas that became the foundation of the American republic. Madison and Jefferson were political allies for over thirty years, but they were not always in complete agreement. During the debate over the federal Constitution, Jefferson favored the addition of a Bill of Rights. Madison, however, argued that a written declaration of rights should be avoided since any such declaration might be construed as *limiting* rights rather than guaranteeing them. His concerns found expression, finally, in the Ninth Amendment, which stated that "the enumeration in the Constitution of certain rights shall not be construed to deny or disparage others retained by the people." (Bowdoin College Museum of Art)

that had served as obstacles to the creation of an effective national government: the question of sovereignty and the question of limiting power.

The question of sovereignty had been one of the chief sources of friction between the American colonies and Great Britain. England had argued that sovereignty could not, by definition, be divided, that it must reside in a single place; and in British eyes, that place had been Parliament, where the authority of king, Lords, and Commons meshed to produce a stable center of power. Thus the colonial assemblies could have no independent power, because that would imply a division of sovereignty—in British eyes, a logical impossibility. Americans themselves were not entirely comfortable with the idea of divided sovereignty, and their reservations had helped shape their first attempts to form a union. Under the Articles of Confederation, virtually all sovereignty resided in the individual states. Congress was simply a creature of the states, with no real sovereignty of its own (and thus without sufficient authority to fulfill its expected functions).

The creation of the federal Constitution had required at the start a resolution of questions associated with sovereignty. How could a national government exercise sovereignty concurrently with state governments? Where did ultimate sovereignty lie? The answer, Madison and his contemporaries decided, was that all power, at all levels of government, flowed ultimately from the people. Thus neither the federal government nor the state governments were truly sovereign. All of them derived their authority from below. The opening phrase of the Constitution (devised by Robert Morris) was "We the people of the United States of America"—an expression of the belief that the new government derived its power not from the states but from the public at large. The logical obstacle to the distribution of authority among different branches or different levels of government was thus removed.

The resolution of the problem of sovereignty made possible one of the distinctive features of the Constitution—its distribution of powers between the national and state governments. It was, Madison wrote at the time, "in strictness, neither a national nor a federal Constitution, but a composition of both." It had many features that were clearly national. The Constitution and the government it created were to be the "supreme law" of the land; no state would have the authority to defy it. The federal government was to have broad powers, including the power to tax, to regulate commerce, to control the currency, and to pass such laws as would be "necessary and proper" for carrying out its other responsibilities. Gone was the stipulation of the Articles that "each State shall retain every power, jurisdiction, and right not *expressly* delegated to the United States in Congress assembled." On the other hand, the Constitution was "federal" in creating a government that accepted the existence of separate states and left certain important powers in their hands.

In addition to solving the question of sovereignty,

the Constitution produced a distinctive solution to a problem that was particularly troubling to Americans: the problem of concentrated authority. Nothing so frightened the leaders of the new nation as the prospect of creating a tyrannical government. Nothing was so important to them as avoiding the problems that had, they believed, turned England into a despotic state. Indeed, that fear had been one of the chief obstacles to the creation of a national government at all.

Drawing from the ideas of the French philosopher Baron de Montesquieu, most Americans had long believed that the best way, perhaps the only way, to avoid tyranny was to keep government close to the people. That meant, according to Montesquieu, that a republic must remain confined to a relatively small area; a large nation would breed corruption and despotism because the rulers would be so distant from most of the people that there would be no way to control them. In the new American nation, these assumptions had led to the belief that the individual states must remain sovereign and that a strong national government would be dangerous.

Madison, however, helped break the grip of these assumptions by arguing that a large republic would be *less,* not more likely to produce tyranny, because it would contain so many different factions that no single group would ever be able to dominate it. (In this, he drew from—among other sources—the Scottish philosopher David Hume.) This idea of many centers of power "checking each other" and preventing any single, despotic authority from emerging not only made possible the idea of a large republic. It also helped shape the internal structure of the federal government. The Constitution's most distinctive feature was its "separation of powers" within the government, its creation of "checks and balances" among the legislative, executive, and judicial branches. (Here again, the new idea of sovereignty was crucial. Since ultimate authority resided in the people, there need be no single, ultimate center of authority within the government.)

It was a system designed to prevent any one person, any one faction, any one element of government from exercising excessive power. The array of forces within the government would constantly compete with (and often frustrate) one another. Congress would have two chambers—the Senate and the House of Representatives, each with members elected in a different way and for different terms—each checking the other, since both would have to agree before any law could be passed. The president would have the power to veto acts of Congress; and the executive's

independence from the legislature would be assured by the special process by which a president would be elected. Electors would be chosen in whatever way the separate states might designate, and the sole duty of this electoral college would be to cast votes for president and vice president. If no one received an electoral majority, then the final selection among the leading candidates would be up to the House of Representatives, with each state casting a single vote. The federal courts would be protected from both the executive and the legislature. Justices would be appointed by the president and confirmed by the Senate, but once in office they would serve for life.

The "federal" structure of the government, which divided power between the states and the nation, and the system of "checks and balances," which divided power among various elements within the national government itself, was designed to protect the United States from the kind of despotism that Americans believed had emerged in England. But it was also designed to protect the nation against another kind of despotism, perhaps more menacing: the tyranny of the people. Fear of the "mob," of an "excess of democracy" was at least as important to the framers as fear of a single tyrant. Shays's Rebellion had been only one example, they believed, of what could happen if a nation did not defend itself against the unchecked exercise of popular will. Thus in the new government, only the members of the House of Representatives would be elected directly by the people. Senators, the president, federal judges—all would be insulated in varying degrees from the public.

But in Madison's view, at least, the new system provided an even more fundamental protection against unrestrained popular will. The competition among the many factions within the federal system would permit no faction to attain genuine dominance. Real authority, Madison believed, would come to be lodged in a small group of particularly talented and virtuous people, who would look out for the interests of society as a whole.

The Constitution did not satisfy everyone. Edmund Randolph, the governor of Virginia and the man who had originally introduced the Virginia Plan, was so unhappy about how far the final version had departed from the initial proposal that he refused to sign the document. Several delegates from the smaller states also withheld their approval. Most members of the convention, however, were willing to overlook their reservations. On September 17, 1787, thirty-nine delegates signed the Constitution, doubtless sharing the feelings that Benjamin Franklin expressed at the end: "Thus I consent, Sir, to this Constitution,

WHERE HISTORIANS DISAGREE

The Background of the Constitution

The debate among historians about the motives of those who framed the American Constitution mirrors in many ways the debate about the causes of the American Revolution. To some, the creation of the federal system was an effort to preserve the ideals of the Revolution by eliminating the disorder and contention that threatened the new nation. To others, supporters of the Constitution appear to have been men attempting to protect their own economic interests, even at the cost of betraying the principles of the Revolution.

The first and most influential exponent of the former view was John Fiske, whose book *The Critical Period of American History* (1888) painted a grim picture of political life under the Articles of Confederation. The nation was, Fiske argued, reeling under the impact of a business depression, the weakness and ineptitude of the national government, the threats to American territory from Great Britain and Spain, the inability of either the Congress or the state governments to make good their debts, the interstate jealousies and barriers to trade, the widespread use of inflation-producing paper money, and the lawlessness that culminated in Shays's Rebellion. Only the timely adoption of the Constitution, Fiske claimed, saved the young republic from disaster.

Fiske's view met with little dissent until 1913, when Charles A. Beard, published a powerful challenge to it in *An Economic Interpretation of the Constitution of the United States*. According to Beard, the 1780s had been a "critical period" not for the nation as a whole but for certain conserva-

tive business interests who feared that the decentralized political structure of the republic imperiled their financial position. Such men, he claimed, wanted a government able to promote industry and trade, protect private property, and perhaps most of all, make good the public debt—much of which was owed to them. The Constitution was, Beard claimed, "an economic document drawn with superb skill by men whose property interests were immediately at stake" and who won its ratification over the opposition of a majority of the people. Were it not for their impatience and determination, he argued in a later book (1927), the Articles of Confederation might have formed a perfectly satisfactory, permanent form of government. The Beard view of the Constitution influenced more than a generation of historians. As late as the 1950s, for example, Merrill Jensen argued in *The New Nation* (1950) that the 1780s were not years of chaos and despair, but a time of hopeful striving and that only the economic interests of a small group of wealthy men can account for the creation of the Constitution.

But the 1950s also produced a series of powerful and persuasive challenges to the Beard thesis. Robert E. Brown, for example, argued in 1956 that "absolutely no correlation" could be shown between the wealth of the delegates to the Constitutional Convention and their position on the Constitution. Forrest McDonald, in *We the People* (1958), looked beyond the convention itself to the debate between the Federalists and the Antifederalists and concluded similarly that there was no con-

because I expect no better, and because I am not sure that it is not the best."

Adoption and Adaptation

The delegates at Philadelphia had greatly exceeded their instructions from Congress and the states. Instead of making simple revisions in the Articles of Confederation, they had produced a plan for a completely different form of government. They had rea-

son to doubt, therefore, whether the Constitution would ever be ratified under the procedures laid down in the Articles of Confederation, which required unanimous approval of any alterations in the Articles by the state legislatures. So the convention changed the rules. The Constitution specified that the new government would come into existence among the ratifying states when only nine of the thirteen had ratified. It recommended to Congress that the Constitution be submitted to state *conventions,* called specifically to consider the document, rather than to the legislatures of the states.

──────WHERE HISTORIANS DISAGREE──────

sistent relationship between wealth and property on the one hand and support for the Constitution on the other. Instead, opinion on the new system was far more likely to reflect local and regional interests. Areas suffering social and economic distress were likely to support the Constitution; states that were stable and prosperous were likely to oppose it. There was no intercolonial class of monied interests operating in concert to produce the Constitution.

The cumulative effect of these attacks has been virtually to destroy Beard's argument; hardly any historians any longer accept his thesis without reservation. By the 1960s, however, a new group of scholars was beginning to revive an economic interpretation of the Constitution—one that differed from Beard's in important ways but that nevertheless emphasized social and economic factors as motives for supporting the federal system. Jackson Turner Main argued, in *The Antifederalists* (1961), that supporters of the Constitution, while not perhaps the united creditor class that Beard described, were nevertheless economically distinct from critics of the document. The Federalists, he argued, were "cosmopolitan commercialists," eager to advance the economic development of the nation; the Antifederalists, by contrast, were "agrarian localists," fearful of centralization. Gordon Wood's important study, *The Creation of the American Republic* (1969), de-emphasized economic grievances but nevertheless suggested that profound social divisions found reflection in the debate over the state constitutions in the 1770s and

1780s; and that those same divisions helped shape the argument over the federal Constitution. The Federalists, he suggested, were largely traditional aristocrats. They had become deeply concerned by the instability of life under the Articles of Confederation and were particularly alarmed by the decline in popular deference toward social elites. The creation of the Constitution was part of a larger search to create a legitimate political leadership based on the existent social hierarchy; it reflected the efforts of elites to contain what they considered the excesses of democracy.

Other historians have stressed not so much class divisions or economic interests as regional or generational differences. H. James Henderson argued in 1974, in *Party Politics in the Continental Congress*, that the debate over the Constitution was part of a larger argument over the integration of different regions into a single nation. Stanley Elkins and Eric McKitrick contended in a 1961 article ("The Founding Fathers," *Political Science Quarterly*) that the Federalists tended to be younger men than the Antifederalists and saw the development of a strong, united nation as the key to their own future. Pauline Maier, in *The Old Revolutionaries* (1980), offered portraits of early leaders of the resistance to Britain toward the end of their lives and argued that their passage from the scene made it possible for new ideas about the nature of the Revolution—ideas that found reflection in the Constitution—to emerge among the leaders of the next generation.

Federalists and Antifederalists

The Congress in New York was completely overshadowed by the events in Philadelphia, and it passively accepted the convention's work and submitted it to the states for approval. All the state legislatures (with the exception of Rhode Island) elected delegates to ratifying conventions, most of which had begun meeting by early 1788. Even before the ratifying conventions adjourned, however, a great national debate on the new Constitution had begun—in the legislatures, in mass meetings, in the columns of newspapers, and in the daily conversations of many

men and women. The debate was intense, but it was generally peaceful and deliberative. Occasionally, however, passions rose to the point that opposing factions came to blows. In at least one place—Albany, New York—such clashes resulted in injuries and death.

Although the preamble made reference to "We the people," the whole people of the United States did not become involved in the ratification process. Most women and blacks and some unpropertied white males had no voice at all in the process. And approximately three-fourths of the adult white males eligible to vote for delegates to the ratifying conventions failed to do so, mainly because of indifference. Of those who did vote, a large majority apparently favored ratification; but because the Constitution was such a complex document, embodying so many different ideas, its real standing among the people at large remained in doubt.

The friends of the Constitution had a number of advantages. They were the better-organized group, and they had the weight of fame and superior leadership on their side. They could point to the support of the two most eminent men in America, Franklin and Washington. (Washington, for example, had declared that the nation faced a choice between the Constitution and disunion.) And they seized control of an appealing label for themselves: "Federalists"— the term that opponents of centralization had once used to described themselves—thus implying that they were less commited to a "nationalist" government than in fact they were. They called their critics "Antifederalists" and implied in the process that the opposition stood for nothing constructive, that it stood for chaos itself. The Constitution's opponents protested the name, and tried to call themselves "Federal Republicans" instead. But the pejorative "Antifederalist" label stuck.

The Federalists also had the support of the ablest political philosophers of their time: Alexander Hamilton, James Madison, and John Jay. And those three men, under the joint pseudonym "Publius," wrote a series of essays—widely published in newspapers throughout the nation—explaining the meaning and virtues of the Constitution. The essays were later issued as a book, and they are known today as *The Federalist Papers*. They constitute the single most authoritative commentary on the Constitution and perhaps the greatest American contribution to political theory.

The opponents of ratification produced no comparable writings, no "Antifederalist Papers." They tried to make a vigorous case for themselves in speeches, pamphlets, and newspaper propaganda; but much of the press simply ignored them. Perhaps inevitably, the Antifederalists resorted mainly to negative argument. They insisted that the Constitution was illegal—as indeed it was if judged by the terms of the Articles of Confederation. The new government, they claimed, would increase taxes, obliterate the states, wield dictatorial powers, favor the "well born" over the common people, and put an end to individual liberty. Above all, they protested, the Constitution lacked a bill of rights.

The Antifederalist concern about inclusion of a bill of rights revealed one of the most important sources of their opposition to the new Constitution: a basic mistrust of human nature and of the capacity of human beings to wield power. (They have, on occasion, been described as "men of little faith.") They echoed the early Revolutionary fears of corruption and tyranny, and they argued that any government that centralized authority in the hands of the powerful would inevitably produce despotism. The Federalists shared many of these fears, but they believed that the Constitution provided ample protection against tyranny. The Antifederalists did not. The idea of a bill of rights, therefore, reflected a belief that no government could be trusted not to infringe on the liberties of its citizens; only by enumerating the natural rights of the people could there be any certainty that those rights would be protected.

Despite the efforts of the Antifederalists, ratification proceeded reasonably smoothly during the winter of 1787–1788. The Delaware convention was the first to act and ratified the Constitution unanimously, as did New Jersey and Georgia. In the larger states of Pennsylvania and Massachusetts, the Antifederalists put up a more determined struggle but lost in the final vote. New Hampshire ratified the document in June 1788—the ninth state to do so. It was now theoretically possible for the Constitution to go into effect.

A new government could not hope to succeed, however, without the participation of Virginia and New York, whose conventions remained closely di-

Ratification of the Constitution

STATE	DATE	VOTE FOR/AGAINST
Delaware	December 1787	30/0
Pennsylvania	December 1787	46/23
New Jersey	December 1787	38/0
Georgia	January 1788	26/0
Connecticut	January 1788	128/40
Massachusetts	February 1788	187/168
Maryland	April 1788	63/11
South Carolina	May 1788	149/73
New Hampshire	June 1788	57/47
Virginia	June 1788	89/79
New York	July 1788	30/27
North Carolina	November 1789	194/77
Rhode Island	May 1790	34/32

vided. But by the end of June, Virginia and then New York had consented to the Constitution by narrow margins. The New York convention yielded to expediency—even some of the most staunchly Antifederalist delegates feared that the state's commercial interests would suffer if, once the other states gathered under the "New Roof," New York were to remain outside. Massachusetts, Virginia, and New York all ratified, on the assumption—although not on the express condition—that certain desired amendments would be added to the Constitution, above all a bill of rights. Deciding to wait and see what became of these hopes for amendment, the North Carolina convention adjourned without taking action. Rhode Island did not even call a convention to consider ratification.

Completing the Structure

The first elections under the Constitution were held in the early months of 1789, and the results showed that the new government was to be in the hands of its friends. Few of the newly elected congressmen and senators had been committed Antifederalists; almost all had favored ratification, and many had served as delegates to the Philadelphia convention.

There was never any real doubt about who would be the first president. George Washington had presided at the Constitutional Convention, and many who had favored ratification did so only because they expected him to preside over the new government as well. Washington received the votes of all the presidential electors, whom the states, either by legislative action or by popular election, had named. John Adams, a leading Federalist (although he had not been a member of the convention, being the American minister to London at the time), received the next highest number of electoral votes and became vice president.

Congressmen were so slow to reach New York (which was, for the time being, to remain the national capital) that not until April was a quorum on hand to make an official count of the electoral vote and send a messenger to notify General Washington of his election. After a journey from Mount Vernon marked by elaborate celebrations along the way, Washington was inaugurated on April 30.

The responsibilities facing the first president and the first Congress were in some ways greater than those facing any president or Congress to follow. The leaders of the new government had the Consti-

tution as a guide, but it provided only a general plan and left many questions unanswered. What, for example, should be the rules of the two houses of Congress for the conduct of their business? What code of etiquette should govern the relations between the president on the one hand and Congress and the people on the other? Should the chief executive have a lofty title, such as "His Highness the President of the United States and Protector of Their Liberties"? (John Adams believed that he should.) What was the true meaning of the many ambiguous phrases in the Constitution? In answering these and other questions, Washington and his colleagues knew they were setting precedents that, in many cases, would give lasting direction to the development of the new government.

Thus the first Congress served in many ways almost as a continuation of the Constitutional Convention, as it acted to fill various gaps in the Constitution. Most conspicuous was the drafting of a bill of rights, which proponents of the Constitution had promised in order to conciliate the Antifederalists. By early 1789, even Madison had come to agree that some sort of bill of rights would be essential to legitimize the new government in the eyes of its opponents. Dozens of amendments had been proposed in the state ratifying conventions, and Congress (led by Madison, a member of the House of Representatives) undertook the task of sifting through them, reducing them to a manageable number, and sending them to the states for ratification. They approved twelve amendments on September 25, 1789; ten of them were ratified by the states by the end of 1791. (Thus what we know as the Bill of Rights is, in legal terms, simply the first ten amendments to the Constitution.)

Nine of those amendments placed limitations on Congress by forbidding it to infringe on certain basic rights: freedom of religion, speech, and the press; immunity from arbitrary arrest; trial by jury; and others. The Tenth Amendment reserved to the states all powers except those specifically withheld from them or delegated to the federal government.

In regard to the structure of the federal courts, the Constitution had only this to say: "The judicial power of the United States shall be vested in one Supreme Court, and in such inferior courts as the Congress may from time to time ordain and establish." Thus the convention had left to Congress the number of Supreme Court judges to be appointed and the kinds of lower courts to be organized. In the Judiciary Act of 1789, Congress provided for a Supreme Court of six members, with a chief justice and five associate justices; for thirteen district courts with one judge apiece; and for three circuit courts of appeal, each to consist of one of the district judges sitting with two of the Supreme Court justices. In the same act, Congress gave the Supreme Court the power to make the final decision in cases involving the constitutionality of state laws. If the Constitution was in fact to be the "supreme law of the land," the various state courts could not be left to decide for themselves whether the state legislatures were violating that supreme law.

As for executive departments, the Constitution referred indirectly to them but did not specify what or how many there should be. The first Congress created three such departments—state, treasury, and war—and also established the offices of the attorney general and postmaster general. In appointing department heads and other high officials, Washington selected men who were generally well disposed toward the Constitution and who as a group would provide a balanced representation of the different sections of the country. To the office of secretary of the treasury he appointed Alexander Hamilton of New York, who at age thirty-two was an acknowledged expert in public finance. For secretary of war he chose a Massachusetts Federalist, General Henry Knox. As attorney general he named Edmund Randolph of Virginia, sponsor of the plan on which the Constitution had been based. As secretary of state he chose another Virginian, Thomas Jefferson, who had been away from the country as minister to France (and thus, like Adams, had not been a delegate to the Constitutional Convention).

From time to time, Washington called on these four men for advice, usually as individuals; but the department heads did not yet operate as a "cabinet." Washington assumed at first that the Senate would serve as an advisory council, since according to the Constitution the Senate was to give its advice and consent for the appointment of high officials and for the ratification of treaties. With only twenty-two members in the beginning, the Senate was small enough so that Washington could expect to consult personally with it. He changed his mind, however, after he took the draft of a treaty to the senators for their advice. They demanded that he leave the document for them to inspect and change at their leisure; Washington refused and resolved never again to submit a treaty to the senators until its negotiation had been completed. Thus he set a precedent in treaty making that his successors have generally followed.

Federalists and Republicans

The resolution of these initial issues stopped far short, however, of resolving the disagreements about the nature of the new government. On the contrary, for the first twelve years under the Constitution, American politics was characterized by a level of acrimony seldom matched in any period since. The framers of the Constitution had dealt with many disagreements not by solving them but by papering them over with a series of vague compromises; as a result, the disagreements survived to plague the new government.

At the heart of the controversies of the 1790s was the same basic difference in philosophy that had lain at the heart of the debate over the Constitution. On one side stood a powerful group that believed America required a strong, *national* government: that the country's mission was to become a genuine nation-state, with centralized authority, a complex commercial economy, and a proud standing in world affairs. On the other side stood another group—a minority at first, but gaining strength during the decade—that envisioned a far more modest central government. It would be stronger than that under the Confederation, to be sure; but it would remain a far weaker instrument than the European equivalents. Moreover, American society should not, this group believed, aspire to be highly commercial or urban. It should remain predominantly rural and agrarian. The centralizers became known as the Federalists and gravitated to the leadership of Alexander Hamilton. Their opponents acquired the name Republicans and gathered under the leadership of James Madison and Thomas Jefferson.

Hamilton and the Federalists

Control of the new government lay from the beginning largely in the hands of the Federalists. It remained there for twelve years. One reason was George Washington, who had always envisioned a strong national government and who during his eight years as president did little to hamper the efforts of those attempting to consolidate its power. Yet Washington's role in enacting the Federalist program was in many respects a passive one, a result of his concept of the office he held. The president, Washington believed, should not be directly involved in political controversies. He should be an almost Olympian figure, above the fray—a symbol of American nationhood. Washington thus avoided any personal involvement in the deliberations of Congress; he made few efforts to mediate among contending factions; he remained aloof.

As a result, the dominant figure in his administration became his talented secretary of the treasury, Alexander Hamilton, a man who exerted more influence than anyone else on domestic and foreign policy both during his term of office and, to an almost equal extent, after his resignation in 1794. Of all the leading men of his time, Hamilton was one of the most aristocratic in personal tastes and political philosophy—ironically, perhaps, since his own origins had been exceedingly humble. Far from embracing republican ideals of the virtue of the people, he believed that a stable and effective government required an elite ruling class; authority should be lodged in the hands of the "enlightened few." As a result, he hoped to adapt the British system of rule by the king and the aristocracy as closely as possible to the United States. The alternative, he was certain, would be continuing disorder.

The new government could best be strengthened,

Hamilton believed, by attracting the support of the wealthy. And the best way to do that was to give them a stake in its success. Thus Hamilton first proposed that the existing public debt be "funded," that the miscellaneous, uncertain, depreciated certificates of indebtedness that the old Congress had issued during and since the Revolution—many of them now in the possession of wealthy speculators—be called in and exchanged for uniform, interest-bearing bonds, payable at definite dates. Next, he recommended that the Revolutionary state debts be "assumed," taken over by the United States, his object being to cause state as well as federal bondholders to look to the central government for eventual payment. Hamilton did not, in other words, envision paying off and thus eliminating the debt. He wanted instead to create a large and permanent national debt, new bonds being issued as old ones were paid off. The result, he believed, would be that creditors—the wealthy classes most likely to lend money to the government—would have a permanent stake in seeing the government survive.

Hamilton also planned the establishment of a national bank. At the time, there were only a few banks

The First Bank of the United States

Alexander Hamilton's dream of creating a powerful national financial center culminated in the establishment of the First Bank of the United States. The bank's grand and dignified classical building in Philadelphia, completed in 1795 (and shown here in a 1799 engraving by William Birch), symbolized Hamilton's hopes for a strong and stable federal government.

in the country, located principally in Boston, Philadelphia, and New York. A new, national bank would serve several purposes. It would provide loans and currency to businesses. It would give the government a safe place for the deposit of federal funds. It would facilitate the collection of taxes and the disbursement of the government's expenditures. It would keep up the price of government bonds through judicious bond purchases. The bank was to be chartered by the federal government, was to have a monopoly of the government's own banking business, and was to be controlled by directors of whom one-fifth would be appointed by the government.

The funding and assumption of the debts, together with the payment of regular interest on them, would cost a great deal of money, and so Hamilton had to find adequate sources of revenue. He thought the government should depend mainly on two kinds of taxes (in addition to the receipts to be anticipated from the sales of public land). One of these was an excise to be paid by distillers of alcoholic liquors. This tax would hit most heavily the whiskey distillers of the back country, especially in Pennsylvania, Virginia, and North Carolina—small farmers who converted part of their corn and rye crop into whiskey.

The other tax on which Hamilton planned to rely was the tariff on imports. Such a tax would not only raise revenue but would also protect and encourage American manufacturing by raising the price of competing manufactured goods brought in from abroad. One of the first acts of the new Congress, in 1789, was the passage of a tariff law; but the level of duties under this law was extremely low. Hamilton advocated a higher and more decidedly protective tariff. In his famous "Report on Manufactures" of 1791, he laid out a grand scheme for stimulating the growth of industry in the United States and glowingly described the advantages that such growth would bring to the nation. Factories, he said, would make the nation more nearly self-sufficient in wartime, would increase prosperity by creating a home market for the produce of the farms, and would make possible the fuller utilization of all kinds of labor.

The Federalists, in short, offered more than a vision of how to ensure the stability of the new government. They offered a vision of the sort of nation America should become—a nation with a wealthy, enlightened ruling class; one possessing a vigorous, independent commercial economy with a thriving industrial sector; a country able to play a prominent role in world economic affairs.

Enacting the Federalist Program

Hamilton faced fervent opposition to many aspects of his program, and from 1789 to 1792 he and his supporters found themselves involved in continuous and often bitter debates. In the end, however, he won passage of almost all the measures he proposed.

Very few members of Congress objected to Hamilton's plan for funding the national debt; they agreed that the government must make its credit good. But many did oppose his proposal to fund the debt *at par,* that is, to exchange new bonds for old certificates of indebtedness on a dollar-for-dollar basis. The old certificates had been issued to merchants and farmers in payment for war supplies during the Revolution, or to officers and soldiers of the Revolutionary army in payment for their services. Many of these holders had been forced to sell their bonds during the hard times of the 1780s to speculators, who had bought them at a fraction of their face value.

Thus while almost everyone agreed that the government should pay what it owed, there was wide disagreement over *whom* it should pay the money to. Many congressmen believed that the original holders deserved some consideration, and James Madison, now a representative from Virginia, argued for a plan by which the new bonds would be divided between the original purchasers and the speculators. But the friends of Hamilton insisted that such a plan was impracticable and that the honor of the government required a literal fulfillment of its earlier promises to pay. Congress finally passed the funding bill in the form that Hamilton desired.

His proposal that the federal government assume the state debts encountered even greater difficulty. Its opponents had a strong case, for if the federal government took over the state debts, the people of one state would have to pay federal taxes for servicing the debts of other states. Some states' debts were much larger than others; Massachusetts, for example, owed far more money than did Virginia. Naturally, Virginia's representatives in Congress balked at the assumption bill. Only by striking a bargain with the Virginians were Hamilton and his supporters able to win passage of the bill.

The deal involved the location of the national capital. The Virginians wanted to create a new capital near them in the South. Hamilton met with Thomas Jefferson (after Jefferson's return from France) and agreed over dinner to provide Northern support for placing the capital in the South in exchange for Virginia's votes for the assumption bill. The capital had moved from New York back to Philadelphia in

1790. But the new bargain called for the construction of a new capital city on the banks of the Potomac River, on land to be selected by Washington himself. The government would move its operations by the beginning of the new century.

The thorny issue of assumption was thus settled reasonably easily. It was Hamilton's bank bill that sparked the first of many debates over the proper interpretation of the Constitution. Hamilton, of course, argued that establishment of a national bank was compatible with the intent of the Constitution, even though the document did not explicitly authorize it. But Madison, Jefferson, Randolph, and others argued that the Constitution should be construed in a strict sense and that Congress should exercise no powers that the document had not clearly assigned it. Both the House and the Senate finally agreed to Hamilton's bill; and although Washington initially displayed some uncertainty about its legality, he finally signed it. The Bank of the United States began operations in 1791, under a charter that granted it the right to continue for twenty years. Hamilton also had his way with the excise tax, although protests from farmers later forced revisions to reduce the burden on the smaller distillers. He failed to win passage of a tariff as highly protective as he had hoped for, but the tariff law of 1792 did raise the rates somewhat.

Once enacted, Hamilton's program had many of the effects he had intended and won the support of influential segments of the population. Public credit was quickly restored; the bonds of the United States were soon selling at home and abroad at prices even above their par value. Speculators (among them many members of Congress) reaped large profits as a result. Merchants in the seaports profited from the tariffs and benefited from the new banking system.

Others, however, found the Hamilton program less appealing. Small farmers in particular, who formed the vast majority of the population, complained that they had to bear a disproportionate burden of taxation. Not only did they owe property taxes to their state governments, but they bore the brunt of the excise tax and, indirectly, of the tariff. A feeling grew that the Federalist program served the interests not of the people but of small, wealthy elites. Out of this feeling an organized political opposition arose.

The Republican Opposition

The Constitution had made no reference to political parties, and the omission had been no oversight. Most of the framers—and George Washington in particular—believed that organized parties were evil and should be avoided. It was inevitable that men would disagree on particular issues, but most believed that such disagreements need not lead to the formation of permanent factions. "The public good is disregarded in the conflicts of rival parties," Madison had written in *The Federalist Papers* (in Number 10, perhaps the most influential of all the essays), "and . . . measures are too often decided, not according to the rules of justice and the rights of the minor party, but by the superior force of an interested and overbearing majority."

Yet not many years had passed after the ratification of the Constitution before Madison and others became convinced that Hamilton and his followers had become just such an "interested and overbearing majority." Not only had the Federalists enacted a program that many of these leaders opposed. More ominously, Hamilton himself had, in their eyes, worked to establish a national network of influence that embodied all the worst features of a party. The Federalists had used their control over appointments and the awarding of government franchises, and all the other powers of their offices, to reward their supporters and win additional allies. They had encouraged the formation of local associations—largely aristocratic in nature—to strengthen their standing in local communities. They were doing many of the same things, their opponents believed, that the corrupt British governments of the early eighteenth century had done.

Because the Federalists appeared to their critics to be creating such a menacing and tyrannical structure of power, there was no alternative but to organize a vigorous opposition. And the result was the emergence of an alternative political party: the Republicans. By the late 1790s, the Republicans were going to even greater lengths than the Federalists to create an apparatus of partisan influence. In every state they had formed committees, societies, and caucuses; Republican groups were corresponding with one another across state lines; they were banding together to influence state and local elections. And they were justifying their actions by claiming that they and they alone represented the true interests of the nation— that they were fighting to defend the people against a corrupt conspiracy by the Federalists. Just as Hamilton believed that the network of supporters he was creating represented the only legitimate interest group in the nation, so the Republicans believed that their party organization represented the best interests

The Jeffersonian Idyll

American artists in the early nineteenth century were drawn to tranquil rural scenes, symbolic of the Jeffersonian vision of a nation of small, independent farmers. Well before 1822, when Francis Alexander painted this pastoral landscape, the simple agrarian republic it depicts was already disappearing in the face of rapid economic growth.
(National Gallery of Art, Washington)

of the people. Neither side was willing to admit that it was acting as a party; nor would either concede the right of the other to exist.

From the beginning, the preeminent figures among the Republicans were Thomas Jefferson and James Madison. Indeed, the two men were such intimate collaborators with such similar political philosophies that it is sometimes difficult to distinguish the contributions of one from those of the other. But Jefferson, as the more magnetic personality of the two, gradually emerged as the most prominent spokesman for the Republicans.

Jefferson, himself a farmer, believed that farmers were God's chosen people and that an ideal republic would consist of sturdy citizens, each tilling his own soil. He was an aristocrat by birth, but he had faith in the good intentions of the ordinary farmer-citizens and believed that they could, if properly educated, be trusted to govern themselves through the election of able and qualified men. Urban people, by contrast, posed a danger to the republic; Jefferson feared city mobs as "sores upon the body politic." Thus he opposed the development of extensive manufactures because they would lead to the growth of cities packed

with propertyless workers. Jefferson envisioned, in short, a decentralized society, dominated by small property owners engaged largely in agrarian activities. He did not scorn commercial activity; farmers would, he assumed, market their crops through national and even international trade. Nor did he oppose industrial activity; Americans should, he believed, develop a certain amount of manufacturing capacity. But Jefferson did believe that the nation should avoid a highly urbanized, industrial economy and that the abundance of land in America was the society's greatest economic resource.

As a member of President Washington's official circle, Jefferson differed so strongly with his colleague Hamilton on particular issues such as the Bank that he soon offered to resign. But Washington, eager to preserve at least the appearance of national unity, persuaded him to remain as secretary of state. Although the two secretaries continued to serve the same president, they worked increasingly against each other. Each began to organize a following in Congress as well as in the country at large.

On the surface, the debate between the Federalists and the Republicans mirrored the earlier battle between Federalists and Antifederalists. In fact, however, the Republicans attracted support from some of those who had been most fervent in their support of the Constitution—among them Madison. The new Republicans did not denounce the Constitution. On the contrary, they professed to be its special friends and champions and accused their opponents of violating it.

Although both parties had supporters in all parts of the country and among all classes, there were regional and economic differences. The Federalists were most numerous in the commercial centers of the Northeast and in such Southern seaports as Charleston; the Republicans were most numerous in the rural areas of the South and the West. The factions differed in their social philosophies as well—as their reactions to the progress of the French Revolution suggest. As that revolution grew increasingly radical in the 1790s, with its attacks on organized religion, the overthrow of the monarchy, and eventually the guillotining of the king and queen, the Federalists watched in horror. The Republicans, in contrast, applauded the democratic, antiaristocratic spirit they believed the French Revolution embodied. Some even imitated the French radicals (the Jacobins) by cutting their hair short, wearing pantaloons, and addressing one another as "Citizen" and "Citizeness."

When the time came for the nation's second presidential election in 1792, both Jefferson and Hamilton urged Washington to run for a second term. The president would have preferred to retire to his plantation at Mount Vernon, but he agreed to serve for another four years. Almost all Americans viewed Washington as a figure above the partisan battle, and as long as he was president the factional dispute remained relatively contained. But Washington was, in reality, far more in sympathy with the Federalists than with the Republicans. And during his presidency, Hamilton managed to remain the dominant figure in government. Indeed, he once referred to Washington as "an aegis very necessary to me."

Asserting National Sovereignty

The Federalists consolidated their position—and attracted wide public support for the new national government—by dealing effectively with two problems that the old Confederation had been unable fully to resolve. They helped stabilize the Western frontier,

and they improved America's position in world affairs.

Securing the Frontier

Despite its success in winning passage of the Northwest Ordinance, the old Congress had been largely unable to tie the outlying Western areas of the country firmly to the government. Farmers in western Massachusetts had risen in revolt; settlers in Vermont, Kentucky, and Tennessee had toyed with the idea of separating from the Union. At first, the new government under the Constitution faced similar problems.

In 1794, farmers in western Pennsylvania raised a major challenge to federal authority when they refused to pay a whiskey excise tax and began terrorizing the tax collectors (much as colonists had done throughout America at the time of the Stamp Act.) But the federal government did not leave settlement of the so-called Whiskey Rebellion to the authorities of Pennsylvania as Congress had left Shays's Rebellion to the authorities of Massachusetts. At Hamilton's urging, Washington took drastic steps. He called out the militias of three states; he raised an army of nearly 15,000, a larger force than he had commanded against the British during most of the Revolution; and he personally accompanied the army into Pennsylvania. At the approach of the militiamen, the farmers around Pittsburgh, where the rebellion centered, either ran for cover or stayed home and claimed to be law-abiding citizens. The rebellion quickly collapsed.

The federal government won the allegiance of the whiskey rebels through intimidation. It won the loyalties of other frontiersmen by accepting new states as members of the Union. The last of the original thirteen colonies joined the union once the Bill of Rights had been appended to the Constitution—North Carolina in 1789 and Rhode Island in 1790. Then Vermont, which had had its own state government since the Revolution, was accepted as the fourteenth state in 1791 after New York and New Hampshire finally agreed to give up their claims to sovereignty over it. Next came Kentucky, in 1792, when Virginia gave up its claim to that region. When North Carolina finally ceded its Western lands to the Union, Tennessee achieved territorial status and in 1796 became a state.

In the more remote areas of the Northwest and the Southwest, meanwhile, the government had to contend with Indians and their European allies, Brit-

Washington in Command, 1794

Washington remembered with horror how the ineffectual response of the Confederation government to Shays's Rebellion in 1786 had threatened the unity of the nation. When Pennsylvania farmers rose up in the Whiskey Rebellion in 1794, the President decided at once on a strong military response and personally took command of the army he ordered into the field. This painting, credited to Frederick Kemmelmeyer, shows Washington reviewing troops in Cumberland, Maryland, as they prepare to march against the insurgents.   (Metropolitan Museum of Art)

ish and Spanish, in order to get a firm grasp on all the territory belonging to the United States. In the Southwest, four tribes—the Cherokees, Creeks, Choctaws, and Chickasaws—continued to resist the expansion of white settlement into their lands. The mixed-blood Creek chieftain Alexander McGillivray, who had fought with the British during the Revolution, led the Indian resistance to the advance of frontiersmen into the lower Mississippi Valley and received support and encouragement from Spain. In 1790, Washington tried to buy peace with the Southwestern Indians; he invited McGillivray to New York and agreed to pay him $100,000 in exchange for a cessation of hostilities. Other Indians, however, continued to accept subsidies from the Spaniards and to raid American settlements along the border. Finally, in 1793–1794, white Tennesseans called up the militia

and invaded Indian country, crushing the native resistance for a time.

In the Northwest, the federal government risked a conflict with Great Britain by sending three armed expeditions into the Ohio country to crush Indian resistance. General Anthony Wayne, a careful and effective commander (despite his nickname "Mad Anthony"), led 4,000 men into the region, moved cautiously toward the Maumee River, and built forts as he went. The British officials in Canada, who were providing the Indians with supplies, themselves ordered the construction of a fort about twenty miles from the mouth of the river, well within the boundary of the United States. Near the British fort, at a place where trees had been blown over by a windstorm, Wayne in the summer of 1794 met and decisively defeated the Indians in the Battle of Fallen

Timbers. The British garrison prudently kept out of the fight. The following summer, the Indians agreed in the Treaty of Greenville to abandon most of what later became the state of Ohio.

Maintaining Neutrality

Not until 1791 did Great Britain send a minister to the United States, and then only because Madison and the Republicans were threatening to place special trade restrictions on British ships. That was only one symbol of the difficulty the new government had in establishing its legitimacy in the eyes of the British.

A crisis in Anglo-American relations emerged in 1793 when the French revolutionary government, after executing King Louis XVI, went to war with Great Britain and its allies. The new federal government was uncertain how to respond. Should the United States recognize the radical government of France by accepting a diplomatic representative from it? Was the United States obligated by the alliance of 1778 to go to war on the side of France? Washington (responding to advice from both Hamilton and Jefferson) recognized the French government and issued a proclamation in 1793 announcing the determination of the United States to remain at peace and (although it did not use the word) neutral. A year later, Congress passed a neutrality act forbidding American citizens to participate in the war and prohibiting the use of American soil as a base of operations for either side.

The first challenge to American neutrality came from France, when its first diplomatic representative, the youthful and brash Edmond Genêt, arrived in America. Instead of landing at Philadelphia and presenting himself immediately to the president, Genêt disembarked at Charleston. There he made plans for using American ports to outfit French warships, issued letters of marque and reprisal authorizing American shipowners to serve as French privateers, and commissioned the aging George Rogers Clark to undertake an overland expedition against the possessions of Spain, an ally of Great Britain and an enemy of France. In all of this, Genêt was brazenly ignoring Washington's proclamation and flagrantly violating the Neutrality Act. His conduct infuriated Washington (who provided "Citizen Genêt," as he was known, with an icy reception in Philadelphia) and the Federalists; it also embarrassed all but the most ardent Francophiles among the Republicans. At last, Washington demanded that the French government

recall him; but by then Genêt's party, the Girondins, was out of power in France and the still more extreme Jacobins were in control, so it would not have been safe for him to return. The president granted him political asylum in the United States, and he settled with his American wife on a Long Island farm. The neutrality policy had survived its first great test.

A second challenge, an even greater one, came from Great Britain. Early in 1794, the Royal Navy began seizing hundreds of American ships engaged in trade in the French West Indies. At the news of the seizures, opinion in the United States became as strongly anti-British as it had recently been anti-French. Anti-British feeling rose still higher at the report that the governor general of Canada had delivered a warlike speech to the Indians on the Northwestern frontier. Hamilton was deeply concerned. War would mean an end to imports from England, and most of the revenue for maintaining his financial system came from duties on those imports.

Jay's Treaty

Hamilton and the other Federalists believed, therefore, that this was no time for ordinary diplomacy. They could not, they knew, rely on the State Department in their quest for a settlement with Britain. Jefferson had resigned as secretary of state in 1793 to devote more time to his political activities; but his successor, Edmund Randolph, was even more ardently pro-French than Jefferson had been. Hence the Federalists persuaded Washington to name a special commissioner to England: the staunch New York Federalist, former secretary for foreign affairs under the old Confederation, and current chief justice of the Supreme Court, John Jay. Jay was instructed to secure compensation for the recent British assaults on American shipping, to demand withdrawal of British forces from the frontier posts, and to negotiate a commercial treaty that would not violate America's existing treaty with France, signed at the time of the alliance in 1778.

Jay negotiated a long and complex treaty in 1794, and in the process he yielded more to Great Britain and obtained less for the United States than he had been instructed to do. But there was much to be said for the agreement. By settling the conflict with Britain, it gave the United States valuable time for peaceful development. It also provided for undisputed American sovereignty over the entire Northwest; and it produced a reasonably satisfactory commercial relationship with a nation whose trade was important to the United States. Nevertheless, when the terms were published, the treaty was bitterly denounced and Jay himself was burned in effigy in various parts of the country. The Republicans condemned the treaty virtually unanimously as a surrender to Britain and an assault on France. Even some Federalists were outraged. Opponents of the treaty went to extraordinary lengths to defeat it in the Senate; French agents aided them and cheered them on. The American minister to France, James Monroe, and even the secretary of state, Edmund Randolph, cooperated closely with the French in a desperate attempt to prevent ratification. But in the end the Senate, after making some amendments, consented to what was by then known as Jay's Treaty.

The treaty led directly to a settlement of America's important conflict with Spain. Fearing a joint Anglo-American challenge to Spanish possessions in North America, the Spanish government was now eager to appease the United States. Thus when Thomas Pinckney arrived in Spain as a special negotiator, he had no difficulty in gaining nearly everything that the United States had sought from the Spaniards for more than a decade. Under Pinckney's Treaty (signed in 1795), Spain recognized the right of Americans to navigate the Mississippi to its mouth and to deposit goods at New Orleans for reloading on ocean-going ships; agreed to fix the northern boundary of Florida where Americans always had insisted it should be, along the 31st parallel; and required Spanish authorities to prevent the Indians in Florida from raiding across the border.

The Downfall of the Federalists

The Federalists' impressive triumphs did not ensure their continued dominance in the national government. On the contrary, success seemed to produce problems of its own—problems that eventually led to their downfall.

Since almost everyone in the 1790s agreed that there was no place in a stable republic for an organized opposition, the emergence of the Republicans as powerful contenders for popular favor seemed to the Federalists a grave threat to national stability. When, beginning in the late 1790s, major international perils confronted the government as well, the temptation to move forcefully against the opposition became too great to resist. Facing what they believed was a stark choice between respecting individual liberties and preserving stability, the Federalists chose stability. The result was political disaster. After 1796, the Federalists never won another election. The popular respect for the institutions of the federal government, which they had worked so hard to produce among the people, survived. But the Federalists themselves gradually vanished as a meaningful political force.

The Election of 1796

As the time approached for the election of 1796, some friends of Washington urged him to run again. Already twice elected without a single vote cast against him in the electoral college, he could be counted on to hold the Federalist party together and carry it to a third great victory. But Washington, weary of the burdens of the office and disgusted with the partisan abuse that was now being heaped on him, was determined to retire to Mount Vernon. With Hamilton's assistance, he composed a long letter to the American people and had it published in a Philadelphia newspaper. The letter became known as Washington's "Farewell Address." Its reference to the "insidious wiles of foreign influence" was not just a warning against international entanglements; it was a denunciation of those Republicans who had been conspiring with the French to frustrate the Federalist diplomatic program.

There was no doubt that Jefferson would be the candidate of the Republicans in 1796, and he chose as his running mate the New York Republican leader, Aaron Burr. The Federalists faced a more difficult choice. Hamilton, the very personification of Federalism, was not "available" because his forthright views had created too many enemies. John Jay was too closely identified with his unpopular treaty. And Thomas Pinckney, although *his* treaty had been enthusiastically received, had the handicap of being a South Carolinian at a time when party leaders thought the next candidate should be a Northerner. John Adams, who as vice president was directly associated with none of the Federalist measures, finally received the party's nomination for president at a caucus of the Federalists in Congress; Pinckney received the nomination for vice president.

The Federalists were still clearly the dominant party, and there was little doubt of their ability to win a majority of the presidential electors. But with-

John Adams
Adams was America's leading diplomat in 1783, when he posed for this portrait by John Singleton Copley. His own illustrious career marked the beginning of four generations of great public distinction among members of his family.   (Fogg Art Museum, Harvard University)

ing and became vice president. (The Constitution provided for the candidate receiving the second highest number of electoral votes to become vice president—hence the awkward result of men from different parties serving in the nation's two highest offices. The Twelfth Amendment, adopted in 1804, reformed the electoral system to prevent such situations.)

Adams assumed the presidency, therefore, under inauspicious circumstances. He presided over a divided party, which faced a strong and resourceful Republican opposition committed to its extinction. And Adams himself was not the dominant figure in his own party; Hamilton remained the most influential Federalist, and Adams was never able to challenge him effectively. The new president was one of the country's most accomplished and talented statesman, but he had few skills as a politician. Austere, rigid, aloof, he showed no ability to conciliate differences, to solicit support, or to inspire enthusiasm. He was a man of enormous, indeed intimidating rectitude; and he seemed to assume that his own virtue and the correctness of his positions would alone be enough to sustain him. He was wrong.

The Quasi War with France

American relations with Great Britain and Spain improved as a result of Jay's and Pinckney's treaties. But the nation's relations with France, now under the government of the Directory, went from bad to worse. French vessels captured American ships on the high seas and at times imprisoned the crews. And when the South Carolina Federalist Charles Cotesworth Pinckney, brother of Thomas Pinckney, arrived in France to replace Monroe, the Directory refused to receive him as the official representative of the United States.

Some of the president's advisers, in particular Secretary of State Timothy Pickering (a rigid New Englander who detested France) favored war. Most (including Hamilton) recommended attempting to reach a peaceful settlement. Adams chose conciliation, and he appointed a bipartisan commission—consisting of Charles Pinckney, the recently rejected minister; John Marshall, a Virginia Federalist, later chief justice of the Supreme Court; and Elbridge Gerry, a Massachusetts Republican but a personal friend of the president—to negotiate with the Directory. When the three Americans arrived in France in 1797, three agents of the Directory's foreign minis-

out Washington to mediate, they fell victim to fierce factional rivalries that almost led to their undoing. Hamilton and many other Federalists (especially in the South) were not reconciled to Adams's candidacy and continued to prefer Pinckney. And when, as expected, the Federalists elected a majority of the presidential electors, some of these Pinckney supporters declined to vote for Adams; he managed to defeat Jefferson by only three electoral votes. Because a still larger number of Adams's supporters declined to vote for Pinckney, Jefferson finished second in the ballotter, Prince Talleyrand, demanded a loan for France and a bribe for French officials before any negotiations could begin. Pinckney delivered the commission's response in a succinct and angry phrase: "No! No! Not a sixpence!"

When Adams received the commissioners' report, he sent a message to Congress in which he urged readiness for war, denounced the French for their insulting treatment of the United States, and vowed he would not appoint another minister to France until he knew the minister would be "received, respected

and honored as the representative of a great, free, powerful and independent nation." The Republicans asked for proof of the president's charge that the United States had been insulted. And Adams responded by turning the commissioners' report over to Congress, after deleting the names of the three French agents and designating them only as Messrs. X, Y, and Z. When the report was published, the "XYZ Affair" provoked an even greater reaction than Adams had expected. There was widespread popular outrage at France's actions and strong popular sup-

Building an American Navy

After the Revolutionary War the United States abandoned the warships it had accumulated in its struggle with Great Britain, and for fifteen years there was no American navy. But when undeclared hostilities broke out with France in 1798, the federal government created a Department of the Navy and began a major shipbuilding program. This engraving shows work on the frigate *Philadelphia* in a Pennsylvania shipyard. The ship was not completed in time to be used against the French, but it saw action in 1803 during the war against Tripoli. When pirates from Tripoli captured the ship, American sailors staged a daring raid and destroyed it.   (New York Historical Society)

port for the Federalists' response. For nearly two years, 1798 and 1799, the United States found itself engaged in an undeclared war with France.

Adams quickly persuaded Congress to cut off all trade with France, abrogate the treaties of 1778, and authorize public and private vessels of the United States to capture French armed ships on the high seas. In 1798, Congress created a Department of the Navy and appropriated money for the construction of new warships. The navy soon won a number of duels with French vessels and captured a total of eighty-five ships, including armed merchantmen.

The United States had not only abandoned neutrality in the war between Britain and France. It was now cooperating so closely with the British as to be virtually a cobelligerent. Adams declined an English offer to lend ships to the United States, preferring that the nation build up a navy of its own. But the British did provide the American navy with shot and shell, furnished officers to help with the training and direction of American crews, and offered signaling information so that British and American ships could communicate readily with one another.

The French, taking notice of all this, finally began to see the wisdom of an accommodation with the Americans. Adams sent a new three-man commission to Paris in 1800; and the new French government (headed now by "first consul" Napoleon Bonaparte) agreed to a treaty with the United States that canceled the old agreement of 1778 and established new commercial arrangements. Federalists in the Senate objected that the agreement failed to provide compensation for American maritime losses at the hands of the French, and they delayed ratification until after Adams had left office. But the "quasi war" nevertheless came to a reasonably peaceful end, and the United States at last freed itself from the entanglements and embarrassments of its "perpetual" alliance with France.

Repression and Protest

The outbreak of hostilities in 1798 had given the Federalists an advantage over the political opposition, and in the congressional elections of that year they increased their majorities in both houses. But their newfound popularity seemed to go to their heads, and they began to consider new ways to weaken and silence the Republicans. Their pretext was the supposed necessity of protecting the nation from dangerous foreign and subversive influences in the midst of the undeclared war. The result was two of the most repressive pieces of legislation in American history: the Alien and Sedition Acts.

The Alien Act was aimed at those critics of the administration who were foreign by birth (many of them Irish and French). It placed new obstacles in the way of foreigners who wished to become American citizens, and it strengthened the president's hand in dealing with aliens. Even more ominous was the Sedition Act, which empowered the government to prosecute those who engaged in sedition against the government. In theory, only libelous or treasonous activities were subject to prosecution. But the law had the capacity to become a potent vehicle for stifling any opposition. The Republicans responded to the new laws with anger and dismay, interpreting them as part of a Federalist campaign to destroy them. The Alien and Sedition Acts became, as a result, the spark that finally ignited the political passions that had been building for nearly a decade.

John Adams signed the new laws, but he was reasonably cautious in implementing them. He did not act to deport any aliens, as he was empowered to do; and he prevented the government from launching a massive crusade against the opposition. Nevertheless, the legislation did have a significant repressive effect, enough to justify the fears of the Republicans that they were tyrannical in intent. The Alien Act, together with the Naturalization Act passed at approximately the same time, discouraged immigration and encouraged some foreigners already in the country to leave. And the administration made use of the Sedition Act to arrest several dozen men; ten were convicted. Most of those prosecuted were Republican newspaper editors whose only crime had been to criticize the Federalists in government.

The Republicans faced an important question as they attempted to decide how to oppose these laws, which they considered clear violations of the Constitution. What agency of government should decide the question of constitutionality? The Supreme Court had never attempted to invalidate an act of Congress; and the Republican leaders Jefferson and Madison concluded that the state legislatures should decide. They ably expressed their view in two sets of resolutions in 1798-1799, one written (anonymously) by Jefferson and adopted by the Kentucky legislature (1798, 1799) and the other drafted by Madison and approved by the Virginia legislature (1798). The Virginia and Kentucky Resolutions, as they were known, used the arguments of John Locke, which had become so familiar during the pre-Revolutionary crisis.

Congressional Pugilists, 1798
This cartoon was inspired by the celebrated fight on the floor of the House of Representatives between Matthew Lyon, a Republican representative from Vermont, and Roger Griswold, a Federalist from Connecticut. Griswold (at right) attacks Lyon with his cane, and Lyon retaliates with fire tongs. Other members of Congress seem to be enjoying the battle. (New York Public Library)

They asserted that the federal government had been formed by a "compact" or contract among the states. It was a limited government, possessing only certain delegated powers. Whenever it exercised any additional and undelegated powers, its acts were "unauthoritative, void, and of no force." The parties to the contract, the states, must decide for themselves when and whether the central government exceeded its powers. And "nullification" by the states was the "rightful remedy" whenever the general government went too far.

The Republicans failed to win wide support for their efforts on behalf of nullification; only Virginia and Kentucky voted to declare the congressional statutes void. They did, however, succeed in elevating their dispute with the Federalists to the level of a national crisis. By the late 1790s, the entire nation was as deeply and bitterly politicized as it would ever be in its history. The partisan divisions reached into every community. Friends and families became bitterly divided. State legislatures at times resembled battlegrounds; loud and angry debates were almost constant, and on several occasions there were rowdy fistfights and brawls in the legislative chambers. Even the United States Congress was plagued with violent disagreements. In one celebrated incident in the chamber of the House of Representatives, Matthew Lyon, a Republican from Vermont, responded to an insult from Roger Griswold, a Federalist from Connecticut, by spitting in Griswold's eye. Griswold attacked Lyon with his cane, Lyon fought back with

a pair of fire tongs, and soon the two men were engaged in a wrestling match on the floor. Such incidents were not only embarrassing to Congress; they served as a disturbing reminder to the public at large of the rancor and instability that had afflicted the nation under the Articles of Confederation. By 1800, it seemed as though the nation was on the verge of dissolving into chaos.

The "Revolution" of 1800

In this troubled atmosphere, Americans went about the task of electing a president in the fall of 1800. The presidential candidates were the same as four years earlier: Jefferson was the Republican nominee, with Aaron Burr again his running mate; Adams campaigned for reelection as a Federalist, with Charles Pinckney as the party's candidate for vice president.

The campaign of that year was probably the ugliest in American history. Adams and Jefferson themselves displayed reasonable dignity; but their supporters showed no such restraint. (It was during this campaign, for example, that the story of Jefferson's alleged romantic involvement with a black slave woman was first widely aired—a story the truth of which scholars continue to debate.) In addition to personal invective, each side argued strenuously that its opponents threatened the very existence of the republic. The Federalists accused Jefferson of being a dangerous radical and his followers of being wild men who, if they should come to power, would bring

---

SIGNIFICANT EVENTS

1783   Continental Congress leaves Philadelphia

1785   Continental Congress settles in New York

1786   Annapolis Conference meets

1787   Constitutional Convention in Philadelphia meets; Constitution adopted (September 17)

1787–1788   States ratify Constitution

1789   First elections held under Constitution
New government assembles in New York
Washington becomes first president
Bill of Rights adopted by Congress
Judiciary Act of 1789 is passed
French Revolution begins

1791   Hamilton issues "Report on Manufactures"
First Bank of the United States chartered
Vermont becomes fourteenth state

1792   Washington reelected without opposition
Kentucky becomes fifteenth state

1793   Citizen Genêt affair challenges American neutrality

1794   Whiskey Rebellion quelled in Pennsylvania
Jay's Treaty signed
Anthony Wayne defeats Indians in Ohio

1795   Pinckney's Treaty signed

1796   John Adams elected president

1798   XYZ Affair precipitates state of quasi war with France
Alien and Sedition acts passed
Virginia and Kentucky resolutions passed

1796   Tennessee becomes sixteenth state

1799   George Washington dies

1800   Jefferson and Burr tie vote in electoral college

1801   Jefferson becomes president after Congress confirms election
Judiciary Act of 1801 passed

---

on a reign of terror comparable to that of the French Revolution at its worst. The Republicans pictured Adams as a tyrant conspiring to become king; and they accused the Federalists of plotting to subvert human liberty and impose slavery on the people—accusations that mirrored the anti-British propaganda of the pre-Revolutionary years.

The election was close, and the crucial contest was in New York. There, Aaron Burr mobilized an organization of revolutionary war veterans, the Tammany Society, to serve as a Republican political machine. And through Tammany's efforts, the party carried the city by a large majority, and with it the state. Jefferson was, apparently, elected.

But an unexpected complication soon jeopardized the Republican victory. The Constitution called for each elector to "vote by ballot for two persons." The normal practice was for an elector to cast one vote for his party's presidential candidate and another for the vice presidential candidate. To avoid a tie, the Republicans had intended for one elector to refrain from voting for Burr. But the plan went awry. When the votes were counted, Jefferson and Burr each had 73. No candidate had a majority, and—in accordance with the Constitution—the House of Representatives was now empowered to choose between the two top

candidates, between Jefferson and Burr. Each state delegation would cast a single vote.

The Federalists controlled a majority of the states' votes in the existing Congress (the new Congress, elected in 1800, did not convene until after the inauguration of the president), and they had the privilege of deciding which of their opponents was to be the next president. Some hoped to use the situation to salvage the election for the Federalists; others wanted to strike a bargain with Burr and elect him. The House met in February 1801 to resolve the election and balloted again and again without mustering a majority for either Jefferson or Burr. Finally, a week before the inauguration, several leading Federalists concluded that Burr (whom many suspected of having engineered the deadlock in the first place) was too unreliable to trust with the presidency. On the thirty-sixth ballot, Jefferson was elected.

As a result of the election of 1800, the Republicans captured not only the presidency but a majority of the seats in both houses of the next Congress as well. The only branch of the government left in Federalist hands was the judiciary, and Adams and his fellow partisans during their last months in office took steps to make their hold on the courts secure. By the Judiciary Act of 1801, passed by the lame duck Congress, the Federalists reduced the number of Supreme Court justiceships by one but at the same time greatly increased the number of federal judgeships as a whole. The act created a separate system of circuit courts of appeal, standing between the federal district courts and the Supreme Court, to replace the old circuit courts on which district judges and Supreme Court justices had served together; and it called for the creation of ten new district judgeships.

Adams quickly appointed Federalists to the newly created positions. Indeed, some claimed that he stayed up until midnight on his last day in office, March 3, 1801, to complete the signing of the judges' commissions; these officeholders became known as the "midnight appointments." Since federal judges held office for life, the Federalists assumed that Jefferson would be powerless as president to remove Adam's appointees.

Despite these last Federalist efforts, the Republicans viewed their victory as almost complete. The nation had, they believed, been saved from tyranny. A new era could now begin, one in which the true principles on which America had been founded would once again govern the land. The exuberance with which the victors viewed the future—and the importance they ascribed to the defeat of the Federalists—was clearly revealed by the phrase Jefferson himself later used to describe his election. He called it the "Revolution of 1800." It remained to be seen how revolutionary it would really be.

SUGGESTED READINGS

General Histories   The framing of the Constitution is discussed in the general histories of the American Revolution listed in the readings for Chapter 5. An overview of the first years of American government under the Constitution is John C. Miller, *The Federalist Era, 1789–1802* (1960)

The Constitution   The fullest documentary account of the Constitutional Convention is Max Farrand (ed.), *Records of the Federal Convention of 1787*, 4 vols. (1911–1937). Farrand is also the author of one of the best accounts of the convention, *The Framing of the Constitution of the United States* (1913). One of the most influential and controversial works of American history is Charles A. Beard, *An Economic Interpretation of the Constitution of the United States* (1913), which argues that the Constitution was the product of conservative economic interests attempting to protect their investment in the national government. Harshly critical of the Beard argument are two works by Forrest McDonald: *We the People: The Economic Origins of the Constitution* (1958) and *E Pluribus Unum: The Formation of the American Republic, 1776–1790* (1965). Also critical of Beard is Robert E. Brown, *Charles Beard and the Constitution* (1956). Clinton Rossiter, *1787: The Grand Convention* (1965), is a careful account of the Constitutional Convention. See also Douglas Adair, *Fame and the Founding Fathers* (1974). Opposition to the Constitution is examined in Jackson Turner Main, *The Anti-Federalists* (1961), and in Alpheus T. Mason, *The States-Rights Debate* (1964). The best source for examining the argument for the Constitution is *The Federalist,* the most complete edition being that edited by J. E. Cooke (1961). Garry Wills, *Explaining America* (1981), is a study of *The Federalist Papers,* emphasizing the influence of the Scottish philosopher David Hume on the Founding Fathers. Linda G. DePauw, *The Eleventh Pillar: New York State and the Federal Constitution* (1966), studies the debate in a single state. Gerald Stourzh, *Alexander Hamilton and the Idea of Republican Government* (1970), is an intellectual portrait of one of the Constitution's chief defenders. See also Robert A. Rutland, *The Ordeal of the Constitution* (1966).

The Federalist Era   A general history of American government during the Federalist period (the 1790s) is John C. Miller, *The Federalist Era, 1789–1801* (1960). Leonard D. White, *The Federalists* (1948), is a valuable history of the process of setting up the administrative structure of the new government. The first administration under the Constitution is examined in Forrest McDonald, *The Presidency of George Washington* (1974). The second is discussed in Ralph Adams Brown, *The Presidency of John Adams* (1975); Stephen Kurtz, *The Presidency of John Adams* (1957); John R. Howe, *The Changing Political Thought of John Adams* (1966); and Manning Dauer, *The Adams Federalists* (1953). More specialized studies of the period include Richard Kohn, *Eagle and Sword: The Federalists and the Creation of the Military Establishment in America, 1783–1802* (1975), and Carl E. Prince, *The Federalists and the Origins of the U.S. Civil Service* (1978). Ralph Ketchum, *Presidents Above Party: The First American Presidency, 1789–1829* (1984), is an overview of the early presidency stressing the ideology underlying the performance of the first chief executives. Leonard Levy, *Legacy of Suppression: Freedom of Speech and Press in Early American History* (1960), discusses some of the controversies over civil liberties of the 1790s, as does James M. Smith, *Freedom's Fetters: The Alien and Sedition Laws and American Civil Liberties* (1956). Leland D. Baldwin, *The Whiskey Rebels* (1939), examines the most prominent challenge to the new government. Irving Brant, *The Bill of Rights* (1965), examines early protections of civil liberties; John C. Miller, *Crisis in Freedom* (1951), discusses early infringements.

The Jeffersonian Republicans   Charles A. Beard, *The Economic Origins of the Jeffersonian Opposition* (1915), is a classic study of the subject and, like his work on the Constitution, highly controversial. Joseph Charles, *The Origins of the*

American Party System (1956), challenges Beard's contention that the Jeffersonian opposition was a continuation of the antifederalism of small farmers in the 1780s. Noble Cunningham, *The Jeffersonian Republicans* (1957), is a good general account of the rise of opposition; Merrill D. Peterson, *Thomas Jefferson and the New Nation* (1970), is a biography of the opposition leader. The most authoritative biography of Jefferson is Dumas Malone, *Jefferson and His Time,* 6 vols. (1948–1981), of which Volume 3, *Jefferson and the Ordeal of Liberty,* examines the 1790s and the election of 1800. The emergence of party competition is examined in Richard Hofstadter, *The Idea of a Party System* (1970); Norman K. Risjord, *Chesapeake Politics, 1781–1800* (1978); Alfred F. Young, *The Democratic-Republicans of New York* (1967); and William N. Chambers, *Political Parties in a New Nation* (1963). Patricia Watlington, *The Partisan Spirit* (1972), examines the ideology of partisan conflict in Kentucky and its relation to national politics. John Zvesper, *Political Philosophy and Rhetoric: A Study of the Origins of American Party Politics* (1977), is a broader study. See also Richard W. Buel, Jr., *Securing the Revolution: Ideology in American Politics, 1789–1815* (1972). Joyce Appleby, *Capitalism and a New Social Order: The Republican Vision of the 1790s* (1984), is an important study of Republican ideology; Drew McCoy, *The Elusive Republic: Political Economy in Jeffersonian America* (1980), traces the efforts of the Jeffersonians (and of Jefferson and Madison in particular) to reconcile their ideology to the realities of the new republic.

Federalist Diplomacy   A classic overview is Felix Gilbert, *To the Farewell Address* (1961). Samuel F. Bemis, in *Jay's Treaty* (1923) and *Pinckney's Treaty* (1926, rev. 1960), examines two of the leading diplomatic episodes of the era. American relations with France are the subject of several important books: Alexander DeConde, *Entangling Alliance* (1958) and *The Quasi-War* (1966); Lawrence S. Kaplan, *Jefferson and France* (1967); Harry Ammon, *The Gênet Mission* (1973); and Louis M. Sears, *George Washington and the French Revolution* (1960). Bradford Perkins, *The First Rapprochement: England and the United States* (1967), and Charles Ritcheson, *Aftermath of Revolution: British Policy Toward the United States, 1783–1795,* examine Anglo-American relations. Paul A. Varg, *Foreign Policies of the Founding Fathers* (1963), is an overview.

The Founders   An unusual number of fine biographies of the major public figures of this period is available. In addition to the Malone biography of Jefferson mentioned above and the Freeman biography of Washington mentioned in the readings for Chapter 5, see Irving Brant, *James Madison* (1950); James T. Flexner, *George Washington,* 4 vols. (1965–1972); Page Smith, *John Adams* (1962); John C. Miller, *Alexander Hamilton* (1959); and Milton Lomask *Aaron Burr,* 2 vols. (1979, 1982).

Thomas Jefferson, **by Rembrandt Peale, 1805** (New-York Historical Society)

Chapter 7

The Jeffersonian Era

Thomas Jefferson and his followers assumed control of the national government in 1801 as the champions of a distinctive vision of America. They envisioned a society of sturdy, independent farmers, happily free from the workshops, the industrial towns, and the city mobs of Europe. They favored a system of universal education that would introduce all Americans to the scientific rationalism of the Enlightenment. They promoted a cultural outlook that emphasized localism and republican simplicity. And above all, they proposed a federal government of sharply limited power, with most authority remaining at the level of the states.

Almost nothing worked out as they had planned, for during their years in power the young republic was developing in ways that made much of their vision obsolete. The American economy in the period of Republican ascendancy became steadily more diversified and complex. Growing cities, expanding commerce, and nascent industrialism made the ideal of a simple, agrarian society impossible to maintain. The quest for universal education foundered, and the nation's institutions of learning remained largely the preserve of privileged elites. American cultural life, far from reflecting localism and simplicity, was dominated by a vigorous and ambitious nationalism reminiscent of (and often encouraged by) the Federalists. And although American religion began, as the Jeffersonians had hoped, to confront and adjust to the spread of Enlightenment rationalism, the new skepticism did not survive unchallenged. A great wave of revivalism, beginning early in the century, ultimately almost submerged the new rational philosophy.

The Republicans did manage to translate some of their political ideals into reality. Jefferson dismantled much of the Federalist power structure that had been erected in the 1790s, and he helped to ensure that in many respects the federal government would remain a relatively unimportant force in American life. Yet at the same time, he frequently encountered situations that required him to exercise strong national authority. On occasion, he used his power more forcefully and arbitrarily than his Federalist predecessors.

The Republicans did not always like these nationalizing and modernizing trends, and on occasion they resisted them. For the most part, however, they had the sense to recognize what could not be changed. And in adjusting to the new realities, they themselves began to become agents of the very transformation of American life they had once strenuously resisted.

The Rising Glory of America

In many respects, American cultural life in the early eighteenth century seemed to reflect the Republican vision of the nation's future. Opportunities for education increased; the nation's literary and artistic life began to free itself from European influences; and American religion came to terms with the ideas of the Enlightenment. In other respects, however, the new culture was posing a serious challenge to Republican ideals.

Education and Professionalism

Central to the Republican vision of America was the concept of a virtuous and enlightened citizenry. An ignorant electorate, the Jeffersonians believed, could not be trusted to preserve democracy; education, therefore, was essential. Jefferson himself called emphatically for a national "crusade against ignorance." Thus Republicans believed in the creation of a nationwide system of public schools, in which all male citizens would receive a free education.

Such hopes were not fulfilled. Although some states endorsed the principle of public education for all, none actually created a working system of free schools. A Massachusetts law of 1789 reaffirmed the colonial laws by which each town was obliged to support a school, but enforcement was so lax as to make it almost meaningless. Even in Boston, there were only seven public schools in 1790, most of them poorly housed. In Virginia, Jefferson had as wartime governor proposed a plan for universal elementary education and for advanced education for the gifted. Neither during nor after the war did the state legislature enact the proposal into law. As late as 1815—after more than a decade of Republican ascendancy in the nation's politics—not a single state had a comprehensive public school system.

Instead, schooling became primarily the responsibility of private institutions, most of which were open only to those who could afford to pay for them. In the South and in the mid-Atlantic states, most schools were run by religious groups; almost every institution required tuition from the parents of prospective students. Poor farmers and workers, therefore, were usually excluded. In New England (and to a lesser extent elsewhere), there were a growing number of private academies available to the children

The One-Room School
Children of many different ages came together in the one-room school. While one group recited, the others studied their lessons. A single teacher—often a recent college graduate supporting himself while preparing for a career in law or politics—had to instruct and discipline the children, tend the fire, and perform various custodial chores.   (Library of Congress)

of the relatively prosperous, but few schools for the less favored. Many of the new academies were modeled on those founded by the Phillips family: at Andover, Massachusetts, in 1778, and at Exeter, New Hampshire, three years later. By 1815, there were thirty such private secondary schools in Massachusetts, thirty-seven in New York, and several dozen more scattered throughout the country. Many were frankly aristocratic in outlook, training their students to become members of the nation's elite.

The Republican enthusiasm for education did not always include a belief in the importance of schooling for women. Private secondary schools such as those in New England generally accepted only male students; even many public schools excluded females from the classroom. No less than other groups of their era, the Republicans clung to a patriarchal vision of society, which envisioned virtuous white males presiding benevolently over a world in which all other groups—slaves, children, and women—would be dependent.

Yet the late eighteenth and early nineteenth centuries did see some important advances. American women in the eighteenth century had received very little education of any kind, and the female illiteracy rate at the time of the Revolution was appallingly high—at least 50 percent. At the same time, Americans had begun to place a new value on the importance of the "republican mother" in training the new generation. That raised an important question. If mothers remained ignorant, how could they raise their children to be enlightened? Such concerns led—beginning as early as the 1770s and accelerating thereafter—to the creation of a network of female academies throughout the nation (usually for the daughters of affluent families). Massachusetts required (beginning in 1789) that its public schools serve females as well as males. Other states (although not all) soon followed.

There were, however, strict limits to this new belief in education for women. Most men, at least, assumed that female education should serve only to make women better wives and mothers. There was no need, therefore, for women to receive advanced or professional training, no reason for colleges and universities to admit female students.

These assumptions did not go entirely unchallenged. In 1784, Judith Sargent Murray published an essay defending the rights of women to education, and defending it in terms very different from those used by most men. Men and women were equal in intellect and equal in potential, Murray argued.

Women, therefore, should have precisely the same educational opportunities as men. What was more, they should have opportunities to earn their own living, to establish a role for themselves in society apart from their husbands and families. Murray's ideas became an inspiration to later generations of women; but during most of her own lifetime (1751–1820), they attracted relatively little support.

The new educational system—whether for men or for women—provided opportunities sharply restricted by wealth. There were some efforts to provide the poor with access to this system of private education or with separate schools of their own. Religious schools and private academies occasionally waived tuition for some who could not afford to pay it. In New York, the Free School Society provided a special institution for the poor. But such efforts fell far short of fulfilling Jefferson's vision of equal and universal education. The institutions available to the poor were not nearly numerous enough to accommodate everyone; and the education they offered was often clearly inferior to that provided more prosperous students. The New York Free School, for example, economized by adopting the so-called Lancastrian method from England, by which teachers taught only a few bright student "monitors," who then drilled their fellow pupils in what they had learned.

There was a similar gap between the Republican ideal and the early eighteenth-century reality in the nature of American higher education. On the one hand, the number of colleges and universities in America grew substantially in the early years of the republic. At the outbreak of the Revolution there had been a total of nine colleges in all the colonies. By 1800, there were twenty-two, and the number continued to increase steadily thereafter. None of the new schools, however, was truly public. Even those established by state legislatures (in Georgia, North Carolina, Vermont, Ohio, and South Carolina, for example, all of which established universities between 1785 and 1805) relied on private contributions and on tuition fees to survive. Scarcely more than one man in a thousand (and no women at all) had access to any college education; and those few who did attend universities were almost without exception members of prosperous, propertied families.

The education that the colleges provided was, moreover, exceedingly limited—narrow training in the classics and a few other areas, and intensive work in theology. Indeed, the clergy was the only profession for which college training was generally required. There were a few institutions that attempted to provide advanced training in other fields to their students. The College of William and Mary in Virginia, the University of Pennsylvania, and Columbia College in New York all created law schools before 1800; but most lawyers continued to train for their profession simply by apprenticing themselves to practicing attorneys.

The University of Pennsylvania created the first American medical school early in the nineteenth century, under the leadership of Benjamin Rush. Most doctors, however, studied medicine by working with an established practitioner. And those such as Rush who believed in applying new scientific methods to medicine continued to struggle against age-old prejudices and superstitions. Efforts to teach anatomy, for example, encountered strong public hostility because of the dissection of cadavers that the study required. Medical knowledge remained so limited that cities were virtually helpless when faced with epidemics; only slowly did urban officials respond to the warnings of Rush and others that lack of adequate sanitation programs were to blame for disease. Individual patients often had more to fear from doctors than from illness itself. George Washington's death in 1799 was probably less a result of the minor throat infection that had afflicted him than of the efforts of his physicians to cure the disease by bleeding and "purging" him.

Education and professional training in the early republic thus fell far short of the Jeffersonian vision. Indeed, efforts to promote education often had the effect of strengthening existing elites rather than eroding them. Nevertheless, the ideal of equal educational opportunity survived, and in later decades it would become a vital force behind universal public education.

Cultural Nationalism

Jeffersonian Americans may have repudiated the belief of the Federalists in political and economic centralization. But they embraced another form of nationalism with great fervor. Having won political independence from Europe, they aspired now to a form of cultural independence. And in the process, they dreamed of an American literary and artistic life that would rival the greatest achievements of Europe. As a "Poem on the Rising Glory of America" had foretold as early as 1772, Americans believed that their "happy land" was destined to become the "seat of empire" and the "final stage" of civilization, with

"glorious works of high invention and of wond'rous art." The United States, one eighteenth-century writer proclaimed, would serve as "the last and greatest theatre for the improvement of mankind."

Such nationalism found expression, among other places, in early American schoolbooks. The Massachusetts geographer Jedidiah Morse, author of *Geography Made Easy* (1784), said the country must have its own textbooks so that the people would not be infected with the aristocratic ideas of England. The Connecticut schoolmaster and lawyer Noah Webster likewise contended that the American schoolboy should be educated as a patriot, his mind filled with nationalistic, American thoughts. "As soon as he opens his lips," Webster wrote, "he should rehearse the history of his own country; he should lisp the praise of liberty, and of those illustrious heroes and statesmen who have wrought a revolution in her favor."

Further to encourage a distinctive American culture and help unify the new nation, Webster insisted on a simplified and Americanized system of spelling—*honor* instead of *honour,* for example. His *American Spelling Book,* first published in 1783 and commonly known as the "blue-backed speller," eventually sold over 100 million copies, to become the best-selling book (except for the Bible) in the entire history of American publishing. Webster also wrote grammars and other schoolbooks. His school dictionary, issued in 1806, was republished in many editions and was eventually enlarged to become (in 1828) *An American Dictionary of the English Language.* His speller and his dictionary established a national standard of words and usages. Although Webster's Federalist political views fell into disfavor in the early nineteenth century, his cultural nationalism remained popular and influential.

Those Americans who aspired to create a more elevated national literary life faced a number of obstacles. There was, to be sure, a large potential audience for a national literature—a reading public developed in large part by the wide circulation of newspapers and political pamphlets during the Revolution. But there were few opportunities for a would-be American author to get his or her work before the public. Printers preferred to publish popular works by British writers (for which they had to pay no royalties); magazine publishers filled their pages largely with items clipped from British periodicals. Only those American writers willing to pay the cost and bear the risk of publishing their own works could compete for public attention.

Yet a growing number of American authors strove to create a strong native literature so that, as the poet Joel Barlow wrote, "true ideas of glory may be implanted in the minds of men here, to take the place of the false and destructive ones that have degraded the species in other countries." Barlow himself, one of a group of Connecticut writers known as the "Hartford Wits," published an epic poem, *The Columbiad,* in 1807, in an effort to convey the special character of American civilization. The acclaim it received helped to encourage other native writers.

Among the most ambitious was the Philadelphia writer Charles Brockden Brown. Like many Americans, he was attracted to the novel, a new literary form that had become popular in England in the late eighteenth century and had been successfully imported to America. But Brown sought to do more than simply imitate English forms; he tried to use his

The Return of Rip Van Winkle
The American artist John Quidor re-created this scene from Washington Irving's famous story, probably in 1849. Rip Van Winkle, awakened after a twenty-year sleep, looks around in bewilderment at the new world (and new nation) he has suddenly entered. Slouching against the tree is Rip's son, now grown, who seems familiar to the old man but whom he cannot quite recognize. This and other stories in Irving's *Sketch Book,* published in 1819, reflected the author's nostalgia for earlier times and his affection for the Hudson Valley region of New York, where he had spent much of his youth.   (National Gallery of Art, Washington)

novels to give voice to distinctively American themes, to convey the "soaring passions and intellectual energy" of the new nation. His obsession with originality led him to produce a body of work characterized by a fascination with horror and deviant behavior—novels that failed to develop a large popular following.

Far more successful was Washington Irving, a resident of New York who won wide acclaim for his satirical histories of early American life and his powerful fables of society in the New World. His popular folk tales, recounting the adventures of such American rustics as Ichabod Crane and Rip Van Winkle, made him the widely acknowledged leader of American literary life in the early nineteenth century and one of the few writers of that era whose works would continue to be read by later generations.

Perhaps the most influential works by American authors in the early republic were not poems, novels, or stories, but works of history that glorified the nation's past. Mercy Otis Warren, the influential pamphleteer and agitator during the 1770s, continued her literary efforts with a three-volume *History of the Revolution,* published in 1805 and emphasizing the heroism of the American struggle. Mason Weems, an Anglican clergyman, published a eulogistic *Life of Washington* in 1806, which became one of the best-selling books of the era. Weems had little interest in historical accuracy. He portrayed the aristocratic former president as a homespun man possessing simple republican virtues. (He also invented the story of the young Washington cutting down a cherry tree.) History, like literature, was serving as a vehicle for instilling a sense of nationalism in the American people.

Religion and Revivalism

The American Revolution had had a disastrous impact on traditional forms of religious practice. Not only had the Anglicans suffered for their alleged British sympathies and the Quakers for their pacifism, but the position of almost all churches had in some ways declined. The detachment of religion from government in the years following independence weakened some established religions—notably Congregationalism in New England. The ideology of individual liberty and reason weakened others. By the 1790s, although most Americans continued to hold strong religious beliefs, only a small proportion (perhaps as few as 10 percent) were members of formal churches. And the evangelical fervor aroused by the Great Awakening of the 1730s had almost entirely vanished. There were ample reasons for the frequent complaints of ministers during the Revolutionary era about the "decay of vital piety" and the luxurious growth of "vice."

Among the most disturbing challenges to religious traditionalists was the emergence of new, "rational" religious doctrines—theologies that attempted to reconcile modern, scientific attitudes with Christian faith. They offered an approach to religion that sharply deemphasized the role of God in the world and challenged much of conventional Christian orthodoxy. Some Americans—including Jefferson and Franklin—embraced "deism," which had originated among Enlightenment philosophers in France. Deists accepted the existence of God, but they considered Him a remote being who, after creating the universe, had withdrawn from direct involvement with the human race and its sins. Such views remained confined to a small group of highly educated people at first; but by 1800, deist ideas were reaching a much wider audience. Books and articles attacking religious "superstitions" were widely read and much discussed. Among the most influential was Thomas Paine's *The Age of Reason,* published between 1794 and 1796. Paine once declared that Christianity was the "strangest religion ever set up," for "it committed a murder upon Jesus in order to redeem mankind from the sin of eating an apple."

Religious skepticism also produced the philosophies of "universalism" and "unitarianism," which emerged at first as dissenting views within the New England Congregational church. Disciples of these new ideas rejected the traditional Calvinist belief in predestination, arguing that salvation was available to all. They rejected, too, the idea of the Trinity. Jesus was only a great religious teacher, they claimed, not the son of God. So wide was the gulf between these dissenters and the Congregationalist establishment that a permanent schism finally occurred. The Universalist church was founded as a separate denomination in Gloucester, Massachusetts, in 1779 (by James Murray, later the husband of Judith Sargent Murray), and the Unitarian church was established in Boston three years later.

Yet although many Americans believed that the spread of rationalism foretold the end of traditional, evangelistic religion in the new nation, nothing could have been further from the truth. Deism, universalism, and unitarianism all seemed more powerful than they actually were, in part because those who clung

The Camp Meeting

Camp meetings became a popular American institution of evangelical religion beginning in 1800. By the 1820s, there were approximately 1,000 such meetings a year, most of them in the South and the West. After one such meeting, in Maryland in 1806, a participant wrote: "Will I ever see anything more like the day of Judgment on this side of eternity—to see the people running, yes, running from every direction to the stand, weeping, shouting, and shouting for joy. . . . O! glorious day they went home singing and shouting." This painting, which dates from approximately 1830, suggests the degree to which women predominated in many religious revivals. (New-York Historical Society)

to more traditional faiths were for a time confused and disorganized, unable to react effectively. Beginning in 1801, however, traditional religion staged a dramatic comeback in the form of a wave of revivalism known as the Second Great Awakening.

The origins of the awakening lay in the efforts of conservative theologians of the 1790s to fight the spread of religious rationalism. Presbyterians strengthened their organization and expanded their efforts on the frontier, with conservatives in the church becoming increasingly militant in response to so-called New Light dissenters. Methodism, authoritarian and hierarchical in structure, was founded in England by John Wesley and spread to America in the 1770s, where it established itself as a formal church in 1784 under the leadership of Francis Asbury. The Methodists sent itinerant preachers throughout the nation to win recruits for the new church, which soon became the fastest-growing denomination in America. Almost as successful were the Baptists, who were themselves relatively new to America; they found an especially fervent following in the South.

By 1800, the revivalist energies of all these congregations were combining to create the greatest surge of evangelical fervor since the first Great Awakening sixty years before. Beginning among Presbyterians in several Eastern colleges (most notably at Yale, under the leadership of President Timothy Dwight), the new awakening soon spread throughout the country, reaching its greatest heights in the Western regions. In only a few years, a large proportion of the American people were mobilized by the movement; and membership in those churches embracing the revival—most prominently the Methodists, the Baptists, and the Presbyterians—was mushrooming. At Cane Ridge, Kentucky, in the summer of 1801, a group of evangelical ministers presided over the nation's first "camp meeting"—an extraordinary revival that lasted several days and impressed all who saw it with its size (some estimated that 25,000 people attended) and its fervor. Such events became common in subsequent years, as the Methodists in particular came to rely on them as a way to "harvest" new members. The Methodist circuit-riding preacher Peter Cartwright won national fame as he traveled from region to region exhorting his listeners to embrace the church. Even Cartwright, however, was often unprepared for the results of his efforts—a religious frenzy that manifested itself at times in convulsions, fits, rolling in the dirt, and the twitching "holy jerks."

The message of the Second Great Awakening was not entirely uniform, but its basic thrust was clear. Individuals must readmit God and Christ into their daily lives, must embrace a fervent, active piety, and must reject the skeptical rationalism that threatened traditional beliefs. Yet the wave of revivalism did not serve to restore the religion of the past. Few denominations any longer accepted the idea of predestination; and the belief that a person could affect his or her own destiny, rather than encouraging irreligion as many had feared, added intensity to the individual's search for salvation. Nor did the awakening work to reestablish old institutional forms of religion. Instead, it reinforced the spread of different sects and denominations and helped to create a general public acceptance of the idea that people could belong to different Protestant churches and still be committed to essentially the same Christian faith. Finally, the new evangelicalism—by spreading religious fervor into virtually every area of the nation, including remote regions where no formal church had ever existed—provided a vehicle for establishing a sense of order and social stability in communities still searching for an identity.

One of the striking features of the awakening was the preponderance of women involved in it. Young women, in particular, were drawn to revivalism; and female converts far outnumbered males. In some areas, church membership became overwhelmingly female as a result. One reason for this was that women were more numerous than men in certain regions during this era. Adventurous young men often struck out on their own and moved west; women, for the most part, had no such options. With their marriage prospects thus diminished, their futures plagued with uncertainty, women discovered in religion a foundation on which to build their lives. But even in areas where there was no shortage of men, women flocked to the revivals in enormous numbers, which suggests that they were responding as well to their changing economic roles. The movement of industrial work out of the home (where women had often contributed to the family economy through spinning and weaving) and into the factory—a process making rapid strides in the early nineteenth century—robbed women of one of their most important social roles. Religious enthusiasm not only helped compensate for that loss; it also provided access to a new range of activities associated with the churches—charitable societies ministering to orphans and the poor, missionary organizations, and others—in which women came to play important roles.

The Second Great Awakening also had significant effects on black Americans and on relations between the races. In many areas, revivals were open to people of all races; and many blacks not only attended, but ardently embraced the new religious fervor. Out of these revivals, in fact, emerged a substantial group of black preachers, who became important figures within the slave community. Some of them translated the apparently egalitarian religious message of the awakening—that salvation was available to all—

into a similarly egalitarian message for blacks in the present world. Out of black revival meetings in Virginia, for example, arose an elaborate plan in 1800 (devised by Gabriel Prosser, the brother of a black preacher) for a slave rebellion and attack on Richmond. The plan was discovered and the rebellion forestalled by whites; but revivalism continued in subsequent years to create racial unrest in the South. In the coming years, fears of such challenges to white supremacy led directly to a strengthening of the laws governing race relations.

The Second Great Awakening also had effects, of course, on the rational "freethinkers," whose skeptical philosophies had done so much to produce it. They did not disappear after 1800, but their influence rapidly declined; and for many years to come they remained a distinct and defensive minority within American Christianity. Instead, the dominant religious characteristic of the new nation was a fervent revivalism, which would survive well into the mid-nineteenth century.

The new religious enthusiasm meshed with the cultural and political optimism of the early republic. Many Americans were coming to believe that their nation had a special destiny: that its political system would serve as a model to the world, that its culture would become a beacon to mankind. Now there were voices arguing that the United States had a religious mission as well: that American revivalism would lead to the salvation of the entire globe. This expansive, at times even arrogant, assumption that Americans had been anointed to lead the world into a new era became one of the most powerful forces in the nation's outlook.

Stirrings of Industrialism

It was not only culturally and religiously that the nation was developing in ways unforeseen by Jefferson and his followers. Economically, the United States was taking the first, tentative steps toward a transformation that would ultimately shatter forever the vision of a simple, agrarian republic.

The Industrial Revolution in England

While Americans were engaged in a revolution to win their independence, an even more important revolution was in progress in England: the emergence of modern industrialism. Historians differ over precisely when the industrial revolution began, but it is clear that by the end of the eighteenth century it was well under way. Its essence was relatively simple: power-driven machines were taking the place of hand-operated tools and were permitting manufacturing to become more rapid and extensive. But however simple the causes, the social and economic consequences of the transformation were complex and profound.

The factory system in England took root first in the manufacture of cotton thread and cloth. There, one invention followed another in quick succession. Improvements in weaving made necessary improvements in spinning; and these changes required new devices for carding (combing and straightening the fibers for the spinner). Water, wind, and animal power continued to be important in the textile industry; but far more important was the emergence of steam power—which began to proliferate after the appearance of James Watt's advanced steam engine (patented in 1769). Cumbersome and inefficient by modern standards, Watt's engine was nevertheless a major improvement over the earlier "atmospheric" engine of Thomas Newcomen. England's textile industry quickly became the most profitable in the world, and it helped encourage comparable advances in other fields of manufacturing as well.

At the same time, England's social system was undergoing a wrenching change. Hundreds of thousands of men and women were moving from rural areas into cities to work in factories; and there they experienced both the benefits and the costs of industrialization. The standard of living of the new working class, when objectively quantified, was significantly higher than that of the rural poor. Most of those who moved from farm to factory, in other words, experienced some improvement in their material circumstances. But the psychological costs of being suddenly uprooted from one way of life and thrust into another, fundamentally different one often outweighed the economic gains. There was little in the prior experience of most workers to prepare them for the nature of industrial labor: disciplined, routinized work on a fixed schedule, which stood in sharp contrast to the varying, seasonal work pattern of the rural economy. Nor were the factory workers often prepared for life in the new industrial towns and expanding cities. They experienced, too, a fundamental change in their relationship with their employers. Unlike the landlords and local aristocrats of rural England, factory owners and managers—the

new class of industrial capitalists, many of them accumulating unprecedented wealth—were usually remote and inaccessible figures. They dealt with their workers impersonally, and the result was a growing schism between the two classes—each lacking access to or understanding of the other.

As a result, English life was being transformed at every level. The middle class was expanding and coming to dominate the economy, although not yet the culture or the nation's politics. Working men and women were beginning to think of themselves as a distinct class, with common goals and interests. And their simultaneous efforts to adjust to their new way of life and to resist its most damaging aspects made the late eighteenth and early nineteenth centuries a time of continuing social turbulence.

Not since the agrarian revolution thousands of years earlier, when humans had turned from hunting to farming for sustenance, had there been an economic change of a magnitude comparable to the industrial revolution. Centuries of traditions, of social patterns, of cultural and religious assumptions, were challenged and often shattered. Almost nothing would ever again be quite the same.

Technology in America

Nothing even remotely comparable to the English industrial revolution occurred in America in the first decade of the nineteenth century. Indeed, it was opposition to the kind of economic growth occurring in England that had helped the Republicans defeat the Federalists in 1800; and Americans continued to view British industrialization with deep ambivalence. Yet even while they warned of the dangers of rapid economic change, Americans of the age of Jefferson were welcoming a series of technological advances that would ultimately help ensure that the United States too would be transformed.

Some of these technological advances were imported from England. The British government attempted to protect the nation's manufacturing preeminence by preventing the export of textile machinery or the emigration of skilled mechanics. But despite such efforts, a number of immigrants arrived in the United States with advanced knowledge of English technology, eager to introduce the new machines to America. Samuel Slater, for example, used the knowledge he had acquired before leaving England to build a spinning mill in Pawtucket, Rhode Island, for the Quaker merchant Moses Brown in

Slater's Mill
Samuel Slater served as an apprentice in England in the 1780s to Richard Arkwright, an inventor of machinery for the new cotton mills that were driving the English industrial revolution. Slater left for America in 1789 disguised as a farm boy, because English law prohibited anyone with knowledge of such technology from emigrating and taking the nation's industrial "secrets" abroad. In 1790 he designed the first successful cotton-spinning mill in the United States at Pawtucket, Rhode Island; and in 1815 he added facilities for weaving woolen cloth. This drawing shows the Pawtucket bridge, falls, and mill as they appeared sometime between 1810 and 1819.   (Rhode Island Historical Society)

1790. It was generally recognized as the first modern factory in America.

More important than imported technology, however, was that of purely domestic origin. America in the early nineteenth century produced several important inventors of its own. Among them was Oliver Evans, of Delaware, who devised a number of ingenious new machines: an automated flour mill, a card-making machine, and others. He worked several important improvements in the steam engine, and in 1795 he published America's first textbook of mechanical engineering: *The Young Mill-Wright's and Miller's Guide*. In his own flour mill, which went into operation in 1787 (the year the Constitutional Convention first met), virtually all operations were mechanized. Only two men were required to operate the mill: one of them emptying a bag of wheat into the machinery, another putting the lid on the barrels of flour and rolling them away.

Even more influential for the future of the nation were the inventions of the Massachusetts-born, Yale-educated Eli Whitney, who revolutionized both cotton production and weapons manufacturing. The growth of the textile industry in England had created an enormous demand for cotton, a demand that planters in the American South were finding it impossible to meet. Their greatest obstacle was the difficulty of separating seeds from cotton fiber—a process that was essential before cotton could be sold. There was one variety of cotton with smooth black seeds and long fibers that was easily cleaned; but this long-staple or Sea Island variety could be grown successfully only along the coast or on the offshore islands of Georgia and South Carolina. There was not nearly enough of it to satisfy the demand. Another variety, short-staple cotton, could be grown almost anywhere in the South; but its sticky green seeds were extremely difficult to remove, and a skilled worker could clean no more than a few pounds a day by hand. Then, in 1793, Whitney, who was working at the time as a tutor on the Georgia plantation of General Nathanael Greene's widow, invented a machine that performed the arduous task quickly and efficiently. It was dubbed the cotton gin ("gin" being a derivative of "engine"); and it would soon transform the life of the South.

Mechanically, the gin was very simple. A toothed roller caught the fibers of the cotton boll and pulled them between the wires of a grating. The grating caught the seeds, and a revolving brush removed the lint from the roller's teeth. With the device, a single operator could clean as much cotton in a few hours as a group of workers had once needed a whole day to do. The results were profound. Soon cotton growing spread into the upland South; and within a decade, the total crop increased eightfold. Black slavery, which with the decline of tobacco production had seemed for a time to be a dwindling institution, was now restored to importance, expanded, and firmly fixed upon the South.

The cotton gin not only changed the economy of the South. It also helped transform the North. The large supply of domestically produced fiber served as a strong incentive to entrepreneurs in New England and elsewhere to develop a native textile industry. Few Northern states could hope to thrive on the basis of agriculture alone; by learning to process cotton, they could become industrially prosperous instead. The manufacturing preeminence of the North, which emerged with the development of the textile industry in the 1820s and 1830s, helped drive a wedge between the nation's two most populous regions and ultimately contributed to the coming of the Civil War. It also helped ensure the eventual Union victory.

Whitney also made a major contribution to the development of modern warfare, and with it a contribution to other industrial techniques. During the two years of undeclared war with France (1798 and 1799), Americans were deeply troubled by their lack of sufficient armaments for the expected hostilities. Production of muskets—each carefully handcrafted by a skilled gunsmith—was distressingly slow. Whitney responded by devising a machine to make each of the parts of a gun according to an exact pattern. Tasks could thus be divided among several workers, and one laborer could assemble a rifle out of parts made by several others. Before long, the same system was being applied to sewing machines, clocks, and many other complicated products.

The new technological advances were relatively isolated phenomena during the early years of the nineteenth century. Not until at least 1820 did the nation begin to develop a true manufacturing economy. But the inventions of this period were crucial in making the eventual transformation possible.

Trade and Transportation

One of the prerequisites for industrialization is a transportation system that allows the efficient conveyance of raw materials to factories and of finished goods to markets. The United States had no such system in the early years of the republic, and thus it had no domestic market extensive enough to justify large-scale production. Yet even then efforts were under way that would ultimately remove the transportation obstacle.

There were several ways to solve the problem of the small American market. One was to develop markets overseas; and American merchants continued their efforts to do that. One of the first acts of the new Congress when it met in 1789 was to pass two tariff bills giving preference to American ships in American ports, helping to stimulate an expansion of shipping. Also helpful was the outbreak of war in Europe in the 1790s, allowing Yankee merchant vessels to take over most of the carrying trade between Europe and the Western Hemisphere. As early as 1793, the young republic had a merchant marine and a foreign trade larger than those of any country except England. In proportion to its population, the United States had more ships and international commerce than any country in the world. And the shipping business was growing fast. Between 1789 and 1810, the total tonnage of American vessels engaged in overseas traffic rose from less than 125,000 to nearly 1 million. Only 30 percent of the country's exports had been carried in American ships in 1789; over 90 percent was being so carried by 1810. The figures for imports increased even more dramatically, from 17.5 percent to 90 percent in the same period.

Another solution to the problem of limited markets was to develop new markets at home, by improving transportation between the states and into the interior. Progress was slower here than in international shipping, but some improvements were occurring nevertheless. In river transportation, a new

Launching the Ship *Fame*, 1802
This painting by the American artist George Ropes shows the launching of a new merchant ship, the *Fame*, at Salem, Massachusetts, in 1802 amid banners and fanfare. Salem was one of several booming American ports whose ships sailed the world trading in exotic goods from Europe and Asia. (Essex Institute, Salem, Massachusetts)

era began with the development of the steamboat. Oliver Evans's high-pressure engine, lighter and more efficient than James Watt's, made steam more feasible for powering boats and, eventually, the locomotive, as well as mill machinery. Even before the high-pressure engine was available, a number of inventors experimented with steam-powered craft, and John Fitch exhibited to some of the delegates at the Constitutional Convention a forty-five-foot vessel with paddles operated by steam. The perfecting of the steamboat was chiefly the work of the inventor Robert Fulton and the promoter Robert R. Livingston. Their *Clermont,* equipped with paddle wheels and an English-built engine, sailed up the Hudson in the summer of 1807, demonstrating the practicability of steam navigation (even though it took the ship thirty hours to go 150 miles). In 1811, a

partner of Livingston, Nicholas J. Roosevelt (a remote ancestor of Theodore Roosevelt), introduced the steamboat to the West by sending the *New Orleans* from Pittsburgh down the Ohio and Mississippi. The next year, this vessel entered on a profitable career of service between New Orleans and Natchez.

Meanwhile, in land transportation, what was to become known as the turnpike era had begun. In 1792, a corporation constructed a toll road running the sixty miles from Philadelphia to Lancaster, with a hard-packed surface of crushed rock. This venture proved so successful that similar turnpikes (so named from the kind of tollgate frequently used) were laid out from other cities to neighboring towns. Since the turnpikes were built and operated for private profit, construction costs had to be low enough and the prospective traffic heavy enough to ensure an early and ample return. Therefore these roads, radiating from Eastern cities, ran for comparatively short distances and through thickly settled areas. Similar highways would not be extended over the mountains until the state governments or the federal government began to participate in the financing of the projects.

Country and City

Despite all the changes and all the advances, America remained in the early nineteenth century an overwhelmingly rural and agrarian nation. Only 3 percent of the population lived in towns of more than 8,000 at the time of the second census in 1800. Ten percent lived west of the Appalachian Mountains, far from what urban centers there were. Much of the country remained a wilderness. Even the nation's largest cities could not begin to compare, either in size or in cultural sophistication, with such European capitals as London and Paris.

Yet here too there were signs that the future might be different from the Jeffersonian vision of rural simplicity. The leading American cities might not yet have become world capitals, but they were large and complex enough to rival the important secondary cities of Europe. Philadelphia, with 70,000 residents, and New York, with 60,000, were becoming major centers of commerce, of learning, and of a distinctively urban culture. So too were the next largest cities of the new nation: Baltimore (26,000 in 1800), Boston (24,000), and Charleston (20,000).

Much remained to be done before this small and still half-formed nation would become a complex modern society. It was still possible in the early nineteenth century to believe that those changes might not ever occur. But forces were already at work that, in time, would lastingly transform the United States. And Thomas Jefferson, for all his commitment to the agrarian ideal, found himself as president obliged to confront and accommodate them.

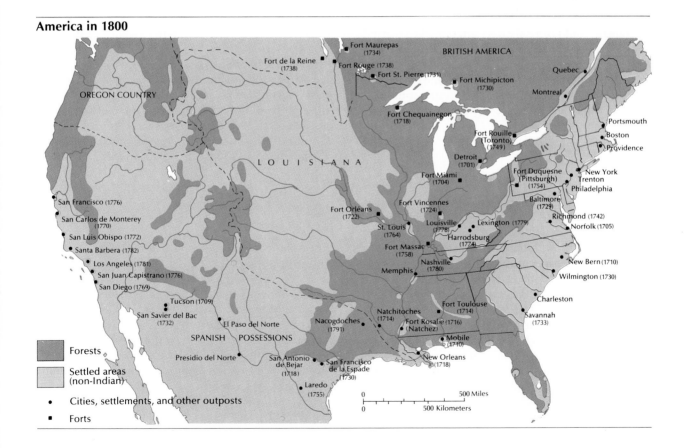

America in 1800

Forests

Settled areas (non-Indian)

• Cities, settlements, and other outposts

■ Forts

Jefferson the President

Privately, Thomas Jefferson may well have considered his victory over John Adams in 1800 to be what he later termed it: a revolution "as real . . . as that of 1776." Publicly, however, he was at the time restrained and conciliatory, attempting to minimize the differences between the two parties and calm the passions that the bitter campaign had aroused. "We are all republicans, we are all federalists," he said in his inaugural address. And during his eight years in office, he did much to prove those words correct. There was no complete repudiation of Federalist policies, no true "revolution." Indeed, at times Jefferson seemed to outdo the Federalists at their own work—most notably in overseeing a remarkable expansion of the territory of the United States.

In some respects, however, the Jefferson presidency did indeed represent a fundamental change in the direction of the federal government. The new administration oversaw a drastic reduction in the powers of some national institutions, and it forestalled the development of new powers in areas where the Federalists would certainly have attempted to expand them. Neither the executive nor the legislative branch of government was willing or able to exercise decisive authority in most areas of national life by the end of the Jeffersonian era. Only the courts continued trying to assert federal power in the ways the Federalists had envisioned.

The Federal City

The relative unimportance of the federal government during the era of Jefferson was symbolized by the character of the newly founded national capital, the city of Washington. John Adams had moved to the new seat of government during the last year of his administration. And there were many at that time who envisioned that the raw, uncompleted town would soon emerge as a great and majestic city, a focus for the growing nationalism that the Federalists were promoting. The French architect Pierre L'Enfant had designed the capital on a grand scale, with broad avenues radiating from the uncompleted Capitol building, which was to adorn one of the area's highest hills. Washington was, many Americans believed, to become the Paris of the United States.

In reality, throughout Jefferson's presidency—indeed throughout most of the nineteenth century—Washington remained little more than a straggling, provincial village. Although the population increased steadily from the 3,200 counted in the 1800 census, it never rivaled that of New York, Philadelphia, and the other major cities of the nation. One problem was the climate: wet and cold in winter, hot and almost unbearably humid in summer, reflecting the marshy character of the site. Another problem, however, was that those in the federal government responsible for the development of the city did little to further its growth. The Republican administrations of the early nineteenth century oversaw the completion of several sections of the present-day Capitol building, of the White House, and of a few other government buildings. Otherwise, they allowed the city to remain a raw, inhospitable community, one whose muddy streets were at times almost impassable, one in which the Capitol and the White House were often cut off from each other by rising creeks and washed-away bridges.

Members of Congress viewed the city not as a home but as a place to visit briefly during sessions of the legislature and leave as quickly as possible. Few owned houses in Washington. Most lived in a cluster of simple boardinghouses in the vicinity of the Capitol. It was not unusual for a member of Congress to resign his seat in the midst of a session to return home if he had an opportunity to accept the more prestigious post of member of his state legislature. During the summers, the entire government in effect packed up and left town. The president, the cabinet, the Congress, and most other federal employees spent the hot summer months far from the uncomfortable capital.

President and Party Leader

From the outset, Jefferson acted in a spirit of democratic simplicity in keeping with the frontierlike character of the unfinished federal city. Although a wealthy and aristocratic planter by background, the owner of more than a 100 slaves, and a man of rare cultivation and sophistication, he conveyed to the public an image of plain, almost crude disdain for pretension. He walked like an ordinary citizen to and from his inauguration at the Capitol, instead of riding in a coach at the head of a procession. In the presidential mansion, which had not yet acquired the name the White House, he disregarded the courtly etiquette of his predecessors (in part, no doubt, because as a widower he had no first lady to take charge of social

Washington, D.C., in the Early Nineteenth Century

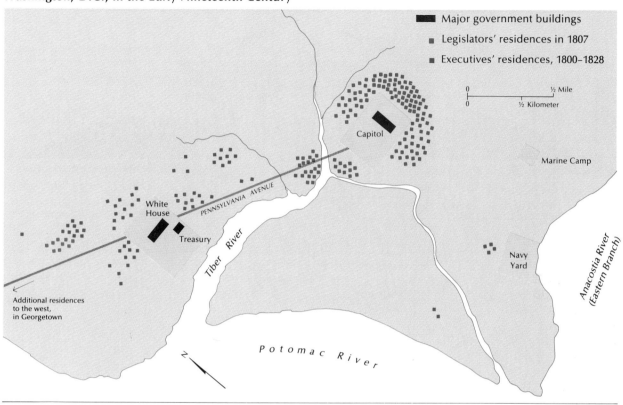

affairs). At state dinners, he let his guests scramble pell-mell for places at the table. He did not always bother to dress up, prompting the fastidious British ambassador to complain on one occasion of being received by the president in coat and pantaloons that were "indicative of utter slovenliness and indifference to appearances." Even when carefully dressed, the tall, freckle-faced, sandy-haired Jefferson did not offer an impressive physical appearance. He was shy. His posture was awkward. He walked with a shambling gait. And he was an ineffective public speaker.

Yet Jefferson managed nevertheless to impress most of those who knew him. He was a brilliant and charming conversationalist, a writer endowed with literary skills unmatched by any president before or since (with the possible exception of Lincoln), and undoubtedly one of the nation's most intelligent and creative men, with a wider range of interests and accomplishments than any public figure in American history. In addition to politics and diplomacy, he was an active architect, educator, inventor, scientific farmer, and philosopher-scientist. He diverted himself with such pastimes as sorting the bones of prehistoric animals or collecting volumes for one of the nation's greatest private libraries (which later became the basis of the original Library of Congress). Many years later, President John Kennedy referred to a White House dinner for Nobel Prize laureates as the greatest collection of genius ever gathered in the building except for those nights when "Thomas Jefferson dined alone."

Jefferson was, above all, a shrewd and practical politician, equaled in that regard perhaps only by Lincoln and Franklin D. Roosevelt. On the one hand, he went to great lengths to eliminate the aura of majesty surrounding the presidency that he believed his predecessors had created. He decided, for example, to submit his messages to Congress not by delivering them in person, as Washington and Adams had done, but by sending them in writing, thus avoiding even the semblance of attempting to dictate to the legislature. (The precedent he established survived for more than a century, until the administration of Woodrow Wilson.) At the same time, however, Jefferson

Jefferson the Architect

Thomas Jefferson drew this sketch of the front elevation of his house at Monticello, in Virginia. The upper portico specified here was never completed; and the octagonal structures on either end of the house are not shown. Jefferson drew elaborate plans for almost every part of Monticello and provided precise specifications down to the last detail. Among his other architectural accomplishments is the splendid central campus of the University of Virginia. (Massachusetts Historical Society)

worked hard to exert influence as the leader of his party, giving direction to Republicans in Congress by quiet and sometimes even devious means.

To his cabinet he appointed members of his own party who shared his philosophy. His secretary of state was James Madison, a long-time friend and neighbor in Virginia whose collaboration with the president throughout Jefferson's administration was so close that it was often difficult to tell who was more responsible for government policy. Secretary of the treasury was Albert Gallatin, a Swiss-born politician with a French accent who, despite a financial expertise that made him the rival of Hamilton, was a staunch opponent of Federalist policies. He had, for

example, once acted as the lawyer defending the tax-resisting western Pennsylvania farmers who were engaged in the Whiskey Rebellion.

Although the Republicans had objected strenuously to the efforts of their Federalist predecessors to build a network of influence through patronage, Jefferson too used his powers of appointment as an effective political weapon. Like Washington before him, he believed that federal offices should be filled with men loyal to the principles and policies of the administration. True, he did not attempt a sudden and drastic removal of Federalist officeholders, possibly because of assurances to the contrary that had been given in his name when Federalist votes in Congress were needed to break the tie with Burr. Yet at every convenient opportunity he replaced the hold-overs from the Adams administration with his own trusted followers. By the end of his first term about half the government jobs, and by the end of his second term practically all of them, were held by loyal Republicans. The president punished Burr and the Burrites by withholding patronage from them; he never forgave the man whom he believed guilty of plotting to frustrate the intentions of the party and the ambitions of its rightful candidate.

The Twelfth Amendment, added to the Constitution in 1804 before the election of that year, ensured that a tie vote between the presidential and vice-presidential candidates of the same party could not occur again. The amendment recognized by implication the function of political parties; it stipulated that the electors should vote for president and vice president as separate and distinct candidates. Burr had no chance to run on the ticket with Jefferson a second time. In place of Burr, the congressional caucus of Republicans nominated his New York factional foe, George Clinton. The Federalist presidential nominee, Charles C. Pinckney, fared poorly against the popular Jefferson, who carried even the New England states (except Connecticut) and was reelected by the overwhelming electoral majority of 162 to 14. The Republican membership of both houses of Congress increased.

Jefferson's popularity faded during his second term, and he had to deal with a revolt within the party ranks. His brilliant but erratic relative John Randolph of Roanoke, the House leader, turned against him, accusing him of acting like a Federalist instead of a states' rights Republican. Randolph mustered a handful of anti-Jefferson factionalists, who called themselves "Quids." Randolph's most importance grievance stemmed from a controversy over Western land claims. The Georgia legislature, before ceding its territorial rights to the federal government, had made and then canceled a grant of millions of acres along the Mississippi to the Yazoo Land Companies. The fate of the so-called Yazoo claims remained a subject of debate for years. Jefferson favored a compromise settlement that would have satisfied both the state of Georgia and the Yazoo investors, many of whom were Northern Republicans whose support he needed. But Randolph insisted that the company's claims were fraudulent and charged the president with complicity in corruption. A number of members of Congress were investors in the land companies or supporters of their claims, and time

and again the tall, skinny Virginian would point his bony finger at one or another of these men and shriek contemptuously, "Yazoo!" He prevented the government from making any settlement of the question until both he and Jefferson were out of office. (See pp. 258–259.)

Dollars and Ships

Despite Jefferson's use of forceful political methods, his administration did move far toward dismantling the federal power structure that the Federalists had attempted to erect. Under Washington and Adams, the Republicans believed, the government had been needlessly extravagant. Yearly federal expenditures had nearly tripled between 1793 and 1800. The public debt had also risen, as Hamilton had intended. And an extensive system of internal taxation, including the hated whiskey excise tax, had been erected.

The Jefferson administration moved deliberately to reverse the trend. In 1802, it persuaded Congress to abolish all internal taxes, leaving customs duties and the sale of Western lands as the only source of revenue for the government. At the same time, Secretary of the Treasury Gallatin carried out a plan for drastic retrenchment in government spending, scrimping as much as possible on expenditures for the normal operations of government, cutting the already small staffs of the executive departments to minuscule levels. Although Jefferson was unable entirely to retire the national debt as he had hoped, he did cut it almost in half (from $83 million to $45 million).

Jefferson also effected a "chaste reformation" of the armed forces. The tiny army of 4,000 men he reduced to 2,500. The navy he pared down from twenty-five ships in commission to seven, cutting the number of officers and sailors accordingly. Anything but the smallest of standing armies, he argued, might menace civil liberties and civilian control of government. And a large navy, he feared, might be misused to promote overseas commerce, which Jefferson believed should remain secondary to agriculture.

Yet despite his claims that "Peace is our passion," Jefferson was not a pacifist. At the same time that he was reducing the size of the army and navy, he was helping to establish the United States Military Academy at West Point, founded in 1802. And when trouble began brewing overseas, he began again to build up the fleet.

The Barbary Wars
The first American naval force to combat the Barbary Coast pirates proved inadequate to defeat the forces of Tripoli, and in 1803 President Jefferson sent reinforcements. Among those joining the war in that year was Lieutenant Stephen Decatur, who was later to win fame as a naval commander in the War of 1812. He is shown here in hand-to-hand combat with Algerians attacking his ship. In 1804 he engineered a daring raid during which Americans destroyed the frigate *Philadelphia,* which had been captured by Tripoli.   (Brown Brothers)

Such trouble appeared first in the Mediterranean, off the coast of northern Africa. For years the Barbary states of North Africa—Morocco, Algiers, Tunis, and Tripoli (now part of Libya)—had made piracy a national enterprise. They demanded protection money from all nations whose ships sailed the Mediterranean. Even the ruler of the seas, Great Britain, gave regular contributions to the pirates. (England did not in fact particularly desire to eliminate a racket that hurt its naval rivals and maritime competitors more seriously than itself.) During the 1780s and 1790s the United States agreed to treaties providing for annual tribute to Morocco and the rest, and from time to time the Adams administration ransomed American sailors who had been captured and were being held as slaves. Jefferson was reluctant to continue this policy of appeasement. "Tribute or war is the usual alternative of these Barbary pirates," he said. "Why not build a navy and decide on war?"

The decision was not left to Jefferson. In 1801, the pasha of Tripoli, dissatisfied with the American response to his extortionate demands, had the flagpole of the American consulate chopped down—his way of declaring war. Jefferson concluded that, as president, he had a constitutional right to defend the United States without a war declaration by Congress; and he sent a naval squadron to relieve American ships already at the scene. Not until 1803, however, was the fleet strong enough to take effective action, under commodores Edward Preble and Samuel Barron. In 1805, the pasha, by threatening to kill captive

Americans, compelled Barron to agree to peace. The agreement ended the payment of tribute to Tripoli by America, but it exacted from the United States a substantial (and humiliating) ransom of $60,000 for the release of the prisoners.

Conflict with the Courts

Having won control of the executive and legislative branches of government, the Republicans looked with suspicion on the judiciary, which remained largely in the hands of Federalist judges. Soon after Jefferson's first inauguration, his followers in Congress launched an attack on this last preserve of the opposition. First, the legislators repealed the Judiciary Act of 1801, thus abolishing the new circuit courts and arranging instead for each of the Supreme Court justices to sit with a district judge on circuit duty. With their energies stretched thin, the Republicans believed, the jurists would be unable to become active or influential foes. Jefferson lacked authority to remove Adams's "midnight appointees" from their newly created jobs; but Congress had achieved the same objective by pulling their benches out from under them, despite Federalist protests that the repeal violated the constitutional provision that judges should hold office for life.

The debate over the Judiciary Act of 1801 led to one of the most important judicial decisions in the history of the nation. Federalists had long maintained that the Supreme Court had the authority to review acts of Congress and to nullify those that were in conflict with the Constitution. Hamilton had argued for such a power in *The Federalist Papers* (although the Constitution said nothing specifically to support him), and the Court itself had actually exercised the review power in 1796 when it upheld the validity of a law passed by the legislature. But the Court's authority would not be secure, it was clear, until it actually declared a congressional act unconstitutional.

In 1803, in the case of *Marbury* v. *Madison,* it did so. William Marbury, one of Adams's "midnight appointments," had been named a justice of the peace in the District of Columbia. But his commission, although duly signed and sealed, had not been delivered to him before Adams left office. Madison, who as Jefferson's secretary of state was responsible for transmitting appointments, then refused to hand over the commission. Marbury applied to the Supreme Court for an order (a writ of mandamus) directing Madison to perform his official duty. In a historic ruling, the Court found that Marbury had a right to his commission but that the Court had no authority to order Madison to deliver it. On the surface, therefore, the decision was a victory for the administration. But of far greater importance than the relatively insignificant matter of Marbury's commission was the Court's reasoning in the decision.

The original Judiciary Act of 1789 had given the Court the power to compel executive officials to act in such matters as the delivery of commissions, and it was on that basis that Marbury had filed his suit. But the Court ruled that Congress had exceeded its authority, that the Constitution had defined the powers of the judiciary, and that the legislature had no right to expand them. The relevant section of the 1789 act was, therefore, void. In seeming to deny its own authority, the Court was in fact radically enlarging it. The justices had repudiated a relatively minor power (the power to force the delivery of a commission) by asserting a vastly greater one (the power to nullify an act of Congress). The administration, recognizing the significance of the ruling, was alarmed. But since the Court had shrewdly encased this assertion of its power within a ruling favorable to the government, there was no way for the Republicans to respond.

The chief justice of the United States at the time of the ruling was (as he would remain until 1835) John Marshall, one of the towering figures in the history of American law. A leading Federalist and prominent Virginia lawyer, he had served John Adams as secretary of state. (It had been Marshall,

ironically, who had neglected to deliver Marbury's commission in the closing hours of the administration.) In 1801, just before leaving office, Adams had appointed him chief justice; and almost immediately Marshall established himself as the dominant figure on the Court, shaping virtually all its most important rulings—including, of course, *Marbury* v. *Madison.* Marshall had served with George Washington's army at Valley Forge during the Revolution, and he retained from the experience a vivid impression of a weak, divided, and inefficient government. Through a succession of Republican presidents, he battled to give the federal government unity and strength. And in so doing, he established the judiciary as a coequal branch of government with the executive and the legislature—a position that the founders of the republic had never clearly indicated it should occupy.

Jefferson recognized the threat that an assertive judiciary could pose to his policies, and even while the *Marbury* case was still pending he was preparing for a renewed assault on the last Federalist stronghold. If he could not remove the judges he considered obnoxious directly, perhaps he could do so indirectly through the process of impeachment. According to the Constitution, the House of Representatives was empowered to bring impeachment charges against any civil officer for "high crimes and misdemeanors," and the Senate sitting as a court was authorized to try the officer on the charges. Jefferson sent evidence to the House to show that one of the district judges, John Pickering of New Hampshire (who was suffering from severe mental illness), was unfit for his position. The House accordingly impeached him, the Senate found him guilty of high crimes and misdemeanors, and Pickering was removed from the bench.

Later the Republicans went after bigger game, a justice of the Supreme Court itself. Justice Samuel Chase, a rabidly partisan Federalist, had in the 1790s applied the Sedition Act with what the Republicans considered particular brutality; and he had delivered political speeches from the bench, insulting President Jefferson and denouncing the Jeffersonian doctrine of equal liberty and equal rights. In so doing, Chase was guilty of no high crime or misdemeanor in the constitutional sense, and he was only saying what thousands of Federalists believed. Some Republicans concluded, however, that impeachment should not be viewed merely as a criminal proceeding and that a judge could properly be impeached for political reasons—for obstructing the other branches of the government and disregarding the will of the people.

At Jefferson's own suggestion, the House of Representatives set up a committee to investigate Chase's conduct. Impeached on the basis of the committee's findings, the justice was brought to trial before the Senate early in 1805. Jefferson did his best to secure a conviction, even temporarily cultivating the friendship of Aaron Burr, who as vice president presided over the trial. But Burr performed his duties with aloof impartiality, and John Randolph as the impeachment manager bungled the prosecution. A majority of the senators finally voted for conviction, but not the necessary two-thirds majority. Chase was acquitted.

In one sense, the effort to impeach Chase was helpful to the Republicans despite the failure, for it pressured federal judges as a whole to be more discreet and less partisan in statements from the bench. Federalist jurists had reason to fear that were they to antagonize the Republicans and the public too greatly, future impeachment efforts might succeed. But in a larger sense, the Republican assault on the judiciary was a failure. Marshall remained secure in his position as chief justice. The duel between the Court and the president continued. And the judiciary survived as a powerful force within the government—more often than not on behalf of the centralizing, expansionary policies that the Republicans had been trying to reverse.

Doubling the National Domain

In the same year that Jefferson was elected president of the United States, Napoleon Bonaparte made himself ruler of France with the title of first consul; and in the year that Jefferson was reelected, Napoleon assumed the name and authority of emperor. The two men had little in common. Yet for a time they were of great assistance to each other in international politics—until Napoleon's ambitions moved from Europe to America and created conflict and estrangement.

Jefferson and Napoleon

Napoleon failed in a grandiose plan to seize India from the British Empire (although he succeeded in the conquest of Italy), and his imperial ambitions began to seek a new target. France, he recalled, had once possessed a vast empire in North America; and he began to dream of extending French power into the New World once again. The French possessions east of the Mississippi had been ceded to Great Britain in 1763 and were now, for the most part, incorporated within the United States. Those territories were lost to France forever. But the lands west of the Mississippi France had ceded to Spain, now a relatively weak neighbor; and those, Napoleon believed, could be recovered. In 1800 (on the day after the French agreed to the settlement with the United States, ending the quasi war), Napoleon reached a secret agreement with Spain (the treaty of San Ildefenso) to reacquire these North American possessions. Thus France once again held title to Louisiana, which included almost the whole of the Mississippi Valley to the west of the river, plus New Orleans to the east of the river near its mouth. Napoleon hoped that Louisiana would form the continental heartland of his proposed North American empire.

Other essential parts of his empire-to-be were the sugar-rich and strategically valuable West Indian islands that still belonged to France—Guadeloupe, Martinique, and above all Santo Domingo. Plans for the islands were threatened, however, by unrest among the Caribbean slaves. Blacks in Santo Domingo had been inspired by the French Revolution to rise in revolt and create a republic of their own, under the remarkable black leader, Toussaint L'Ouverture. Taking advantage of a truce in his war with England, Napoleon sent to the West Indies an army led by his brother-in-law Charles Leclerc, which crushed the insurrection and restored French authority.

Jefferson was for a time unaware of Napoleon's imperial ambitions in America, and he pursued a foreign policy that reflected his well-known admiration for France. He appointed as the American minister to Paris the ardently pro-French Robert R. Livingston. Continuing the peace policy of Adams, he worked to secure ratification of the Franco-American settlement of 1800 and began observing the terms of the treaty even before it was ratified. The Adams administration had joined with the British in recognizing and supporting the rebel regime of Toussaint in Santo Domingo; Jefferson assured the French minister in Washington that the American people, especially those of the slaveholding states, did not approve of the black revolutionary, who was setting a bad example for their own slaves. He even implied that the United States might join with France in putting down the rebellion (although nothing ever came of the suggestion).

UNDER MY WINGS EVERY THING PROSPERS

New Orleans in 1803
Because of its location near the mouth of the Mississippi River, New Orleans was the principal port of western North America in the early nineteenth century. Through it, Western farmers shipped their produce to markets in the East and Europe. This 1803 painting celebrates the American acquisition of the city from France as part of the Louisiana Purchase. (Chicago Historical Society)

Jefferson began to reappraise the whole subject of American relations with France when he heard rumors of the secret retrocession of Louisiana. "It completely reverses all the political relations of the U.S.," he wrote to Minister Livingston on April 18, 1802. Always before, America had looked to France as its "natural friend." But there was on the earth "one single spot" the possessor of which was "our natural and habitual enemy." That spot was New Orleans, the outlet through which the produce of the fast-growing Western regions of the United States was shipped to the markets of the world. If France should actually take and hold New Orleans, Jefferson said, then "we must marry ourselves to the British fleet and nation."

Jefferson was even more alarmed when, in the fall of 1802, he learned that the Spanish intendant at New Orleans (who still governed the city, since the French had not yet taken formal possession of the region) announced a disturbing new regulation. American shippers servicing the Mississippi River had for many years been accustomed to depositing their cargoes in New Orleans for transfer to ocean-going vessels. The intendant now forbade the practice, even though Spain had guaranteed Americans that right in the Pinckney Treaty of 1795. Without such a right, the lower Mississippi would be effectively closed to American shippers.

Westerners suspected that Napoleon himself had ordered the closing of the river for sinister purposes of his own, and they demanded that something be done to reopen it. Some of the more extreme among them clamored for war with France; and they were joined in that clamor by the Federalists of the Northeast, who were not greatly concerned about the specific problems of the Westerners but who believed that by encouraging Western discontent they could embarrass the Jefferson administration. The president faced a dilemma. If he yielded to the frontier clamor and sought satisfaction through force, he would run the risk of a major war with France. If, on the other hand, he ignored the Westerners' demands, he might lose their political support.

Jefferson, however, saw another way out of the dilemma: the purchase of New Orleans from Napoleon. Jefferson was not particularly interested in acquiring the lands of Louisiana to the west of the Mississippi. But he was eager to acquire the vital port city; and almost as soon as he heard the rumors of Napoleon's reacquisition of the Louisiana Territory, he instructed Livingston in Paris to negotiate for the purchase of New Orleans. Livingston on his own authority suggested to the French that they might be glad to be rid of the upper part of Louisiana as well.

Jefferson also persuaded Congress to appropriate funds for an expansion of the army and the construction of a river fleet, and he allowed the impression to emerge that American forces, despite his own desire for peace, might soon descend on New Orleans. At the same time, he dispatched a special envoy to work with Livingston in Paris: James Monroe, who had served as minister to France in the 1790s and was well remembered there, and who was popular among Westerners in the United States. Jefferson told Monroe that if he and Livingston could not reach satisfactory terms with the French, they should cross the Channel and begin discussions with the British government. No one ever had a chance to determine whether Jefferson was serious in his hints of an attack on New Orleans and an alliance with Great Britain or whether he was merely attempting to put pressure on the French. Because even before Monroe arrived in Paris, Napoleon suddenly decided to dispose of the entire Louisiana Territory.

Startling though this decision seemed to some of his advisers, Napoleon had good reasons for it. His plans for an American empire had already gone seriously awry, partly because of misfortunes best described in two words—*mosquitoes* and *ice*. Mosquitoes had brought yellow fever and death to General Leclerc and to thousands of the soldiers whom Napoleon had sent to reconquer Santo Domingo. Ice had locked in a Dutch harbor earlier than anticipated in the winter of 1802. That had delayed the departure of an ex-

peditionary force that Napoleon wished to send to reinforce Leclerc's army and take possession of Louisiana. When the harbor thawed in the spring of 1803, it was too late to send the fleet to America. By then, Napoleon was preparing for a renewed war in Europe and feared that he would not be able to hold Louisiana if the British, with their superior naval power, should attempt to take it. He also realized that, quite apart from the British threat, there was danger from the United States itself. It would be virtually impossible to prevent the Americans, who were pushing steadily into the Mississippi Valley, from overrunning Louisiana sooner or later.

The Louisiana Purchase

Napoleon left the negotiations over Louisiana to his finance minister, Barbé-Marbois, rather than his foreign minister, Talleyrand (since Talleyrand was remembered and distrusted in America for the XYZ Affair). Barbé-Marbois had lived for some time in the United States and had married an American woman; the delegates from the United States considered him trustworthy. Livingston and Monroe had to decide first whether they should even consider making a treaty for the purchase of the entire Louisiana Territory, since they had not been authorized by their government to do so. But they were reluctant to wait for new instructions from home; they feared Napoleon might withdraw his offer as suddenly as he had made it. And so, aware that Jefferson could always reject any treaty they negotiated, they decided to proceed. After some haggling over the price—Barbé-Marbois asked and got somewhat more than Napoleon's minimum—Livingston and Monroe signed the agreement on April 30, 1803.

By the terms of the treaty, the United States was to pay a total of 80 million francs ($15 million), directly or indirectly to the French government. The United States was also to grant certain exclusive commercial privileges to France in the port of New Orleans. Moreover, the United States was to incorporate the residents of Louisiana into the Union and grant them as soon as possible the same rights and privileges as other citizens—an implication that the new territories would soon be admitted as states. The boundaries were not clearly defined; the treaty simply specified that Louisiana would occupy the "same extent" as it had when owned by France and Spain. When Livingston and Monroe appealed to Talleyrand for his opinion about the boundary, he merely replied: "You have made a noble bargain for your-selves, and I suppose you will make the most of it."

In Washington, the president was both pleased and embarrassed when he received the treaty. He was glad to get such a "noble bargain"; but according to his oft-repeated views on the Constitution, the United States government lacked authority to accept it. Jefferson had always insisted that the federal government could rightfully exercise only those powers explicitly assigned to it, and nowhere did the Constitution say anything about the acquisition of new territory. But his advisers argued that his treaty-making power under the Constitution would justify the purchase of Louisiana. Finally the president gave in, trusting, as he said, "that the good sense of our country will correct the evil of loose construction when it shall produce ill effects."

Jefferson called Congress into special session. And despite objections to the treaty from a few die-hard Federalists from New England, the Senate promptly gave its consent and the House soon passed the necessary appropriation bill. Spain was then still administering Louisiana; the French had never taken actual possession. Finally, late in 1803, the French assumed formal control of Louisiana just long enough to turn the territory over to General James Wilkinson, the commissioner of the United States and the commander of a small occupation force. In New Orleans, beneath a bright December sun, the recently raised French tricolor was lowered and the American flag raised.

For the time being, the Louisiana Territory was given a semimilitary government with officials appointed by the president; later it was organized on the general pattern of the Northwest Territory, with the assumption that it would be divided into states. The first of these was admitted to the union as the state of Louisiana in 1812.

Meriwether Lewis
In 1807, when the French painter Charles de Saint-Mémin produced this watercolor, Lewis had returned from his fabled expedition through the Far West with William Clark and had been named governor of the Louisiana Territory by President Jefferson. He had served earlier as a private secretary to Jefferson. (New-York Historical Society)

Exploring the West

Meanwhile, a series of bold explorations were revealing the geography of the far-flung new territory. In 1803, even before Napoleon's offer to sell Louisiana, Jefferson planned an expedition that was to cross the continent to the Pacific Ocean, gather geographical facts, and investigate prospects for trade with the Indians. Congress secretly provided the necessary funds, and Jefferson named as leader of the expedition his private secretary and Virginia neighbor, the thirty-two-year-old Meriwether Lewis, a veteran of

Indian wars skilled in the ways of the wilderness. Lewis chose as a colleague the twenty-eight-year-old William Clark, who—like George Rogers Clark, his older brother—was an experienced frontiersman and Indian fighter.

Lewis and Clark, with a company of four dozen men, set up winter quarters in St. Louis at about the time the United States took formal possession of Louisiana. In the spring of 1804, they started up the Missouri River, and with the Shoshoni woman

Exploration of the Louisiana Purchase, 1803–1807

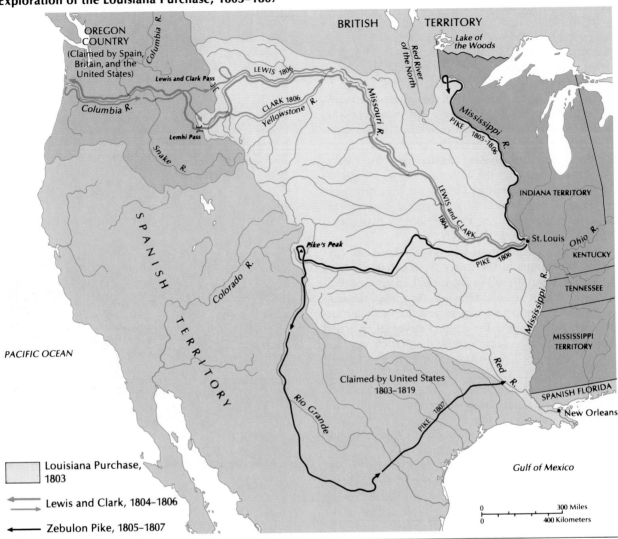

Louisiana Purchase, 1803

Lewis and Clark, 1804–1806

Zebulon Pike, 1805–1807

Sacajawea as their guide, her baby on her back, they eventually crossed the Rocky Mountains, descended the Snake and the Columbia rivers, and in the late autumn of 1805 camped on the Pacific coast. In September 1806, they were back in St. Louis with elaborate records of what they had observed along the way. No longer was the Far West a completely unknown country.

While Lewis and Clark were on their epic journey, Jefferson dispatched other explorers to fill in the picture of the Louisiana Territory. The most important of these was Lieutenant Zebulon Montgomery Pike. Then only twenty-six years old, Pike led an

expedition in the fall of 1805 from St. Louis up the Mississippi River in search of its source. He did not find it, but he learned a great deal about the upper Mississippi Valley. In the summer of 1806, Pike set out again and proceeded up the valley of the Arkansas river and into what later became Colorado, where he discovered, but failed in his attempt to climb, the peak that now bears his name. His account of his Western travels created an enduring (and inaccurate) impression among most Americans that the land between the Missouri and the Rockies was a desert that farmers could never cultivate and that ought to be left forever to the nomadic Indian tribes.

The Burr Conspiracy

In the long run, the Louisiana Purchase prepared the way for the growth of the United States as a great continental power. At first, however, the purchase provoked reactions that seemed to threaten the very existence of the Union.

Jefferson's triumphant reelection in 1804 suggested that most of the nation approved the new acquisition. But some New England Federalists raged against it. They realized that the more the West grew and the more new states joined the Union, the less power the Federalists and their region would retain. In Massachusetts, a group of the most extreme Federalists, known as the Essex Junto, concluded that the only recourse for New England was to secede from the Union and form a separate "Northern Confederacy." To justify their position, they cited states' rights arguments similar to those Jefferson had used only a few years earlier to justify his call for nullification of the Alien and Sedition Acts.

If a Northern Confederacy was to have any hope for lasting success as a separate nation, the Federalists believed, it would have to include New York and New Jersey as well as New England. But the leading Federalist in New York, Alexander Hamilton, refused to support the secessionist scheme. "Dismemberment of our empire," he wrote, "will be a clear sacrifice of great positive advantages without any counterbalancing good, administering no relief to our real disease, which is *democracy*." Hamilton feared that disorders like those of the French Revolution were about to sweep over the United States. If so, the country would need a military dictator, an American Napoleon, to bring order out of chaos—perhaps Hamilton himself, who by now clearly had no future in electoral politics.

Hamilton opposed the secessionists as well because their plans threatened to strengthen his greatest political rival in New York. Vice President Aaron Burr was another politician without prospects, at least within the party of Thomas Jefferson, who had never forgiven him for his role in the 1800 election deadlock. When Federalists approached Burr and offered him their support if he would run for governor in 1804, he agreed. There were rumors that he had agreed as well to support disunion plans and that he would, if elected, lead the state into secession along with New England. There was no evidence to support such rumors. Hamilton, however, accused Burr of plotting treason and made numerous private remarks, widely reported in the press, about Burr's "despicable" character. When Burr lost the election,

he blamed his defeat on Hamilton's malevolence and demanded redress. "These things," he wrote, "must have an end." And he challenged Hamilton to a duel.

Dueling had already fallen into some disrepute in America, but many people still considered it a legitimate institution for settling matters of "honor." Hamilton feared that refusing Burr's challenge would brand him a coward and damage his prospects of future glory. And so, on a July morning in 1804, the two men crossed the Hudson River and met at Weehawken, New Jersey. Hamilton was mortally wounded; he died the next day.

Burr fled New York to escape an indictment for murder and spent months traveling through the South. He returned to Washington to preside over the United States Senate the following winter and then, at the end of his term as vice president, faced a political outlook more hopeless than ever. He was ambitious, resourceful, and enormously charismatic. But he was largely discredited within the existing political organizations of his country. He was, in short, a man in search of a cause.

He found it, apparently, in the wilderness. Even before his duel with Hamilton, it seems Burr had dreamed of glorious exploits in the unsettled lands of the Southwest. (Hamilton had cherished some of the same ambitions, which may have been another reason for Burr's challenge to him.) Both before and after the duel, he corresponded with prominent men of the region, especially with General James Wilkinson, now governor of the Louisiana Territory.

Burr and Wilkinson hoped, it seems clear, to lead an expedition that would capture Mexico from the Spanish. "Mexico glitters in all our eyes," he wrote; "the word is all we wait for." But there were also rumors that they intended to separate the Southwest from the Union, which Burr would rule as an empire of his own. Historians disagree about Burr's real intentions, but there is little evidence that these rumors were true.

Whether true or not, many of Burr's opponents chose to believe the rumors—including, ultimately, Jefferson himself. In the fall of 1806, Burr led a group of armed followers down the Ohio River by boat. Disturbing reports of his activities flowed into Washington throughout the winter, the most alarming from Wilkinson, who, having suddenly turned against Burr, informed the president that treason was afoot, that an attack on New Orleans was imminent. Jefferson ordered the arrest of Burr and his men as traitors; eventually Burr was tracked down and brought to Richmond for trial.

Jefferson was not present in Richmond but, de-

SIGNIFICANT EVENTS

1769	James Watt patents steam engine
1778	Phillips Academy founded in Andover, Massachusetts
1779	Universalist church founded in Gloucester, Massachusetts
1781	Phillips Exeter Academy founded in New Hampshire
1782	Unitarian church founded in Boston
1784	Judith Sargent Murray publishes essay on rights of women American Methodist church formally established
1789	Massachusetts law requires public schools to admit female students
1790	Samuel Slater builds textile mill, first modern factory in America, in Pawtucket, Rhode Island
1792	Toll road constructed from Philadelphia to Lancaster, beginning the turnpike era
1793	Eli Whitney invents cotton gin
1794	First black churches in America established
1794–1796	Thomas Paine's *Age of Reason* attacks traditional religion
1800	United States capital moves to Washington, D.C. Gabriel Prosser's plans for slave rebellion in Virginia foiled
1801–1805	Conflict with Tripoli
1801	Second Great Awakening begins John Marshall appointed chief justice of the Supreme Court
1802	Jefferson administration abolishes all internal federal taxes United States Military Academy founded at West Point
1803	Louisiana Territory purchased from French Supreme Court establishes power of judicial review in *Marbury* v. *Madison*
1804–1806	Lewis and Clark, and Zebulon Pike, explore Louisiana Territory
1804	Aaron Burr kills Alexander Hamilton in duel Thomas Jefferson reelected president
1806	Burr conspiracy uncovered
1807	Fulton and Livingston launch the *Clermont*, first steamboat Burr tried for conspiracy
1828	Webster's *American Dictionary of the English Language* published

termined to secure a conviction, carefully managed the government's case from Washington. The prosecution relied hopefully on its star witness, General Wilkinson—a disreputable character who had been in the pay of the Spaniards during the entire affair and had demanded extra money from them on the grounds that in heading off the Burr expedition, he had saved their territory from attack. Despite the administration's efforts to influence the trial, Chief Justice Marshall, presiding over the case on circuit duty, insisted that Burr receive a fair hearing—for both judicial and political reasons.

In the course of the trial, which continued from May through October 1807, Marshall applied literally the constitutional provision that no one shall be convicted of treason except on the testimony of at least two witnesses to the same "overt act." He excluded all evidence not bearing directly on such an act. Thus the jury had little choice but to acquit Burr, since not even one witness had actually seen him waging war against the United States or giving aid and comfort to its enemies. The trial had given the chief justice another chance to frustrate the president. And it had set a precedent that made it almost impossible to convict anyone of treason against the United States.

Burr was free, but his political reputation was permanently destroyed. For several years, he lived in self-imposed exile in Europe. In 1812, he returned to America and established a successful legal practice in New York. He lived long enough to hail the Texas revolution of 1836 as the fruition of the movement to "liberate" Mexico that he had tried to launch.

The Burr conspiracy was in part the story of a single man's soaring ambitions and flamboyant personality. But it was also a symbol of the larger perils still facing the new nation. With a central government that remained deliberately weak, with vast tracts of land only nominally controlled by the United States, with ambitious political leaders willing, if necessary, to circumvent normal channels in their search for power, the United States remained an imperfectly realized nation. The legitimacy of the federal government was yet to be fully asserted.

SUGGESTED READINGS

General Histories   Henry Adams's nine-volume *History of the United States During the Administration of Jefferson and Adams* (1889–1891) is one of the classics of American historical writing. It is available in a two-volume abridged edition edited by Herbert Agar (1947). More recent surveys include Marcus Cunliffe, *The Nation Takes Shape, 1789–1832* (1959); John Mayfield, *The New Nation* (1981); and Marshall Smelser, *The Democratic Republicans, 1801–1815* (1968).

Cultural Life   Useful surveys include Joseph J. Ellis, *After the Revolution: Profiles of Early American Culture* (1979); Russel B. Nye, *The Cultural Life of the New Nation* (1960); and Kenneth Silverman, *A Cultural History of the American Revolution* (1976). On education, see Lawrence A. Cremin, *American Education: The National Experience* (1981); Carl F. Kaestle, *The Evolution of an Urban School System* (1973); and Harry Warfel, *Noah Webster, Schoolmaster to America* (1936). There are several important studies of religion and revivalism in the young republic. The standard work has long been William W. Sweet, *Revivalism in America* (1944). A more recent study of importance is William G. McLoughlin, *Revivals, Awakenings, and Reform* (1978). Sydney Ahlstrom, *A Religious History of the American People* (1972), is a valuable overview. Whitney R. Cross, *The Burned Over District* (1950), discusses revivalism in upstate New York; and John Boles, *The Great Revival in the South* (1972), examines its influence on that region. Jan Lewis, *The Pursuit of Happiness: Family and Values in Jefferson's Virginia* (1983), examines changing social patterns.

Economic Growth   Stuart Bruchey, *The Roots of American Economic Growth* (1965), and Thomas C. Cochran, *Frontiers of Change: Early Industrialization in America* (1981), are useful introductions to the emergence of industrialization. Douglas C. North, *The Economic Growth of the United States, 1790–1860* (1961), provides an important interpretation; W. Elliot Brownlee, *Dynamics of Ascent* (1979), is a survey of American economic history. Nathan Rosenberg, *Technology and American Economic Growth* (1972), is a broad view of the role technology played in spurring early economic development. Merritt Roe Smith, *Harpers Ferry Armory and the New Technology* (1977), is a skillful local study. Anthony F. C. Wallace, *Rockdale* (1978), examines the impact of industrialization on a Pennsylvania town. Arthur H. Cole, *The American Wool Manufacture*, 2 vols. (1926), and C. F. Ware, *Early New England Cotton Manufacture* (1931), are classic works examining the birth of the textile industry. C. M. Green, *Eli Whitney and the Birth of American Technology* (1956), studies the inventor of the cotton gin. George R. Taylor, *The Transportation Revolution* (1951), examines the economic impact of the growth of the American transportation network. See also P. D. Jordan, *The National Road* (1948), and J. A. Durrenburger, *Turnpikes* (1931). James Henretta, *The Evolution of American Society, 1700–1815* (1973), suggests ways in which economic change affected social arrangements.

Politics and Government   Morton Borden, *Parties and Politics in the Early Republic* (1967), is a useful study of political rivalries, as is Noble Cunningham, *The Jeffersonian Republicans in Power* (1963). James S. Young, *The Washington Community* (1966), is an excellent study of life in the nation's capital during the Jeffersonian era. The Federalist opposition is considered in David Hackett Fischer, *The Revolution of American Conservatism* (1965); Linda Kerber, *Federalists in Dissent* (1970); and James M. Banner, *To the Hartford Convention* (1967). The workings of the Jefferson administration are examined in Noble Cunningham, *The Process of Government Under Jefferson* (1978); Leonard White, *The Jeffersonians* (1951); Alexander Balinky, *Albert Gallatin: Fiscal Theories and Policy* (1958); and Robert M. Johnstone, Jr., *Jefferson and the Presidency* (1978). Two volumes of the great Dumas Malone biography of Jefferson, *Jefferson the President: First Term* (1970) and *Jefferson the President: Second Term* (1974), study the president himself. On Jefferson's conflict with the courts, see Richard Ellis, *The Jeffersonian Crisis* (1971), and Leonard Baker, *John Marshall: A Life in Law* (1974).

Jeffersonian Thought   In addition to the various biographies of leading figures, see Adrienne Koch, *The Philosophy of Thomas Jefferson* (1943); Charles M. Wiltse, *The Jeffersonian Tradition in American Democracy* (1935); Merrill Peterson, *The Jeffersonian Image in the American Mind* (1960); and Leonard W. Levy, *Jefferson and Civil Liberties: The Darker Side* (1963), a critical study. Drew McCoy, *The Elusive Republic: Political Economy in Jeffersonian America* (1980), is a particularly important study of Jeffersonian ideology.

Foreign Policy   Irving Brant, *James Madison: Secretary of State* (1953), and Bradford Perkins, *Prologue to War: England and the United States, 1805–1812* (1961), are useful introductions. On the Louisiana Purchase, consult Alexander DeConde, *The Affair of Louisiana* (1976), and Arthur P. Whitaker, *The Mississippi Question* (1934). George Dangerfield, *Chancellor Robert R. Livingston of New York* (1960), and Harry Ammon, *James Monroe and the Quest for National Identity* (1971), are also useful sources for the diplomacy of the era. Bernard deVoto, *Course of Empire* (1952), examines the travels of Lewis and Clark, as does his edition of *The Journals of Lewis and Clark* (1953). On the Burr conspiracy, see Nathan Schachner, *Aaron Burr* (1937), for a sympathetic biography, and Thomas P. Abernethy, *The Burr Conspiracy* (1954), for an unfriendly account. Milton Lomask, *Aaron Burr*, 2 volumes (1979, 1982), is the most thorough biography.

Indians and the West   B. W. Sheehan, *Seeds of Extinction* (1973), discusses Jeffersonian views of the American Indian. Francis S. Philbrick, *The Rise of the New West* (1965), and Ray Allen Billington, *Westward Expansion* (1967), are overviews of territorial growth.

Appalachian Pass (Corcoran Gallery of Art)

Chapter 8 # Free Seas and Fresh Lands

Two very different conflicts took shape in the early nineteenth century that would, together, draw the United States into a difficult and frustrating war. One was the continuing struggle in Europe (the Napoleonic Wars), which in 1803 escalated once again into a full-scale conflict. At first, the hostilities posed no direct danger to the United States and in many respects worked indirectly to benefit it—by enabling Americans to develop a profitable trade with belligerents on both sides. As the fighting continued, however, both the British and the French took steps to prevent the United States from trading with (and thus assisting) the other. And tensions between the Old and New Worlds rapidly grew.

The other conflict was an older one, on the North American continent itself. The ceaseless westward expansion of white settlement was now stretching to the Mississippi River and beyond, colliding once again with a native population committed to protecting its lands from intruders. In both the North and the South, the threatened tribes mobilized themselves—and began building new and effective alliances—to resist white encroachments. And they began as well to forge connections with British forces in Canada and Spanish forces in Florida. The Indian conflict on land, therefore, became intertwined with the European conflict on the seas. Together they drew the United States into war with Great Britain—the War of 1812.

That war was far from a glorious experience for the United States. America drifted into the conflict with Britain gradually, not in response to a single great event that might have galvanized public opinion behind it. And so it provoked wide domestic opposition, especially from those whose economic fortunes were endangered by it. It also produced several humiliating defeats (including the British capture and burning of Washington) and only a few decisive American victories. It ended with a treaty that fell far short of guaranteeing the nation's war aims—a treaty that signaled, at best, a draw.

But the more important war, in the long run, was the conflict with the Indians. And in that, white America won a series of important, indeed decisive, victories. The most important Indian alliance in the West was destroyed. The most effective Indian leader was killed. Large new territories were opened for white settlement, and the way was paved for the ultimate removal of the tribes to the arid lands farther west. White Americans have long considered the conflict with Great Britain the real war. The conflict with the Indians is generally viewed as a minor "police action," or as a secondary aspect of the larger conflict. But the victories over the tribes had far more lasting effects on the nation than the inconclusive struggle with the British.

The war had other effects on the United States as well. It greatly stimulated American nationalism, helping to diminish for a time the tensions between North and South. And it stimulated manufacturing and economic growth, and thus accelerated progress toward industrialization. It was a Republican administration that presided over the War of 1812, and the conflict ultimately became another factor in consigning to oblivion the Jeffersonian vision of a small, decentralized, agrarian nation.

Causes of Conflict

Politicians at the time disagreed sharply over the causes of the War of 1812. Historians have continued to disagree over them ever since. Some have argued that the question of frontier lands and the conflicts with the Indians lay at the heart of the conflict. Others claim that the real issue was freedom of the seas. In fact, the two matters were closely related to each other. The war cannot be understood without considering both.

Neutral Rights

The early nineteenth century saw a dramatic expansion of American shipping in the Atlantic. Britain's naval superiority prevented France and Spain (constantly at war with the English) from carrying on more than a modest ocean trade. But the British merchant marine was preoccupied with commerce in Europe and Asia and devoted little energy to trade with America. Thus the United States stepped effectively into the void and developed one of the most important merchant marines in the world. Year after year, American shippers assumed a larger and larger proportion of the carrying trade between Europe and the West Indies.

In 1805, at the Battle of Trafalgar, a British fleet virtually destroyed what was left of the French navy. Napoleon continued in the following years to extend his domination over the continent of Europe by land; but Britain remained the undisputed master of the seas. And because France could no longer challenge the British navy, Napoleon was powerless to invade the British Isles. He needed, therefore, to find another way to bring England to terms—through economic, rather than naval, pressure. The result was what he called the Continental System. The British, he reasoned, were a nation of shopkeepers; they depended for their existence on buying and selling in the rest of the world, especially in Europe. If he could close the Continent to their trade, he thought, they ultimately would have to give in. Accordingly, he issued a series of decrees (one in Berlin in 1806 and another in Milan in 1807) barring British ships and neutral ships touching at British ports from landing their cargoes at any European port controlled by France or its allies.

The British government replied to Napoleon's decrees by establishing—through a series of "orders in council"—an unusual blockade of the European coast. The blockade did not keep imported goods out of Napoleon's Europe; it required, rather, that the goods be carried either in British vessels or in neutral vessels stopping at British ports and paying for a special license. The blockade would thus not only frustrate the Continental System but also compel neutral shippers to help England finance its war effort. It would also limit the growth of its maritime rivals, above all the United States.

Caught between Napoleon's Berlin and Milan decrees and Britain's orders in council, American vessels ran a double risk. If they sailed directly for the European continent, they took the chance of being captured by the British navy. If they sailed by way of a British port, they ran the risk of seizure by the French. Both of the warring powers were violating America's rights as a neutral nation. But most Americans considered the British, with their much greater sea power, the worse offender. British ships pounced on Yankee merchantmen all over the wide ocean; the French could do so only in European ports. In particular, British vessels stopped American ships on the high seas and seized sailors off the decks, making them victims of "impressment."

Impressment

The British navy—with its floggings, its low pay, and its dirty and dangerous conditions on shipboard—was a "floating hell" to its sailors. They had to be "impressed" (forced) into the service, and at every good opportunity they deserted. By 1807, many of them had joined the American merchant marine or the American navy. To check this loss of vital manpower, the British claimed the right to stop and search American merchantmen (although not naval vessels) and reimpress deserters. They did not claim the right to take native-born Americans, but they did insist on the right to seize naturalized Americans born on British soil; according to the laws of England, a true-born subject could never give up allegiance to the king. In practice, the British often impressed native as well as naturalized Americans; thousands of sailors claiming the protection of the United States government were thus kidnapped. To these hapless men, impressment was little better than slavery. To their American shipowning employers, it was at least a serious nuisance. And to millions of proud and patriotic Americans, even those living far from the ocean, it was an intolerable affront to the national honor.

In the summer of 1807, the British went to more

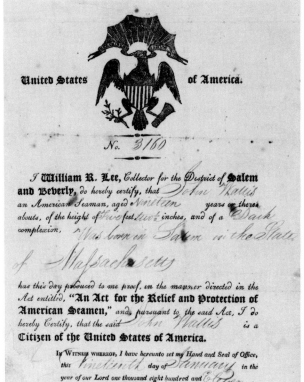

United States of America.

No. 3160

I William R. Lee, Collector for the District of Salem and Beverly, do hereby certify, that John Wallis an American Seaman, aged Nineteen years or thereabouts, of the height of Five feet Two inches, and of a Dark complexion, Was born in Salem in the State

of Massachusetts

has this day produced to me proof, in the manner directed in the Act entitled, "An Act for the Relief and Protection of American Seamen," and, pursuant to the said Act, I do hereby Certify, that the said John Wallis is a Citizen of the United States of America.

In Witness whereof, I have hereunto set my Hand and Seal of Office, this Nineteenth day of January in the year of our Lord one thousand eight hundred and Eleven

William R. Lee Collector.

Protection from Impressment
To protect American sailors from British impressment, the federal government issued official certificates of United States citizenship—known as "protection papers." But British naval officers, aware that such documents were often forged, frequently ignored them. (Essex Institute, Salem, Massachusetts)

provocative extremes in an incident involving not an ordinary merchantman, but a vessel of the American navy. Sailing from Norfolk, with several alleged deserters from the British navy among the crew, the American naval frigate *Chesapeake* was hailed by His Majesty's Ship *Leopard,* which had been lying in wait off Cape Henry, at the entrance to Chesapeake Bay. The American commander, Commodore James Barron, refused to allow the Chesapeake to be searched, so the *Leopard* opened fire. Barron was unprepared for action and was compelled to surrender. A boarding party from the *Leopard* dragged four men off the American frigate.

When news of the *Chesapeake-Leopard* incident reached America, a loud cry arose for a war of re-

venge. Not since the days of Lexington and Concord had Americans been so strongly aroused. Even the "most temperate people and those most attached to England," the British minister reported home, "say that they are bound as a people and that they must assert their honor on the first attack upon it." If Congress had been in session, the country might have stampeded into war. But, as the French minister in Washington informed Talleyrand, "the president does not want war" and "Mr. Madison [the secretary of state] dreads it now still more."

Instead of calling a special session of Congress and demanding a war declaration, Jefferson made a determined effort to maintain the peace. First, he issued an order expelling all British warships from American waters, to lessen the likelihood of future incidents. Then he sent instructions to his minister in England, James Monroe, to demand from the British government the complete renunciation of impressment. The British government was conciliatory—to a degree. It disavowed the action of Admiral Berkeley, the officer primarily responsible for the *Chesapeake-Leopard* affair, and recalled him. It offered to compensate the wounded and the families of those killed in the exchange. And it promised to return three of the captured sailors (one of the original four had been hanged). But the British cabinet refused to concede anything to Jefferson's main point; instead, the cabinet issued a proclamation reasserting the right of search to recover deserting seamen.

The impressment issue therefore prevented any permanent settlement of Anglo-American differences. Even after the British completed a financial settlement, the *Chesapeake* outrage remained an open sore in the relations between the two nations. That incident, and the larger impressment issue it symbolized, was probably the most important single cause of the War of 1812, even though the conflict did not begin for another five years.

"Peaceable Coercion"

Even at the height of the excitement over the *Chesapeake,* Jefferson made no preparations for war. He and Madison believed that the United States could bring Great Britain—and, if necessary, France—to terms through the use of economic pressure instead of military or naval force. Dependent as both nations were on the Yankee carrying trade, they would presumably mend their ways if threatened with the complete loss of it.

Thus when Congress met for its regular session

late in 1807, Jefferson hastily drafted a drastic measure. Madison revised it, and both the House and the Senate, dominated by Republicans, promptly enacted it into law. It was known as the Embargo, and it became one of the most controversial political issues of its time. The Embargo prohibited American ships from leaving the United States for any foreign port anywhere in the world. (If it had specified only British and French ports, Jefferson reasoned, it could have been evaded by means of false clearance papers.) Congress also passed a "force act" to give the government power to enforce the Embargo.

The law was widely evaded, but it was effective enough to have serious repercussions—in France, in Great Britain, and above all in the United States itself. Throughout the nation—except in the frontier areas of Vermont and New York, which soon doubled their overland exports to Canada—the Embargo created a serious depression. The planters of the South and the farmers of the West, although deprived of foreign markets for their crops, were willing to suffer in comparative silence, devoted Jeffersonian Republicans that most of them were. But the Federalist merchants and shipowners of the Northeast, still harder hit by the depression, made no secret of their rabid discontent.

The Northeastern merchants disliked impressment, disliked the British blockade of the European continent, and disliked Napoleon's Continental System. But they hated Jefferson's Embargo much more. Previously, in spite of the risks from Britain and France, they had managed to keep up their business and had earned excellent profits. Now they lost money every day that their ships idled at the wharves. Again, as at the time of the Louisiana Purchase, they concluded that Jefferson had violated the Constitution and had subverted the original purposes of the republic.

The election of 1808 came in the midst of the Embargo-induced depression. James Madison was safely elected to succeed Jefferson as president; but the Federalist candidate, Charles Pinckney, made the most of the Embargo's unpopularity and won a far larger proportion of the popular and electoral votes than he had in 1804. And although the Republicans continued to hold a majority in Congress, the Federalists gained a number of seats in both the House and the Senate. To Jefferson and Madison, the returns plainly indicated that the Embargo was a growing political liability. A few days before leaving office, Jefferson approved a bill terminating his experiment with what he called "peaceable coercion." But Mad-

Dolly Madison
Dolly Payne was born in North Carolina, grew up a Quaker in Virginia, and in 1794 (a year after her first husband had died of yellow fever) married James Madison. He was forty-three; she was twenty-six. A woman of enormous charm and social grace, she became one of her husband's greatest political assets. She acted as hostess for President Jefferson, a widower, while her husband was serving as secretary of state; and she presided over a lively social life at the White House during her eight years as First Lady. (New-York Historical Society)

ison made no basic change in the general policy of attempting to settle differences with Britain through economic rather than military means.

By the time of his inauguration as president, Madison had already ensured himself immortality in his nation's history by his role in the founding of the republic. Now he was faced with preserving it in the face of its greatest threat since the Revolution. He was a stark contrast to his friend and predecessor, Thomas Jefferson. Small, wizened, with a scholarly frown that seemed perpetual, he had little personal charm and few political skills. His greatest political asset may have been his wife, Dolly, a native of North

Carolina and a gracious, energetic, and popular woman. John C. Calhoun wrote of Madison at the time: "Our President tho a man of amiable manners and great talents has not I fear those commanding talents which are necessary to control those about him." Madison's presidency was marked, therefore, by frustration and contention. His diplomatic efforts to resolve the disputes with Europe came to naught; his preparations for war were inadequate; his administration was in constant confusion.

Just before Madison's inauguration, Congress passed a modified Embargo bill known as the Non-Intercourse Act, which reopened trade with all nations but Great Britain and France. A year later, in 1810, the Non-Intercourse Act expired and was replaced by another expedient, commonly called Macon's Bill No. 2. This measure reopened free commercial relations with the whole world, including Great Britain and France, but authorized the president to prohibit intercourse with either belligerent if it should continue its violations after the other had stopped. Napoleon had every incentive to induce the United States to reimpose the Embargo against his enemy; and so he issued a proclamation, the Cadore letter, which announced that France would no longer interfere with American shipping. The Cadore letter was, in fact, nothing but a diplomatic trick; the French continued to confiscate American ships. But Madison fell for Napoleon's bait and announced that an embargo against Great Britain alone would automatically go into effect early in 1811, in accordance with Macon's Bill, unless Britain renounced its restrictions on American shipping.

In time, the new Embargo, although less well enforced than the earlier, all-inclusive one had been, hurt the economy of England enough that the government repealed its blockade of Europe. The repeal would have been too late to prevent war even if the blockade had been the only grievance of the United States. But there were other grievances—not just impressment, but the role of the British in the continuing conflicts with Indian tribes along America's Western frontier.

The "Indian Problem" and the British

Given the ruthlessness with which white settlers had dislodged Indian tribes to make room for expanding settlement, it was hardly surprising that ever since the Revolution most Indians had continued to look to England—which had historically attempted to limit Western expansion—for protection. The British in Canada, for their part, had relied on Indian friendship to keep up their fur trade, even within the territory of the United States, and to maintain potentially useful allies. At one point, in 1794, America had nearly gone to war with Great Britain because of its Indian policy; but Anthony Wayne's victory over the tribes at Fallen Timbers and the conclusion of Jay's Treaty dispelled the danger and brought on a period of comparative peace. Then, in 1807, the border quiet was disturbed by an event occurring far away—the British assault on the *Chesapeake*. The ensuing war crisis greatly aggravated the frontier conflict between Indians and settlers—a conflict that elevated to prominence two important (and very different) leaders: William Henry Harrison and Tecumseh.

In 1799 the Virginia-born Harrison, already at twenty-six years of age a veteran Indian fighter, went to Washington as the congressional delegate from the Northwest Territory. He was a committed advocate of growth and development in the Western lands, and he was largely responsible for the passage in 1800 of the so-called Harrison Land Law, which enabled settlers to acquire farms from the public domain on much easier terms than before. Land in the Northwest Territory soon was selling fast. The growth of population led to a division of the area into the state of Ohio and the territories of Indiana, Michigan, and Illinois. By 1812, Ohio contained 250,000 people and was beginning to resemble an Eastern state. Paths had widened into roads; villages had sprung up and had in some cases grown into cities; and the forests had receded before the spreading cornfields. Michigan still had few settlers in 1812; but Illinois contained a scattered population of about 13,000, and Indiana 25,000. Harrison's vision of the rapid expansion of white settlement westward was well on its way to realization.

In 1801, Jefferson appointed Harrison governor of Indiana Territory; and in that capacity, Harrison devoted himself to carrying out the president's now clearly defined approach to the "Indian problem." Jefferson offered the Indians a stark choice: they could convert themselves into settled farmers and become part of white society or they could migrate west of the Mississippi. In either case, they would have to give up their claims to their tribal lands in the Northwest. Harrison went about enforcing this policy with cold-blooded efficiency and with little regard for propriety. He played off one tribe against another, and he used whatever tactics he felt suited the occasion. Through threats, bribes, and trickery, he concluded treaty after treaty with the separate tribes of the Northwest. By 1807, the United States claimed treaty rights to eastern Michigan, southern Indiana, and most of Illinois. Meanwhile, in the Southwest, white Americans were taking millions of acres from other tribes in the states of Georgia and Tennessee and in Mississippi Territory. Having been forced off their traditional hunting grounds, the Indians throughout the Mississippi Valley seethed with discontent. But the separate tribes were helpless by themselves against the power of the United States. They might have passively accepted their fate if two complicating factors had not arisen.

One complication was the policy of the British authorities in Canada. For years they had neglected their Indian friends across the border to the south. Then came the *Chesapeake* incident and the surge of anti-British feeling throughout the United States. Now the British colonial authorities, expecting an American invasion of Canada, began to take desperate measures for their own defense. "Are the Indians to be employed in case of a rupture with the United States?" asked the lieutenant governor of upper Canada in a letter of December 1, 1807, to Sir James Craig, governor general of the entire province. The governor replied: "If we do not employ them, there cannot exist a moment's doubt that they will be employed against us." Craig at once took steps to renew friendship with the Indians and provide them with increased supplies. Thus the trouble on the sea over the question of impressment intensified the border conflict hundreds of miles inland.

Tecumseh and the Prophet

The second factor intensifying this conflict was the rise of a remarkable native leader, one of the most heroic in Indian history. Tecumseh, "The Shooting Star," chief of the Shawnees, understood, as few other Indian leaders had, that only through united action could the tribes hope to resist the steady advance of white civilization. Tecumseh set out to unite all the tribes of the Mississippi Valley, north and south. Together, he promised, they would halt white expansion, recover the whole Northwest, and make the Ohio River the boundary between the United States and the Indian country. He maintained that Harrison and others, by negotiating treaties with individual tribes, had obtained no real title to land. The land belonged to all the tribes; none of them could rightfully cede any of it without the consent of the others. "The Great Spirit gave this great island to his red children. He placed the whites on the other side of the big water," Tecumseh told Harrison. "They were not contented with their own, but came to take ours from us. They have driven us from the sea to the lakes—we can go no farther."

In his plans for united resistance, Tecumseh had the important assistance of his brother Tenskwatawa, a charismatic orator known as the Prophet. The Prophet had experienced a mystical awakening in the process of recovering from alcoholism. And having freed himself from the evil effects of white culture, he began to speak to his people of the superior virtues of Indian civilization and the sinfulness and corruption

Tecumseh
Tecumseh's efforts to unite the tribes of the Mississippi Valley against further white encroachments on their lands led him ultimately into an ill-fated alliance with the British after his brother, the Prophet, was defeated at the Battle of Tippecanoe in 1811. In the War of 1812, he was commissioned a brigadier general by the British and died in the Battle of the Thames fighting against the Americans. He is shown in this painting (by the daughter of an English officer stationed near Detroit) wearing British military trousers. (Fort Malden National Historic Park)

of the white world. In the process, he helped inspire a religious revival that spread through numerous tribes and helped unite them. The Prophet increased his influence, and convinced his followers of his supernatural powers, when he commanded the sun to be dark on the day of a solar eclipse. (He had learned of the eclipse in advance from Canadian traders.)

The Prophet's town, at the confluence of Tippecanoe Creek and the Wabash River, became the sacred place of the new religion as well as the headquarters of Tecumseh's confederacy. In 1811, Tecumseh left the settlement in the hands of his brother and traveled down the Mississippi to visit the tribes of the South and persuade them to join his alliance. At about the same time, a great earthquake—with its center at New Madrid, Missouri—rumbled up and down the Mississippi Valley, causing much of the river to change its course. Many Indians saw this phenomenon as another sign that a new era was at hand.

During Tecumseh's absence, Governor Harrison saw a chance to destroy the growing influence of the two Indian leaders. With 1,000 soldiers he camped near the Prophet's town; and on November 7, 1811, he provoked an armed conflict. Although the white forces suffered losses as heavy as those of the natives, Harrison succeeded in driving off the Indians and burning the town. The Battle of Tippecanoe disillusioned many of the Prophet's followers, for they had come to believe that his magic would protect them from the white man's bullets. Tecumseh returned to find his confederacy in disarray. But there were still many warriors eager for combat, and by the spring of 1812 they were busy all along the frontier, from Michigan to Mississippi, raiding the white settlements and terrifying the white settlers.

The bloodshed along the frontier was largely at the hands of the Indians, but Britain's agents in Canada had encouraged Tecumseh (used the Prophet as a "vile instrument," as Harrison put it) and had provided the guns and supplies that enabled the Indians to do battle. To Harrison and to most of the frontiersmen, there seemed only one way to make the West safe for Americans. That was to drive the British out of Canada and annex that province to the United States—a goal that many Westerners had long cherished for other reasons as well.

The Lure of Florida

While frontiersmen in the North demanded the conquest of Canada, those in the South looked to the acquisition of Florida (an expanse of land including not only the present state of Florida, but the southern areas of what are now Alabama, Mississippi, and Louisiana as well). Spanish possession of that territory created perpetual nuisances. Slaves escaped from the United States south across the Florida border, and Indians in Florida launched frequent raids north into white settlements along the border. But white Southerners coveted Florida for other reasons as well, for without it they had no direct access to the Gulf of Mexico. Through the territory ran such rivers as the Alabama, the Apalachicola, and others that could provide residents of the Southwest with access to valuable ports on the Gulf. In 1810, American settlers in West Florida (the area presently part of Mississippi and Louisiana) took matters into their own hands. They seized the Spanish fort at Baton Rouge, and they sent a request to the federal government that the territory be annexed to the United States. President Madison unhesitatingly proclaimed its annexation and then began scheming to get the rest of Florida too. With Madison's connivance, George Mathews, a former governor of Georgia, attempted in 1811 to foment a revolt in East Florida. Spain protested, and Madison backed down; but the desire of Southern frontiersmen for all of Florida did not abate. That desire became yet another motivation for war with Britain. Spain was Britain's ally, and a war would give these frontiersmen an excuse for taking Spanish as well as British territory.

By 1812, therefore, war fever was raging on both the northern and southern frontiers. The white residents of these outlying regions were not numerous in comparison with the population of the country as a whole. For the most part, moreover, they were represented in Congress by only a few, nonvoting territorial delegates. Their demands, however, found substantial support in Washington among a group of determined young congressmen who soon earned the name of "war hawks."

The War Hawks

Three days before the Battle of Tippecanoe, a new Congress met in Washington for the session of 1811–1812. In the congressional elections of 1810, voters had indicated their impatience with the temporizing measures of both Republicans and Federalists by electing a large number of representatives eager for war with Britain. A new generation had arrived on the political scene—aggressive and impatient young men, the most influential of whom came from the new states in the West or from the back country of the old states in the South.

Two of their natural leaders, both recently elected to the House of Representatives, were Henry Clay and John C. Calhoun, men who would loom large in American politics for the next four decades. The tall, magnetic Clay, barely thirty-four when he arrived in Washington in 1811, was a Virginian by birth but had made Kentucky his home. He had already served briefly in the United States Senate in 1806 and 1807. Calhoun was only twenty-nine years old, the son of Scotch-Irish pioneers in the South Carolina hills. He was as striking in appearance as Clay but lacked the Kentuckian's personal magnetism. Calhoun's great strength was his powerful intellect and his equally powerful ambition.

When Congress organized itself in 1811, the war faction of young Republicans won control of both the House and the Senate. Clay was elected Speaker of the House, a position of influence then second only to that of the president, and he filled the committees with those who believed as he did in the necessity of preparing for war. He appointed Calhoun to the crucial Committee on Foreign Affairs, and he began agitating immediately for the conquest of Canada. Madison, who still hoped to maintain the peace, was losing control of his government.

The War of 1812

For a time, Great Britain was eager to avoid an open conflict with the United States. Preoccupied with the Napoleonic Wars in Europe, it hoped to avoid a distracting conflict in America. And so, in 1812, the British attempted to conciliate the United States. In an effort to restore peaceful commerce with America, the British moved on June 16, 1812, to remove their restrictions on American shipping in the Atlantic. But they acted too late. On June 14, 1812, the United States had declared war.

Even then, however, the British were unable to devote much attention (or many resources) to the American conflict. But in the fall of 1812, the course of battle—and of European history—changed. Napoleon launched a catastrophic campaign against Russia; before the winter was over his army was in disarray, his power in Europe was greatly diminished, and his empire was well on the way to its final defeat. With the threat from France diminishing,

Britain was able by late 1813 to turn its military attention to America.

The Course of Battle

Thomas Jefferson believed that an American conquest of Canada, which so many Westerners were by 1812 demanding, would be a "mere matter of marching." It was not. American forces tried repeatedly to conquer the British territories to the north; all such efforts ended in frustration. In the summer of 1812, the elderly General William Hull, governor of Michigan Territory, led American forces into Canada by way of Detroit, as part of a planned three-pronged invasion. He was soon forced to retreat to Detroit, and in August he surrendered the fort there. Other invasion efforts also failed and Fort Dearborn (Chicago) fell before an Indian attack.

In the face of these disasters and defeats on land, the Madison administration and its supporters took what consolation they could from the news of American successes on the sea. American frigates engaged British warships in a series of duels and won some spectacular victories, one of the most renowned being the victory of the *Constitution* over the *Guerrière*. American privateers destroyed or captured one British merchant ship after another, occasionally braving the coastal waters of the British Isles and burning vessels within sight of the shore. But these acts of bravado soon provoked an angry and effective British counterattack. By 1813, the British navy was driving the American frigates to cover and imposing a close blockade on the United States.

While British sea power dominated the ocean, American fleets seized control of the Great Lakes. First, the Americans took command of Lake Ontario, enabling troops to cross over to York (Toronto), the capital of Canada. At York, on April 27, 1813, the invaders ran upon a cunningly contrived land mine, the explosion of which killed more than fifty, including General Zebulon M. Pike. Some of the enraged survivors, without authorization, set fire to the capital's public buildings, which burned to the ground. After destroying some ships and military stores, the Americans departed to their own lands across the lake.

American forces next seized control of Lake Erie, mainly through the work of the youthful Oliver Hazard Perry. Having constructed a fleet at Presque Isle (Erie, Pennsylvania), Perry took up a position at Put-in Bay, near a group of islands off the mouth of

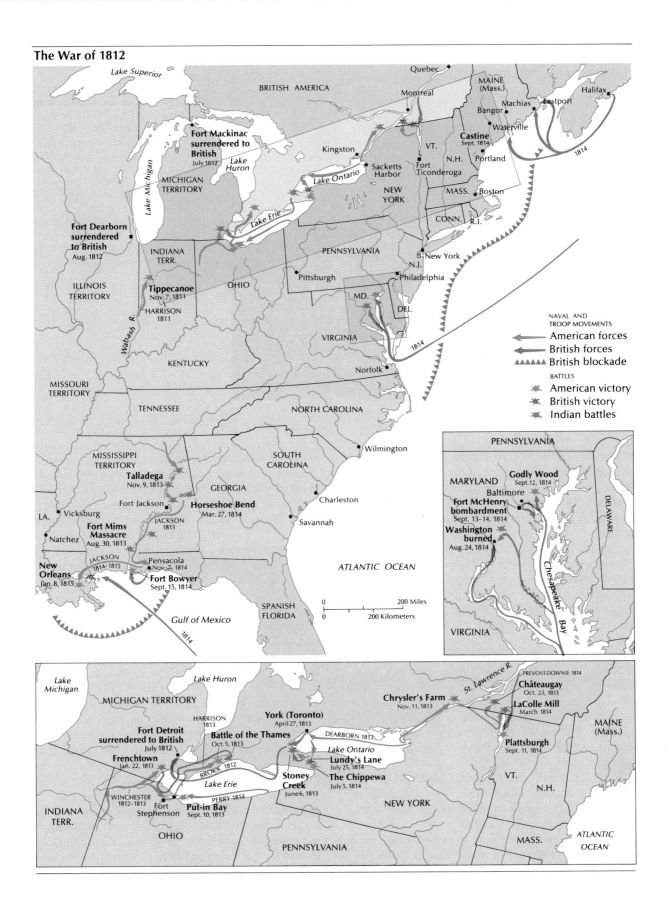

The War of 1812

Lake Superior

BRITISH AMERICA

Quebec

Montreal

MAINE (Mass.)

Machias

Bangor

Eastport

Halifax

Waterville

Fort Mackinac surrendered to British
July 1812

Lake Huron

Lake Michigan

MICHIGAN TERRITORY

Kingston

Sacketts Harbor

Lake Ontario

Castine
Sept. 1814

VT.

N.H.

Portland

Fort Ticonderoga

1814

Fort Dearborn surrendered to British
Aug. 1812

Lake Erie

NEW YORK

MASS.

Boston

INDIANA TERR.

CONN.

R.I.

ILLINOIS TERRITORY

Tippecanoe
Nov. 7, 1811

HARRISON 1811

OHIO

PENNSYLVANIA

Pittsburgh

New York

N.J.

Philadelphia

Wabash R.

KENTUCKY

MD.

DEL.

VIRGINIA

NAVAL AND TROOP MOVEMENTS

American forces

British forces

British blockade

Norfolk

1814

MISSOURI TERRITORY

TENNESSEE

NORTH CAROLINA

BATTLES

American victory

British victory

Indian battles

Wilmington

MISSISSIPPI TERRITORY

Talladega
Nov. 9, 1813

GEORGIA

SOUTH CAROLINA

Charleston

Fort Jackson

Horseshoe Bend
Mar. 27, 1814

JACKSON 1813

LA.

Vicksburg

Savannah

Fort Mims Massacre
Aug. 30, 1813

Natchez

JACKSON 1814-1815

Pensacola
Nov. 7, 1814

New Orleans
Jan. 8, 1815

Fort Bowyer
Sept. 15, 1814

ATLANTIC OCEAN

SPANISH FLORIDA

Gulf of Mexico

1814

0   200 Miles

0   200 Kilometers

PENNSYLVANIA

MARYLAND

Godly Wood
Sept. 12, 1814

Baltimore

DELAWARE

Fort McHenry bombardment
Sept. 13–14, 1814

Washington burned
Aug. 24, 1814

Chesapeake Bay

VIRGINIA

Lake Michigan

Lake Huron

St. Lawrence R.

PREVOST-DOWNIE 1814

Châteaugay
Oct. 23, 1813

MICHIGAN TERRITORY

HARRISON 1813

York (Toronto)
April 27, 1813

Chrysler's Farm
Nov. 11, 1813

LaColle Mill
March 1814

Fort Detroit surrendered to British
July 1812

Battle of the Thames
Oct. 5, 1813

DEARBORN 1813

MAINE (Mass.)

Frenchtown
Jan. 22, 1813

BROCK 1812

Lake Ontario

Lundy's Lane
July 25, 1814

Plattsburgh
Sept. 11, 1814

Stoney Creek
June 6, 1813

The Chippewa
July 5, 1814

VT.

N.H.

WINCHESTER 1812-1813

Lake Erie

PERRY 1813

Fort Stephenson

Put-in Bay
Sept. 10, 1813

NEW YORK

INDIANA TERR.

OHIO

PENNSYLVANIA

MASS.

ATLANTIC OCEAN

The Battle of Lake Erie
In the Battle of Lake Erie twenty-eight-year-old Captain Oliver Hazard Perry maneuvered a British fleet into a decisive engagement—one of the bloodiest naval battles of the war and a major triumph for the United States. After the battle Perry sent a message to General William Henry Harrison that read: "We have met the enemy and they are ours." The victory gave the United States control of Lake Erie and forced the British to evacuate their strongholds at Malden and Detroit. (New York State Historical Association, Cooperstown)

the Maumee River. With the banner "Don't Give Up the Ship" flying on his flagship, he awaited the British fleet, whose intentions he had learned from a spy. When the fleet arrived on September 10, 1813, he dispersed it and established American dominance of the lake.

This made possible, at last, an American invasion of Canada by way of Detroit. The post had been hard to reach overland; but after Perry's victory at Put-in Bay, supplies as well as men could be quickly and easily transported by water. William Henry Harrison, who had replaced Hull in the Western command, now pushed up the river Thames into upper Canada and on October 5, 1813, won a victory chiefly notable for the death of Tecumseh, who had been commissioned a brigadier general in the British army. The Battle of the Thames resulted in no lasting occupation of Canada, but it weakened and disheartened the Indians of the Northwest and greatly diminished their ability to defend their claims to the region.

While Harrison was harrying the tribes of the Northwest, another Indian fighter was striking an even harder blow at the Creeks in the Southwest. The Creeks, aroused by Tecumseh on his Southern visit and supplied by the Spaniards in Florida, had fallen upon Fort Mims, on the Alabama River just north of the Florida border and had massacred the frontier families taking shelter within its stockade. Andrew Jackson, a wealthy Tennessee planter and a general in the state's militia, temporarily abandoned plans for an invasion of Florida and set off in pursuit of the Creeks instead. On March 27, 1814, in the Battle of Horseshoe Bend, Jackson's men took frightful vengeance on the Indians— slaughtering women and children along with warriors. Jackson's victory broke the resistance of the Creeks; the tribe agreed to cede most of its lands to the United States and retreated westward, farther into the interior. The battle also won Jackson a commission as major general in the United States Army, and in that capacity he led his men further south into Florida and, on November 7, 1814, seized the Spanish fort at Pensacola.

Until 1814, the British had committed few forces of their own to the struggle on land and had restricted themselves largely to aiding the Indians. But after the Battles of the Thames and Horseshoe Bend, the Indians were no longer a major factor in the conflict, and the British approach to the war now shifted. The surrender of Napoleon made it possible for England to transfer part of its European army to America to dispose of what they called the "dirty shirts," the unkempt Americans. And so in 1814, the British prepared to invade the United States from three approaches—Chesapeake Bay, Lake Champlain, and the mouth of the Mississippi.

An armada under Admiral Sir George Cockburn sailed up the Patuxent River from Chesapeake Bay and landed an army that marched a short distance overland to Bladensburg, on the outskirts of Washington. A much more numerous force of American militiamen opposed the British, but they had been hastily assembled and poorly trained. Unnerved by the repeated assaults of the well-disciplined redcoats, they finally broke formation and ran. The British marched into Washington on August 24, 1814, and put the government to flight. Then they set fire to the public buildings, including the White House, in retaliation for the earlier American burning of the Canadian capital at York. The sack of Washington marked the low point of American fortunes in the war.

Leaving Washington in partial ruins, the invading army proceeded up the bay toward Baltimore. But Baltimore, guarded by Fort McHenry, was ready. To block the river approach, the garrison had stretched a chain across the Patapsco and had sunk several boats in the river, forcing the British to bombard the fort from a distance. Through the night of September 13, Francis Scott Key (a Washington lawyer who was on board one of the British ships on a mission to secure the release of an American prisoner) watched the bombardment. The next morning, "by the dawn's early light," he could see the flag on the fort still flying; he recorded his pride in the moment by scribbling a poem—"The Star-Spangled Banner"—on the back of an envelope. The British withdrew from Baltimore. Key's words were set to the tune of an old English drinking song and established lasting fame as an American patriotic anthem. (In 1931, it became the official national anthem.)

Meanwhile, another British invasion force was descending on northern New York. The British navy had gathered a fleet on Lake Champlain about the size of the American fleet drawn up in opposition; and they had an army nearby three times as large as the mixed force of American regulars and militia facing it. Despite the odds, however, the American defenders destroyed the invading fleet; the British army then retreated to Canada. This important victory—the Battle of Plattsburgh, on September 11, 1814—secured the northern border of the United States.

Far to the south, the most serious threat of all soon materialized. In December 1814, a formidable array of battle-hardened British veterans, fresh from the duke of Wellington's peninsular campaign against the French in Spain, landed below New Orleans. On Christmas Day, Wellington's brother-in-law, Sir Edward Pakenham, arrived to take command. (Neither he nor anyone else in America knew that a treaty of peace between the British and American governments had been signed in faraway Belgium the day before.) Awaiting Pakenham's advance up the Mississippi was Andrew Jackson with a motley collection of Tennesseans, Kentuckians, Creoles, blacks, and pirates drawn up behind earthen breastworks. On January 8, 1815, the redcoats advanced on the American fortifications. For all their discipline and bravery, the exposed British forces were no match for Jackson's well-protected men. After the Americans had repulsed several waves of attackers, the British finally retreated, while an American band struck up "Hail, Columbia!" Left behind were 700 British dead, including Pakenham himself, 1,400 wounded, and 500 other prisoners. Jackson's losses: 8 killed, 13 wounded.

The Revolt of New England

With a few notable exceptions, such as the Battle of New Orleans, the military operations of the United States between 1812 and 1815 consisted of a series of bungled, humiliating failures. In retrospect, these frustrations seem unsurprising. The American government was woefully unprepared for the war at the outset, and it faced increasing popular opposition as the contest dragged on. In some areas, in fact, the opposition went to such extremes that it became almost a part of the British war effort. That was nowhere more true than in New England, where some Federalists celebrated British victories, deliberately sabotaged their own country's war effort, and even plotted disunion and a separate peace. Once again, the Federalists—who were beginning to regain some of their political strength because of dissatisfaction with Madison's handling of the war—destroyed their own prospects through extremism.

Until 1814, the British blockade of the American coast did not extend north of Newport, Rhode Island. The British government was deliberately cultivating the New England trade, and the merchants of New England happily responded. Goods carried in Yankee ships helped to feed British troops in Canada as well as in Spain, and for a time many New England shipowners grew rich by trading with the enemy while denouncing Madison and the war (although eventually the business of the shipowners

The Battle of New Orleans

The Battle of New Orleans was the last major engagement and the greatest American victory on land of the War of 1812. General Andrew Jackson commanded about 4,500 troops and fended off superior British forces under the command of Sir Edward Pakenham (who was killed in the fighting). The artist Hyacinthe de Laclotte drew the sketch that became the basis of this painting while standing above the battlefield during the decisive engagement. The British suffered over 2,000 casualties in the battle, the Americans 21. But the American triumph was more tragic than glorious. Unknown to the commanders in Louisiana, the Peace of Ghent, which brought an official end to the war, had been signed in Europe two weeks before. (New Orleans Museum of Art)

as a whole fell far below the level of the prosperous prewar years).

Although most of the money in the nation was concentrated in New England, the government was unable to sell more than a very few war bonds there. One Treasury bond issue, desperately needed to keep soldiers in the field, almost fell through because of the refusal of the New England banks to make loans. Secretary of the Treasury Albert Gallatin had to turn to his friend John Jacob Astor of New York and to two foreign-born bankers of Philadelphia for the necessary funds.

In Congress, the Republicans had continual trouble with the Federalist opposition. John C. Calhoun, leader of the administration forces, faced New England obstructionists in every effort to win approval of measures in support of the war. Foremost among the obstructionists was a young congressman from New Hampshire, Daniel Webster. Introducing resolution after resolution to embarrass the administration, Webster demanded to know the reasons for the war and intimated (correctly) that Napoleon had tricked the president into antagonizing England. Every measure to finance the fighting—by loans, taxes, tariffs, or a national bank—Webster and his Federalist allies vehemently denounced. At a time when voluntary enlistments were lagging and the army was seriously undermanned, he opposed a bill to encourage enlistments. In desperation, the administration proposed to draft men into the regular army from the state militias. (On several occasions, the governors of New England states had refused to allow their state militias to take orders from the president or to fight outside the country.) Webster declared that no such law could be enforced in his part of the country and thus helped doom the conscription bill to defeat.

As new states in the South and West, all strongly Republican, had joined the Union, the Federalists had become more and more hopelessly a minority party in the country as a whole. But they were still the majority party in New England. And some of them began to dream of creating a separate nation in that region, which they could dominate and in which they could escape the dictation of slaveholders and backwoodsmen. The talk of secession, heard before at the time of the Louisiana Purchase and again at the time of Jefferson's Embargo, revived during the war and reached a climax in the winter of 1814–1815, when the republic appeared to be on the verge of ruin.

On December 15, 1814, while the British were beginning their invasion by way of New Orleans, delegates from the New England states met in Hartford, Connecticut, to consider the grievances of their section against the Madison administration. The would-be seceders were overruled by the comparatively moderate men, who were in the overwhelming majority at the Hartford Convention. The convention's report reasserted the right of nullification but only hinted at secession, observing that "the severance of the Union by one or more States, against the will of the rest, and especially in time of war, can be justified only by absolute necessity." But the report proposed seven amendments to the Constitution (presumably as the condition of New England's remaining in the Union)—amendments designed to protect New England from the growing influence of the South and the West.

The Federalists believed they were in a strong bargaining position. The war was going badly, and the government was becoming desperate. The New Englanders assumed, therefore, that the Republicans would have to give in to the Hartford Convention terms. Soon after the convention adjourned, however, the news of Jackson's smashing victory at New Orleans reached the cities of the Northeast. While most Americans rejoiced, the Federalists were plunged into gloom. A day or two later, reports arrived from abroad of a treaty of peace. The treaty, of course, had been signed before the Battle of New Orleans. But the public—which first heard the news of the battle and then the news of the treaty—re-

ceived the impression that the United States had won the war. "Peace is signed in the arms of victory!" the magazine *Niles's Register* exclaimed. In the euphoria of this presumed triumph, the Hartford Convention and the Federalist party came to seem futile, irrelevant, even treasonable.

The Peace Settlement

Peace talks between the United States and Britain had begun even before the first battles of the War of 1812 were fought. President Madison, who had never really wanted a declaration of war and who regretted "the necessity that had produced it," hoped for an early end to hostilities even after the war began.

The British government, eager to liquidate the minor war and concentrate on the major one, against Napoleon, sent an admiral to Washington in the fall of 1812 with proposals for an armistice; but the negotiations failed because of Madison's continued insistence that the British renounce impressment and Britain's continued refusal to do so. Twice Russia offered to mediate the conflict; twice the British declined. Finally, however, the British agreed to meet the Americans in direct negotiations on neutral ground. After prolonged delays, diplomats from the two countries met in Ghent, Belgium, on August 8, 1814.

The American peace delegation at Ghent was composed of men of exceptional ability, representing both parties and all regions of their country. John Quincy Adams, an experienced diplomat (and son of the former president) who had recently been minister to Russia, headed the delegation; a former Federalist, he had broken with his party in order to support Jefferson's Embargo. Serving with him was Henry Clay, once a war hawk, now eager for peace; and Albert Gallatin, secretary of the treasury in both Jefferson's and Madison's administrations. A natural diplomat, Gallatin held the delegation together by moderating the disputes between Adams and Clay.

At Ghent, the two delegations began by presenting extreme demands, then gradually backed down, and finally agreed to a compromise. The Americans originally demanded not only that Britain renounce impressment, but also that it cede all or part of Canada to the United States. They also demanded British aid in acquiring Florida from Spain. The English diplomats presented an ultimatum requiring the United States to cede territory in the Northwest for the formation of an Indian buffer state. Then, when London refused to sustain them in the ultimatum, they withdrew it and proposed that peace be made on the principle of *uti possidetis*. This meant that each of the belligerents would keep the territory it actually held whenever the fighting stopped. Expecting large territorial gains from the invasion of America, the English diplomats at Ghent tried to delay negotiations so as to maximize the gains. But the government in London, still principally concerned with developments in Europe, decided to hasten the settlement with the United States and recommended peace on the basis of the *status quo ante bellum*, a return to things as they had been before the war began. President Madison, in the meantime, had advised his delegates that they need no longer insist on the renunciation of impressment. A treaty providing for the status quo, hastily drawn up, was signed on Christmas Eve 1814.

According to the Treaty of Ghent, the war was to end as soon as the document had been ratified on both sides. Each of the belligerents was to restore its wartime conquests to the other. Four commissions, composed of both Americans and Britons, were to be appointed to agree on disputed or undetermined segments of the boundary between Canada and the United States.

The Treaty of Ghent was followed by other settlements that contributed to the improvement of Anglo-American relations. A separate commercial treaty in 1815 gave Americans the right to trade freely with England and the British Empire except for the West Indies. A fisheries convention in 1818 renewed the privileges of Americans to catch and dry fish at specified places along the shores of British North America. The Rush-Bagot agreement of 1817 provided for mutual disarmament on the Great Lakes. Gradually disarmament was extended to the land, and eventually (although not until 1872) the Canadian-American boundary became the longest "unguarded frontier" in the world.

Although the British had not renounced impressment in principle, they ceased to apply it in practice after 1815. With the final end of the Napoleonic Wars after the Battle of Waterloo, the nations of Europe entered upon a century of comparative peace, broken only by wars of limited scale. So the British no longer felt the need to violate American sovereignty on the high seas, and the government and people of the United States could afford to devote their energies primarily to affairs at home.

Free Seas Again

No sooner had peace come in 1815 than Congress declared war again, this time against Algiers, which had taken advantage of the War of 1812 to loose its pirates once more against American shipping in the Mediterranean. Two American squadrons now proceeded to North African waters. One of the two, under the command of Stephen Decatur, a naval hero of the late war with England, captured a number of enemy ships, blockaded the coast of Algiers, and forced the dey (the Algerian ruler) to accept a treaty that not only ended the payment of tribute by the United States but required Algiers to pay reparations to America. Decatur then sailed on to Tunis and Tripoli and collected additional indemnities. This naval action in the Mediterranean did more to provide Americans with free access to the seas than the War of 1812 itself had done.

Postwar Expansion

With the international conflict settled, Americans could once again turn their attention to their internal affairs. The aftermath of the war made clear how far the nation had already moved from its simple, agrarian origins. Commerce, which had become central to the American economy, revived and expanded. Industry, which had made a few tentative beginnings in the first years of the century, advanced rapidly. Westward expansion, deterred for a time by the conflicts with the Indians and the British, now accelerated dramatically. The period following the war, in short, was one of rapid growth and progress—too rapid, as it turned out, for the boom was followed in 1819 by a disastrous bust. The collapse proved to be only a temporary obstacle to economic expansion, but it revealed clearly that the United States continued to lack some of the basic institutions necessary to sustain long-term growth.

Banking and Currency

The War of 1812 may have stimulated the growth of manufactures. But it also produced chaos in shipping and banking; and it exposed dramatically the inadequacy of the existing transportation system. The aftermath of the war, therefore, saw the emergence of a series of political issues connected with national economic development: reestablishing the Bank of the United States (the first Bank's charter had not been renewed when it expired in 1811), protecting the new industries, and providing a nationwide net-

The United States Capitol in 1824
The slightly idealized view by the American artist Charles Burton shows the approach to the west front of the United States Capitol along Pennsylvania Avenue. The rotunda that today rises above the building was built in the 1860s to replace the lower dome shown in this painting. Other later additions included the two wings containing the present chambers of the Senate and the House of Representatives. (Metropolitan Museum of Art)

work of roads and waterways. On these issues, the former war hawks Clay and Calhoun became the leading advocates of economic nationalism. Republicans both, they were now sponsoring measures of a kind once championed by the party of Hamilton. In regard to the Bank and the tariff, the new nationalists were fully successful; in regard to internal improvements, only partly so.

The wartime experience seemed to underline the need for another national bank. After the expiration of the first Bank's charter, a large number of state banks had sprung up. They issued vast quantities of bank notes (promises to pay, which then served much the same purpose as bank checks were later to do). But the state banks did not always bother to retain a large enough reserve of gold or silver to redeem the notes on demand. The notes passed from hand to hand more or less as money; but their actual value depended on the reputation of the bank that issued them. There was, therefore, a wide variety of notes, of widely differing value, in circulation at the same time. The result was a confusion that made honest business difficult and counterfeiting easy. In legal terms, bank notes were not genuine currency and thus did not technically violate the clause of the Constitution giving Congress the exclusive power to regulate the currency and forbidding the states to emit bills of credit. But the use of bank notes as money clearly challenged the spirit of that clause.

Congress struck at the currency problem not by prohibiting the bank notes but by chartering a second Bank of the United States in 1816. It was essentially the same institution as the one founded under Hamilton's leadership in 1791 except that it had more capital than its predecessor. The national bank could not forbid state banks from issuing notes; but its size and power gave it the ability to control the state banks. It could, if it chose, accumulate the state bank notes, present them to the local banks, and demand payment either in cash or in the national bank's own notes, which were as good as gold. Once the Bank of the United States began to exercise its power, as it did within a few years of its creation, the state banks had to stay on a specie-paying basis or risk being forced out of business.

Protecting Industry

Solving the problems of the currency was, for a time at least, less controversial than solving the problems that the end of the war created for American manufacturing. During the war, manufacturing had flourished, in large part because of the decline of American shipping. Between 1811 and 1814, American exports had dropped from $61 million to $7 million, and

imports had fallen from $53 million to $13 million. The total tonnage of American vessels engaged in foreign trade had declined from about 950,000 to fewer than 60,000. America's principal export was agricultural goods, and the decline of the carrying trade had been disastrous for farmers, who were unable to get their produce to the markets of the world. But America's principal import was manufactured goods; and with imports effectively blocked, manufacturers prospered. Much of the capital and labor formerly employed in commerce and shipbuilding was diverted to manufacturing. Goods were so scarce that, even with comparatively unskilled labor and poor management, new factories could be started with an assurance of quick profits.

The American textile industry had experienced a particularly dramatic growth. The first census of manufacturing, in 1810, revealed 269 cotton and 24 woolen mills in the country. But the Embargo of 1807 and the War of 1812 had spurred a tremendous expansion. Between 1807 and 1815, the total number of cotton spindles increased more than fifteenfold, from 8,000 to 130,000. Until 1814, the textile factories—most of them in New England—produced only

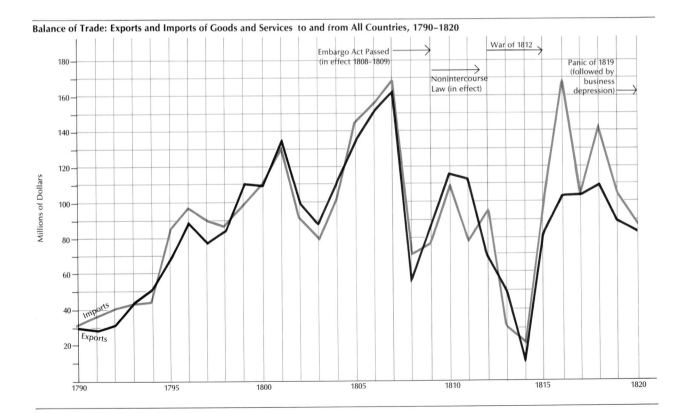

Balance of Trade: Exports and Imports of Goods and Services to and from All Countries, 1790–1820

yarn and thread; the weaving of cloth was left to families operating handlooms at home. Then the Boston merchant Francis Cabot Lowell, after examining textile machinery in England, developed a power loom even better than its English counterpart. In 1813, Lowell organized the Boston Manufacturing Company and, at Waltham, Massachusetts, founded the first mill in America to carry on the processes of spinning and weaving under a single roof. Lowell's company was an important step in revolutionizing American manufacturing.

As the War of 1812 came to an end, however, the prospects for American industry suddenly dimmed. British ships swarmed into American ports and unloaded cargoes of manufactured goods to be sold at cut-rate prices, even below cost. As Lord Brougham explained to Parliament, it was "well worth while to incur a loss upon the first exportation, in order, by the glut, to stifle in the cradle those rising manufactures in the United States, which war had forced into existence, contrary to the natural course of things." The "infant industries" cried out for protection against these tactics, arguing that they needed time to grow strong enough to withstand the foreign competition. In 1816, protectionists in Congress won passage of a tariff law that effectively limited competition from abroad on a broad range of items, among the most important of which was cotton cloth. There were objections from agricultural interests, who stood to pay higher prices for manufactured goods. But the nationalist dream of creating an important American industrial economy prevailed.

Transportation

The nation's most pressing economic need in the aftermath of the war, however, was for improvements in its transportation system. Without a better transportation network, manufacturers would not have access to the raw materials they needed and would not be able to send their finished goods to markets. So an old debate resumed: Should the federal government help to finance roads and other "internal improvements"?

The idea of using government funds to finance road building was not a new one. When Ohio entered the Union in 1803, the federal government had agreed that part of the proceeds from its sale of public lands there should be used for building roads. And in 1807, Jefferson's secretary of the treasury, Albert Gallatin, had proposed that a national road, financed

partly by the Ohio land sales, be built from the Potomac to the Ohio. Both Congress and the president had approved. The next year, Gallatin presented a comprehensive plan of internal improvements that required an appropriation of $20 million. Work on the new roads did not begin until 1811 (partly because of Jefferson's doubts about the constitutionality of such expenditures). Finally, however, construction of the National Road got under way at Cumberland, Maryland, on the Potomac; and by 1818, this highway—with a crushed stone surface and massive stone bridges—was completed to Wheeling, Virginia, on the Ohio River. Meanwhile the state of Pennsylvania gave $100,000 to a private company that extended the Lancaster pike westward to Pittsburgh.

Over both of these roads moved a heavy traffic of stagecoaches, Conestoga wagons, private carriages, and other vehicles, as well as droves of cattle. Despite high tolls, freight rates across the mountains were now lower than ever before. They were not low enough to permit the long-distance hauling of such bulky loads as wheat or flour. But commodities with a high value in proportion to their weight, especially manufactures, moved from the Atlantic seaboard to the Ohio Valley in unprecedented quantities.

At the same time, on the rivers and the Great Lakes, steam-powered shipping was experiencing rapid expansion. The development of steamboat lines was already well under way before the War of 1812, thanks to the technological advances introduced by Robert Fulton and others. (See pp. 246–249.) The war had retarded expansion of the system for a time; but by 1816, river steamers were beginning to journey up and down the Mississippi to the Ohio River, and up the Ohio as far as Pittsburgh, for the first time. Within a few years, steamboats were carrying far more cargo on the Mississippi than all the earlier forms of river transport—flatboats, barges, and others—combined. They stimulated the agricultural economy of the West and the South, by providing much readier access to markets at greatly reduced cost. And they enabled Eastern manufacturers to send their finished goods west much more readily.

But despite the progress with steamboats and turnpikes, there remained serious gaps in the transportation network of the country, as experience during the War of 1812 had shown. Once Atlantic shipping was cut off by the British blockade, the coastal roads became choked by the unaccustomed volume of north-south traffic. At the river ferries, long lines of wagons waited for a chance to cross.

Deck Life on the *Paragon*, 1811–1812

The *North River Steamboat Clermont,* launched in 1806 by the inventor Robert Fulton and propelled by an engine he had developed, traveled from Manhattan to Albany (about 150 miles) in thirty-two hours. That was neither the longest nor the fastest voyage to date, but the *Clermont* proved to be the first steam-powered vessel large and reliable enough to be commercially valuable. Within a few years Fulton and his partner Robert R. Livingston had several steamboats operating profitably around New York. The third vessel in their fleet, the *Paragon,* shown here in a painting by the Russian diplomat and artist Pavel Petrovich Svinin, could carry 150 people and contained an elegant dining salon fitted with bronze, mahogany, and mirrors. Svinin called it "a whole floating town," and Fulton told a friend that the *Paragon* "beats everything on the globe, for made as you and I are we cannot tell what is in the moon." (Metropolitan Museum of Art)

Oxcarts, pressed into emergency service, took six or seven weeks to go from Philadelphia to Charleston. In some areas there were serious shortages of goods normally carried by sea, and prices rose to new heights. Rice cost three times as much in New York as in Charleston, flour three times as much in Boston as in Richmond. There were military consequences as well. On the Northern and Western frontiers, the American campaigns were frustrated partly by the absence of good roads.

With this wartime experience in mind, President Madison in 1815 called the attention of Congress to the "great importance of establishing throughout our country the roads and canals which can be best executed under the national authority," and he suggested that a constitutional amendment would resolve any doubts about the authority of Congress to provide for the construction of canals and roads. Representative Calhoun promptly introduced a bill that would have used the funds owed the government by the Bank of the United States to finance internal improvements. "Let us, then, bind the republic together with a perfect system of roads and canals," Calhoun urged. "Let us conquer space."

Congress passed the internal improvements bill, but President Madison, on his last day in office (March 3, 1817), returned it with his veto. He supported the purpose of the bill, he explained, but he still believed that Congress lacked authority to fund the improvements without a constitutional amendment. And so on the issue of internal improvements, at least, the nationalists fell short of their goals. The tremendous task of building the transportation network necessary for the growing American economy was left to the state governments and to private enterprise.

The Great Migration

One reason for the growing interest in internal improvements was the sudden and dramatic surge in westward expansion in the years following the War of 1812. "Old America seems to be breaking up and moving westward," wrote an English observer at the time. By the time of the census of 1820, settlers had pushed well beyond the Mississippi River, and the population of the Western regions was increasing more rapidly than that of the nation as a whole. Almost one of every four Americans lived west of the Appalachians in 1820; ten years before, only one in seven had resided there. There were several important reasons for this expansion. Population pressures and economic pressures pushed many Americans from the East; the availability of new lands and the removal of old dangers drew them to the West.

The pressures driving Americans out of the East came in part from the continued growth of the American population—both through natural increase and through immigration. Between 1800 and 1820, the nation's population nearly doubled—from 5.3 million to 9.6 million. The growth of the nation's cities absorbed some of that increase; but most Americans were still farmers, and the agricultural lands of the East were by now largely occupied. Some of the farmland in the East, moreover, was now exhausted. And in the South, the spread of the plantation system, and of a slave labor force, limited opportunities for new settlers.

Meanwhile, the West itself was becoming increasingly attractive. The War of 1812 had helped diminish one of the traditional obstacles to Western expansion: Indian opposition. And in the aftermath of the war, the federal government continued its policy of pushing the remaining tribes farther and farther west. A series of treaties in 1815 wrested still more land from the Indians. And in the meantime,

the government was erecting a chain of stockaded forts along the Great Lakes and the upper Mississippi, to protect the frontier. It also created a "factory" system, by which government factors or agents supplied the Indians with goods at cost. This not only worked to drive Canadian traders out of the region; it also helped create a situation of dependency that made the Indians themselves easier to control.

The fertile lands now made secure for white settlement drew migrants from throughout the East to what was then known as the Old Northwest (now part of the Midwest). For many of them, the Ohio River was the main route—the "grand track"— westward, until the completion of the Erie Canal in 1825. The pioneers reached the river by traveling along the turnpike to Pittsburgh or along the National Road to Wheeling, or by sailing down one of its tributaries—such as the Kanawha, the Cumberland, or the Tennessee. Once on the Ohio, they floated downstream on flatboats bearing all their possessions, then left the river (often at Cincinnati, which was becoming one of the region's—and the nation's— principal cities) and pressed on overland with wagons, handcarts, packhorses, cattle, and hogs.

Once having arrived at their destination, preferably in the spring or early summer, the settlers built a lean-to or cabin, then hewed a clearing out of the forest and put in a crop of corn to supplement the wild game they caught and the domestic animals they had brought with them. It was a rough existence, often plagued by loneliness, poverty, dirt, and disease. Men, women, and children worked side by side in the fields—and at times had virtually no contact for weeks or months at a time with anyone outside their own families.

Life on the frontier was not, however, as solitary and individualistic as later myth suggested. Migrants often journeyed westward in groups, which at times became the basis of new communities where schools, churches, stores, and other community institutions were built. The labor shortage in the interior meant that neighbors developed systems of mutual aid, gathering periodically to raise a barn, clear land, harvest crops, or make quilts. Gradually, the settlers built a thriving farm economy based largely on family units of modest size and committed to the cultivation of grain and the raising of livestock.

Another common feature of life in the Northwest (and indeed in much of early nineteenth-century America) was mobility. Individuals and families were constantly on the move, settling for a few years in one place, then selling their land (often at a significant

Prairie Life in Illinois, 1833
Americans flocked to the open lands of the West in the 1830s in search of economic opportunity. Many found it, but some also discovered that life in the sparsely settled prairies could be bleak, lonely, and at times perilous. This painting by the Swiss artist Carl Bodmer of a farm in Illinois suggests both the isolation of life in the West and the abundance of land available to settlers.   (by Joslyn Art Museum, Omaha, Nebraska)

profit, given the rapidly rising price of farm properties in the region) and settling again somewhere else. When new areas for settlement opened farther to the west, it was often the people on the frontier—rather than those who remained in the East—who flocked to them first.

In the Southwest, the new agricultural economy emerged along different lines—just as the economy of the Old South had long been different from that of the Northeast. The principal attraction there was cotton. The cotton lands in the uplands of the Old South had lost much of their fertility through overplanting and erosion. But the market for cotton continued to grow, and so there was no lack of ambitious farmers seeking fresh soil in a climate suitable for the crop. In the Southwest, around the end of the Appalachian range, stretched a broad zone within which cotton

could thrive—including what was to become known as the Black Belt of central Alabama and Mississippi, a vast prairie with a productive soil of rotted limestone.

The advance of the Southern frontier meant the spread of cotton and slavery. Usually the first arrivals were ordinary frontiersmen like those farther north, small farmers who made rough clearings in the forest. Then came wealthier planters, who bought up the cleared or partially cleared land, while the original settlers moved farther west and started over again. The large planters made the westward journey in a style quite different from that of the first pioneers. Over the alternately dusty and muddy roads came great caravans consisting of herds of livestock, wagonloads of household goods, long lines of slaves, and—bringing up the rear—the planter's family riding in carriages. Success in the wilderness was by no means assured, even for the wealthiest settlers. But many planters soon expanded small clearings into vast fields white with cotton. They replaced the cabins of the pioneers with more sumptuous log dwellings and ultimately with imposing mansions that demonstrated the rise of a newly rich class.

The rapid growth of the West resulted in the admission of four new states to the Union in the immediate aftermath of the War of 1812: Indiana in 1816, Mississippi in 1817, Illinois in 1818, and Alabama in 1819.

The Far West

Not many Americans were yet much interested in the Far Western areas of the continent. Except for New Englanders engaged in Pacific whaling or in the China trade, few Americans were familiar with the Oregon coast. Only fur traders and trappers had any knowledge of the land between the Missouri and the Pacific.

Before the War of 1812, John Jacob Astor's American Fur Company had established Astoria as a trading post at the mouth of the Columbia River in Oregon. But when war came, Astor sold his interests to the Northwestern Fur Company, a British concern operating out of Canada; and after the war he centered his own operations in the Great Lakes area, from which he eventually extended them westward to the Rockies. Other companies carried on operations up the Missouri and its tributaries and in the Rocky Mountains. At first, fur traders did most of their business by purchasing pelts from the Indians. But beginning with Andrew and William Ashley's Rocky Mountain Fur Company, founded in 1822, more and more traders dispatched white trappers into the wilderness to capture animals themselves.

The trappers or "mountain men" explored the Far West and gained an intimate knowledge of it; but although such men as Jedediah S. Smith ultimately became famous for their exploits, they did not write books or draw maps, and thus their knowledge did not spread widely. Public awareness of the region increased as a result of the explorations of Major Stephen H. Long. In 1819 and 1820, with instructions from the War Department to find the sources of the Red River, Long led nineteen soldiers on a journey up the Platte and South Platte rivers through what is now Nebraska and eastern Colorado (where he discovered the peak named for him), and then returned eastward along the Arkansas River through what is now Kansas.

Long's expedition failed to find the headwaters of the Red River. But Long wrote an influential report on his trip and assessed the region's potential for future settlement and development. "In regard to this

Jim Butler, Mountain Man

Well before most Americans were interested in settling the lands of the Far West, a small group of solitary trappers and explorers—known in popular legend as "mountain men"—moved through the region in search of wealth and solitude. This pencil sketch by an unknown artist shows one of these early pioneers. (Gilcrease Institute of Art)

extensive section of country between the Missouri River and the Rocky Mountains," he said, "we do not hesitate in giving the opinion that it is almost wholly unfit for cultivation, and of course uninhabitable by a people depending upon agriculture for their subsistence." On the published map of his expedition, he labeled the Great Plains the "Great American Desert"—giving increased currency to the idea earlier advanced by Pike and others that the land beyond the Missouri River was unfit for cultivation.

The "Era of Good Feelings"

The expansion of the economy, the growth of the West, the creation of new states—all reflected the rising spirit of nationalism that was permeating the United States in the years following the war. That spirit found reflection, for a time, in the course of American politics.

Ever since 1800, the presidency seemed to have been the special possession of Virginians, who had passed it from one to another in unvarying sequence. After two terms in office Jefferson named his secretary of state, James Madison, to succeed him; and after two more terms, Madison secured the presidential nomination for *his* secretary of state, James Monroe. Many in the North already were expressing their impatience with the so-called Virginia Dynasty, but the Republicans had no difficulty in electing their candidate in the remarkably listless campaign of 1816. Monroe received 183 ballots in the electoral college; his opponent, Rufus King of New York, only 34—from the states of Massachusetts, Connecticut, and Delaware.

Monroe was sixty-one years old when he became president, and he seemed in many respects a relic of an earlier age. Tall and dignified, he wore the old-fashioned garb of his youthful days, including knee-length pantaloons and white-topped boots. In the course of his long and varied career, he had served as a soldier in the Revolution, as a diplomat, and most recently as a cabinet officer. He had once been regarded as impulsive and changeable, but he was by now noted for his caution and patience.

Monroe entered office under what seemed to be remarkably favorable circumstances. With the decline of the Federalists, his party faced no serious opposition. With the conclusion of the War of 1812, the nation faced no important international threats. American politicians had dreamed since the first days of the republic of a time in which partisan divisions and factional disputes might come to an end, a time in which the nation might learn to exhibit the harmony and virtue that the founders had envisioned. The postwar years seemed, at last, to provide an opportunity; and Monroe attempted to use his office to realize that dream.

He made that clear, above all, in the selection of his cabinet. For secretary of state, the first and most important position, he chose the New Englander and former Federalist John Quincy Adams. Jefferson, Madison, and Monroe had all served as secretary of state before becoming president; Adams, therefore, immediately became the heir apparent, suggesting that the Virginia Dynasty would soon come to an end. Monroe offered the office of secretary of war to Henry Clay, but Clay turned him down and remained Speaker of the House. So he chose instead the forceful South Carolinian John C. Calhoun. In his other appointments as well, Monroe seemed to go out of his way to include both Northerners and Southerners, Federalists and Republicans—to harmonize the various interests and sections of the country in a government of national unity.

Soon after his inauguration, Monroe did what no other president since Washington had done: He made a goodwill tour through the country, eastward to New England, westward as far as Detroit. In New England, so recently the scene of rabid Federalist discontent, he was greeted everywhere with enthusiastic demonstrations. The *Columbian Centinel*, a Federalist newspaper in Boston, commenting on the "Presidential Jubilee" in that city, observed that an "era of good feelings" had arrived. This phrase soon spread throughout the country and became a popular label for the presidency of Monroe.

In 1817, there seemed every reason to expect the "era of good feelings" to be just that—a time of happy national unity. And on the surface, at least, those expectations were realized. In 1820, when Monroe was a candidate for reelection to the presidency, only one elector voted against him; and he did so only to ensure that Washington would remain the only unanimously elected president. The Federalists did not even bother to put up an opposing candidate. For all practical purposes, the opposition party had now ceased to exist.

But beneath this surface calm, serious social and political divisions were emerging. Indeed, the years of Monroe's presidency became in the end a time of very bad feelings—a time in which the dream of a harmonious republic unsullied by party and faction was shattered forever.

John Quincy Adams and Florida

Whatever problems there were, however, did not seem to affect Monroe's secretary of state, John Quincy Adams. Like his father, the second president of the United States, Adams had spent much of his life in diplomatic service. He had represented the United States in Britain, Russia, the Netherlands, and Prussia. He had helped negotiate the Treaty of Ghent. And he had demonstrated in all his assignments a calmness and firmness that made him one of the great diplomats in American history.

He was also a committed nationalist; and when he assumed the office of secretary of state, he considered his most important task to be the promotion of American expansion. His first major challenge was Florida. The United States had already annexed West Florida, but most Americans still believed the nation should gain possession of the entire peninsula. Even the claim to West Florida was under dispute. Spain still claimed the whole of the province, East and West, and actually occupied most of it. In 1817, Adams began negotiations with the Spanish minister, Luis de Onís, in hopes of resolving the dispute and gaining the entire colony for the United States.

In the meantime, however, events were taking their own course in Florida itself. Andrew Jackson, now in command of American troops along the Florida frontier, had orders from Secretary of War Calhoun to "adopt the necessary measures" to put a stop to the continuing raids on American territory by the Seminole Indians south of the Florida border. Jackson (with, he later claimed, tacit encouragement from Washington) used those orders as an excuse to invade Florida, seize the Spanish forts at St. Marks and Pensacola, and order the hanging of two British subjects on the charge of supplying the Indians and inciting them to hostilities.

Instead of condemning Jackson or disavowing the raid, Adams urged the government to assume complete responsibility for it, for he saw in it a chance to win an important advantage in his negotiations with Spain. The United States, he told the Spanish, had the right under international law to defend itself against threats from across its borders. Since Spain was unwilling or unable to curb those threats, America had simply done what was necessary. And he implied that the nation might consider even more drastic action in the future.

Jackson's raid had demonstrated to the Spanish that the United States could easily take Florida by force. Onís realized, therefore, that he had little choice but to come to terms with the Americans, although he was determined to make the most of a bad situation. Under the terms of the Adams-Onís Treaty of 1819, Spain ceded all of Florida to the United States. In return, the American government assumed $5 million in outstanding claims by its citizens against Spain. The United States also gave up its claims to Texas, and Spain its claims to territory north of the 42nd parallel from the Rockies to the Pacific. Thus a line was drawn from the Gulf of Mexico northwestward across the continent establishing the northern border of the Spanish Empire and transferring to the United States the Spanish title to the West Coast north of California. Adams and Onís had concluded something more than a Florida agreement; it was a "transcontinental treaty."

The Panic of 1819

But the Monroe administration had little time to revel in its diplomatic successes. At the same time that Adams was completing his negotiations with Onís, the nation was falling victim to a serious economic crisis that helped revive many of the political disputes that the "era of good feelings" had presumably settled.

In part, the Panic of 1819 was a delayed reaction to the War of 1812 and to the preceding years of warfare in Europe. Ever since 1793, the continual fighting had drawn manpower from European fields, disrupted European business and agriculture, and created an abnormally high foreign demand for the produce of American plantations and farms. The whole period was one of exceptionally high prices for American producers, and although some prices fell with the decline of trade in 1814, they recovered with the resumption of exports to Europe after the war.

The rising prices for farm products stimulated a land boom in the United States, particularly in the West. After the war, the government land offices did a bigger business than ever before, a level of business they would maintain for twenty years. In 1815, sales totaled about 1 million acres; in 1819, more than 5 million. Many settlers bought on credit; under the land laws of 1800 and 1804 they could pay as little as $80 down, and then, they hoped, raise the remaining three installments within four years from the proceeds of their farming. Speculators bought large tracts of choice land, hoping to resell it at a profit to incoming settlers. At the land-office auctions, bidding became so spirited that much of the public land sold for prices far above the minimum of $2 an acre, some

SIGNIFICANT EVENTS

1803	Napoleonic Wars escalate in Europe
1805	British defeat French at Trafalgar
1806–1807	Napoleon issues Berlin and Milan decrees
1807	*Chesapeake-Leopard* incident nearly precipitates war with Great Britain Embargo Act passed Congress approves construction of National Road
1808	Economy plunges into depression Madison elected president
1809	Embargo is repealed Non-Intercourse Act passed
1810	Macon's Bill No. 2 reopens trade with Britain and France United States annexes west Florida
1811	Harrison is victorious in Battle of Tippecanoe: destroys Tecumseh's Indian confederacy First Bank of the United States closes after charter is not renewed
1812	United States declares war on Great Britain (June 14) Madison reelected president
1813	British erect naval blockade
1813	American forces burn York (Toronto), Canadian capital Perry defeats British fleet at Put-in Bay on Lake Erie Harrison defeats British and Tecumseh at Battle of the Thames Lowell establishes textile mill at Waltham, Massachusetts
1814	Jackson, at Battle of Horseshoe Bend, slaughters Creek Indians British troops capture and burn Washington Americans win Battle of Plattsburgh Hartford Convention meets Treaty of Ghent signed
1815	Jackson wins Battle of New Orleans Naval war fought with Algiers
1816	Second Bank of the United States is chartered Monroe elected president
1818	Jackson invades Florida, ends first Seminole War Rush-Bagot agreement signed
1819	Commercial panic destabilizes economy Spain cedes Florida to United States in Adams-Onís Treaty
1820	Monroe reelected president

in the Black Belt of Alabama and Mississippi going for $100 and more. Optimistic real estate promoters often paid still higher prices and then laid out town sites, even in swamps, hoping to make fortunes through the sale of city lots.

The availability of easy credit helped fuel the speculative boom. Until the refounding of the Bank of the United States in 1817, settlers and speculators could borrow readily from state banks and pay the government for the land with bank notes. Even after 1817, wildcat banks continued to provide easy credit for a few years. Indeed, the Bank of the United States itself at first offered easy loans. But in 1819, new management took over. Concerned that the Bank was endangering its stability by extending too much credit, the new governors called in loans and foreclosed mortgages, thus acquiring thousands of acres of mortgaged land in the West. They also gathered up state bank notes and presented them to the state

banks for payment in cash. And since state banks often had too little cash on hand to meet the demand, many were forced to close their doors. That started a financial panic, with depositors flooding even the comparatively sound state banks with notes to be cashed, forcing many of them out of business as well. Many Americans, particularly those in the West, blamed the Bank of the United States for the crisis—the beginning of a process that would ultimately make the Bank's existence one of the nation's most burning political issues.

Six years of depression followed. Prices for both manufactured goods and agricultural produce fell rapidly. Manufacturers demanded protection from foreign competition and ultimately secured passage of a new tariff in 1824. Farmers who had bought land on credit could no longer earn enough from sale of their crops to keep up their payments, and they too demanded relief. Congress responded with the land law of 1820 and the relief act of 1821. The new land law required new purchasers to buy their farms outright, without credit, but made land much cheaper than before. The relief act allowed existing landowners to pay off their debts at a reduced price and gave them more time to meet their installments.

The Panic of 1819 and the widespread distress that followed seemed to some Americans to confirm fears that rapid economic growth and territorial expansion would destabilize the nation and threaten the nation's survival. But those who continued to embrace the Jeffersonian vision of a simple, agrarian re-public had become a tiny minority, even within the Republican party. Most Americans by 1820 were irrevocably committed to economic growth and rapid expansion. And public debate in the future would revolve less around the question of whether such growth was good or bad, and more around the question of how it should be encouraged and controlled. That debate, which the Panic of 1819 did much to encourage, created new factional divisions within the Republican party and ultimately brought the era of nonpartisanship—the "era of good feelings"—to an acrimonious end.

SUGGESTED READINGS

The War of 1812   The most thorough account is J. C. A. Stagg, *Mr. Madison's War: Politics, Diplomacy, and Warfare in the Early American Republic, 1783–1830* (1983). Julius W. Pratt, *Expansionists of 1812* (1925), is a standard account of the causes of the conflict, which should be supplemented with Reginald Horsman, *The Causes of the War of 1812* (1962); Bradford Perkins, *Prologue to War: England and the United States, 1805–1812* (1961); and A. L. Burt, *The United States, Great Britain, and British North America* (1940). Roger H. Brown, *The Republic in Peril: 1812* (1964), examines the outbreak of hostilities. For the war itself, see four books, all entitled *The War of 1812,* by the following authors: Harry L. Coles (1965), Reginald Horsman (1969), F. F. Beirne (1949), and J. K. Mahon (1975). William Wood, *The War with the United States* (1915), examines the Canadian viewpoint. Irving Brant, *James Madison: Commander-in-Chief* (1961), is a sympathetic study of the president's role in the conflict; Robert V. Remini, *Andrew Jackson and the Course of American Empire* (1977), is a study of one of the nation's leading generals. Alfred T. Mahan, *Sea Power in Its Relation to the War of 1812,* 2 vols. (1905), is a classic military study. Samuel F. Bemis, *John Quincy Adams and the Foundations of American Foreign Policy* (1949), and Bradford Perkins, *Castlereagh and Adams* (1964), examine the peace negotiations.

Postwar Expansion   The general story of American nationalism and expansion in the postwar era is well told in George Dangerfield, *The Awakening of American Nationalism* (1965) and *The Era of Good Feelings* (1952). Shaw Livermore, Jr., *The Twilight of Federalism* (1962), is a study of the ideas behind nationalism. Bray Hammond, *Banks and Politics in America from the Revolution to the Civil War* (1957), examines economic policy. Murray Rothbard, *The Panic of 1819* (1962), examines the economic crisis.

The West   Frederick Jackson Turner, *The Rise of the New West* (1906), emphasizes the importance of the West in the early nineteenth century. Francis S. Philbrick, *The Rise of the West, 1745–1830* (1965), challenges many of Turner's views. Thomas P. Abernethy, *The South in the New Nation* (1961), examines the influence of expansionism on the slave states. The classic work on the influence of the West in American history is Frederick Jackson Turner, *The Frontier in American History* (1920). On the westward migration, see Ray Billington, *The Far Western Frontier* (1965) and *Westward Expansion* (1974); John A. Hawgood, *America's Western Frontier* (1967); David J. Wishart, *The Fur Trade of the American West* (1979); Frederick Merk, *History of the Westward Movement* (1978); and Dale Van Every, *The Final Challenge* (1964).

P·A·R·T T·H·R·E·E

Expansion and Disunion, 1820–1860

Rapid growth and rapid change have been constant features of American history. But in few periods of national life were growth and change more sudden or profound than in the years from 1820 to 1860. During those four decades, the United States experienced a remarkable expansion of the size of its population, of the area of its settlement, and of the extent and complexity of its economy. Together, these changes transformed American life. And together, they helped produce a great national crisis that threatened to destroy the Union forever.

The American population had already, in 1820, nearly tripled in size since the end of the Revolution. Over the next forty years it more than tripled again—from just under 10 million to just over 31 million. And the population fanned out during those years to inhabit an expanse of territory that would make the United States one of the largest countries in the world. Americans were not only pouring into the regions that the nation had acquired in the first years of the century—the vast Louisiana Purchase and the great Florida accession. They were also pressuring their government to acquire, and on one occasion to go to war for, still more land—Texas, Oregon, the Southwest. It was the nation's destiny, many Americans argued, to span the North

P·A·R·T T·H·R·E·E

American continent. And some continued to dream of adding Canada and Mexico to the national realm as well.

Of equal importance, the American economy transformed itself in those years. Agriculture—in the North, in the South, and in the newly settled regions of the West—grew dramatically in both extent and productivity. Commerce—domestic and international—expanded steadily. And industry, which had its tentative beginnings as early as the eighteenth century, emerged as a major part of the national economy—not yet the dominant force it would eventually become, but strong enough to reshape the social, economic, and political lives of millions of men and women.

Much of this growth was a result of the energy and resourcefulness of the American people, who displayed in the mid-nineteenth century courage, vision, and remarkable entrepreneurial and technological talents. Indeed, the United States became in these years one of the marvels of the world, a society that served as a model for many Western nations. But American growth was a result, too, of ruthless exploitation: of land, of resources, and of people.

Americans exploited their land and their natural resources with reckless abandon, always aware that a vast, largely untouched continent still awaited them. In much the same spirit, the growing nation exploited people. Indians were ruthlessly driven from their ancestral homes, as they had been since the first years of European and African settlement in the seventeenth century, to make room for the onward march of white settlement. In the South, American growth rested on the exploitation of another group of people: black slaves. Southern agriculture, which experienced a booming prosperity through much of the mid-nineteenth century as a result of the expanding world market for cotton, was based largely on slave labor. Thus, while in some other nations the institution of slavery was in decline during these years, in the United States it was growing stronger. And in the North, economic growth rested in part on the exploitation of white men and women—the new labor force that developed in response to the needs of industrial capitalism. White factory workers were not in bondage; indeed, many of them found in industrial labor an avenue to economic advancement. But the rise of the factory system did require a large number of people—some of them native-born Americans, but a growing number of them, as the century progressed, immigrants from Europe—to adapt to a new way of life. For many, the adjustment was a harsh one—so harsh that some critics of the factory system likened it to the condition of Southern blacks and called it "wage slavery."

With changes so sudden and so vast, political and social tensions were inevitable. And that these changes were occurring within a nation still only a few decades old, a nation still in many ways only half-formed, meant that the tensions could become a threat to American unity. At first, the political struggles of the mid-nineteenth century involved issues that largely transcended regional differences. In the 1820s and 1830s, much of the nation's political energy was devoted to defining the position of elites—to debating how to balance the need for stability and order with the desire for expanding individual opportunity. Slowly, however, another set of concerns—related to the first, but different in impact—came to the fore. Most prominent among them was the issue of slavery. As territorial expansion forced the nation time and again to confront the question of whether new areas of settlement were to be slave or free, as the power of the South in national politics began slowly to decline, as residents of both North and South began to see in the social structure of the other a threat to their own way of life, the conflict between sections grew to menacing proportions. For a time, the forces of nationalism were strong enough to counterbalance the divisive issues of sectionalism. By the 1850s, however, those unifying forces were in decline; and the pressures for disunion, no longer contained, were leading rapidly to the greatest domestic crisis in American history.

Fourth of July Picnic at Weymouth Landing, **by Susan Merrett, c. 1845**
(Art Institute of Chicago)

Chapter 9 A Resurgence of Nationalism

Like a "fire bell in the night," as Thomas Jefferson put it, the issue of slavery arose only five years after the end of the War of 1812 to threaten the unity of the nation. The specific question was whether the territory of Missouri should be admitted to the Union as a free or as a slaveholding state. But the larger issue, one that would arise again and again to plague the republic, was the question of whether the vast new Western regions of the United States would ultimately be controlled by the North or by the South.

Yet the Missouri crisis, which was settled by a compromise in 1820, was significant at the time not only because it augured the sectional crises to come but because it stood in such sharp contrast to the rising American nationalism of the 1820s. Whatever forces might be working to pull the nation apart, far stronger ones were acting for the moment to draw it together. The American economy was experiencing revolutionary growth. And while ultimately the industrialization of the North would contribute to sectional tensions, economic progress—which brought with it new systems of transportation and communication—seemed likelier for the moment to link the nation more closely together. The federal government, in the meantime, was acting in both domestic and foreign policy to assert a vigorous nationalism— through the judicial decisions of John Marshall's Supreme Court; through congressional legislation encouraging economic growth; and through James Monroe's foreign policy, which attempted to assert the nation's rising stature in the world.

Above all, perhaps, the United States was held together in the 1820s by a set of shared sentiments and ideals, the "mystic bonds of union," as they were occasionally described. The memory of the Revolution, the veneration of the Constitution and its framers, the widely held sense that America had a special destiny in the world—all combined to obscure sectional differences and arouse a vibrant, even romantic, patriotism. Every year, Fourth of July celebrations reminded Americans of their common struggle for independence, as fife and drum corps and flamboyant orators appealed to patriotism and nationalism. When the Marquis de Lafayette, the French general who had aided the United States during the Revolution, revisited the country in 1824, the glorious past was revived as never before. Everywhere Lafayette traveled, crowds without distinction of section or party cheered him in frenzied celebration.

And on July 4, 1826—the fiftieth anniversary of the adoption of the Declaration of Independence— there occurred an event which seemed to many to confirm that the United States was a nation specially chosen by God. On that special day, Americans were to learn, two of the greatest of the country's founders and former presidents—Thomas Jefferson, author of the Declaration, and John Adams, "its ablest advocate and defender" (as Jefferson had said)—died within hours of each other. Jefferson's last words, those at his bedside reported, were "Is it the Fourth?" And Adams comforted those around him moments before his death by saying, "Thomas Jefferson still survives."

Events would prove that the forces of nationalism were not, in the end, strong enough to overcome the emerging sectional differences. For the time being, however, they permitted the republic to enter an era of unprecedented expansion confident and united.

America's Economic Revolution

There had been signs for many years that the United States was poised for a period of dramatic economic growth. In the 1820s and 1830s, that period finally began. Improvements in transportation and the expanding range of business activity created, for the first time, a national market economy. Each area of the country could concentrate on the production of a certain type of goods, relying on other areas to buy its surplus production and to supply it with those things it no longer produced itself. This regional specialization enabled much of the South, for example, to concentrate on growing its most lucrative crop: cotton. And it enabled the North to develop a new factory system—to begin an industrial revolution that would, in time, become even greater than the one that had begun in England some forty years before. By the mid-1820s, the nation's economy was growing more rapidly than its population.

Many factors combined to produce this dramatic transformation. The American population was growing and spreading across a far greater expanse of territory, providing both a labor supply for the production of goods and a market for the sale of them. A "transportation revolution"—based on the construction of roads, canals, and eventually railroads—was giving merchants and manufacturers access to new markets and raw materials. New entrepreneurial techniques were making a rapid business expansion possible. And technological advances were helping to spur industry to new levels of activity. Equally important, perhaps, Americans in the 1820s embraced an ethic of growth that was based on a commitment to hard work, individual initiative, thrift, and ambition. The results of their efforts seemed, to many people at least, to confirm the value of such a commitment.

The Population, 1820–1840

During the 1820s and 1830s, as during virtually all of American history, three trends of population were clear: rapid increase, migration to the West, and movement to towns and cities.

Americans continued to multiply almost as fast as they had in the colonial period. The population still doubled roughly every twenty-five years. The population had stood at only 4 million in 1790. By 1820, it had reached 10 million; by 1830, nearly 13 million; and by 1840, 17 million. The United States was growing much more rapidly in population than the

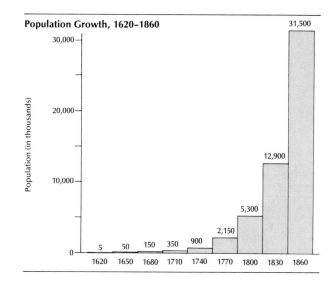

Population Growth, 1620–1860

British Isles or Europe. By 1860 it had moved ahead of the United Kingdom and had nearly overtaken Germany and France.

The black population increased more slowly than the white. After 1808, when the importation of slaves became illegal, the proportion of blacks to whites in the nation as a whole steadily declined. In 1820, there was one black to every four whites; in 1840, one to every five. The slower increase of the black population was a result of its comparatively high death rate, not of a low birth rate. Slave mothers had large families, but life was shorter for both slaves and free blacks than for whites—a result of the enforced poverty in which virtually all blacks lived.

The mortality rate for whites slowly declined, and life expectancy gradually increased. Epidemics continued to take their periodic toll, among them a cholera plague that swept the country in 1832; but public health efforts gradually improved and reduced the number and ferocity of such outbreaks. The population increase was, however, a result less of lengthened life than of the maintenance of a high birth rate.

From the time of independence, immigration had accounted for little of the nation's population growth. The long years of war in Europe, from 1793 to 1815, had kept the number of newcomers to America down to not more than a few thousand a year, and then the Panic of 1819 checked the immigrant tide that had risen after the restoration of peace. During the 1820s, arrivals from abroad averaged about 14,000 annually. Of the total population of nearly 13 million in 1830, the foreign-born numbered fewer than 500,000, most of them naturalized citizens. Soon, however, immi-

The Family at Home, c. 1845
This painting by Henry F. Darby of a minister, his wife, and their six children is an indication of how large American families often were in the early nineteenth century. Unlike in colonial times, a woman in the 1840s could expect not only to bear many children but to see most of them live to maturity.   (Museum of Fine Arts, Boston)

gration began to grow once again. It reached a total of 60,000 for 1832 and nearly 80,000 for 1837.

Since the United States exported more goods than it imported, ships returning to America from Europe often had vacant space and took on immigrants to fill it. Competition among shipping lines reduced fares so that, by the 1830s, immigrants could get passage across the Atlantic for as little as $20 or $30. No longer did they need to sell their services to a temporary master in America in order to pay for the voyage. And so the system of indentured servitude, which had dwindled steadily after the Revolution, disappeared entirely after the Panic of 1819.

Until the 1830s, most of the new arrivals came from the same sources as had the bulk of the colonial population—from England and the northern (predominantly Protestant) counties of Ireland. In the 1830s, however, the number of immigrants arriving from the southern (Catholic) counties of Ireland began to grow, the beginning of a tremendous influx of Irish Catholics that was to occur over the next two decades. Generally, the newcomers—Irish as well as others—were welcomed in the United States. They were needed to provide labor for building canals and railroads, manning ships and docks, and performing other heavy work essential to the expanding economic system. But the Irish, as Roman Catholics, excited Protestant prejudices in some communities. In 1834, an anti-Catholic mob set fire to a convent in Charlestown, Massachusetts. The next year, Samuel

Sources of Immigration, 1820–1840

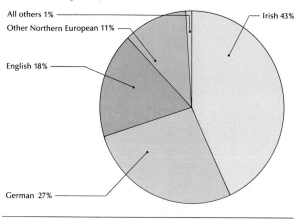

All others 1%
Other Northern European 11%
English 18%
German 27%
Irish 43%

Total Immigration, 1820–1840

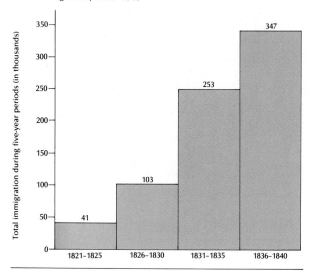

Total immigration during five-year periods (in thousands)

1821–1825	41
1826–1830	103
1831–1835	253
1836–1840	347

lost nearly as many people through migration as they gained by natural increase, so that their populations remained almost static. The same was true of Vermont and New Hampshire. Many villages in these two states were completely depopulated, their houses and barns left to rot, as their people scattered over the country in search of a better life than the infertile granite hills afforded.

Not all the migrating villagers and farmers sought the unsettled frontier: some moved instead to the increasingly crowded population centers. Cities (defined as communities of 8,000 or more) grew faster than the nation as a whole. In 1820 there were more than twice as many cities, and in 1840 more than seven times as many, as there had been in 1790. While the vast majority of Americans continued to reside in the open country or in small towns, the number of city dwellers increased remarkably. In 1790, one person in thirty lived in a community of 8,000 or more; in 1820, one in twenty; and in 1840, one in twelve.

The rise of New York City was phenomenal. By 1810 it had surpassed Philadelphia as the largest city in America. New York steadily increased its lead in both population and trade. Its growth was based in large part on its superior natural harbor. But it was also a result of several commercial and political decisions, by New Yorkers themselves and by others, following the War of 1812. After the war, the British chose New York as the chief place to "dump" their manufactured goods and thus helped make it the nation's leading center for imports. Liberal state laws regarding auction sales encouraged inland merchants to do their buying in New York. The first packet line, with regularly scheduled monthly sailings between England and the United States, made New York its American terminus in 1816. And the Erie Canal (completed in 1825) gave the city unrivaled access to the interior.

F. B. Morse (who is better remembered as a portrait painter and as the inventor of the telegraph) published his *Foreign Conspiracy,* which served thereafter as a textbook for those crusading against what they imagined was a popish plot to gain control of the United States.

The Northwest and the Southwest continued to grow much more rapidly than the rest of the country. By 1830, more than a fourth of the American people lived west of the Appalachians; by 1850, nearly half. As a result, some of the seaboard states suffered a serious loss of human resources (as well as of the material goods that departing migrants took with them). Year after year the Carolinas, for example,

The Canal Age

The so-called turnpike era, which lasted from 1790 to about 1830, saw the construction of an important network of roads that did much to link the nation together and to open access to new markets and sources of materials. Roads alone, however, were not sufficient to provide the system of transportation necessary for a growing industrial society. And so, in the 1820s and 1830s, Americans began to construct other means of transportation as well. As in colonial times, they looked first to water routes.

The Port of New York, 1828
This view of South Street in Manhattan shows the East River lined with docks. Other docks, similarly busy, lined the Hudson River on the opposite side of the island. The population of New York City was approaching 150,000 by 1828. (New York Public Library)

The larger rivers, especially the Mississippi and the Ohio, became increasingly useful, as steamboats grew in number and improved in design. A special kind of steamboat evolved to meet the problems of navigation on the Mississippi and its tributaries. These waters were shallow, with strong and difficult currents, shifting bars of sand and mud, and submerged logs and trees. So the boat needed a flat bottom, paddle wheels rather than screw propellers, and a powerful, high-pressure—and thus dangerously explosive—engine. (The river boats were, therefore, prone to deadly, spectacular accidents.) To accommodate as much cargo and as many passengers as possible, the boat was triple-decked, its superstructure rising high in the air. These river boats carried to New Orleans the corn and other crops of Northwestern farmers and the cotton and tobacco of South-

western planters. From New Orleans, ocean-going ships took the cargoes on to Eastern ports.

But neither the farmers of the West nor the merchants of the East were completely satisfied with this pattern of trade. Farmers knew they would be able to get better prices for their crops if they could ship them directly eastward to market, rather than by the roundabout river-sea route; and merchants knew they would be able to sell larger quantities of their manufactured goods if they could transport them more directly and economically to the West.

The highways across the mountains, such as the Philadelphia-Pittsburgh turnpike and the National Road, provided a partial solution to the problem. But the costs of hauling goods overland, although lower than before the roads were built, were too high for anything except the most compact and valuable merchandise. It took four horses a full day to pull a wagon weight of one ton twelve miles over an ordinary road; on a turnpike, four horses could haul one and a half tons eighteen miles in a day. But the same four horses could draw a boatload of a hundred tons twenty-four miles a day on a canal. Thus interest quickly grew in expanding the nation's water routes.

Canal building was a task too expensive for the existing institutions of private enterprise. Sectional jealousies and constitutional scruples prevented the federal government from financing the projects. So the job of digging extensive canals fell to the various states. New York was the first to act. It had the natural advantage of a comparatively level route be-tween the Hudson River and Lake Erie through the only break in the Appalachian chain. Yet the engineering tasks were still imposing. The distance from the Hudson to Lake Erie was more than 350 miles, several times as long as any of the existing canals in America. There were high ridges to cross and a wilderness of woods and swamps to penetrate. For many years, New Yorkers debated whether the scheme was practical. The canal advocates finally won the debate after De Witt Clinton, a late but ardent convert to the cause, became governor in 1817. Digging began on July 4, 1817.

The building of the Erie Canal was by far the greatest construction project that Americans had ever

The Erie Canal

In this contemporary pencil sketch, canal boats—loaded with migrants on their way to the West and pulled by horse teams moving along the towpath—arrive at a landing at Little Falls, New York. The boats moved so slowly that passengers often lightened the tedium by going ashore and walking alongside.   (New York Historical Society)

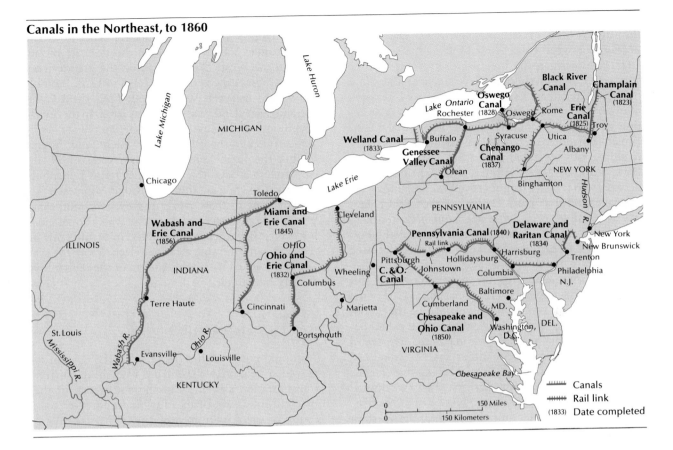

Canals in the Northeast, to 1860

undertaken. It was the work of self-made engineers. One of them had made a careful study of English canals, but he and his associates did more than merely copy what they had seen abroad. They devised ingenious arrangements of cables, pulleys, and gears for bringing down trees and uprooting stumps. Instead of the usual shovels and wheelbarrows, they used specially designed plows and scrapers for moving earth. To make watertight locks they produced cement from native limestone. The canal itself was of simple design: basically a ditch, forty feet wide and four feet deep, with towpaths along the banks for the horses or mules that were to draw the canal boats. (Steamboats were not to be used: the churning of a paddle wheel or propeller would cave in the earthen banks.) Cuts and fills, some of them enormous, enabled the canal to pass through hills and over valleys; stone aqueducts carried it across streams; and eighty-eight locks, of heavy masonry, with great wooden gates, took care of the necessary ascents and descents.

Not only was the Erie Canal an engineering triumph; it quickly proved a financial success as well. It opened for through traffic in October 1825, amid elaborate ceremonies and celebrations. Governor Clinton headed a parade of canal boats that made the trip from Buffalo to the Hudson and then downriver to New York City, where he emptied a keg of Erie water into the Atlantic to symbolize the wedding of the lake and the ocean. Traffic was soon so heavy that, within about seven years, the tolls had brought in enough money to repay the whole cost of construction.

The profitability of the Erie encouraged the state to enlarge its canal system by building several branches. An important part of the system was the Champlain Canal, begun at about the same time as the Erie and completed in 1822, which connected Lake Champlain with the Hudson River. Some of the branches did not fully pay for themselves, but all provided valuable water connections between New York City and the larger towns of the state. The main line, by providing access to the Great Lakes, led beyond the state's borders, to the West.

The system of water transportation extended farther when the states of Ohio and Indiana, inspired by the success of the Erie Canal, provided water connections between Lake Erie and the Ohio River. In 1825, Ohio began the building of two canals, one between Portsmouth and Cleveland and the other between Cincinnati and Toledo, both of which were in use by 1833. In 1832, Indiana started the construction of a canal to connect Evansville with the Cincinnati-Toledo route. These canals made it possible to ship goods by inland waterways all the way from New York to New Orleans, although it was still necessary to transfer cargoes several times among canal, lake, and river craft. By way of the Great Lakes, it was possible to go by water from New York to Chicago. After the opening of the Erie Canal, shipping on the Great Lakes by sail and steam increased rapidly.

The consequences of the development of this transportation network were far-reaching. One of the immediate results was the stimulation of the settlement of the Northwest, not only because it had become easier for migrants to make the westward journey but also, and more important, because it had become easier for them, after establishing their farms, to ship their produce to markets. Towns boomed along the Erie and other canals. New York City benefited the most of all. Although much of the Western produce, especially corn, continued to go downriver to New Orleans, an increasing proportion of it (including most of the wheat of the Northwest) went to New York. And manufactured goods from throughout the East now moved in growing volume through New York and then via the comparatively direct and economical new routes to the West.

Rival cities along the Atlantic seaboard took alarm at the prospect of New York's acquiring so vast a hinterland, largely at their expense. If they were to hold their own, they knew that they too would have to find ways of tapping the Western market. Boston, its way to the Hudson River blocked by the Berkshire Mountains, did not try to connect itself to the West by canal. Its hinterland would remain confined largely to New England itself. Philadelphia and Baltimore had the still more formidable Allegheny Mountains to contend with, but they nevertheless made a serious effort at canal building. Beginning in 1834, Pennsylvania invested in a complicated and costly system of waterways and railways—with an arrangement of "inclined planes," stationary engines, and cable cars to take canal boats over the mountains—in an effort to connect Philadelphia with Pittsburgh. But the

"Pennsylvania system" was a financial and technological failure. Baltimore planned a canal to ascend the Potomac Valley and tunnel through the mountains to the West. Work began on the grandly conceived Chesapeake and Ohio Canal in 1828, but only the stretch between Washington, D.C., and Cumberland, Maryland, was ever completed. In the South, Richmond and Charleston also aspired to build water routes to the Ohio Valley; Richmond, hoping to link the James and Kanawha rivers, eventually constructed a canal that reached as far as Lynchburg but failed to traverse the Blue Ridge Mountains.

For none of these rivals of New York did canals provide a satisfactory way to the West. Some cities, however, saw their opportunity in a different and newer means of transportation. Even before the canal age had reached its height, the era of the railroad was already beginning.

The Early Railroads

Through most of the 1820s and 1830s, railroads played a relatively secondary role in the nation's transportation system. But the emergence of these first rail lines was of inestimable importance to the future of the American economy. The tentative beginnings of these early years led, by the time of the Civil War, to a great surge of railroad building, linking the nation together as no previous system of transportation had ever done. Railroads eventually became the primary means of transportation for the United States and remained so until the creation of the interstate highway system in the mid-twentieth century.

It is difficult to identify the precise date of the invention of the railroad. It emerged from a combination of innovations, each of which had its own history. One of these innovations was the invention of railroad tracks: rails, wooden or iron, laid on a prepared roadbed to make a fairly straight and level track. Another was the employment of steam-powered locomotives. A third was the operation of trains as public carriers of passengers and freight.

For nearly 200 years before the nineteenth century opened, small railways—wheeled vehicles running along fixed tracks—with cars pulled by men and women or by animals had been used to haul coal from English mines; and in the early 1800s similar railways had appeared in the United States. But it took the development of steam power to make rail-

Racing on the Railroad

Peter Cooper, who in later years was best known as a philanthropist and as the founder of the Cooper Union in New York City, was also a successful iron manufacturer. Cooper designed and built the first steam-powered locomotive in America in 1830 for the Baltimore and Ohio railroad. On August 28 of that year, he raced his locomotive (the "Tom Thumb") against a horse-drawn railroad car. This sketch depicts the moment when Cooper's engine overtook the horsecar. (Museum of the City of New York)

roads viable as a general transportation method. By 1804, both English and American inventors had experimented with steam engines for propelling land vehicles as well as boats. In 1820, John Stevens ran a locomotive and cars around a circular track on his New Jersey estate. Finally, in 1825, the Stockton and Darlington Railroad in England began to operate with steam power over a short length of track. It became the first line to carry general traffic. All earlier rail lines had been operated by particular companies to service only their own needs.

This news quickly aroused the interest of American businessmen, especially in those seaboard cities that sought better communication with the West. The first to organize a railroad company was a group of New Yorkers, who in 1826 obtained a charter for the Mohawk and Hudson, and five years later began running trains along the sixteen miles between Schenectady and Albany. The first company to begin actual operations was the Baltimore and Ohio; the only living signer of the Declaration of Independence, Charles Carroll of Carrollton, dug a spadeful of earth in the ceremonies in Maryland to start the work on July 4, 1828; and a thirteen-mile stretch opened for business in 1830. Not only the seaboard but also the Mississippi Valley became the scene of railroad building. By 1836, a total of more than 1,000 miles of track had been laid in eleven states.

There did not yet exist what could properly be called a railroad system. Even the longest of the lines was comparatively short in the 1830s, and most of them served to connect water routes and otherwise to supplement water transportation. Even when two lines did connect the tracks might differ in gauge (width), so that cars from the one line often could not fit onto the tracks of the other. Schedules were erratic, and since roadbeds and bridges were often of shoddy construction, wrecks were frequent.

In response to these deficiencies, railroad pioneers produced a series of important technological developments in the 1830s. Roadbeds were improved through the introduction of heavier iron rails attached to wooden ties resting on crushed rock—a system that enabled tracks to withstand the shock of use far better than the earlier methods. American manufacturers began to produce steam locomotives more flexible and powerful than the engines of the past, which had usually been imported from Europe. Passenger cars, originally mere stagecoaches, were redesigned after 1840 as elongated boxes with two rows of reversible seats and a center aisle—thus making more room for people.

Railroads and canals were soon competing bitterly with each other. For a time, the Chesapeake and Ohio Canal Company blocked the advance of the Baltimore and Ohio Railroad through the narrow gorge of the upper Potomac, and the state of New York prohibited railroads from hauling freight in competition with the Erie Canal and its branches. But railroads had the advantages of speed and year-round operation (canals had to close for the winter freeze) and could be located almost anywhere, regardless of terrain and the availability of water. Where free competition existed, railroads gradually took over most of the passenger traffic and the light freight. The future, in fact, belonged to the towns and cities along the path of the "iron horse," not to those that continued to depend exclusively on waterways.

The Expansion of Business

The rapid expansion of business activity in the 1820s and 1830s was in part a result of the growth in population and improvements in the means of transportation. It was also, however, the result of daring and imagination on the part of new generations of businessmen and their employees. Two industries, one old and one new, illustrated the capacities of American enterprise. One was the whaling industry, which was reaching its heyday in the 1830s. From New Bedford and other New England ports, bold skippers and their crews, having driven most of the whales from the Atlantic, voyaged far into the Pacific in their hazardous tracking of the source of spermaceti for candles, whale oil for lamps, and whalebone for corset stays and other uses. Another example of Yankee enterprise was the ice industry. For years, Northeastern farmers had harvested winter ice from ponds and stored it for the summer; but the large-scale transportation and sale of ice as a commodity began in the 1830s. The New England ice harvest then found a ready market in Northern cities, on Southern plantations, and halfway around the world in India, where it was carried in fast-sailing ships; a voyage was considered highly successful if no more than half the cargo melted on the way.

Retail distribution of goods, whether of foreign or domestic origin, remained somewhat haphazard by the standards of later times; but it was becoming far more systematic than it had ever been before. Stores specializing in groceries, dry goods, hardware, and other lines appeared in the larger cities. Smaller towns and villages depended on the general store. Storekeepers did much of their business by barter, taking country eggs and other produce in exchange for such things as pins and needles, sugar, and coffee. Many customers, living remote from any store, welcomed the occasional visits of peddlers, who came on foot or by horse.

The organization of business was undergoing a gradual change. Most business continued to be operated by individuals or partnerships operating on a limited scale. The dominating figures were the great merchant capitalists, who controlled much of the big business of the time. They owned their own ships. They organized certain industries on the putting-out system: providing materials to individual craftsmen, directing the work, and selling the finished product.

In larger enterprises, however, the individual merchant capitalist was giving way before the advance of the corporation. Corporations had the advantage of combining the resources of a large number of shareholders, and they began to develop particularly rapidly in the 1830s, when certain legal obstacles to their formation were removed. In the past, a corporation had had to obtain a charter, which at first could be granted only by a special act of the state legislature. By the 1830s, however, states were beginning to pass general incorporation laws. No longer did each corporation need to obtain specific legislative approval. A group could now secure a charter merely by paying a fee. Moreover, the laws began to grant the privilege of limited liability. This meant that individual stockholders risked losing the value of their own investment if a corporation should fail, but they were not liable (as they had been in the past) for the corporation's larger losses.

Corporations made possible the accumulation of larger and larger amounts of capital for manufacturing enterprises as well as for banks, turnpikes, and railroad companies. Some of this capital came from the profits of wealthy merchants who turned from shipping to newer ventures. Some came from the savings of people of only moderate means. Some came from tax collections, since state governments often bought shares in turnpike, canal, and railroad companies. A considerable part was supplied by foreign, especially English, investors.

But these sources provided too little capital to meet the demands of the ambitious schemes of some businesses, and they relied on an expansion of credit—some of it by dangerously unstable means. Credit mechanisms remained highly underdeveloped in the early nineteenth century. The government alone was permitted to issue currency, but it issued no paper—only gold and silver coins—and the amount of official currency in circulation was thus too small to support the demand for credit. Under pressure from corporate promoters, many banks issued large quantities of bank notes to provide capital for expanding business ventures. The notes rested on a bank's promise to redeem them in gold and silver on demand; but many institutions issued notes far in excess of their own reserves. As a result, bank failures were frequent and bank deposits often insecure.

The Rise of the Factory

All of these changes—increasing population, improved transportation, and the expansion of business activity—contributed to perhaps the most profound economic development in mid-nineteenth-century America: the rise of factory manufacturing. Although it was in the 1840s that industry experienced its most spectacular surge of growth in the antebellum period, it was in the 1820s and 1830s that the factory system established itself as an integral part of the national economy.

Before the War of 1812, most of what manufacturing there was in the United States took place within households or in small, individually operated workshops. Most goods were produced by hand; most were sold in local markets. Gradually, however, improved technology and increased opportunities for commerce stimulated the beginnings of a fundamental change. It came first in the New England textile industry. There, even before the war and the Embargo, some farsighted entrepreneurs were beginning to make use of the region's extensive waterpower and of the new machines (some imported from England, some developed at home) to bring textile operations together under a single roof. This factory system, as it was to be called, spread rapidly in the 1820s. Spinning and weaving in the home remained for a time the principal means of producing cloth, but factories were beginning to make serious inroads into the old process of production.

In the shoe industry as well, mass production through the specialization of tasks was expanding and was by the 1830s becoming an important force in the industry. Most of the work in shoe factories continued to be done by hand, but manufacturing in the newer establishments was increasingly divided among men and women who, in a careful division of labor, specialized in one or another of the various tasks involved in production. Private cobblers continued to produce shoes for individual customers; and the artisanal workshops, where groups of shoemakers worked under a single roof but did not divide up the tasks, remained the largest source of shoe manufacturing. But the future of the industry was more clearly suggested by factories producing large numbers of identical shoes in ungraded sizes and without

distinction as to rights and lefts. As with textiles, the new shoe factories emerged first in eastern Massachusetts.

By the 1830s, factory production was spreading from textiles and shoes into other industries as well; and manufacturing was moving beyond Massachusetts and New England to become an important force throughout the American Northeast.

From the beginning, American industry relied heavily on technology for its growth. Because labor was scarce in the United States, at least in comparison to other industrializing countries, there was great incentive for entrepreneurs to improve the efficiency of their productive enterprises by introducing new labor-saving devices. Machine technology advanced more rapidly in the United States in the mid-nineteenth century than in any other country in the world. Change was so rapid, in fact, that some manufacturers built their new machinery out of wood; by the time the wood wore out, they reasoned, improved technology would have made the machine obsolete. By the end of the 1830s, so advanced had American technology—particularly in textile manufacturing—become that industrialists in Britain and Europe were beginning to travel to the United States to learn new techniques, instead of the other way around.

Men and Women at Work

However advanced their technology, manufacturers still relied above all on a supply of labor. In later years, much of that supply would come from great waves of immigration from abroad. In the 1820s and 1830s, however, labor had to come primarily from the native population. Recruitment was not an easy task. Ninety percent of the American people still lived and worked on farms. City residents, although increasing in number, were relatively few, and the potential workers among them even fewer. Many urban laborers were skilled artisans who owned and managed their own shops as small businessmen; they were not likely to flock to factory jobs. The available unskilled workers were not numerous enough to form a reservoir from which the new industries could draw.

What did produce the beginnings of an industrial labor supply was the transformation of American agriculture in the nineteenth century. The opening of vast, fertile new farmlands in the Midwest, the improvement of transportation systems, the development of new farm machinery—all combined to increase food production dramatically. No longer did each region have to feed itself entirely from its own farms; it could import food from other regions. Thus in the Northeast, and especially in New England, where poor land had always placed harsh limits on farm productivity, the agricultural economy began slowly to decline, freeing up rural people to work in the factories.

Two systems of recruitment emerged to bring this new labor supply to the expanding textile mills. One, common in the mid-Atlantic states and in parts of New England, brought whole families from the farm to the mill. Parents and children, even some who were no more than four or five years old, worked together tending the looms. The second system, common in Massachusetts, enlisted young women—mostly the daughters of farmers—in their late teens and early twenties. It was known as the Lowell or Waltham system, after the factory towns in which it first emerged. Most of these women worked for several years in the factories, saved their wages, and ultimately returned home to marry and raise chil-

dren. They did not form a permanent working class.

Labor conditions in these early years of the factory system were significantly better than those in English industry, better too than they would ultimately become in the United States. The employment of young children entailed undeniable hardships. But the evils were fewer than in Europe, since working children in American factories remained under the supervision of their parents. In England, by contrast, asylum authorities often hired out orphans to factory employers who showed little solicitude for their welfare.

Even more distinctive from the European labor system was the lot of working women in the mills in Lowell and factory towns like it. In England, as a parliamentary investigation revealed, woman workers were employed in coal mines in unimaginably wretched conditions. Some had to crawl on their hands and knees, naked and filthy, through cramped, narrow tunnels, pulling heavy coal carts behind them. It was little wonder, then, that English visitors to America considered the Lowell mills a female para-

Specialized Manufacturing Towns: Lowell, Massachusetts, 1832

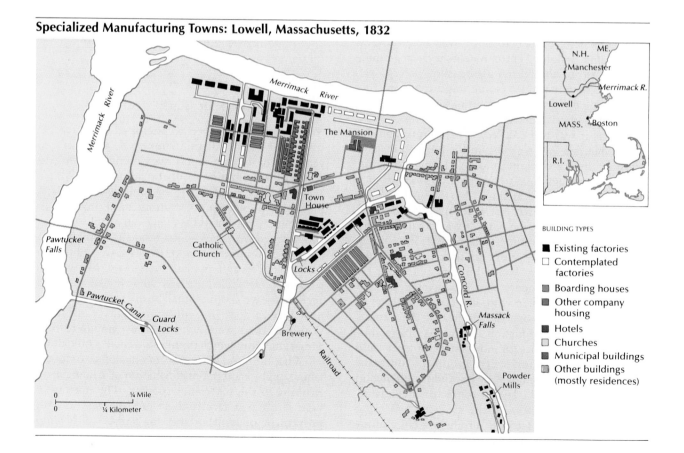

BUILDING TYPES

- ■ Existing factories
- □ Contemplated factories
- ▨ Boarding houses
- ■ Other company housing
- ■ Hotels
- □ Churches
- ■ Municipal buildings
- ▨ Other buildings (mostly residences)

dise by contrast. The Lowell workers lived in clean boardinghouses and dormitories maintained for them by the factory owners. They were well fed and carefully supervised. Because many New Englanders considered the employment of women to be vaguely immoral, the factory owners placed great emphasis on maintaining an upright environment for their employees, enforcing strict curfews and requiring regular church attendance. Factory girls suspected of immoral conduct were quickly dismissed. Wages for the Lowell workers, modest as they were, were nevertheless generous by the standards of the time. The women even found time to write and publish a monthly magazine, the *Lowell Offering.*

Yet even these relatively well-treated workers often found the transition from farm life to factory work difficult, even traumatic. Uprooted from everything familiar, forced to live among strangers in a regimented environment, many women suffered from loneliness and disorientation. Still more had difficulty adjusting to the nature of factory work—to the repetition of fixed tasks hour after hour, day after day. That the women had to labor from sunrise to sunset was not in itself always a burden; many of them had worked similarly long days on the farm. But that they now had to spend those days performing tedious, unvarying chores, and that their schedules did not change from week to week or season to season, made the adjustment to factory work a painful one.

Female mill workers suffered, moreover, from a special disadvantage. They were, like male workers, generally products of a farm economy in decline and were forced to find nonagricultural work by which to support themselves and contribute to the maintenance of their families. But unlike men, they had very few options. They had no access to construction work; they could not become sailors or dockworkers; it was considered unthinkable for women to travel the country alone, as many men did, in search of opportunities. Work in the mills was in many cases virtually the only option available to them.

The relative powerlessness of woman workers was one reason for the gradual breakdown of the paternalistic factory system. In the competitive textile market as it developed in the 1830s and 1840s—a market prey to the booms and busts that afflicted the American economy as a whole—manufacturers found it difficult to maintain the high living standards and reasonably attractive working conditions with which they had begun. Wages declined; the hours of work lengthened; the conditions of the boardinghouses de-

The *Lowell Offering*
The "factory girls" of the Lowell mills published a small literary magazine, which included poems and stories written by the workers themselves. The cover of this 1845 edition portrays a young mill worker standing in pastoral surroundings, holding a book, with the mill visible in the background. (Massachusetts Historical Society)

teriorated as the buildings decayed and overcrowding increased. In 1834, mill girls in Lowell organized a union—the Factory Girls Association—which staged a strike to protest a 25 percent wage cut. Two years later, the association struck again—against a rent increase in the boardinghouses. Both strikes failed, and a recession in 1837 virtually destroyed the organization. Eight years later, led by the militant Sarah

Bagley, the Lowell women created the Female Labor Reform Association and began agitating for a ten-hour day and for improvements in conditions in the mills. The new association not only made demands of management; it turned to state government and asked for legislative investigation of conditions in the mills. By then, however, the character of the factory work force was changing. Textile manufacturers were turning to a less demanding labor supply: immigrants. The mill girls were gradually moving into other occupations: teaching, domestic service, or marriage.

The increasing supply of immigrant workers was a boon to manufacturers and other entrepreneurs. At last they had access to a cheap and plentiful source of labor. These new workers, because of their growing numbers and because of unfamiliarity with their new country, had even less leverage than the women they at times displaced; and thus they often encountered far worse working conditions. Construction gangs, made up increasingly of Irish immigrants, performed the heavy, unskilled work on turnpikes, canals, and railroads under often intolerable conditions. Because most of these workers had no marketable skills and because of native prejudice against them, they received wages so low—and received them so intermittently, since the work was seasonal and uncertain—that they generally did not earn enough to support their families in even minimal comfort. Many of them lived in flimsy, unhealthy shanties.

By the 1840s, the Irish workers (men and women) predominated in the New England textile mills as well; and their arrival accelerated the deterioration of working conditions there. There was far less social pressure on owners to provide a decent environment for Irish workers than for native women. Employers began paying piece rates rather than a daily wage and employed other devices to speed up production and exploit the labor force more efficiently. By the mid-1840s, the town of Lowell—once a model for foreign visitors of enlightened industrial development—had become a squalid slum. Similarly miserable working-class neighborhoods were emerging in other Northeastern cities.

It was not only the unskilled workers who suffered from the transition to the modern factory system. It was the skilled artisans whose trades the factories were displacing. Threatened with obsolescence, faced with increasing competition from industrial capitalists, craftsmen began early in the nineteenth century to form organizations—the first American labor unions—to protect their endangered position. As early as the 1790s, printers and cordwainers took the lead. The cordwainers—makers of high-quality boots and shoes—suffered from the competition of merchant capitalists. These artisans sensed a loss of security and status with the development of mass-production methods, and so did members of other skilled trades: carpenters, joiners, masons, plasterers, hatters, and shipbuilders. In such cities as Philadelphia, Baltimore, Boston, and New York, the skilled workers of each craft formed societies for mutual aid. During the 1820s and 1830s, the craft societies began to combine on a city-wide basis and set up central organizations known as trade unions. Since, with the widening of the market, workers of one city competed with those at a distance, the next step was to federate the trade unions or to establish craft unions of national scope. In 1834, delegates from six cities founded the National Trades' Union; and in 1836, the printers and the cordwainers set up their own national craft unions.

This early labor movement soon collapsed. Labor leaders struggled against the handicap of hostile laws and hostile courts. By the common law, as interpreted by judges in the industrial states, a combination among workers was viewed as, in itself, an illegal conspiracy. But adverse court decisions did not alone halt the rising unions. The death blow came from the Panic of 1837 and the ensuing depression.

Sectionalism and Nationalism

For a brief but alarming moment, the increasing differences between the nation's two leading sections threatened in 1819 and 1820 to damage the unity of the United States. But once a sectional crisis was averted with the Missouri Compromise, the forces of nationalism continued to assert themselves; and the federal government began to assume the role of promoter of economic growth.

The Missouri Compromise

When Missouri applied for admission to the Union as a state in 1819, slavery was already well established there. The French and Spanish inhabitants of the Louisiana Territory (including what became Missouri) had owned slaves, and in the Louisiana Purchase treaty of 1803 the American government promised to maintain and protect the inhabitants in the free enjoyment of their property as well as their liberty and religion. By 1819, approximately 60,000 people resided in Missouri Territory, of whom about 10,000 were slaves.

In that year, while Missouri's application for statehood was being considered in Congress, Representative James Tallmadge, Jr., of New York, proposed an amendment that would prohibit the further introduction of slaves into Missouri and provide for the gradual emancipation of those already there. The Tallmadge Amendment provoked a controversy that was to rage for the next two years.

Although the issue arose suddenly, the sectional jealousies that produced it had long been accumulating. Already the concept of a balance of power between the Northern and Southern states was well developed. From the beginning, partly by chance and partly by design, new states had come into the Union more or less in pairs, one from the North, another from the South. With the admission of Alabama in 1819, the Union contained an equal number of free and slave states, eleven of each. If Missouri were to be admitted as a slave state, not only would the existing sectional balance be upset but a precedent would be established that in the future would increase the political power of the South still further.

This concern about the balance of power among the states was not yet accompanied by a widespread or fervent opposition to slavery itself. There were groups, in both the North and the South, opposed to slavery on moral grounds and committed to its destruction. On the eve of the dispute over Missouri, for example, the Manumission Society of New York was busy with attempts to rescue runaway slaves; and Quakers were conducting a campaign to strengthen the laws against the African slave trade and to protect free blacks from kidnappers who sold them into slavery. But most Northern opponents of slavery were affluent philanthropists and reformers associated with the Federalist party; and for many of them, humanitarian concerns were secondary to political ones.

The Missouri controversy provided the opportunity for which Federalist leaders such as Rufus King had long waited: the opportunity to attempt a revival and reinvigoration of their party. By appealing to the Northern people on the issue of slavery extension, the Federalists hoped to win many of the Northern Republicans away from their allegiance to the Republican party's Southern leadership. In New York, the De Witt Clinton faction of the Republicans, who

had joined with the Federalists in opposition to the War of 1812 and were outspoken in their hostility to "Virginia influence" and "Southern rule," were more than willing to cooperate with the Federalists again. The cry against slavery in Missouri, Thomas Jefferson wrote, was "a mere party trick." He explained: "King is ready to risk the union for any chance of restoring his party to power and wriggling himself to the head of it, nor is Clinton without his hopes nor scrupulous as to the means of fulfilling them."

The Missouri question was soon complicated by the application of Maine for admission as a state. Massachusetts had earlier consented to the separation of this northern part of the commonwealth, but only on the condition that Maine be granted statehood before March 4, 1820. The Speaker of the House, Henry Clay, now informed Northerners that if they refused to consent to Missouri's becoming a slave state, Southerners would deny the application of Maine. Despite the warning, the Northern majority in the House continued to insist on the principle of the Tallmadge Amendment; but in the Senate, a few Northerners sided with the Southerners and prevented its passage.

The Maine question, however, ultimately produced a way out of the impasse. The Senate finally agreed to combine the Maine and Missouri proposals into a single bill. Maine would be admitted as a free state, Missouri as a slave state. Then, to make the package more acceptable to the House, Senator Jesse B. Thomas of Illinois proposed an amendment prohibiting slavery in all the rest of the Louisiana Purchase territory north of the southern boundary of Missouri (latitude 36° 30′). The Senate adopted the Thomas Amendment, and Speaker Clay, with great difficulty, guided the amended Maine-Missouri bill through the House.

Nationalists in both North and South hailed the Missouri Compromise as a happy resolution of a danger to the Union. Others, however, were less optimistic. Thomas Jefferson, for example, saw in the controversy a "speck on our horizon" which might ultimately "burst on us as a tornado." And he added, "The line of division lately marked out between the different portions of our confederacy is such as will never, I fear, be obliterated." (That was one reason why Jefferson, in his last years, devoted so much attention to the construction of the University of Virginia—an institution that would, he hoped, confirm Southern students in the values of their own region and protect them against the taint of "anti-Missourianism" that he believed pervaded the

The Missouri Compromise, 1820

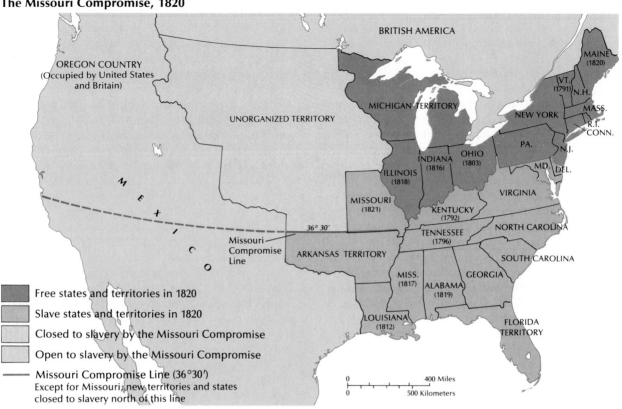

Free states and territories in 1820

Slave states and territories in 1820

Closed to slavery by the Missouri Compromise

Open to slavery by the Missouri Compromise

—— Missouri Compromise Line (36°30′)
Except for Missouri, new territories and states
closed to slavery north of this line

Northern universities.) The Missouri Compromise revealed, in short, a strong undercurrent of sectionalism that competed with—although at the moment failed to derail—the powerful tides of nationalism.

Marshall and the Court

John Marshall served as chief justice of the United States for almost thirty-five years, from 1801 to 1835. He was a man of practical and penetrating mind, of persuasive and winning personality, and of strong will; and he dominated the Court as no one else before or since. During his years as chief justice, Republican presidents filled vacancies with Republican justices, one after another; and yet Marshall continued to carry a majority with him in most of the Court's decisions. The members of the Court boarded together, without their families, during the winter months when the Court was in session, and Marshall had abundant opportunity to influence his younger associates.

But Marshall's achievements went beyond the narrow one of influencing his colleagues. He literally molded the development of the Constitution itself. The net effect of the hundreds of opinions delivered by the Marshall Court was to strengthen the judicial branch at the expense of the other two branches of the government; increase the power of the United States and lessen that of the states themselves; and advance the interests of the propertied classes, especially those engaged in commerce.

No state, the Constitution says, shall pass any law "impairing the obligation of contracts." The first Supreme Court case involving this provision was that of *Fletcher* v. *Peck* (1810), which arose out of the notorious Yazoo land frauds (see p. 201). The Court had to decide whether the Georgia legislature of 1796 could rightfully repeal the act of the previous legislature granting lands under shady circumstances to the Yazoo Land Companies. In the unanimous decision, Marshall held that a land grant was a contract and therefore, regardless of any corruption involved, the repeal was invalid. This was the first time the

Supreme Court had voided a state law on the ground that it conflicted with a provision of the United States Constitution, although the Court had previously declared state laws unconstitutional because they were inconsistent with federal laws or treaties.

Dartmouth College v. *Woodward* (1819) expanded further the meaning of the contract clause. The case had originated in a quarrel between the trustees and the president of the college, and it became a major political issue in New Hampshire when the Republicans championed the president and the Federalists took the side of the trustees. Having gained control of the state government, the Republicans undertook to revise Dartmouth's charter (granted by King George III in 1769) so as to convert the private college into a state university. When the case came before the Supreme Court in Washington, Daniel Webster, a Dartmouth graduate, represented the trustees in opposing the charter revision. The Court, he reminded the judges, had decided in *Fletcher* v. *Peck* that "a *grant* is a contract." The Dartmouth charter, he went on, "is embraced within the very terms of that decision," since "a grant of corporate powers and privileges is as much a *contract* as a grant of land." Then, according to legend, he brought tears to the eyes of the justices with an irrelevant peroration that concluded: "It is, sir, as I have said, a small college. And yet there are those who love it." A year later, the Court gave its decision in favor of Webster and the trustees. The ruling had a significant bearing on the development of business corporations. It proclaimed that corporation charters were contracts and that contracts were inviolable; this doctrine placed important restrictions on the ability of state governments to control corporations.

The *Dartmouth College* case raised another important constitutional question as well. Did the Supreme Court have the power to override the decisions of state courts? The Judiciary Act of 1789 and the *Dartmouth College* decision itself both seemed to have established that the Court did have that right. But some advocates of states' rights, notably in the South, continued to argue otherwise. In *Cohens* v. *Virginia* (1821), Marshall provided a ringing reaffirmation of the constitutionality of federal review of state court decisions. The states no longer were sovereign in all respects, he wrote, since they had given up part of their sovereignty in ratifying the Constitution. The state courts, he insisted, must submit to federal jurisdiction; otherwise the government would be prostrated "at the feet of every state in the Union."

Meanwhile, in *McCulloch* v. *Maryland* (1819),

Marshall had confirmed the "implied powers" of Congress by upholding the constitutionality of the Bank of the United States. The Bank, with headquarters in Philadelphia and branches in various cities throughout the country, had become so unpopular in the South and the West that several of the states tried to drive the branches out of business by outright prohibition or by prohibitory taxes. Maryland, for example, laid a heavy tax on the Baltimore branch of the Bank. This case presented two constitutional questions to the Supreme Court: Could Congress charter a bank? And if so, could one of the states thus tax it? As one of the Bank's attorneys, Webster first repeated the arguments used originally by Hamilton to prove that the establishment of such an institution came within the "necessary and proper" clause. Then, to dispose of the tax issue, Webster added an ingenious argument of his own. The power to tax, he said, involved a "power to destroy," and if the states could tax the Bank at all, they could tax it to death. Since the Bank with its branches was an agency of the federal government, the power to tax it was the power to destroy the United States itself. Marshall adopted Webster's words in deciding for the Bank.

The case of *Gibbons* v. *Ogden* (1824) raised the question of the powers of Congress, as against the powers of the states, in regulating interstate commerce. The state of New York had granted Robert Fulton and Robert Livingston's steamboat company the exclusive right to carry passengers on the Hudson River to New York City. From this monopoly, Aaron Ogden obtained the business of navigation across the river between New York and New Jersey. Thomas Gibbons, with a license granted under an act of Congress, went into competition with Ogden, who brought suit against him and was sustained by the New York courts. When Gibbons appealed to the Supreme Court, the justices faced the twofold question whether "commerce" included navigation and whether Congress alone or Congress and the states together could regulate interstate commerce. Marshall replied that "commerce" was a broad term embracing navigation as well as the buying and selling of goods. Although he did not say that the states had no authority whatever regarding interstate commerce, he asserted that the power of Congress to regulate such commerce was "complete in itself" and might be "exercised to its utmost extent." He concluded that the state-granted monopoly was void.

The decision, the last of Marshall's great pronouncements, was the first conspicuous one in which the Marshall Court appeared to be on the popular

John Marshall
Marshall became Chief Justice of the United States Supreme Court in 1801 after establishing himself as one of the leaders of the Federalist party. He served on the Court for thirty-five years, longer than anyone else in American history. And despite the frequent opposition of a series of Republican presidents, he used his position to make the judiciary a vigorous instrument for asserting and strengthening American nationalism.   (Boston Athenaeum)

side. Most people, then as always, hated monopolies, and he had declared this particular monopoly unconstitutional. But the lasting significance of *Gibbons* v. *Ogden* was that it freed internal transportation from restraints by the states and thus prepared the way for the unfettered economic development of the nation by private capitalism.

More immediately, however, the decision had the effect of helping to head off a movement that was under way to weaken the Supreme Court. For some time, such Virginia Republicans as Thomas Jefferson, Spencer Roane, and John Taylor had argued against the views of their fellow Virginian John Marshall. In *Construction Construed and Constitutions Vindicated,* published in 1820, Taylor argued that Marshall and his colleagues were not merely interpreting but were actually changing the nature of the Constitution, which should properly be changed only by the amending process. In Congress some critics of the Court, mostly from the South and the West, proposed various means of curbing what they called judicial tyranny. A Kentucky senator suggested making the Senate, not the Court, the agency to decide the constitutionality of state laws and to settle interstate disputes. Other senators and congressmen introduced bills to increase the membership of the Court (from seven to ten) and to require more than a mere majority to declare a state law unconstitutional.

Still others argued for "codification," that is, for making legislative statutes the basis of the law, rather than the common-law precedents that judges used. Such a reform, codifiers argued, would limit the power of the judiciary and prevent "judge-made" law. The Court reformers did not succeed, however, in passing any of their various panaceas; and after the *Gibbons* v. *Ogden* decision, the hostility to the judicial branch of the government gradually died down.

The decisions of the Marshall Court had a profound cumulative influence on the future development both of American government and of the American economy. They established the primacy of the federal government over the states in exercising control over the economy. They opened the way for an increased federal role in promoting economic growth. And they created or affirmed protection for corporations and other private economic institutions from local government interference, hence facilitating the growth of the new industrial capitalist economy. They were, in short, highly nationalistic decisions, designed to promote the growth of a strong, unified, and economically developed United States.

The Latin American Revolution

Just as the Supreme Court was asserting American nationalism in the shaping of the country's economic life, so the Monroe administration was expressing nationalism in the shaping of foreign policy. As in earlier and later years, the central concern of the United States was its position in relation to Europe. But in defining that position, Americans were forced in the 1820s to develop a policy toward Latin America, which was suddenly winning its independence.

To most citizens of the United States, South and Central America had long seemed to constitute a "dark continent." After the War of 1812, however, they suddenly emerged into the light, and Americans looking southward beheld a gigantic spectacle: the Spanish Empire struggling in its death throes, a whole continent in revolt, new nations in the making with a future no one could foresee.

Already a profitable trade had developed between the ports of the United States and those of the Rio de la Plata (Argentina), Chile, and above all Cuba. Americans exported flour and other staples and received in return sugar, gold, and silver. Great Britain remained the principal trading nation in Latin America, but American commerce was growing steadily. Many believed that trade would increase much faster once the United States established regular diplomatic and commercial relations with the countries in revolt.

In 1815, the United States proclaimed its neutrality in the wars between Spain and its rebellious colonies. This neutrality was in itself advantageous to the rebels, since it implied a partial recognition of their status as nations. It meant, for example, that their warships would be treated as bona-fide belligerent vessels, not as pirate ships. Moreover, even though the neutrality law was revised and strengthened in 1817 and 1818, it still permitted the revolutionists to obtain unarmed ships and supplies from the United States. In short, the United States was not a strict and impartial neutral but a nonbelligerent whose policy, though cautious, was intended to help the insurgents and actually did.

Secretary of State John Quincy Adams and President James Monroe hesitated at first to take the risky step of recognition unless Great Britain would agree to do so at the same time. In 1818 and 1819, the United States made two bids for British cooperation, and both were rejected. Finally, the nationalist impulses so strong in the United States of the 1820s prevailed. In 1822, President Monroe decided to proceed alone. He informed Congress that five nations—La Plata, Chile, Peru, Colombia, and Mexico—were ready for recognition, and he requested an appropriation to send ministers to them. The United States would be the first country formally to recognize the new governments, in defiance of the rest of the world.

The Monroe Doctrine

In 1823, Monroe stood forth as an even bolder champion of America against Europe and an even more forthright champion of American nationalism. Presenting to Congress his annual message on the state of the Union, he announced a policy that would ultimately be known (beginning some thirty years later) as the "Monroe Doctrine." One part of this policy had to do with the role of Europe in America. "The American continents," Monroe declared, ". . . are henceforth not to be considered as subjects for future colonization by any European powers." Further-

James Monroe

This portrait of the fifth president of the United States, by Rembrandt Peale, was painted in the White House during Monroe's presidency. Peale was best known for his idealized portraits of George Washington, painted after Washington's death.

(James Monroe Museum and Memorial Library)

more, "we should consider any attempt on their part to extend their system to any portion of this hemisphere as dangerous to our peace and safety." And the United States would consider any "interposition" against the sovereignty of existing American nations as an unfriendly act. A second aspect of the pronouncement had to do with the role of the United States in Europe. "Our policy in regard to Europe," said Monroe, ". . . is not to interfere in the internal concerns of any of its powers."

How did the president happen to make these statements at the time he did? What specific dangers, if any, did he have in mind? Against what powers in particular was his warning directed? To answer these questions, it is useful to consider first the relations of the United States with the European powers as of 1823, and then the process by which the Monroe administration reached its decision to announce the new "doctrine."

After Napoleon's defeat, the powers of Europe combined in a "concert" to uphold the "legitimacy" of established governments and to prevent the overthrow of existing regimes from within or without. When Great Britain withdrew, the concert became a quadruple alliance, with Russia and France the strongest of its four members. In 1823, after assisting in the suppression of other revolts in Europe, the European allies authorized France to intervene in Spain to restore the Bourbon dynasty that revolutionists had overthrown. Some observers in England and the Americas wondered whether the allies next would back France in an attempt to retake by force the lost Spanish Empire in America. In fact, such concerns were almost certainly groundless. France was still a relatively weak power, not yet recovered from the long and exhausting Napoleonic Wars. It did, to be sure, try to promote the establishment of friendly kingdoms in Latin America by means of intrigue, but it dared not challenge British sea power with an expedition to subvert the new governments by force.

In the minds of most Americans, and certainly in the mind of their secretary of state, Great Britain seemed an even more serious threat to American interests. Adams was much concerned about supposed British designs on Cuba. Like Jefferson and others before him, Adams feared the transfer of Cuba from a weak power such as Spain, its present ruler, to a strong power such as Great Britain. He thought Cuba eventually should belong to the United States; for the "Pearl of the Antilles" had great economic and strategic value and, because of its location, was virtually a part of the American coastline. Adams did not de-

sire to seize the island; he wanted only to keep it in Spanish hands until, by a kind of political gravitation, it should fall naturally to the United States. Despite his worries over the supposed British threat to Cuba, he and other American leaders were pleased to see the rift between Great Britain and the concert of Europe. He was willing to cooperate with Britain, but only to the extent that its policies and his own coincided.

Those policies did not always coincide, however, as the British demonstrated when they rejected the American overtures for joint recognition of Latin American independence in 1818 and 1819. The Americans demonstrated the same thing by their reaction to a British proposal for a joint statement in 1823. That summer, the British secretary for foreign affairs, George Canning, suggested to the American minister in London, Richard Rush, that Great Britain and the United States should combine in announcing to the world their opposition to any European movement against Latin America. But Canning's refusal to join the United States in recognizing the Latin American nations forestalled agreement. And in the fall, after receiving assurances from France that it had no plans to intervene militarily in Latin America, the British abandoned the proposal altogether.

Even before Canning changed his mind about cooperation with the United States, Monroe and Adams were developing grave reservations about a joint pronouncement. Adams, in particular, argued that the American government should act alone instead of following along like a "cock-boat in the wake of a British man-of-war." Canning's loss of interest, therefore, only strengthened an already growing inclination within the administration to make its own pronouncement.

Although Canning's overture led to Monroe's announcement, the message was directed against all the powers of Europe, including Great Britain, which seemed at least as likely as Russia to undertake further colonizing ventures in America. Monroe and Adams hoped the message would rally the people of Latin America to look to their own security. They also hoped it would stir the people of the United States. America was mired in a business depression, divided by sectional politics, and apathetic toward the rather lackluster administration of Monroe. In the rumors of European aggression against the Western Hemisphere lay a chance for the president to arouse and unite the people with an appeal to national pride. The Monroe Doctrine was, then, in one sense a culmination of the growing spirit of unity and nationalism that had been emerging in the United States for over a decade. But it was also an expression of concern about the forces that were already gathering to threaten that spirit.

The Revival of Opposition

For a time during the "era of good feelings," it seemed that the dream of the founders of the republic—of a nation free of party strife—had been realized. After 1816, the Federalist party offered no presidential candidate. Soon it ceased to exist as a national political force. Presidential politics was now conducted wholly within the Republican party, which considered itself not a party at all but an organization representing the whole of the population.

Yet the policies of the federal government during and after the War of 1812, and particularly the nationalizing policies of the 1820s, continued to spark opposition. At first, criticism remained contained within the existing one-party structure. But by the late 1820s, partisan divisions were emerging once again. In some respects, the division mirrored the schism that had produced the first party system in the 1790s. The Republicans had in many ways come to resemble the early Federalist regimes in their promotion of economic growth and centralization. And the opposition, like the opposition in the 1790s, stood opposed to the federal government's expanding role in the economy. There was, however, a crucial difference. At the beginning of the century, the opponents of centralization had also often been opponents of economic growth. Now, in the 1820s, the controversy involved not whether but how the nation should continue to expand.

The "Corrupt Bargain"

From 1796 to 1816, presidential candidates had been nominated by caucuses of the members of each of the two parties in Congress. In 1820, when the Federalists declined to oppose his candidacy, Monroe ran unopposed as the Republican nominee without the necessity of a caucus nomination. If the caucus system had prevailed in 1824, the nominee of the Republicans in Congress would have run unopposed again. But it did not prevail. Several men aspired to the presidency, and they and their followers were

unwilling to let a small group of congressmen and senators determine which one of them was to win the prize.

In 1824, therefore, "King Caucus" was overthrown. Fewer than a third of the Republicans in Congress even bothered to attend the gathering. The caucus did go through the motions of nominating a candidate: William H. Crawford of Georgia, the secretary of the treasury. Other candidates received nominations from state legislatures and endorsements from irregular mass meetings throughout the country.

John Quincy Adams, secretary of state for two terms, had made a distinguished record in the conduct of foreign affairs, and he held the office that had become the traditional stepping stone to the presidency. But as he himself ruefully realized, he was a man of cold and forbidding manners, not a candidate with strong popular appeal. Crawford, in contrast, was an impressive giant of a man who had the backing not only of the congressional caucus but also of the extreme states' rights faction of the Republican party. In midcampaign, however, he was stricken by a paralyzing illness.

Challenging the two cabinet contenders was Henry Clay, the Speaker of the House. The tall, black-haired, genial Kentuckian had a personality that gained him a devoted following. He also stood for a definite and coherent program, which he called the "American System." His plan, attractive to citizens just recovering from a business depression, was to create a great home market for factory and farm producers by raising the tariff to stimulate industry, maintaining the national bank to facilitate credit and exchange, and spending federal funds on internal improvements to provide transportation between the cities and the farms.

Andrew Jackson, the fourth major candidate, offered no such clear-cut program. Although Jackson had served briefly as a representative in Congress and was a member of the United States Senate, he had no significant legislative record. Nevertheless, he had the advantages of a military hero's reputation and a campaign shrewdly managed by the Tennessee politician friends who had put him forward as a candidate. To some of his contemporaries he seemed a crude, hot-tempered frontiersman and Indian fighter. Actually, although he had arisen from a humble background as an orphan in the Carolinas, he had become a well-to-do planter who lived in an elegant mansion ("The Hermitage") near Nashville.

Once the returns were counted, there was no

John Quincy Adams

This photograph of the former president was taken shortly before his death in 1848—almost twenty years after he had left the White House—when he was serving as a congressman from Massachusetts. During his years as president, he was—as he had been throughout his life—an intensely disciplined and hard-working man. He rose at four in the morning and built a fire long before the servants were awake; then, in the predawn hours, he made a long entry in his diary for the previous day. He wrote so much that his right hand at times became paralyzed with writer's cramp, so he taught himself to write with his left hand as well. (Brown Brothers)

doubt that the next vice president was to be John C. Calhoun, of South Carolina, who ran on both the Adams and the Jackson tickets. But there was considerable doubt as to who the next president would be. Jackson received a plurality, although not a majority, of the popular vote. In the electoral college too he came out ahead, with 99 votes to Adams's 84, Crawford's 41, and Clay's 37. Again, however, he lacked a majority. So, in accordance with the Twelfth Amendment, the final decision was left to the House of Representatives, which was to choose among the three candidates with the highest electoral vote. Clay was out of the running.

But while Clay could not be elected president in 1824, he was in a strong position to determine who would be. As Speaker, he had indirect influence throughout the House of Representatives. And as a candidate for the presidency whose electors had won in three states—Kentucky, Ohio, and Missouri—he was in a position to influence those state delegations directly.

Before Congress made its decision, supporters of Jackson, Crawford, and Adams approached Clay on behalf of their respective candidates. Jackson's followers insisted that Jackson, with his popular and electoral pluralities, was really the people's choice and that Congress had no rightful alternative but to ratify the people's will. But Jackson was Clay's most dangerous rival for the political affections of the West; and Jackson, moreover, had demonstrated no support for Clay's nationalistic legislative program. Crawford was out of the question, for he was now a paralytic, incapable of discharging the duties of the presidency. Adams was no friend of Clay and had clashed with him repeatedly when both were peace delegates at Ghent and afterward. But alone among the candidates, Adams was an ardent nationalist and a likely supporter of the American System. Thus Clay finally gave his support to Adams, and the House elected him.

The Jacksonians were angry enough at this, but they became far angrier when the new president announced that Clay was to be his secretary of state. The State Department was the well-established route to the presidency, and Adams thus appeared to be naming Clay as his own successor. To the Jacksonians, it seemed clear that Clay and Adams must have agreed to make each other president—Adams now, Clay next; and they claimed to be horrified by this "corrupt bargain." Very likely there had been some sort of understanding; and though there was nothing corrupt, or even unusual, about it, it proved to be politically costly for both Adams and Clay.

Soon after Adams's inauguration as president, Jackson resigned from the Senate to accept a renomination for the presidency from the Tennessee legislature and to begin a three-year campaign for election in 1828. Politics now overshadowed all else. Throughout his term in the White House, Adams and his policies were to be thoroughly frustrated by the political bitterness arising from the "corrupt bargain."

The Second President Adams

The career of John Quincy Adams divides naturally into three parts. In the first part, as befitted the son of John Adams, he was a brilliant diplomat, serving as the American minister in one foreign capital after another and then as one of the most successful of all secretaries of state. In the second phase of his career, as president from 1825 to 1829, he endured four unhappy and ineffectual years that amounted to a mere interlude between the periods of his greatness. In the third, as a congressman from Massachusetts, he served with high distinction, gaining fame as "Old Man Eloquent," the foremost congressional champion of free speech. His frustration in the White House shows that the presidency demands more than exceptional ability and high-mindedness, for John Quincy Adams possessed both. The presidency also requires political skill and political luck, and these he did not have.

In his inaugural address and in his first message to Congress, Adams gave voice to his own nationalistic vision of the powers and duties of the federal government. He recommended "laws promoting the improvement of agriculture, commerce, and manufactures, the cultivation of the mechanic and of the elegant arts, the advancement of literature, and the progress of the sciences, ornamental and profound." He had no chance of getting an appropriation from Congress for most of these goals. All he actually did get was a few million dollars to improve rivers and harbors and to extend the National Road westward from Wheeling. Still, this was more than Congress had appropriated for internal improvements under all his predecessors together.

Even in the field of diplomacy, where Adams had more experience than any other president before or since, he failed in the major efforts of his administration. Yielding to Secretary of State Clay's wish for cooperation with the Latin American governments, Adams appointed two delegates to attend an international conference that the Venezuelan liberator, Simón Bolívar, had called to meet at Panama in 1826. Objections arose in Congress for two reasons. One was that Southerners opposed the idea of white Americans mingling in Panama with black delegates from Haiti, a country whose independence the United States refused to recognize. The other reason for obstruction was simply politics—the determination of Jacksonians to discredit the administration. They charged that Adams aimed to sacrifice American interests and involve the nation in an entangling alliance. While the Jacksonians filibustered, Congress delayed the Panama mission so long that by the time it was finally approved it was too late. One of the American delegates died on the way to the conference; the other arrived after it was over. Adams had hoped to offset British influence, which prevailed in Latin America, by having the United States play an active role at the conference. Those hopes were dashed.

Adams was also bested in a contest with the state of Georgia, which wished to remove the remaining Creek and Cherokee Indians from the state so as to gain additional soil for cotton planters. The United States government, in a 1791 treaty, had guaranteed the Creeks possession of the land they occupied. But the Georgians extracted a new treaty from the tribe in 1825, by which the Creeks ceded the land to the state. Adams was convinced that the new treaty had been fraudulently obtained and refused to enforce it, setting up a direct conflict between the president and the leaders of the state. The governor of Georgia defied the president and went ahead with plans for Indian removal. The conflict was finally resolved in 1827, when the Creeks agreed to still another treaty, in which they again yielded their land, thus undercutting Adams's position. The affair was memorable in one sense: Adams became one of the few major American public figures firmly to oppose the continuing displacement of the Indians. But at the time, it served mainly as a political embarrassment.

Even more damaging to the administration was its support for a new tariff on imported goods in 1828. This measure originated in the demands of Massachusetts and Rhode Island woolen manufacturers, who complained that the British were dumping woolens on the American market at prices with which the domestic mill owners could not compete. The New Englanders were frustrated at first by Southern opposition in Congress, but eventually they com-

Choctaws in Louisiana
The Choctaws were among the many Mississippi Valley tribes to experience forced relocation at the hands of the United States in the 1830s. Originally located in central Mississippi, the tribe marched through Louisiana and Arkansas and into Indian Territory (now Oklahoma) beginning in 1830. Some members of the tribe remained behind at various points along the way, living alongside the white community and adopting many of its ways. The French artist Alfred Boisseau painted this scene of a group of them walking along a bayou in Louisiana in 1845.   (New Orleans Museum of Art)

bined with the middle and Western states to create political pressures that could not be resisted.

But the 1828 bill, the result of these efforts, contained provisions attractive to the West that antagonized its original New England supporters. It established high duties not only on woolens, as the New Englanders had wanted, but also on a number of other items, such as flax, hemp, iron, lead, molasses, and raw wool, some of which the West produced and for which they wanted protection from foreign rivals. That distressed New England manufacturers; the benefits of protecting their manufactured goods from foreign competition now had to be weighed against the prospects of having to pay more

for raw materials. Indeed, a story arose that the bill had taken its shape from a Jacksonian plot to embarrass and discredit Adams. The bill related to "manufactures of no sort or kind but the manufacture of a president of the United States," John Randolph said. The bill would present Adams with a dilemma, for he would lose friends whether he signed or vetoed it. To sign the bill would lose him support in both the South and the Northeast. To veto it would lose him support from the farmers and manufacturers of the West.

When Congress considered the bill item by item, Southerners voted against proposals to reduce the tariff rates, in the hope that some of its outrageous duties would so antagonize New Englanders that they would help defeat it. But when it came to a final test, Daniel Webster voted for it despite its duties on raw materials, and he carried with him enough New England votes to enable the bill to pass. Adams signed it. The tactics of the Southerners had backfired, and they were left cursing the bill as the "tariff of abominations."

Jackson Triumphant

By 1828, the schism within the Republican party was complete. Once again, as in 1800, two parties offered candidates in the presidential election. On one side stood the supporters of John Quincy Adams, who called themselves the National Republicans. They supported the economic nationalism of the preceding years. Opposing them were the followers of Andrew Jackson, who took the name Democratic Republicans. They argued for a dispersal of public authority, an assault on privilege, and a widening of opportunity. Adams attracted the support of most of the remaining Federalists (among whose number he had once counted himself); Jackson appealed to a broad coalition that stood opposed to the "economic" aristocracy.

Issues seemed to count for little in the campaign of 1828. There was much talk of the "corrupt bargain" and frequent rhetorical references to the "tariff of abominations." But while Adams's position on the tariff was a matter of record (he had signed the bill), nobody knew where Jackson stood. Again, as in 1824, personalities became a more important factor than policies. Indeed, the tone of the campaign was such as to suggest that two criminals were running for the highest office in the land.

The Jacksonians charged that Adams as president had been guilty of gross waste and extravagance and had used public funds to buy gambling devices (a chess set and a billiard table) for the White House. But that was not the worst of Adams's alleged crimes. While Adams had been minister to Russia, the Jacksonians falsely claimed, he had tried to procure a beautiful American girl for the sinful pleasures of the czar.

Adams's supporters directed even worse accusations at Jackson. He was, they claimed in speeches, handbills, and pamphlets, a murderer and an adulterer. A "coffin handbill" listed, within coffin-shaped

---

SIGNIFICANT EVENTS

1808	Importation of slaves to United States banned
1817–1825	Erie Canal constructed
1819	Supreme Court hears *Dartmouth College* and *McCulloch* v. *Maryland*
1820	Missouri Compromise enacted Monroe reelected president without opposition
1823	Monroe Doctrine is proclaimed
1824	John Quincy Adams wins disputed presidential election Supreme Court rules in *Gibbons* v. *Ogden*
1826	Thomas Jefferson and John Adams die on July 4
1827	Creek Indians cede lands to Georgia
1828	"Tariff of abominations" passed Andrew Jackson elected president
1830	Baltimore & Ohio becomes first American railroad to begin operations
1830s	Major immigration from southern (Catholic) Ireland begins Factory system spreads in textile and shoe industries First craft unions founded
1831	Cyrus McCormick invents mechanical reaper
1832	Cholera plague
1834	Woman workers at Lowell mills stage strike
1837	Commercial panic
1845	Female Labor Reform Association established at Lowell

Election of 1828 (57.6% of electorate voting)

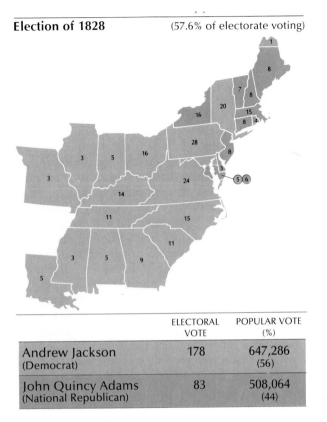

	ELECTORAL VOTE	POPULAR VOTE (%)
Andrew Jackson (Democrat)	178	647,286 (56)
John Quincy Adams (National Republican)	83	508,064 (44)

outlines, the names of militiamen whom Jackson was said to have shot in cold blood during the War of 1812. (The men had been deserters who were executed after due sentence by a court-martial.) It was also rumored that Jackson had knowingly lived in sin with the wife of another man. Actually, he had married the woman, his beloved Rachel, at a time when the pair apparently believed her first husband had divorced her.

Jackson's victory was decisive, if sectional. He won 56 percent of the popular vote and an electoral majority of 178 votes to Adams's 83. But the Jacksonians made few inroads into the National Republican strongholds of the Northeast. Adams swept virtually all of New England, and he showed significant strength in the mid-Atlantic region. Nevertheless, the Jacksonians considered their victory complete, and they hailed it as an event as important as the victory of Jefferson in 1800. Once again, the forces of privilege had been ejected from Washington. Once again, a champion of democracy would occupy the White House and restore liberty to the society and the economy. America had entered, many claimed, the "era of the common man." And Andrew Jackson, the people's champion, departed for Washington determined to transform the federal government.

SUGGESTED READINGS

The Economic Revolution: General Histories Many of the books cited in the readings for Chapter 7 as sources for American economic and technological growth are useful as well for the period described in this chapter. In addition, see W. Elliot Brownlee, *Dynamics of Ascent* (1974), and Stuart Bruchey, *The Growth of the Modern American Economy* (1975), which are useful overviews.

Transportation George R. Taylor, *The Transportation Revolution* (1951), is a valuable source for the construction of roads, canals, and railroads. Nathan Miller, *The Enterprise of a Free People* (1962), examines New York during the Canal Age, as does R. E. Shaw, *Erie Water West* (1966). Harry N. Scheiber, *Ohio Canal Era* (1969), examines the government's role in transportation and in the economy in general in the mid-nineteenth century. Albert Fishlow, *American Railroads and the Transformation of the Ante-Bellum Economy* (1965), examines early railroad building.

Business and Technology E. P. Douglas, *The Coming of Age of American Business* (1971), examines early entrepreneurs, as does Thomas C. Cochran and William Miller, *The Age of Enterprise* (1942). Thomas C. Cochran, *Business in American Life* (1972), is an overview of the subject. Richard D. Brown, *Modernization: The Transformation of*

American Life, 1600–1865 (1976), examines business development in a much larger context; Diane Lindstrom, *Economic Development in the Philadelphia Region, 1810–1850* (1978), is a useful study of that growth in a particular area. Merritt Roe Smith, *Harpers Ferry Armory and the New Technology* (1977), is a local study of technological change. David J. Jeremy, *Transatlantic Industrial Revolution: The Diffusion of Textile Technologies Between Britain and America, 1790–1830* (1981), examines the diffusion of technology in a particular industry. H. J. Habbakuk, *American and British Technology in the Nineteenth Century* (1962), and Nathan Rosenberg, *Technology and American Economic Growth* (1972), adopt a somewhat broader focus.

Factories and Workers Classic studies of the early factory system include Arthur H. Cole, *The American Wool Manufacture*, 2 vols. (1926), and Caroline Ware, *The Early New England Cotton Manufacture* (1931). Thomas Dublin, *Women at Work* (1979), is an important study of industrialization and labor in Lowell. Alan Dawley, *Class and Community* (1977), examines the shoe industry and its workers in Lynn, Massachusetts. Other more recent examples of important work in the field of nineteenth-century labor history are Alice Kessler-Harris, *Out to Work: A History of Wage-Earning Women in the United States* (1982); Bruce Laurie, *Working*

People of Philadelphia (1980); Susan E. Hirsch, *Roots of the American Working Class: The Industrialization of Crafts in Newark, 1800–1860* (1978); Jonathan Prude, *The Coming of Industrial Order: Town and Factory Life in Rural Massachusetts, 1810–1860* (1983); and Steven J. Ross, *Workers on the Edge: Work, Leisure, and Politics in Industrializing Cincinnati, 1788–1890* (1985). Sean Wilentz, *Chants Democratic: New York City and the Rise of the American Working Class, 1788–1850* (1984), explores the connection between working class formation and Jacksonian politics.

Political Affairs Two good overviews of the political life of the era following the War of 1812 are by George Dangerfield: *The Awakening of American Nationalism* (1965) and *The Era of Good Feelings* (1952). Glover Moore, *The Missouri Compromise* (1953), is a basic work on the sectional crisis of 1819–1820. Paul C. Nagle, *One Nation Indivisible: The Union in American Thought, 1815–1828* (1965), discusses the intellectual background of postwar nationalism. Biographies of leading nationalists of the era also shed light on the phenomenon. See particularly Glyndon Van Deusen, *The Life of Henry Clay* (1937), a study of the architect of the Missouri Compromise; Harry Ammon, *James Monroe: The Quest for National Identity* (1971); and Charles M. Wiltse, *John C. Calhoun: American Nationalist* (1944). Wesley Frank Craven, *The Legend of the Founding Fathers* (1956), discusses the influence of the past on nationalism in the nineteenth century. Shaw Livermore, *The Twilight of Federalism* (1962), is a valuable study of the decline of the Federalists after the War of 1812. Samuel F. Bemis, *John Quincy Adams and the Union* (1956), recounts the troubled administration of the second President Adams. Robert V. Remini, *The Election of Andrew Jackson* (1963), examines the revival of partisan opposition and the eventual triumph of it. See also Norman K. Risjord, *The Old Republicans: Southern Conservatism in the Age of Jefferson* (1965).

The Courts Albert J. Beveridge, *The Life of John Marshall,* 4 vols. (1916–1919), is the classic study of the Supreme Court in the early national period. Leonard Baker, *John Marshall: A Life in Law* (1974), and Francis N. Stites, *John Marshall: Defender of the Constitution* (1981), are more recent studies. Likewise useful are Richard E. Ellis, *The Jeffersonian Crisis: Courts and Politics in the Young Republic* (1971); R. Kent Newmyer, *The Supreme Court Under Marshall and Taney* (1968); Charles G. Haines, *The Role of the Supreme Court in American Government and Politics, 1789–1835* (1970); and D. O. Dewey, *Marshall Versus Jefferson: The Political Background of* Marbury *v.* Madison (1970). Alexander M. Bickel, *Justice Joseph Story and the Rise of the Supreme Court* (1971), and James McClellan, *Joseph Story and the American Constitution* (1971), examine one of the most influential of Marshall's judicial contemporaries.

The Monroe Doctrine Arthur P. Whitaker, *The United States and the Independence of Latin America* (1941), examines the background of the Monroe Doctrine. The standard study of the shaping of the doctrine itself is Dexter Perkins, *The Monroe Doctrine* (1927); a later study by Perkins, *Hands Off: A History of the Monroe Doctrine* (1941), summarizes his earlier work. Ernest R. May, *The Making of the Monroe Doctrine* (1975), is a provocative reexamination of policymaking. Samuel F. Bemis, *John Quincy Adams and the Foundations of American Foreign Policy* (1949), is a biography of the architect of the Monroe Doctrine. See also Bradford Perkins, *Castlereagh and Adams: England and the United States, 1812–1823* (1964), and Frank Thistlethwaite, *The Anglo-American Connection in the Early Nineteenth Century* (1959).

Detail from _The Verdict of the People,_ by George Caleb Bingham, 1855 (Boatmen's National Bank of St. Louis)

Chapter 10 # Democracy in America

special right, benefit *settle oneself in a firmly position.*

When the French aristocrat Alexis de Tocqueville visited the United States in 1831, one feature of American society struck him as "fundamental": the "general equality of condition among the people." Unlike older societies, in which privilege and wealth were passed from generation to generation within an entrenched upper class, America had no rigid distinctions of rank. "The government of democracy," he wrote in his classic study *Democracy in America* (1835–1840), "brings the notion of political rights to the level of the humblest citizens, just as the dissemination of wealth brings the notion of property within the reach of all the members of the community."

Yet Tocqueville also wondered how long the fluidity of American society could survive in the face of the growth of manufacturing and the rise of the factory system. Industrialism, he feared, would create a large class of dependent workers and a small group of new aristocrats. For, as he explained it, "at the very moment at which the science of manufactures lowers the class of workmen, it raises the class of masters."

Americans, too, pondered the future of their democracy in these years of economic and territorial expansion. Some feared that the nation's rapid growth would produce social chaos and insisted that the country's first priority must be to establish order and a clear system of authority. Others argued that the greatest danger facing the nation was privilege and that society's goal should be to eliminate the favored status of powerful elites and make opportunity more widely available. The advocates of this latter vision seized control of the federal government in 1829 with the inauguration of Andrew Jackson.

Jackson and his followers were not egalitarians. They did nothing to challenge the existence of slavery; they supervised one of the most vicious assaults on American Indians in the nation's history; and they accepted the necessity of economic inequality and social gradation. Jackson himself was a frontier aristocrat, and most of those who served him were themselves people of wealth and standing. They were not, however, usually aristocrats by birth. They had, they believed, risen to prominence on the basis of their own talents and energies; and their goal in public life was to ensure that others like themselves would have the opportunity to do the same.

The "democratization" of government over which Andrew Jackson presided was permeated with the rhetoric of equality and aroused the excitement of working people. To the national leaders who promoted that democratization, however, its purpose was less to aid the farmers and laborers who were Jackson's greatest champions than to challenge the power of Eastern elites for the sake of the rising entrepreneurs of the South and the West.

consider carefully

The Advent of Mass Politics

On March 4, 1829, an unprecedented throng—thousands of Americans from all regions of the country, including farmers, laborers, and others of humble rank—crowded before the Capitol in Washington, D.C., to witness the inauguration of Andrew Jackson. After the ceremonies, the boisterous crowd

271

The Inaugural Levee, 1829
Even in the relatively rustic days of the early republic, presidential inaugurations often took place amid almost monarchical grandeur. But when Andrew Jackson entered office in 1829, having won election as the champion of democratic simplicity, he avoided formal trappings and threw the White House open to the public. Frontier settlers and common people of all kinds had flocked to Washington to witness the inauguration of their hero, and the result was an invasion of the White House by an enormous and—in the view of some conservative observers—cretinous horde. Jackson's critics described the inaugural levee as the triumph of "King Mob." (Library of Congress)

poured down Pennsylvania Avenue, following their hero to the White House. And there, at a public reception open to all, they filled the state rooms to overflowing, trampling one another, soiling the carpets, ruining the elegantly upholstered sofas and chairs in their eagerness to shake the new president's hand. "It was a proud day for the people," wrote Amos Kendall, one of Jackson's closest political associates. "General Jackson is *their own* President." To other observers, however, the scene was less appealing. Justice of the Supreme Court Joseph Story, a friend and colleague of John Marshall, looked on the inaugural levee, as it was called, and remarked with disgust: "The reign of King 'Mob' seems triumphant."

In a sense, both Kendall and Story were correct. For if what some have called the "age of Jackson" did not mark the elevation of all Americans to prosperity and equality, it did mark a transformation of American politics that extended power widely to new groups. Formerly the preserve of a relatively small group of property owners, politics now became the province of virtually all the nation's citizens (that is, all its white males; for few Jacksonians were willing to contemplate the participation of women or blacks in the electoral process). In a political sense at least, the era well earned its title "the age of the common man."

President of the Common Man

Unlike Thomas Jefferson, Jackson was no democratic philosopher. Nevertheless, in his own plain, straight-

Ships Takeapart

forward way, he too expressed a distinct theory of democracy. Government, he insisted, should offer "equal protection and equal benefits" to all the people. It should provide special favors to no one. Once in office, he set about to dismantle those institutions and policies that he believed worked to protect special privileges and restrict opportunity.

His first target was the personnel procedures of the federal government. For a generation, ever since the downfall of the Federalists in 1800, there had been no change of party in the national administration. Officeholders in Washington, therefore, had stayed on year after year, many of them growing gray and some of them growing corrupt. "Office is considered as a species of property," Jackson told Congress in a bitter denunciation of the entrenched "class" of permanent officeholders, "and government rather as a means of promoting individual interests than as an instrument created solely for the service of the people." Official duties, he believed, could be made "so plain and simple that men of intelligence may readily qualify themselves for their performance." Offices belonged to the people, he argued, not to the entrenched officeholders. Or, as one of his henchmen, William L. Marcy of New York, more cynically put it, "To the victors belong the spoils."

In actual practice, Jackson did not do nearly as much as his partisan critics claimed to remove existing government employees and replace them with appointees of his own. During the entire eight years of his presidency he removed a total of no more than one-fifth of the federal officeholders; and many of them he removed for cause, such as misuse of government funds. Proportionally, Jackson dismissed no more of the jobholders than Jefferson had done. Nevertheless, by embracing the philosophy of the "spoils system," a system already well entrenched in a number of state governments, the Jackson administration fixed it firmly upon American politics.

Eventually the Jacksonians adopted another instrument of democratic politics: the national nominating convention. Jackson supporters had long resented the process by which presidential candidates were selected by congressional caucus, a process that they believed was designed to restrict access to the office to those favored by entrenched elites. Jackson himself had achieved office without resort to the caucus; and in 1832, to renominate him for the presidency, his followers staged the first national convention of a major party. Although in later generations the party convention would be seen by many as the source of corruption and political exclusivity,

in the 1830s it was viewed as a great triumph of the people. Power in the party would, through the convention, arise directly from the populace, circumventing established political institutions.

Despite the rhetoric, however, the acceptance of the spoils system and the creation of the political convention exposed not only the extent but the limits of Jacksonian political democracy. Both served to limit the power of entrenched elites—permanent officeholders and the exclusive party caucus. Yet neither really transferred power to the common people. Appointments to office almost always went to prominent political allies of the president and his associates. Delegates to national conventions were less often common men than members of local party elites. Political opportunity within the party was expanding, but within narrow limits.

The Expanding Electorate

In other ways, however, Jacksonian politics did indeed transfer power to the population at large. For it was in this era that a true mass electorate emerged. The expansion of the franchise began in Ohio and other new states of the West, which, on joining the Union, adopted constitutions that guaranteed all adult white males the right to vote and permitted all voters the right to hold public office. Older states, concerned about the loss of their population to the West, began slowly and haltingly to grant additional political rights to their people so as to encourage them to stay. Even before the War of 1812 a few of the Eastern states had permitted white men to vote whether or not they owned property or paid a tax. Eventually, all the states (although some of them not until after the Civil War) changed their constitutions in the direction of increased democracy.

Change provoked resistance, and at times the democratic trend fell short of the aims of the more radical reformers, as when Massachusetts held its constitutional convention in 1820. Reform-minded delegates complained that in the Massachusetts government the rich were better represented than the poor, both because of the restrictions on voting and officeholding and because of the peculiar system of property representation in the state senate. But Daniel Webster, one of the conservative delegates, opposed democratic changes on the grounds that "power *naturally* and *necessarily* follows property" and that "property as such should have its weight and influence in political arrangement." Webster and the rest of the conservatives could not prevent the reform of senate representation, nor could they prevent elimination of the property requirement for voting. But, to the dismay of the radicals, the new constitution required that every voter be a taxpayer and that the governor be the owner of considerable real estate.

More often, however, it was the forces of democratization that prevailed in the states. In the New York convention of 1821, for example, conservatives led by Chancellor James Kent insisted that a taxpaying requirement for suffrage was not enough and that, at least in the election of state senators, the property qualification should be retained. Kent argued that society "is an association for the protection of property as well as of life" and that "the individual who contributes only one cent to the common stock ought not to have the same power and influence in directing the property concerns of the partnership as he who contributes his thousands." But reformers, citing the Declaration of Independence, maintained that life, liberty, and the pursuit of happiness, not property, were the main concerns of society and government. The property qualification was abolished.

The wave of state reforms was generally peaceful, but in Rhode Island democratization efforts created considerable instability. The Rhode Island constitution in the 1830s was still the old colonial charter, little changed; and under its terms, more than half the adult males of the state were disqualified as voters. The conservative legislature, representing this restricted electorate, consistently blocked all efforts at reform. In 1840, the lawyer and activist Thomas L. Dorr and a group of his followers formed a "People's party," held a convention, drafted a new constitution, and submitted it to a popular vote. It was overwhelmingly approved. The existing legislature, however, refused to accept the Dorr constitution and submitted one of its own to the voters; it was narrowly voted down. The Dorrites, in the meantime, had begun to set up a new government, under their own constitution, with Dorr as governor; and so, in 1842, two governments were laying claims to legitimacy in Rhode Island. The old state government proclaimed that Dorr and his followers were rebels and began to imprison them. The Dorrites, in the meantime, made a brief and ineffectual effort to capture the state arsenal. The Dorr Rebellion, as it was known, quickly failed, and Dorr himself surrendered and was briefly imprisoned. But the episode helped spur the old guard finally to draft a new constitution, which greatly expanded the suffrage.

In the South, democratization moved more

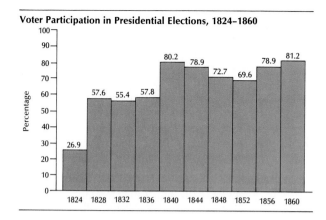

Voter Participation in Presidential Elections, 1824–1860

slowly. Reformers in several states criticized the overrepresentation of the tidewater areas and the underrepresentation of the back country in the legislatures. The Virginia constitutional convention, which met in 1829, granted some slight concessions to the western counties, but not enough to satisfy the residents of the area. Elsewhere in the Southeast the planters and politicians of the older counties continued to dominate the state governments.

Other limitations on democratization survived as well. With few exceptions, free blacks could not vote anywhere in the South and hardly anywhere in the North. Pennsylvania at one time allowed black suffrage, but in 1838 it amended the state constitution to prohibit it. Women could vote in neither the North nor the South, regardless of the amount of property they might own. Everywhere the ballot was open, not secret, and often it was cast as a spoken vote rather than a written one. The lack of secrecy meant that voters could be, and often were, bribed or intimidated.

Despite the persisting limitations, however, the number of voters increased far more rapidly than did the population as a whole. And the result was a significant increase in political participation in both state and national elections. Indeed, one of the most striking political trends of the early nineteenth century was the change in the method of choosing presidential electors and the dramatic increase in popular participation in the process. In 1800, the legislature had chosen the presidential electors in ten of the states, and the people in only six. By 1828, electors were chosen by popular vote in every state but South Carolina, which had no popular presidential elections until after the Civil War. In the presidential election of 1824, fewer than 27 percent of adult white males had voted. In the election of 1828, the figure rose to about

58 percent—more than twice that in the preceding election. In 1832 and 1836, the proportion remained approximately the same as in 1828. But then, in 1840, people flocked to the polls as never before, 80 percent of white men casting their ballots. The multiplication of voters was only in part the result of a widening of the electorate. It was in greater measure the result of a heightening of interest in politics and a strengthening of party organization.

The Legitimation of Party

At the same time that the electorate was expanding and the number of elective offices was increasing, another, equally profound political development was in progress: the establishment of the idea of party as a legitimate part of American public life. Even at the peak of the first party system in 1800, virtually no one had been willing to accept the *idea* of a party system. There was wide agreement that parties were evils to be avoided, that the nation should strive for a broad consensus in which permanent factional lines would not exist. But in the 1820s and 1830s, those assumptions gave way to a new view: that permanent, institutionalized parties were a desirable part of the political process, that indeed they were essential to democracy.

Like so many other American political developments, the elevation of the idea of party occurred first at the state level, most prominently in New York. There a dissident political faction under the leadership of Martin Van Buren (known as the "Bucktails" or the "Albany Regency") began in the years after the War of 1812 to challenge the political oligarchy—led by the aristocratic governor, De Witt Clinton—that had been dominating the state for years. In itself, the challenge was nothing new; factional rivalries occurred in virtually every state. What was new was the way in which Van Buren and his followers posed their challenge. Refuting the traditional view of a political party as undemocratic, they argued that only an institutionalized party, based in the populace at large, could ensure genuine democracy. The alternative was the sort of oligarchy that Clinton had created. In this new kind of party, ideological commitments would be less important than loyalty to the party itself. Preservation of the party as an institution—through the use of favors, rewards, and patronage—would be the principal goal of the leadership. Above all, for a party to survive, it must have a permanent opposition. The existence of two competing parties would give each political faction a sense of purpose and would force politicians to remain continually attuned to the will of the people. The opposing parties would check and balance each other in much the same way that the different branches of government checked and balanced one another.

By the late 1820s, this new idea of party was emerging in other states beyond New York—in Pennsylvania, for example, where the spoils system was introduced well before it was transplanted to the federal government. The election of Jackson in 1828, the result of a popular movement apparently removed from the usual political elites, seemed further to legitimize the idea of party. And finally, in the 1830s, a fully formed two-party system began to operate at the national level, with each party committed to its own existence as an institution and willing to accept the legitimacy of its opposition. "Parties of some sort must exist," said a New York newspaper. "'Tis in the nature and genius of our government."

"Our Federal Union"

True to the new concept of party, Andrew Jackson had won election on the basis of no clearly articulated program. His followers—who soon began to call themselves Democrats (no longer Democratic Republicans), thus giving a permanent name to what would become the nation's oldest political party—had interests so diverse that a statement of precise aims would have alienated many of them at the outset. Yet Jackson entered office with certain strong convictions about the purposes of government and about the nature of the presidency. He believed that the federal government should work on behalf of the common man, eliminating the privileges of established elites. In general, that meant reducing the functions of government, since a concentration of power in Washington would, he believed, almost inevitably produce a restriction of opportunity to those favored few with political connections. But Jackson believed, too, in forceful presidential leadership. And although he spoke frequently of the importance of states' rights, he was strongly committed to the preservation of the Union. Thus at the same time that Jackson was contemplating an economic program to reduce the power of the national government, he was forced to assert the supremacy of the Union in the face of a potent challenge. For he had no sooner entered office than his own vice president—John C. Calhoun—began to assert a dangerous new constitutional theory: what became known as nullification.

Calhoun and Nullification

Calhoun was forty-six years old in 1828, a man with a distinguished past and what seemed to be a promising future. He had been a congressional leader during the War of 1812; he had served for eight years as head of the War Department (compiling a record as one of the few truly great secretaries of war); he had been vice president in John Quincy Adams's administration. And now, he was running for another term as vice president, this time with Andrew Jackson. Presumably he could look forward to the presidency itself.

But the tariff question confronted Calhoun with a dilemma. Once he had been a forthright protectionist, coming out strongly for the tariff of 1816. But since that time many South Carolinians had changed their minds on the subject. Carolina cotton planters were disturbed because their plantations were less profitable than they thought they should be. The whole state appeared to be stagnating, its population remaining almost stationary, its countryside showing signs of ruin and decay. One reason was the exhaustion of the South Carolina soil, which could not compete effectively with the newly opened fertile lands of the Southwest. But the Carolinians blamed their trouble on another cause—the "tariff of abominations" of 1828. They argued that protective duties raised the prices of the things they had to buy, whether they bought them at home or from abroad. Some exasperated Carolinians were ready to seek escape from the hated law through revolution—that is, through secession. This was a challenge Calhoun had to meet in order to maintain his leadership in the

Charleston, 1831
The little-known South Carolina artist S. Bernard painted this view of Charleston's East Battery in 1831. Then as now, residents and visitors liked to stroll along the battery and watch the activity in the city's busy harbor. But Charleston in the 1830s was a less important commercial center than it had been a few decades earlier. By then, overseas traders were increasingly avoiding Southern ports and doing more and more business in New York. (Yale University Art Gallery)

state and make a future for himself in national politics.

Quietly he worked out a theory to justify state action in resisting the tariff law—action that would be effective yet that would stop short of secession. Because he wanted any such plan to be legal and constitutional, not revolutionary, he had to find a basis for it in the Constitution itself. And he did so by following the lines laid down by Madison and Jefferson in their Virginia and Kentucky Resolutions of 1798–1799.

Calhoun began with the assumption that sovereignty, the ultimate source of power, lay in the states, which were separate political communities. These separate peoples had created the federal government through their conventions that had ratified the Constitution in the 1780s. In the American political system, therefore, the states were the "principals," and the federal government was their "agent." The Constitution was a "compact" containing instructions within which the agent was to operate.

From these assumptions, the rest of his theory followed more or less logically. The Supreme Court was not competent to judge whether acts of Congress were constitutional, since the Court, like the Congress, was only a branch of an agency created by the states. The principals must decide, each for itself, whether their instructions had been violated. If Congress enacted a law of doubtful constitutionality— say, a protective tariff—a state could "interpose" to frustrate the law. That is, the people of the state could hold a convention, and if (through their elected delegates) they decided that Congress had gone too far, they could declare the federal law null and void within their state. In that state, the law would remain inoperative until three-fourths of the whole number of states should ratify an amendment to the Constitution specifically assigning Congress the power in question. The nullifying state would then submit to the will of the nation; or, if unwilling to do that, it could secede from the Union. The legislature of South Carolina published Calhoun's first statement of his theory in 1828, anonymously, in a document entitled *The South Carolina Exposition and Protest*. This paper condemned the "tariff of abominations" as unconstitutional, unfair, and unendurable—a law fit to be nullified.

Calhoun's real hope, however, was that the theory of nullification would never be put to the test, that it would simply serve to pressure the federal government to respond to South Carolina's grievances. He hoped in particular that Jackson as president would persuade Congress to make drastic reductions in tariff rates. But Calhoun did not, he soon discovered, have as much influence in the new administration as he had hoped. He had a powerful rival for Jackson's favor in the person of Martin Van Buren.

The Rise of Van Buren

Van Buren was about the same age as Calhoun and equally ambitious. But he was very different in background and personality. Born of Dutch ancestry in the village of Kinderhook, near Albany, New York, he advanced himself through skillful maneuvering to the position of United States senator, a position he held from 1820 to 1828. He also made himself the party boss of his state by organizing and leading the Albany Regency, the Democratic machine of New York. Though he supported Crawford for president in 1824, he afterward became one of the most ardent of Jacksonians, doing much to carry his state for Jackson in 1828 while getting himself elected governor. By this time he had a reputation as a political wizard. Short and slight, with reddish-gold sideburns and a quiet manner, he gained a variety of revealing nicknames, such as "the Sage of Kinderhook," "the Little Magician," and "the Red Fox." Never giving or taking offense, he was in temperament just the opposite of the choleric Jackson. But the two were soon to become the closest of friends. Van Buren promptly resigned the governorship and went to Washington in 1829 when Jackson called him to head the new cabinet as secretary of state.

Except for Van Buren, Jackson's cabinet contained no one of more than ordinary talent. It was assembled largely to represent and harmonize the sectional and factional interests within the party. The cabinet was not intended to form a council of advisers, and Jackson did not even call cabinet meetings. Instead, he relied on an unofficial circle of political allies who came to be known as the "Kitchen Cabinet." Noteworthy in this group were several newspaper editors, among them Isaac Hill, from New Hampshire, and Amos Kendall and Francis P. Blair, from Kentucky. After 1830, Blair edited the administration's official organ, the Washington *Globe*. Also influential was Jackson's old Tennessee friend and political manager William B. Lewis, who lived at the White House and had ready access to the president. But the most important of all was Van Buren, a member of both the official and the unofficial cabinets.

Martin Van Buren
As leader of the so-called Albany Regency in New York in the 1820s, Van Buren had helped create one of the first modern party organizations in the United States. Later, as Andrew Jackson's secretary of state and (after 1832) vice president, he helped bring party politics to the national level. So it was perhaps ironic that in 1840, when he ran for reelection to the presidency, he should lose to William Henry Harrison, whose Whig party made effective use of many of the techniques of mass politics that Van Buren himself had pioneered. (Library of Congress)

Vice President Calhoun, to his dismay, saw signs of Van Buren's growing influence when he viewed the division of the spoils. Not only did Van Buren get cabinet places for himself and his friends; he also secured the appointment of his followers to most of the lesser offices. Already, beneath the surface, there

was the beginning of a rift between the vice president and the president. Then Calhoun and Jackson were further estranged, and Jackson and Van Buren were brought closer together, through a curious quarrel over a woman and etiquette.

Margaret O'Neale (generally known as Peggy) was the attractive and vivacious daughter of a Washington tavern keeper with whom both Andrew Jackson and his friend John H. Eaton had taken lodgings while serving as senators from Tennessee. Peggy was married at a young age to a navy purser and was the mother of two children; but rumors began to circulate in Washington in the mid-1820s that she and Senator Eaton had become "familiar." In 1828, Peggy's husband died, and she and Eaton were soon married, with Jackson's blessing. Only weeks after the wedding, Jackson named his friend Eaton to be his secretary of war and thus made the new Mrs. Eaton a cabinet wife. The rest of the administration wives, led by Mrs. Calhoun, were incensed and refused to receive her. Jackson was furious. His own wife, Rachel, now dead, had been slandered by his political enemies; and he was confident that Peggy Eaton too was an innocent victim of dirty politics. He not only defended her virtue; he demanded that his secretaries and associates treat her with respect and accept her into their social world. Calhoun, however, bowed to his wife's adamant demands and refused, thus taking sides against the president. Van Buren, who was a widower, befriended the Eatons and thus ingratiated himself with Jackson.

By 1831, partly as a result of the repercussions of the Peggy Eaton affair, Jackson had settled on Van Buren as his choice to succeed him in the White House. Calhoun's dreams of the presidency had all but vanished.

The Webster-Hayne Debate

If there had been only personal differences between Jackson and Calhoun, their parting would have been less significant. But there were also differences of principle. At the height of the Eaton affair, a great debate emerged on the nature of the Constitution that dramatically revealed the gulf between them.

The debate received its most dramatic and public expression in the United States Senate in January 1830. The controversy grew out of a seemingly routine Senate discussion of federal policy toward the public lands in the West. In the midst of the discussion, a senator from Connecticut suggested that all land sales and surveys be temporarily discontinued. Senator Thomas Hart Benton of Missouri, the Jacksonian leader in the Senate and a sturdy defender of the West, charged that the proposal to stop land sales was intended to keep New England workers from going West and would serve to choke off the growth and prosperity of the frontier.

Robert Y. Hayne, a young and eloquent senator from South Carolina, took up the argument after Benton. Hayne and other Southerners had no direct interest in the Western lands. But they hoped to win Western support for their drive to lower the tariff, and so they were willing to back the Westerners on this issue. Hayne suggested in his speech before the Senate that the South and the West were both victims of the tyranny of the Northeast, and he hinted that the two regions might well combine in self-defense against that tyranny.

Daniel Webster, now a senator from Massachu-setts, had once been an advocate of states' rights and himself an opponent of tariffs—in the waning days of the Federalist party. But like Calhoun, he had changed his position with the changing interests of his section. The day after Hayne's speech, Webster took the floor. Ignoring Benton, he directed his remarks to Hayne and, through him, to Calhoun in the vice president's chair. He reviewed much of the history of the republic, with occasional disregard for historical facts, to prove that New England always had been the friend of the West. Referring to the tariff of 1816, he said that New England was not responsible for the protectionist policy but had accepted it after other sections had fixed it upon the nation. Then, changing the subject, he spoke gravely of disunionists and disunionism in South Carolina.

Webster was, in effect, challenging Hayne to a debate not on the original grounds of the public lands and the tariff but on the issue of states' rights versus

The Webster-Hayne Debate

This scene from the famous Webster-Hayne debate in 1830 shows Webster replying to South Carolina Senator Robert Hayne's defense of states' rights. Webster's speeches during the debate were read, admired, and often memorized and repeated throughout the North for years. This painting, by G. P. A. Healy, hangs today in Faneuil Hall in Boston, where Webster once spoke.   (Frick Art Reference Library)

national power. Hayne, coached by Calhoun, responded with a defense of the theory of nullification. Webster listened and then spent two full afternoons delivering his remarkable second reply to Hayne, a speech that Northerners quoted and revered for years to come. "I go for the Constitution as it is, and for the Union as it is," he proclaimed, in a description of the "true principles" of the Constitution. "It is, Sir, the people's Constitution, the people's government, made for the people, made by the people, and answerable to the people." He concluded with the ringing appeal: "Liberty *and* Union, now and for ever, one and inseparable!"

Calhoun's followers were sure that Hayne had the better of the argument. The important question at the moment, however, was what President Jackson thought and what side, if any, he would take. The answer soon became clear at the annual banquet in honor of Thomas Jefferson, whom the Democrats considered the founder of their party. As was customary at such affairs, the guests settled down after dinner to hear a series of toasts. The president, urged on by Van Buren, had arrived with a prepared toast, which he had written down, underscoring certain words. When his turn came to speak, he stood up and proclaimed: "Our *Federal* Union—*It must be preserved.*" While he spoke he looked sternly and directly at Calhoun. The diminutive Van Buren, who stood on his chair to see better from the far end of the table, thought he saw Calhoun's hand shake and a trickle of wine run down the outside of his glass. Calhoun responded to the president's toast with his own: "The Union—next to our liberty most dear. May we always remember that it can only be preserved by distributing evenly the benefits and the burthens of the Union." Both in the Congress and in the executive branch, sharp lines had been drawn.

The Nullification Crisis

For more than two years, the sectional tensions aroused by the Webster-Hayne debate and the nullification doctrine continued without producing a direct confrontation between the federal government and the South. In 1832, however, the state of South Carolina precipitated a crisis. Having waited four years for Congress to repeal the "tariff of abominations," South Carolinians watched with anger as Congress enacted a new tariff that year which offered them virtually no relief. Some of the more militant

South Carolinians were now ready for revolt. Had it not been for Calhoun, they might have attempted to withdraw the state from the Union. Having lost the confidence of Jackson, Calhoun was now an open advocate of nullification; and in the aftermath of the 1832 tariff, he persuaded extremists in South Carolina to adopt that doctrine—not secession—as their remedy. The question of whether to nullify the tariff act was the leading issue in the state elections of 1832, and the result was a ringing victory for the nullifiers (although opponents of nullification—the Unionists—constituted a sizable minority; a referendum question on the issue passed 23,000 to 17,000).

Without delay, the newly elected legislature called for the election of delegates to a state convention. And the convention, once assembled, voted to declare null and void the tariffs of 1828 and 1832 and to forbid the collection of duties within the state. The legislature then passed laws to enforce the ordinance and make preparations for military defense. The nullifiers needed strong leaders, they believed, to take command at home and to present the South Carolina case in Washington. They elected Hayne governor of the state; and they chose Calhoun to replace Hayne as senator. Calhoun resigned the vice presidency to defend his state's position in the Senate.

Andrew Jackson was outraged. Privately, he threatened to hang Calhoun. Publicly, he insisted that nullification was treason and that its adherents were traitors. Cooperating closely with the Unionists of South Carolina, he took steps to strengthen the federal forts in the state, ordering General Winfield Scott and a warship and several revenue cutters to Charleston.

When Congress convened early in 1833, the president asked for new and specific authority with which to handle the crisis. His followers introduced a "force bill" authorizing him to use the army and navy to see that acts of Congress were obeyed. Violence seemed a real possibility early in 1833, as Calhoun took his place in the Senate. He introduced a set of resolutions on the "constitutional compact" and then spoke out in opposition to the force bill.

Webster's reply to Calhoun on February 16, 1833, was less colorful and dramatic than his reply to Hayne three years earlier. But it dealt more fully and cogently with the constitutional issues at stake. The Constitution, Webster argued, was no mere compact among sovereign states. It was an "executed contract," an agreement to set up a permanent government, supreme within its allotted sphere and acting directly upon the people as a whole. Webster dismissed secession as a revolutionary but not a constitutional right, then denounced nullification as no right at all. The nullifiers, he said, rejected "the first great principle of all republican liberty; that is, that the majority must govern." They pretended to be concerned about minority rights, but they did not practice what they preached. "Look to South Carolina, at the present moment. How far are the rights of minorities there respected?" Obviously the nullificationist majority was proceeding with a "relentless disregard" for the rights of the Unionist minority—"a minority embracing, as the gentleman himself will admit, a large portion of the worth and respectability of the state."

At the moment Calhoun was in a predicament. South Carolina was standing alone. Not a single state had come to its support. It was itself divided, and it could not hope to prevail if a showdown with the federal government should come. If the nullifiers meekly yielded, however, they would lose face and their leader would be politically ruined. Calhoun was saved by the timely intervention of the "Great Pacificator," Henry Clay, who had been newly elected to the Senate. Clay consulted with Calhoun to devise a compromise by which the tariff would be lowered year after year, until in 1842 it would reach approximately the same level as in 1816. The compromise and the force bill were passed on the same day, March 1, 1833. Webster consistently opposed any concessions to the nullifiers, but Jackson was satisfied. He signed the new tariff measure as well as the force bill.

In South Carolina, the convention reassembled and repealed its ordinance of nullification as applied to the tariffs of 1828 and 1832. But unwilling to allow Congress to have the last word, the convention adopted a new ordinance nullifying the force act. Both the force act itself and the nullification of it were, however, purely symbolic. The original tariff, against which the force act was directed, had already been repealed. Calhoun and his followers claimed a victory for nullification, which had, they insisted, forced the revision of the tariff. But the episode taught Calhoun and his allies an important lesson: No state could assert and maintain its rights by independent action. Calhoun continued in the following years to talk of states' rights and nullification. But he devoted himself primarily to building up a sense of Southern solidarity so that when another trial should come, the whole section might be prepared to act as a unit in resisting federal authority.

Jackson and States' Rights

Despite his ringing defense of the authority of the federal government in the nullification crisis, Andrew Jackson was not an opponent of the rights of the states. On the contrary, some of his most important decisions as president reflected his view that, as he had declared in his inaugural address, none but "constitutional" undertakings should be pursued by the federal government. Thus throughout his administration, he frequently vetoed laws that he considered to exceed the powers originally granted to Congress by the states.

The Maysville Road Bill of 1830 prompted the most significant of Jackson's vetoes. The bill authorized the government to buy stock in a private company so as to provide a federal subsidy for the construction of a turnpike from Maysville to Lexington, within the state of Kentucky. The Maysville pike was a segment of a projected highway that was to form a great southwestern branch of the National Road. Nevertheless, since the pike itself was an intrastate and not an interstate project, Jackson doubted whether Congress constitutionally could give aid to it. Earlier (in 1822) President Monroe had declared in a veto message that the federal government should support only those improvements that were of general rather than local importance. Now, with Van Buren's assistance, Jackson prepared a veto message based on similar grounds. He also urged economy, denounced the selfish "scramble for appropriations," and stressed the desirability of paying off the national debt. Although Jackson also refused to sign other appropriation bills, he did not object to every proposal for federal spending to build roads or improve rivers and harbors. During his two terms such expenditures continued to mount, far exceeding even those of the John Quincy Adams administration.

The Maysville veto was not popular in the West, where better transportation was a never-ending demand. Others of Jackson's policies, however, met with wholehearted approval in both the South and the West—most prominently, his use of federal powers to remove all Indian tribes from the areas of white settlement.

The Removal of the Indians

There had never been any doubt about Andrew Jackson's attitude toward the Indian tribes that continued to live in the Eastern states and territories of the United States. He wanted them to move west, beyond the Mississippi, out of the way of expanding white settlement. Jackson's antipathy toward the Indians had a special intensity because of his own earlier experiences leading military campaigns against tribes along the Southern border. But in most respects, his views were little different from those of the majority of white Americans. They considered the Indians uncivilized (and probably uncivilizable) savages, who could not coexist with whites and whose cultures and societies were unworthy of respect. They feared that continued contact between the expanding white set-

Black Hawk

After his defeat in the Black Hawk War in 1832, the Sac chief (whose Indian name was Muck-a-tah-mish-a-kah-kaik) was captured and taken to Washington, where he met with Andrew Jackson. The president then ordered him returned to his tribe, where Black Hawk lived until his death in 1838. He published a classic autobiography in 1833. This portrait is the work of the American painter George Catlin, who spent nearly eight years among the trans-Mississippi Indians in the 1830s. (Gilcrease Institute of Art)

tlements and the Indian tribes would produce endless conflict and violence; and so they wanted the Indians to be separated from the whites to avoid future clashes. Most of all, however, white Americans favored Indian removal because of their own insatiable desire for land. The tribes possessed valuable acreage in the path of expanding white settlement; whites wanted that territory.

The federal government had already taken significant strides toward removing the Indians from the East by the time Jackson entered the White House. But substantial tribal enclaves remained. In the Old Northwest, the long process of expelling the woodland Indians culminated in a last battle, in 1831–1832, between an alliance of Sac and Fox Indians under the fabled warrior Black Hawk and white settlers in Illinois. The Indians had previously been resettled west of the Mississippi but had found life there difficult. Hungry and resentful, 1,000 of them crossed the Mississippi and reoccupied vacant lands in Illinois that another tribe had earlier ceded. White settlers in the region feared that the resettlement was the beginning of a sizable invasion; and they employed the Illinois state militia and regular army troops to repel the "invaders." The Black Hawk War, as it became known, drove the tribes back across the Mississippi. But unsatisfied with that, white troops pursued the Indians as they fled and slaughtered most of them. (Abraham Lincoln served as a captain of the militia but saw no action in the Black Hawk War; Jefferson Davis was a lieutenant in the regular army.)

More troubling to the government in the 1830s were the remaining Indian tribes in the South: in western Georgia, Alabama, Mississippi, and Florida. There lived what were known as the "Five Civilized Tribes"—the Cherokee, Creek, Seminole, Chickasaw, and Choctaw—most of whom had established settled agricultural societies with successful economies. The Cherokee in Georgia had formed a particularly stable and sophisticated culture, with its own written language and a formal constitution (adopted in 1827), which created an independent Cherokee Nation. They were, therefore, more reluctant to abandon their lands than many of the more nomadic tribes to the north. Even some whites argued that the Cherokee, unlike other tribes, should be allowed to retain their Eastern lands, since they had become such a successful and civilized society.

The federal government, to which the Constitution had delegated the power to negotiate with the Indian tribes, had worked steadily through the first decades of the nineteenth century to make treaties with the Southern Indians that would remove them to the West and open their lands for white settlement. But the negotiating process often did not proceed fast enough to satisfy the region's whites. The state of Georgia's independent effort to dislodge the Creek Indians, over the objection of President Adams, was one example of this impatience. (See p. 265.) That same impatience became evident early in Jackson's administration, when the legislatures in Georgia, Alabama, and Mississippi began extending their laws over the tribes remaining in their states. They received assistance in these efforts from Congress, which in 1830 passed the Removal Act (with Jackson's approval), a measure that appropriated funds for negotiating treaties with the Southern tribes and relocating them to the west. The president quickly dispatched federal officials to negotiate nearly 100 new treaties with the remaining tribes. Thus the Southern tribes faced a combination of pressures from both the state and federal governments. Most tribes were too weak to resist such pressures, and they ceded their lands in return for only token payments. Some, however, resisted.

In Georgia, the Cherokee realized that they had no chance to stop these white encroachments militarily, and so they sought to stop them legally. They hired a prominent lawyer and appealed to the Supreme Court. In the case of *Cherokee Nation* v. *Georgia* (1831), Chief Justice Marshall refused to recognize the Cherokee as a truly independent nation; they were, he said in his majority opinion, "domestic dependents," "wards" of the federal government, which served as their "guardian." Nevertheless, Marshall also ruled that the Cherokee had a right to the land they occupied until they voluntarily ceded it to the United States. In another case, *Worcester* v. *Georgia* (1832), Marshall and the Court declared that the Cherokee Nation was a political community over which the laws of Georgia had no authority and into which Georgians could not enter without permission.

Jackson did not sympathize with the Cherokee as Adams had done with the Creek. By now, moreover, the debate over Indian removal had become entwined with the larger partisan battles over the direction of his administration's policies. Congressional opponents of the Removal Act of 1830 and subsequent Indian legislation had been motivated as much by a desire to frustrate and embarrass the president as by any real concern about the fate of the tribes. (The 1830 act had passed Congress by a perilously slim margin.) Jackson's support of the removal demands had been motivated in part by his desire to retain the allegiance of Southerners and Westerners on other issues. Thus the president had vigorously supported (and even actively encouraged) Georgia's efforts to remove the Cherokee prior to the Court decision. And his reaction to Marshall's rulings reflected his belief that the justices, too, were using the issue to express their own hostility to the larger aims of his presidency. When the chief justice announced the decision in *Worcester* v. *Georgia,* Jackson reportedly responded with contempt: "John Marshall has made his decision," he is said to have stated. "Now let him enforce it." The decision was not enforced.

In 1835, the government extracted a treaty from a minority faction of the Cherokee, none of whose members was a chosen representative of the Cherokee Nation. The treaty ceded to Georgia the tribe's land in that state in return for $5 million and a reservation west of the Mississippi. The great majority of the 17,000 Cherokee did not recognize the treaty as legitimate and refused to leave their homes. But Jackson was not to be thwarted. He sent an army of 7,000 under General Winfield Scott to round them up and drive them westward at bayonet point.

About 1,000 Cherokee fled across the state line to North Carolina, where eventually the federal government provided a reservation for them in the Smoky Mountains, which survives today. But most of the rest made the long, forced trek to Oklahoma, beginning in the winter of 1838. Along the way a Kentuckian observed: "Even aged females, apparently nearly ready to drop in the grave, were travelling with heavy burdens attached to their backs, sometimes on frozen ground and sometimes on muddy streets, with no covering for their feet." Thousands, perhaps a quarter or more of the émigrés, perished before reaching their unwanted destination. In the new reservations in which they were now forced to live, the survivors were never to forget the hard journey. They called their route "The Trail Where They Cried," the Trail of Tears.

The Cherokee were not alone in experiencing the hardships of the Trail of Tears. Between 1830 and 1838, virtually all the Five Civilized Tribes were expelled from the Southern states and forced to relocate in the "Indian Territory" (formally created by the Indian Intercourse Act of 1834) in what later became Oklahoma. The new territory seemed safely removed from existing white settlements and embraced land that most whites considered undesirable. It had the additional advantage, the government believed, of

The Expulsion of Indians from the South, 1830–1835

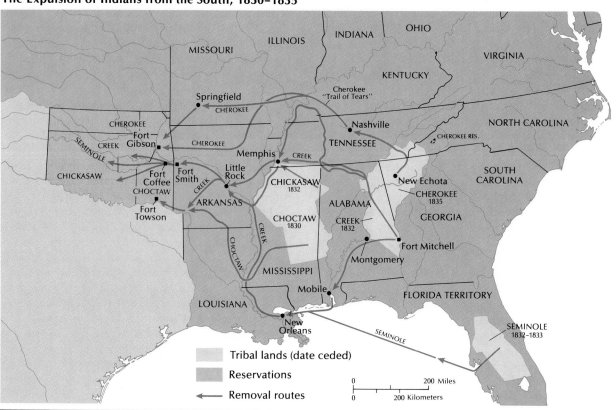

Tribal lands (date ceded)

Reservations

← Removal routes

being bordered on the west by what explorers such as Lewis and Clark and Stephen H. Long had christened the "Great American Desert," land deemed unfit for white habitation. It seemed unlikely that whites would ever seek to settle along the western borders of the Indian Territory; thus the danger of whites surrounding the reservation and producing further conflict could be avoided.

The Choctaw of Mississippi and western Alabama were the first to make the trek, beginning in 1830. The Creek of eastern Alabama and western Georgia were moved out by the army in 1836. The Chickasaw in northern Mississippi began the long march westward a year later.

Only the Seminole in Florida managed effectively to resist the pressures, and even their success was limited. Like other tribes, the Seminole had agreed under pressure to a settlement (the 1832–1833 treaties of Payne's Landing and Fort Gibson) by which they ceded their lands and agreed to move to the Indian Territory within three years. Most did move west, but a substantial minority—under the leadership of

the chieftain Osceola—refused to leave and staged an uprising beginning in 1835 to defend their lands. (Joining the Indians in their struggle was a group of runaway black slaves who had been living with the tribe.) The Seminole War dragged on for years. Jackson sent troops to Florida, but the Seminole with their black associates were masters of guerrilla warfare in the jungly Everglades. Even after Osceola had been treacherously captured under a flag of truce and had died in prison; even after white troops had engaged in a systematic campaign of extermination against the resisting Indians and their black allies; even after 1,500 white soldiers had died and the federal government had spent $20 million on the struggle: even then, followers of Osceola remained in Florida. Finally, in 1842, the government abandoned the war. By then, many of the Seminole had been either killed or forced westward. But the relocation of the Seminole, unlike the relocation of most of the other tribes, was never complete.

By the end of the 1830s, virtually all the important Indian societies east of the Mississippi (with a few exceptions such as the Seminole) had been removed to the West. The tribes had ceded over 100 million acres of Eastern land to the federal government; they had received in return about $68 million and 32 million acres in the far less hospitable lands west of the Mississippi between the Missouri and Red rivers. There they lived, divided by tribe into a series of sharply defined reservations, in a territory surrounded by a string of United States forts to keep them in (and to keep most whites out), in a region whose climate and topography bore little relation to anything they had known before. Eventually, even this forlorn enclave would face encroachments from white civilization. But by then, the once-proud tribes would be reduced to such poverty and desolation that they would have little strength to resist.

Jackson and the Bank War

How far Jackson was willing to go to destroy the power of what he considered institutions of centralized elite power was clearly revealed in one of the most celebrated episodes of his presidency: the war against the Bank of the United States. His opponents in this case, he believed, were the same Eastern aristocrats he had battled throughout his political career. So he approached his battle with them with special fervor.

The Bank of the United States was a private corporation chartered by the federal government, which owned one-fifth of the Bank's stock. The Bank was a monopoly, with the exclusive right to hold the government's own deposits. With its headquarters in Philadelphia and its branches in twenty-nine other cities, it also did a tremendous business in general banking, totaling about $70 million a year. Its services were important to the national economy because of the credit it provided for profit-making enterprises; because of its bank notes, which circulated throughout the country as a dependable medium of exchange; and because of the restraining effect that its policies had on the less well managed banks chartered by the various states. Nevertheless, Andrew Jackson was determined to destroy it.

Biddle's Institution

Nicholas Biddle, president of the Bank from 1823 on, had done much to put the institution on a sound and prosperous basis. A member of an aristocratic Philadelphia family, Biddle was educated at the University of Pennsylvania and pursued, in addition to his financial interests, a number of intellectual activities, including poetry. He personally owned a large proportion of the Bank's stock, so much of it that together with two other large stockholders he controlled the Bank. He could and did choose the officials of the branches, decide what loans were to be made, and set the interest rates. For several years after he took charge, he made these decisions according to financial considerations. A banker, not a politician, he had no desire to mix in politics. But he finally concluded it was necessary to do so in self-defense when, with the encouragement of Jackson, popular opposition to the Bank rose to a threatening pitch.

Opposition came from two very different groups: "soft money" people and "hard money" people. Advocates of soft money consisted largely of state bankers and their allies. They objected to the Bank of the United States because it restrained the state banks from issuing notes as freely as some of them would have liked. The Philadelphia bank inhibited the issue of such notes by collecting them and presenting them for payment in cash, thus forcing the local banks to retain sufficient reserves to redeem the paper. The other set of critics, the hard-money people, had the opposite complaint. They believed that coin was the only safe currency, and they condemned all banks of issue—that is, all banks issuing bank notes—whether chartered by the states or (as in the case of the Bank of the United States) by the federal government. The soft-money advocates were believers in rapid economic growth, speculation, the "main chance." The hard-money forces tended to cling to older ideas of "public virtue" and to look with suspicion on reckless expansion and speculation.

Jackson himself supported the hard-money position. Many years before, he had been involved in grandiose land and mercantile speculations based on paper credit. His business had been ruined and he himself had fallen deeply into debt as a result of the Panic of 1797. Thereafter he was suspicious of all banks. Once he became president, he expressed that suspicion by suggesting that the charter of the Bank of the United States should not be renewed. Unless renewed, it would expire in 1836.

To preserve the institution, Biddle began to grant banking favors to influential men in the hope of winning them to his side. At first he sought to cultivate Jackson's supporters, with some success in a few in-

Election of 1832

(55.4% of electorate voting)

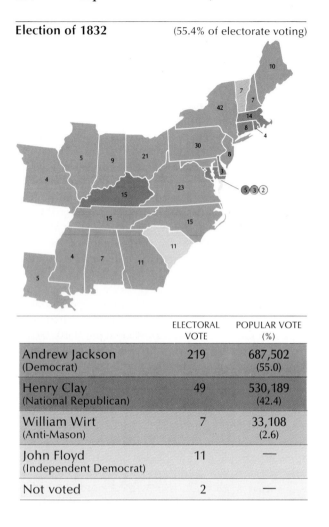

	ELECTORAL VOTE	POPULAR VOTE (%)
Andrew Jackson (Democrat)	219	687,502 (55.0)
Henry Clay (National Republican)	49	530,189 (42.4)
William Wirt (Anti-Mason)	7	33,108 (2.6)
John Floyd (Independent Democrat)	11	—
Not voted	2	—

stances. Then he turned more and more to Jackson's opponents. He extended loans on easy terms to several prominent newspaper editors, to a number of important state politicians, and to more than fifty congressmen and senators. In particular, he relied on Senators Clay and Webster, the latter of whom was connected with the Bank in various ways—as legal counsel, director of the Boston branch, frequent and heavy borrower, and Biddle's personal friend.

Clay, Webster, and other advisers persuaded Biddle to apply to Congress for a recharter bill in 1832, four years ahead of the expiration date. After investigating the Bank and its business, Congress passed the recharter bill. Jackson at once vetoed it, sending it back to Congress with a stirring message in which he denounced the Bank as unconstitutional, undemocratic, and un-American. The Bank's friends

in Congress failed to obtain the two-thirds majority necessary to override the veto. And the Bank question emerged as the paramount issue of the coming election, just as Clay had hoped.

In 1832, Clay ran as the unanimous choice of the National Republicans, who had held a nominating convention in Baltimore late in the previous year. Jackson, with Van Buren as his running mate, sought reelection as the candidate of the Democrats). Still another candidate was in the field, representing a third party for the first time in American history. He was William Wirt, a prominent Baltimore lawyer and man of letters, the nominee of the Anti-Mason party. (See pp. 290–291.) Wirt drew more votes from Clay than from Jackson (although he opposed the president far more bitterly than he did Clay). But he was not a major factor in the election; he carried only the state of Vermont. The legislature of South Carolina gave that state's electoral vote in protest to a man who was not even a candidate, John Floyd, one of Calhoun's Virginia followers. Despite this varied opposition, Jackson won reelection overwhelmingly. He received 55 percent of the popular vote and 219 electoral votes (more than four times as many as Clay). If the Bank was the issue, Jackson's stance had received a ringing public endorsement.

The "Monster" Destroyed

Jackson, at least, interpreted his reelection as a mandate to continue his war on the bank. As soon as the nullification crisis was resolved, he determined to strike a decisive blow at the "monster." He could not abolish the institution before the expiration of its charter, but he could lessen its power in the meantime. He resolved to remove the government's deposits from the Bank. Under the law establishing the Bank, the secretary of the treasury had to give the actual order to remove them. The incumbent secretary, who believed that such an action would destabilize the financial system, refused to give the order. Jackson removed him and appointed a replacement. When the new secretary similarly procrastinated, Jackson named a third: Roger B. Taney, the attorney general, a close friend and ally of the president. Taney was more than willing to cooperate.

With Taney at the head of the Treasury Department, the process of removing the government's deposits began immediately. The government stopped putting new funds in the Bank but continued paying its bills by drawing on its existing deposits, which steadily dwindled. Meanwhile the government opened accounts with a number of state banks, depositing its incoming receipts with them. These banks, including one in Baltimore with which Taney himself was associated, were chosen presumably on the basis of their financial soundness but not always without consideration of their political leanings. Jackson's enemies called them his "pet banks." By 1836 there were eighty-nine of them.

The proud and poetic Biddle, "Czar Nicholas" to Jacksonians, was not a man to give in without a fight. "This worthy President," he wrote sarcastically, "thinks that because he has scalped Indians and imprisoned Judges, he is to have his way with the Bank. He is mistaken." When the administration began to transfer funds directly from the Bank of the United States to the pet banks (as opposed to the earlier practice of simply depositing new funds in those banks), Biddle struck back. The loss of these government deposits, amounting to several millions, made it necessary, he claimed, to call in loans and raise interest rates, since the government deposits had served as the basis for much of the Bank's credit. He realized that by making borrowing more difficult, he was bound to hurt business and cause unemployment; but he consoled himself with the belief that a short depression would help to bring about a recharter of the Bank. "Nothing but the evidence of suffering," he told the head of the Boston branch, would "produce any effect in Congress."

During the winter of 1833–1834, with interest high and money scarce, there was suffering indeed, as many businesses failed and thousands of workers lost their jobs. All over the country, friends of the Bank organized meetings to adopt petitions begging for relief from Congress, petitions that delegates then brought in person to Washington and that pro-Bank senators or representatives introduced with appropriately gloomy speeches. But Jackson and the Jacksonians denied responsibility. When distressed citizens appealed to the president he answered, "Go to Biddle."

The banker finally carried his contraction of credit too far to suit his own friends among the anti-Jackson business interests of the Northeast, and some of them did go to Biddle. A group of New York and Boston merchants protested (as one of them reported) that the business community "ought not and would not sustain him in further pressure, which he very well knew was not necessary for the safety of the bank, and in which his whole object was to coerce a char-

ter." To appease the business community, Biddle at last reversed himself and began to grant credit in abundance and on reasonable terms. His hopes of winning a recharter of the Bank died in the process.

The "Bank War" was over, and Jackson had won it. But with the passing of the Bank of the United States, on the expiration of its charter in 1836, the country lost an indispensable financial institution. Economic troubles lay ahead.

The Taney Court

The discouraging aftermath of the Bank War did not weaken Jackson's commitment to "democratizing" the nation's political and economic life. On the contrary, he continued to move forcefully against what he perceived to be institutions of aristocratic privilege and excessive federal power. And in 1835, he moved against the most powerful institution of economic nationalism of all: the Supreme Court. When John Marshall died in 1835, the president appointed as the new chief justice his trusted ally in the Bank War, Roger B. Taney—a man fervently committed to Jacksonian democracy.

Taney never dominated the Court in the way Marshall had managed to do, nor did he preside over a sharp break in constitutional interpretation. But he did help produce a marked change in emphasis. Taney and the majority of his colleagues were moderate agrarian liberals; in general, they tended to support the right of the people, acting through state legislatures, to regulate private property rights and the activities of corporations. Although they stopped far short of accepting Calhoun's extreme states' rights philosophy, the justices were modifying Marshall's vigorous nationalism.

Perhaps the clearest indication of the new judicial mood was the celebrated case of *Charles River Bridge* v. *Warren Bridge* of 1837. The case involved a dispute between two Massachusetts companies over the right to build a bridge across the Charles River between Boston and Cambridge. One company had a longstanding charter from the state to operate a toll bridge for a specified number of years, a charter that guaranteed it, the firm claimed, a monopoly of the bridge traffic. The second company had applied to the legislature for authorization to construct a second, competing bridge that would—since it would be toll-free—greatly reduce the value of the first company's charter. The first company contended that in granting the second charter the legislature was engaging in a breach of contract.

"The Downfall of Mother Bank"
This 1832 Democratic cartoon celebrates Andrew Jackson's destruction of the Bank of the United States. The president is shown here driving away the Bank's corrupt supporters by ordering the withdrawal of government deposits.
(New-York Historical Society)

The Marshall Court, in the *Dartmouth College* case and other decisions, had ruled clearly that states had no right to abrogate contracts. But now Taney, speaking for the Democratic majority on the Court, supported the right of Massachusetts to award the second charter. Although he advanced elaborate legal precedents to support the decision, the ruling reflected less the influence of the law than the influence of Jacksonian social theory. The object of government, Taney maintained, was to promote the general happiness, an object that took precedence over the rights of property. A state, therefore, had the right to amend or abrogate a contract if such action was necessary to advance the well-being of the community.

In the *Charles River Bridge* case, he maintained, such abrogation had been clearly necessary. The original bridge company, by exercising a monopoly, was benefiting from unjustifiable privilege. (It did not help the first company that its members were largely Boston aristocrats and that it was closely associated with elite Harvard College; the challenging company, by contrast, was composed largely of newer, aspiring entrepreneurs—the sort of people with whom Jackson and his allies instinctively identified.) The decision was another indication of one of the cornerstones of Jacksonian philosophy. The key to democracy was an expansion of economic opportunity, which would not occur if older corporations could maintain monopolies and choke off competition from newer companies.

The Emergence of the Second Party System

Jackson's forceful—some claimed tyrannical—tactics in crushing first the nullification movement and then the Bank of the United States helped galvanize a growing opposition coalition that by the mid-1830s was ready to assert itself in national politics. It began as a gathering of national political leaders opposed to Jackson's use of power. Denouncing the president as "King Andrew I," they began to refer to themselves as Whigs, after the party in England that traditionally worked to limit the power of the king. As the new party began to develop as a national organization with constituencies in every state, its appeal became more diffuse. Nevertheless, both in philosophy and in the character of its adherents, the Whig party offered a discernible contrast to the party of Jackson.

The partisan competition of the 1820s and 1830s produced what has come to be known as the "second party system." The first party system—the system that began in the 1790s between the Federalists and the Republicans—had begun to collapse early in the nineteenth century. By 1816, the Federalist party was virtually extinct, and nothing had emerged to replace it. Political battles revolved for a time not around parties, but around shifting and usually temporary factional alignments. But in the 1820s, divisions began to emerge that seemed more lasting—divisions that ultimately produced a new two-party system consisting of the Whigs and the Democrats. And also in the 1820s, Americans began to admit for the first time that parties had a legitimate role to play in national politics.

Party Philosophies

Even before the election of Jackson in 1828, those who would ultimately form the Democratic party had stood for a certain general approach to government and society; and during the years of the Jackson administration, that approach began to take the form of something similar to a philosophy. To the Democrats, America's future was to be one of steadily expanding opportunities. To that end, the federal government should be limited in power, the rights of states should be protected, and the nation should work to eliminate all social and economic arrangements that served to entrench privilege and stifle the common man. Jacksonians tended to romanticize the "honest workers," the "simple farmers," and the "forthright businessmen" who stood, they believed, in sharp contrast to the corrupt, monopolistic, aristocratic forces of established wealth. As Jackson himself said in his farewell address, the society of America should be one in which "the planter, the farmer, the mechanic, and the laborer, all know that their success depends on their own industry and economy," in which no man's opportunity would be stifled by artificial privilege.

There was no necessary connection between this philosophy of a fluid, open society and opposition to economic development; and indeed, many Jacksonians believed wholeheartedly in the necessity of material progress. Yet in practice, Democrats were far more likely than others to look with suspicion on proposals for stimulating modern commercial and industrial growth. They tended to associate such growth with the creation of menacing institutions of power—the Bank of the United States, for example; and they often spoke yearningly of a simpler era in which no such concentrations of privilege had existed. Both in Washington and in state governments, Democratic legislators, much more often than their Whig counterparts, opposed such modernizing institutions as chartered banks and corporations, state-supported internal improvements, even public schools. Rather than economic development and consolidation, Democrats favored territorial expansion, which would, they believed, widen opportunities for aspiring Americans. And among the most radical members of the party—the so-called Locofocos, mainly workingmen and small businessmen and professionals in the Northeast—sentiment was strong for a vigorous, ultimately perhaps even violent, assault on monopoly and privilege far in advance of anything Jackson himself ever contemplated.

The political philosophy that became known as Whiggery, by contrast, looked far more favorably on expanding the power of the federal government, encouraging industrial and commercial development, and knitting the country together into a consolidated economic system. While Democrats often looked with suspicion on such technological advances as railroads, telegraphs, and manufacturing machinery, Whigs embraced such material progress enthusiastically. And where Democrats advocated rapid geographic expansion, Whigs urged a more prudent, cautious movement into the West, fearful that too rapid territorial growth would produce instability.

Their vision of America was of a nation embracing the industrial future, of a nation rising to world greatness as a commercial and manufacturing power. And although Whigs insisted that their vision would result in increasing opportunities for all Americans, they tended to attribute particular value to the enterprising, modernizing forces in their society—the entrepreneurs and institutions that most effectively promoted economic growth. Thus while Democrats were inclined to oppose legislation establishing banks, corporations, and other modernizing institutions, Whigs generally favored such measures.

Party Constituencies

To some extent, the constituencies of the two major parties were reflections of these diffuse philosophies. The Whigs were strongest among the more substantial merchants and manufacturers of the Northeast; the wealthier planters of the South (those who favored commercial development and the strengthening of ties with the North); and the ambitious farmers and rising commercial class of the West—usually migrants from the Northeast—who advocated internal improvements, expanding trade, and rapid economic progress. The Democrats drew more support from the smaller merchants and the workingmen of the Northeast; from those Southern planters who looked with some suspicion on Northern industrial growth; and from those Westerners—usually with Southern roots—who favored a predominantly agrarian economy and opposed the development of powerful economic institutions in their region. Whigs, in short, tended to be wealthier than Democrats, tended to have more aristocratic backgrounds, and tended to be more commercially ambitious.

But party divisions were not always so simple. For one thing, although Democrats tended to be people of more modest means than Whigs, they did not include those most conspicuously excluded from economic opportunity. Some of the poorest residents of the Northeast—unskilled laborers, recent Protestant immigrants, and others—gravitated toward the Whigs. To them, the Democrats, often representatives of the lower middle class that stood one rung above them on the social ladder, seemed more menacing and hostile than the Whigs.

Furthermore, Whigs and Democrats alike were more interested in winning elections than in maintaining philosophical purity. And both parties made adjustments from region to region in order to attract the largest possible number of voters, so that often the original ideology of the party appeared to be almost lost. In New York, for example, the Whigs—under the leadership of party boss Thurlow Weed—developed a large popular following by turning the Democrats' own tactics against their opponents. Their vehicle was a movement known as Anti-Masonry. The so-called Anti-Mason party had emerged in the 1820s in response to widespread resentment against the secret and exclusive, hence supposedly undemocratic, Society of Freemasons. Such resentments rose to new heights when, in 1826, a former Mason, William Morgan, mysteriously disappeared from his home in Batavia, New York, shortly before he was scheduled to publish a book purporting to expose the secrets of Freemasonry. The assumption was widespread that Morgan had been abducted and murdered by the vengeful Masons. Weed and other opponents of Jackson seized on the Anti-Mason frenzy to launch spirited attacks on Jackson and Van Buren (both Freemasons), implying that the Democrats were connected with the antidemocratic conspiracy. The excitement soon spread to other states—most notably Pennsylvania; and in 1831, some Anti-Masons broke with the Whigs and held their own national convention in Harrisburg to nominate a presidential candidate—William Wirt—for the next year's campaign. (Their campaign, ironically, benefited Andrew Jackson above all; see p. 286.)

By embracing Anti-Masonry, Whigs discovered a vehicle that permitted them to portray themselves to the public as opponents of aristocracy and exclusivity. They were, in other words, attacking the Democrats with the Democrats' own issues. Both parties, therefore, were adopting the rhetoric of democracy and equality; and the specific issues that divided them in their legislative battles were often obscured in actual campaigns.

Religious and ethnic divisions also played an important role in determining the constituencies of the two parties. Irish Catholics, one of the largest of the recent immigrant groups, tended to support the Democrats, who appeared to reflect their own vague aversion to commercial development and entrepreneurial progress. And not only Irish but German Catholics found the Democrats far more willing than the Whigs to respect and protect their cultural values and habits. Catholics resented such Whiggish reform movements as temperance, public education, and enforced Sabbath observance, seeing them as attempts to impose Protestant moral standards on them.

Evangelical Protestants gravitated toward the

Whigs for the same reasons that Catholics opposed the new party. Such Protestants embraced a religious and cultural outlook that encouraged constant development and improvement. They envisioned a society progressing steadily toward unity and order, and they looked on the new immigrant communities as a threat to that progress—as groups that needed to be disciplined and taught "American" ways. They liked to claim that immigrants supported the Democratic party because the Democrats engaged in shameless vote buying and other frauds. But their own cultural outlook was far more to blame for their failure to attract support from such groups. In many communities, these and other local ethnic, religious, and cultural tensions were far more influential in determining party alignments than any concrete political or economic proposals.

Party Leadership

If presidential politics were indicative of popular favor, it would be fair to say that the Whigs, in the more than twenty years of their existence as a party, enjoyed relatively little public support. Only in 1840 and 1848 were Whig candidates able to capture the White House, and in each of those elections the winning contestant was a popular military hero. Yet when elections at every level—congressional, state, and local, as well as presidential—are considered, the balance between the two parties appears much more even.

The Democrats maintained their edge over the Whigs at the level of national leadership largely because of the popularity of a single man. Throughout the 1830s, the Democratic party was the party of Andrew Jackson—beloved war hero, champion of the people, a political figure of such magnetism that no opponent could hope to match him. The Whigs, on the other hand, rallied behind three national leaders—each a powerful and charismatic figure in his own right, but each, too, a man with significant political limitations. Henry Clay, Daniel Webster, and John C. Calhoun all brought their own formidable constituencies into the Whig coalition. (All also brought their own intense ambitions for the presidency.) But none was ever able to forge a truly national constituency capable of winning a presidential election.

The glamorous Clay, "Harry of the West," won many supporters throughout the country through his support for internal improvements and economic de-

Daniel Webster
"The great god Webster," as he was occasionally known, was the most passionately admired public figure of his age. Crowds of up to 100,000 turned out at times for his speeches, even though many of them, in an age before amplification, presumably could not even hear him. Yet Webster inspired contempt as well as admiration among his contemporaries. His shady connections with influential businessmen tarnished his reputation among many Americans. So did his consuming (and unfulfilled) ambition for the presidency and his often embarrassing affection for brandy.   (The Library of Congress)

velopment—the American System. But his image as a devious political operator and his regional identification with the West proved an insuperable liability. He ran for president three times and never won. Daniel Webster, the greatest orator of his era, gained fame and respect for his passionate speeches in defense of the Constitution and the Union. Some of his admirers, of whom a large number were wealthy businessmen, considered him a greater man than any president. But Webster's close connection with the Bank of the United States and the protective tariff,

WHERE HISTORIANS DISAGREE

Jacksonian Democracy

Andrew Jackson was not only one of the most powerful political figures of the nineteenth century; he also became the symbol of a political philosophy and a social spirit that seemed to be gaining strength in America in the 1820s and 1830s. Historians have taken a particular interest, therefore, both in Jackson and in the set of social and political ideas he has come to represent. And they have disagreed markedly both about the man himself and about the social and ideological movement that has come to be known as "Jacksonian Democracy." As with many other issues on which historians differ, their views of Jackson have often reflected the political climate of their own day.

In the late nineteenth century, when the historical profession was dominated by aristocratic Easterners with Whiggish political views, studies of Jackson were largely hostile. Conservative biographers such as James Parton (*Life of Andrew Jackson*, 1860) denounced the Jacksonians as "barbarians" who had turned government over to the "rabble." By embracing the spoils system, such historians argued, Jackson had paved the way for the rampant corruption in government of later years. By destroying the Bank of the United States, he had struck a heavy blow against American financial stability.

By the early twentieth century, the writing of history, and with it the historical view of the Jacksonians, had begun to experience an important transformation. Under the influence of Frederick Jackson Turner, historians began to emphasize the role of the West in American life and to see in the frontier a healthy, democratic influence on the nation. Turner and his disciples, most of them Westerners or Southerners themselves, rejected the view of Whiggish historians that the Jacksonians had been ill-bred rabble. Instead, they argued, the Democrats of Jackson's time had been the freedom-loving frontiersmen of the West, challenging the conservative aristocracy of the East, which was attempting to restrict opportunity. Jackson himself, they claimed, was much like the progressives

of their own time: a true democrat who strove to make government responsive to the will of the people rather than to the desires of special interests. Dissenters such as Thomas P. Abernethy (*From Frontier to Plantation in Tennessee*, 1932) argued that Jackson had himself been a frontier aristocrat and had opposed the democratic trend in his own state. For the most part, however, the view of Jacksonianism as "frontier democracy" (as Turner had argued in his famous essay "The Significance of the Frontier in American History," 1893) prevailed through the first half of the twentieth century.

A new era in Jacksonian scholarship began in 1945 with the publication of the celebrated study by Arthur M. Schlesinger, Jr., *The Age of Jackson*. Like Turner and others, Schlesinger admired Jackson for bringing a healthy democratic influence to American politics and saw the Jacksonian era as one of steadily expanding political opportunity. He did not, however, share the view of earlier historians that the roots of Jacksonianism lay in the West. Instead, Schlesinger claimed, the conflict between Democrats and Whigs was a conflict "not of sections, but of classes." Jacksonian Democracy was an effort "to control the power of the capitalist groups, mainly Eastern, for the benefit of noncapitalist groups, farmers and laboring men, East, West, and South." Emphasizing the role of the urban working classes in the Jacksonian coalition, he saw in the 1830s an early version of modern reform efforts to "restrain the power of the business community."

Other historians have accepted Schlesinger's view that classes were more important than sections, but they have disagreed with him about which class Jackson represented. Richard Hofstadter's influential essay in *The American Political Tradition* (1948) portrayed Jackson as the spokesman of rising entrepreneurs—aspiring businessmen who saw the road to opportunity blocked by the monopolistic power of the Eastern aristocracy. Thus the Jacksonians were opposed to special

WHERE HISTORIANS DISAGREE

privileges only to the extent that those privileges blocked their own road to success. They were less sympathetic to the aspirations of those below them—workers and small farmers. Bray Hammond, in *Banks and Politics in America from the Revolution to the Civil War* (1957), argued similarly that the Jacksonian cause was "one of enterpriser against capitalist, of banker against regulation, and of Wall Street against Chestnut"—that is, of the rising bankers of New York City against the established bankers of the Philadelphia-based Bank of the United States.

Still another view of Jacksonianism emerged in the 1950s from historians concerned with the ideological origins of the movement. Marvin Meyers, in *The Jacksonian Persuasion* (1957), emphasized the appeal of the Jeffersonian heritage to the Jacksonians. Jackson and his followers looked with mistrust on the new industrial society emerging around them and yearned instead for a restoration of the agrarian, republican virtues of an earlier time. In destroying the Bank, limiting federal economic activities, and emphasizing states' rights, they were attempting to restore a simpler, more decentralized world. Ironically, their actions contributed instead to the expansion of unregulated capitalism.

Lee Benson, in *The Concept of Jacksonian Democracy* (1961), a study of political parties in New York, used new quantitative techniques to challenge virtually all previous interpretations of Jacksonianism. There was no consistent difference—in class, occupation, or region—between the Jacksonians and anti-Jacksonians, Benson argued. Both parties contained big as well as small businessmen, farmers, and city workers. Nor were there any significant ideological differences. Both parties used the same "agrarian" rhetoric; both were in favor of greater equality of opportunity and greater political democracy. Local and cultural factors—religion and ethnicity, for example—were the crucial determinants of party divisions, not economic interests or ideology. Because the movement toward democracy was much broader than the Democratic party, he suggested, the "age of Jackson" should be renamed the "age of egalitarianism."

Other historians have continued Benson's deemphasis of party divisions in the Jacksonian period and have cited instead social and economic developments that transcended partisan concerns. Edward Pessen, in *Jacksonian America* (1969), portrayed the mid-nineteenth century as a time of widespread and increasing social and economic inequality but suggested that party divisions did not reflect the broader stratification of American society. Richard McCormick (1966) and Glyndon Van Deusen (1963) similarly emphasized the pragmatism of Jackson and the Democrats and de-emphasized clear ideological or social party divisions.

More recent historians have begun to turn the discussion of early nineteenth-century politics back to the question of class. Among the new studies is Sean Wilentz's *Chants Democratic* (1984), which traces the emergence in New York City of an industrial work force with an increasingly powerful class identity. The grievances of such people, he argues, were important in reshaping the way Americans defined the concept of republicanism. "Republicanism" is a concept that has attracted the interest of many scholars in recent years. It describes an ideology, stretching back to the eighteenth century and forward into the twentieth, that many historians believe has been central to American history: the belief that citizens in a republic should have unobstructed opportunities to advance toward ownership of their own land or their own enterprises. Workers in New York, Wilentz argues, waged an attack on the emerging system of laissez-faire capitalism and the wage system, which together threatened to choke off their chances for advancement. The degree to which the new industrial system threatened republican ideals helped create a radical tradition in American public life that found reflection, for a time, in at least some parts of the Jacksonian constituency.

his reliance on rich men for financial support, and his unfortunate and often embarrassing fondness for brandy—all prevented him from developing enough of a national constituency to win him the office he so desperately wanted.

John C. Calhoun, the third member of what became known as the Great Triumvirate, was equally controversial. He never considered himself a true Whig, and his identification with the nullification controversy in effect disqualified him from national leadership in any case. Yet he sided with Clay and Webster on the issue of the national bank. And he shared with them a strong animosity toward Andrew Jackson. Calhoun did not embrace the belief of most Southern Whigs in the importance of commercial development. He did, however, produce reasons of his own for advocating an alliance between the upper classes of the two regions. In his *South Carolina Exposition and Protest* of 1828 and in later writings, he presented a critique of modern capitalism that in its frank predictions of class struggle resembled much of what Karl Marx and Friedrich Engels would say in later decades—although Calhoun drew from those predictions very different prescriptions for social action than Marx and Engels would produce. Capitalist society would, Calhoun predicted, inevitably become divided into two classes: "capitalists" and "operatives." The former, he argued, would expropriate and impoverish the latter; and unless steps were taken to prevent it, a revolutionary struggle would ensue. "There is and always has been in an advanced stage of wealth and civilization," he insisted in 1837, "a conflict between labor and capital." Northern businessmen had a common interest with Southern planters, therefore, in working to prevent the revolutionary danger by protecting their position against threats from below. Such views found scant sympathy among Northern Whigs. Webster, for example, admitted that "in the old countries of Europe there is a clear and well-defined line between capital and labor"; but he declared that there was no line so "broad, marked, and visible" in the United States.

The Whigs, in other words, were able to marshal an imposing array of national leaders, each with his own powerful constituency. Yet for many years they were unable to find a way to merge those constituencies into a single winning combination. The result was that the Democrats for a time, as in the election of 1836, appeared far more dominant than they actually were.

The Crowded Campaign of 1836

The importance of incumbency in the age of party politics became abundantly clear in 1836. Despite the growing power of the Whigs, Jackson and the Democrats continued to control federal appointments and contracts; and they made liberal use of their patronage powers to bolster the fortunes of their candidates. The party also benefited from Jackson's continuing popularity and from its elaborate party organization. With little debate, the party convention nominated Jackson's personal favorite, Martin Van Buren, as its candidate for president.

The Whigs in 1836 could boast no such unity and discipline. Indeed, they could not even agree on a single candidate. Their strategy, masterminded by Biddle, was to run several candidates, each of them supposedly strong in one part of the country. Webster would represent them in New England; Hugh Lawson White of Tennessee would seek the votes of the South; and the former Indian fighter and hero of the War of 1812 from Ohio, William Henry Harrison, would attract support in the middle states and in the West. As Biddle advised: "This disease is to be treated as a local disorder—apply local remedies—if General Harrison will run better than anybody else in Pennsylvania, by all means unite upon him." None of the three candidates could expect to get a majority in the electoral college, but separately they might draw enough votes from Van Buren to prevent his getting a majority. The decision would then rest, as in 1824–1825, with the House of Representatives, where the Whigs might be better able to elect one of their candidates. But the three Whigs proved to be no match for the one Democrat. When the returns were in, Van Buren had 170 electoral votes to 124 for all his opponents.

Post-Jacksonian Politics

Andrew Jackson retired from public life in 1837, the most beloved political figure of his age. He left the presidency in the hands of a friend and ally dedicated to continuing his policies and sustaining the political party he had helped to create. But Martin Van Buren was a different man from his predecessor, and also far less fortunate. Never was he able to establish the great personal popularity that had sustained Jackson during the bleaker moments of his presidency. And unlike Jackson, Van Buren was plagued throughout his administration with economic difficulties that contributed to the strengthening of the Whigs. For the next eight years, party politics would be highly competitive and often deeply embittered.

Economic Dilemmas

Van Buren's success in the 1836 election was a result in part of a nationwide economic boom that was reaching its height in that year. Canal and railroad builders were at a peak of activity. Prices were rising as people indulged in an orgy of spending and speculating. Money was plentiful—most of it manufactured by the banks, which multiplied their loans and notes with little regard to their reserves of cash. By 1837, bank loans outstanding amounted to five times as much as in 1830. Never had the nation seemed so prosperous.

Land as usual was a favorite target of speculation, especially the land sold by the federal government. After congressional legislation in 1821 had abolished installment buying and set the minimum price at $1.25 an acre, sales of public lands had slowed. They averaged 300,000 to 400,000 acres a year in the late 1820s and early 1830s. Then the business suddenly boomed. Between 1835 and 1837 nearly 40 million acres were disposed of, and the expression "doing a land-office business" came into use to describe fast selling of any kind. Nearly three-fourths of the land being sold went to speculators, who acquired large tracts in the hope of reselling at a profit, and only about one-fourth of it to actual settlers. Speculators generally borrowed from the banks to make payment at the land offices.

For the moment, the government enjoyed great profits from the booming business. Receipts from land sales, which had averaged less than $2.4 million annually for the ten years preceding 1835, rose to more than $24 million in 1836. These land sales, when combined with the revenues the government received from the compromise tariff of 1833, created a series of substantial federal budget surpluses and made possible a steady reduction of the national debt (something Jackson had always advocated). Finally, from 1835 to 1837, the government for the first and only time in its history was out of debt, with a substantial surplus in the Treasury.

The question for Congress and the administration was how to get rid of the Treasury surplus. Tampering with the tariff was out of the question; few people wanted to reopen that touchy subject so soon after the compromise that had put it to rest. Instead, support began to build for returning the federal surplus to the states. In 1836, Congress passed and Jackson signed a distribution act, which required the federal government to pay whatever surplus had accumulated by the end of the year (estimated at $40 million) to the states in four quarterly installments as a loan without security or interest. Each state would receive a share proportional to its representation in Congress. No one seriously expected the "loan" to be repaid. As the states began to receive their shares, they promptly spent the money, mainly to encourage the construction of highways, railroads, and canals. The distribution of the surplus thus gave further stimulus to the economic boom. At the same time the withdrawal of federal funds strained the pet banks, for they had to call in a large part of their own loans in order to make the transfer of funds to the state governments.

Congress did nothing to check the speculative fever, with which many congressmen themselves were badly infected. Webster, for one, was buying up thousands of acres in the West. But Jackson was concerned. Although money continued to pour into the Treasury from the land offices, most of it was paper of dubious value. The government was selling good land and was receiving in return a miscellaneous collection of state bank notes, none of them worth any more than the credit of the issuing bank. Jackson finally decided to act. In 1836, he issued the "specie circular," which announced that in the future only hard money or the notes of specie-paying banks (that is, notes backed by gold or silver) would be accepted in payment for public lands.

Jackson had been correct in fearing that the speculative fever was reaching dangerous proportions and that the banking system was seriously unstable. He was wrong, however, in thinking his specie circular would forestall further difficulties. Van Buren had been president less than three months when panic struck. The banks of New York, followed by those of the rest of the country, suddenly suspended specie payments (that is, they stopped paying gold and silver on demand for their bank notes and other obligations). During the next few years, hundreds of banks failed, and so did hundreds of other business firms. As unemployment grew, bread riots occurred

"The Times," 1837
This savage caricature of the economic troubles besetting the United States in 1837 illustrates, among other things, popular resentment of the hard-money orthodoxies of the time. A sign on the Custom House reads: "All bonds must be paid in Specie." Next door, the bank announces: "No specie payments made here." Women and children are shown begging in the street, while unemployed workers stand shoeless in front of signs advertising loans and "grand schemes." (New-York Historical Society)

in some of the larger cities. Prices fell, especially the price of land. Webster was only one of a great many who all at once found themselves "land poor." Many railroad and canal schemes were abandoned; several of the debt-burdened state governments ceased to pay interest on their bonds, and a few repudiated their debts, at least temporarily. The depression, the worst the American people had ever experienced, lasted for five years and proved catastrophic for Van Buren and the Democrats.

The Whigs blamed Jackson for the depression. It had come, they said, because of his destruction of the national bank and his mismanagement of public finance. But the whigs were also in part to blame. The

distribution of the Treasury surplus had been a Whig measure, although Jackson had signed it. (With the onset of the panic, the distribution was halted before the entire surplus had been transferred to the states.) Distribution, by weakening the pet banks, helped to bring on the crash. So did Jackson's specie circular, which started a general run on the banks as land buyers rushed to trade in their bank notes for specie with which to make land-office payments. Distribution of the surplus and the specie circular only precipitated the depression, however; they did not cause it.

While the Bank of the United States, if continued, could have lessened the overexpansion of credit, a period of financial stringency doubtless would have come sooner or later. For this was an international depression, affecting England and Western Europe as well. English investors faced a financial crisis at home, and they began to withdraw funds from America; that accounted for part of the strain on American banks. Then a succession of crop failures on American farms not only reduced the purchasing power of farmers but also necessitated the import of foodstuffs; and payment for these imports drew additional money out of the country.

The Panic of 1837 had significant consequences beyond its immediate financial impact. Hard times increased social, sectional, and economic tensions. In the economically troubled cities, fears were rising that a real and dangerous class conflict was taking shape in America. Southern planters suffered heavy losses and became confirmed in their conviction that national policies worked to their disadvantage. The decline of business profits in the North intensified the belief of manufacturers that the compromise of 1833 must be undone and the tariff raised. Defaults on interest payments and outright repudiation of state bonds, many of them held by the English, added to difficulties in relations between the United States and Great Britain. And these accumulated grievances soon translated into dissatisfaction with the administration. Thus in 1840, the predominance of the Democrats came temporarily to an end.

The Van Buren Program

The modern concept that government can successfully fight depressions, and that it has an obligation to do so, did not exist in Van Buren's time. The only tradition of government intervention in economic matters was the Federalist–National Republican–Whig program of aid to business, to which Democrats were fiercely opposed. Consequently, Van Buren recommended but few direct antidepression measures. He advised Congress to authorize the borrowing of $10 million to meet expenses during the emergency, and Congress did so. He also urged that the government accept only specie for taxes and other payments.

In formulating a program of permanent legislation, the administration clearly reflected the wishes of the dominant farmer-labor segment of the party. The president urged Congress to reduce the price of public lands, and he recommended passage of a general "preemption" bill giving settlers already in an area the right to buy 160 acres at a set minimum price

before land in that area was opened for public sale. A bill graduating land prices downward passed the Senate three times but was blocked in the House. A similar fate befell the preemption bill.

Stymied by legislative opposition, Van Buren resorted to executive action to please his urban followers. By presidential order he established a ten-hour workday on all federal projects. For the first time in the nation's history, the government thus took direct action to aid the rising labor class.

The most important measure in the president's program, and the most controversial, was his proposal for a new fiscal system. With the Bank of the United States destroyed and with Jackson's expedient of pet banks discredited, some kind of new system was urgently needed. Van Buren's fiscal ideas demonstrated both his ingenuity and his commitment to Democratic principles. The plan he suggested, known as the "independent treasury" or "subtreasury" system, was simplicity itself. Government funds would be placed in an independent treasury at Washington and in subtreasuries in specified cities throughout the country. Whenever the government had to pay out money, its own agents would handle the funds. No bank or banks would have the government's money or name to use as a basis for speculation. The government and the banks would be "divorced."

Van Buren placed the independent treasury proposal before Congress in a special session he called in 1837. It encountered the immediate and bitter opposition of most Whigs and of many conservative Democrats. Twice a bill to establish an independent treasury passed the Senate only to fail in the House. Not until 1840, the last year of Van Buren's presidency, did the administration succeed in driving the measure through both houses of Congress.

The Log Cabin Campaign

As the campaign of 1840 approached, the Whigs scented victory. The effects of the depression still gripped the country, and the Democrats, the party in power, were thus vulnerable to attack. The Whigs now realized that a party representing the upper-income groups must, if it expected to win, pose as a party of the people.

The Whigs also realized that they would have to achieve more unity and a stronger organization than they had demonstrated in 1836. They would have to settle on one candidate who could appeal to all segments of the party and to all sections of the country.

Obviously, the easiest way to coordinate the party was through the new mechanism of the national nominating convention, already used by the Democrats. Accordingly, the Whigs held their first convention in Harrisburg, Pennsylvania, in December 1839. Their veteran leader, Henry Clay, expected the nomination; but the party bosses decided otherwise. Clay had too definite a record; he had been defeated too many times; he had too many enemies. Passing him over, the convention nominated William Henry Harrison of Ohio, and for vice president, John Tyler of Virginia.

William Henry Harrison was a descendant of the Virginia aristocracy, but he had spent all his adult life in the Northwest, where he first went as a young army officer in General Wayne's campaign against the Indians. (See pp. 217.) Although he had little experience in government, he was a renowned Indian fighter (like Jackson) and a popular national figure.

The Democrats, meeting in national convention at Baltimore, nominated Van Buren, pointed proudly to their record (especially the independent treasury), and condemned all the works of the Whigs (especially the Bank of the United States). Demonstrating that their party was, in some respects, no more united than the Whigs, the Democrats failed to nominate a vice-presidential candidate, declaring vaguely that they would leave the choice of that office to the wisdom of the voters.

The campaign of 1840 displayed in full the effects of an established party system on American politics and, in so doing, established a new pattern for presidential contests. The Whigs—who had emerged as a party largely because of their opposition to Andrew Jackson's common-man democracy, who in most regions represented the more affluent elements of the population, who stood for government policies that would aid business—were in the 1840 campaign almost indistinguishable from their opponents. Democrats and Whigs used the same techniques of mass voter appeal; the same evocation of simple, rustic values; the same identification with the common people. What mattered now was not the philosophical purity of the party but its ability to win votes.

Thus it was that the eager Whigs depicted themselves as the party of the people, the party able to save the nation from depression; and thus it was that they used against Martin Van Buren the same tactics that the Democrats had so often used against them. They accused the president of being an aloof aristocrat who used cologne, drank champagne, ate off gold plates, and otherwise engaged in undemocratic

A Whig Banner, 1840
This campaign banner sustains the popular fiction, created by the leaders of the Whig party, that their presidential candidate, William Henry Harrison, had been born in a log cabin and was a devotee of hard cider. In fact, Harrison was from a prosperous Virginia family, had attended college, and had studied law before entering the army. Nevertheless, the rustic image assigned to him in 1840 was an effective tool in ridding the Whig party of its elitist image. (New-York Historical Society)

and un-American practices. In retaliation, a Democratic newspaper unwisely sneered that Harrison was a simple soul who would be glad to retire to a log cabin if provided with a pension and plenty of hard cider. In a country where many people lived or had lived in log cabins, this was an unwise line of attack; and the Whigs took full advantage. Yes, their candidate was a simple man of the people, they proclaimed, and he loved log cabins and cider. (Actually he was a man of substance and lived in a large and well-appointed house.)

Thereafter, the log cabin was an established symbol at every Whig meeting, and hard cider an established beverage. Against such techniques and the lingering effects of the depression the Democrats could not win. When the votes were counted in November, Harrison had 234 electoral votes to 60 for Van Buren. But the Whig victory was not as sweeping as it seemed; of the popular vote, Harrison had 1,275,000 to Van Buren's 1,128,000, a majority of less than 150,000.

The Frustration of the Whigs

Despite their decisive victory, the Whigs were to find the next four years frustrating and divisive ones. In large part, that was because their appealing new president, "Old Tippecanoe," William Henry Harrison, never had a chance to demonstrate what sort of leader he might become. Sixty-eight years old in 1841, he had appeared to be in good health. But the strain of the campaign, of the inauguration (after which he rode bareheaded through the streets of Washington to the White House in bitter cold), and of the pressing demands of grasping job seekers apparently became too much for him. Shortly after taking office, he contracted a cold. It soon turned into pneumonia; and Harrison died on April 4, 1841, exactly one month after he had been inaugurated.

Harrison was the first president to die in office, and there was momentary uncertainty as to what should happen next. The Constitution clearly stated that the "Powers and Duties" of the highest office would "devolve on the Vice President" in the event of a president's death. But there were some who believed that the "Powers and Duties" were not the same thing as the office, that the vice president could become only an "acting president," that his authority might in some way be compromised. This potentially critical constitutional problem was resolved by Vice President Tyler, who calmly took the oath of office as president and left no doubt that he considered himself a legitimate chief executive. The question of the legal status of a vice president who succeeded to the presidency was never raised again.

More troubling to the leaders of the Whig party than such constitutional questions was that with Harrison gone, control of government had fallen to a man with whom they had much weaker ties. Harrison in his brief weeks in office had generally deferred to Henry Clay and Daniel Webster, confirming the predictions of those who had foretold that the Whig chieftains would be the real powers in government. Webster had become secretary of state; four of Clay's allies had taken other positions in the cabinet. Under Tyler, things were to change.

Tyler was a member of an aristocratic Virginian family. Originally a Democrat, he had left the party in reaction to what he considered Jackson's excessively egalitarian program and his imperious methods. One reason the Whigs had included him on their ticket was to attract the votes of similarly disenchanted conservative Democrats. But while Tyler had certain attitudes in common with the Whig leadership, there were still signs of his Democratic past in

his approach to public policy. Clay apparently had the impression that the new president would support the restoration of a national bank and other Whig projects, but Tyler soon indicated otherwise. A break occurred between the president and Clay that was never to heal.

There were, to be sure, some elements of Clay's ambitious program that Tyler was willing to accept. The president signed a bill abolishing the independent treasury system. He agreed to a bill raising tariff rates to nearly the same level as 1832 (although he displayed little enthusiasm for the proposal). And he approved a measure—the Preemption Act of 1841—to increase the appeal of the Whigs to Western settlers and farmers. The bill was virtually identical to the one the Whigs had defeated when Van Buren proposed it. This "log cabin bill," as the Whigs called it, was promoted as a measure to relieve the suffering caused by the depression and to prove the party's devotion to the welfare of the common man.

Although Tyler supported Whig measures designed to appeal to Democratic voters, he was less willing to cooperate with the party leadership in pursuing the heart of the Whig program—the creation of a national financial system similar to the Bank of the United States. Tyler favored a national bank, but one very different from that proposed by Clay. His was to be a "states' rights national bank," one that would confine its operations to the District of Columbia and establish branches in the states only with the consent of those states. Twice he vetoed bills that would have set up what the Whigs tried to disguise as a "fiscal corporation."

Lacking a sufficient majority to override the veto, the Whigs fumed with rage at the president, who added to their anger by vetoing a number of internal improvement bills. In an unprecedented action, a conference of congressional Whigs read Tyler out of the party. All the cabinet members resigned except Webster. To fill their places, the president appointed five men of his own stripe—former Democrats. When the office of secretary of state became vacant in 1844, Tyler appointed John C. Calhoun, who had now rejoined the Democratic party that he had left in the 1830s.

A portentous new political alignment was taking shape. Tyler and a small band of conservative Southern Whigs who followed him were preparing to rejoin the Democrats. Into the common man's party of Jackson and Van Buren was arriving a group of men with decidedly aristocratic political ideas, who thought that government had an obligation to protect and even expand the institution of slavery, and who believed in states' rights with a single-minded, almost fanatical devotion.

Whig Diplomacy

In the midst of these domestic controversies, a series of incidents brought Great Britain and the United States to the brink of war in the late 1830s.

One such incident occurred in upstate New York. In 1837, a rebellion against the British colonial government broke out in the eastern provinces of Canada; many Americans applauded the rebels and furnished them with material aid. The rebels chartered a small American steamship, the *Caroline,* to carry supplies across the Niagara River from New York. One night while the ship was moored at a wharf on the American side, Canadian authorities sent over a force that took possession of the *Caroline* and burned it. In the melée one American was killed. Excitement flared on both sides of the border. President Van Buren issued a proclamation asking Americans to abide by the neutrality laws, and he sent General Winfield Scott to the border to act as a pacifier. The State Department demanded an apology and reparations from Great Britain, but the British government neither disavowed the attack nor offered compensation for it.

While the *Caroline* affair simmered, another troublesome issue began to plague Anglo-American relations: the issue of the boundary between Canada and Maine. The Treaty of 1783 had left the boundary ill defined, and all subsequent attempts to fix it by mutual agreement and by arbitration had failed. In 1838, groups of Americans and Canadians, mostly lumberjacks, began to move into the Aroostook River region in the disputed area. A head-smashing brawl between the two groups—the "Aroostook War"—threatened more trouble between England and America.

Eventually a Canadian named Alexander McLeod was arrested in New York and charged with the murder of the American who had died in the *Caroline* incident. The British government reacted with majestic rage, contending that McLeod could not be accused of murder because he had acted under official orders. The foreign secretary, the bellicose Lord Palmerston, demanded McLeod's release and threatened that his execution would bring "immediate and frightful" war. Webster as secretary of state did not

think McLeod was worth a war but could do nothing to release him. The prisoner was under New York jurisdiction and had to be tried in the state courts, a peculiarity of American jurisprudence that the British did not seem to understand. Fortunately for the cause of peace—and for himself—McLeod was acquitted.

Festering points of disagreement still remained. In an attempt to stamp out the African slave trade, Great Britain had long sought the right to search American merchant ships suspected of carrying black cargoes. This was a sensitive subject to the American government, which remembered well the events that had precipitated the War of 1812. The United States had steadfastly refused the British request. As a result, slavers of other nations frequently sought to avoid capture by hoisting the American flag. Complicating the issue was the domestic slave trade, in which slaves were carried by sea from one American port to another. Sometimes the ships in this trade were blown off their course to the British West Indies, where the authorities, acting under English law, freed the slaves. In 1841, an American brig, the *Creole,* sailed from Virginia for New Orleans with more than 100 slaves aboard. En route the slaves mutinied, took possession of the ship, and took it to the Bahamas. Here British officials declared the bondsmen free. Although Webster protested, England refused to return the slaves. Many Americans, especially Southerners, were infuriated.

At this critical juncture a new government came to power in Great Britain, one that was more disposed to conciliate the United States and to settle the outstanding differences between the two countries. The new ministry sent to America an emissary, Lord Ashburton, to negotiate an agreement on the Maine boundary and other matters. Ashburton liked Americans, and Webster admired the English. To avoid war, both were willing to compromise. The result of their deliberations was the Webster-Ashburton Treaty of August 9, 1842.

By the terms of this arrangement, the United States received about seven-twelfths of the disputed area. Minor rectifications were made in other areas, and the boundary was now established as far west as the Rocky Mountains. It was agreed that both Great Britain and the United States would maintain naval squadrons off the African coast, the American ships being charged with chasing slavers using the American flag.

Through the exchange of notes that were not part of the treaty, Webster and Ashburton also eased the

SIGNIFICANT EVENTS

1820–1840 State constitutions revised	**1832–1833** Nullification crisis brews
1823 Nicholas Biddle becomes president of Bank of the United States	**1834** Indian Intercourse Act passed
1826 William Morgan disappearance inflames Anti-Masonry	**1835** Roger Taney succeeds Marshall as chief justice of the Supreme Court Federal debt retired
1828 Calhoun's *South Carolina Exposition and Protest* outlines nullification doctrine	**1835–1840** Tocqueville publishes *Democracy in America*
1829 Andrew Jackson inaugurated	**1835–1842** Seminole War
1830 Webster and Hayne debate Jackson vetoes Maysville Road bill Indian Removal Act passed	**1836** Jackson issues "specie circular" Martin Van Buren elected president
1830–1838 Indians expelled from Southeast	**1837** Supreme Court rules in *Charles River Bridge* case
1831 Anti-Mason party established Supreme Court rules in *Cherokee Nation* v. *Georgia*	**1837–1844** Commercial panic and depression
1832 Democrats hold first national party convention Jackson vetoes bill to recharter Bank of the United States Jackson reelected president	**1838** "Aroostook War" fought in Maine and Canada
	1839 Whigs hold their first national convention
	1840 William Henry Harrison elected president Independent Treasury Act passed
1833 Jackson and Taney remove federal deposits from Bank of the United States Commercial panic disrupts economy	**1841** Harrison dies; John Tyler succeeds
	1842 Dorr Rebellion hastens reform in Rhode Island Webster-Ashburton Treaty signed

memory of the *Caroline* and *Creole* affairs. Ashburton expressed "regret" for the raid on the *Caroline,* and he pledged that in the future there would be no "officious interference" with American ships forced by "violence or accident" to enter British ports. Webster used secret funds to inspire newspaper propaganda favorable to his arrangements with Ashburton, and the treaty proved quite popular. War talk faded, and Anglo-American relations suddenly looked better than they had for many years.

During the Tyler administration, the United States established diplomatic relations with China. In 1842, Britain forced China to open certain ports to foreign trade. Eager to share the new privileges, American mercantile interests persuaded Tyler and Congress to send a commissioner—Caleb Cushing—to China to negotiate a treaty giving the United States some part in the China trade. In the Treaty of Wang Hya, concluded in 1844, Cushing secured most-

favored-nation provisions giving Americans the same privileges as the English. He also won for Americans the right of "extraterritoriality"—the right of Americans accused of crimes in China to be tried by American, not Chinese, officials. In the next ten years, American trade with China steadily increased.

In their diplomatic efforts, at least, the Whigs were able to secure some important successes. But by the end of the Tyler administration, the party could look back on few other victories. Having elected a president in 1840, they had watched as the policies of the administration (and the political allegiances of its principal figures, including the president himself) became steadily more Democratic. And in the election of 1844, the Whigs lost even nominal control of the White House. They were to win only one more national election in their history—in 1848—before a great sectional crisis arose that would shatter their party and, for a time, the Union.

SUGGESTED READINGS

General Histories   Surveys of the Jacksonian era emphasizing political developments include Glyndon Van Deusen, *The Jacksonian Era* (1959); John Mayfield, *The New Nation, 1800–1845* (1981); James C. Curtis, *Andrew Jackson and the Search for Vindication* (1976); and Edward Pessen, *Jacksonian America*, rev. ed. (1979).

Democracy   Alexis de Tocqueville, *Democracy in America*, 2 vols. (1835), initially published in French but available in many subsequent English editions, is a masterpiece of American literature and political analysis. Moisie Ostrogorskii, *Democracy and the Organization of Political Parties*, 2 vols. (1902), is another classic study of democratic trends in the era. Chilton Williamson, *American Suffrage from Property to Democracy, 1760–1860* (1960), is an important study of the expansion of the franchise; Louis Hartz, *The Liberal Tradition in America* (1955), is a sweeping interpretation of American political philosophy, which includes observations about the intellectual climate of the Jacksonian era. Marvin E. Gettleman, *The Dorr Rebellion* (1973), and Patrick T. Conley, *Democracy in Decline* (1977), offer contrasting views of democratic controversies in Rhode Island.

Jacksonian Society   Edward Pessen, *Riches, Class, and Power Before the Civil War* (1973), offers observations about the distribution of wealth and power in the Jacksonian period. Douglas T. Miller, *Jacksonian Aristocracy* (1967), is a case study of social stratification in New York. Sean Wilentz, *Chants Democratic: New York City and the Rise of the American Working Class, 1788–1850* (1984), examines class formation.

Jacksonian Politics   Important works attempting to explain the meaning of "Jacksonian Democracy" abound. One of the most influential is Arthur M. Schlesinger, Jr., *The Age of Jackson* (1945). Marvin Meyers, *The Jacksonian Persuasion* (1960), stresses ideology. Richard Hofstadter's important essay on Jackson in *The American Political Tradition* (1948) was especially influential in shaping later views of Jacksonianism. John William Ward, *Andrew Jackson: Symbol for an Age* (1955), examines the way in which Americans used the image of Jackson. Lee Benson, *The Concept of Jacksonian Democracy* (1961), is a quantitative study of politics in New York that challenges earlier ideas about how political alignments took shape. More specialized studies of the Jackson administration include Leonard White, *The Jacksonians: A Study in Administrative History* (1954), and Richard B. Latner, *The Presidency of Andrew Jackson: White House Politics, 1829–1837* (1979). Party politics in the Jacksonian era is the subject of Richard B. McCormick, *The Second American Party System: Party Formation in the Jacksonian Era* (1966), and Ronald P. Formisano, *The Birth of Mass Political Parties: Michigan, 1827–1861* (1971). Harry L. Watson, *Jacksonian Politics and Community Conflict: The Emergence of the Second Party System in Cumberland County, North Carolina* (1981), links political alignments to economic and social developments.

Andrew Jackson   The leading modern biographer of Jackson is Robert V. Remini, author of *Andrew Jackson and the Course of American Empire: 1767–1821* (1977), *Andrew Jackson and the Course of American Freedom: 1822–1832* (1981), and *Andrew Jackson and the Course of American Democracy* (1984). Remini has also written a briefer study, *Andrew Jackson* (1966). Marquis James, *Andrew Jackson*, 2 vols. (1933–1937), is an earlier major biography, which in turn succeeded James Parton, *Life of Andrew Jackson*, 3 vols. (1860), the first major study.

Nullification   William V. Freehling, *Prelude to Civil War: The Nullification Controversy in South Carolina* (1966), is a vivid narrative account of the crisis. A broader study is Charles S. Sydnor, *The Development of Southern Sectionalism 1819–1848* (1948). Merrill D. Peterson, *Olive Branch and Sword: The Compromise of 1833* (1983), examines the resolution of the crisis.

Indian Policies   Ronald N. Satz, *American Indian Policy in the Jacksonian Era* (1975), provides an overview. A controversial analysis of Jackson's attitudes and behavior toward Indians, using psychohistorical methods, is Michael Rogin, *Fathers and Children: Andrew Jackson and the Destruction of American Indians* (1975). Angie Debo, *A History of the Indians of the United States* (1970), and Wilcomb E. Washburn, *The Indian in America* (1975), are general studies containing observations about the Jackson years, as is William Brandon, *The Last Americans* (1974). B. W. Sheehan, *Seeds of Extinction: Jeffersonian Philanthropy and the American Indian* (1973), provides background for later Indian policies; F. P. Prucha, *American Indian Policy in the Formative Years* (1962), examines the policies themselves. Two additional works by Angie Debo—*The Road to Disappearance: A History of the Creek Indians* (1941) and *And Still the Waters Run: The Betrayal of the Five Civilized Tribes* (1973)—provide detailed analyses of the effects of white policies on the Eastern tribes. Cecil Elby, *"That Disgraceful Affair"* (1973), is a history of the Black Hawk War.

The Bank War   Robert V. Remini, *Andrew Jackson and the Bank War* (1967), is a good account of the political aspects of the controversy over the Bank of the United States; Bray Hammond, *Banks and Politics in America from the Revolution to the Civil War* (1957), is an important study of some of the economic aspects. Peter Temin, *The Jacksonian Economy* (1969), and J. M. McFaul, *The Politics of Jacksonian Finance* (1972), provide background to the controversy. William G. Shade, *Banks or No Banks: The Money Issue in Western Politics, 1832–1865* (1972), provides a regional perspective. J. A. Wilburn, *Biddle's Bank* (1967), examines public support for the Bank of the United States; and T. P. Govan, *Nicholas Biddle; Nationalist and Public Banker* (1959), makes a case for its subject. Reginald C. McGrane, *The Panic of 1837* (1924), studies the aftermath of the "Bank War"; and J. R. Sharp, *The Jacksonians Versus the Banks* (1970), looks at state banks after the panic.

The Courts and the Law C. B. Swisher, *Roger B. Taney* (1936), is a good biography of Jackson's Treasury secretary and later chief justice of the Supreme Court. Morton Horwitz, *The Transformation of American Law, 1780–1860* (1977), is an important study of the role of the courts and the legal process in nineteenth-century America, with particular emphasis on the Jackson period and the period immediately following it.

Post-Jacksonian Politics Useful works on Van Buren and his administration include Robert V. Remini, *Martin Van Buren and the Making of the Democratic Party* (1959); James C. Curtis, *The Fox at Bay; Martin Van Buren and the Presidency* (1970); and John Niven, *Martin Van Buren: The Romantic Age of American Politics* (1983). In addition to the works by McCormick and Van Deusen cited above, there are several works that give specific attention to the rise of the Whig party. E. M. Carroll, *Origins of the Whig Party* (1925), is a classic standard work. Daniel Walker Howe, *The Political Culture of the American Whigs* (1979), examines party ideology. Daniel Webster has been the subject of several major biographies, among them Claude M. Fuess, *Daniel Webster,* 2 vols. (1930); Richard N. Current, *Daniel Webster and the Rise of National Conservatism* (1955); and Irving Bartlett, *Daniel Webster* (1978). Other studies of Webster include Norman D. Brown, *Daniel Webster and the Politics of Availability* (1969); Sydney Nathans, *Daniel Webster and Jacksonian Democracy* (1973); Robert Dalzell, *Daniel Webster and the Trial of American Nationalism* (1973); and Maurice C. Baxter, *One and Inseparable: Daniel Webster and the Union* (1984). On Henry Clay, in addition to the Van Deusen biography mentioned above, see Clement Eaton, *Henry Clay and the Art of American Politics* (1957), and George R. Poage, *Henry Clay and the Whig Party* (1936). Thomas H. O'Connor, *Lords of the Loom: The Cotton Whigs and the Coming of the Civil War* (1968), follows the party into its last days. William Preston Vaughn, *The Anti-Masonic Party in the United States, 1826–1843* (1983), examines one of the challenges to Whig survival. Oscar D. Lambert, *Presidential Politics in the United States, 1841–1844* (1936), examines the Tyler administration. R. G. Gunderson, *The Log Cabin Campaign* (1957), is a study of the contest that put the Whigs in power. Oliver P. Chitwood, *John Tyler: Champion of the Old South* (1939), examines Tyler himself. On Whig foreign policy, see Howard Jones, *To the Webster-Ashburton Treaty* (1977); A. B. Corey, *The Crisis of 1830–1842 in Canadian-American Relations* (1941); and John B. Brebner, *North Atlantic Triangle* (1945).

Steamboats at the Sugar Levee, New Orleans, **by Hippolyte Victor Valentin Sebron, 1853** (Tulane University)

Chapter 11 The North and the South: Diverging Societies

mericans in the mid-nineteenth century liked to believe that theirs was a nation specially ordained by God, that their Union represented a beacon of liberty and stability that would serve as a model to the rest of the world. In fact, however, the United States in these years was in many respects not truly a nation at all—at least not in the way nations would be defined in later times. It was, rather, a highly decentralized confederation of states, many of which had little in common with one another. Those states remained together in part because the union was so loose, and the central authority of the nation so weak, that the differences among them did not often have to be confronted.

When the United States began to move in the direction of greater national unity, as it did in the 1840s, it encountered a series of major obstacles. And one obstacle, in particular, became so powerful that it soon threatened to tear the nation apart: sectionalism. The rivalry of one part of the country with another was not, of course, new to the mid-nineteenth century. There had been sectional differences as early as the seventeenth century among the colonies of the South, the mid-Atlantic, and New England.

By the 1840s and 1850s, however, sectionalism had changed both in its nature and in its intensity. In many respects, there were now four quite distinct regions: the Northeast, with a growing industrial and commercial economy and an increasing density of population; the Northwest, a rapidly expanding agricultural region; the Southeast, with a settled plantation system and (in some areas) declining economic fortunes as well; and the Southwest, a booming frontierlike region with an expanding cotton econ-

omy. As the sectional crisis grew more intense, however, many Americans came to view their nation as divided into two sections, each with a distinctive and relatively homogeneous culture: the North and the South.

The most obvious aspect of this division was a basic difference in the labor systems of the sections. The South was not only maintaining but, as its plantation economy expanded into new areas of the Southwest, intensifying its commitment to slavery as its primary source of labor. The Northeast and the Northwest were committed to a free-labor economy. But slavery was only part of a much larger difference between the sections. In the North, a modern, diversified economy was developing, with an important manufacturing sector, a flourishing commercial life, and an expanding range of urban services and activities. Between the North and the Northwest, moreover, close economic and cultural ties were developing. And the South, as a result, was becoming—or at least sensed itself becoming—isolated, left behind. Increasingly dependent on the North for manufactured goods, for commercial services, for many of the most basic necessities of life; increasingly cut off from the flourishing agricultural regions of the Northwest; increasingly committed to a way of life that much of the rest of the nation considered obsolete: the South was coming to seem a colonial appendage of the powerful regions to the north. In the 1840s and 1850s, this schism between Northern and Southern societies greatly intensified. Ultimately, it produced tensions and conflicts that contributed to the disruption of the Union.

The Developing North

The most conspicuous change in American life in the 1840s and 1850s was the rapid development of the economy and society of the Northeast. Industrialization, which had begun slowly in the years immediately following the War of 1812 and had gathered force in the 1820s and 1830s, now burst forth as a major factor in the Northern economy. Urban centers, in the past relatively few and relatively small, now grew rapidly. Class divisions became more visible and pronounced. New industrial capitalists and financiers accumulated fortunes only rarely seen in earlier times; a growing urban middle class became an ever more important factor in American society; and a rapidly expanding industrial labor force created an increasingly distinct working class. The Northeast, and with it in many ways its new economic ally the Northwest, was developing a complex, modern society, one that would greatly increase the differences that had always existed between that region and the South.

Northeastern Industry

Between 1840 and 1860, American industry experienced a steady and, in some fields, spectacular growth. In 1840, the total value of manufactured goods produced in the United States stood at $483 million; ten years later the figure had climbed to over $1 billion; and in 1860 it reached close to $2 billion. For the first time, the value of manufactured goods was approximately equal to that of agricultural products.

Industrial growth was greatest in the states of the Northeast. Of the approximately 140,000 manufacturing establishments in the country in 1860, 74,000 were located in the Northeast. They included, moreover, most of the larger enterprises. Although the Northeast had only a little more than half the mills and factories of the nation, it produced more than two-thirds of the manufactured goods. Of the 1,311,000 workers in manufacturing in the United States, about 938,000 were employed in the mills and factories of New England and the middle states.

Even the most highly developed industries still showed qualities of immaturity and were far from the production levels they would later attain. Cotton manufacturers, for example, produced goods of coarse grade; fine items continued to be imported from England. The woolens industry suffered from a limited supply of domestic raw wool and could not even produce enough coarse goods to satisfy the home market. American industry exported little; it was unable to meet fully the demands of American consumers. But technology and industrial ingenuity were preparing the way for future American industrial supremacy.

The machine tools used in the factories of the Northeast—such as the turret lathe, the grinding machine, and the universal milling machine—were by the 1840s already better than those in European factories. The principle of interchangeable parts, first applied decades earlier in gun factories by Eli Whitney and Simeon North, was by the 1840s being introduced into many other industries. Coal was replacing wood as an industrial fuel, particularly in the smelting of iron. Coal was also being used in increasing amounts to generate power in steam engines, which were replacing the water power that had in the past driven most of the factory machinery in the Northeast. The production of coal, most of it mined in the Pittsburgh area of western Pennsylvania, leaped from 50,000 tons in 1820 to 14 million tons in 1860. The new power source made it possible to locate mills away from running streams and thus permitted industry to expand still more widely.

The great technical advances in American industry owed much to American inventors. Patent records give some indication of the extent of Yankee ingenuity in these years. In 1830, the number of inventions patented was 544; in 1850, the figure rose to 993; and in 1860, it stood at 4,778. Several industries provide particularly vivid examples of how a technological innovation could produce a major economic change. In 1839, Charles Goodyear, a New England hardware merchant, discovered a method of vulcanizing rubber; his process had been put to 500 uses by 1860 and had succeeded in establishing a major American rubber industry. In 1846, Elias Howe of Massachusetts constructed a sewing machine; Isaac Singer made improvements on it, and the Howe-Singer machine was soon employed in the manufacture of ready-to-wear clothing. A few years later, during the Civil War, it would supply the Northern troops with uniforms.

In an earlier period, the dominant economic figures in the Northeast had been the merchant capitalists—entrepreneurs who engaged in foreign or domestic trade, who invested their surplus capital in banks, and who sometimes financed small-scale domestic manufacturers. The merchant capitalists remained figures of importance in the 1840s. In such cities as New York, Philadelphia, and Boston, important and influential mercantile groups operated shipping lines to Southern ports—carrying away cotton, rice, and sugar—or dispatched fleets of trading vessels to the ports of Europe and the Orient. Many of these vessels were the famous clippers, the most beautiful and the fastest sailing ships afloat. In their heyday in the late 1840s and early 1850s, the clippers were capable of averaging 300 miles a day, which compared favorably with the best time then being made by steamships.

Nevertheless, merchant capitalism was entering a state of decline by the middle of the century. Although the value of American exports, still largely agricultural, increased from $124 million in 1840 to $334 million in 1860, American merchants in the 1850s saw much of their carrying trade fall into the hands of British competitors, who enjoyed the advantages of steam-driven iron ships and government subsidies.

Foreign competition was not, however, the principal cause of the decline of the merchant capitalist. It was the rise of the factory system in the United States. Merchants now saw greater opportunities for profit in manufacturing than in trade. They shifted their capital from mercantile investments to industry. They became owners and operators of factories or invested their money in factories operated by others. Indeed, one reason that industries developed soonest in the Northeast was that an affluent merchant class already existed there and had the money and the will to finance them.

As in the past, many business concerns continued to be owned by individuals, by families, or by small groups of partners. But by the 1840s, particularly in the textile industry, the corporate form of organization was spreading rapidly. In their overseas ventures, merchants had been accustomed to diversifying their risks by buying shares in a number of vessels and voyages. They employed the same device when they moved their capital from trade to manufacturing. They tended to purchase shares in several textile companies. Ownership of American enterprise, in other words, was moving away from individuals and families and toward its highly dispersed modern form: many stockholders, each owning a relatively small proportion of the total. The discovery of new and more flexible forms of financing was, along with the technological innovations of the era, a crucial factor in the advancement of industrialization.

Whatever the form of business organization, and

there continued to be many different forms, industrial capitalists soon became the new ruling class, the aristocrats of the Northeast. And just as they had sought and secured economic dominance, they reached for and often achieved political influence. In local or national politics, the capitalists liked to be represented by highly literate lawyers who could articulate their prejudices and philosophy. Their ideal of a representative was Daniel Webster of Massachusetts, whom the business leaders of the section, at considerable financial cost to themselves, supported for years in the United States Senate.

Transportation and Communications

The new industrial economy could not have developed without an adequate transportation system. New forms of transportation were essential for moving raw materials to the factories and for moving finished goods out. And they were essential, above all, in forging ties between the industrial Northeast and the growing agricultural regions of the Northwest—an alliance that became crucial not only to the growth of the American economy but also to the sectional tensions that would soon rise to threaten the Union.

In the 1830s, most of the goods exchanged between the two sections were carried on the Erie Canal. But after 1840, railroads gradually supplanted canals and all other modes of transport. The railroads enabled the Western farmers to ship their products cheaply and quickly to Eastern markets and thus helped to force many Eastern farmers out of business.

In 1840, the total railroad trackage of the country was only 2,818 miles; by the end of the decade, the trackage figure had risen to 9,021 miles. But an outburst of railroad construction without previous parallel occurred in the 1850s. The amount of trackage tripled between 1850 and 1860. The Northeast developed the most comprehensive and efficient system, with twice as much trackage per square mile as the Northwest and four times as much as the South. Railroads were reaching even west of the Mississippi, which at several points was spanned by iron bridges. One line ran from Hannibal to St. Joseph on the Missouri River, and another was being built from St. Louis to Kansas City.

In the South, such towns as Charleston, Atlanta, Savannah, and Norfolk had direct connections with Memphis, and thus with the Northwest; and Rich-

An 1850s Railroad
Artists pose on the "cowcatcher" of a Baltimore and Ohio Company locomotive during an excursion from Baltimore to Wheeling, West Virginia in 1858. By the 1850s locomotives in the United States had become largely standardized in design. But track widths (gauges) continued to vary from one region to another. (Baltimore and Ohio Railroad Company)

mond was connected, via the Virginia Central, with the Memphis and Charleston railroad. In addition, several independent lines furnished a continuous connection between the Ohio River and New Orleans. The South, however, remained generally unconnected to the national railroad system. Most lines in the region were short, local ones. And the absence of a major railroad system became another factor isolating the South from the rest of the nation.

A new feature in railroad development—one that would profoundly affect the nature of sectional alignments—was the trend toward the consolidation of short lines into trunk lines. By 1853, four major railroad trunk lines had surmounted the Appalachian barrier to connect the Northeast with the Northwest. Two, the New York Central and the New York and Erie, gave New York City access to the Lake Erie ports. The Pennsylvania road linked Philadelphia and Pittsburgh, and the Baltimore and Ohio connected Baltimore with the Ohio River at Wheeling. From the terminals of these lines, other railroads into the interior touched the Mississippi River at eight points. Chicago became the rail center of the West, served by fifteen lines and more than a hundred daily trains. The appearance of the great trunk lines tended to divert traffic from the main water routes—the Erie Canal and the Mississippi River. By lessening the dependence of the West on the Mississippi, the rail-roads helped to weaken further the connection between the Northwest and the South.

Capital to finance the railroad boom came from various sources. Private American investors provided part of the necessary funding; and railroad companies borrowed large sums from abroad. But local governments—states, cities, towns, counties—also often contributed capital, because they were eager to have railroads to serve their needs. This support took the form of loans, stock subscriptions, subsidies, and donations of land for rights of way. The railroads obtained additional assistance from the federal government in the shape of public land grants. In 1850, Senator Stephen A. Douglas of Illinois and other railroad-minded politicians persuaded Congress to grant federal lands to the state of Illinois to aid the Illinois Central, then building toward the Gulf of Mexico; Illinois then transferred the land to the railroad company as an incentive to build lines in the state. Other states and their railroad promoters demanded the same privileges; and by 1860, Congress had allotted over 30 million acres to eleven states.

Facilitating the operation of the railroads was another important technological innovation: the magnetic telegraph. Its lines extended along the tracks, connecting one station with another and aiding the scheduling and routing of the trains. But the telegraph had an importance to the nation's economic development all its own. It permitted instant communication between distant cities, tying the nation together as never before. And yet, ironically, it also helped reinforce the schism between the two sections. As with railroads, telegraph lines were far more extensive in the North than in the South; and they helped similarly to link the North more closely to the Northwest (and thus to separate that region further from the South).

The telegraph had burst into American life in 1844, when Samuel F. B. Morse, after several years of experimentation, succeeded in transmitting from Baltimore to Washington the news of James K. Polk's nomination for the presidency. The Morse telegraph seemed, because of the relatively low cost of constructing wire systems, the ideal answer to the problems of long-distance communication. By 1860, more than 50,000 miles of wire connected most parts of the country; and a year later, the Pacific telegraph, with 3,595 miles of wire, was opened between New York and San Francisco. Nearly all of the independent lines had been absorbed into one organization, the Western Union Telegraph Company.

New forms of journalism also served to draw communities together into a common communications system, as well as to reveal more clearly to different regions their differences from one another. In 1846, Richard Hoe invented the steam cylinder rotary press, making it possible to print newspapers rapidly and cheaply. The development of the telegraph, together with the introduction of the rotary press, made possible much speedier collection and distribution of news than ever before. In 1846, the Associated Press was organized for the purpose of cooperative news gathering by wire; no longer did publishers have to depend on an exchange of newspapers for out-of-town reports. Major metropolitan newspapers began to appear in the larger cities of the Northeast. Horace Greeley's *Tribune,* James Gordon Bennett's *Herald,* and Henry J.Raymond's *Times* were all published in New York; but all gave serious attention to national and even international events and had substantial circulations beyond the city. Southern newspapers, by contrast, tended to have smaller budgets and reported largely local news. Few had any impact outside their immediate communities.

The Growth of the Railroads, 1850–1860

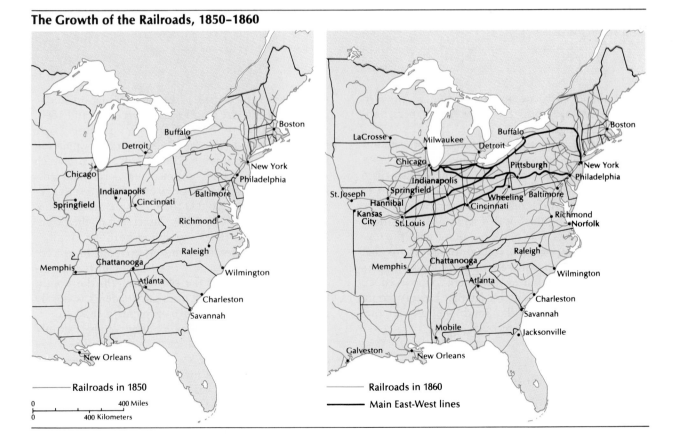

Population Density, 1820

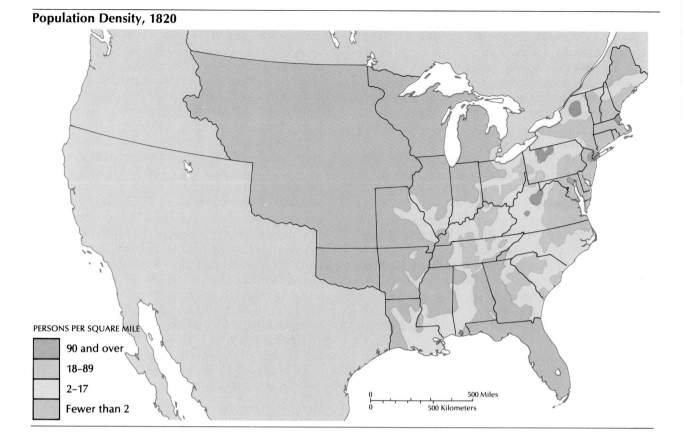

PERSONS PER SQUARE MILE

- 90 and over
- 18–89
- 2–17
- Fewer than 2

0 — 500 Miles
0 — 500 Kilometers

The combined circulation of the *Tribune* and the *Herald* exceeded that of all the daily newspapers published in the South.

In the long run, journalism would become an important unifying factor in American life. In the 1840s and 1850s, however, the rise of the new journalism helped to feed the fires of sectional discord. Most of the major magazines and newspapers were in the North, reinforcing the South's sense of subjugation. Above all, the news revolution—along with the revolutions in transportation and communications that accompanied it—contributed to a growing awareness within each section of how the other section lived, an awareness of the deep differences that had grown up between the North and the South—differences that would ultimately seem irreconcilable.

Cities and Immigrants

One of the most profound changes in the nature of Northeastern society in the antebellum period was in the character and distribution of the population, above all the growing size of cities. Between 1840 and 1860, the population of New York, for example, rose from 312,000 to 805,000. (New York's population numbered 1.2 million in 1860 if Brooklyn, which was then a separate municipality, is included.) Philadelphia's population grew over the same twenty-year period from 220,000 to 565,000; Boston's from 93,000 to 177,000. By 1860, 26 percent of the population of the free states was living in towns or cities (places of 2,500 people or more), up from 14 percent in 1840; that percentage was even higher for the industrializing states of the Northeast. (In the South, by contrast, the increase of urban residents was only from 6 percent in 1840 to 10 percent in 1860.)

The enlarged urban population was in part simply a reflection of the growth of the national population as a whole, which rose by more than a third—from 23 million to over 31 million—in the decade of the 1850s alone. But it was also a result of the flow of people into the cities from two sources in particular. The first and for a time larger source was the native farming classes of the Northeast, whose members were being forced off their lands by Western competition. The second and ultimately at least equally important source was immigration from Europe. Between 1830 and 1840, only a relatively small number of foreigners had moved to the United States, about 500,000 in all. Beginning in 1840, however, the floodgates opened. The number of immigrants arriving in 1840—84,000—was the highest for any one year so far in the century. But in the ensuing years, even that number would come to seem insignificant. Between 1840 and 1850, more than 1.5 million Europeans moved to America; in the last years of the decade, the average number arriving annually was almost 300,000. Of the 23 million people in the United States in 1850, 2,210,000 (approximately 10 percent) were foreign-born. Still greater numbers arrived in the 1850s—over 2.5 million. Almost half of the population of New York City in the 1850s consisted of recent immigrants. And in St. Louis, Chicago, and Milwaukee, the foreign-born outnumbered those of

native birth. Few immigrants settled in the South. Only 500,000 lived in the slave states in 1860, and a third of these were concentrated in Missouri.

The newcomers came from many different countries and regions: England, France, Italy, Scandinavia, Poland, and Holland. But the overwhelming majority came from Ireland and Germany. In 1850, the Irish constituted approximately 45 percent and the Germans over 20 percent of the foreign-born in America. By 1860, there were more than 1.5 million Irish and approximately 1 million Germans in the United States. Several factors accounted for the prevalence of immigrants from Ireland and Germany: widespread poverty caused by the economic dislocations of the industrial revolution, famines resulting from the failure of the potato and other crops, dislike of English rule by the Irish, and the collapse of the liberal revolution of 1848 in Germany. The great majority of the Irish settled in Eastern cities, where they swelled the ranks of unskilled labor. The Germans tended to arrive with more money than the Irish,

Population Density, 1860

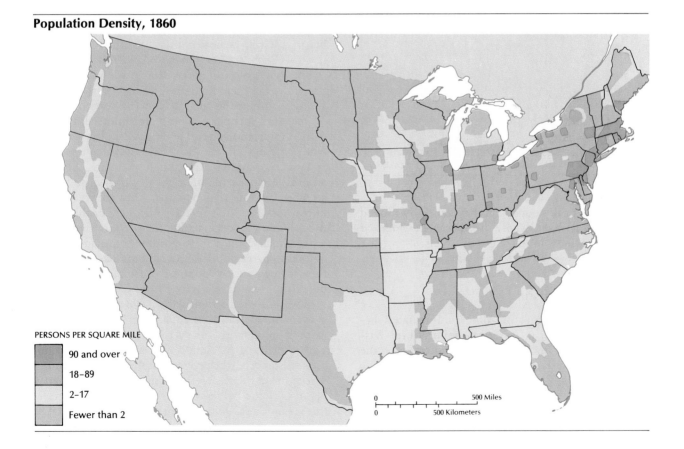

PERSONS PER SQUARE MILE

- 90 and over
- 18–89
- 2–17
- Fewer than 2

0   500 Miles

0   500 Kilometers

Sources of Immigration, 1840–1860

Sources of Immigration, 1840–1860

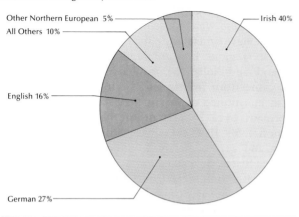

Other Northern European 5%
All Others 10%
Irish 40%
English 16%
German 27%

Total Immigration, 1840–1860

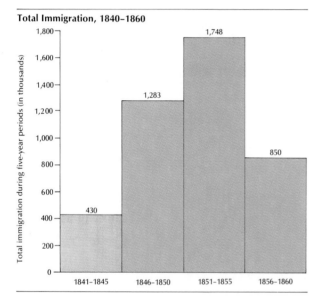

politicians saw in the immigrant population a source of important potential support; and they eagerly courted the new arrivals for their ballots. Others, however, viewed the growing foreign population with alarm. Among the results of their fears were the first important organized nativist movements in American history.

The emerging nativism took many forms. Some critics argued that the immigrants were mentally and physically defective, that they bred urban slums, that they corrupted politics by selling their votes. Others complained that because the aliens were willing to work for low wages, they were stealing jobs from the native work force. Protestants took note of the Irish Catholics' aptitude for politics and claimed that the church of Rome was attaining an undue power in American government. Whig politicians were outraged because so many of the newcomers voted Democratic. Many Americans of older stock feared the immigrants would inject new and radical philosophies into national thought.

Out of these tensions and prejudices emerged a number of secret societies to combat the "alien menace." Most of them originated in the Northeast, and some later spread to the West and even to the South. The first of these, the Native American Association, began agitating against immigration in 1837. In 1845, nativists held a convention in Philadelphia and formed the Native American party. But anti-immigrant sentiment crested in the 1850s. Many of the nativist groups combined in 1850 to form the Supreme Order of the Star-Spangled Banner. It endorsed a list of demands that included banning Catholics or aliens from holding public office, more restrictive naturalization laws, and literacy tests for voting. The order adopted a strict code of secrecy, which included the secret password, used in lodges across the country, "I know nothing." Ultimately, members of the movement became known as the "Know-Nothings."

Gradually, the Know-Nothings turned their attention to party politics, and after the election of 1852 they created a new political organization that they called the American party. In the East, the new organization scored an immediate and astonishing success in the elections of 1854: The Know-Nothings cast a large vote in Pennsylvania and New York and won control of the state government in Massachusetts. Elsewhere, the progress of the Know-Nothings was more modest. Western members of the party, because of the presence of many German voters in the area, found it expedient to proclaim that they were not opposed to naturalized Protestants. After 1854, however, the strength of the Know-Nothings

who had practically none, and they generally moved on to the Northwest, where they became farmers or went into business in the Western towns.

The Rise of Nativism

The new foreign population almost immediately became a major factor in American political life. Wisconsin, from the moment of its admission to the Union in 1848, permitted aliens to become voters as soon as they had declared their intention of seeking citizenship and had resided in the state for a year. Other states followed Wisconsin's lead in liberalizing voting laws, and in most places the polling officials were even more generous than the law allowed. Many

"Americans Shall Rule America"
Thomas Swann, a Maryland railroad
magnate, was elected mayor of
Baltimore in 1856 as the candidate of
the American (or "Know Nothing")
party after a campaign characterized by
widespread violence and disorder. This
cartoon lambasting the American
party's activities in Baltimore conveys
the opponents' image of the Know
Nothings as a party of drunken
hooligans.   (Maryland Historical Society)

declined; and the party's most lasting impact was its
contribution to the collapse of the second party system and the creation of new national political alignments. (See pp. 387–388.)

Labor in the Northeast

The increasing migration of farmers into the cities,
and the great rise in immigration from abroad, became another essential factor in the promotion of industrialization. It provided a labor force.

In the early years of industrial growth, the work
force of the Northeastern factories had remained both
small and for the most part impermanent. Because
mills had been relatively few, manufacturers had
made do with a modest, largely female labor supply—for example, the mill girls of Waltham and
Lowell, who generally worked only temporarily in
the factories before returning home. (See pp. 254–
255.) By the 1840s, however, the need for factory
workers was such that a large, permanent laboring
class was beginning to emerge, drawn from the new
urban population.

It had also been possible in the early years for mill
owners to treat their workers with a paternal solicitude that at times softened the conditions of living

and working in a new and alien environment. But
with the expansion of industry, such niceties were
quickly forgotten. No longer did workers live in neat
boardinghouses or dormitories carefully maintained
and patrolled by their employers. Instead, they were
generally left to their own devices, to find whatever
accommodations they could in the cheerless, ugly
factory towns that were rapidly growing up. No
longer were the conditions of factory labor monitored so as to reduce the hardship of the workers.
Instead, factories were becoming large, noisy,
unsanitary, and often dangerous places to work; the
average workday was extending to twelve, often
fourteen hours; and wages were declining, so that
even skilled male workers could hope to earn only
from $4 to $10 per week, while unskilled laborers
were likely to earn only about $1 to $6 per week.
Women and children, whatever their skills, also
earned less than most men. Conditions were still not
as bad as in most factory towns in England and Europe; but neither were American factories the models
of cleanliness, efficiency, and human concern that
many people had once believed them to be.

Workers faced with the arduous conditions of the
new factory complexes made a number of efforts to
improve their lot. They tried, with little success, to
persuade state legislatures to pass laws setting a max-

imum workday. Two states—New Hampshire in 1847 and Pennsylvania in 1848—actually passed ten-hour laws, limiting the workday unless the workers agreed to an "express contract" calling for more time on the job. Such measures were virtually without impact, however, because employers could simply require prospective employees to sign the "express contract" as a condition of hiring. Three states—Massachusetts, New Hampshire, and Pennsylvania—passed laws regulating child labor. But again, the results were minimal. The laws simply limited the workday to ten hours for children unless their parents agreed to something longer; employers had little difficulty compelling parents to consent to additional hours.

Perhaps the greatest legal victory of industrial workers came in Massachusetts in 1842, when the supreme court of the state, in *Commonwealth* v. *Hunt*, declared that unions were lawful organizations and that the strike was a lawful weapon. Other state courts gradually accepted the principles of the Massachusetts decision. But the union movement of the 1840s and 1850s remained, on the whole, generally feeble and ineffective. Partly because many workers were reluctant to think of themselves as members of a permanent laboring force, resistance to organization remained strong. And those unions that did manage to establish a foothold in industry were usually not strong enough to stage strikes, and even less frequently strong enough to win them.

What organization there was among workers usually occurred at the local level and among limited groups of skilled workers. These early unions often had more in common with preindustrial guilds than with modern labor organizations. Their primary purpose was in most cases to protect the favored position of their members in the labor force by restricting admission to the skilled trades. As early as the 1830s, a few local craft unions had begun to associate with one another to form national organizations. (See p. 256.) More such associations emerged in the 1850s, among them the National Typographical Union, founded in 1852, followed by the Stone Cutters in 1853, the Hat Finishers in 1854, and the Molders and the Machinists, both in 1859.

Despite these modest efforts at organization and protest, what was most notable about the American working class in the 1840s and 1850s was its relative passivity. In England, workers were becoming a powerful, united, and often violent economic and political force. They were creating widespread social turmoil and helping to transform the nation's political structure. In America, nothing of the sort happened.

Many factors combined to inhibit the growth of effective labor resistance. Among the most important was the flood of immigrant laborers into the country. The newcomers were usually willing to work for lower wages than native workers; and because they were so numerous, manufacturers had little difficulty replacing disgruntled or striking workers with eager immigrants. Ethnic divisions and tensions—both between natives and immigrants, and among the various immigrant groups themselves—often caused working-class resentments to be channeled into internal bickering rather than complaints against employers. There was, too, the sheer strength of the industrial capitalists, who had not only economic but political and social power and could usually triumph over even the most militant challenges. But a full understanding of the nature of the working-class response to industrialism requires an examination of the emerging social and economic structure of antebellum America.

Wealth and Mobility

The commercial and industrial growth of the United States greatly increased national wealth in the 1840s and 1850s. It elevated, too, the average income of the American people. But what evidence there is—and it is admittedly sketchy—suggests that this increasing wealth was not being widely distributed. Some groups of the population, of course, shared virtually not at all in the economic growth: slaves, Indians, landless farmers, and many of the unskilled workers on the fringes of the manufacturing system. But even among the rest of the population, disparities of income were becoming so marked as to be impossible to ignore. Wealth had always been unequally distributed in the United States, to be sure. Even in the era of the Revolution, according to some estimates, 45 percent of the wealth was concentrated in the hands of about 10 percent of the population. But by the mid-nineteenth century, that concentration had become far more pronounced. In Boston in 1845, for example, 4 percent of the citizens are estimated to have owned more than 65 percent of the wealth; in Philadelphia in 1860, 1 percent of the population possessed more than half the wealth. Among the American people at large in 1860, 5 percent of the families possessed more than 50 percent of the wealth.

On the surface, such figures would seem likely to

have encouraged a far greater level of class conflict than actually occurred. But a number of factors operated to quell resentments. There was, first, the fact that however much the *relative* economic position of American workers may have been declining, the *absolute* living standard of most laborers was improving. Life, in material terms at least, was usually better for factory workers than it had been on the farms or in the European societies from which they had migrated. They ate better, they were often better clothed and housed, and they had greater access to consumer goods.

There was also a significant amount of mobility within the working class, which helped to limit discontent. Opportunities for *social* mobility, for working one's way up the economic ladder, were limited; but opportunities did exist. A few workers did manage to move from poverty to riches by dint of work, ingenuity, and luck—a very small number, but enough to support the dreams of those who watched them. And a much larger number of workers managed to move at least one notch up the ladder—for example, becoming in the course of a lifetime a skilled, rather than an unskilled, laborer. Such people could envision their children and grandchildren moving up even further.

More important than social mobility was *geographical* mobility. Unlike European nations, America had a huge expanse of unsettled land in the West, much of it being opened for settlement for the first time in the 1840s and 1850s. To some workers, therefore, the dream of saving money to move out to the frontier could become a reality—thus creating what the historian Frederick Jackson Turner called a "safety valve" for discontent. For most workers, however, the expense and expertise required for a move to the agricultural frontier made such a step impossible. Far more frequent was the movement of laborers from one industrial town to another. Restless, questing, these "people in motion," as some scholars have described them, were often the victims of layoffs, looking for better opportunities elsewhere. Their search may seldom have led to a marked improvement in their circumstances; but the rootlessness of this large segment of the work force—perhaps the most distressed segment—made effective organization and protest far more difficult.

There was, finally, another "safety valve" for working-class discontent: politics. Economic opportunity may not have greatly expanded in the nineteenth century, but opportunities to participate in politics did. And to many working people, access to the ballot seemed to offer a way to help guide their society and to feel like a significant part of their communities.

Women and the "Cult of Domesticity"

The new industrializing society of the Northern regions of the United States produced a profound change in the nature and function of the family. At the heart of the transformation was the shift of income-earning work out of the home and into the shop, mill, or factory. In the early decades of the nineteenth century (and for many years before that), the family itself had been the principal unit of economic activity. Family farms, family shops, and family industries were the norm throughout most of the United States. Men, women, and children worked together, sharing tasks and jointly earning the income that sustained the family.

Among the farming population, which continued to constitute the majority of the American people, the family generally remained a unit of joint economic activity. But in the industrial economy of the rapidly growing cities, the traditional economic function of the family suffered a gradual erosion. The urban household itself became increasingly less important as a center of production. Instead, most income earners left home each day to work elsewhere. A sharp distinction began to emerge between the public world of the workplace—the world of commerce and industry—and the private world of the family—a world now dominated by housekeeping, child rearing, and other primarily domestic concerns.

Among members of the growing middle class, at least, the emerging distinction between the public and private worlds, between the workplace and the home, was accompanied by the emergence of an equally sharp distinction between the roles of men and women. There had, of course, always been important differences between the male and female spheres in American society. Women had long been denied many legal and political rights enjoyed by men; it was widely assumed that within the family, the husband and father ruled and the wife and mother bowed to his demands and desires. It was practically impossible for most women to obtain a divorce, although divorces initiated by men were often easier to arrange. (Men were also far more likely than women to win custody of children in case of a divorce.) In most states, husbands retained almost absolute authority over both the property and persons of their wives; wife beating was illegal in only a few areas. And women traditionally had very little access to the worlds of business or politics. Indeed, women generally were forbidden by custom to speak in public before mixed audiences.

Women traditionally also had far less access to education than men, a situation that survived into the mid-nineteenth century. Although they were encouraged to attend school at the elementary level, they were strongly discouraged—and in most cases effectively barred—from pursuing higher education. Oberlin in Ohio became the first college in America to accept woman students; it permitted four to enroll in 1837, despite criticism that coeducation would become a rash experiment approximating free love. Oberlin authorities were confident that "the mutual influence of the sexes upon each other is decidedly happy in the cultivation of both mind & manners." But few other institutions shared their views. Coeducation remained extraordinarily rare until long after the Civil War; and only a very few women's colleges—such as Mount Holyoke, founded in Massachusetts by Mary Lyon in 1837—emerged.

But however unequal the positions of men and women in the preindustrial era, those positions had generally been defined within the context of a household in which all members played crucial roles in the generation of family income. In the middle-class family of the new industrial society, however, the husband was assumed to be the principal, usually the only, income producer. The wife was now expected to remain in the home and to engage in largely domestic activities.

The result was an important shift in the concept of the woman's place within the family and of the family's place within the larger society. Women in the mid-nineteenth century came to be seen as guardians of the "domestic virtues." Their role as mothers, entrusted with the nurturing of the young, came to be seen as far more central to the family than it had in the past. And their role as wives—as companions and helpers to their husbands—grew more important as well. Middle-class women, no longer producers, now became more important as consumers. They learned to place a high value on keeping a clean, comfortable, and well-appointed home; on entertaining; on dressing elegantly and stylishly.

Occupying their own, separate sphere, women began to develop a distinctive female culture. Friendships among women became increasingly intense; women began to form their own social networks (and, ultimately, to form female clubs and associations that were of great importance to the advancement of various reforms). A distinctive feminine literature began to emerge to meet the demands of middle-class women. There were romantic novels (many of them by female writers), which focused on the private sphere that women now inhabited. There were women's magazines, of which the most prominent was *Godey's Lady's Book,* edited after 1837 by Sarah Hale, who had earlier founded a women's magazine of her own. The magazine scrupulously avoided dealing with public controversies or political issues and focused instead on fashions, shopping and homemaking advice, and other purely domestic concerns. Politics and religion were inappropriate for the magazine, Hale explained in 1841, because "other subjects are more important for our sex and more proper for our sphere."

By the standards of a later era, the increasing isolation of women from the public world seems to be a form of oppression and discrimination. And it is true that few men considered women fit for business, politics, or the professions. On the other hand, most middle-class men—and many middle-class women as well—considered the new female sphere a vehicle for expressing special qualities that made women in many ways superior to men. Women were to be the custodians of morality and benevolence, just as the home—shaped by the influence of women—was to be a refuge from the harsh, competitive world of the marketplace. It was the responsibility of women to provide religious and moral instruction to their children and to counterbalance the acquisitive, secular impulses of their husbands. Thus the "cult of domesticity," as some scholars have called it, brought both benefits and costs to middle-class women. It allowed them to live lives of greater material comfort than in the past, and it placed a higher value on their "female virtues" and on their roles as wife and mother. At the same time, it left women increasingly detached from the public world, with fewer outlets for their interests and energies.

The costs of that detachment were particularly clear among unmarried women of the middle class. By the 1840s, the ideology of domesticity had grown so powerful that few genteel women would any longer consider working (as many had in the past) in shops or mills (and few employers would consider hiring them). But unmarried women nevertheless required some income-producing activity. They had few choices. They could become teachers or nurses, professions that seemed to call for the same female qualities that made women important within the home; and both those professions began in the 1840s and 1850s to attract large numbers of women. Oth-

New England Textile Workers

Women continued to constitute the majority of the work force in the cotton mills of New England even after the carefully monitored life of the "Lowell girls" became a thing of the past—as this 1868 engraving by Winslow Homer suggests. About 58 percent of the textile industry work force were female in the 1860s. Approximately 7 percent were children under twelve (shown here carrying their lunch pails alongside the adults). (Library of Congress)

erwise, unmarried females were largely dependent on the generosity of relatives.

Except for teaching and nursing, work by women outside the household gradually came to be seen as a lower-class preserve. Working-class women could not afford to stay home and cultivate the "domestic virtues." They had to produce income for their families. They continued to work in factories and mills, but under conditions far worse than those that the original, more "respectable" woman workers had enjoyed. They also frequently found employment in middle-class homes. Domestic service became one of the most frequent sources of female employment. In other words, now that production had moved outside the household, women who needed to earn

money had to move outside their own households to do so.

Accompanying (and perhaps in part caused by) the changing economic function of the family was a decline in the birth rate. In 1800, the average American woman could be expected to give birth to approximately seven children during her childbearing years. By 1860, women bore an average of five children apiece. The birth rate fell most quickly in urban areas and among middle-class women. Mid-nineteenth-century Americans had access to certain birth control devices, which undoubtedly contributed in part to the change. There was also a significant rise in abortions, which remained legal in some states until after the Civil War and which, according to some estimates, may have terminated as many as 20 percent of all pregnancies in the 1850s. But the most important cause of the declining birth rate was almost certainly a change in sexual behavior—including increased abstinence.

The deliberate effort among middle-class men and women to limit family size was a reflection of a much larger shift in the nature of society in the mid-nineteenth-century North. In a world in which the economy was becoming increasingly organized, in which production was moving out of the home, in which individuals were coming to expect more from the world, in which more emphasis was being placed on calculations about the future, the idea of making careful, rational decisions about bearing children was of particular appeal. It expressed the increasingly secular, rationalized, and progressive orientation of the rapidly developing American North.

Northeastern Agriculture

The story of agriculture in the Northeast after 1840 is one of decline and transformation. The reason for the decline was simple: the farmers of the section could no longer compete with the new and richer soil of the Northwest. Centers of production were gradually shifting westward for many of the farm goods that had in the past been most important to Northeastern agriculture: wheat, corn, grapes, cattle, sheep, and hogs. In 1840, the leading wheat-growing states were New York, Pennsylvania, Ohio, and Virginia; in 1860, they were Illinois, Indiana, Wisconsin, Ohio, and Michigan. In the case of corn, Illinois, Ohio, and Missouri supplanted New York, Pennsylvania, and Virginia. In 1840, the most important cattle-raising areas in the country were New York, Pennsylvania, and New England; but by the 1850s, the leading cattle states were Illinois, Indiana, Ohio, and Iowa in the West, and Texas in the South.

Some Eastern farmers responded to these changes by moving west themselves and establishing new farms. Still others moved to mill towns and became laborers. Some farmers, however, remained on the land and managed to hold their own against, at times even to surpass, the Northwest in certain lines of agriculture. As the Eastern urban centers increased in population, many farmers turned to the task of supplying food to the city masses; they engaged profitably in truck gardening (vegetables) or fruit raising. New York, for example, led all other states in apple production. The rise of cities also stimulated the rise of dairy farming. The profits to be derived from supplying milk, butter, and cheese to local markets attracted many farmers in central New York, southeastern Pennsylvania, and various parts of New England. Approximately half of the dairy products of the country were produced in the East; most of the rest came from the West, where Ohio was the leading dairy state. Partly because of the expansion of the dairy industry, the Northeast led other sections in the production of hay. New York was the leading hay state in the nation, and large crops were grown in Pennsylvania and New England. The Northeast also exceeded other areas in producing potatoes.

Nevertheless, while agriculture in the region remained an important part of the economy, it was steadily becoming less important relative both to the agriculture of the Northwest and to the industrial growth of the Northeast itself. As a result, the rural population in many parts of the Northeast continued to decline.

The Old Northwest

Life was different in the states of what was known as the Northwest—now the Midwest—in the mid-nineteenth century. There was some industry in this region, more than in the South; and in the two decades before the Civil War, the section experienced steady industrial growth. By 1860, it had 36,785 manufacturing establishments employing 209,909 workers. Along the southern shore of Lake Erie was a flourishing industrial and commercial area of which Cleveland was the center. Another manufacturing region was in the Ohio River valley, with the meat-packing city of Cincinnati as its nucleus. Farther west, the rising city of Chicago, destined to become the great metropolis of the section, was emerging as the national center of the agricultural machinery and meat-packing industries. The most important industrial products of the West were farm machinery, flour, meat, distilled whiskey, and leather and wooden goods.

On the whole, however, industry was far less important in the Northwest than in the Northeast. The Northwest remained primarily an agricultural region. Its rich and plentiful lands made farming there a lucrative and expanding activity, in contrast to the Northeast. Thus the typical citizen of the Northwest was not the industrial worker or the poor, marginal farmer but the owner of a reasonably prosperous family farm. The average size of Western farms was 200 acres, the great majority of them owned by the people who worked them.

Pastoral America, 1848
This painting by the American artist Edward Hicks suggests the degree to which Americans continued to admire the "Peaceable Kingdom" (the name of another, more famous Hicks work) of the agrarian world. Hicks entitled this work *An Indian Summer view of the Farm w. Stock of James C. Cornell of Northampton Bucks county Pennsylvania. That took the Premium in the Agricultural Society, October the 12, 1848*. It portrays the diversified farming of a prosperous Pennsylvania family, shown here in the foreground with their cattle, sheep, and workhorses. In the background stretches a field ready for plowing and another ready for harvesting. (National Gallery of Art, Washington)

In concentrating on corn, wheat, cattle, sheep, and hogs, the Western farmer was motivated by sound economic reasons. As the Northeast became more industrial and urban, it enlarged the domestic market for farm goods. At the same time, England and certain European nations, undergoing the same process, started to import larger amounts of food. This growing worldwide demand for farm products resulted in steadily rising farm prices. For the farmers, the 1840s and early 1850s were years of increasing prosperity.

The expansion of agricultural markets had profound effects on sectional alignments in the United States. The Northwest sold by far the greatest part of its products to the residents of the Northeast; only the surplus remaining after domestic needs were sat-

isfied was exported abroad. The new well-being of Western farmers, then, was sustained in large part by Eastern purchasing power. Eastern industry, in turn, found an important market for its products in the prospering West. Between the two sections a strong economic relationship was emerging that was profitable to both—and that was increasing the isolation of the South within the Union.

To meet the increasing demand for its farm products, the Northwest worked strenuously, and often frantically, to increase its productive capacities. One way it did so was by taking advantage of the large areas of still unoccupied land and enlarging the area under cultivation during the 1840s. By 1850, the growing Western population had settled the prairie regions east of the Mississippi and was pushing beyond the river. But another way the Northwest increased production was by adopting agricultural techniques designed to produce the largest possible crop in the shortest possible time. The average Western farmer engaged, therefore, in wasteful, exploitive methods of farming that often resulted in rapid exhaustion or the region's rich soil.

At the same time, however, Northwestern farmers were discovering improved agricultural techniques. New varieties of seed, notably Mediterranean wheat, which was hardier than the native type, were introduced in some areas; better breeds of animals, such as hogs and sheep from England and Spain, were imported to take the place of native stock. Of greater importance were the improvements that Americans continued to introduce in farm machines and tools. During the 1840s, more efficient grain drills, harrows, mowers, and hay rakes were placed in wide use. The cast-iron plow, devised earlier, continued to be popular because its parts could be replaced when broken. An even better implement appeared in 1847, when John Deere established at Moline, Illinois, a factory to manufacture plows with steel moldboards, which were more durable than those made of iron.

Two new machines heralded a coming revolution in grain production. The most important was the automatic reaper, invented by Cyrus H. McCormick of Virginia. The reaper took the place of sickle, cradle, and hand labor and enabled a crew of six or seven men to harvest in a day as much wheat (or any other small grain) as fifteen men could harvest using the older methods. McCormick, who had patented his device in 1834, established a factory at Chicago, in the heart of the grain belt, in 1847. By 1860, more than 100,000 reapers were in use on Western farms. Almost as important to the grain grower was the thresher—a machine that separated the grain from the wheat stalks. Threshers appeared in large numbers after 1840. Before that time, grain was generally flailed by hand (seven bushels a day was a good average for a farm) or trodden by farm animals (twenty bushels a day on the average). A threshing machine could thresh twenty-five bushels or more in an hour. Most of the threshers were manufactured at the Jerome I. Case factory in Racine, Wisconsin.

The Northwest was the most self-consciously democratic section of the country. But its democracy was of a relatively conservative type—capitalistic, property conscious, middle-class. Abraham Lincoln, an Illinois Whig, voiced the economic opinions of many of the people of his section. "I take it that it is best for all to leave each man free to acquire property as fast as he can," said Lincoln. "Some will get wealthy. I don't believe in a law to prevent a man from getting rich; it would do more harm than good. . . . When one starts poor, as most do in the race of life, free society is such that he knows he can better his condition; he knows that there is no fixed condition of labor for his whole life."

The Expanding South

The South, like the North, experienced dramatic growth in the middle years of the nineteenth century. Southerners fanned out into the new territories of the Southwest and established new communities, new states, and new markets. The Southern agricultural economy grew increasingly productive and increasingly prosperous. Trade in such staples as sugar, rice, tobacco, and above all cotton made the South a major force in international commerce and created substantial wealth within the region. Southern society, Southern culture, Southern politics—all were affected by these important demographic and economic changes. The South in the 1850s was a very different place from the South of the first years of the century.

Yet for all the expansion and all the changes, the South experienced a much less fundamental transformation in these years than did the North. It had begun the nineteenth century a primarily rural and agricultural region; it remained overwhelmingly agrarian in 1860. It began the century with few important cities and little industry; and so it remained sixty years later. In 1800, the economy of the South had been dominated by a plantation system dependent on slave labor; by 1860, that system had only strengthened its grip on the region. As one historian has written, "The South *grew,* but it did not *develop.*" And as a result, it became increasingly unlike the North and increasingly sensitive to what it considered to be threats to its distinctive way of life.

The Rise of King Cotton

The most important economic development in the South of the mid-nineteenth century was the shift of economic power from the "upper South," the original Southern states along the Atlantic coast, to the "lower South," the expanding agricultural regions in

Slavery and Cotton: The South in 1820 and 1860

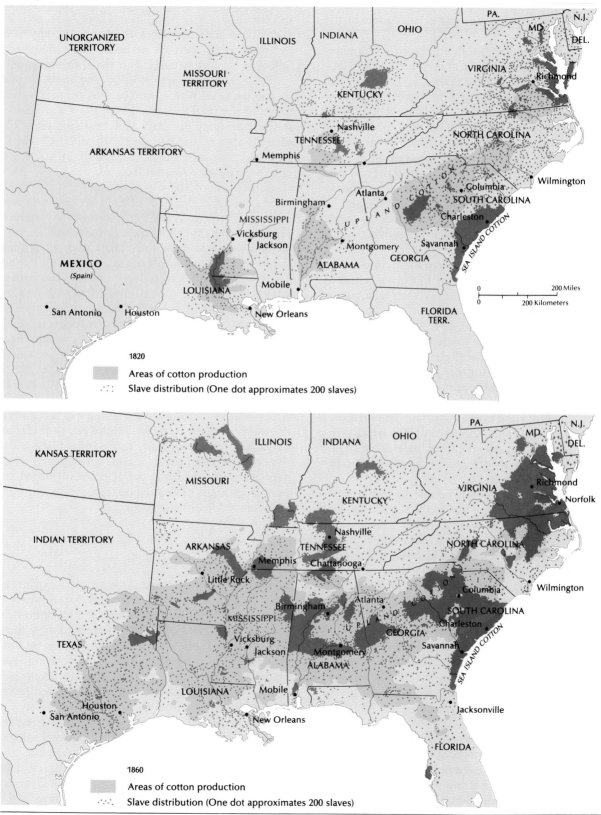

1820

- Areas of cotton production
- ·∷· Slave distribution (One dot approximates 200 slaves)

1860

- Areas of cotton production
- ·∷· Slave distribution (One dot approximates 200 slaves)

the new states of the Southwest. That shift reflected above all the growing dominance of cotton in the Southern economy.

Much of the upper South continued in the nineteenth century to rely, as it always had, on the cultivation of tobacco. But the market for that crop was notoriously unstable, subject to recurrent depressions, including a prolonged one that began in the 1820s and extended into the 1850s. And tobacco rapidly exhausted the land on which it was grown, which made it difficult for most growers to remain in business in the same place for very long. By the 1830s, therefore, many farmers in the old tobacco-growing regions of Virginia, Maryland, and North Carolina were shifting to other crops—notably wheat—while the center of tobacco cultivation was moving westward, into the piedmont area.

The southern regions of the coastal South—South Carolina, Georgia, and parts of Florida—continued to rely on rice production, a more stable and lucrative crop. But rice demanded substantial irrigation and needed an exceptionally long growing season (nine months), so cultivation of that staple remained restricted to a relatively small area. Sugar growers, similarly, enjoyed a reasonably profitable market for their crop; but sugar cultivation, too, required special conditions and a long growing time and thus did not spread much beyond a small area in southern Louisiana and eastern Texas. Long-staple (Sea Island) cotton was another lucrative crop; but like rice and sugar, it could be grown only in a limited area—the coastal regions of the Southeast.

The decline of the tobacco economy in the upper South, and the inherent limits of the sugar, rice, and long-staple cotton economies farther south might have forced the region to shift its attention to other, nonagricultural pursuits in the nineteenth century had it not been for the growing importance of a new product, which soon overshadowed all else: short-staple cotton. This was a hardier and coarser strain of cotton, which could be grown effectively in a variety of climates and in a variety of soils. It was more difficult to process than the long-staple variety; its seeds were far more difficult to remove from the fiber. But the invention of the cotton gin (see pp. 194–195) had largely solved that problem, and by the 1820s cotton production was spreading rapidly. From the western areas of South Carolina and Georgia, production moved steadily—first into Alabama and Mississippi, then into northern Louisiana, Texas, and Arkansas. By the 1850s, cotton had come to be the linchpin of the Southern economy. In 1820, the South had produced only about 500,000 bales of cotton. By 1850, it was producing nearly 3 million bales a year, and by 1860 nearly 5 million. There were periodic fluctuations in cotton prices, resulting generally from overproduction; periods of boom were frequently followed by abrupt busts. But the cotton economy continued to grow, even if in fits and starts. By the time of the Civil War, cotton constituted nearly two-thirds of the total export trade of the United States and was bringing in nearly $200 million a year. The annual value of the rice crop, in contrast, was $2 million. It was little wonder that Southern politicians now proclaimed: "Cotton is king!"

Settlement of the cotton kingdom bore certain resemblances to the rush of gold seekers to a new frontier. The prospect of tremendous profits quickly drew settlers by the thousands. Some who came were wealthy planters from the older states who transferred their assets and slaves to a cotton plantation. Most were small slaveholders or slaveless farmers who intended to become planters. A similar shift occurred in the slave population. In the period 1820–1860, the number of slaves in Alabama leaped from 41,000 to 435,000, and in Mississippi from 32,000 to 436,000. In the same period, the increase in Virginia was only from 425,000 to 490,000. It has been estimated that between 1840 and 1860, 410,000 slaves moved from the upper South to the cotton states—either accompanying masters who were themselves migrating to the Southwest, or (more often) sold to planters already there. Indeed, the sale of slaves to the Southwest became an important economic activity in the upper South and helped the troubled planters of that region to compensate for the declining value of their crops.

Southern Trade and Industry

In the face of this booming agricultural expansion, other forms of economic activity developed slowly in the South. The business classes of the region—the manufacturers and merchants—were not without importance. There was growing activity in flour milling and in textile and iron manufacturing, particularly in the upper South. The Tredegar Iron Works in Richmond, for example, compared favorably with the best iron mills in the Northeast. But industry remained an insignificant force in comparison with the agricultural economy. The total value of Southern textile manufactures in 1860 was $4.5 million—a threefold increase over the value of those goods twenty years before, but only about 2 percent of the value of the cotton exported that year.

The New Orleans Cotton Exchange

Edgar Degas, the great French artist, painted this scene of cotton traders examining samples in the New Orleans cotton exchange in 1873. By this time the cotton trade was producing profits far less impressive than those that made it the driving force of the booming Southern economy of the 1850s. Degas's mother came from a Creole family of cotton brokers in New Orleans; and two of the artist's brothers (depicted here reading a newspaper and leaning against a window) joined the business in America.   (Giraudon/Art Resource)

To the degree that the South developed a nonfarm commercial sector, it was largely to serve the needs of the plantation economy. Particularly important were the brokers, or factors, who marketed the planters' crops. These merchants were centered in such towns as New Orleans, Charleston, Mobile, and Savannah, where they worked to find buyers for cotton and other crops and where they purchased needed goods for the planters they served. The South had only a very rudimentary financial system, and the factors often also served the planters as bankers,

providing them with credit. Planters frequently accumulated substantial debts, particularly during periods when cotton prices were in decline; and the Southern merchant-bankers thus became figures of considerable influence and importance in the region. There were also substantial groups of professional people in the South—lawyers, editors, doctors, and others; they too, however, were closely tied to and dependent on the plantation economy.

However important these manufacturers, merchants, and professionals might have been to Southern society, they were relatively unimportant in comparison with the manufacturers, merchants, and professionals of the North, on whom Southerners were coming more and more (and increasingly unhappily) to depend. Perceptive Southerners recognized the economic subordination of their region. "From the rattle with which the nurse tickles the ear of the child born in the South to the shroud that covers the cold form of the dead, everything comes to us from the North," exclaimed the Arkansas journalist Albert Pike.

Perhaps the most prominent advocate of Southern economic independence was James B. D. De Bow, a resident of New Orleans. He published a magazine advocating Southern commercial and agricultural expansion: *De Bow's Review,* which survived from its founding in 1846 until 1880. De Bow made his journal into a tireless advocate of Southern economic independence from the North, warning constantly of the dangers of the "colonial" relationship between the sections. One writer noted in the pages of his magazine: "I think it would be safe to estimate the amount which is lost to us annually by our vassalage to the North at $100,000,000. Great God!" Yet *De Bow's Review* was itself clear evidence of the dependency of the South on the North. It was printed in New York, because no New Orleans printer had facilities adequate to the task; it was filled with advertisements from Northern manufacturing firms; and its circulation was always modest in comparison

with those of Northern publications. In Charleston, for example, it sold an average of 173 copies per issue, while *Harper's Magazine* of New York regularly sold 1,500 copies to Carolinians.

Despite this awareness of the region's "colonial dependency," the South made few serious efforts to develop an economy that might challenge that dependency. An important question about antebellum Southern history, therefore, is why the region did so little to develop a larger industrial and commercial economy of its own.

Part of the reason was the great profitability of the region's agricultural system, and particularly of cotton production. Another reason was that wealthy Southerners had so much capital invested in their land and in their slaves that they had little left for other investments. Some historians have suggested that the Southern climate—with its long, hot, steamy summers—was less suitable for industrial development than the climate of the North. Still others have gone so far as to claim that Southern work habits impeded industrialization; white Southerners appeared—at least to many Northern observers—not to work very hard, to lack the strong work ethic that fueled Northern economic development.

But the Southern failure to create a flourishing commercial or industrial economy was also in part the result of a set of values distinctive to the South that discouraged the growth of cities and industry. White Southerners liked to think of themselves as

Life on the Mississippi
Shown here is the "saloon," or main cabin, of one of the great Mississippi steamboats, the *Princess,* as painted by the French artist Marie Adrien Persac. Steamboats not only carried cotton and other freight up and down the Mississippi; they also provided affluent Southerners with a lavish form of transportation and entertainment, as the elegant appointments of this room suggest. (Anglo-American Art Museum, Louisiana State University)

representatives of a special way of life: one based on traditional values of chivalry, leisure, and elegance. Southerners were, they argued, "cavaliers"—people happily free from the base, acquisitive instincts of Northerners, people more concerned with a refined and gracious way of life than with rapid growth and development. But appealing as the "cavalier" image was to Southern whites, it conformed to the reality of Southern society in strictly limited ways.

Plantation Society

Only a minority of Southern whites owned slaves. In 1850, when the total white population of the South was over 6 million, the number of slaveholders was only 347,525. In 1860, when the white population was just above 8 million, the number of slaveholders had risen to only 383,637. These figures are, of course, somewhat misleading, since each slaveholder was normally the head of a family averaging five members. But even with all members of slaveowning families included in the figures, those owning slaves still amounted to perhaps no more than one quarter of the white population. And of the minority of whites holding slaves, only a small proportion owned them in substantial numbers.

How, then, did the South come to be seen—both by the outside world and by many Southerners themselves—as a society dominated by great plantations and wealthy landowning planters? In large part, it was because the planter aristocracy—the cotton magnates, the sugar, rice, and tobacco nabobs, the whites who owned at least forty or fifty slaves and 800 or more acres—exercised power and influence far in excess of their numbers. They stood at the apex of society, determining the political, economic, and even social life of their region. Enriched by vast annual incomes, dwelling in palatial homes, surrounded by broad acres and many black servants, they became a class to which all others paid a certain deference. Southerners liked to compare their planter class to the old upper classes of England and Europe: true aristocracies long entrenched. In fact, however, the Southern upper class was in most cases not at all similar to the landed aristocracies of the Old World.

In some areas of the upper South—the tidewater region of Virginia, for example—the great aristocrats were sometimes people whose families had occupied positions of wealth and power for generations. In most of the South, however, a longstanding landed aristocracy, though central to the "cavalier" image, was largely a myth. Even the most important planters in the cotton-growing areas of the region were,

typically, new to their wealth and power. As late as the 1850s, the great landowners in the lower South were still often first-generation settlers, who had arrived with only modest resources, who had struggled for many years to clear land and develop a plantation in what was at first a rugged frontier, and who had only relatively recently begun to live in the comfort and luxury for which they were now famous. Large areas of the "Old South" (as Americans later called the South of the pre–Civil War era) had been settled and cultivated for less than two decades at the time of the Civil War. Nor was the world of the planter nearly as leisured and genteel as the "cavalier" myth would suggest. Growing staple crops was a business—often a big and highly profitable business—which was in its own way just as competitive and just as risky as the industrial enterprises of the North. Planters had to supervise their operations carefully if they hoped to make a profit. They were, in many respects, just as much competitive capitalists as the industrialists of the North whose life styles they claimed to hold in contempt.

Indeed, it may have been the newness and precariousness of the plantation way of life, and the differences between the reality of that life and the image of it, that made many Southern planters determined to portray themselves as genteel aristocrats. Having struggled so hard to reach and maintain their position, they were all the more determined to defend it. (It was perhaps no accident that the defense of slavery and of the South's "rights" was stronger in the new, booming regions of the lower South and weaker in the more established and less flourishing areas of the tidewater.)

Wealthy Southern whites sustained their image of themselves as aristocrats in many ways. They adopted an elaborate code of "chivalry," which obligated white men to defend their "honor" (often through dueling). They avoided such "coarse" occupations as trade and commerce; those who did not become planters often gravitated toward the military, a "suitable" career for men raised in a culture in which medieval knights (as portrayed in the novels of Walter Scott) were a powerful and popular image. Above all, perhaps, the aristocratic ideal found reflection in the definition of a special role for Southern white women.

The Southern Lady

In some respects, affluent white women in the South occupied roles very similar to those occupied by middle-class white women in the North. Their lives

French Long Lot Landscape in Iberville Parish, Louisiana, 1858

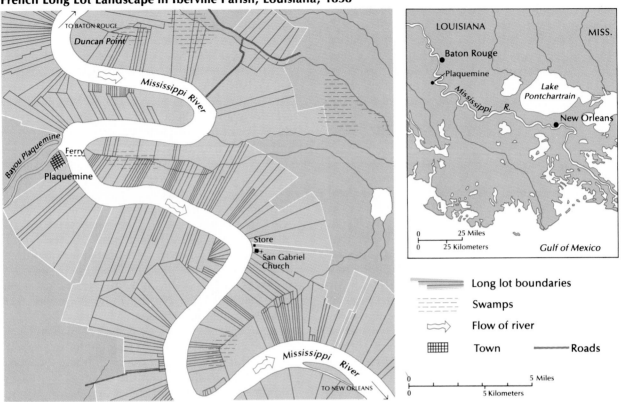

were expected to be centered in the home, where they would serve as companions to (and hostesses for) their husbands and as nurturing mothers for their children. Even less frequently than in the North did "genteel" Southern white women engage in public activities or find income-producing employment.

But the life of the "Southern lady" was also in many ways very different from that of her Northern counterpart. For one thing, the cult of honor in the region meant that Southern white men gave particular importance to the "defense" of women. In practice, this generally meant that white men were even more dominant and white women even more subordinate in Southern culture than they were in the North. George Fitzhugh, one of the South's most important social theorists, wrote in the 1850s: "Women, like children, have but one right, and that is the right to protection. The right to protection involves the obligation to obey."

More important in determining the role of Southern white women, however, were the social realities in which they lived. The vast majority of females in the region lived on farms, relatively isolated from people outside their own families, with virtually no

access to the "public world" and thus few opportunities to look beyond their roles as wives and mothers. For many women, living on farms of modest size meant a fuller engagement in the economic life of the family than was becoming typical for middle-class women in the North. These women engaged in spinning, weaving, and other production; they participated in agricultural tasks; they helped supervise the slave work force. On the larger plantations, however, even these limited roles were often considered unsuitable for white women; and the "plantation mistress" became, in some cases, more an ornament for her husband than a meaningful part of the economy or the society.

Southern women also had far less access to education than their Northern counterparts. Nearly a quarter of all white women over twenty were completely illiterate; relatively few women had more than a rudimentary exposure to schooling. Even wealthy planters were not much interested in extensive schooling for their daughters. The few female "academies" in the South were designed largely to train women to be suitable wives.

Southern white women had other special burdens

Hopeton Plantation, Georgia

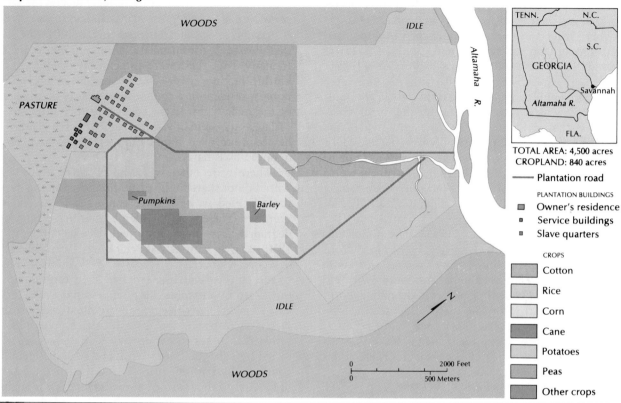

TOTAL AREA: 4,500 acres
CROPLAND: 840 acres

— Plantation road

PLANTATION BUILDINGS
- Owner's residence
- Service buildings
- Slave quarters

CROPS
- Cotton
- Rice
- Corn
- Cane
- Potatoes
- Peas
- Other crops

as well. The Southern birth rate remained nearly twenty percent higher than that of the nation as a whole, and infant mortality in the region remained higher than elsewhere; nearly half the children born in the South in 1860 died before they reached five years of age. And the slave labor system created particular problems. Male slaveowners had frequent sexual relationships with the female slaves on their plantations; the children of those unions became part of the plantation labor force and served as a constant reminder to white women of their husbands' infidelity. Resentment of such relationships ran deep among Southern women, and yet the social code under which they lived generally prevented them from venting their anger, or even openly acknowledging that the relationships existed at all.

A few Southern white women rebelled against their roles and against the prevailing assumptions of their region. Some became outspoken abolitionists and joined Northerners in the crusade to abolish slavery. (See pp.355–360.) Some agitated for other reforms within the South itself. Most white women, however, found few outlets for whatever discontent they felt with their lot. Instead, they generally con-

vinced themselves of the benefits of their position and—like Southern white men—defended the special virtues of the Southern way of life.

The Plain Folk

The typical white Southerner was not a great planter and slaveholder, but a modest yeoman farmer. Some owned a few slaves, with whom they worked and lived far more closely than did the larger planters. Most (in fact, two-thirds of all white families) owned no slaves at all. These "plain folk," most of whom owned their own land, devoted themselves largely to subsistence farming. During the 1850s, the number of nonslaveholding landowners increased much faster than the number of slaveholding landowners. While there were occasional examples of poor farmers moving into the ranks of the planter class, such cases were rare. Most yeomen knew that they had little prospect of substantially bettering their lot.

One reason was the Southern educational system, which provided poor whites with few opportunities to learn and thus limited their chances of advancement. For the sons of wealthy planters, however, the system provided ample opportunities to gain an education. In 1860 there were 260 Southern colleges and universities, public and private, with 25,000 students enrolled in them, or more than half the total number of students in the United States. The lower South had 11,000 students in its institutions of higher learning, while New England, with approximately the same population, could boast of only 3,748. College was within the reach of only the upper class, however. And below the college level, where the white lower classes more often looked, the schools of the South were not only fewer but also inferior to those of the Northeast (although not much worse than the crude schools of the Northwest). The South had more than 500,000 white illiterates, or over half of the country's total.

That a majority of the South's white population consisted of modest farmers largely excluded from the dominant plantation society presents an important question about the antebellum South. Why did the plain folk have so little power in the public world of the Old South? Why did they not oppose the aristocratic social system in which they shared so little? Why did they not resent the system of slavery, from which they generally did not benefit? There is no single answer to such questions.

Some nonslaveowning whites did oppose the slaveholding oligarchy, but for the most part in limited ways and in a relatively few, isolated areas. These were the Southern highlanders, the "hill people," who lived in the Appalachian ranges east of the Mississippi and in the Ozarks to the west of the river. Of all Southern whites, they were the most set apart from the mainstream of the region's life. They practiced a crude form of subsistence agriculture, owned practically no slaves, and had a proud sense of seclusion. They held to old ways and old ideals, which included the ideal of loyalty to the nation as a whole. Such whites frequently expressed animosity toward the planter aristocracy of the other regions of the South and misgivings about (although seldom moral objections to) the system of slavery. The mountain region was the only part of the South to defy the trend toward sectional conformity; and it was the only part to resist the movement toward secession when it finally developed. Even during the Civil War itself, many refused to support the Confederacy; some went so far as to fight for the Union.

Far greater in number, however, were the nonslaveowning whites who lived in the midst of the plantation system. Many, perhaps most of them, accepted that system because they were tied to it in important ways. Small farmers depended on the local plantation aristocracy for many things: for access to cotton gins, for markets for their modest crops and their livestock, for financial assistance in time of need. In many areas, there were also extensive networks of kinship linking lower- and upper-class whites. The poorest resident of a county might easily be a cousin of the richest aristocrat. Taken together, these mutual ties—a system of vaguely paternal relationships—helped mute what might otherwise have been pronounced class tensions.

There were other white Southerners, however, who did not share in the plantation economy in even these limited ways and yet continued to accept its premises. These were the members of that tragic and degraded class—numbering perhaps a half-million in 1850—known variously as "crackers," "sand hillers," or "poor white trash." Occupying the infertile lands of the pine barrens, the red hills, and the swamps, they lived in miserable cabins amid almost unbelievable squalor. Their degradation resulted partly from dietary deficiencies and disease. These poor whites resorted at times to eating clay; and they were afflicted by pellagra, hookworm, and malaria. Held in contempt by both the planters and the small farmers of the South, they formed a true underclass. In many ways, their plight was worse than that of the black slaves (who themselves often looked down on the poor whites).

Even among these Southerners—the true outcasts of white society in the region—there was no real opposition to the plantation system or slavery. In part, undoubtedly, this was because these men and women were so benumbed by poverty that they had little strength to protest. But it resulted also from perhaps the single greatest unifying factor among the Southern white population—the one force that was most responsible for reducing tensions among the various classes. That force was race. However poor and miserable white Southerners might be, they could still consider themselves members of a ruling race; they could still look down on the black population of the region and feel a bond with their fellow whites born of a determination to maintain their racial supremacy. As Frederick Law Olmsted, a Northerner who visited the South and chronicled Southern society in the 1850s, wrote: "From childhood, the one thing in their condition which has made life valuable to the mass of whites has been that the niggers are yet their inferiors."

The "Peculiar Institution"

White Southerners often referred to slavery as the "peculiar institution." By that, they meant not that the institution was odd but that it was distinctive, special. The description was an apt one, for American slavery was indeed distinctive. The South in the mid-nineteenth century was the only area in the entire Western world—except for Brazil and Cuba—where slavery still existed; and Southern slavery differed even from its Caribbean and Latin American counterparts. Slavery, more than any other single factor, isolated the South from the rest of American society. And as that isolation increased, so did the commitment of Southerners to defend the institution. William Harper, a prominent South Carolina politician in the 1840s, wrote: "The judgment is made up. We can have no hearing before the tribunal of the civilized world. Yet, on this very account, it is more important that we, the inhabitants of the slave-holding States, insulated as we are by this institution, and cut off, in some degree, from the communion and sympathies of the world by which we are surrounded, . . . and exposed continually to their animadversions and attacks, should thoroughly understand this subject, and our strength and weakness in relation to it."

Within the South itself, the institution of slavery had paradoxical results. On the one hand, it isolated blacks from whites, drawing a sharp and inviolable line between the races. As a result, blacks under slavery began to develop a society and culture of their own, one that was in many ways unrelated to the white civilization around them. On the other hand, slavery created a unique bond between blacks and whites—masters and slaves—in the South. The two races may have maintained separate spheres, but each sphere was deeply influenced by, indeed dependent on, the other.

Varieties of Slavery

Slavery was an institution established by law and regulated in detail by law. The slave codes of the Southern states forbade slaves to hold property, to leave their masters' premises without permission, to be out after dark, to congregate with other slaves except at church, to carry firearms, or to strike a white person even in self-defense. The codes prohibited whites from teaching slaves to read or write, and they denied to slaves the right to testify in court against

white people. They contained no provisions to legalize slave marriages or divorces. If an owner killed a slave while punishing him, the act was generally not considered a crime. Slaves, however, faced the death penalty for killing or even resisting a white person and for inciting to revolt. The codes also contained extraordinarily rigid provisions for defining a person's race. Anyone with even a trace of African ancestry was considered black. And anyone thought to possess any such trace was presumed to be black unless he or she could prove otherwise.

These and dozens of other restrictions and impositions indicate that the slaves lived under a uniformly harsh and dismal regime. Had the laws been rigidly enforced, that might have been the case. In fact, however, they were applied unevenly. Sometimes slaves did acquire property, were taught to read and write, and did assemble with other slaves, in spite of laws to the contrary. Although major slave offenses were generally referred to the courts (and thus to the jurisdiction of the slave codes), most transgressions were handled by the master, who might inflict punishments ranging from some mild disciplinary action to flogging or branding for running away. In other words, despite the rigid provisions of law, there was in reality considerable variety within the slave system. Some blacks lived in almost prisonlike conditions, rigidly and harshly controlled by their masters. Many (probably most) others enjoyed a certain flexibility and (at least in comparison to the regimen prescribed by law) a striking degree of autonomy.

The nature of the the relationship between masters and slaves depended in part on the size of the plantation. Thus the typical master had a different image of slavery from that of the typical slave. Most masters possessed very few slaves, and their experience with (and image of) slavery was therefore shaped by the special nature of slavery on the small farm. Small farmers generally supervised their workers directly and often worked closely alongside them. On such farms, blacks and whites developed a form of intimacy unknown on larger plantations. The paternal relationship between such masters and their slaves could, like relationships between fathers and children, be warm and in many ways benevolent. It could also be tyrannical and cruel. In general, the evidence suggests, blacks themselves preferred to live on larger plantations, where they had more opportunities for privacy and for a social world of their own.

Although the majority of slaveowners were small farmers, the majority of slaves lived on plantations of

Returning from the Cotton Field
In this photo, South Carolina field workers return after a day of picking cotton, their harvest carried in bundles on their heads. A black slave driver leads the way.   (New-York Historical Society)

medium or large size, with sizable slave work forces. There the relationship between master and slave was usually far less intimate. Substantial planters often hired overseers and even assistant overseers to represent them. "Head drivers," trusted and responsible slaves often assisted by several subdrivers, acted under the overseer as foremen. Larger planters generally used one of two methods of assigning slave labor. One was the task system, most widely used in rice culture, under which slaves were assigned a particular task in the morning, for example, hoeing one acre; after completing the job, they were free for the rest of the day. The other, far more common, was the gang system, employed on the cotton, sugar, and tobacco plantations, under which slaves were simply divided into groups, each of them directed by a driver, and worked for as many hours as the overseer considered a reasonable workday.

Slaves were provided with at least enough necessities to enable them to live and work. They were furnished with an adequate if rough diet, consisting mainly of corn meal, salt pork, and molasses. Many were allowed to raise gardens for their own use and were issued fresh meat on special occasions. They received issues of cheap clothing and shoes. They lived in rude cabins, called slave quarters, usually clustered together in a complex near the master's house. Medical care was provided by the plantation mistress or by a doctor retained by the owner. Slaves worked hard, beginning with light tasks as children; and their workday was longest at harvest time. Slave women worked particularly hard. They generally shared the labor in the fields with the men, and they assumed as well the traditional women's chores of cooking, cleaning, and child rearing in the slave family.

Some historians have argued that the material conditions of slavery were, in fact, superior to those of Northern industrial workers. Whether or not that is true (and the evidence for this conclusion is at least

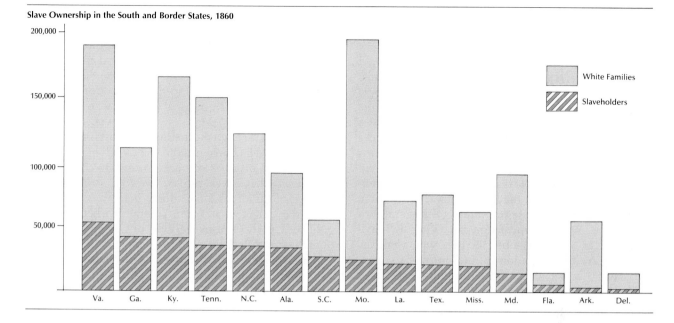

Slave Ownership in the South and Border States, 1860

White Families

Slaveholders

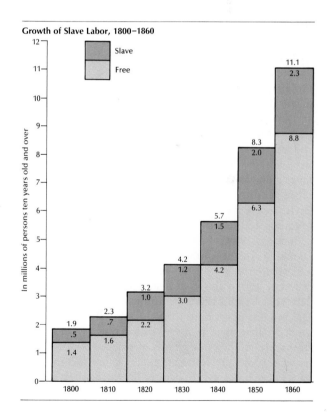

Growth of Slave Labor, 1800–1860

Slave

Free

debatable), the conditions of American slavery were undoubtedly less severe than those of slavery in the Caribbean and South America. There the slave supply was constantly replenished well into the nineteenth century by the African slave trade, giving owners less incentive to protect their existing laborers. Working and living conditions there were arduous, and masters at times literally worked their slaves to death. In the United States, in contrast, there were strong economic incentives to maintain a healthy slave population. One result of this was that America became the only country where a slave population actually increased through natural reproduction.

One example of the solicitude with which masters often treated their slaves was the frequent practice of using hired labor, when available, for the most unhealthy or dangerous tasks. A traveler in Louisiana noted, for example, that Irishmen were employed to clear malarial swamps and to handle cotton bales at the bottom of chutes extending from the river bluff down to a boat landing. If an Irishman died of disease or was killed in an accident, the master could hire another for a dollar a day or less. But he would lose perhaps $1,000 or more if he lost a prime field hand. Still, cruel masters might forget their pocketbooks in the heat of momentary anger. And slaves were often left to the discipline of overseers, who had no pecuniary stake in their well-being; overseers were paid in proportion to the amount of work they could get out of the slaves they supervised.

Household servants had a somewhat easier life—physically at least—than did field hands. On a small plantation, the same slaves might do both field work and house work; but on a large one, there would generally be a separate domestic staff: nursemaids, housemaids, cooks, butlers, coachmen. These people lived close to the master and his family, eating the leftovers from the family table and in some cases even sleeping in the "big house." Between the blacks and whites of such households affectionate, almost familial relationships might develop. More often, however, house servants resented their isolation from their fellow slaves and the lack of privacy that came with living in such close proximity to the family of the master. When emancipation came after the Civil War, it was often the house servants who were the first to leave the plantations of their former owners.

Slavery in the cities differed significantly from slavery in the country. On the relatively isolated plantations, slaves had little contact with free blacks and lower-class whites, and masters maintained a fairly direct and effective control; a deep and unbridgeable chasm yawned between slavery and freedom. In the city, however, a master often could not supervise his slaves closely and at the same time use them profitably. Even if they slept at night in carefully watched backyard barracks, they went about by day on errands of various kinds. Others—particularly skilled workers such as blacksmiths or carpenters—were hired out; and after hours they often fended for themselves, neither their owners nor their employers bothering to supervise them. Thus urban slaves gained numerous opportunities to mingle with free blacks and with whites. In the cities, the line between slavery and freedom remained, but it became less and less distinct.

Indeed, white Southerners generally considered slavery to be incompatible with city life; and as Southern cities grew, the number of slaves in them declined, relatively if not absolutely. The reasons were social rather than economic. Fearing conspiracies and insurrections, urban slaveowners sold off much of their male property to the countryside. The cities were left with an excess of black women while they continued to have an excess of white men (a situation that helped to account for the birth of many mulattoes). While slavery in the cities declined, segregation of blacks both free and slave increased. Segregation was a means of social control intended to make up for the loosening of the discipline of slavery itself.

The Continuing Slave Trade

The transfer of slaves from one part of the South to another was one of the most important demographic consequences of the development of the Southwest. Sometimes slaves moved to the new cotton lands in the company of their original owners, who were migrating themselves. More often, however, the transfer occurred through the medium of professional slave traders. Traders transported slaves over long distances on trains or on river or ocean steamers. On shorter journeys, the slaves moved on foot, trudging in coffles of hundreds along dusty highways. Eventually they arrived at some central market such as Natchez, New Orleans, Mobile, or Galveston, where purchasers collected to bid for them. At the auction, the bidders checked the slaves like livestock, watching them as they were made to walk or trot, inspecting their teeth, feeling their arms and legs, looking for signs of infirmity or age. It paid to be careful, for traders were known to deceive buyers by blacking gray hair, oiling withered skin, and concealing physical defects in other ways. A sound young field hand would fetch a price that, during the 1840s and 1850s, varied from $500 to $1,700, depending mainly on fluctuations in the price of cotton. The average figure was about $800, a substantial sum given the value of the dollar at the time. An attractive woman, desirable as a concubine, might bring several times that much.

The domestic slave trade was essential to the growth and prosperity of the whole system. It was also one of the most horrible aspects of it. The trade dehumanized all who were involved in it. It separated children from parents, and parents from each other. Even families kept together by scrupulous masters might be broken up in the division of the estate after the master's death. Planters condoned the trade and eased their consciences by holding the traders in contempt and assigning them a low social position.

The foreign slave trade was as bad or worse. Although federal law had prohibited the importation of slaves from 1808 on, they continued to be smuggled in as late as the 1850s. The numbers can only be guessed at. There were not enough such imports to satisfy all planters, and the Southern commercial conventions, which met annually to consider means of making the South economically independent, began to discuss the legal reopening of the trade. "If it is right to buy slaves in Virginia and carry them to New Orleans," William L. Yancey of Alabama asked his fellow delegates at the 1858 meeting, "why is it

The Slave Market
The trans-Atlantic slave trade was abolished long before 1852, the year of this painting. Slave auctions such as this one, therefore, almost always involved blacks being sold from one plantation to another. Younger men and women, capable of hard field work, were in particular demand and were thus especially likely to be separated from their families by sale. (Chicago Historical Society)

not right to buy them in Cuba, Brazil, or Africa and carry them there?" The convention that year voted to recommend the repeal of all laws against slave imports. Only the delegates from the states of the upper South, which profited from the domestic trade, opposed the foreign competition.

Slave Resistance

Few issues have sparked as much debate among historians as the effects of slavery on the blacks themselves. (See "Where Historians Disagree," pp. 334–335.) Slaveowners, and many white Americans for generations to come, liked to argue that the slaves were generally content, "happy with their lot." That may well have been true in some cases. But it is clear that the vast majority of Southern blacks were not content with being slaves, that they yearned for freedom even though most realized there was little they could do to secure it. Evidence for that conclusion comes, if from nowhere else, from the reaction of slaves when emancipation finally came. Virtually all Southern blacks reacted to freedom with joy and celebration; relatively few chose to remain in the service of the whites who had owned them before the Civil

WHERE HISTORIANS DISAGREE

The Nature of Plantation Slavery

Few subjects have produced so rich a historical literature in recent years as the nature of American slavery. And in that literature is lodged one of the liveliest of all scholarly debates. Even more vividly than other historical controversies, the argument over slavery illustrates the extent to which historians are influenced by the times in which they write. Popular attitudes about race have always found reflection in historical examinations of slavery. Never has that been more true than in the past two decades.

The first accounts of slavery, written before the Civil War by contemporaries of the institution, were usually stark expressions of the political beliefs of their authors. Southern chroniclers emphasized the benevolent features of the system, the paternalism with which masters cared for their slaves (a stark contrast, they implied, to the brutal impersonality of Northern factory owners and their "wage slaves"), and the carefree, happy demeanor of the slaves themselves. From Northern writers (many of them abolitionists) came a picture of slavery as a brutal, savage institution that dehumanized all who were touched by it. Theodore Dwight Weld's *American Slavery as It Is* (1839), for many years a widely cited book, depicted a system so horrible in its impact, it was little wonder the book inspired many of its readers to political action.

By the end of the nineteenth century, however, the political climate had changed. White Americans were now eager to foster a spirit of sectional reconciliation; and in both North and South, there was emerging—in popular literature, in folktales and myths, and increasingly in scholarship—a romantic vision of the Old South as a graceful and serene civilization. It was a receptive climate for the publication in 1918 of the most influential study of slavery of the time (and for many years thereafter): Ulrich B. Phillips's *American Negro Slavery*. Phillips portrayed slavery as an essentially benign institution, in which kindly masters looked after submissive, childlike, and generally contented blacks. Black people, he suggested, were for the most part lazy and irresponsible; and the occasional harshness of the slave system was simply a necessary part of supervising a backward labor force. The book was, in effect, an apology for the Southern slaveowner; and for nearly thirty years, it remained the authoritative work on the subject.

Beginning in the 1940s, when the nation began finally to confront forthrightly its legacy of racial injustice, new approaches to slavery started to emerge. As early as 1941, Melville J. Herskovits was challenging one of Phillips's assumptions: that slaves had retained little if any of their African cultural inheritance. In fact, Herskovits argued, many Africanisms survived in slave culture for generations. Two years later, Herbert Aptheker attacked another of Phillips's claims: that slaves were submissive and content. "Discontent and rebelliousness," he wrote in *American Negro Slave Revolts,* "were not only exceedingly common, but, indeed, characteristic of American Negro slaves."

But for a time, at least, the more influential challenge to Phillips came from those who claimed that he had neglected the brutality of the system and the damage it did to those who lived under it. Kenneth Stampp's *The Peculiar Institution* (1956), the first comprehensive study of slavery since Phillips, emphasized the harshness of the system—not only its physical brutality but its psychological impact on men and women kept in a virtual prison, with little room to develop their own social and cultural patterns. An even more devastating portrait of slavery came from Stanley Elkins, whose *Slavery* (1959) argued that many slaves had, indeed, displayed childlike, submissive, "Sambo"

War (although most blacks, of course, remained for many years subservient to whites in one way or another).

Rather than contented acceptance, the dominant response of blacks to slavery was a complex one: a combination of adaptation and resistance. At the extremes, slavery could produce two opposite reactions—each of which served as the basis for a powerful stereotype in white society. One extreme was what became known as the "Sambo"—the shuffling, grinning, head-scratching, deferential slave who acted out the role that he recognized the white expected of him.

WHERE HISTORIANS DISAGREE

personalities, as Phillips had suggested. But to Elkins, such personalities were evidence of the terrible damage the institution had inflicted on them. Comparing the slave system to Nazi concentration camps in World War II, he cited the effects on the individual of enforced "adjustment to absolute power" and the tragic distortions of character that resulted.

Stampp and Elkins reflected the general belief of white liberals in the 1950s and early 1960s that their society bore a large measure of guilt for the injustices it had inflicted on blacks, that whites must work to undo the damage they had done in the past. By the early 1970s, however, racial attitudes had changed again, with the emergence of the "black power" ideology and the widespread belief among blacks and some whites that blacks themselves should determine their own future. The new emphasis on black pride and achievement, therefore, helped produce a new view of the black past, emphasizing the cultural and social accomplishments of blacks under slavery. John Blassingame, in *The Slave Community* (1973), echoed the approach of Herskovits thirty years before in arguing that "the most remarkable aspect of the whole process of enslavement is the extent to which the American-born slaves were able to retain their ancestors' culture." Herbert Gutman, in *The Black Family in Slavery and Freedom, 1750–1925* (1976), provided voluminous evidence to support his claim that the black family, far from being weakened and destroyed by the slave system, survived with remarkable strength—although with some differences from the prevailing form of the white family. The slave community, Gutman claimed, was so successful in preserving and developing its own culture that the master class was unable, despite its great legal power, to affect it in any significant way.

This emphasis on the ability of blacks to maintain their own culture and society under slavery, and on their remarkable achievements within the system, formed the basis of two studies in 1974 that claimed to present comprehensive new portraits of the entire system. *Time on the Cross,* by Robert Fogel and Stanley Engerman, used quantitative methods to show not only that slaves were skilled and efficient workers, not only that the black family was strong and healthy, but that the institution of slavery was a prosperous one that benefited masters and slaves alike. Slave workers, Fogel and Engerman claimed, were generally better off than Northern industrial workers. Slaves often rose to managerial positions on plantations. Whippings were few, and families were rarely broken up. The findings of *Time on the Cross* soon came under harsh attack—both from those who were offended by what they considered its apology for slavery and, more important, from historians who claimed to have discovered crucial flaws in Fogel and Engerman's methods. More influential in the long run was Eugene Genovese's *Roll, Jordan, Roll: The World the Slaves Made.* Genovese revived the idea of "paternalism" as the central element of the slave system. But in his view, paternalism was not an expression of white generosity; it was a powerful instrument of control. And it worked in two directions, enabling blacks to make demands of whites as well as the other way around. Moreover, within this paternal system, Genovese claimed, blacks retained a large cultural "space" of their own within which they developed their own family life, traditions, social patterns, and above all religion. Indeed, slaves had by the mid-nineteenth century developed a sense of themselves as part of a separate black "nation"—a nation tied to white society in important ways, but nevertheless powerful and distinct.

More often than not, the "Sambo" pattern of behavior was a charade, a façade assumed in the presence of whites. In some cases, however, it might have represented more than that—the tragic distortion of personality that the rigors of slavery inflicted on its victims. The other extreme was the slave rebel—the

black who could not bring himself or herself to either acceptance or accommodation but harbored an unquenchable spirit of rebelliousness. Here, too, there may at times have been personality disorders at work (as is suggested by newspaper advertisements for runaways who were described as having stutters or other behavioral quirks). It was, after all, a somewhat abnormal act to rise up in rebellion against odds so overwhelming that there existed virtually no chance of success. Yet to attribute slave rebellions to mental disorder is to accept a largely white point of view. It is also possible to see in the rebellious slave signs of a strength and courage far greater than most white Southerners were disposed to admit black people could possess.

Actual slave revolts were extremely rare, but the knowledge that they were possible struck terror into the hearts of white Southerners everywhere. In 1800, Gabriel Prosser gathered 1,000 rebellious slaves outside Richmond, but two blacks gave the plot away, and the Virginia militia was called out in time to head it off. Prosser and 35 others were executed. In 1822, the Charleston free black Denmark Vesey and his followers—rumored to total 9,000—made preparations for revolt; but again the word leaked out, and retribution followed. In 1831, Nat Turner, a slave preacher, led a band of blacks who armed themselves with guns and axes and, on a summer night, went from house to house in Southampton County, Virginia. They slaughtered sixty white men, women, and children before being overpowered by state and federal troops. More than a hundred blacks were put to death in the aftermath. Nat Turner's was the only actual slave insurrection in the nineteenth-century South, but slave conspiracies and threats of renewed violence continued throughout the section as long as slavery lasted.

For the most part, however, resistance to slavery took other, less drastic forms. In some cases, slaves worked "within the system" to free themselves from it—earning money with which they managed to buy their own and their families' freedom. Some had the good fortune to be set free by their master's will after his death—for example, the more than 400 slaves belonging to John Randolph of Roanoke, freed in 1833. From the 1830s on, however, state laws made it more and more difficult, and in some cases practically impossible, for an owner to manumit his slaves. The laws, when permitting manumission, often required the removal of the freed slaves from the state. Slaveowners objected to the very presence of free blacks, who by their existence set a disturbing example for the slaves.

By 1860, there nevertheless were about 250,000 free blacks in the slaveholding states, more than half of them in Virginia and Maryland. A few (generally on the northern fringes of the slaveholding regions) attained wealth and prominence. Some owned slaves themselves, usually relatives whom they had bought in order to ensure their ultimate emancipation. Most, however, lived in abject poverty, under conditions worse than those afflicting blacks in the North. Law or custom closed many occupations to them, forbade them to assemble without white supervision, and placed numerous other restraints on them. They were only quasi-free, and yet they had all the burdens of freedom: the necessity to support themselves, to find housing, to pay taxes. Yet great as were the hardships of freedom, blacks usually preferred them to slavery.

Some blacks attempted to resist slavery by escaping from it, by running away. A small number managed to escape to the North or to Canada, especially after sympathetic whites began organizing the so-called underground railroad to assist them in flight. But the odds against a successful escape, particularly from the Deep South, were almost impossibly great. The hazards of distance and the slaves' ignorance of geography were serious obstacles. So were the white "slave patrols," which stopped wandering blacks on sight throughout the South demanding to see travel permits. Without such a permit, slaves were presumed to be runaways and were taken captive. For blacks who attempted to escape through the woods, slave patrols often employed bloodhounds. Despite all the obstacles to success, however, blacks continued to run away from their masters in large numbers. Some did so repeatedly, undeterred by the whippings and other penalties inflicted on them when captured.

But perhaps the most important method of resistance was simply a pattern of everyday behavior by which blacks defied their masters. That whites so often considered blacks to be lazy and shiftless suggests one means of resistance: refusal to work hard. Slaves might also steal from their masters or from neighboring whites. They might perform isolated acts of sabotage: losing or breaking tools (Southern planters gradually began to buy unusually heavy hoes because so many of the lighter ones got broken) or performing tasks improperly. In extreme cases, blacks might make themselves useless by cutting off their fingers or even committing suicide. Or, despite the terrible consequences, they might on occasion turn on their masters and kill them. The extremes, however, were rare. For the most part, blacks resisted by building into their normal patterns of behavior subtle methods of rebellion.

Harriet Tubman with Escaped Slaves
Harriet Tubman (c. 1820–1913) was born into slavery in Maryland. In 1849, when her master died, she escaped to Phila-delphia to avoid being sold out of state. Over the next ten years, she assisted first members of her own family and then up to 300 other slaves to escape from Maryland to freedom. During the Civil War, she served alternately as a nurse and as a spy for Union forces in South Carolina. She is shown here, on the left, with some of the slaves she had helped to free. (Smith College)

Slave Religion and the Black Family

But resistance was only part of the slave response to slavery. The other was an elaborate process of adap-tation—a process that did not imply contentment with bondage but a recognition that there was no realistic alternative. One of the ways blacks adapted was by developing a rich and complex culture, one that en-abled them to keep a sense of racial pride and unity. In many areas, they retained a language of their own, sometimes incorporating African speech patterns into English. They developed a distinctive music, estab-lishing in the process what was perhaps the most impressive of all American musical traditions. The most important features of black culture, however, were the development of two powerful institutions: religion and the family.

A separate slave religion was not supposed to ex-ist. Almost all blacks were Christians, and their mas-ters expected them to worship under the supervision of white ministers—often in the same chapels as whites. Indeed, autonomous black churches were banned by law. Nevertheless, blacks throughout the South developed their own version of Christianity, at times incorporating such African practices as voo-doo, but more often simply bending religion to the special circumstances of bondage. Natural leaders emerging within the slave community rose to the

SIGNIFICANT EVENTS

1831 Nat Turner slave rebellion breaks out in Virginia

1834 Cyrus McCormick patents mechanical reaper

1837 Oberlin becomes first men's college to accept woman students

Mount Holyoke Seminary for women founded

1842 Massachusetts supreme court, in *Commonwealth* v. *Hunt,* declares unions and strikes legal

1844 Samuel F. B. Morse sends first telegraphic message

1845 Irish potato famine begins, spurring major emigration to America

1846 Rotary press invented, making possible rapid printing of newspapers

Associated Press organized

1848 Failed revolution in Germany spurs emigration to America

1849 Rise in cotton prices spurs production boom

1852 American party (Know-Nothings) formed

---

rank of preacher; and when necessary, blacks would hold services in secret, often at night.

Black religion was far more emotional than its white counterparts, and it reflected the influence of African customs and practices. Slave prayer meetings routinely involved fervent chanting, spontaneous exclamations from the congregation, and ecstatic conversion experiences. Black religion was also more joyful and affirming than that of many white denominations. And above all, black religion emphasized the dream of freedom and deliverance. In their prayers and songs and sermons, black Christians talked and sang of the day when the Lord would "call us home," "deliver us to freedom," "take us to the Promised Land." And while their white masters generally chose to interpret such language merely as the expression of hopes for life after death, blacks themselves were undoubtedly using the images of Christian salvation to express their own dream of freedom in the present world.

The slave family was the other crucial institution of black culture in the South. Like religion, it suffered from certain legal restrictions—most notably the lack of legal marriage. Nevertheless, the nuclear family consistently emerged as the dominant kinship pattern among blacks. Such families did not always operate precisely according to white customs. A black couple would often begin living together before declaring any intent to marry; and a black woman would often bear a child before becoming wed. But family ties were generally no less strong than those of whites,

and many slave marriages lasted throughout the course of long lifetimes.

When marriages did not survive, it was often because of circumstances over which blacks had no control. Up to a third of all black families were broken up by the slave trade. And that accounted for some of the other distinctive characteristics of the black family, which adapted itself to the cruel realities of its own uncertain future. Networks of kinship—which grew to include not only spouses and their children, but aunts, uncles, grandparents, even distant cousins—remained strong and important and often served to compensate for the breakup of nuclear families. A slave suddenly moved to a new area, far from his or her family, might create "fictional" kinship ties and become "adopted" by a family in the new community. Even so, the impulse to maintain contact with a spouse and children remained strong long after the breakup of a family. One of the most frequent causes of escape from the plantation was a slave's desire to find a husband, wife, or child who had been sent elsewhere. It was not only by breaking up families through sale that whites intruded on black family life. Black women, usually powerless to resist the sexual advances of their masters, often bore the children of whites—children whom the whites seldom recognized as their own and who were consigned to slavery from birth.

In addition to establishing social and cultural institutions of their own, slaves adapted themselves to slavery by forming complex relationships with their masters. However much blacks resented their lack of freedom, they often found it difficult to maintain an entirely hostile attitude toward their owners. Not only were they dependent on whites for the material means of existence—food, clothing, and shelter; they also often derived from their masters a sense of security and protection. There was, in short, a paternal relationship between slave and master—sometimes harsh, sometimes kindly, but almost invariably important. That paternalism, in fact, became (even if not always consciously) a vital instrument of white control. By creating a sense of mutual dependence, whites helped to reduce resistance to an institution that, in essence, was designed solely for the benefit of the ruling race.

SUGGESTED READINGS

The Northern Economy Most of the books on economic development cited in the readings for Chapters 7 and 9 are relevant for the changes described in this chapter as well. In particular, see the works by Brownlee, Bruchey, and North for useful overviews. See also Thomas C. Cochran, *Frontiers of Change: Early Industrialization in America* (1981), and David A. Hounshell, *From the American System to Mass Production, 1800–1932: The Development of Manufacturing Technology in the United States* (1985). For the expansion of agriculture, see Paul W. Gates, *The Farmer's Age* (1960). Peter Temin, *Iron and Steel in Nineteenth-Century America* (1964), examines one of the growing industries of the antebellum period. Alfred D. Chandler, Jr., *The Visible Hand: The Managerial Revolution in American Business* (1977), is an important study of the origins of modern business management, beginning in the 1850s. James Norris, *R. G. Dun & Co., 1841–1900* (1978), is a study of the growth of a single company; and Joseph E. Walker, *Hopewell: A Social and Economic History of an Ironmaking Community* (1966), is an examination of a single town. On the growth of railroads, see, in addition to the books cited in the readings for Chapter 9, Robert W. Fogel, *Railroads and American Economic Growth* (1964), a controversial quantitative study that questions the centrality of railroads to American economic growth. Carter Goodrich, *Government Promotion of Canals and Railroads, 1800–1890* (1960), examines the role of the state in building transportation systems. See also two works by John F. Stover: *The Life and Decline of the American Railroad* (1970), a broadly focused work, and *Iron Road to the West: American Railroads in the 1850s* (1978), narrower in scope. R. L. Thompson, *Wiring a Continent* (1947), studies the early growth of the telegraph system.

Immigration Two books by Marcus Hansen—*The Immigrant in American History* (1940) and *The Atlantic Migration, 1607–1860* (1940)—are valuable surveys, along with Maldwyn A. Jones, *American Immigration* (1960). Several studies examine the experiences of immigrants on their arrival in the United States: Oscar Handlin, *The Uprooted* (1951, rev. 1973); Charlotte Erickson, *Invisible Immigrants* (1972); Philip Taylor, *The Distant Magnet* (1971); Robert Ernst, *Immigrant Life in New York City, 1825–1863* (1949); Kathleen N. Conzen, *Immigrant Milwaukee: 1836-1860* (1976); and Carl Wittke, *We Who Built America*, rev. ed.

(1964). On particular immigrant groups, see Oscar Handlin, *Boston's Immigrants* (1941), which focuses largely on the Irish; Harold Runblom and Hans Norman, *From Sweden to America* (1976); Carl Wittke, *Refugees of Revolution: The German Forty-Eighters in America* (1952) and *The Irish in America* (1956); Theodore C. Blegen, *Norwegian Migration to America*, 2 vols. (1931–1940); Stuart C. Miller, *The Unwelcome Immigrant* (1969), on the Chinese; and Rowland T. Berthoff, *British Immigrants in Industrial America, 1790–1950* (1953). Jay P. Dolan, *The Immigrant Church: New York's Irish and German Catholics* (1975), examines immigrant religion. On mid-nineteenth-century nativism, see Ray Billington, *The Protestant Crusade, 1800–1860* (1938), a valuable study of anti-Catholicism. I. M. Leonard and R. D. Parmet, *American Nativism, 1830-1860* (1971), is a more general view, as is T. J. Curran, *Xenophobia and Immigration* (1975). Allan Nevins, *The Ordeal of the Union*, 2 vols. (1947), also contains an analysis of antebellum nativism.

Labor In addition to works cited in the readings for Chapter 9, useful studies of antebellum labor include Susan E. Hirsch, *Roots of the American Working Class: The Industrialization of Crafts in Newark, 1800–1860* (1978); Bruce Laurie, *Working People of Philadelphia* (1980); Norman Ware, *The Industrial Worker, 1840–1860* (1924), a pioneering work that remains valuable; Henry Pelling, *American Labor* (1960), a concise survey; and Hannah Josephson, *The Golden Threads* (1949), a study of mill girls and their employers in New England.

Northern Society and Culture Many community studies examine society and culture in industrializing America, as well as the conditions of labor and immigrants. Among the most valuable are Alan Dawley, *Class and Community: The Industrial Revolution in Lynn* (1977); Michael Frisch, *Town into City: Springfield, Massachusetts, and the Meaning of Community, 1840–1880* (1972); Peter Knights, *The Plain People of Boston, 1830–1860* (1971); Don Doyle, *The Social Order of a Frontier Community: Jacksonville, Illinois, 1825–1870* (1978); and Stuart Blumin, *The Urban Threshold: Growth and Change in a Nineteenth-Century Community* (1976). Sam Bass Warner, Jr., *The Urban Wilderness* (1972), examines urban growth, as does Richard C. Wade, *The Urban Frontier, 1790–1830* (1957). Raymond A. Mohl, *Poverty in New York,*

1783–1825 (1971), and Edward Pessen, *Riches, Classes, and Power Before the Civil War* (1973), explore economic stratification and poverty. Stephan Thernstrom, *Poverty and Progress* (1964), is an important study of social mobility in nineteenth-century Newburyport, Massachusetts. A good introduction to the skimpy literature on the history of journalism is Frank Luther Mott, *American Journalism* (1950). Glyndon Van Deusen, *Horace Greeley* (1953), examines a leading nineteenth-century editor.

The Southern Mind   The question of what distinguished the South from the rest of the nation has produced a large literature and a wide range of viewpoints. A classic analysis, one that has been the source of much later theorizing and has spawned great controversy, is W. J. Cash, *The Mind of the South* (1941). Avery Craven, *The Growth of Southern Nationalism* (1953), emphasizes political developments but includes discussion of social and cultural factors. John McCardell, *The Idea of a Southern Nation* (1979), considers the social and intellectual roots of Southern nationalism; Charles S. Sydnor, *The Development of Southern Sectionalism, 1819–1848* (1948), examines an earlier period. Two works by Clement Eaton—*Freedom of Thought in the Old South* (1940) and *The Growth of Southern Nationalism, 1848–1861* (1961)—discuss the intellectual history of the region. William R. Taylor, *Cavalier and Yankee: The Old South and American National Character* (1961), is an important study of Southern culture, viewed largely through its literary products. Rollin G. Osterweis, *Romanticism and Nationalism in the Old South* (1949), and John Hope Franklin, *The Militant South* (1956), take contrasting views of the Southern outlook. Two works by Drew Gilpin Faust—*A Sacred Circle: The Dilemma of the Intellectual in the Old South* (1977) and *James Henry Hammond and the Old South: A Design for Mastery* (1982)—examine Southern intellectuals. Bertram Wyatt-Brown, *Southern Honor: Ethics and Behavior in the Old South* (1982), and Edward L. Ayers, *Vengeance and Justice* (1984), examine the values of Southern white male culture. On Southern white religion, see Donald G. Mathews, *Religion in the Old South* (1977), and Ann C. Loveland, *Southern Evangelicals and the Social Order, 1800–1860* (1980). Frank Freidel, *Francis Lieber* (1947), is a biography of a prominent antebellum Southern educator and reformer.

The Plantation Economy   The economy of the plantation South is examined in Gavin Wright, *The Political Economy of the Cotton South: Households, Markets, and Wealth in the Nineteenth Century* (1978). Earlier studies of importance include Lewis C. Gray, *History of Agriculture in the Southern United States to 1860*, 2 vols. (1933); Ulrich B. Phillips, *Life and Labor in the Old South* (1929); and R. R. Russel, *Economic Aspects of Southern Sectionalism, 1840–1861* (1924). Frank L. Owsley, *Plain Folk of the Old South* (1949), and Ralph A. Wooster, *Politicians, Planters, and Plain Folk* (1975), examine the economy and society of poor Southern whites.

The Planters   Several collections of letters and diaries by white Southerners themselves offer particularly vivid portraits of life in the Old South. See especially Robert Manson Myers (ed.), *The Children of Pride* (1972); Mary D. Robertson (ed.), *Lucy Breckinridge of Grove Hill* (1979); Carol Bleser, *The Hammonds of Redcliffe* (1981); and Frances Ann Kemble, *Journal of a Residence on a Georgian Plantation in 1838–1839* (1863). The world of the slaveowners themselves is examined in two books by Eugene Genovese—*The Political Economy of Slavery* (1965) and *The World the Slaveholders Made* (1969)—and in James Oakes, *The Ruling Race: A History of American Slaveholders* (1982).

Southern White Women   Anne Firor Scott, *The Southern Lady* (1970), and Catherine Clinton, *The Plantation Mistress: Woman's World in the Old South* (1982), offer contrasting views of the position of white women in antebellum Southern society; Mary Boykin Chesnut, *A Diary from Dixie* (1981, ed. by C. Vann Woodward), is an eloquent record of the views of a prominent Southern woman as her society began to crumble. Suzanne Lebsock, *The Free Women of Petersburg: Status and Culture in a Southern Town* (1984), examines the role of women in a Southern community. Jane Turner Censer, *North Carolina Planters and Their Children, 1800–1860* (1984), challenges the claims of other historians that the Southern white family was fundamentally different from the Northern family.

Slavery   The nature of American slavery is the subject of a vast literature. An influential early study of the subject is Ulrich B. Phillips, *American Negro Slavery* (1918), a work of scholarship flawed by the apparent proslavery bias of its author. Kenneth Stampp, *The Peculiar Institution* (1956), and Stanley Elkins, *Slavery* (1959), are more hostile studies written from the perspective of liberals in the 1950s. Studies emphasizing black culture and achievement, as well as resistance to slavery, began to emerge in the 1940s with Herbert Aptheker, *American Negro Slave Revolts* (1943), and Melville J. Herskovits, *The Myth of the Negro Past* (1941). Such studies proliferated in the 1970s, beginning with John Blassingame, *The Slave Community* (1973). Eugene Genovese, *Roll, Jordan, Roll: The World the Slaves Made* (1974), is one of the most important studies of slave society and the roots of black culture. Herbert Gutman, *The Black Family in Slavery and Freedom, 1750–1925* (1976), is a major study of one of the most important elements of slave culture. Other studies of slave culture include Judith Chase, *Afro-American Art and Craft* (1971), which emphasizes black artistic achievement; and Dena Epstein, *Sinful Tunes and Spirituals* (1977), and Lawrence W. Levine, *Black Culture and Black Consciousness: Afro-American Folk Thought from Slavery to Freedom* (1977), which emphasize music and folk culture. Michael P. Johnson and James L. Roark, *Black Masters* (1984), examines the rare phenomenon of free blacks owning slaves. G. P. Rawick, *From Sundown to Sunup: The Making of the Black Community* (1973), examines plantation life. Leslie Howard Owens, *This Species of Property* (1976), is a useful survey employing recent scholarship. A controversial quantitative study of the slave economy is Robert Fogel and Stanley Engerman, *Time on the Cross,* 2 vols. (1974), which has been attacked by, among others, Herbert Gutman, *Slavery and the Numbers Game* (1975), and P. A. David et al., *Reckoning with Slavery* (1976). Jacqueline Jones, *Labor of Love, Labor of Sorrow* (1985), is an important study of black women. Robert Starobin, *Industrial Slavery in the Old South* (1970), and Richard C. Wade, *Slavery in the Cities* (1964), examine the institution away from the plantation. Stephen B. Oates, *The Fires of Jubilee* (1974), examines the Nat Turner uprising; and Robert Starobin, *Denmark Vesey* (1970), discusses the Vesey conspiracy. Carl Degler, *Neither Black nor White* (1971), is a comparative study of race relations in Brazil and the United States. Joel Williamson, *New People: Miscegenation and Mulattoes in the United States* (1980), is a study of the sensitive subject of race mixture. Ira Berlin, *Slaves Without Masters* (1974), considers free blacks in the antebellum South; Leon Litwack, *North of Slavery* (1961), examines free blacks in the North. Orlando Patterson, *Slavery and Social Death: A Comparative Study* (1982), examines slavery in different cultures and different eras. David Brion Davis, *Slavery and Human Progress* (1984), is an important intellectual study of changing white attitudes toward slavery.

***Girls' Evening School,* Anonymous, c. 1840**   (Museum of Fine Arts, Boston)

Chapter 12

An Age of Reforms

The American people in the mid-nineteenth century lived in a society in transition. Their nation was growing rapidly in geographical extent, in the size and diversity of its population, and in the dimensions and complexity of its economy. And like any people faced with such rapid and fundamental alterations in their surroundings, Americans reacted with ambiguity. On the one hand, they were excited by the new possibilities that economic growth was providing. On the other hand, they were painfully aware of the dislocations that it was creating: the challenges to traditional values and institutions, the social instability, the uncertainty about the future.

The result of these conflicting attitudes was the emergence of a bewildering array of movements intended to adapt society to its new realities, to "reform" the nation. These reform efforts took so many different shapes that generalizations about them are difficult, but in general they reflected one of two basic impulses, and at times elements of both. Many of these movements rested on an optimistic faith in human nature, a belief that within every individual resided a spirit that was basically good and that society should attempt to unleash. This assumption—which spawned in both Europe and America a movement known, in its artistic aspects at least, as romanticism—stood in marked contrast to the traditional Calvinist assumption that human impulses and instincts were evil and needed to be repressed. Instead, reformers now argued, individuals should strive to give full expression to the inner spirit, should work to unleash their capacity to experience joy and to do good.

A second impulse, which appeared directly to contradict the first but in practice often existed alongside it, was a desire for order and control. With their society changing so rapidly, with their traditional values and institutions being challenged and eroded, many Americans yearned above all for a restoration of stability and discipline to their nation. Often, this impulse embodied a conservative nostalgia for better, simpler times. But it also inspired efforts to create new institutions of social control, suited to the realities of the new age.

The reforms that flowed from these two impulses came in many guises and embraced many different groups within the population. But the heart of reform activity remained always the Northeast, in particular New England; and in the course of the 1840s, the focus of this core group of reformers began to shift to one issue that came to overshadow all others: slavery. Not all Northern reformers agreed on how precisely to deal with the existence of slavery in their nation, but virtually all came to believe that the institution was an evil that must ultimately be eliminated. And in taking this position, they added another powerful force to the many that were driving a wedge between America's two major sections.

Culture and Liberation

"In the four quarters of the globe," wrote the English wit Sydney Smith in 1820, "who reads an American book? or goes to an American play? or looks at an American picture or statue?" The answer, he assumed, was obvious: no one.

American intellectuals were painfully aware of the low regard in which their culture was held by Europeans; and they continued in the middle decades of the century to work for a liberation of their nation's culture—for the creation of an American artistic life independent of Europe, one that would express their own nation's special virtues. At the same time, however, the nation's cultural leaders were beginning to strive for another kind of liberation, one that would gradually come almost to overshadow their self-conscious nationalism. That impulse, which was—ironically—largely an import from Europe, was the spirit of romanticism. In literature, in philosophy, in art, even in politics and economics, American intellectuals were committing themselves to the liberation of the human spirit.

A Literary Flowering

The effort to create a distinctively American literature, which Washington Irving and others had advanced in the first decades of the century, bore important fruit in the 1820s with the emergence of the first great American novelist: James Fenimore Cooper. The author of over thirty novels in the space of three decades, Cooper was known to his contemporaries as a master of adventure and suspense. What most distinguished his work, however, was its evocation of the American frontier. Cooper had grown up in central New York, at a time when the wilderness was not far away; and he retained throughout his life a fascination with man's relationship to nature and with the challenges (and dangers) of America's expansion westward. His most important novels—the "Leatherstocking Tales," among them *The Last of the Mohicans* (1826) and *The Deerslayer* (1841)—explored the American frontiersman's experience with Indians, pioneers, violence, and the law.

Cooper's novels were a continuation, in many ways a culmination, of the early nineteenth-century effort to produce a truly American literature. But they also served as a link to the concerns of later intellectuals. For in the "Leatherstocking Tales" could be seen not only a celebration of the American spirit and landscape but an evocation, through the character of Natty Bumppo, of the ideal of the independent individual, with a natural inner goodness. There was also evidence of the second impulse that would motivate American reform: the fear of disorder. In portraying other characters, who exemplified the vicious,

Leatherstocking

James Fenimore Cooper published *The Pathfinder* in 1840, fourteen years after *The Last of the Mohicans,* the previous volume in his "Leatherstocking" series. The period between the two novels had been a generally unsuccessful one for Cooper. It included a restless seven-year absence from the United States and, after his return, several years devoted largely to ill-tempered criticism of American society, which, Cooper claimed, had become vulgar and materialistic. The "Leatherstocking" series—which also included *The Pioneers* (1823), *The Prairie* (1827), and *The Deerslayer* (1841)—chronicled the life of Natty Bumppo, a fictional "natural man" comfortable only in the wilderness. (Bumppo bore at least some similarity to the legendary Daniel Boone, who had died in 1820.) (Culver Pictures) grasping nature of some of the nation's Western settlers, Cooper was suggesting a need for social discipline even in the wilderness.

Emerging on the heels of Cooper was another group of important American writers who displayed even more clearly the grip of romanticism on the nation's intellectual life. Walt Whitman, the self-proclaimed poet of American democracy, was the son of a Long Island carpenter and lived for many years roaming the country doing odd jobs. Finally, in 1855, he hired a printer and published a first, thin volume of work: *Leaves of Grass.* His poems were an unrestrained celebration of democracy, of the liberation of the individual, and of the pleasures of the flesh as well as of the spirit. In these poems, as well as in a large body of other work spanning nearly forty more years until his death in 1892, Whitman not only helped liberate verse from traditional, restrictive conventions but helped express the questing spirit of individualism that characterized his age.

But the new literary concern with the unleashing of human emotions did not always produce optimistic and exuberant works. Herman Melville is a case in point. Born in New York in 1819, Melville ran away to sea as a youth and spent years sailing the world (including the South Seas) before returning home to become the greatest American writer of his era. The most important of his novels was *Moby Dick,* published in 1851. His portrayal of Ahab, the powerful, driven captain of a whaling vessel, was a story of courage and of the strength of individual will; but it was also a tragedy of pride and revenge. Ahab's maniacal search for a great white whale, Moby Dick, who had maimed him, suggested how the search for personal fulfillment and triumph could not only liberate but destroy. The result of Ahab's great quest was the annihilation of Ahab himself.

Similarly bleak were the works of one of the few Southern writers of the time to embrace the search for the essence of the human spirit: Edgar Allan Poe. In the course of his short and unhappy life (he died in 1849 at the age of forty), Poe produced stories and poems that were primarily sad and macabre. His first book, *Tamerlane and Other Poems* (1827), received little recognition. But later works, including his most famous poem, "The Raven" (1845), established him as a major, if controversial, literary figure. Through it all, Poe evoked images of individuals rising above the narrow confines of intellect and exploring the deeper world of the spirit and the emotions. Yet that world, he seemed to say, was one of pain and horror.

Other American writers were contemptuous of Poe's work and his message, but he was ultimately to have a profound effect on European poets such as Baudelaire.

Poe, however, was something of an exception in the world of Southern literature. The South experienced a literary flowering of its own in the mid-nineteenth century, and it produced writers and artists who were, like their Northern counterparts, concerned with defining the nature of American society and of the American nation. But Southerners tended to produce very different images of what that society was and should be.

Southern novelists of the 1830s (among them Beverly Tucker, William Alexander Caruthers, and John Pendleton Kennedy), some of them writers of great talent, many of them residents of Richmond, produced historical romances or romantic eulogies of the plantation system of the upper South. In the 1840s, the Southern literary capital moved to Charleston, home of the most distinguished of the region's men of letters: William Gilmore Simms. For a time, his work expressed a broad nationalism that transcended his regional background; but by the 1840s he had become a strong defender of Southern institutions—especially slavery—against the encroachments of the North. There was, he believed, a unique quality to Southern life that it was the duty of intellectuals to defend.

One group of Southern writers, however, produced works that were more distinctively American and less committed to a glorification of the peculiarities of Southern life. These were the writers of the frontier, who depicted the society of the backwoods rural areas. Writers such as Augustus B. Longstreet, Joseph G. Baldwin, and Johnson J. Hooper focused not on aristocratic "cavaliers," but on ordinary people and poor whites. Instead of romanticizing their subjects, they were deliberately and sometimes painfully realistic. And they seasoned their sketches with a robust, vulgar humor that was something new in American literature. These Southern realists established a tradition of American regional humor that was ultimately to find a supreme exponent in Mark Twain.

The Transcendentalists

The outstanding expression of the romantic impulse in America came from a group of New England writers and philosophers known as the transcendentalists. Borrowing heavily from German philosophers such as Kant, Hegel, and Schelling, and from the English writers Coleridge and Carlyle, the transcendentalists embraced a theory of the individual that rested on a distinction (first suggested by Kant) between what they called "reason" and "understanding." Reason, as they defined it, was the highest human faculty; it was the individual's innate capacity to grasp beauty and truth by giving full expression to the instincts and emotions. Understanding, by contrast, was the use of intellect in the narrow, artificial ways imposed by society; it involved the repression of instinct and the victory of externally imposed learning. Every person's goal, therefore, should be liberation from the confines of "understanding" and cultivation of "reason." Each individual should strive to "transcend" the limits of the intellect and allow the emotions, the "soul," to create an "original relation to the Universe."

Transcendentalist philosophy emerged first among a small group of intellectuals centered in Concord, Massachusetts. Their leader and most eloquent voice was Ralph Waldo Emerson. A Unitarian minister in his youth, Emerson left the church in 1832 to devote himself entirely to writing and teaching the elements of transcendentalism. He produced a significant body of poetry, but he was most renowned for his essays and lectures. In "Nature" (1836), one of his best-known essays, Emerson wrote that in the quest for self-fulfillment, individuals should work for a communion with the natural world: "in the woods, we return to reason and faith. . . . Standing on the bare ground,—my head bathed by the blithe air, and uplifted into infinite space,—all mean egotism vanishes. . . . I am part and particle of God." In other essays, he was even more explicit in advocating a commitment of the individual to the full exploration of inner capacities. "Nothing is at last sacred," he wrote in "Self-Reliance" (1841), perhaps his most famous essay, "but the integrity of your own mind." The quest for self-reliance, he explained, was really a search for communion with the unity of the universe, the wholeness of God, the great spiritual force that he described as the "Oversoul." Each person's innate capacity to become, through his or her private efforts, a part of this essence was perhaps the classic expression of the romantic belief in the "divinity" of the individual.

Almost as influential as Emerson was another leading Concord transcendentalist, Henry David Thoreau. Thoreau went even further than his friend Emerson in repudiating the repressive forces of society, which produced, he said, "lives of quiet desperation." Each individual should work for self-realization by breaking all ties with organized civilization, by attempting to create a private world in which he or she communed only with nature. Thoreau's own effort to create such a world—immortalized in his most famous book, *Walden* (1854)—led him to build an isolated cabin in the Concord woods on the edge of Walden Pond, where he lived for two years as simply as he could. "I went to the woods," he explained, "because I wished to live deliberately, to front only the essential facts of life, and see if I could not learn what it had to teach, and not, when I came to die, discover that I had not lived." Thoreau's rejection of what he considered the artificial constraints of society extended as well to his relationship with government. In 1846, he went to jail (briefly) rather than agree to pay a poll tax. He would not, he insisted, give financial support to a government that permitted the existence of slavery. In his 1849 essay "Resistance to Civil Government," he explained his refusal by claiming that the individual's personal morality had the first claim on his or her actions, that a government which required violation of that morality had no legitimate authority. The proper response was "civil disobedience," or "passive resistance"—a public refusal to obey unjust laws.

Visions of Utopia

Although transcendentalism was above all an individualistic philosophy, it helped to spawn the most famous of all nineteenth-century experiments in communal living: Brook Farm. The dream of the Boston transcendentalist George Ripley, Brook Farm was established as an experimental community in West Roxbury, Massachusetts, in 1841. There, according to Ripley, individuals would gather to create a new form of social organization, one that would permit every member of the community full opportunity for self-realization. All residents would share equally in the labor of the community so that all could share too in the leisure; for it was leisure that was the first necessity for cultivation of the self. (Ripley was one of the first Americans to attribute positive connotations to the idea of leisure; most of his contemporaries equated it with laziness and sloth.) Participation in manual labor served another purpose as well: It helped individuals bridge the gap between the world of the intellect and the world of the flesh, thus aiding them to become whole people. The obvious tension between the ideal of individual freedom and the demands of a communal society took their toll on Brook Farm. Increasingly, individualism gave way to a form of socialism. Many residents became disenchanted and left; when a fire destroyed the central building of the community in 1847, the experiment dissolved.

Among the original residents of Brook Farm was the writer Nathaniel Hawthorne, who expressed his disillusionment with the experiment and, to some extent, with transcendentalism in a series of notable novels. In *The Blithedale Romance* (1852), he wrote scathingly of Brook Farm itself, portraying the disastrous consequences of the experiment on the individuals who submitted to it. In other novels—most notably *The Scarlet Letter* (1850) and *The House of Seven Gables* (1851)—he wrote equally passionately about the price individuals pay for cutting themselves off from society. Egotism, he claimed (in an indirect challenge to the transcendentalist faith in the self), was the "serpent" that lay at the heart of human misery.

The failure of Brook Farm did not, however, prevent the formation of other experimental communities. Some borrowed, as Ripley had done, from the ideas of the French philosopher Charles Fourier, whose ideas of socialist communities organized as cooperative "phalanxes" received wide attention in America. Others drew from the ideas of the Scottish industrialist and philanthropist Robert Owen. Owen himself founded an experimental community in Indiana in 1825, which he named New Harmony. It was to be a "Village of Cooperation," in which every resident worked and lived in total equality. The community was an economic failure, but the vision that had inspired it continued to enchant Americans. Dozens of other "Owenite" experiments began in other locations in the ensuing years.

Redefining Sexual Roles

One of the principal concerns of many of the new utopian communities (and of the new social philosophies on which they rested) was the relationship between men and women. In transcendentalism and other movements of this period can be seen expressions of a kind of feminism that would not gain a secure foothold in American society until the late twentieth century. Margaret Fuller, a leading transcendentalist, suggested the important relationship between the discovery of the "self" that was so central to antebellum reform and the questioning of sexual roles: "Many women are considering within themselves what they need and what they have not," she wrote in 1845. "I would have Woman lay aside all thought, such as she habitually cherishes, of being taught and led by men."

A redefinition of sexual roles was crucial to one of the most enduring of the utopian colonies of the nineteenth century: the Oneida Community, established in 1848 in upstate New York by John Humphrey Noyes. The Oneida "Perfectionists," as residents of the community called themselves, rejected traditional notions of family and marriage. All residents, Noyes declared, were "married" to all other residents; there were to be no permanent conjugal ties. But Oneida was not, as its horrified critics often claimed, an experiment in unrestrained "free love." It was a place where the community carefully monitored sexual behavior; where women were to be protected from unwanted childbearing; in which children were raised communally, often seeing little of their own parents. The Oneidans took special pride in what they considered the liberation of their women from the demands of male "lust" and from the traditional bonds of family.

The Shakers, even more than the Oneidans, made a redefinition of traditional sexual roles central to their society. Founded by "Mother" Ann Lee in the 1770s, the society of the Shakers survived throughout the nineteenth century and into the twentieth. (A small remnant survives today.) But the Shakers attracted a particularly large following in the antebellum period and established more than twenty communities throughout the Northeast and Northwest in the 1840s. They derived their name from a unique religious ritual—a sort of dance, in which members of a congregation would "shake" themselves free of sin while performing a loud chant.

The most distinctive feature of Shakerism, however, was its commitment to complete celibacy—which meant, of course, that no one could be born to Shakerism; all Shakers had voluntarily to choose the faith. Shaker communities attracted about 6,000 members in the 1840s, more women than men, and they lived in communities in which contacts between men and women were very limited. They openly endorsed the idea of sexual equality; they even embraced the idea of a God who was not clearly male or female. Within the Shaker society as a whole, it was women who exercised the most power. Mother Ann Lee was succeeded as leader of the movement by Mother Lucy Wright. Shakerism, one observer wrote

Shakers Near Lebanon, Pennsylvania
The Shakers always welcomed visitors to their strikingly simple farms and shops and to their distinctive worship services. Outsiders were often astonished by the singing, shaking, shouting, and ecstatic movement these otherwise dignified and restrained men and women displayed during their ritualistic dances. The lithographer Nathaniel Currier produced this view of a Shaker service in about 1838 and gave evidence of the contempt with which many Americans viewed the sect. The dancers (separated by sex, as befitted the celibate Shaker community) look awkward and even grotesque here, even though in reality—according to most accounts—they moved with rhythm and grace. The elegance of a visitor (at left) stands in sharp contrast to the simple attire and spare surroundings of the Shakers themselves.
(New York Public Library)

in the 1840s, was a refuge from the "perversions of marriage" and "the gross abuses which drag it down."

The Shakers were not, however, motivated only by a desire to escape the burdens of traditional sexual roles. They were trying as well to create a society separated and protected from the chaos and disorder that they believed had come to characterize American life as a whole. They were less interested in personal freedom than in social discipline. And in that, they were much like other dissenting religious sects and other utopian communities of their time. Another example was the Amana Community, founded by German immigrants in 1843, which moved to Iowa in 1855; the Amanas attempted to realize Christian ideals by creating an ordered, socialist society.

The Mormons

But the most important of all efforts to create a new and more ordered society within the old was that of the Church of Jesus Christ of Latter Day Saints—the Mormons. Mormonism began in upstate New York as a result of the efforts of Joseph Smith, a young, energetic, but economically unsuccessful man, who had spent most of his twenty-four years moving restlessly through New England and the Northeast. Then, in 1830, he published a remarkable document—the Book of Mormon—which was, he claimed, a translation of a set of golden plates he had found in the hills of New York, revealed to him by an angel of God. The Book of Mormon told the story of an ancient civilization in America, whose now vanished kingdom could become a model for a new holy community in the United States.

Gathering a small group of believers around him, Smith began in 1831 an effort to find a sanctuary for his new community of "saints," an effort that would continue, unhappily, for more than twenty years. Time and again, the Mormons attempted to establish their "New Jerusalem." Time and again, they met with persecution from surrounding communities suspicious of the radical religious doctrines—which included polygamy (the right of men to take several wives), a rigid form of social organization, and most damaging of all, an intense secrecy, which gave rise to wild rumors among their critics of conspiracy and depravity.

Driven from their original settlements in Independence, Missouri, and Kirtland, Ohio, the Mormons moved on to the new town of Nauvoo, Illinois, which in the early 1840s became an imposing and economically successful community. In 1844, however, Joseph Smith was arrested, charged with treason (for conspiring against the government to win foreign support for a new Mormon colony in the Southwest), and imprisoned in Carthage, Illinois. There an angry mob attacked the jail, forced Smith from his cell, and shot and killed him. The Mormons now abandoned Nauvoo and, under the leadership of Smith's successor, Brigham Young, traveled across the desert—a society of 12,000 people, in one of the largest group migrations in American history—and established a new community in Utah, the present Salt Lake City. There, at last, the Mormons were able to create a permanent settlement. And although they were not always to remain as completely isolated from the rest of American society as they were at the beginning, never again were they to be dislodged.

Like other experiments in social organization of the era, Mormonism reflected a belief in human perfectibility. God had once been a man, the church taught; and thus every man or woman could aspire to become—as Joseph Smith had done—a god. But unlike other new communities, the Mormons did not embrace the doctrine of individual liberty. Instead, they created a highly organized, centrally directed, even militarized social structure, a refuge against the disorder and uncertainty of the secular world. The original Mormons were, for the most part, men and women who felt displaced in their rapidly changing society—economically marginal people left behind by the material growth and social progress of their era. In the new religion, they found security and order.

Remaking Society

The simultaneous efforts to liberate the individual and impose order on a changing world did not simply produce efforts to escape from society and create alternatives to it. They also helped to create a wide range of new movements to remake society—movements in which, to a striking degree, women formed the real rank and file and often the leadership as well. By the 1830s, such movements had taken the form of organized reform societies. "In no country in the world," Tocqueville had observed, "has the principle of association been more successfully used, or more unsparingly applied to a multitude of different objects, than in America. . . . for there is no end which the human will, seconded by the collective exertions of individuals, despairs of attaining."

The new organizations did indeed work on behalf of a wide range of goals: temperance; education; peace; the care of the poor, the handicapped, and the mentally ill; the treatment of criminals; the rights of women; and many more. Few eras in American history have witnessed as wide a range of reform efforts. And few eras have exposed more clearly the simultaneous attraction of Americans to the ideas of personal liberty and social order.

Revivalism, Morality, and Order

The philosophy of reform arose from two distinct sources. One was the optimistic vision of those who, like the transcendentalists, rejected Calvinist doctrines and preached the divinity of the individual. These included not only Emerson, Thoreau, and their followers, but a much larger group of Americans who embraced the doctrines of Unitarianism and Universalism and absorbed European romanticism.

The second, and in many respects more important, source was Protestant revivalism—the movement that had begun with the Second Great Awakening early in the century and had, by the 1820s, evolved into a powerful force for social reform. Although the New Light revivalists were theologically far removed from the transcendentalists and Unitarians, they had come to share the optimistic belief that every individual was capable of salvation. According to Charles Grandison Finney, a Presbyterian minister who became the most influential revival evangelist of the 1820s and 1830s, traditional Calvinist doctrines of predestination and individual human helplessness were both obsolete and destructive. Each person, he preached, contained within himself or herself the capacity to experience spiritual rebirth and achieve salvation. A revival need not depend on a miracle from God; it could be created by individual effort.

Finney enjoyed particular success in upstate New York, where he helped launch a series of passionate revivals in towns along the Erie Canal—a region so prone to religious awakenings that it was known as

the "burned-over district." It was no coincidence that the new revivalism should prove so powerful there, for this region of New York was experiencing—largely as a result of the construction of the canal—a major economic transformation. And with that transformation had come changes in the social fabric so profound that many men and women felt baffled and disoriented. (It was in roughly this same area of New York that Joseph Smith first organized the Mormon church.)

Finney's doctrine of personal regeneration appealed strongly to those who felt threatened by change. In Rochester, New York, the site of his greatest success, he staged a series of emotionally wrenching religious meetings that aroused a large segment of the community—particularly the relatively prosperous citizens, who were enjoying the economic benefits of the new commercial growth but who were also uneasy about the introduction into their community of a new, undisciplined pool of

The Drunkard's Progress

This 1846 lithograph by Nathaniel Currier shows what temperance advocates argued was the inevitable consequence of alcohol consumption. Beginning with an apparently innocent "glass with a friend," the young man rises step by step to the summit of drunken revelry, then declines to desperation and suicide while his abandoned wife and child grieve. (Library of Congress)

transient laborers. For them, revivalism became not only a means of personal salvation but a mandate for the reform (and control) of the larger society. In particular, Finney's revivalism became a call for a crusade against personal immorality. "The church," he maintained, "must take right ground on the subject of Temperance, and Moral Reform, and all the subjects of practical morality which come up for decision from time to time."

Evangelical Protestantism added major strength, therefore, to one of the most influential reform movements of the era: the crusade against drunkenness. No social vice, argued some reformers (including, for example, many of Finney's converts in cities such as Rochester), was more responsible for crime, disorder, and poverty than the excessive use of alcohol. Women, who were particularly active in the temperance movement, claimed that alcoholism placed a particular burden on them: men spent money needed by their families on alcohol, and drunken husbands often beat and abused their wives. Although advocates of temperance had been active since the late eighteenth century, the new reformers gave the movement an energy and influence it had never known. In 1826, the American Society for the Promotion of Temperance emerged as a coordinating agency among various groups; it attempted to use many of the techniques of revivalism in preaching abstinence. Then, in 1840, six reformed drunkards in Baltimore organized the Washington Temperance Society and began to draw large crowds to hear their impassioned and intriguing confessions of past sins. By then, temperance advocates had grown dramatically in numbers; more than a million people had signed a formal pledge to forgo hard liquor.

As the movement gained in strength, it also became divided in purpose. Some temperance advocates now urged that abstinence include not only liquor but beer and wine; not everyone agreed. Others began to demand state legislation to restrict the sale and consumption of alcohol (Maine passed such a law in 1851); but others insisted that temperance must rely on the conscience of the individual. Whatever their disagreements, however, most temperance advocates shared similar motives. By promoting abstinence, reformers were attempting to promote individual moral self-improvement; but they were also trying to impose discipline on society.

The latter impulse was reflected particularly clearly in the battle over prohibition laws, which pitted established Protestants against new Catholic immigrants. The arrival of the immigrants was profoundly disturbing to established residents of many communities; and the restriction of alcohol seemed to them a way to curb the disorder that they believed the new population was creating.

Education and Rehabilitation

One of the outstanding reform movements of the mid-nineteenth century was the effort to produce a system of universal public education. As of 1830, no state could yet boast such a system, although some—such as Massachusetts—had supported a limited version for many years. Now, however, interest in public education grew rapidly—a reflection of the new belief in the innate capacity of every person and of society's obligation to tap that capacity; but a reflection, too, of the desire to expose students to stable social values as a way to resist instability.

The greatest of the educational reformers was Horace Mann, the first secretary of the Massachusetts Board of Education, which was established in 1837. To Mann and his followers, education was the only way to "counterwork this tendency to the domination of capital and the servility of labor." It was also the only way to protect democracy, for an educated electorate was essential to the workings of a free political system. Mann reorganized the Massachusetts school system, lengthened the academic year (to six months), doubled teachers' salaries (although he did nothing to eliminate the large disparities between the salaries of male and female teachers), enriched the curriculum, and introduced new methods of professional training for teachers. Other states experienced similar expansion and development: building new schools, creating teachers' colleges, and offering vast new groups of children access to education. Henry Barnard helped produce a new educational system in Connecticut and Rhode Island. Pennsylvania passed a law in 1835 appropriating state funds for the support of universal education. Governor William Seward of New York extended public support of schools throughout the state in the early 1840s. By the 1850s, the principle of tax-supported elementary schools had been accepted in all the states; and all, despite continuing opposition from certain groups, were making at least a start toward putting the principle into practice.

Yet the quality of the new education continued to vary widely. In some places—Massachusetts, for example, where Mann established the first American state-supported teachers' college in 1839, and the first

The Emerson School, Boston, 1850
This daguerreotype (or early photograph) shows a classroom in a Boston school named for Ralph Waldo Emerson, who years before had been a student there. A stern male teacher oversees a class of young women, who not many years before had been considered unfit subjects for advanced education. (Metropolitan Museum of Art)

professional association of teachers was created in 1845—educators were usually capable men and women, often highly trained, and with an emerging sense of themselves as career professionals. In other areas, however, teachers were often barely literate, and funding for education was so limited as to restrict opportunities severely. In the newly settled regions of the West, where the population was highly dispersed, many children had no access to schools at all. In the South, the entire black population was barred from education (although approximately 10 percent of the slaves managed to achieve literacy anyway); and only about a third of all white children of school age were actually enrolled in schools in 1860. In the North, the percentage was 72 percent; but even there,

many students attended classes only briefly and casually.

Despite all the limitations and inequities, the achievements of the school reformers were impressive by any standard. By the beginning of the Civil War, the United States had the highest literacy rate of any nation in the world: 94 percent of the population of the North and 83 percent of the white population of the South (58 percent of the total population).

The conflicting impulses that underlay the movement for school reform were visible in some of the different institutions that emerged. In New England, for example, the transcendentalist Bronson Alcott established an experimental school in Concord that reflected his strong belief in the importance of complete self-realization. He urged children to learn from their own inner wisdom, not from the imposition of values by the larger society. Children were to teach themselves, rather than relying on teachers. A similar emphasis on the potential of the individual sparked the creation of new institutions to help the handicapped, institutions that formed part of a great network of charitable activities known as the Benevolent Empire. Among them was the Perkins School for the Blind in Boston, the first such school in America. Nothing better exemplified the romantic impulse of the era than the belief of those who founded Perkins that even society's least-favored members—the blind and otherwise handicapped—could be helped to discover an inner strength and wisdom. One teacher at the school expressed such attitudes when he described to the visiting English writer Charles Dickens the case of a blind, deaf, and speechless young woman who had been taught to communicate with the world. Although the "darkness and the silence of the tomb were around her," the teacher explained, "the immortal spirit which had been implanted within her could not die, nor be maimed nor mutilated." Gradually, she had learned to deal with the world around her, even to sew and knit, and most importantly, to speak through sign language. No longer was she a "dog or parrot." She was "an immortal spirit, eagerly seizing upon a new link of union with other spirits!"

Far more typical of educational reform, however, were efforts to use schools to impose a set of social values on children—the values that reformers believed were appropriate for their new, industrializing society. These values included thrift, order, discipline, punctuality, and respect for authority. Horace Mann, for example, spoke frequently of the role of public schools in extending democracy and expanding individual opportunity. But he spoke, too, of their role in creating social order. "The unrestrained passions of men are not only homicidal, but suicidal," he said in words that directly contradicted the emphasis of Alcott and other transcendentalists on instinct and emotion. "Train up a child in the way he should go, and when he is old he will not depart from it."

Similar impulses helped stir another powerful movement of reform: the creation of "asylums," as they were now called for the first time, for criminals and for the mentally ill. On the one hand, in advocating prison and hospital reform, Americans were reacting against one of society's most glaring ills. Criminals of all kinds, debtors unable to pay their

A Pennsylvania Asylum

In 1843 the United States had only thirteen mental hospitals. Most communities locked the mentally ill in jails with common criminals and often confined them to the worst quarters. By the 1880s, largely as a result of the work of the Massachusetts reformer Dorothea Dix, who worked tirelessly prodding states to build new facilities, there were over 120 asylums for the insane—including this one in Berks County, Pennsylvania, which served as well as an almshouse for the poor.   (Historical Society of Berks County, Reading, Pennsylvania)

debts, the mentally ill, even senile paupers—all were crowded together indiscriminately into prisons and jails, which in some cases were literally holes; one jail in Connecticut was an abandoned mine shaft. Beginning in the 1820s, numerous states replaced these antiquated facilities with new penitentiaries and mental institutions designed to provide a proper environment for inmates. New York built the first penitentiary at Auburn in 1821; in Massachusetts, the reformer Dorothea Dix began a national movement for new methods of treating the mentally ill. Imprisonment of debtors and paupers was gradually eliminated, as were such traditional practices as public hangings.

But the creation of asylums for social deviants was not simply an effort to curb the abuses of the old system. It was also an attempt to reform and rehabilitate the inmates. New forms of rigid prison discipline were designed to rid criminals of the "laxness" that had presumably led them astray. Solitary confinement and the imposition of silence on work crews (both instituted in Pennsylvania and New York in the 1820s) were meant to give prisoners the opportunity to meditate on their wrongdoings. Some reformers argued that the discipline of the asylum could serve as a model for other potentially disordered environments—for example, factories and schools. But penitentiaries and even many mental hospitals soon fell victim to overcrowding, and the original reform ideal was gradually lost. Most prisons ultimately degenerated into little more than warehouses for criminals, with scant emphasis on rehabilitation. The idea, in its early stages, had envisioned far more.

The Rise of Feminism

The reform ferment of the antebellum period had a particular meaning for American women. They played central roles in a wide range of reform movements and a particularly important role in the movement on behalf of the abolition of slavery. In the process, they expressed their awareness of the problems that women themselves faced in a male-dominated society. The result was the creation of the first important American feminist movement, one that laid the groundwork for more than a century of agitation for women's rights.

Women in the 1830s and 1840s suffered not only all the traditional restrictions imposed on members of their sex by society but a new set of barriers that had emerged from the transformation of the family. (See pp.315–318.) Those women who began to involve themselves in reform movements in the 1820s and 1830s came to look on such restrictions with rising resentment. Some began to defy them. Sarah and Angelina Grimké, sisters born in South Carolina who had become active and outspoken abolitionists, ignored attacks by men who claimed that their activities were inappropriate for their sex. "Men and women were CREATED EQUAL," they argued. "They are both moral and accountable beings, and whatever is right for man to do, is right for women to do." Other reformers—Catharine Beecher, Harriet Beecher Stowe (her sister), Lucretia Mott, Elizabeth Cady Stanton, and Dorothea Dix—similarly pressed at the boundaries of "acceptable" female behavior, chafing at the restrictions placed on them by men.

Finally, in 1840, the patience of several women snapped. A group of American female delegates arrived at a world antislavery convention in London, only to be turned away by the men who controlled the proceedings. Angered at the rejection, several of the delegates—notably Lucretia Mott and Elizabeth Cady Stanton—became convinced that their first duty as reformers should now be to elevate the status of women. Over the next several years, Mott, Stanton, and others began drawing pointed parallels between the plight of women and the plight of slaves; and in 1848, they organized in Seneca Falls, New York, a convention to discuss the question of women's rights. Out of the meeting emerged a "Declaration of Sentiments and Resolutions" (patterned on the Declaration of Independence), which stated that "all men and women are created equal," that women no less than men are endowed with certain inalienable rights. Their most prominent demand was for the right to vote, thus launching a movement for woman suffrage that would survive until the battle was finally won in 1920. But the document was in many ways more important for its rejection of the whole notion that men and women should be assigned separate "spheres" in society.

Progress toward these feminist goals was limited in the antebellum years, but certain individual women did manage to break the social barriers to advancement. Elizabeth Blackwell, born in England, gained acceptance and fame as a physician. Her sister-in-law Antoinette Brown Blackwell became the first ordained woman minister in the United States; and another sister-in-law, Lucy Stone, took the revolutionary step of retaining her maiden name after marriage. She became a successful and influential lecturer on women's rights. Emma Willard, founder of the Troy Female Seminary in 1821, and Catharine Beecher, who founded the Hartford Female Seminary in 1823, worked on behalf of women's education. Some women expressed their feminist sentiments even in their choice of costume—by wearing a distinctive style of dress (introduced in the 1850s) that combined a short skirt with full length pantalettes—an outfit that allowed freedom of movement without loss of modesty. Introduced by the famous actress Fanny Kemble, it came to be called the "bloomer" costume, after one of its advocates, Amelia Bloomer. (It provoked so much controversy that feminists finally abandoned it, believing that the furor was drawing attention away from their more important demands.)

Yet there was an irony in this rise of interest in the rights of women. Feminists benefited greatly from their association with other reform movements, most notably abolitionism; but at the same time, they suffered as a result. For the demands of women were usually assigned—even by some women themselves—a secondary position to what many considered the far greater issue of the rights of slaves.

The Crusade Against Slavery

The antislavery movement was not new to the mid-nineteenth century. There had been efforts even before the Revolution to limit, and even eliminate, the institution, efforts that had helped remove slavery from most of the North by the end of the eighteenth century. There were powerful antislavery movements in England and Europe that cried out forcefully against human bondage. But American antislavery sentiment remained relatively muted in the first decades after independence. Not until 1830 did it begin to gather the force that would ultimately enable it to overshadow virtually all other efforts at social reform.

Early Opposition to Slavery

In the early years of the nineteenth century, those who opposed slavery were, for the most part, a calm and genteel lot, expressing moral disapproval but engaging in few overt activities. To the extent that there was an organized antislavery movement, it centered on the concept of colonization—an effort to encourage the resettlement of American blacks in Africa or the Caribbean. In 1817, a group of prominent white Virginians organized the American Colonization Society (ACS), which worked carefully to challenge slavery without challenging property rights or Southern sensibilities. The ACS proposed a gradual manumission of slaves, with masters receiving compensation (through funds raised by private charity or appropriated by state legislatures). The liberated blacks were then to be transported out of the country and helped to establish a new society of their own. The ACS was not without impact. It received some funding from private donors, some from Congress, some from the legislatures of Virginia and Maryland. And it arranged the shipment of several groups of blacks out of the country, some of them to the west coast of Africa, where in 1830 they established the nation of Liberia (which became an independent black republic in 1846, with its capital, Monrovia, named for the American president who had presided over the initial settlement). But the ACS was in the end a negligible force. Neither private nor public funding was nearly enough to carry out the vast projects its supporters envisioned. In the space of a decade, they managed to "colonize" fewer slaves than were born in the United States in a month. Nothing, in fact, would have been enough; there were far too many blacks in America in the nineteenth century to be transported to Africa by any conceivable program. And the ACS met resistance, in any case, from blacks themselves, many of whom were now three or more generations removed from Africa and had no wish to move to an alien land. (The Massachusetts free black Paul Cuffe had met similar resistance from members of his race in the early 1800s when he proposed a colonization scheme of his own.)

By 1830, in other words, the early antislavery movement was rapidly losing strength. Colonization was proving not to be a viable method of attacking the institution, particularly since the cotton boom in the Deep South was increasing the commitment of planters to their "peculiar" labor system. Those opposed to slavery had reached what appeared to be a dead end.

Garrison and Abolitionism

It was at this crucial juncture, with the antislavery movement seemingly on the verge of collapse, that a new figure emerged to transform it into a dramatically different phenomenon. He was William Lloyd Garrison. Born in Massachusetts in 1805, Garrison

William Lloyd Garrison

Garrison was the first member of the antislavery movement to call publicly for "immediate and complete emancipation" of blacks. That was in 1831, and for the next three decades he remained a stern and uncompromising enemy of slavery. After the Civil War, however, Garrison displayed little interest in the plight of the blacks he had tried to emancipate. In the last years before his death in 1879, he worked on behalf of woman suffrage, Indian rights, and the prohibition of alcohol. (Wichita State University Library, Wichita, Kansas)

was in the 1820s an assistant to the New Jersey Quaker Benjamin Lundy, who published the leading antislavery newspaper of the time—the *Genius of Universal Emancipation*—in Baltimore. Garrison shared Lundy's abhorrence of slavery, but he soon grew impatient with his employer's moderate tone and mild proposals for reform. In 1831, therefore, he returned to Boston to found his own weekly newspaper, the *Liberator*.

Garrison's philosophy was so simple as to be genuinely revolutionary. Opponents of slavery, he said, should view the institution from the point of view of the black man, not the white slaveowner. They should not, as earlier reformers had done, talk about the evil influence of slavery on white society; they should talk about the damage the system did to blacks. And they should, therefore, reject "gradualism" and demand the immediate, unconditional, universal abolition of slavery. Garrison spoke with particular scorn about the advocates of colonization. They were not emancipationists, he argued; on the contrary, their real aim was to strengthen slavery by ridding the country of those blacks who were already free. The true aim of foes of slavery, he insisted, must be to extend to blacks all the rights of American citizenship. As startling as the drastic nature of his proposals was the relentless, uncompromising tone with which he promoted them. "I am aware," he wrote in the very first issue of the *Liberator*, "that many object to the severity of my language; but is there not cause for severity? I *will* be as harsh as truth, and as uncompromising as justice. . . . I am in earnest—I will not equivocate—I will not excuse—I will not retreat a single inch—AND I WILL BE HEARD."

Garrison soon attracted a large group of followers throughout the North, enough to enable him to found the New England Antislavery Society in 1832 and a year later, after a convention in Philadelphia, the American Antislavery Society. Membership in the new organizations mushroomed. By 1835, there were more than 400 societies; by 1838, there were 1,350, with more than 250,000 members. Antislavery sentiment was developing a strength and assertiveness greater than at any point in the nation's history.

This success was in part a result of the similarity between abolitionism and other reform movements of the era. Like reformers in other areas, abolitionists were calling for an unleashing of the individual human spirit, the elimination of artificial social barriers to fulfillment. Who, after all, was more in need of assistance in realizing individual potential than the enslaved blacks? Theodore Dwight Weld, a prominent abolitionist (and husband of Angelina Grimké), expressed this belief in an 1833 letter to Garrison. Slavery was a sin, Weld wrote, because "no condition of birth, no shade of color, no mere misfortune of circumstances can annul the birthright charter, which God has bequeathed to every being upon whom he has stamped his own image, by making him a *free moral agent*."

Black Abolitionists

Abolitionism had a particular appeal, needless to say, to the free black population of the North, which in 1850 numbered about 250,000, mostly concentrated in cities. These free blacks lived in conditions of poverty and oppression often far worse than their slave counterparts in the South. An English traveler who had visited both sections of the country wrote in 1854 that he was "utterly at a loss to imagine the source of that prejudice which subsists against [the black man] in the Northern states, a prejudice unknown in the South, where the relations between the Africans and the European [white American] are so much more intimate." This confirmed an earlier observation by Tocqueville that "the prejudice which repels the Negroes seems to increase in proportion as they are emancipated." Northern blacks were often victimized by mob violence; they had virtually no access to education; they could vote in only a few states; and they were barred from all but the most menial of occupations. Most worked either as domestic servants or as sailors in the American merchant marine, and their wages were such that they lived, for the most part, in squalor. Some were kidnapped by whites and forced back into slavery.

For all their problems, however, Northern blacks were aware of, and fiercely proud of, their freedom. And they remained acutely sensitive to the plight of those members of their race who remained in bondage, aware that their own position in society would remain precarious as long as slavery existed. Many in the 1830s came to support Garrison. But there were also important black leaders who expressed the aspirations of their race. One of the most militant was David Walker, a resident of Boston, who in 1829 published a harsh pamphlet: *Walker's Appeal . . . to the Colored Citizens.* In it he declared: "America is more our country than it is the whites'—we have enriched it with our *blood and tears.*" He warned: "The whites want slaves, and want us for their slaves, but some of them will curse the day they ever saw us." Slaves should, he declared, cut their masters' throats, should "kill, or be killed!"

Most black critics of slavery, however, were less violent in their rhetoric. The greatest of them all—one of the most electrifying orators of his time, black or white—was Frederick Douglass. Born a slave in Maryland, Douglass escaped to Massachusetts in 1838, became an outspoken leader of antislavery sentiment, and spent two years lecturing in England, where he was lionized by members of that country's vigorous antislavery movement. On his return to the United States in 1847, Douglass purchased his freedom from his Maryland owner and founded an antislavery newspaper, the *North Star,* in Rochester, New York. He achieved wide renown as well for his autobiography, *Narrative of the Life of Frederick Douglass* (1845), in which he presented a damning picture of slavery. Douglass demanded for blacks not only freedom but full social and economic equality. Black abolitionists had been active for years; they had held their first national convention in 1830. But with Douglass's leadership, they became a far more influential force; and they began, too, to forge alliances with white antislavery leaders such as Garrison.

Antiabolitionism

The rise of abolitionism was a powerful force, but it provoked a powerful opposition as well. Almost all

Frederick Douglass

Frederick Douglass was the most prominent black American of the nineteenth century. Born in Maryland to an unknown white father and a slave mother, he escaped from slavery into the North in 1838. He quickly became a leader in the abolitionist movement—lecturing widely, editing a newspaper (*The North Star*), and in 1845 publishing his own autobiography, which became an important document in advancing the antislavery cause. Douglass was particularly popular among antislavery groups in England, where he spent two years in the 1840s. (UPI/ Bettmann Newsphotos)

white Southerners, of course, looked on the movement with fear and loathing. But so too did many Northern whites. Indeed, even in the North, abolitionists were never more than a small, dissenting minority. To its critics, the abolitionist crusade was a dangerous and frightening threat to the existing social system. It would, warned some whites (including many substantial businessmen), produce a destructive war between the sections. It might, others feared, lead to a great influx of free blacks into the North. And whatever the long-range consequences, this strident, outspoken movement seemed to many Northern whites a sign of the disorienting social changes that their society was experiencing. It was yet another threat to stability and order.

The result was an escalating wave of violence directed against abolitionists in the 1830s. When Prudence Crandall attempted to admit several black girls to her private school in Connecticut, local citizens had her arrested, threw filth into her well, and forced her to close down the school. A mob in Philadelphia attacked the abolitionist headquarters, the "Temple of Liberty," in 1834, burned it to the ground, and began a bloody race riot. Another mob seized Garrison on the streets of Boston in 1835 and threatened to hang him. He was saved from death only by being locked in jail. Elijah Lovejoy, the editor of an abolitionist newspaper in Alton, Illinois, was victimized repeatedly by mob violence. Three times angry whites invaded his offices and smashed his presses. Three times Lovejoy installed new machines and began publishing again. When a mob attacked his office a fourth time, late in 1837, he tried to defend his press. The attackers set fire to the building and, as Lovejoy fled, shot and killed him.

That so many men and women continued to embrace abolitionism in the face of such vicious opposition from within their own communities suggests much about the nature of the movement. Abolitionists were not people who made their political commitments lightly or casually. They were strongwilled, passionate crusaders, displaying enormous courage and moral strength, and displaying too at times a level of fervency that many of their contemporaries (and some later historians) found disturbing. Abolitionists were widely attacked, even by some who shared their aversion to slavery, as wild-eyed fanatics bent on social revolution. The antiabolitionist mobs, in other words, were only the most violent expression of a sentiment that many other white Americans shared.

Abolitionism Divided

By the mid-1830s, the abolitionist crusade had gained such influence that it was impossible to ignore. It had also begun to experience serious internal strains and divisions. One reason was the violence of the antiabolitionists, which persuaded some members of the movement that a more moderate approach was necessary. Another reason was the growing radicalism of William Lloyd Garrison, who shocked even many of his own allies (including Frederick Douglass) by attacking not only slavery but the government itself. The Constitution, he said, was "a covenant with death and an agreement with hell." The nation's churches, he claimed, were bulwarks of slavery. In 1840, finally, Garrison precipitated a formal division within the American Antislavery Society by insisting that women be permitted to participate in the movement on terms of full equality. He continued after 1840 to arouse controversy with new and even more radical stands: an extreme pacifism that rejected even defensive wars; opposition to all forms of coercion—not just slavery but prisons and asylums; and finally, in 1843, a call for Northern disunion from the South. The nation could, he suggested, purge itself of the sin of slavery by expelling the slave states from the Union.

From 1840 on, therefore, abolitionism moved in many channels and spoke with many different voices. The Garrisonians remained influential, with their uncompromising moral stance. Others operated in more moderate ways, arguing that abolition could be accomplished only as the result of a long, patient, peaceful struggle—"immediate abolition gradually accomplished," as they called it. At first, they depended on "moral suasion." They would appeal to the conscience of the slaveholders and convince them that their institution was sinful. When that produced no results, they turned to political action, seeking to induce the Northern states and the federal government to aid the cause wherever possible. They helped runaway slaves find refuge in the North or in Canada through the so-called underground railroad (although their efforts were never as highly organized as the term suggests). After the Supreme Court (in *Prigg* v. *Pennsylvania,* 1842) ruled that states need not aid in enforcing the 1793 law requiring the return of fugitive slaves to their owners, abolitionists secured the passage of "personal liberty laws" in several Northern states. These laws forbade state officials to assist in the capture and return of runaways. Above all, the antislavery societies petitioned Congress to abolish slavery in places where the federal government had jurisdiction—in the territories and in the District of Columbia—and to prohibit the interstate slave trade. But political abolitionism had severe limits. Few members of the movement believed that Congress could constitutionally interfere with a "domestic" institution such as slavery within the individual states themselves.

While the abolitionists engaged in pressure politics, they never formed a political party with an abolition platform. Antislavery sentiment underlay the formation in 1840 of the Liberty party, which offered the Kentucky antislavery leader James G. Birney as its presidential candidate. But this party, and its successors, never campaigned for outright abolition (an illustration of the important fact that "antislavery" and "abolitionism" were not always the same thing). They stood instead for "free soil," for keeping slavery out of the territories. Some free-soilers were concerned about the welfare of blacks; others were racists who cared nothing about slavery but simply wanted to keep the West a country for whites. Garrison dismissed free-soilism as "white-manism." But the free-soil position would ultimately do what abolitionism never could accomplish: attract the support of large numbers, even a majority, of the white population of the North. (See pp. 385–386.)

The frustrations of political abolitionism drove some critics of slavery to embrace more drastic measures. A few began to advocate violence; it was a group of prominent abolitionists in New England, for example, who funneled money and arms to John Brown for his bloody uprisings in Kansas and Virginia. (See pp. 384, 391.) Others attempted to arouse widespread public anger through propaganda. Abolitionist descriptions of slavery (for example, Theodore Dwight Weld and Angelina Grimké's *American Slavery as It Is: Testimony of a Thousand Witnesses* of 1839) presented what the authors claimed were careful, factual pictures of slavery but what were in fact highly polemical, often wildly distorted images.

The most powerful of all abolitionist propaganda, however, was a work of fiction: Harriet Beecher Stowe's *Uncle Tom's Cabin*. It appeared first, in 1851–1852, as a serial in an antislavery weekly. Then, in 1852, it was published as a book. It rocked the nation. It sold more than 300,000 copies within a year of publication and was later issued again and again to become one of the most remarkable best sellers in American history. And it succeeded, as a result, in

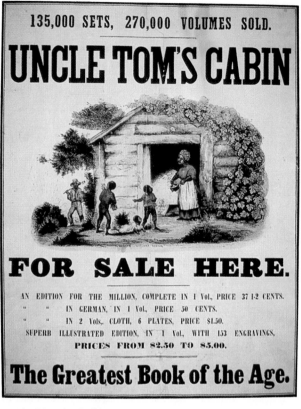

Uncle Tom's Cabin
This poster (advertising, among other things, a German edition of Harriet Beecher Stowe's novel) did not exaggerate when it described *Uncle Tom's Cabin* as "The Greatest Book of the Age." There were, to be sure, greater literary accomplishments; but no American book of the nineteenth century had so profound a political impact. Abraham Lincoln, who was introduced to Stowe in the White House, reportedly said to her: "So you are the little lady who has brought this great war." Stowe was a wife and mother in Brunswick, Maine, when she began writing the novel in 1851. It was, she claimed, a response to a "vision" that came to her while she was taking Communion; but the greater inspiration was likely several abolitionist works she had recently read describing the horrors of the slave system. (Bettmann Archive)

bringing the message of abolitionism to an enormous new audience—not only those who read the book but those who watched dramatizations of its story by countless theater companies throughout the nation. The novel's emotional portrayal of good, kindly blacks victimized by a cruel system; of the loyal, trusting Uncle Tom; of the vicious overseer Simon

SIGNIFICANT EVENTS

1817   American Colonization Society founded

1821   New York constructs first penitentiary

1823   Catharine Beecher founds Hartford Female Seminary

1825   Robert Owen founds New Harmony community in Indiana

1826   James Fenimore Cooper publishes *The Last of the Mohicans*

American Society for the Promotion of Temperance founded

1829   David Walker publishes *Appeal . . . to the Colored Citizens*

1830   Joseph Smith publishes the Book of Mormon

1831   William Lloyd Garrison begins publishing *The Liberator*

1833   American Antislavery Society founded

1837   Horace Mann becomes first secretary of Massachusetts Board of Education

Elijah Lovejoy killed by antiabolitionist mob in Illinois

1840   Garrison demands admission of women into American Antislavery Society, precipitating schism

1840   Liberty party formed

1841   Brook Farm founded in Roxbury, Massachusetts

1843   Amana Community founded

1844   Joseph Smith killed

1845   Frederick Douglass publishes autobiography

1847   Brook Farm dissolved

Mormons found Salt Lake City

1848   Women's rights convention held at Seneca Falls, New York

Oneida Community founded in New York

1850   Nathaniel Hawthorne publishes *The Scarlet Letter*

1851   Herman Melville publishes *Moby Dick*

1852   Harriet Beecher Stowe publishes *Uncle Tom's Cabin*

1854   Henry David Thoreau publishes *Walden*

1855   Walt Whitman publishes *Leaves of Grass*

Legree (described as a New Englander so as to prevent the book from seeming to be an attack on Southern whites); of the escape of the beautiful Eliza; of the heart-rending death of Little Eva: all became a part of American popular legend. Reviled throughout the South, Stowe became a hero to many in the North. And in both regions, her novel helped to inflame sectional tensions to a new level of passion. Few books in American history have had so great an impact on the course of public events.

Even divided, therefore, abolitionism remained a powerful influence on the life of the nation. Only a relatively small number of people before the Civil War ever accepted the abolitionist position that slavery must be entirely eliminated in a single stroke. But the crusade that Garrison had launched, and that thousands of committed men and women kept alive for three decades, was a constant, visible reminder of how deeply the institution of slavery was dividing America.

SUGGESTED READINGS

Antebellum Literature   The literary flowering of the antebellum period is examined in the stimulating, if partially discredited, work of Vernon L. Parrington, *The Romantic Revolution in America, 1800–1860* (1927). More durable has been the remarkable work of F. O. Matthiessen, *American Renaissance* (1941). Leo Marx, *The Machine and the Garden* (1964), considers the tension in literature between the pastoral tradition and the growth of a modern economy. Henry F. May, *The Enlightenment in America* (1976), is a good overview of cultural trends; Van Wyck Brooks, *The Flow-ering of New England, 1815–1865* (1936), examines the region that produced much of the most important literature of the period. Neil Harris, *Humbug: The Art of P. T. Barnum* (1973), is revealing of trends in popular culture.

Social Philosophies and Utopias   On the transcendentalists, see—in addition to the works by Matthiessen and Brooks cited above—P. F. Boller, Jr., *American Transcendentalism, 1830–1860: An Intellectual Inquiry* (1974). Biographies of individual transcendentalists include Gay Wilson

Allen, *Waldo Emerson* (1981); Arthur M. Schlesinger, Jr., *Orestes A. Brownson: A Pilgrim's Progress* (1939); Henry Steele Commager, *Theodore Parker* (1936); and Richard Lebeaux, *Young Man Thoreau* (1977). Perry Miller considers the transcendentalists in a collection of their writings, *The Transcendentalists* (1950), as well as in relevant sections of *The Life of the Mind in America: From the Revolution to the Civil War* (1966). Arthur Bestor, *Backwoods Utopias: The Sectarian and Owenite Phases of Communitarian Socialism in America, 1663–1829* (1950), M. L. Carden, *Oneida: Utopian Community to Modern Corporation* (1971), Raymond Muncy, *Sex and Marriage in Utopian Communities* (1973), and R. D. Thomas, *The Man Who Would Be Perfect: John Humphrey Noyes and the Utopian Impulse* (1977), consider several antebellum utopian experiments. Fawn Brodie, *No Man Knows My Name* (1945), is a valuable biography of Mormon founder Joseph Smith. Klaus J. Hansen, *Quest for Empire* (1967), examines Mormon theology and politics. Wallace Stegner, *The Gathering of Zion* (1964), is a vivid account of the Mormon trek westward.

Antebellum Reforms A standard overview of the reform agitation of the mid-nineteenth century is Alice Felt Tyler, *Freedom's Ferment* (1944); a more recent survey, better attuned to current scholarship, is Ronald G. Walters, *American Reformers, 1815–1860* (1978). William G. McLoughlin, *Revivals, Awakenings, and Reform* (1978), is a valuable study of the relationship between reform and religious revivals. Whitney R. Cross, *The Burned-Over District* (1950), examines the revival-prone region of upstate New York; Paul Johnson, *A Shopkeeper's Millennium* (1978), is a fine study of the relationship between revivalism and socioeconomic forces in the community of Rochester, New York. Timothy L. Smith, *Revivalism and Social Reform in Mid-Nineteenth Century America* (1957), and William W. Sweet, *Revivalism in America* (1949), are general studies; Charles A. Johnson, *The Frontier Camp Meeting* (1955), is more specialized. C. C. Cole, Jr., *The Social Ideas of the Northern Evangelists, 1826–1860* (1954), links revivalism and reform. W. J. Rorabaugh, *The Alcoholic Republic* (1979), discusses American drinking habits, and Ian R. Tyrrell, *Sobering Up: From Temperance to Prohibition in Antebellum America, 1800–1860* (1979), examines efforts to curb alcohol consumption. David Rothman, *The Discovery of the Asylum* (1971), is an examination of prison and hospital reform that reveals much about the broader reform spirit. Estelle Freedman, *Their Sisters' Keepers: Women's Prison Reform in America, 1830–1930* (1981), sees society's attitudes towards the incarceration of women as a reflection of its larger assumptions about woman's social sphere.

Education Michael Katz, *The Irony of Early School Reform* (1968), is a provocative and iconoclastic view of the most widely praised of the antebellum reform movements. Lawrence A. Cremin's sweeping study, *American Education: The National Experience* (1980), includes valuable information about school reform; while Stanley K. Schultz, *The Culture Factory: Boston's Public Schools, 1789–1860* (1973), examines a particular community. Paul Monroe, *The Founding of the American Public School System* (1949), and Carl Bode, *The American Lyceum* (1956), are earlier

studies. Jonathan Messerli, *Horace Mann* (1972), is a biography of the leading exponent of educational reform.

Feminism On antebellum feminism, see Barbara J. Berg, *The Remembered Gate: Origins of American Feminism. The Woman and the City* (1977); Ellen C. Du Bois, *Feminism and Suffrage: The Emergence of an Independent Women's Movement in America, 1848–1869* (1978); Nancy Cott, *The Bonds of Womanhood: "Woman's Sphere" in New England, 1780–1835* (1977); Ann Douglas, *The Feminization of American Culture* (1977), a provocative literary and cultural study; Lois Banner, *Elizabeth Cady Stanton* (1980); William L. O'Neill, *Everyone Was Brave: The Rise and Fall of Feminism in the United States* (1970); and Eleanor Flexner, *Century of Struggle*, rev. ed. (1975), a standard study of the women's rights movement. Barbara Leslie Epstein, *The Politics of Domesticity: Women, Evangelism, and Temperance in Nineteenth-Century America* (1981), examines the interaction between feminism and other reforms. Carl Degler, *At Odds: Women and the Family in America from the Revolution to the Present* (1980), is a valuable social history of the role of women in American life.

Antislavery and Abolitionism Surveys of the antislavery movement and abolitionism include Louis Filler, *The Crusade Against Slavery* (1960), and Gerald Sorin, *Abolitionism* (1972). See also M. L. Dillon, *The Abolitionists* (1974), and J. B. Stewart, *Holy Warriors* (1976). Peter F. Walker, *Moral Choices: Memory, Desire, and Imagination in Nineteenth Century Abolition* (1978), is a psychological study of abolitionists. Lawrence J. Friedman, *Gregarious Saints: Self and Community in American Abolitionism* (1982), also explores the motives of abolitionists. Lewis Perry and Michael Fellman (eds.), *Antislavery Reconsidered: New Perspectives on the Abolitionists* (1979), is a collection of essays reflecting recent scholarship. Aileen Kraditor, *Means and Ends in American Abolitionism: Garrison and His Critics on Strategy and Tactics, 1834–1850* (1967), is a valuable study of the first important abolitionist. G. H. Barnes, *The Antislavery Impulse* (1933), stresses the role of Theodore Dwight Weld in the movement. Gerda Lerner, *The Grimké Sisters of South Carolina: Rebels Against Slavery* (1967), is a good study of two of the leading feminist abolitionists. John L. Thomas, *The Liberator* (1963), is a standard biography of Garrison. Other biographies of abolitionist figures are Bertram Wyatt-Brown, *Lewis Tappan and the Evangelical War Against Slavery* (1969); Robert Abzug, *Theodore Dwight Weld* (1980); Irving Bartlett, *Wendell Phillips* (1962); and Betty Fladelan, *James Gillespie Birney* (1955). Martin Duberman (ed.), *The Anti-Slavery Vanguard* (1965), is a collection of admiring essays about the abolitionists. Benjamin Quarles, *Black Abolitionists* (1969), and William H. Pease and Jane H. Pease, *They Would Be Free* (1974), consider the contributions of blacks themselves to the struggle. Arna Bontemps, *Free at Last: The Life of Frederick Douglass* (1971), and Nathan Huggins, *Slave and Citizen* (1980), are biographies of the leading black antislavery spokesman. Leonard Richards, *Gentlemen of Property and Standing* (1970), examines anti-abolition mobs; George Fredrickson, *The Black Image in the White Mind: The Debate on Afro-American Character and Destiny, 1817–1914* (1971), considers American racial attitudes.

The Lincoln-Douglas Debates, Illinois, 1858   (Granger Collection)

Chapter 13 # The Impending Crisis

Until the 1840s, the sectional tensions between North and South had remained relatively contained. On two occasions, serious crises had emerged that had threatened the Union; but neither had been permitted to develop very far. The first was resolved in 1819 by the Missouri Compromise. The second, the nullification crisis of the 1830s, was not so much resolved as allowed quietly to die.

Throughout these early decades, the nation generally avoided confronting its sectional differences. This was in part because the Union was so loose and the federal government so weak and unobtrusive that open conflicts seldom arose; and in part because people of all sections had certain shared sentiments (memories of the Revolutionary past, respect for the Constitution, dreams of national glory) and certain common institutions (the vigorous two-party system, an increasingly interdependent economy) that held them together. Had no new sectional issues arisen, it is possible that the United States would have avoided a civil war, that the two sections might have resolved their differences peaceably over time.

But new issues did arise, and almost without exception they centered around the question of slavery. From the North came the strident and increasingly powerful abolitionist movement, which kept the matter alive in the public mind and greatly increased sectional animosities. And from the West, more important, came a series of controversies that would ultimately destroy the fragile Union. For ironically, the vigorous nationalism that was in some ways helping to keep the United States together was also producing a desire for territorial expansion that would tear the nation apart. As America annexed extensive

new lands—Texas, the Southwest, California, the Oregon Country, and more—the question continually arose: What would be the status of slavery in the territories?

Only the most fervent abolitionists believed that anything could be done to eliminate slavery in the states where it already existed; but a powerful coalition of Northerners began to insist that slavery be banned from new acquisitions. White Southerners, in the meantime, began to argue that slavery extension was essential to protect the future status of their region in the nation. Unless the Southern economic system expanded, they came to believe, it would be consigned to a helpless minority position.

By the late 1840s, these differences had grown to create a dangerous and enduring crisis. Twice—first in 1850 and again in 1854—national leaders attempted to settle the issue by means of a great compromise. But after each such effort, the sectional question arose again in more virulent form, until finally, in 1861, the American people took up arms against one another.

Expansion and War

In the course of the 1840s, more than a million square miles of new territory came under the control of the United States—the greatest wave of expansion since the Louisiana Purchase nearly forty years before. By the end of the decade, the nation possessed nearly all the territory of the present-day United States—ev-

Expanding Settlement, 1810–1850

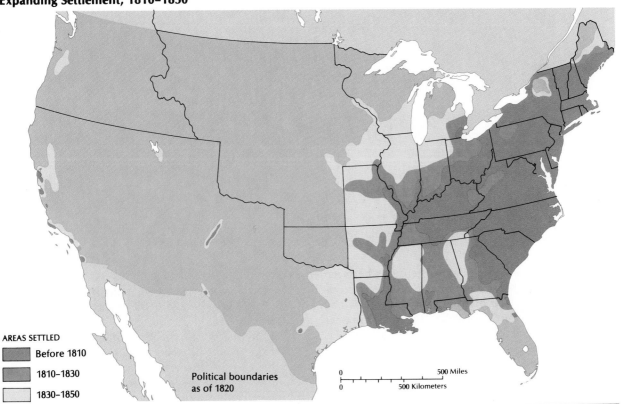

AREAS SETTLED

- Before 1810
- 1810–1830
- 1830–1850

Political boundaries
as of 1820

0   500 Miles

0   500 Kilometers

erything except Alaska, Hawaii, and a few relatively small areas acquired later through border adjustments.

What accounted for this great new wave of expansion after a lull of nearly four decades? In part, it was a result of simple growth—growth of population and growth in the economy—which created pressures to extend the borders westward. In part, too, it was a result of American fears that European nations might somehow extend their influence into the Western lands. But neither of these factors was alone sufficient to explain the new thrust westward. America had not yet even approached developing all the lands it already held; and the threat of European intervention on the continent was limited to a few areas. What gave the decisive push to the nation's quest for new territory was a set of ideas—an ideology that acquired the name "Manifest Destiny."

Manifest Destiny

Manifest Destiny emerged out of a combination of the vigorous nationalism of the 1830s and the reform sentiment of the same era, for it reflected both national pride and an idealistic vision of social perfection. It was the idea that America was destined by God to expand its boundaries over a vast area—an area not clearly defined but certainly including much of the continent of North America. The motive for this expansion, advocates of Manifest Destiny maintained, was not a selfish desire for economic gain but an altruistic attempt to extend American liberty to new realms. John L. O'Sullivan, the influential Democratic editor who gave the movement its name, wrote in 1845 that the American claim to new territory

> . . . is by the right of our manifest destiny to overspread and to possess the whole of the continent which Providence has given us for the development of the great experiment of liberty and federative self government entrusted to us. It is a right such as that of the tree to the space of air and earth suitable for the full expansion of its principle and destiny of growth.

By the 1840s, the idea of Manifest Destiny had spread throughout the nation, publicized by the new "penny press," which had made newspapers available to a far greater proportion of the population than ever before, and fanned by the rhetoric of nationalist politicians. The sentiment was strongest in the North and West, but there were advocates in the South as well.

Devotees of Manifest Destiny disagreed among themselves, however, as to how far and by what means the nation should expand. Some had relatively limited territorial goals; others envisioned a vast new American "empire of liberty" extending north into Canada and south into Mexico, and including islands in the Caribbean and in the Pacific. A few visionaries dreamed of the United States becoming a federation of much of the entire world. There was disagreement too over whether the nation could be justified in using force to achieve its goals. Democratic politicians such as O'Sullivan implied that it could. Others, especially among the Whigs, believed that only peaceful methods should be used to acquire new territory. Daniel Webster, for example, said: "I have always wished that this country should exhibit to the nations of the earth the example of a great, rich, and powerful republic which is not possessed by a spirit of aggrandizement." America should, in other words, encourage other areas to join the nation through the strength of its example, not through force.

And there were other politicians—men such as Henry Clay—who were hesitant about any further expansion at all. They feared, correctly as it turned out, that the acquisition of new territories would re-open the painful controversy over slavery and threaten the stability of the Union. Their voices, however, were all but drowned out in the enthusiasm over expansion in the 1840s, which began with the issues of Texas and Oregon.

The Question of Texas

Southwest of the United States stretched the northern provinces of Mexico—Texas, New Mexico, and Upper California—once parts of Spain's colonial empire in North America but, since 1822, states in the independent republic of Mexico. Under Spanish rule, the provinces had been subject to only the lightest supervision from the government of the viceroyalty in Mexico, and only a few thousand whites had settled in them. The same conditions prevailed under the Mexican republic, which lacked the power and the population to govern and settle such distant areas. The United States had once claimed Texas as a part of the Louisiana Purchase, but it had renounced the claim in 1819. Twice thereafter, however, in the presidencies of John Quincy Adams and Andrew Jackson, the United States had offered to buy Texas, only to meet with indignant Mexican refusals.

But the Mexican government itself soon invited difficulties in Texas. In the early 1820s it encouraged American immigration by offering land grants to Stephen Austin and other men who promised to colonize the land. The motive of the government was to

Promoting the West
Cyrus McCormick was one of many American businessmen with an interest in the peopling of the American West. The reaper he invented was crucial to the cultivation of the new agricultural regions of the West; and the rapid settlement of those regions was, in turn, essential to the health of his company. In this idealized poster, the McCormick Reaper Company presents a romantic image of vast, fertile lands awaiting settlement, an image that drew many settlers westward.
(Chicago Historical Society)

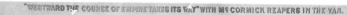

build up the economy of Texas, and hence its own tax revenues, by increasing the population with foreigners. But the experiment was to result in the loss of Texas to the United States. Thousands of Americans, attracted by reports of the rich soil in Texas, took advantage of Mexico's welcome. The great majority came from the Southern states, sometimes bringing slaves with them. By 1835, approximately 35,000 Americans were living in Texas.

Almost from the beginning, there was friction between the settlers and the Mexicans. Finally the Mexican government, realizing that its power over Texas was being challenged by the settlers, moved to exert control. A new law reduced the powers of the various states of the republic, a measure that white Texans took to be aimed specifically at them. In 1836, the American settlers defiantly proclaimed the independence of Texas.

The Mexican dictator, Antonio de Santa Anna, advanced into Texas with a large army. Even with the aid of volunteers, money, and supplies from private groups in the United States, the Texans were having difficulty in organizing a resistance. Their garrison at the Alamo mission in San Antonio was exterminated after a famous, if futile, defense by a group of Texas "patriots," a group that included, among others, the renowned frontiersman Davy Crockett; another garrison at Goliad suffered substantially the same fate when the Mexicans murdered most of the force after it had surrendered. But General Sam Houston, emerging as the national hero of Texas, kept a small army together, and at the Battle of San Jacinto (April 23, 1836, near present-day Houston), he defeated the Mexican army and took Santa Anna prisoner. Although the Mexican government later refused to recognize officially the captured dictator's vague promises to withdraw Mexican authority from Texas, it made no further attempt to subdue the province. Texas had won its independence.

The new republic desired to join the United States and through its new president, Sam Houston, immediately asked for recognition, to be followed by annexation. Although President Andrew Jackson favored annexation, he proceeded cautiously. Many Northerners opposed the annexation of a large new slave territory. Others were opposed to incorporating a region that would add to Southern votes in Congress and in the electoral college. Jackson feared that annexation might cause an ugly sectional controversy and even lead to a war with Mexico. He did not, therefore, propose annexation and did not even extend recognition to Texas until just before he left

office in 1837. His successor, Martin Van Buren, also refrained, for similar reasons, from pressing the issue.

Spurned by the United States, Texas sought recognition, support, and money in Europe. Texan leaders talked about creating a vast southwestern nation, stretching to the Pacific, which would be a rival to the United States. It was the kind of talk that Europe, particularly England (which already saw in the United States a potential rival in world trade and naval influence), was pleased to hear. An independent Texas would be a counterbalance to the United States and a barrier to further American expansion; it would supply cotton for European industry and provide a market for European exports. England and France hastened to recognize and conclude trade treaties with Texas. Observing all this, and also eager to increase Southern power, President Tyler persuaded Texas to apply again, and Secretary of State Calhoun submitted an annexation treaty to the Senate in April 1844. Unfortunately for Texas, Calhoun presented annexation as if its only purpose were to extend and protect slavery. The treaty was soundly defeated.

By now, however, the issue of Texas had become one of the major concerns of advocates of Manifest Destiny. And the rejection of the treaty of annexation only spurred them to greater efforts toward their goal. The Texas question would soon become the central issue in the election of 1844.

The Question of Oregon

American interest in what was known as the Oregon Country had, like the interest in Texas, a long history. And like Texas, Oregon became in the 1840s a major political issue. The ownership of the territory had long been in dispute, but its boundaries were clearly defined—on the north the latitude line of 54°40′, on the east the crest of the Rocky Mountains, on the south the 42nd parallel, and on the west the Pacific. Its half-million square miles included the present states of Oregon, Washington, and Idaho, parts of Montana and Wyoming, and half of British Columbia.

At various times in the past, the Oregon Country had been claimed by Spain, Russia, France, England, and the United States. By the 1820s, Spain, Russia, and France had withdrawn and surrendered their rights to Britain or to the United States or to both. For years after that, both nations claimed sovereignty over the region. Each could assert title on the basis of the activities of its explorers, maritime traders, and fur traders. The English had one solid advantage:

They were in actual possession of a part of the area. In 1821, the powerful British fur trading organization, the Hudson's Bay Company, under the leadership of its factor, John McLoughlin, established a post at Fort Vancouver, north of the Columbia River.

Several times the English government proposed the Columbia as a suitable line for dividing Oregon: Great Britain would retain possession of the regions to the north of the river, the United States would control the land to the south of it. The United States, also showing a desire to compromise, countered by suggesting the 49th parallel. This difference in official views prevented a settlement of the Oregon question in the treaty of 1815, which ended the War of 1812. Unable to agree on a demarcation line, the diplomats of the two powers provided in the treaty that citizens of each were to have equal access to Oregon for ten years. This arrangement, called joint occupation, was renewed in 1827 for an indefinite period, with either nation empowered to end it on a year's notice.

The first real American interest in Oregon came as a result of the activities of missionaries, notably Jason Lee, Marcus Whitman, and Father Pierre Jean de Smet. All the missionaries located their posts east or south of the Columbia River, mostly in the fertile Willamette Valley. They described their work in reports and letters that were published in the United States in influential religious journals and widely reprinted in secular newspapers. These reports dwelt as much on the rich soil and lovely climate of Oregon as on the spiritual condition of the Indians.

Beginning in 1841, thousands of American pioneers set out for Oregon in a display of what became known as "Oregon fever." Two thousand miles in length, the Oregon Trail penetrated Indian country and crossed mountains and semidesert regions. To the emigrants, traveling in caravans of covered wagons and accompanied by huge herds of cattle, the trail presented enormous problems in transportation. The average period required for the journey was from May to November. Some never lived to complete it. But the great majority got through. By 1845, 5,000 Americans were living south of the Columbia—and demanding that their government take possession of Oregon. Their cries were echoed by the supporters of Manifest Destiny within the United States.

Polk and Expansion

The election of 1844 was widely expected to be a contest between two old foes: Henry Clay, the anticipated presidential candidate of the Whigs (President Tyler having been driven out of the party), and

Settlement of the Oregon Boundary Dispute, 1846

RUSSIAN POSSESSIONS
54° 40'
NORTHERN LIMIT OF AMERICAN CLAIM
Fort Simpson
Fraser R.
Columbia R.
ROCKY MOUNTAINS
BRITISH AMERICA
Vancouver Island
49°
Fort Victoria
Puget Sound
Fort Colville
Missouri R.
PACIFIC OCEAN
Fort Walla Walla
Spokane
UNITED STATES
Astoria
Fort Vancouver
Snake R.
Portland
Columbia R.
Willamette R.
OREGON TRAIL
Fort Boise
Fort Hall
42°
SOUTHERN LIMIT OF BRITISH CLAIM
Fort Bridger
MEXICO

Primary area in dispute
To Britain, 1846
To United States, 1846
1846 treaty line

0   300 Miles
0   300 Kilometers

former president Martin Van Buren, assumed to be the favorite for the Democratic nomination. Both men wished to avoid taking a stand on the heated issue of the annexation of Texas, because whatever stand they took was certain to lose them some votes. Consequently, they issued separate statements on the question so similar in tone as to suggest that they had consulted with one another in advance: Both favored annexation, but only with the consent of Mexico. Since such consent was unlikely at best, the statements had little or no meaning.

Sentiment for expansion was relatively mild within the Whig party, and Clay had no difficulty securing the nomination despite his noncommittal position. The Whig platform discreetly omitted any reference to Texas. Among the Democrats, however, sentiment for annexation had grown to major proportions, particularly among party members in the South. They were enraged by Van Buren's equivocal stand on Texas, and their opposition destroyed the former president's chance of regaining the White House. Instead, the Democratic convention nominated James K. Polk.

Polk's supporters had skillfully exploited their

Western Trails to 1860

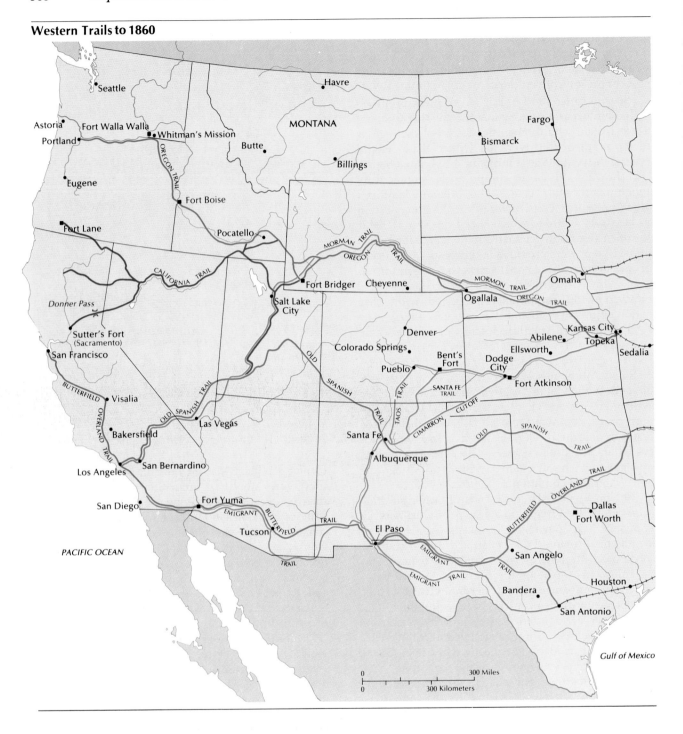

candidate's backing for the annexation of Texas to generate votes for him at the convention. And in doing so, they won a victory for the first "dark horse" to win the presidential nomination of his party. Polk was not as obscure as his Whig critics suggested when they asked sarcastically during the campaign, "Who is James K. Polk?" Neither, however, was he a genuinely major figure within his party. Born in North Carolina, he had in his mid-twenties moved to Tennessee (following the pattern of the man who would become his political mentor, Andrew Jackson). For fourteen years, beginning in 1825, he had served in the U.S. House of Representatives, four of them as its Speaker. Most recently, he had been governor of Tennessee. But in 1844, he had been out of public office—and for the most part out of the public mind—for three years. Hence his nomination was unexpected.

The sentiment that had made his victory possible could be seen in the key resolution of the Democratic platform: "that the re-occupation of Oregon and the re-annexation of Texas at the earliest practicable period are great American measures." The words "*re-occupation*" and "*re-annexation*" were intended to imply that in taking Oregon and Texas, the United States would only be confirming its claim to territories that had already belonged to it. By combining the Oregon and Texas questions, the Democrats hoped to appeal to both Northern and Southern expansionists.

Too late, Clay realized that he had mishandled the expansion issue. In midcampaign he announced that under certain circumstances he might be for the acquisition of Texas. His tardy straddling probably cost him more votes than it gained. Polk carried the election by 170 electoral votes to 105, although his popular majority was less than 40,000. The Liberty party, running James G. Birney a second time, polled 62,000 votes (as compared with 7,000 in 1840), mainly from antislavery Whigs who had turned against Clay.

The new president was an ordinary-looking man: short, thin, and grim of expression, with public manners that matched his appearance. But Polk was both intelligent and energetic, and he entered office with a clear idea of what he wished to accomplish and a firm grasp of the means necessary to attain it. Perhaps no president in American history was as successful in fulfilling his stated goals as James K. Polk.

One of those goals was achieved for him even before he took office. John Tyler, who remained in the White House until March 1845, interpreted the election returns as a mandate for annexation of Texas. He proposed to Congress that the territory be accepted into the Union by a joint resolution of both houses, a device that would eliminate the necessity of obtaining a two-thirds majority in the Senate for a treaty. In February 1845, Congress complied. There were conditions. Texas could be subdivided into no more than four additional states (in fact, it was never subdivided at all); it would retain responsibility for paying the debts that it had acquired as an independent nation (although it was permitted to retain its public lands as well, rather than ceding them to the federal government); and it had to submit to the United States any boundary disputes in which it be-

came involved. After the inauguration of Polk, Texas accepted the conditions; and in December 1845, it became a state.

Polk himself resolved the perplexing question of Oregon, although not without difficulty and not to the thorough satisfaction of his supporters. In his inaugural address, the new president seemed to reassert American title to all of the Oregon Country. In reality, however, he was willing to compromise—to effect a division on the line of the 49th parallel. The British minister in Washington was less conciliatory. He rejected Polk's offer without even referring it to London.

Abruptly, Polk took a more militant attitude. Saying America should look John Bull "straight in the eye" and hinting at war, he asserted again the American claim to all of Oregon. In his annual message to Congress in December 1845, he asked for approval to give notice to England that joint occupation was to end in a year. Citing the Monroe Doctrine (which had been largely forgotten during the previous twenty years), he insisted that the United States would permit no further European colonization. Congress, despite the dissent of some Whigs, complied with the president's request.

There was loose talk of war on both sides of the Atlantic—talk that in the United States often took the form of the bellicose slogan "Fifty-four forty or fight!" Neither nation, however, genuinely wished to resort to force. Finally, the British government offered to divide Oregon at the 49th parallel—that is, to accept Polk's original proposal. The president pretended to believe that the offer should be rejected, but with little resistance he allowed himself to be persuaded by the cabinet to submit the proposal to the Senate for advice. The result was that responsibility for the decision now shifted, no doubt to the president's great relief, from the White House to the Capitol. The Senate accepted the proposed agreement, and on June 15, 1846, a treaty was signed fixing the boundary at the 49th parallel, where it remains today. The United States had secured the larger and better part of the Oregon Country. It had certainly obtained all that it could reasonably have expected to get without war.

The Southwest and California

One of the reasons the Senate and the president had agreed so readily to the British proposal for settling the Oregon question was that new tensions were emerging in the Southwest—tensions that threatened to lead (and ultimately did lead) to a war with Mexico. The moment the United States admitted Texas to statehood in 1845, the Mexican government broke diplomatic relations with Washington. To make matters worse, a dispute now developed over the boundary between Texas and Mexico (which was now, of course, the southern boundary of the United States). The Texans claimed that the Rio Grande constituted the western and southern border, an assertion that included much of what is now New Mexico within Texas. Mexico, still refusing formally to concede the loss of Texas, nevertheless argued that the border had always been the Nueces River, well to the north of the Rio Grande. Polk recognized the Texas claim, and in the summer of 1845 he sent a small army under General Zachary Taylor to the Nueces line—to protect Texas, he claimed, against a possible Mexican invasion.

The semiprimitive economy of New Mexico, part of the area in dispute, supported a scanty population. The trade center of the region was the small metropolis of Santa Fe, 300 miles from the nearest settlements to the south and more than 1,000 miles from Mexico City and Vera Cruz, the economic centers on which New Mexico had relied during Spanish rule. This geographical isolation from Mexico helped produce a social and cultural isolation as well; for after Mexico had won its independence, the new government did for New Mexico much the same thing as it did for Texas—it invited American traders into the region. The Mexicans hoped that the new trade with the United States would enhance the development of their province. It did. But it also, although on a more limited scale than in Texas, started a process by which New Mexico began to become more American than Mexican.

Soon a flourishing commerce—inaugurated in 1821 by William Becknell—developed between Santa Fe and Independence, Missouri, with long caravans moving back and forth along the Santa Fe Trail, carrying manufactured goods west and bringing back gold, silver, furs, and mules. The Santa Fe trade, as it was called, increased the American presence in New Mexico, and it signaled to advocates of expansion another direction for their efforts.

Americans were similarly increasing their interest in an even more distant province of Mexico: California. In this vast region lived perhaps 7,000 Mexicans, descendants of Spanish colonists, who engaged in agricultural pursuits, chiefly ranching, and carried on a skimpy trade with the outside world. Gradually, however, Americans began to arrive: first maritime traders and captains of Pacific whaling ships, who stopped to barter goods or buy supplies; then merchants, who established stores, imported merchandise, and developed a profitable trade with the Mexicans and Indians. Some of these new settlers began to dream of bringing California into the United States. Thomas O. Larkin, for example, set up a business in Monterey in 1832, quickly became a leading citizen of the region, and in 1844 accepted an appointment as American consul, with instructions to arouse sentiment among the Californians for annexation.

As reports spread of the rich soil and mild climate, immigrants began to enter California from the east by land. These were pioneering farmers, men of the type that were penetrating Texas and Oregon in search of greener pastures. By 1845, there were 700 Americans in California, most of them concentrated in the valley of the Sacramento River. The overlord of this region was John A. Sutter, once of Germany and Switzerland, who had moved to California in 1839 and had become a Mexican citizen. His headquarters at Sutter's Fort was the center of a magnificent domain where the owner ranched thousands of cattle and horses and maintained a network of small manufacturing shops to supply his armed retainers.

President Polk feared that Great Britain would try to acquire or dominate California as well as Texas—a suspicion that was given credence by the activities of British diplomatic agents in the province. His dreams of expansion thus began to extend beyond the Democratic platform. He was determined to acquire for his country New Mexico and California and possibly other parts of northern Mexico.

At the same time that he sent Taylor to the Nueces, Polk also sent secret instructions to the commander of the Pacific naval squadron to seize the California ports if he heard that Mexico had declared war. A little later, Consul Larkin was informed that, if the people wanted to revolt and join the United States, they would be received as brethren. Still later, an exploring expedition led by Captain John C. Frémont, of the army's corps of topographical engineers, entered California. The Mexican authorities, alarmed by the size of the party and its military character, ordered Frémont to leave. He complied, but moved only over the Oregon border.

After appearing to prepare for war, Polk resolved on a last effort to achieve his objectives by diplomacy. He dispatched to Mexico a special minister, John Slidell, a Louisiana politician, with instructions to settle with American money all the questions in dispute between the two nations. If Mexico would acknowledge the Rio Grande boundary for Texas,

Sutter's Fort
John Sutter, who migrated to the United States fom Switzerland in 1834, settled in northern California several years later and persuaded the Mexican governor to grant him a large piece of land in the Sacramento River valley (the site of the California state capital today). There he built a fortified town, surrounded by eighteen-foot walls, to protect against unfriendly Indians and established himself as one of the leading ranchers of the region. When gold was discovered on his property in 1848, his own workers quickly deserted him to join the search for instant wealth; his livestock was stolen; and his land was occupied by squatters. Four years later Sutter declared bankruptcy. (Library of Congress)

the United States would assume the damage claims, amounting to several millions, which Americans held against Mexico. If Mexico would cede New Mexico, the United States would pay $5 million. And for California, the United States would pay up to $25 million. Slidell soon notified his government that his mission had failed. Immediately after receiving Slidell's report, on January 13, 1846, Polk ordered Taylor's army to move across the Nueces to the Rio Grande.

If Polk was hoping for trouble, he was disappointed for months. Finally, in May, he decided to ask Congress to declare war on the grounds that Mexico had refused to honor its financial obligations and had insulted the United States by rejecting the Slidell mission. While Polk was working on a war message, the news arrived from Taylor that Mexican troops had crossed the Rio Grande and attacked a unit of American soldiers. Polk now revised his message. He declared: "Mexico has passed the boundary of the United States . . . and shed American blood upon the American soil. . . . War exists by the act of Mexico herself." Congress accepted Polk's interpretation of events and on May 13, 1846, declared war by votes of 40 to 2 in the Senate and 174 to 14 in the House.

The Mexican War

The war was never popular in the United States. Whig critics charged from the beginning that Polk had deliberately maneuvered the country into the conflict, that the border incident that had precipitated the declaration had been staged. Many argued that the hostilities with Mexico were draining resources and attention away from the far more important issue of Oregon; when the United States finally reached its agreement with Britain, opponents claimed that Polk had settled for less than he should have because he was preoccupied with Mexico. This opposition, limited at first to a relatively few Whigs in Congress, increased and intensified as the war continued and as the public became aware of the level of casualties and of the expense. Whigs in Congress generally supported military appropriation bills, not wishing to face accusations of obstructing the war effort. But they became ever bolder and more bitter in denouncing "Mr. Polk's war" as an aggressive and unnecessary conflict.

The president himself, in the meantime, was finding it more difficult than he had thought to achieve his goals. Although American forces were generally successful in their campaigns against the

Mexicans, final victory did not come nearly as quickly as Polk had hoped. In the opening phases of the war, the president assumed the planning of grand strategy, a practice that he continued almost to the end of the war. His basic idea was to seize key areas on the Mexican frontier and then force the Mexicans to make peace on American terms. Accordingly, he ordered Taylor to cross the Rio Grande and occupy northeastern Mexico, taking as his first objective the city of Monterrey. Polk seems to have had a vague idea that from Monterrey Taylor could advance southward, if necessary, and menace Mexico City. Taylor, known as "Old Rough and Ready," beloved by his soldiers for his courage and easy informality but ignorant of many of the technical aspects of war, attacked Monterrey in September 1846. After a hard fight he captured it, but at the price of agreeing to let the garrison evacuate without pursuit. Although the country hailed Taylor as a hero, Polk concluded that he did not possess the ability to lead an offensive against Mexico City. Also, Polk began to realize that an advance south through the mountains would involve impossible problems of supply.

Polk launched two other offensives against New Mexico and California. In the summer of 1846, a small army under Colonel Stephen W. Kearny made the long march to Santa Fe and occupied the town with no opposition. Kearny sent part of his army (Missouri volunteers under Colonel A. W. Doniphan) south to join Taylor, and ordered other troops under his command to remain in the province and defend it. Then, under instructions from Polk, Kearny proceeded with a few hundred soldiers to California to take charge of operations there. In California a combined revolt and war was being staged by the settlers, Frémont's exploring party, and the American navy. The settlers had proclaimed California an independent nation in the "Bear Flag Revolution." Frémont had returned from Oregon to lead the rebels, and the navy had landed forces and annexed California to the United States. When Kearny arrived, the Americans were fighting under the direction of Commodore R. F. Stockton of the navy. With some difficulty, Kearny brought the disparate American elements under his command, and by the autumn of 1846 completed the conquest of California.

In addition to northeastern Mexico, the United States now had possession of the two provinces for which it had gone to war. In a sense, the original objectives of the war had been achieved. Mexico, however, refused to recognize realities and would not agree to a peace or cede the conquered territory.

At this point, Polk turned to General Winfield Scott, the commanding general of the army and its finest soldier, for help. Together, the two men devised a plan to force peace on the Mexicans—and, perhaps, gain even more new territory for the United States. Scott was to assemble an army at Tampico made up partly of troops from Taylor's army and partly of other forces. The navy would transport this new army down the coast to Vera Cruz, which the Americans would seize and make into a base. From Vera Cruz, Scott would move west along the National Highway to Mexico City. Late in 1846, Scott went to Mexico to organize his forces. Taylor, about half of whose army was transferred to Scott's command, was instructed to stand on the defensive.

While Scott was assembling his army off the coast, General Santa Anna, the Mexican dictator, decided to take advantage of the division of American forces by marching northward, crushing Taylor, and then returning to deal with Scott. With an army much larger than Taylor's, Santa Anna attacked the Americans at Buena Vista in February 1847. But he could not break the American line and had to return to defend Mexico City.

In the meantime, Scott had taken Vera Cruz by siege and was moving inland, in one of the most brilliant campaigns in American military annals. With an army that never numbered more than 14,000, he advanced 260 miles into enemy territory, conserved the lives of his soldiers by using flanking movements instead of frontal assaults, and finally achieved his objective without losing a battle. At Cerro Gordo, in the mountains, he inflicted a smashing reverse on the Mexicans. He met no further resistance until he was within a few miles of Mexico City. After capturing the fortress of Chapultepec in a hard fight, the Americans occupied the enemy capital. A new Mexican government came into power, one that recognized defeat and was willing to make a peace treaty.

President Polk was now growing thoroughly unclear about his objectives. He continued to encourage those who demanded that the United States annex much of Mexico itself. At the same time, concerned about the approaching presidential election, he was growing anxious to get the war finished quickly. Along with the invading army, Polk had sent a special presidential agent authorized to negotiate a settlement with Mexico. The agent—Nicholas Trist, one of those obscure figures who occasionally have a major impact on history—concluded a treaty with the new Mexican government on February 2, 1848: the Treaty of Guadalupe Hidalgo. Mexico agreed to cede

The Mexican War, 1846–1848

TROOP MOVEMENTS
→ American forces
← Mexican forces

BATTLES
✳ American victory
✳ Mexican victory

Capture of Mexico City September 1847

California and New Mexico to the United States and acknowledge the Rio Grande as the boundary of Texas. In return, the United States contracted to assume the claims of its citizens against Mexico and pay to the Mexicans $15 million. When the treaty reached Washington, Polk faced a dilemma. Trist had obtained for the United States most of Polk's original demands, but he had stopped far short of the expan-

sive dreams the president had come to harbor of acquiring more territory in Mexico. Polk angrily claimed that Trist had violated his instructions; he soon realized, however, that he had no choice but to accept the treaty. Some ardent expanionists were demanding that he hold out for annexation of—in a phrase widely bandied about at the time—"All Mexico!" Antislavery leaders, in the meantime, were

Scott's Army in Mexico City
General Winfield Scott leads an American army into the capital of Mexico in September 1847, the culminating triumph of the Mexican War. George W. Kendall of the New Orleans *Picayune* was one of the first war correspondents to accompany an army on its campaigns and was with Scott throughout the assault on the city. This print appeared in a history of the war Kendall published several years later. (Library of Congress)

charging that the demands for acquisition of Mexico were part of a Southern scheme to extend slavery to new realms (although other antislavery people, convinced that slavery could never be established in Mexico, were among those arguing for taking the whole country). To silence this bitter and potentially destructive debate, Polk submitted the Trist treaty to the Senate, which approved it by a vote of 38 to 14. The war was over, and America had gained a vast new territory. But it had also acquired a new set of troubling and divisive issues.

A New Sectional Crisis

James Polk tried during his presidency to be a leader whose policies transcended sectional issues. Thus he responded to the expansionist demands of both Northerners and Southerners. And he pursued economic policies designed similarly to strengthen the Democratic party as an organization with strong national support. He persuaded Congress, for example, to reestablish the independent treasury system—the Van Buren plan of 1840 to stabilize the nation's banks without resorting to another Bank of the United States. The Tyler administration had dismantled the system two years earlier, and Polk now delighted Democrats throughout the country by restoring it. He also delighted the South by fulfilling his campaign pledge to lower tariff rates—through the tariff of 1846, which achieved support as well from Northwestern Democrats.

Yet Polk was not to find it so easy to conciliate the sections. Although he acquired territory both in the Northwest and in the Southwest, Northerners continued to accuse him of having made Oregon a second priority so as to favor the expansionists of the South. The tariff bill, moreover, not only alienated

manufacturers and merchants in the Northeast. It encouraged those Northwesterners who had supported it to believe that the president should, in return for their backing, now support internal improvements in their region. When Polk vetoed two bills providing federal funds for construction of roads and other improvements in the West, arguing that the national government had no authority to fund such projects, Westerners charged again that the administration was sacrificing their interests to those of the South.

The Sectional Debate

Sectional tensions were already rising, therefore, when a much more dangerous issue emerged. In August 1846, while the war was still in progress, Polk had asked Congress to provide him with $2 million that he could use to purchase peace with Mexico. When the appropriation was introduced in the House, David Wilmot of Pennsylvania, an antislavery Democrat from a high-tariff state, moved an amendment that slavery should be prohibited in any territory secured from Mexico. The so-called Wilmot Proviso passed the House but failed in the Senate. It would be called up again and be debated and voted on repeatedly for years.

Diametrically opposed to the Wilmot Proviso was the formula of the Southern extremists. They contended that the states jointly owned the territories and that the citizens of each state possessed equal rights in them, including the right to move to them with their property, particularly slave property. According to this view, Congress had no power to prohibit the movement of slavery into the public domain or to regulate it in any way except by extending protection. Neither could a territorial legislature, which was a creature of Congress, take any action to ban slavery.

Two compromise plans were presented. One, which numbered President Polk among its advocates, proposed to run the Missouri Compromise line of 36°30′ through the new territories to the Pacific coast, banning slavery north of the line and permitting it south of the line. The other, first prominently supported by Lewis Cass, Democratic senator from Michigan, was originally called "squatter sovereignty." Some years later, when taken up by Stephen A. Douglas, an Illinois senator of the same party, it was given the more dignified title of "popular sovereignty." According to this formula, the question of slavery in each territory should be left to the people there, acting through the medium of their territorial legislature.

Congress and the country debated the various formulas, but at the end of Polk's administration a decision had still not been reached. No territorial government had been provided for California or New Mexico (New Mexico included most of present New Mexico and Arizona, all of Utah and Nevada, and parts of Colorado and Wyoming). Even the organization of Oregon, so far north that slavery obviously would never enter it, was held up by the controversy. Southern members of Congress, hoping to gain some advantage in the regions farther south, blocked a territorial bill for Oregon until August 1848, when a free-soil government was finally authorized.

The debate was partially stilled by the presidential campaign of 1848. Both the Democrats and the Whigs tried to avoid provocative references to the slavery question. When Polk declined to run for a second term, the Democrats nominated as their candidate Lewis Cass of Michigan, an elderly, honest, dull party wheel horse—and, according to most accounts (and portraits), a man of stunning physical unattractiveness. Although the platform was purposely vague, it could be interpreted as an endorsement of squatter

American Expansion into the Southwest, 1845–1853

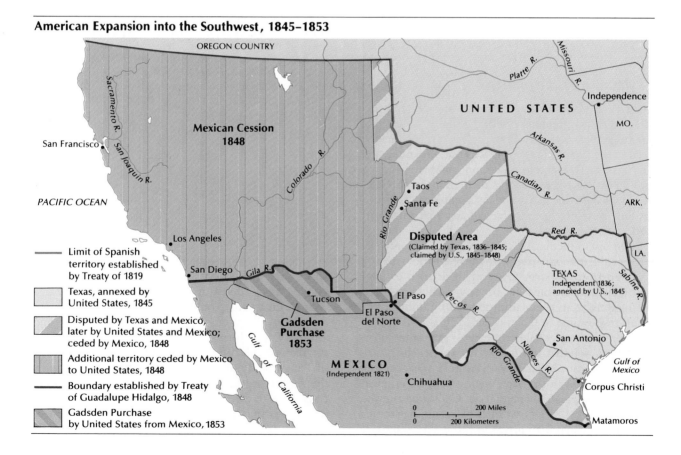

sovereignty. The Whigs adopted no platform and presented as their candidate a military hero with no political record, General Zachary Taylor of Louisiana.

Ardent abolitionists and even moderates who merely opposed the expansion of slavery found it difficult to swallow either Cass or Taylor. The situation was ripe for the appearance of a powerful third party. The potential sources for such a group were the existing Liberty party and the antislavery Whigs and Democrats. Late in the campaign, third-party promoters held a national convention, adopted a platform endorsing the Wilmot Proviso, free homesteads (free land for migrants to the West), and a higher tariff, and nominated former president Van Buren for the presidency. Thus was launched the Free Soil party—a major step toward what would ultimately be a dissolution of the existing party system and its replacement with another.

Taylor won a narrow victory. Although Van Buren failed to carry a single state, he polled an impressive 291,000 votes (10 percent of the total), and the Free-Soilers elected ten members to Congress. It is probable that Van Buren pulled enough Democratic votes away from Cass, particularly in New York, to throw the election to Taylor.

Taylor and the Territories

Zachary Taylor was the first man to be elected president with no previous political training or experience. He was also the first professional soldier to occupy the White House. (He was not, of course, the first general. Washington, Jackson, and Harrison had all attained that rank during their military service.) Taylor was a Southerner and a slaveholder, but from his long years in the army he had acquired a national outlook.

Almost immediately, the new president encountered problems connected with the territories recently acquired from Mexico. Congress had failed to provide a civil government for the new possessions, and the regions were being administered by military officials responsible to the president. There was particular pressure to establish a new government in California, for that territory was experiencing a remarkable boom. In January 1848, gold was accidentally discovered in the Sacramento Valley. As word of the strike spread, inhabitants of California and the whole Far West, fired by hopes of becoming immediate millionaires, stampeded to the area to stake out claims. By the end of summer the news had reached

Gold Mining in California in the 1850s
This photograph shows a sluice, used in placer mining. A "placer" was a deposit of sand, dirt, or clay—often in the bed of a stream—that contained fine particles of gold, which could be mined by washing. The "sluice" was a wooden trough into which miners shoveled the earth and then ran a steady stream of water over it. Heavy particles (such as gold) would sink to the bottom, where they were caught by cleats (known as "riffles"). Placer mining was one of the simplest and cheapest methods of extracting gold from the land, but it seldom produced large strikes. (Bettmann Archive)

the Eastern states and Europe. Then the gold rush really started.

From the United States and throughout the world, thousands of "forty-niners" poured into California. Those who left from the older states could choose among three routes of travel: overland by covered wagon, inexpensive but involving a long journey over the Great Plains and across the Rockies; by ship around Cape Horn, quicker but more expensive; or the dangerous, difficult shortcut across the Isthmus of Panama. By all three routes, disdaining hunger, thirst, disease, and even death, the seekers after gold came—more than 80,000 of them in 1849 alone. By the end of that year, California had a population of approximately 100,000, more than enough to entitle it to statehood.

President Taylor believed that statehood would serve as the solution not only to the inadequacy of the military government in California but to the whole issue of slavery in the territories. Let California and New Mexico both frame state constitutions and apply for admission to the Union, he declared. Once they had become states, no one could deny their right to dispose of slavery as they wished. So Taylor directed military officials in the territories to expedite statehood movements.

California promptly ratified a constitution in which slavery was prohibited. When Congress assembled in December 1849, Taylor proudly described his efforts. He recommended that California be admitted as a free state and that New Mexico, when it was ready, be permitted to come in with complete freedom to decide the status of slavery as it wished. But Congress was not about to accept the president's program.

Complicating the situation was the emergence of side issues generated by the conflict over slavery in the territories. One such issue concerned slavery in the District of Columbia. Antislavery people, charging that human servitude in the capital was a national disgrace, demanded that it be abolished there. Southerners angrily replied that the institution could not be touched without the consent of Maryland, which had originally donated the land.

Another disturbing issue was the question of fugitive slaves. Northern personal liberty laws, forbidding courts and police officers to assist in the return of runaways, provoked Southerners to call for a new, more stringent *national* fugitive slave law.

A third issue related to the boundary between Texas and New Mexico. Texas claimed the portion of New Mexico east of the Rio Grande, although the federal government during the Mexican War had assigned this region to New Mexico. To Texans, it seemed that Washington was trying to steal part of their territory. They also resented the government's refusal to assume the Texas war debt. Southern extremists supported the pretensions of Texas, while Northerners, eager to cut down the size of a slave state, upheld New Mexico.

But the biggest obstacle in the way of the president's program was the South—angered and frightened by the possibility that two new free states would be added to the Northern majority. Only in the Senate did the South still maintain equality. The number of free and slave states was equal in 1849—fifteen of each. But now the admission of California would upset the balance, with New Mexico, Oregon, and Utah still to come.

Responsible Southern leaders declared that if California was to be admitted, and if slavery was to be prohibited in the territories, the time had come for the South to secede from the Union. At the suggestion of Mississippi, a call went out for a Southern-rights convention to meet in June 1850 at Nashville, Tennessee, to consider whether the South should resort to the ultimate act of secession. In the North excitement ran equally high. Every Northern state legislature but one adopted resolutions demanding that slavery be barred from the territories. Public meetings all through the free states called for the passage of the Wilmot Proviso and the abolition of slavery in the District of Columbia. Such was the crisis that confronted Congress and the country as the tense year of 1850 opened.

The Compromise of 1850

Moderates and lovers of the Union turned their thoughts, during the winter of 1849–1850, to the framing of a great congressional compromise that would satisfy both sections and restore tranquillity. The venerable statesman from Kentucky, Henry Clay, headed the forces of conciliation. In Clay's view, no compromise would have any lasting effect unless it settled all the issues in dispute between the sections. Accordingly, he took a number of separate measures, which had been proposed before, combined them into one set of resolutions, and on January 29, 1850, presented them to the Senate. He recommended (1) that California be admitted as a free state; (2) that, in the rest of the Mexican cession, territorial governments be formed without restrictions as to slavery; (3) that Texas yield in its boundary dispute with New Mexico and be compensated by the federal government's taking over its public debt; (4) that the slave trade, but not slavery itself, be abolished in the District of Columbia; and (5) that a new and more effective fugitive slave law be passed. These resolutions launched a debate that raged for seven months—both in Congress and throughout the nation. The debate occurred in two phases, the differences between which revealed much about how American politics was changing in the 1850s.

In the first phase of the debate, the dominant voices in Congress were those of old men—national leaders who still remembered Jefferson, Adams, and other founders—who argued for or against the compromise on the basis of broad ideals. Clay himself, seventy-three years old in 1850, was the most prominent of these spokesmen. He opened the oratorical tournament with a defense of his measures and a broad plea to both North and South to be mutually conciliatory. It was the Union, he claimed, and the shared sentiments of nationalism that had emerged from America's glorious past, that should be the primary concern of the lawmakers.

Early in March, another of the older leaders—John C. Calhoun, sixty-eight years old and so ill that he had to sit grimly in his seat while a colleague read his speech for him—made his contribution to the debate. Almost ignoring Clay's proposals, he devoted his argument to what to him was the larger, in fact the only subject: the minority status of the South; and he asked more for his section than any realistic observer believed could be given. Like Clay, however, Calhoun spoke emotionally of the bonds holding the nation together. Because of Northern aggressions, the cords that bound the Union were snapping. What could save it? The North, he insisted, must admit that the South possessed equal rights in the territories, must agree to observe the laws concerning fugitive slaves, must cease attacking slavery, and must accept an amendment to the Constitution guaranteeing a balance of power between the sections. The amendment would provide for the election of dual presidents, one from the North and one from the South, each possessing a veto power. In short, nothing would satisfy Calhoun but a comprehensive, permanent solution to the sectional problem. His proposal, however, would have required an abject surrender by the North.

After Calhoun came the third of the elder statesmen, the sixty-eight-year-old Daniel Webster. His "Seventh of March Address" was probably the greatest forensic effort of his long oratorical career. Still nourishing White House ambitions, he now sought to calm angry passions and to rally Northern moderates to support Clay's compromise.

After six months of debate, however—six months dominated by ringing appeals to the memory of the founders, to nationalism, to idealism—the effort to win approval of the compromise failed. In July, Congress defeated the Clay proposal. And with that, the controversy moved into its second phase, in which a very different cast of characters would predominate. Clay, ill and tired, left Washington to spend the summer resting in the mountains. He would return, but never with his old vigor; he died in 1852. Calhoun had died even before the vote in July. And Webster in the course of the summer accepted a new appointment as secretary of state, thus removing himself from the Senate and from the debate.

In place of these leaders, a new, younger group now emerged as the dominant voices. There was William H. Seward of New York, forty-nine years old, a wily political operator who staunchly opposed the proposed compromise. The ideals of Union were to him clearly less important than the issue of eliminating slavery. Emerging as the new voice of the South was Jefferson Davis of Mississippi, forty-two years old, a representative not of the old aristocratic South of Calhoun but of the new, cotton South—a hard, frontierlike country that was growing rapidly and prospering. To him, and to those he represented, the slavery issue was not only one of principles and ideals but also one of economic self-interest.

Most important of all, there was Stephen A. Douglas, the thirty-seven-year-old senator from Illinois. More than any of the others, Douglas represented the new generation of politicians coming to dominate national life. A Westerner from a rapidly growing frontier state, a man unpolished in manner, he was an open spokesman for the economic needs of his section—and especially for the new railroads. His was a career devoted not to any broad national goals, as Clay's, Webster's, and even Calhoun's had often been, but one devoted frankly to sectional gain and personal self-promotion.

The new leaders of the Senate were able, where the old leaders were not, to arrive at a compromise in 1850. In part, they were aided by a shift in popular sentiment. The country was entering a period of prosperity—the result of an expanding foreign trade, the flow of gold from California, and a boom in railroad construction—reminiscent of the flush days of the 1830s. Conservative economic interests everywhere wanted to end the sectional dispute and concentrate on internal expansion. Even in the South, excitement seemed to be abating. The Nashville convention met in June, adopted a few tame resolutions, and then quietly adjourned to await final action by Congress.

Progress toward the compromise was also furthered by the removal of the most powerful obstacle to it: the president. Zachary Taylor had been unyielding in his stand that the admission of California and possibly New Mexico must come first, that only then could other measures be discussed. Taylor had threatened not only to veto any measure that diverged from this proposal but to use force against the South (even to lead the troops in person) if they attempted to secede. But on July 9, Taylor suddenly died—the victim of a violent stomach disorder following an attack of heat prostration. He was succeeded by his vice president, Millard Fillmore of New York—a handsome and dignified man of no particular ability, but one who understood the political importance of flexibility. He ranged himself on the side of the compromise and used his powers of persuasion to swing Northern Whigs into line.

The new leaders benefited, however, not just from the shift in sentiment and the change in presidents, but also from their own pragmatic tactics. Douglas's first step, after the departure of Clay, was to break up the "omnibus bill" that Clay had envisioned as a great, organic solution to the sectional crisis and introduce instead a series of separate measures to be voted on one by one. Thus representatives of different sections could support those elements of the compromise favorable to them and could abstain from voting on or could vote against those they opposed. Douglas also gained support by avoiding the grand appeals to patriotism of Clay and Webster and resorting instead to complicated backroom maneuverings and deals—linking the compromise to such nonideological matters as the sale of government bonds and the construction of railroads. As a result of his efforts, by mid-September all the components of the compromise had been enacted by both houses of Congress and signed by the president.

The outcome was a great victory for Douglas and the forces of conciliation; but it was a clouded victory. For the passage of the Compromise of 1850, unlike the creation of the Missouri Compromise thirty years before, had not resulted from any widespread agreement on common national ideals. It was, rather, a victory largely of self-interest that had not resolved the underlying problems. Nevertheless, leaders in Congress hailed the event as a great triumph; and Millard Fillmore, signing the measure, called it a just settlement of the sectional problem, "in its character final and irrevocable."

It was one thing to pass the compromise through Congress and another to persuade the country to accept it. In the North, the most objectionable of the measures was the Fugitive Slave Act. By this law, blacks accused of being runaways were denied trial by jury and the right to testify in their own behalf.

Slave and Free Territories According to the Compromise of 1850

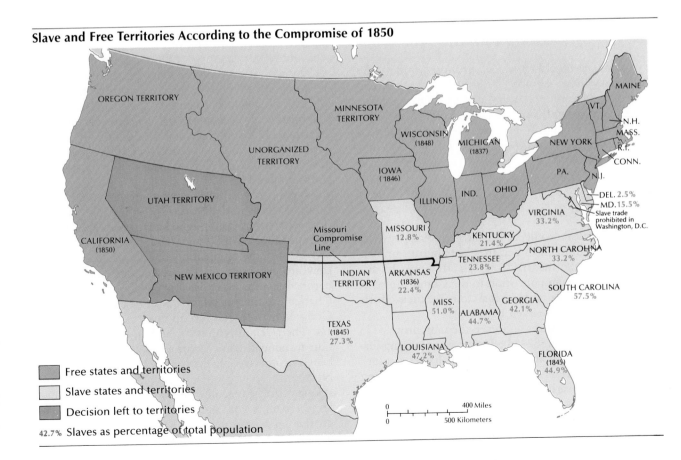

Free states and territories

Slave states and territories

Decision left to territories

42.7% Slaves as percentage of total population

Their status was to be decided by a federal judge or by a special commissioner appointed by the federal circuit courts. They could be remanded to slavery simply on the evidence of affidavits presented by those who claimed to be their owners.

But the Fugitive Slave Act was the only part of the compromise that most Southerners could ungrudgingly approve. The Nashville convention met again in November 1850 (with only about a third of the original delegates present) and condemned the compromise. Eventually the South brought itself to accept the settlement, but only after much agonizing, and then only conditionally. Epitomizing such feelings was the "Georgia Platform," which declared that Georgia would acquiesce in the compromise—but that if the North disregarded the Fugitive Slave Act or attempted to abolish slavery in the District of Columbia or denied admission to a state because it wished to have slavery, then Georgia would consider the compact broken and would protect its rights even to the point of seceding from the union.

The Crises of the 1850s

For a few years after the Compromise of 1850, the sectional conflict seemed briefly to be forgotten, and much of the nation concentrated on enjoying prosperity and growth. But the tensions between North and South remained, and the crisis continued to smolder until—in 1854—it once more burst into flames.

The Uneasy Truce

How difficult it would be for the nation to put aside its sectional differences became clear almost immediately. For while the major parties attempted to display an unswerving devotion to the Compromise of 1850, events in the nation began to make their efforts seem unrealistic and even irrelevant.

Both major parties endorsed the Compromise in their platforms in 1852—the Democrats pledging fervently to avoid all attempts in any "shape or color" to renew agitation over slavery, the Whigs making the same promise in somewhat milder language. Both parties, similarly, nominated presidential candidates who were moderates on the sectional issue and were unlikely to arouse passionate opposition in either

North or South. The Democrats chose the obscure New Hampshire politician Franklin Pierce (although not until after wrangling through forty-nine ballots, with the convention deadlocked among the three leading contenders—Lewis Cass, Stephen Douglas, and James Buchanan of Pennsylvania). The Whigs chose as their nominee the military hero General Winfield Scott, a man whose political views were so undefined that no one even knew whether or not he approved of the Compromise of 1850.

Yet the gingerly way in which party leaders dealt with the sectional question could not prevent its divisive influence from intruding on the election. The Whigs, in particular, suffered from their attempts to straddle the issue. Already plagued by the defections of those antislavery Northerners who had formed the Free Soil party in 1846, they alienated still more party members—the "Conscience" Whigs—by refusing to take an open stand against slavery now. Partly as a result of these divisions, Scott was the last presidential candidate the Whigs were ever to nominate. In the meantime, the Free Soil party was gaining in numbers and influence in the North; its presidential candidate, John P. Hale, repudiated the Compromise of 1850.

The divisions among the Whigs, and the vagueness of the party's support of the compromise, helped produce a victory for the Democrats in 1852. The new president, Franklin Pierce, was forty-nine years old when inaugurated the following March—the youngest man to serve in the office to that date. A charming, amiable man of no great distinction, he attempted to maintain party—and national—harmony by avoiding divisive issues. But those issues arose despite him.

Partly, they arose because there remained active political forces in the North—most notably the abolitionist organizations—who had never supported the Compromise of 1850 and who continued to work actively for the elimination of slavery. Partly, too, they arose because of the presence of eloquent and combative antislavery leaders in Congress—Senator Charles Sumner of Massachusetts, elected in 1850; Congressman Joshua R. Giddings of Ohio; and others. Their denunciations of the South and its institution resounded from a national forum. Most of all, however, the sectional tensions continued because of Northern response to the Fugitive Slave Act. Always strong, that opposition intensified after 1850 when Southerners began appearing in Northern states to pursue fugitives or to claim as slaves blacks who had been living for years in Northern communities. So fervently did many opponents of slavery resent such efforts that mobs formed in city after city to prevent enforcement of the law. In 1851, a crowd in Boston took a runaway named Shadrach from a federal marshal and sent him on his way to Canada; in Syracuse, New York, later in the same year, another crowd rescued a slave named Jerry McHenry. In 1854, a Boston mob led by respectable and prominent citizens attempted, unsuccessfully, to seize the escaped slave Anthony Burns from federal officers.

Northern states tried to undermine the Fugitive Slave Act through legal means as well. Several states passed new personal liberty laws, designed to interpose state authority between the accused fugitive and the federal government. In Wisconsin and Massachusetts, such laws directed state courts to grant all fugitives a judicial hearing (heavily weighted in the fugitives' favor) before they could be deported from the state. The supreme court of Wisconsin, in *Ableman* v. *Booth* (1857), went so far as to declare the federal Fugitive Slave Act void and to ignore the U.S. Supreme Court when it overruled the Wisconsin ruling.

White Southerners watched all this with growing anger and alarm. The Fugitive Slave Act had been the one element of the Compromise of 1850 they had considered a victory. Now they had to watch while the North, through the extralegal device of mobs and through legal efforts of dubious constitutionality, made that victory meaningless.

"Young America"

The Pierce administration tried to avoid taking a position on most domestic issues likely to produce controversy. And in foreign policy as well, the Democrats tried to revive a sense of cross-sectional nationalism. Here, too, however, their efforts created more problems than they resolved.

Spearheading the revival of nationalist diplomacy was a group of Democrats who organized what they called the Young America movement. Aware of the great liberal and nationalist revolutions of 1848 in Europe, these adventurous Democrats were stirred by the vision of a republican Europe with governments based on the model of the United States. They continued to dream as well of expanding American commerce in the Pacific and of extending the sweep of Manifest Destiny with new acquisitions in the Western Hemisphere. The sentiments they aroused had a profound effect on the nation's foreign policy.

Those sentiments were first felt in the second half of the Whig administration, under the new president, Millard Fillmore, and his new secretary of state, Daniel Webster. One example of their approach to international relations was Webster's defiance of the powerful government of Austria by supporting the effort of Hungary to win its independence. The Fillmore administration also sponsored an expedition into the Pacific under Commodore Matthew C. Perry, who began efforts to open Japan—for nearly two centuries all but totally closed to the West—to American trade. Perry's efforts resulted in 1854 in a treaty giving Americans access to two Japanese ports.

Few Americans in either section objected to these displays of nationalism. But efforts by both the Fillmore and Pierce administrations to extend the nation's domain in its own hemisphere produced new problems. First Fillmore and then Pierce sanctioned a series of ill-considered and ultimately unsuccessful attempts to wrest Cuba from the Spanish Empire. Frustrated in efforts to acquire the island through open diplomacy, Pierce turned to more devious means—authorizing his minister to Spain, the impetuous Pierre Soulé, to try to "detach" Cuba from the empire by subterfuge. Soulé's clumsy efforts only widened the gap between Spain and the United States, particularly when he collaborated with several other American diplomats in Europe (John Y. Mason, minister to France, and James Buchanan, minister to Great Britain) to produce a preposterous document, the so-called Ostend Manifesto. In it, Soulé and the others declared that all parties—Spain, Cuba, and the United States—would benefit from the annexation of Cuba by America. What was more, if disturbances there became a threat to American security, the United States would be justified "by every law human and divine" in "wresting" the island from Spain. The document was meant to be confidential, but its contents soon became public, enraging many antislavery Northerners, who charged the administration with conspiring to bring a new slave state into the Union even at the risk of war.

The South, for its part, opposed all efforts to acquire new territory that would not support a slave system. The kingdom of Hawaii agreed to join the United States in 1854, but the treaty had no chance in the Senate because it contained a clause prohibiting slavery in the islands. A powerful movement to annex Canada to the United States—a movement that had the support of many Canadians eager for access to American markets—similarly foundered, at least in part because of slavery. Southerners eager to prevent the addition of free territory to the Union supported an 1854 treaty providing trade reciprocity between the two nations—a treaty that undercut pressures for annexation.

The Kansas-Nebraska Controversy

Controversy over the return of fugitive slaves and the efforts to extend American dominion abroad kept sectional tensions alive in the early 1850s. But what fully revived the crisis between North and South was the same issue that had produced it in the first place: slavery in the territories. By the 1850s, the line of frontier settlement had moved west to the great bend of the Missouri River. Beyond the boundaries of Minnesota, Iowa, and Missouri stretched a great expanse of plains, which most Americans had always believed was unfit for cultivation (it was widely known as the Great American Desert) and which the nation had thus assigned to the Indian tribes it had dislodged from the more fertile lands to the east. Now it was becoming apparent that large sections of this region were, in fact, suitable for farming. In the states of the Old Northwest, therefore, pressure began to build for efforts to extend settlement westward once again. Prospective settlers urged the government to open the area to them, provide territorial governments, and—despite the solemn assurance the United States had earlier given the Indians of the sanctity of their reservations—to dislodge the tribes so as to make room for white settlers. There was relatively little opposition from any segment of white society to the violation of Indian rights proposed by these demands. But the interest in further settlement raised two issues that did prove highly divisive and that gradually became entwined with each other: railroads and slavery.

As the nation expanded westward, the problem of communication between the older states and the so-called trans-Mississippi West (those areas west of the Mississippi River) became more and more critical. As a result, the idea of building a transcontinental railroad gradually gained favor both in and out of Congress. The problem, however, was where to place it—in particular, where to locate the railroad's eastern terminus. Northerners favored Chicago, the growing capital of the free states of the Northwest. Southerners supported St. Louis, Memphis, or New Orleans—all located in slave states. The transcontinental railroad, in other words, was—like nearly everything else in the 1850s—becoming entangled in sectionalism. It had become a prize that both North and South were struggling to secure.

Indians Near Fort Laramie
This 1859 painting of Fort Laramie is by Albert Bierstadt, who at the time was serving as an artist-illustrator for a team of government surveyors charting Western lands. The fort was the site of a great conference in 1851 between agents of the United States government and over 10,000 representatives of nine tribes. After nearly three weeks of talks, the tribal leaders agreed to a treaty that gave the United States the right to build more roads and forts in Indian territory.
(Museum of Fine Arts, Boston)

One argument against a southern route had been removed through the foresight of Pierce's secretary of war, Jefferson Davis, a Mississippian. Surveys had indicated that a road with a southern terminus would probably have to pass through an area south of the Gila River, in Mexican territory. At Davis's suggestion, Pierce appointed James Gadsden, a Southern railroad builder, to negotiate with Mexico for the sale of this region. In 1853 Gadsden persuaded the Mexican government to dispose of a strip of land that today comprises a part of Arizona and New Mexico, the so-called Gadsden Purchase; the United States paid Mexico $10 million for the land.

Particularly interested in a transcontinental railroad was Senator Stephen A. Douglas, and his interest influenced him to introduce in Congress a fateful legislative act, one that accomplished the final destruction of the Compromise of 1850. As a senator from Illinois, a resident of Chicago, and above all, the acknowledged leader of the Northwestern Democrats, Douglas naturally wanted the transcontinental railroad for his own city and section. He realized too the potency of the principal argument urged against the northern route: that west of the Mississippi it would run largely through unsettled Indian country. In January 1854, as chairman of the Committee on Territories, he acted to forestall this argument. He introduced a bill to organize a huge new territory, to be known as Nebraska, west of Iowa and Missouri.

Douglas seemed to realize that this bill would encounter the opposition of the South, partly because it would prepare the way for a new free state, the proposed territory being in the Louisiana Purchase area north of the 36°30' line of the Missouri Compromise and hence closed to slavery. In an effort to make the measure acceptable to Southerners, Douglas inserted a provision that the status of slavery in the territory would be determined by the territorial legislature—that is, according to popular sovereignty. Theoretically, at least, this would open the region to slavery. The concession was not enough to satisfy extreme Southern Democrats, particularly those from Missouri, who feared that their state would be surrounded by free territory. They demanded more, and Douglas had to give more to get their support. He agreed to two additions to his bill: a clause specifically repealing the antislavery provision of the Missouri Compromise, and another creating two territories, Nebraska and Kansas, instead of one. Presumably Kansas would become a slave state. In its final form the measure was known as the Kansas-Nebraska Act.

Douglas persuaded President Pierce to endorse his bill, and so it became an official Democratic measure. But even with the backing of the administration, it encountered stiff opposition and did not become a law until May 1854. Nearly all the Southern members of Congress, whether Whigs or Democrats, supported the bill, and nearly all the Northern Whigs opposed it. The Northern Democrats in the House split evenly.

Of greater importance than the opposition to the Kansas-Nebraska Act in Congress was the reaction against it in the Northern states. The effort to repeal the Missouri Compromise—a measure that many Northerners believed had a special sanctity, almost as if it were a part of the Constitution—was particularly alarming. The whole North seemed to blaze with fury at this latest demonstration of the power of the slavocracy, and much of the fury was directed at Douglas, who, in the eyes of many Northerners, had acted as a tool of the slaveholders. No other piece of legislation in congressional history produced so many immediate, sweeping, and ominous changes as the Kansas-Nebraska Act. It destroyed the Whig party in

the South except in the border states. At the same time, as many Southern Whigs became Democrats, it increased Southern influence in the Democratic party. It destroyed the popular basis of Whiggery in the North, with the result that by 1856 the national Whig party had disappeared and a conservative, nationalistic influence in American politics had been removed. It divided the Northern Democrats and drove many of them from the party. Most important of all, it called into being a new party that was frankly sectional in composition and creed.

People in both the major parties who opposed Douglas's bill began to call themselves Anti-Nebraska Democrats and Anti-Nebraska Whigs. In 1854, they formed a new party and began to call themselves "Republicans." The party had its beginnings in a series of spontaneous popular meetings throughout the Northwest, and the movement soon spread to the East. In the elections of 1854, the Republicans, often cooperating with the Know-Nothings, elected a majority to the U.S. House of Representatives and won control of a number of Northern state governments.

At first, the Republican party was a one-idea organization: It simply opposed the expansion of slavery into the territories. Its original members were mostly former Whigs and Free-Soilers but also included a substantial number of former Democrats. In part, it represented the democratic idealism of the North. But it also represented the agricultural and business interests of the section. Soon the party gained additional support from advocates of federal aid to economic activity—advocates of high tariffs, homesteads, and internal improvements—who blamed the South for blocking such aid and thus hindering Northern development. When the Know-Nothing organization broke up, the Republicans absorbed most of its members. Thus the new party inherited the taint of nativism that once had clung to the Whigs. Like the Whigs, the Republicans repelled the Roman Catholics among the German, Irish, and other foreign-born groups. Yet the Republicans succeeded in attracting Protestants among German and Scandinavian, as well as British, immigrants.

"Bleeding Kansas"

The pulsing popular excitement aroused in the North by the Kansas-Nebraska Act was sustained by events during the next two years in Kansas. Almost immediately, settlers moved into this territory. Those from the North were encouraged by press and pulpit and the powerful organs of abolitionist propaganda. Of-

FREE STATE CONVENTION!

All persons who are favorable to a union of effort, and a permanent organization of all the Free State elements of Kansas Territory, and who wish to secure upon the broadest platform the co-operation of all who agree upon this point, are requested to meet at their several places of holding elections, in their respective districts on the 25th of August, instant, at one o'clock, P. M., and appoint five delegates to each representative to which they were entitled in the Legislative Assembly, who shall meet in general Convention at

Big Springs, Wednesday, Sept. 5th '55,

at 10 o'clock A. M., for the purpose of adopting a Platform upon which all may act harmoniously who prefer Freedom to Slavery.

The nomination of a Delegate to Congress, will also come up before the General Convention.

Let no sectional or party issues distract or prevent the perfect co-operation of Free State men. Union and harmony are absolutely necessary to success. The pro-slavery party are fully and effectually organized. No jars nor minor issues divide them. And to contend against them successfully, we also must be united.—Without prudence and harmony of action we are certain to fail. Let every man then do his duty and we are certain of victory.

All Free State men, without distinction, are earnestly requested to take immediate and effective steps to insure a full and correct representation for every District in the Territory. "United we stand; divided we fall."

By order of the Executive Committee of the Free State Party of the Territory of Kansas, as per resolution of the Mass Convention in session at Lawrence, Aug 15th and 16th, 1855.

J. K. GOODIN, Sec'y.   **C. ROBINSON,** Chairman.

Herald of Freedom, Print.

Free-Soilers Organize in Kansas

In 1855 proslavery elements in Kansas, with the aid of "border ruffians" from Missouri, succeeded in electing a territorial legislature committed to legalizing slavery. In response, Kansas Free-Soilers called a convention to organize an antislavery government. This broadside announcing the meeting was widely distributed throughout the territory. (Kansas State Historical Society, Topeka)

---

ten they received financial help from such organizations as the New England Emigrant Aid Company. Those from the South often received financial contributions from the communities they left.

In the spring of 1855, elections were held for a territorial legislature. Thousands of Missourians, some traveling in armed bands, moved into Kansas and voted. Although there were probably only some 1,500 legal votes in the territory, more than 6,000 votes were counted. With such conditions prevailing, the proslavery forces elected a majority to the legislature, which proceeded immediately to enact a series of laws legalizing slavery. The outraged free-staters, convinced that they could not get fair treatment from the Pierce administration, resolved on extralegal action. Without asking permission from Congress or the territorial governor, they elected delegates to a constitutional convention that met at Topeka and adopted a constitution excluding slavery. They then chose a governor and legislature and petitioned Congress for statehood. Pierce called their movement unlawful and akin to treason. The full weight of the government, he announced, would be thrown behind the proslavery territorial legislature.

A few months later a proslavery federal marshal assembled a huge posse, consisting mostly of Missourians, to arrest the free-state leaders in Lawrence. The posse not only made the arrests but sacked the town. Several free-staters died in the melee. Retribution came immediately. Among the more extreme opponents of slavery in Kansas was a fierce, fanatical man named John Brown, who considered himself an instrument of God's will to destroy slavery. Brown estimated that five antislavery people had been murdered, and he decided that it was his sacred duty to take revenge. He gathered six followers, and in one night murdered five proslavery settlers, leaving their mutilated bodies to discourage other supporters of slavery from entering Kansas. The episode was known as the Pottawatomie Massacre; and its result was more civil strife in Kansas—irregular, guerrilla warfare conducted by armed bands, some of them more interested in land claims or loot than in ideologies.

In both North and South, the belief was widespread that the aggressive designs of the other section were epitomized by (and responsible for) what was happening in Kansas. Whether or not such beliefs were entirely correct is less important than that they became passionately held articles of faith in both sections. Thus "Bleeding Kansas" became a symbol of the sectional controversy.

Another symbol soon appeared, in the United States Senate. In May 1856, Charles Sumner of Massachusetts rose to discuss the problems of the strife-torn territory. He entitled his speech "The Crime Against Kansas." Handsome, humorless, eloquent, and passionately doctrinaire, Sumner embodied the most extreme element of the political antislavery movement. And in his speech, delivered with the righteous eloquence for which he was becoming famous, he bemoaned the fate of "bleeding Kansas" and fiercely denounced the Pierce administration, the South, and the institution of slavery. He singled out for particular attention his colleague in the Senate Andrew P. Butler of South Carolina, an outspoken defender of slavery. It was an age in which orators were accustomed to indulging in personal invective; but in his discussion of Butler, Sumner far exceeded the normal bounds. The South Carolinian was, Sumner claimed, the "Don Quixote" of slavery, having "chosen a mistress . . . who, though ugly to others, is always lovely to him, though polluted in the sight of the world, is chaste in his sight . . . the harlot slavery."

The pointedly sexual references and the general viciousness of the speech enraged Butler's nephew, Preston Brooks, a member of the U.S. House of Representatives from South Carolina. Brooks resolved to punish Sumner for his insults by a method approved by the Southern gentleman's code—a public, physical chastisement. Several days after the speech, Brooks approached Sumner at his desk in the Senate chamber during a recess, raised a heavy cane, and began beating him repeatedly on the head and shoulders. Sumner, trapped behind his desk, rose in agony with such strength that he tore the table from the bolts holding it to the floor, then collapsed, bleeding and unconscious. So severe were his injuries that he was unable to return to the Senate for four years, during which time his state refused to replace him. He became a potent symbol throughout the North—a martyr to the barbarism of the South.

Preston Brooks became a symbol too. Censured by the House, he resigned his seat, returned to South Carolina, and stood for reelection. He won the virtually unanimous support of his state. Brooks's assault had made him a Southern hero. And as a result, he, like Sumner, served as evidence of how deep the antagonism between North and South had become.

The Free-Soil Ideology

What had happened to produce such deep hostility between the two sections? There were, obviously, important differences between the North and the South; but many of these differences had always existed. There were real issues—above all the question of slavery in the territories—dividing them; but these issues alone are not a sufficient explanation. Despite the passions generated by the conflict in Kansas, neither the North nor the South really seemed to believe that there was ever a genuine prospect of slavery becoming established there. At the height of the struggle between pro- and antislavery forces in the territory, there were almost no blacks in Kansas at all. Similarly, few of the remaining territories seemed likely ever to support flourishing slave systems. And despite the fervor of the abolitionists, relatively few Northerners were yet willing to advocate an end to slavery where it presently existed.

Slavery and other issues attained such destructive importance among most Americans largely because they served as symbols for a set of larger concerns on both sides. As the nation expanded and political power grew more dispersed, the North and the South each became concerned with ensuring that its vision of America's future would be the dominant one. And those visions were becoming—partly as a result of internal developments within the sections themselves, partly because of each region's conceptions (and misconceptions) of what was happening outside it—increasingly distinct and increasingly rigid.

In the North, assumptions about the proper structure of society came to center on the belief in "free soil" and "free labor." The abolitionists generated some support for their argument that slavery was a moral evil and must be eliminated. Theirs, however, was never the dominant voice of the North. Instead, an increasing number of Northerners, gradually becoming a majority, came to believe that the existence of slavery was dangerous not because of what it did to blacks but because of what it threatened to do to whites. At the heart of American democracy, they believed, was the right of all citizens to own property, to control their own labor, and to have access to opportunities for advancement. The ideal society, in other words, was one of small-scale capitalism, with everyone entitled to a stake and with the chance of upward mobility available to all.

According to this vision, the South was the antithesis of democracy. It was a closed, static society, in which the slave system preserved an entrenched aristocracy and the common whites had no opportunity to improve themselves. More than that, the South was a backward society—decadent, lazy, dilapidated. While the North was growing and prospering, displaying thrift, industry, and a commitment to progress, the South was stagnating, rejecting the Northern values of individualism and growth. The South was, Northern free-laborites further maintained, engaged in a conspiracy to extend slavery throughout the nation and thus to destroy the openness of Northern capitalism and replace it with the closed, aristocratic system of the South. This "slave power conspiracy," as it came to be known, threatened the future of every white laborer and property owner in the North. The only solution was to fight the spread of slavery and work for the day when the nation's democratic (i.e., free-labor) ideals extended to all sections of the country—the day of the victory of what Northerners called "Freedom National."

This was the ideology that lay at the heart of the new Republican party. There were abolitionists and others in the organization who sincerely believed in the rights of blacks to freedom and citizenship. Far more important, however, were those who cared less about blacks than about the threat that slavery posed to white labor and to individual opportunity. This ideology also strengthened the commitment of Republicans to the Union. Since the idea of continued growth and progress was central to the free-labor vision, the prospect of dismemberment of the nation—a diminution of America's size and economic power—was unthinkable.

The Proslavery Argument

In the South, in the meantime, a very different ideology was emerging—one that was entirely incompatible with the vision of America's future being promoted by the defenders of free labor in the North. It was an ideology that emerged out of a rapid hardening of position among Southern whites on the issue of slavery.

As late as the early 1830s, there had been a substantial number of Southern whites who had harbored deep reservations about slavery. Between 1829 and 1832, for example, a Virginia constitutional convention, and then the state legislature, responding to demands from nonslaveholders in the western part of the state, had seriously considered ending slavery through compensated emancipation. They had chosen not to do so in large part because of the tremendous expense it would have entailed. There had been, moreover, many antislavery societies in the South—more there in 1827 than there were in the North, most of them in the border states. And there were prominent Southern politicians who spoke openly in opposition to slavery—among them Cassius M. Clay of Kentucky.

By the mid-1830s, however, this ambivalence about slavery was beginning to be replaced by a militant defense of the system. In part, the change was a result of events within the South itself. The Nat Turner uprising terrified whites throughout the region. They had always been uneasy, always mindful of the horrors of the successful slave uprising in Santo Domingo in the 1790s. Now they were reminded again of their insecurity, and they were especially horrified because there had been long-trusted house servants among Turner's followers who, ax in hand, had suddenly turned on their masters' sleeping families. Many slaveowners blamed Garrison and the abolitionists for the slaves' defection, and they grew more determined than ever to make slavery secure against all dangers. There was, too, an economic incentive to defend the system. With the expansion of the cotton economy into the Deep South, slavery—which had begun to seem unprofitable in many areas of the original South—now suddenly became lucrative once again.

But the change was also a result of events in the North, and particularly of the growth of the abolitionist movement, with its strident attacks on Southern society. Harriet Beecher Stowe's *Uncle Tom's Cabin* was perhaps the most glaring example of such an attack, a book that enraged the South and increased its resentment of the North. But other abolitionist writings had been antagonizing white Southerners for years.

In response to these pressures, a growing number of white Southerners began to elaborate an intellectual defense of slavery. It began as early as 1832, when Professor Thomas R. Dew of the College of William and Mary published a pamphlet outlining the slavery case. In subsequent years, many others added their contributions to the cause; and in 1852, the defense was summed up in an anthology that gave the philosophy its name: *The Pro-Slavery Argument*.

The essence of the argument, as John C. Calhoun boasted in 1837, was that Southerners should cease apologizing for slavery as a necessary evil and defend it as "a good—a positive good." Slavery was, according to such theorists, good for the slaves because they were inferior creatures. They needed the guidance of white masters, and they were better off—better fed, clothed, and housed, and more secure—than Northern factory workers. It was good for Southern society because it was the only way the two races could live together in peace. It was good for the country as a whole because the Southern economy, dependent on slavery, was the key to the prosperity of the nation. And it was good in itself because it was sanctioned by the Bible—did not the Hebrews of the Old Testament own bondsmen, and did not the New Testament apostle Paul advise, "Servants, obey your masters"?

Above all, Southern apologists argued, slavery was good because it served as the basis for the Southern way of life—a way of life superior to any other in the United States, perhaps in the world. White Southerners looking at the North saw a society that they believed was losing touch with traditional American values and replacing them with a spirit of greed, debauchery, and destructiveness. "The masses of the North are venal, corrupt, covetous, mean and selfish," wrote one Southerner. Others wrote with horror of the exploitation of the factory system, the growth of crowded, pestilential cities filled with unruly immigrants. The South, in contrast, was a stable, orderly society, operating at a slow and human pace. It had a labor system that avoided the feuds between capital and labor plaguing the North, a system that protected the welfare of its workers, a system that allowed the aristocracy to enjoy a refined and accomplished cultural life. It was, in short, as nearly perfect as any human civilization could become, an ideal social order in which all elements of the population were secure and content. Proslavery theoreticians—and the vast number of white Southerners, slaveowners, and nonslaveowners alike, who were coming to accept their arguments—were creating a dream world as a defense against the growing criticism from the North. It was, as one historian has described it, an "affirmation of Southern perfection."

Some proslavery propagandists went so far as to argue that slavery was such a good thing that it should be extended to include white workers in the North as well as black laborers in the South. George Fitzhugh of Virginia—in *Sociology for the South, or the Failure of Free Society* (1854), *Cannibals All* (1857), and other writings—claimed that all society lived on forced labor and that in the South masters at least acknowledged responsibility for those whose labor they were exploiting. Slavery, therefore, was the only workable form of socialism—a system that all societies should adopt as the sole cure for class conflict and the other ills of competitive society. (Such arguments fueled the fears of those Northern free-labor advocates who argued that the South was plotting to extend slavery everywhere, even into the factory system.)

Southern leaders had, by the 1850s, not only committed themselves to a militant proslavery ideology. They had also become convinced that they should silence advocates of freedom. Southern critics of slavery found it advisable to leave the region, among them Hinton Rowan Helper, whose *Impending Crisis of the South* (1857) contended that slavery hurt the welfare of the nonslaveholder and made the whole region backward. Beginning in 1835 (when a Charleston mob destroyed sacks containing abolitionist literature in the city post office), Southern postmasters generally refused to deliver antislavery mail. Southern state legislatures passed resolutions demanding that Northern states suppress the "incendiary" agitation of the abolitionists. Southern representatives even managed for a time to force Congress to honor a "gag rule" (adopted in 1836), according to which all antislavery petitions would be tabled without being read. Only the spirited protests of such Northerners as John Quincy Adams led to the repeal of the gag rule in 1844. Southern defenders of slavery, in other words, were not only becoming more militant about its virtues; they were becoming less tolerant of criticism of it—further encouraging those Northerners who warned of the "slave power conspiracy" against their liberties.

Buchanan and Depression

It was in this unpromising climate—with the country convulsed by the Brooks assault and the continuing violence in Kansas, and with each section becoming increasingly militant in support of its own ideology—that the presidential campaign of 1856 began. The Democrats adopted a platform that endorsed the Kansas-Nebraska Act and defended popular sovereignty. The leaders wanted a candidate who had not made many enemies and who was not closely associated with the explosive question of "Bleeding Kansas." So the nomination went to James Buchanan of Pennsylvania, a reliable party stalwart who as minister to England had been safely out of the country during the recent troubles, although he was a signer of the highly controversial Ostend Manifesto.

The Republicans, engaging in their first presidential contest, faced the campaign with confidence. They denounced the Kansas-Nebraska Act and the expansion of slavery but also approved a program of internal improvements, thus combining the idealism of antislavery with the economic aspirations of the North. Just as eager as the Democrats to present a safe candidate, the Republicans nominated John C. Frémont, who had made a national reputation as an explorer of the Far West and who had no political record.

The Native American, or Know-Nothing, party was beginning to break apart on the inevitable rock of sectionalism. At its convention, many Northern delegates withdrew because the platform was not sufficiently firm in opposing the expansion of slavery. The remaining delegates nominated former president Millard Fillmore. His candidacy was endorsed by the sad remnant of another party, the few remaining Whigs who could not bring themselves to support either Buchanan or Frémont.

The campaign was the most frenzied since the tempestuous election of 1840. It generated excitement largely as a result of the fervor of the Republicans, who shouted for "Free Soil, Free Speech, Free Men, and Frémont"; who depicted "Bleeding Kansas" as a sacrifice to the evil ambitions of the slavocracy; and who charged that the South, using Northern dupes such as Buchanan as its tools, was plotting to extend slavery into every part of the country.

The returns suggested that the prevailing mood of the country was still relatively conservative but that opinion was relatively narrowly divided. Buchanan, the winning candidate, polled 1,833,000 popular votes to 1,340,000 for Frémont and 872,000 for Fillmore. A slight shift of votes in Pennsylvania and Illinois, however, would have thrown those states into the Republican column and elected Frémont. More significant, perhaps, was that Frémont, who attracted virtually no votes at all in the South, nevertheless received a third of all votes cast. In the North, he had outpolled all other candidates.

The election of Buchanan was a disaster for the nation. He had been in public life for more than forty years at the time of his inauguration, and he was at age sixty-five the oldest president, except for William Henry Harrison, ever to have taken office. Whether because of his age and physical infirmities or because of a more fundamental weakness of character, he became a painfully timid and indecisive president in a time when the nation cried out as perhaps never before for strong, effective leadership.

In the year Buchanan took over, a financial panic struck the country, followed by several years of stringent depression. Europe had shown an unusual demand for American food during the Crimean War of 1854–1856. When that demand fell off, agricultural prices declined. The depression sharpened sectional differences. The South was not hit as hard as the North (since the region depended less on food crops than other agricultural areas), and Southern leaders thus found what they believed was confirmation for their claim that their economic system was superior to that of the free states. Smarting under previous Northern criticisms of Southern society, they loudly boasted of their superiority to the North.

In the North, the depression strengthened the Republican party. Distressed economic groups—manufacturers and farmers—came to believe that the hard times were the result of the unsound policies of Southern-controlled Democratic administrations. These groups thought that prosperity could be restored by a high tariff (the tariff had been lowered again in 1857), a homestead act, and internal improvements—all measures the South opposed. In short, the frustrated economic interests of the North were being drawn into an alliance with the antislavery elements and thus into the Republican party.

The Dred Scott Decision

The Supreme Court of the United States now projected itself into the sectional controversy with one of the most controversial decisions in its history—its ruling in the case of *Dred Scott* v. *Sanford,* handed down two days after Buchanan was inaugurated.

Dred Scott was a Missouri slave, once the property of an army surgeon who on military pilgrimages had carried Scott to Illinois, a free state, and to the Wisconsin Territory, where slavery was forbidden by the Missouri Compromise. Scott was persuaded by some abolitionists to bring suit in the Missouri courts for his freedom on the ground that residence in a free territory had made him a free man. The state supreme court decided against him. Meanwhile, the surgeon had died and his widow had married an abolitionist; and ownership of Scott had been transferred to her brother, J. F. A. Sanford, who lived in New York. Now Scott's lawyers could get the case into the federal courts on the ground that the suit lay between citizens of different states. Regardless of the final decision, Scott would be freed; his abolitionist owners would not keep him a slave. The case was intended less to determine Scott's future than to secure a federal decision on the status of slavery in the territories.

Of the nine justices of the Supreme Court, seven were Democrats (five of them from the South), one was a Whig, and one was a Republican. The Court was so divided that it was unable to issue a single ruling on the case and issued separate decisions on each of the major issues it raised. Each of the justices, moreover, wrote a separate opinion. The thrust of the rulings, however, was a defeat for Dred Scott and an affirmation of the South's argument that the Constitution guaranteed the existence of slavery. Chief Justice Roger Taney, who wrote one of the majority opinions, declared that Scott was not a citizen of Missouri or of the United States and hence could not bring a suit in the federal courts. According to Taney, no black could qualify as a citizen. So far as the Constitution was concerned, he added, blacks had no rights that white men were bound to respect. Having said this, Taney could simply have declined jurisdiction over the case. Instead, he went on to argue that Scott's sojourn in Minnesota had not affected his status as a slave. Slaves were property, said Taney, and the Fifth Amendment prohibited Congress from taking property without "due process of law." Consequently, Congress possessed no authority to pass a law depriving persons of their slave property in the territories. The Missouri Compromise, therefore, had always been null and void.

The ruling did nothing to challenge the right of an individual state to prohibit slavery within its borders, but the statement that the federal government was powerless to act on the issue was a drastic and startling one. Few judicial opinions have stirred as much popular excitement. Southern whites were elated: The highest tribunal in the land had sanctioned the extreme Southern argument. On behalf of abolitionists, black and white, Frederick Douglass declared: "This very attempt to blot out forever the hopes of an enslaved people may be one necessary link in the chain of events preparatory to the complete overthrow of the whole slave system." Republicans claimed that the decision deserved as much consideration as any pronouncement by a group of political hacks "in any Washington bar room." They threatened that when they secured control of the national government, they would reverse the decision—by altering the personnel of the Court and "packing" it with new members.

Deadlock over Kansas

President Buchanan endorsed the decision and concluded that the best solution for the troubles over Kansas was to force the admission of that territory as a slave state. The existing proslavery territorial legislature called an election for delegates to a constitutional convention. The free-state residents refused to participate. As a result, the proslavery forces won control of the convention, which met in 1857 at Lecompton and framed a constitution establishing slavery. When an election for a new territorial legislature was called, the antislavery groups turned out to vote and won a majority. Promptly the legislature

moved to submit the Lecompton constitution to the voters. The document was rejected by more than 10,000 votes.

Although both sides had resorted to fraud and violence, the Kansas picture was clear enough. The majority of the people in the territory did not want to see slavery established. Buchanan, however, ignored the evidence. He urged Congress to admit Kansas under the Lecompton constitution, and he tried to force the party to back his proposal. Stephen A. Douglas and other Western Democrats refused to accept this perversion of popular sovereignty. Openly breaking with the administration, Douglas denounced the Lecompton proposition. And although Buchanan's plan passed the Senate, Western Democrats helped to block it in the House. Partly to avert further division in the party, a compromise measure, the English bill (proposed by Indiana Democrat William English) won approval from Congress in April 1858. It provided that the Lecompton constitution should be submitted to the people of Kansas for the third time. If the document was approved, Kansas was to be admitted and given a federal land grant; if it was disapproved, statehood would be postponed until the population reached 93,600, the legal ratio for a representative in Congress. Again, and for the last time, the Kansas voters decisively rejected the Lecompton constitution. Not until the closing months of Buchanan's administration in 1861, when a number of Southern states had withdrawn from the Union, would Kansas enter the Union—as a free state.

The Emergence of Lincoln

The congressional elections of 1858 were of greater interest and importance than most midterm contests. Not only did they have an immediate and powerful influence on the course of the sectional controversy, but they projected into the national spotlight the man who was to be the dominating figure in the tragic years just ahead.

The senatorial election in Illinois attracted particularly wide attention throughout the nation. There Stephen A. Douglas, the most prominent Northern Democrat, was a candidate for reelection; and he was fighting for his political life. Since Douglas, or his successor, would be chosen by a legislature that was yet to be elected, the control of that body became a matter of paramount importance. To punish Douglas for his resistance to the Lecompton constitution, the

Buchanan administration entered Democratic candidates opposed to him in many legislative districts. But Douglas's greatest worry was that he faced Abraham Lincoln, the ablest campaigner in the Republican party.

Lincoln had been the leading Whig in Illinois. He was now the leading Republican in the state, although hardly a national figure, for his reputation still could not compare with that of the famous Douglas. Lincoln challenged the senator to a series of seven debates. Douglas accepted, and the two candidates argued their cases before huge crowds. The Lincoln-Douglas debates were widely reported by the nation's press, and before their termination the Republican who had dared to challenge the "Little Giant of Democracy" was a man of national prominence.

Douglas, in the course of defending popular sovereignty, accused the Republicans of promoting a war of sections, of wishing to interfere with slavery in the South, and of advocating social equality of the races. Lincoln denied these charges (properly, since neither he nor his party had ever advocated any of these things). He, in turn, accused the Democrats and Douglas of conspiring to extend slavery into the territories and possibly, by means of another Supreme Court decision, into the free states as well (a charge that was equally unfounded). Lincoln was particularly effective in making it appear that Douglas did not regard slavery as morally wrong. He quoted Douglas as saying he did not care whether slavery was "voted up, or voted down."

Lincoln was opposed to slavery—on moral, political, and economic grounds. He believed that it contradicted the American ideal of democracy. Let the idea be established that blacks were not created with an equal right to earn their bread, he said, and the next step would be to deny the right to certain groups of whites, such as immigrant laborers. Thus it was his solicitude for the economic well-being of the white masses—his commitment to the ideology of free labor—that impelled Lincoln to oppose the introduction of slavery into the territories. He maintained that the national lands should be preserved as places for poor white people to go to better their condition.

Yet as much as he opposed the extension of slavery, Lincoln did not share the views of the abolitionists. The physical fact of slavery, he believed, must be taken into account. "We have a due regard to the actual presence of it amongst us and the difficulties of getting rid of it in any satisfactory way and all

the constitutional obligations thrown about it." He and his party would "arrest the further spread of it," that is, prevent its expansion into the territories; he would not directly challenge it where it already existed. Yet the implications of Lincoln's argument were far greater than this relatively moderate formula suggests, for both he and other Republicans believed that by restricting slavery to the South, they would be consigning it to its "ultimate extinction." As he said in the most famous speech of the campaign:

> A house divided against itself cannot stand. I believe this government cannot endure permanently half slave and half free. I do not expect the Union to be dissolved—I do not expect the house to fall—but I do expect it will cease to be divided. It will become all one thing, or all the other.

In the debate at Freeport, Lincoln asked Douglas: Can the people of a territory exclude slavery from its limits prior to the formation of a state constitution? Or in other words, is popular sovereignty still a legal formula despite the *Dred Scott* decision? The question was a deadly trap, for no matter how Douglas answered it, he would lose something. If he disavowed popular sovereignty, he would undoubtedly be defeated for reelection and his political career would be ended. But if he reaffirmed his formula, Southern Democrats would be offended, the party split deepened, and his chances of securing the Democratic nomination in 1860 damaged if not destroyed.

Douglas met the issue boldly. The people of a territory, he said, could, by lawful means, shut out slavery prior to the formation of a state constitution. Slavery could not exist a day without the support of "local police regulations": territorial laws recognizing the right of slave ownership. The mere failure of a legislature to enact such laws would have the practical effect of keeping slaveholders out. Thus despite the *Dred Scott* decision, a territory could exclude slavery. Douglas's reply became known as the Freeport Doctrine or, in the South, as the Freeport Heresy. It satisfied his followers sufficiently to win him reelection to the Senate, but throughout the North it aroused little enthusiasm.

Elsewhere, the elections went heavily against the Democrats, who lost ground in almost every Northern state. The administration retained control of the Senate but lost its majority in the House, where the Republicans gained a plurality. In the holdover or short session of 1858–1859, in which the Democrats were in the majority, and in the regular session of

1859 (elected in 1858), every demand of the Republicans and Northern Democrats was blocked by Southern votes or by presidential vetoes. These defeated measures included a tariff increase, a homestead bill, a Pacific railroad, and federal land grants to states for the endowment of agricultural colleges. The 1859 session was also marked by an uproarious struggle over the election of a Speaker of the House.

The controversies in Congress, however, were almost entirely overshadowed by another event in the fall of 1859: an event that enraged and horrified the entire South and greatly hastened the rush toward disunion.

John Brown's Raid

John Brown, the antislavery zealot whose bloody actions in Kansas had done so much to inflame the crisis there, made an even greater contribution to sectional conflict through a grim and spectacular episode that had major national implications. Still convinced that he was God's instrument to destroy slavery, he decided to transfer his activities from Kansas to the South itself. With encouragement and financial aid from some Eastern abolitionists, he made plans to seize a mountain fortress in Virginia from which he could make raids to liberate slaves. He would arm the freedmen, set up a black republic, and eventually force the South to concede emancipation. Because he needed guns, he chose Harpers Ferry, where a United States arsenal was located, as his base of operations. In October, at the head of eighteen followers, he descended on the town and captured the arsenal. Almost immediately he was attacked by citizens and local militia companies, who were shortly reinforced by a detachment of U.S. Marines sent to the scene by the national government. With ten of his men killed, Brown had to surrender. He was promptly tried in a Virginia court for treason against the state, found guilty, and sentenced to death by hanging. Six of his followers met a similar fate.

Probably no other event had so much influence as the Harpers Ferry raid in convincing Southerners that their section was unsafe in the Union. Despite all their praise of slavery, one great fear always secretly gnawed at their hearts: the possibility of a general slave insurrection. Southerners now jumped to the conclusion that the Republicans were responsible for Brown's raid. This was, of course, untrue; prominent Republicans such as Lincoln and Seward condemned Brown as a criminal. But Southerners were

John Brown
Even in this formal photographic portrait (taken in 1859, the last year of his life), John Brown conveys the fierce sense of righteousness that fueled his extraordinary activities in the fight against slavery. (Library of Congress)

more impressed by the words of such abolitionists as Wendell Phillips and Ralph Waldo Emerson, who now glorified Brown as a new saint. His execution made him a martyr to thousands of Northerners.

The Election of Lincoln

The election of 1860, judged by its consequences, was the most momentous in American history.

The Democrats gathered in convention at Charleston, South Carolina, in April; and most of the Southern delegates arrived determined to adopt a platform providing for federal protection of slavery in the territories—that is, an official endorsement of the principles of the *Dred Scott* decision. The Western Democrats, arriving with bitter memories of how Southern influence had blocked their legislative demands in the recent Congress, resented the rule-or-ruin attitude of the Southerners. The Westerners hoped, however, to negotiate a face-saving statement on slavery so as to hold the party together. They vaguely endorsed popular sovereignty and proposed that all questions involving slavery in the territories be left up to the Supreme Court. By now, however, passions in the South had risen to a point where compromise was no longer possible. When the convention adopted the Western platform, the delegations from eight states of the lower South withdrew from the hall. The remaining delegates then proceeded to the selection of a candidate. Stephen A. Douglas led on every ballot, but he could not muster the two-thirds majority (of the original number of delegates) required by party rules. Finally the managers adjourned the convention to meet again in Baltimore in June. At the Baltimore session, most of the Southerners reappeared, only to walk out again. Other Southerners, meanwhile, had assembled at Richmond. The decimated convention at Baltimore nominated Douglas. The Southern bolters at Baltimore joined the Democrats in Richmond to nominate John C. Breckinridge of Kentucky. Sectionalism had at last divided the Democratic party.

The Republicans held their convention in Chicago in May. Although the divisions developing in the Democratic ranks seemed to spell a Republican triumph, the party managers took no chances. They were determined that the party, in both its platform and its candidate, should appear to the voters to represent conservatism, stability, and moderation rather than radical idealism. No longer was the Republican party a one-idea organization composed of crusaders against slavery. It now attempted to embrace every major interest group in the North that believed the South, the champion of slavery, was blocking its legitimate economic aspirations.

The platform endorsed such measures as a high tariff, internal improvements, a homestead bill, and a Pacific railroad to be built with federal financial assistance. On the slavery issue, the platform affirmed the right of each state to control its own institutions. The Republicans were saying, in other words, that they did not intend to interfere with slavery in the South. But they also claimed that neither Congress nor territorial legislatures could legalize slavery in the territories. This was the equivalent of saying that they would still oppose the expansion of slavery.

The leading contender for the nomination was Senator William H. Seward of New York, who faced competition from a number of favorite-son candidates. But Seward's prominence and his long, con-

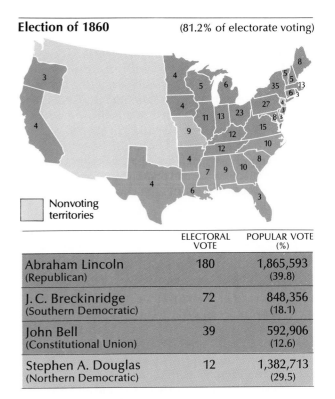

Election of 1860   (81.2% of electorate voting)

Nonvoting territories

	ELECTORAL VOTE	POPULAR VOTE (%)
Abraham Lincoln (Republican)	180	1,865,593 (39.8)
J. C. Breckinridge (Southern Democratic)	72	848,356 (18.1)
John Bell (Constitutional Union)	39	592,906 (12.6)
Stephen A. Douglas (Northern Democratic)	12	1,382,713 (29.5)

troversial political record damaged his chances. Passing him and other aspirants over, the convention nominated on the third ballot Abraham Lincoln, who was prominent enough to be respectable but obscure enough to have few foes, radical enough to please the antislavery faction in the party but conservative enough to satisfy the ex-Whigs. The vice-presidential nomination went to Hannibal Hamlin of Maine, a former Democrat.

As if three parties were not enough, a fourth entered the lists—the Constitutional Union party. Although posing as a new organization, it was really the last surviving remnant of the oldest conservative tradition in the country; its leaders were elder statesmen, and most of its members were former Whigs. Meeting in Baltimore in May, this party nominated John Bell of Tennessee and Edward Everett of Massachusetts. Its platform favored the Constitution, the Union, and enforcement of the laws; it avoided taking a clear stand on the issue of slavery.

In the North, the Republicans conducted a campaign reminiscent of the exciting Harrison-Van Buren contest of 1840, with parades, symbols, and mass meetings. For the most part, they stressed the economic promises in their platform and subordinated the slavery issue. Lincoln, following the customary

SIGNIFICANT EVENTS

1822	Mexico wins independence from Spain	1853	Gadsden Purchase
1836	Texas declares independence from Mexico	1854	Kansas-Nebraska Act passed
1844	James K. Polk elected president		Republican party formed
1845	Texas admitted to Union		Commodore Matthew Perry opens Japan to American trade
1846	Oregon boundary dispute settled	1855–1856	Violence breaks out in "Bleeding Kansas"
	United States declares war on Mexico	1856	Preston Brooks canes Charles Sumner
	Congress approves tariff reduction		James Buchanan elected president
	Wilmot Proviso introduced in Congress	1857	George Fitzhugh publishes *Cannibals All*
	Antislavery Free Soil party formed		Hinton Rowan Helper publishes *Impending Crisis of the South*
1848	Treaty of Guadalupe Hidalgo settles Mexican War		Supreme Court hands down *Dred Scott* decision
	Zachary Taylor elected president	1858	Proslavery Lecompton constitution defeated by popular referendum in Kansas
	Gold discovered in Sacramento Valley, California, sparking gold rush		Lincoln and Douglas debate
1850	Compromise of 1850 enacted	1859	John Brown raids Harpers Ferry
	Taylor dies; Millard Fillmore succeeds him	1860	Democratic party splits
1852	Franklin Pierce elected president		Lincoln elected president
	The Pro-Slavery Argument published		Process of secession begins
	Harriet Beecher Stowe publishes *Uncle Tom's Cabin*		

practice of presidential candidates, made no speeches. Lesser party luminaries addressed rallies and party meetings. Unlike previous candidates, Lincoln refused to issue any written statements of his views, claiming that anything he said would be seized on by Southerners and misrepresented. In the November election, Lincoln won a majority of the electoral votes and the presidency, but only about two-fifths of the popular votes. The Republicans had elected a president, but they had failed to secure a majority in Congress; and of course they did not control the Supreme Court.

Nevertheless, the election of Lincoln served as the final signal to many Southerners that their position in the Union was hopeless. Throughout the campaign, various Southern leaders had warned that if the Republicans should win, they would secede from the Union. Within a few weeks of Lincoln's victory, this process of disunion began—a process that would quickly lead to a prolonged and bloody war between two groups of Americans, both heirs of more than a century of struggling toward nationhood, each now convinced that it shared no common ground with the other.

SUGGESTED READINGS

Westward Expansion Several good surveys of westward expansion are available, of which two of the most prominent are Frederick Merk, *History of the Westward Movement* (1978), and Ray Allen Billington, *Westward Expansion*, rev. ed. (1974). John D. Unruh, *The Plains Across: The Overland Emigrants and the Trans-Mississippi West, 1840–1860* (1979), is an important study of the migrations westward in the antebellum period, revising earlier interpretations. On the expansionist impulse, which became known as Manifest Destiny, see above all Frederick Merk, *Manifest Destiny and Mission in American History* (1963). Merk is also the author

of *The Monroe Doctrine and American Expansionism, 1843–1849* (1966), which examines some of the diplomatic aspects of expansionism. Albert K. Weinberg, *Manifest Destiny* (1935), is an important study that Merk's book revises. William H. Goetzmann, *Exploration and Empire* (1966), examines the roles of explorers and scientists in the expansionist efforts. Henry Nash Smith, *Virgin Land* (1950), examines the image of the West in American literature. Other works of value on Manifest Destiny include Ray Allen Billington, *The Far Western Frontier, 1830–1860* (1956); Norman A. Graebner, *Empire of the Pacific* (1955);

and Frederick Merk, *Fruits of Propaganda in the Tyler Administration* (1971). The Texas question is considered by Merk in *Slavery and the Annexation of Texas* (1972). Other standard works include E. C. Barker, *Mexico and Texas, 1821–1835* (1928), and William C. Binkley, *The Texas Revolution* (1952). Francis Parkman, *The Oregon Trail* (1849, and many later editions), is a classic account of the migration to the Far West. R. L. Duffus, *The Santa Fe Trail* (1930), examines expansion into the Southwest. R. G. Cleland, *From Wilderness to Empire: A History of California, 1542–1900* (1944), R. W. Paul, *California Gold* (1947), and J. S. Holliday, *The World Rushed In* (1981), describe the settlement of California. Frederick Merk, *The Oregon Question* (1967), examines some of the political and diplomatic controversies arising from American expansion into the Northwest. O. O. Winther, *The Great Northwest*, rev. ed. (1950), describes the actual settlement of the region.

Expansion and the Mexican War   David J. Weber, *The Mexican Frontier, 1821–1846: The American Southwest Under Mexico* (1982), surveys the Southwest from the point of view of Mexico. The role of James K. Polk in the expansionism of the 1840s is examined in Charles G. Sellers, *James K. Polk: Continentalist, 1843–1846* (1966); J. S. Reeves, *American Diplomacy Under Tyler and Polk* (1907); and David M. Pletcher, *The Diplomacy of Annexation: Texas, Oregon, and the Mexican War* (1973). G. M. Brack, *Mexico Views Manifest Destiny, 1821–1846* (1975), examines the other side of the controversy. On the Mexican War itself, see K. Jack Bauer, *The Mexican-American War, 1846–1848* (1974); John H. Schroeder, *Mr. Polk's War: American Opposition and Dissent* (1973); Otis A. Singletary, *The Mexican War* (1960); and S. V. Conner and O. B. Faulk, *North America Divided* (1971). Holman Hamilton, *Zachary Taylor, Soldier of the Republic* (1941), and C. W. Elliott, *Winfield Scott* (1937), are biographies of two of the military heroes of the war. Diplomacy following the Mexican War is examined in Samuel F. Bemis (ed.), *American Secretaries of State*, vols. 5 and 6 (1928); Basil Rauch, *American Interest in Cuba, 1848–1855* (1948); and Robert E. May, *The Southern Dream of a Caribbean Empire, 1854–1861* (1973).

The Sectional Crisis: General Studies   Two works by Allan Nevins constitute a basic source: *The Ordeal of the Union*, 2 vols. (1947) and *The Emergence of Lincoln*, 2 vols. (1950). Other useful overviews include Michael Holt, *The Political Crisis of the 1850s* (1978); Roy F. Nichols, *The Disruption of American Democracy* (1948); Avery Craven, *The Coming of the Civil War* (1942); and David Potter, *The Impending Crisis, 1848–1861* (1976), a work of particular importance. Two works by William J. Cooper, *The South and the Politics of Slavery, 1828–1856* (1978) and *Liberty and Slavery* (1983), examine the changing political climate of the South. James G. Randall and David Donald, *The Civil War and Reconstruction*, rev. ed. (1969), and James M. McPherson, *Ordeal by Fire* (1981), are excellent overviews of the entire era of crisis, war, and reunion.

The Compromise of 1850   For the immediate background to the controversy, see Holman Hamilton, *Prologue to Conflict: The Crisis and Compromise of 1850* (1964); Chaplain W. Morrison, *Democratic Politics and Sectionalism: The Wilmot Proviso Controversy* (1973); and Kinley J. Brauer, *Cotton Versus Conscience: Massachusetts Whig Politics and Southern Expansion, 1843–1848* (1967). Biographies of some of the principals in the political debate are also useful sources of information. Among them are Robert W. Johannsen, *Stephen A. Douglas* (1973); Charles M. Wiltse, *John C. Calhoun: Sectionalist, 1840–1850* (1951); Charles B. Going, *David Wilmot, Free-Soiler* (1924); Holman Hamilton, *Zachary Taylor: Soldier in the White House* (1951); Richard N. Current, *Daniel Webster and the Rise of National Conservatism* (1955); and Robert F. Dalzell, Jr., *Daniel Webster and the Trial of American Nationalism, 1843–1852* (1973).

Sectional Crises in the 1850s   Gerald Wolff, *The Kansas-Nebraska Bill* (1977), and James C. Malin, *The Nebraska Question* (1953), examine the crisis of 1854; and Paul W. Gates, *Fifty Million Acres: Conflict over Kansas Land Policy, 1854–1890* (1954), examines its aftermath. On John Brown, see Stephen Oates, *To Purge This Land with Blood* (1970), an excellent biography, and R. O. Boyer, *The Legend of John Brown* (1973). Truman Nelson, *The Old Man: John Brown at Harper's Ferry* (1973), examines the last episode in Brown's career, as does J. C. Furnas, *The Road to Harpers Ferry* (1959). Benjamin Quarles, *Allies for Freedom* (1974), describes black views of Brown. Eric Foner, *Free Soil, Free Labor, Free Men* (1970), is the outstanding study of Northern free-labor ideology. See also his collection of essays, *Politics and Ideology in the Age of the Civil War* (1980). David Donald, *Charles Sumner and the Coming of the Civil War* (1960), is an important biography of one of the important figures in the early Republican party. Dale Baum, *The Civil War Party System: The Case of Massachusetts, 1848–1876* (1984), examines the impact of the Republican party on political alignments in a Northern state. On the proslavery ideology, see William Jenkins, *Pro-Slavery Thought in the Old South* (1935), and Harvey Wish, *George Fitzhugh: Propagandist of the Old South* (1943). Don E. Fehrenbacher, *The Dred Scott Case* (1978), is the definitive account of the Supreme Court decision that exacerbated sectional tensions.

Lincoln   On the emergence of Lincoln, see the Nevins volumes of that title mentioned above. Other works in the vast literature on Lincoln that are useful for these years are Richard N. Current, *The Lincoln Nobody Knows* (1958); David Donald, *Lincoln Reconsidered* (1956); Don E. Fehrenbacher, *Prelude to Greatness: Lincoln in the 1850's* (1962); and George B. Forgie, *Patricide in the House Divided* (1979), a provocative psychological portrait of Lincoln and his contemporaries. Carl Sandburg, *Abraham Lincoln: The Prairie Years* (1929), a one-volume abridgment of his larger biography, is a romantic and appealing (if often inaccurate) view of the young Lincoln.

War and Reunion, 1860–1877

To most of the South, and even to much of the North, the election of Abraham Lincoln to the presidency in 1860 marked the ultimate failure of compromise. The nation's highest office was now to be in the possession of a man unanimously opposed by the residents of one of the sections. No longer, apparently, were there leaders or programs capable of appealing across regional lines to a common national interest. Sentiment on both sides had hardened to the point where there no longer seemed any way for North and South to exist in amicable union. And so the war came.

Yet despite the apparent irreconcilability of the sections, the war came as something of a surprise to both sides. The Southern states, when they began late in 1860 to secede from the Union, assumed at first that the North would not in the end use force to oppose them. The national government in Washington, for its part, believed that secession was a momentary aberration, that the rebellious states could be made to come to their senses and return to their proper relation to the Union. Even after the first shots over Fort Sumter had signaled the beginning of hostilities, both sides expected at most a brief and limited conflict.

As the fighting continued, however, year after murderous year, killing more than 600,000 people, maiming and injuring many more, and devastating large portions of the nation, Americans on both sides were forced finally to confront the real price of their inability to settle their differences. The Civil War was like no conflict in the nation's history, perhaps like no conflict in the history of the human race to that point. Waged on a scale hitherto unknown, employing horrible new technology that made widespread slaughter the new norm of combat, the war did not so much settle the differences between North and South as exhaust both sides. When, at last, General Robert E. Lee surrendered the last major force of the once great Confederate army to General Ulysses S. Grant in 1865, only two issues were effectively settled. The Union was to survive, and the institution of slavery was to be abolished. Other questions—the future economic relationship between the sections, the distribution of political power, the status of freed blacks in the nation—remained unanswered. The Civil War had determined that the United States would remain a single nation. It had not, however, determined what kind of a nation it would be.

Nor was the troubled aftermath of the fighting successful in resolving the difficult sectional issues that remained. The spirit of compromise that had died so painfully in the 1850s did not quickly revive; and both North and South remained intransigent in many ways after the war. White Southerners quickly attempted to rebuild a social order that resembled their antebellum society as closely as possible. Above all, they attempted to reduce the now emancipated black population to a level of economic bondage hardly distinguishable from slavery. Northerners—motivated partly by bitterness and a desire for revenge, partly by a genuine commitment to protecting the freed slaves—responded by imposing their own system of government on the South, a system that greatly restricted the power of the region's traditional ruling class and so deeply embittered the white residents of the section that even a century later they would refer to Reconstruction as an "outrage" and an "abomination." When finally, in 1877, the last Reconstruction governments began to be replaced and conservative white

Southerners once again gained control of their region, they rejoiced that the South had been "redeemed," that the long nightmare of Northern tyranny was over.

There were others, however, who looked on the end of Reconstruction with less enthusiasm. Black Americans had viewed the postwar policies in a very different light from whites. They saw in the actions of the federal government the first systematic effort in the history of their nation to provide them with the elemental rights of citizenship. Only federal protection, they believed, could effectively guard them from the determination of the Southern white population to keep blacks isolated and demeaned. The withdrawal of this federal support, the result of a series of political bargains between the whites of both regions, consigned black Southerners to another century of poverty and discrimination. It had been the issue of race that had helped to produce the Civil War in the first place. Now, after four years of bloodshed and twelve more years of political acrimony, the issue remained unresolved. Instead, white Americans in both regions of the nation had returned to the spirit of compromise that had permitted the Union to survive during the first half of the nineteenth century. And in the 1870s, as in the 1830s and 1840s, compromise meant abandoning the difficult effort to resolve the status of blacks. It meant leaving the question unsettled to confront and frustrate future generations of Americans.

***The Flag of Sumter, October 20, 1863,* by Conrad Wise Chapman, c. 1863**   (Museum of the Confederacy, Richmond)

Chapter 14

The War of the Rebellion

By the end of 1860, the cords that had once bound the Union together appeared to have snapped. The almost mystical veneration of the Constitution and its framers was no longer working to unite the nation; residents of the North and South—particularly after the controversial *Dred Scott* decision—now differed fundamentally over what the Constitution said and what the framers had meant. The romantic vision of America's great national destiny had ceased to be a unifying force; the two sections now defined that destiny in different and apparently irreconcilable terms. The stable two-party system could not dampen sectional conflict any longer; that system had collapsed in the 1850s, to be replaced by a new one that accentuated rather than muted regional controversy. Above all, the federal government was no longer the remote, unthreatening presence it once had been; the need to resolve the status of the territories had made it necessary for Washington to deal with sectional issues in a direct and forceful way. And thus, beginning in 1860, the divisive forces that had always existed within the United States were no longer counterbalanced by unifying forces; and the Union began to dissolve.

To the South, the war that ensued was a legitimate struggle for independence, a conflict no less glorious than the American Revolution of nine decades before. Ultimately, they would call it the "War Between the States," as if to imply that it had reflected a constitutional exercise of states' rights. To the North, however, the conflict was nothing more than a criminal insurrection—illegal, unjustifiable, even treasonous. And the Union government, therefore, assigned to the struggle an official name that

attributed far less dignity to the Southern cause: the "War of the Rebellion."

Despite the differences in outlook between the sections, however, both sides encountered very similar experiences. Both were forced to mobilize a high proportion of their resources for victory; both were required to confront problems of production and organization never before encountered in a modern society; and by the end, both found themselves fighting a war that had resulted from supposedly fundamental regional differences in markedly similar ways.

The Secession Crisis

Almost as soon as the news of Abraham Lincoln's election reached the South, the militant leaders of the region—the champions of the new concept of Southern "nationalism," men known both to their contemporaries and to history as the "fire-eaters"—began to demand an end to the Union. The Southern states, they argued, should withdraw from the federal system and form a new nation of their own; and their vehicle should be a device that had, they claimed, firm legal grounding in the Constitution: secession.

The Withdrawal of the South

The concept of secession was rooted in the political philosophy that the South had developed over the course of several decades to protect its minority sta-

The Process of Secession

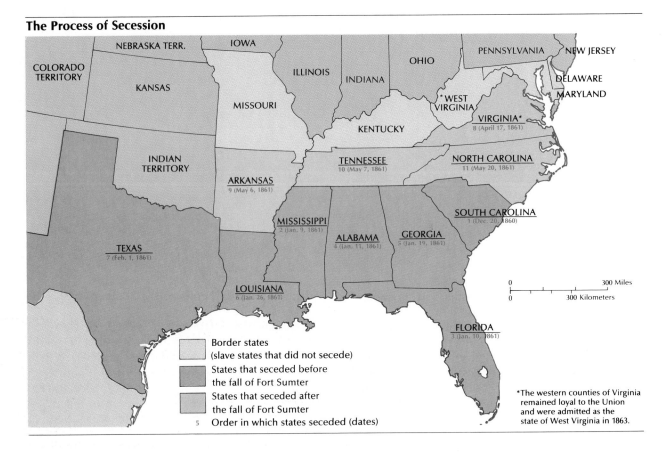

Border states
(slave states that did not secede)

States that seceded before
the fall of Fort Sumter

States that seceded after
the fall of Fort Sumter

5   Order in which states seceded (dates)

*The western counties of Virginia
remained loyal to the Union
and were admitted as the
state of West Virginia in 1863.

tus in the nation. According to this doctrine, the Union was an association of sovereign states. The individual states had once joined the Union; they could, whenever they wished, dissolve their connections with it and resume their status as separate sovereignties. It was a momentous act to leave the Union, supporters of secession believed. But it was a lawful act.

The Constitution did not, of course, specify a method by which a state could secede; but most of the Southern states came to agree that the proper course was to follow the same procedures they had used when they originally ratified the federal Constitution. The governor would call an election for delegates to a special state convention, which could then pass an ordinance of secession. South Carolina, long the hotbed of Southern separatism, led off the secession parade. Its convention took the state out of the Union on December 20, 1860, by a unanimous vote. Even before Lincoln assumed the presidency, six other Southern states—Mississippi (January 9, 1861), Florida (January 10), Alabama (January 11), Georgia (January 19), Louisiana (January 26), and Texas (Feb-

ruary 1)—had left the Union. And in February 1861, representatives of the seven seceded states met at Montgomery, Alabama, and formed a new, Southern nation—the Confederate States of America.

Many Northerners reacted at first with confused indecision, no one more so than President James Buchanan. In a message to Congress in December 1860, Buchanan declared that no state had the right to secede from the Union. At the same time, he questioned whether the federal government had the authority to force a state back into the Union. Buchanan's real goal at this point, however, was not to resolve these difficult questions. He simply wanted to avoid an open conflict and to maintain the symbolic authority of the national government until his successor could take office.

Among the first acts of the seceding states was to take possession of federal property—forts, arsenals, offices—within their boundaries. But they did not at first have sufficient military power to seize two important offshore forts: Fort Sumter, on an island in the harbor of Charleston, South Carolina, garrisoned by a small force under Major Robert Anderson; and

Fort Pickens in the harbor of Pensacola, Florida. South Carolina sent commissioners to Washington to ask for the surrender of Sumter; but Buchanan, fearful though he was of provoking a clash, refused to yield the fort. In January 1861, he decided to reinforce it. He ordered an unarmed merchant ship, the *Star of the West,* to proceed to Fort Sumter with additional troops and supplies. When the vessel attempted to enter the harbor, it encountered fire from Confederate guns on shore and turned back. The first shots between the North and the South had been fired. Even so, neither section was ready to admit that a war had begun. And in Washington, attention turned once more to efforts to resolve the controversy through compromise.

The Failure of Compromise

As the situation in South Carolina deteriorated, President Buchanan urged Congress to try again to find a peaceful solution to the crisis that might hold the Union together. The Senate and the House appointed committees to study various plans of adjustment; and gradually—in the Senate at least—attention began to center on a proposal submitted by Senator John J. Crittenden of Kentucky. The Crittenden Compromise, as it was known, called for a series of constitutional amendments. One would have guaranteed the permanence of slavery in the states; others were designed to satisfy Southern demands on such matters as fugitive slaves and slavery in the District of Columbia. But the heart of Crittenden's plan dealt with slavery in the territories. He proposed to reestablish the Missouri Compromise line of 36°30′ in all the territory that the United States then held or *thereafter acquired.* Slavery was to be prohibited north of the line and permitted south of it. Southern members of a Senate committee appointed to draft the compromise indicated they would accept this territorial division if the Republicans would. The Republicans, after conferring with President-elect Lincoln in Illinois, voted against the proposal. Lincoln maintained that the restoration of the Missouri Compromise line would encourage the South to embark on imperialist adventures in Latin America. It also, of course, would have represented an abandonment by the Republicans of their most basic position: that slavery could not be allowed to expand.

There was one notable attempt outside Congress to produce a compromise. The legislature of Virginia called for a national peace conference at Washington.

Representatives from twenty-one of the thirty-four states assembled early in February and produced a series of proposals that closely resembled the Crittenden scheme. The convention submitted the plan to the Senate, but the proposal received almost no support.

And so nothing had been resolved when Abraham Lincoln arrived in Washington for his inauguration—sneaking into the city in disguise by train in the dead of night, to avoid assassination as he passed through the slave state of Maryland en route. The country was now divided into two hostile nations, waiting for what was coming to seem an inevitable war.

In his eloquent inaugural address, Lincoln laid down several basic principles. The Union, he said, was older than the Constitution; hence no state could of its own volition leave the Union. The ordinances of secession were illegal, and acts of violence to support secession were insurrectionary or revolutionary. Of most immediate significance, given the ongoing struggle over Fort Sumter, Lincoln declared that he would enforce the laws and would "hold, occupy, and possess" federal property in the seceded states.

Conditions at Fort Sumter quickly forced Lincoln to translate his words into action. Major Anderson was running short of supplies; unless he received fresh provisions, the fort would have to be evacuated. Lincoln was convinced that if he surrendered Sumter, the South (and perhaps also the North) would never believe that he meant to sustain the Union. After much deliberation, therefore, he dispatched a naval relief expedition to the fort. At the same time, he carefully informed the authorities in South Carolina that ships were on the way, with supplies, and that there would be no attempt to send troops or munitions to the fort unless the supply ships met with resistance. The new Confederate government now faced a dilemma. If it permitted the expedition to land, it would appear to be bowing tamely to federal authority and would lose credibility among its own people. If it fired on the ships or the fort, it would appear (to the North, at least) to be the aggressor. After hours of anguished discussion, the government in Montgomery decided that to appear cowardly would be worse than to appear belligerent. It ordered General P. G. T. Beauregard, commander of Confederate forces at Charleston, to demand Anderson's surrender and, if the demand was refused, to attack the fort. Beauregard made the demand; Anderson rejected it. The Confederates then bombarded the fort for two days, April 12–13, 1861. On April 14, Anderson surrendered. The Civil War had begun.

In both the North and the South, events moved quickly. Lincoln immediately requested an expansion of the regular army and called for the states to raise their own forces to contribute to the struggle for the Union. In the South, four more slave states seceded and joined the Confederacy: Virginia (April 17, 1861), Arkansas (May 6), Tennessee (June 8), and North Carolina (May 20). The mountain counties in northwestern Virginia refused to accept the decision of their state, established their own "loyal" government, and in 1863 secured admission to the Union as the new state of West Virginia. The four remaining slave states, Maryland, Delaware, Kentucky, and Missouri, cast their lot with the Union, although not without considerable controversy (and in large part because of heavy pressure from Washington). These border states were crucial to the Union's hopes, and Lincoln kept a close watch on their actions. In two of them, Maryland and Missouri, he used military force to ensure that secessionists would have no opportunity to prevail.

The Question of Inevitability

Was the outbreak of war inevitable? Was there anything that Lincoln (or those before him) could have done to settle the sectional conflict peaceably? Those questions have preoccupied historians for more than a century without resolution. (See "Where Historians Disagree," pp. 404–405.)

In one sense, of course, the war was not inevitable. If the nation had not acquired new Western lands in the 1840s, if Douglas had not presented the Kansas-Nebraska Act to Congress in 1854, if the Supreme Court had chosen not to rule on the *Dred Scott* case, if John Brown had not raided Harpers Ferry, if Lincoln had not rejected the Crittenden Compromise, or if the North had agreed (as some urged) to let the Southern states leave in peace—if any number of things that did happen had not happened, then there might not have been a war. Even after Lincoln's election, even after the secession of the South, it would have been technically possible for the nation to avoid armed conflict.

The real question, however, is not what hypothetical situations might have reversed the trend toward war but whether the preponderance of forces in the nation were acting to hold the nation together or to drive it apart. And by 1861, it seems clear that in both the North and the South, sectional antagonisms—whether justified or not—had risen to such a point that the existing terms of union had become untenable. People in both regions of the country had come to believe that two distinct and incompatible civilizations had developed in the United States and that those civilizations were incapable of living together in peace. Ralph Waldo Emerson, speaking for much of the North, said at the time: "I do not see how a barbarous community and a civilized community can constitute one state." And a slaveowner, expressing the sentiments of much of the South, said shortly after the election of Lincoln: "These [Northern] people hate us, annoy us, and would have us assassinated by our slaves if they dared. They are a different people from us, whether better or worse, and there is no love between us. Why then continue together?"

That the North and the South had come to believe these things may have made secession and war virtually inevitable. Whether these things were actually true—whether the North and the South were really as different and incompatible as they thought—is another question, one that the preparations for and conduct of the war helped to answer.

The Opposing Sides

A comparison of the combatants on the eve of war reveals that in one crucial area, at least, there were indeed basic differences between the sections. All the great material factors were on the side of the North.

These advantages, important from the beginning, became more significant as the conflict continued and the superior economy of the North became geared for war production. The North had a larger manpower reservoir from which to draw its armed forces. There were twenty-three states still in the Union, with a population of approximately 22 million. There were only eleven Confederate states, with a population of about 9 million, of whom 3.5 million were slaves.

The North had an even greater advantage in its levels of industrial production. Southern industry, particularly in those areas necessary for the conduct of a war, was almost nonexistent; the North already possessed an advanced industrial system. In the first year of the war, before Northern factories had converted to war production, both sides had to purchase large amounts of supplies, particularly arms, from Europe. After 1862, however, the North was able to manufacture practically all of its war materials.

The South, on the other hand, had to rely on

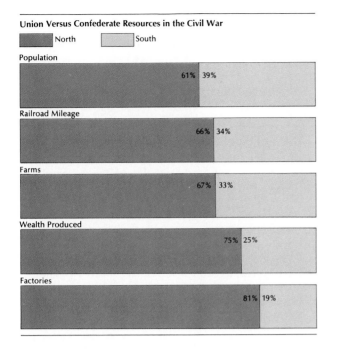

Union Versus Confederate Resources in the Civil War

■ North   □ South

Population
61% 39%

Railroad Mileage
66% 34%

Farms
67% 33%

Wealth Produced
75% 25%

Factories
81% 19%

Europe throughout the war. It tried desperately to expand its own industrial facilities. The brilliant Confederate chief of ordnance, Josiah Gorgas, accomplished wonders in building arsenals and in supplying the armies with weapons and munitions. Nevertheless, both the quantity and the quality of Confederate firearms were inferior to those of the North. The Southern economic system was also unable to pro-

vide its soldiers with the other necessities of modern war: clothes, boots, blankets, medical supplies, and the like. The Northern armies (and Northern society in general) had more of everything after 1862 than the armies or the society of the South; and that was one reason why Confederate morale began rapidly to deteriorate by the end of 1863.

In addition, the transportation system of the North was superior in every respect to that of the South. The North had more and better means of inland water transportation (steamboats, barges), more surfaced roads, more wagons and animals. Above all, the North had approximately 20,000 miles of railroads, while the Confederacy, which comprised at least as large a land area, had only 10,000 miles. The trackage figures, however, do not tell the whole story of Southern railroad inferiority. There were important gaps between key points in the South, which required supplies to make detours over long distances or to be carried between rail lines by wagon. As the war continued, the Confederate railroad system steadily deteriorated, and by the last year and a half of the struggle it had almost collapsed.

The enormous imbalance in the material forces of the two sides suggests that the South had absolutely no chance to win the war. But in the beginning, at least, the material strengths of the North were not as decisive as they appear. The South was, for the most part, fighting a defensive war on its own land and thus had the advantage of local support and familiarity with the territory. The South also had an advan-

War by Railroad
Union soldiers pose beside a mortar mounted on a railroad car in July 1864, during the siege of Petersburg, Virginia. Six days after this photograph was taken, Union forces exploded a huge mine in a futile effort to take the city. After that, Grant dug in for a nine-month siege. Petersburg did not fall until April 2, 1865, only a week before the end of the war.
(National Archives)

WHERE HISTORIANS DISAGREE

The Causes of the Civil War

The debate over the causes of the Civil War began even before the war itself. In 1858, Senator William H. Seward of New York took note of the two competing explanations of the sectional tensions that were then inflaming the nation. On one side, he claimed, stood those who believed the sectional hostility to be "accidental, unnecessary, the work of interested or fanatical agitators." Opposing them stood those who believed there to be "an irrepressible conflict between opposing and enduring forces." Although he did not realize it at the time, Seward was drawing the outlines of a debate that would survive among historians for more than a century to come.

The "irrepressible conflict" argument was the first to dominate historical discussion. In the first decades after the fighting, histories of the Civil War generally reflected the views of Northerners who had themselves participated in the conflict. To them, the war appeared to be a stark moral conflict in which the South was clearly to blame, a conflict that arose inevitably as a result of the threatening immorality of slave society. Henry Wilson's *History of the Rise and Fall of the Slave Power* (1872–1877) was (as the title suggests) a particularly vivid version of this moral interpretation of the war, which argued that Northerners had fought to preserve the Union and a system of free labor against the aggressive designs of the "slave power."

A more temperate interpretation, but one that reached generally the same conclusions, emerged in the 1890s, when the first serious histories of the war began to appear. Preeminent among them was the seven-volume *History of the United States from the Compromise of 1850 . . .* (1893–1900) by James Ford Rhodes. Like Wilson and others, Rhodes identified slavery as the central, indeed virtually the only, cause of the war. "If the Negro had not been brought to America," he wrote, "the Civil War could not have occurred." And because the North and the South had reached positions on the issue of slavery that were both irreconcilable and unalterable, the conflict had become "inevitable."

Although Rhodes placed his greatest emphasis on the moral conflict over slavery, he suggested, too, that the struggle reflected fundamental differences between the Northern and Southern economic systems. Not until the 1920s, however, did the idea of the war as an irrepressible *economic* rather than *moral* conflict receive full expression. As on so many other issues, it was the great historians Charles and Mary Beard who most clearly expressed this viewpoint, in *The Rise of American Civilization* (2 vols., 1927). Slavery, the Beards claimed, was not so much a social or cultural institution as an economic one, a labor system. There were, they insisted, "inherent antagonisms" between Northern industrialists and Southern planters. Each group sought to control the federal government so as to protect its own economic interests. Both groups used arguments over slavery and states' rights only as a smoke screen.

The economic determinism of the Beards influenced a generation of historians in important ways, but ultimately most of those who believed the Civil War to have been "irrepressible" returned to an emphasis on social and cultural factors. Allan Nevins argued as much in his great work, *The Ordeal of the Union* (8 vols., 1947–1971). The North and the South, he wrote, "were rapidly becoming separate peoples." At the root of these cultural differences was the "problem of slavery"; but "fundamental assumptions, tastes, and cultural aims" of the regions were diverging in other ways as well.

More recent proponents of the "irrepressible conflict" argument have taken more hostile views of the Northern and Southern positions on the conflict but have been equally insistent on the role of culture and ideology in creating them. Eric Foner, in *Free Soil, Free Labor, Free Men* (1970) and other writings, emphasized the importance of the "free-labor ideology" to Northern opponents of slavery. The moral concerns of the abolitionists were not the dominant sentiments in the North, he claimed. Instead, most Northerners (including Abraham Lincoln) opposed slavery largely because they feared it might spread to the North and threaten the position of free white laborers. Convinced that Northern society was superior to that of the South, increasingly persuaded of the South's

—————WHERE HISTORIANS DISAGREE———

intentions to extend the "slave power" beyond its existing borders, Northerners were embracing a viewpoint that made conflict inevitable. Eugene Genovese, writing of Southern slaveholders in *The Political Economy of Slavery* (1965), emphasized their conviction that the slave system provided a far more humane society than industrial labor, that the South had constructed "a special civilization built on the relation of master to slave." Just as Northerners were becoming convinced of a Southern threat to their economic system, so Southerners believed that the North had aggressive and hostile designs on the Southern way of life. Like Foner, therefore, Genovese saw in the cultural outlook of the section the source of an all but inevitable conflict.

Historians who argue that the conflict emerged naturally, even inevitably, out of a fundamental divergence between the sections have, therefore, disagreed markedly over whether moral, cultural, social, ideological, or economic issues were the primary causes of the Civil War. But they have been in general accord that the conflict between North and South was deeply embedded in the nature of the two societies, that the crisis that ultimately emerged was irrepressible. Other historians, however, have questioned that assumption and have argued that the Civil War could have been avoided, that the differences between North and South were not important enough to have necessitated a war. Like proponents of the "irrepressible conflict" school, advocates of the war as a "repressible conflict" emerged first in the nineteenth century. President James Buchanan, for example, believed that extremist agitators were to blame for the conflict; and many Southerners writing of the war in the late nineteenth century claimed that only the fanaticism of the Republican party could account for the conflict.

But the idea of the war as avoidable did not gain wide recognition among historians until the 1920s and 1930s, when a group known as the "revisionists" began to offer new accounts of the prologue to the conflict. One of the leading revisionists was James G. Randall, who saw in the social and economic systems of the North and the South no

differences so fundamental as to require a war. Slavery, he suggested, was an essentially benign institution; it was, in any case, already "crumbling in the presence of nineteenth century tendencies." Only the political ineptitude of a "blundering generation" of leaders could account for the Civil War, he claimed. Avery Craven, another leading revisionist, placed more emphasis on the issue of slavery than had Randall. But in *The Coming of the Civil War* (1942), he too argued that slave laborers were not much worse off than Northern industrial workers, that the institution was already on the road to "ultimate extinction," and that war could, therefore, have been averted had skillful and responsible leaders worked to produce compromise.

More recent students of the war have kept elements of the revisionist interpretation alive by emphasizing the role of political agitation in the coming of the war. David Herbert Donald, for example, argued in 1960 that the politicians of the 1850s were not unusually inept but that they were operating in a society in which traditional restraints were being eroded in the face of the rapid extension of democracy. Thus the sober, statesmanlike solution of differences was particularly difficult. Michael Holt, in *The Political Crisis of the 1850s* (1978), similarly emphasized the actions of politicians, rather than the irreconcilable differences between sections, in explaining the conflict, although he avoided placing blame on any one group. "Much of the story of the coming of the Civil War," he wrote, "is the story of the successful efforts of Democratic politicians in the South and Republican politicians in the North to keep the sectional conflict at the center of the political debate."

Like the proponents of the "irrepressible conflict" interpretation, the "revisionist" historians have differed among themselves in important ways. But the explanation of the Civil War has continued, even a century later, to divide roughly into the same two schools of thought that William Seward identified in 1858. And while the idea of the war as inevitable remains, as it has always been, the dominant interpretation, it has yet to establish unchallenged dominance.

tage among its own people: It was fighting for something concrete, something easy for its people to understand. It simply wanted to be independent, to be left alone; it had no aggressive designs on the North.

The North, on the other hand, faced a more difficult task, both militarily and politically. Its armies were fighting largely within the South. They had to maintain long lines of communications, deal with hostile local populations, and rely on the South's own inadequate transportation system. The Northern public, moreover, was far less united in support of the war than that of the South. Union war aims were more difficult to define, especially since many Northerners so disliked the South that they saw no reason to fight to keep the Union together. As late as 1864, Northern sentiment often wavered. Thus a major Southern victory at any one of several crucial moments might have proved decisive by breaking the North's will to continue the struggle.

There was, moreover, one additional factor that Southerners at first thought would virtually guarantee them a victory: cotton. The rapidly growing textile industries of England and France were, the South believed, dependent on their cotton. They would have no choice but to intervene in the conflict on the side of the Confederacy and force the North to acquiesce in the South's independence.

The Mobilization of the North

For the North, the war years were a time of political and social discord, of frustration, and of the inevitable suffering that accompanies battle. Yet they were also a period of prosperity and expansion. The war provided a major stimulus to both industry and agriculture. Not only did the rising productivity of the North contribute to its ultimate victory; it also ensured that the region would be more highly developed at the end of the war than at the start.

Economic Measures

The expanding Northern economy received a powerful stimulant during the war from the economic legislation of the now dominant Republican party. With Southern opposition removed, the Republicans proceeded to enact an aggressively nationalistic program to promote economic development.

The Homestead Act and the Morrill Land Grant Act, both passed in 1862, were measures that the West had long sought. The Homestead Act entitled any citizen, or anyone who intended to become a citizen, to claim 160 acres of public land and to purchase it for a small fee after living on it for five years. The Morrill Act gave every state 30,000 acres of public land for each of its congressional representatives. The states were to use the proceeds from the sale of that acreage to finance public education in agriculture, engineering, and military science. This provided a basis for the development of many new state colleges and universities, the so-called land-grant institutions.

A few days before President Buchanan left office, Congress passed the Morrill Tariff Act, which moderately increased duties and brought the rates up to approximately what they had been before 1846. Later measures, in 1862 and 1864, were even more frankly protective. By the end of the war, customs duties were, on average, the highest in the nation's history, and more than double the prewar rate.

Business achieved other victories in promoting railroads and immigration. One of the great dreams of those who believed in industrial growth was a railroad link between the Atlantic and Pacific coasts. Two laws, passed in 1862 and 1864, paved the way to realization of that dream. Congress created two new federally chartered corporations: the Union Pacific Railroad Company, which was to build westward from Omaha, and the Central Pacific, which was to build eastward from California. The two companies were to meet somewhere in the middle and complete the link. The government would provide free public lands and generous loans to the companies.

Immigration from Europe fell off in the first years of the war, partly because of the unsettled conditions in America. That decrease, coupled with the military's demand for manpower, threatened to produce a serious labor shortage. Business leaders, with the support of the president, persuaded Congress to pass new legislation to encourage immigration: a contract labor law, enacted in 1864, which authorized employers to import laborers and collect the costs of transportation from future wages.

Perhaps the most important measure affecting the business and financial worlds was the National Bank Act, passed in 1863 and amended in 1864. The act created a national banking system, which survived without serious modification until 1913. Under the new system, existing state banks or newly formed corporations were entitled to apply for federal charters and become national banks. To qualify for such charters, an institution had to possess a minimum amount of capital and had to invest one-third of that capital in government securities. In return, it would receive U.S. Treasury notes that it could issue as currency. In addition, Congress (in 1865) placed a tax on all state bank notes, which forced state notes out of existence and induced reluctant state banks to seek federal charters. At the outbreak of the war, 1,500 banks chartered by twenty-nine states had been issuing bank notes. The new system eliminated much of the chaos and uncertainty in the nation's currency and created a new, uniform system of national bank notes.

But reforming the currency did not alone solve one of the North's principal problems: financing the war. The government raised funds in three ways. It levied taxes, it borrowed money, and it issued paper currency.

Not until 1862, when war expenses began rapidly to mount, did Congress face the necessity of raising substantial new taxes. It passed the Internal Revenue Act, which placed duties on practically all goods and most occupations. For the first time, in 1861, the government levied an income tax: a duty of 3 percent on incomes above $800. Later, the rates were increased to 5 percent on incomes between $600 and $5,000 and 10 percent on incomes above $5,000. Through the medium of the various war taxes, the hand of the government was coming to rest on most individuals in the country. The United States was in the process of acquiring a national internal revenue system—in fact, a national tax system—one of the many nationalizing effects of the war. Even so, taxation never raised more than a small proportion of the funds necessary for financing the war—$667 million in all (including tariff revenues); and strong popular resistance prevented the government from raising the rates. Other methods, therefore, became increasingly important.

The most significant of these was borrowing. In America's previous wars, the government had sold bonds only to banks and to a few wealthy investors. Now, however, the Treasury employed the services of Jay Cooke, a Philadelphia banker, to persuade ordinary citizens to buy bonds. Through high-pressure propaganda techniques, Cooke disposed of $400 million worth of bonds—the first example of mass financing of a war in American history. In all, the United States borrowed $2.6 billion.

The most controversial method of financing (and the least productive of revenue) was the printing of paper currency, or "greenbacks." The new currency paid no interest and was not supported by a specie reserve (gold or silver). Holders of greenbacks had only the good faith of the government (and its ability to win the war) to rely on. The value of the greenbacks fluctuated, therefore, according to the fortunes of the Northern armies. Early in 1864, with the war effort bogged down, a greenback dollar, in relation to a gold dollar, was worth only 39 cents. Even at the close of the war, its value had advanced to only 67 cents. The uncertain value of greenbacks made it difficult for the government to use them to pay many of its expenses. The Treasury issued only $450 million worth of paper currency in all. That was, however, enough to produce serious problems of inflation in the later years of the war.

Raising the Union Armies

When hostilities began, there were only about 16,000 troops in the regular army of the United States, many of them scattered throughout the West to keep order between whites and Indians along the frontier. Lincoln realized, therefore, that the Union would have to rely heavily on state militias if it hoped to suppress the rebellion. Shortly after assuming office, he called 75,000 militiamen into service for three months, the usual period of service set for state troops by existing militia laws. The president quickly recognized that the war would last longer than three months; and (without clear legal sanction) he called up 42,000 state volunteers for national service for three years and authorized an increase of 23,000 in the regular army. When Congress convened in July 1861, it passed legislation that not only endorsed Lincoln's previous acts but called for enlisting 500,000 volunteers to serve for three years.

For a time, this voluntary system brought out enough men to fill the armies. But after the first flush of enthusiasm had subsided, enlistments declined. Finally, in March 1863, Congress enacted the first national draft law in its history. (The Confederacy had begun conscription almost a year earlier.) Few exemptions were permitted: only high national and state officials, ministers, and men who were the sole support of dependent families. But a drafted man could escape service by hiring someone to go in his place or by paying the government a fee of $300.

Supporters of the law hoped that the threat of conscription would spur voluntary enlistments. Each state was assigned a quota of men to be raised. If a

Sending the Boys Off to War
In this painting by Thomas Nast, New York's Seventh Regiment parades down Broadway in April 1861, to the cheers of exuberant, patriotic throngs, shortly before departing to fight in what most people then assumed would be a brief war. Thomas Nast is better known for his famous political cartoons of the 1870s. (Seventh Regiment Armory, New York City)

state could fill its quota, it would escape the draft completely; if it did not, the draft would make up the difference. Although only about 46,000 men were ever actually conscripted, the draft greatly increased voluntary enlistments. A total of approximately 1.5 million men served in the Union armies. (The Confederate armies had the services of about 900,000.)

To a people accustomed to a government that had hardly touched their daily lives, conscription seemed a strange and ominous thing. Opposition to the law was widespread, particularly from laborers, immigrants, and Democrats opposed to the war (known as "Peace Democrats"). In places it erupted into violence. Demonstrators against the draft rioted in New York City for four days in July 1863, killed several hundred people, mostly blacks, and burned down homes and businesses, again mostly those of free blacks. (Some Northern opponents of the war believed that blacks were responsible for the conflict.) Only the arrival of federal troops managed to subdue the rioters. Some Democratic governors (Horatio Seymour of New York among them) supported the war but contended that the national government had no constitutional power to conscript; they openly challenged the Lincoln administration on the issue.

Political Challenges

When Abraham Lincoln arrived in Washington early in 1861, most national leaders considered him a mi-

nor politician from the prairies. Lincoln's folksy, unpretentious demeanor helped strengthen some in their conviction that he was unfit for his position. But the new president had few doubts about his own abilities, as he demonstrated when he selected his cabinet. He assembled a group of men representing every faction of the Republican party and every segment of Northern opinion—men of extraordinary prestige and political influence, as difficult a set of prima donnas as any president had ever attempted to manage. Three of the secretaries, William Seward, Salmon P. Chase, and Edwin Stanton, were men of great ability—and no one was more certain of that than they themselves. Seward and Chase were convinced that they, not Lincoln, should be president. For a time early in the administration, Seward tried to dominate Lincoln. He failed and ultimately became the president's loyal supporter. Chase never ceased trying to outshine the president and enhance his own political prospects.

Lincoln demonstrated confidence as well by his bold exercise of the war powers of his office. In order to accomplish his purposes, he ignored certain parts of the Constitution. It would be foolish, he explained, to lose the whole by being afraid to disregard a part. He called for troops to repress the rebellion without asking Congress for a declaration of war. He increased the size of the regular army without legislative authority to do so. He unilaterally proclaimed a naval blockade of the South.

Lincoln's greatest political problems, however, came not from legal obstacles, but from widespread popular opposition to the war. The opposition came principally from two sources: from Southern sympathizers in the slave states that had remained in the Union, and from the peace wing of the Democratic party. Many Democrats did support the war and even accepted office from the administration. But Peace Democrats (or, as their enemies called them, "Copperheads") feared that agriculture and the Northwest were being subordinated to industry and the East, and that Republican nationalism was threatening states' rights. Some Peace Democrats called for a truce in the fighting and proposed a national convention to amend the Constitution in ways that would satisfy Southern demands. Some advocated the formation of an independent Western confederacy. Some joined such secret societies as the Knights of the Golden Circle and the Sons of Liberty, which many people believed conspired to aid the Southern rebels.

Lincoln used extraordinary methods to suppress opposition to the war. He ordered military arrests and suspended the right of habeas corpus. Suspected offenders could, therefore, be arrested and held without trial. Those who were tried appeared before military courts, where they would not have the benefit of sympathetic local juries. At first, Lincoln used these methods only in particularly sensitive areas, such as the border states; but in 1862, he proclaimed that all persons who discouraged enlistments or engaged in disloyal practices would be subject to martial law. In all, more than 13,000 persons were arrested and imprisoned for varying periods. The most prominent Copperhead in the country—Clement L. Vallandigham, a member of Congress from Ohio—was seized by military authorities and exiled to the Confederacy. Lincoln defied all efforts to curb his authority to suppress opposition. He even defied the Supreme Court. When Chief Justice Taney issued a writ (*Ex parte Merryman*) requiring him to release an imprisoned Maryland secessionist leader, Lincoln simply ignored it. (After the war, in 1866, the Supreme Court held, in *Ex parte Milligan,* that military trials in areas where the civil courts were capable of functioning were unconstitutional.)

Early in the war, and particularly after the election of 1862, in which the Republicans suffered heavy losses, leaders of the party began working to create a broad coalition of all the groups that supported the war. In particular, they tried to attract the War Democrats. They called the new organization the Union

party; but it was, in reality, little more than the Republican party and a small fringe of War Democrats. It encountered its major political test in the presidential election of 1864.

The Union convention met in June 1864 and nominated Lincoln for another term as president and Andrew Johnson of Tennessee, a War Democrat who had opposed his state's decision to secede, for the vice presidency. In August, the Democratic convention nominated George B. McClellan, a celebrated former Union general who had been relieved of his command by Lincoln. The peace faction won approval of a plank in the party platform denouncing the war as a failure and calling for a truce and a settlement with the South. McClellan repudiated the plank, but the Democrats stood before the country as the peace party—ready to profit from the growing war weariness of the nation and from the dismal state of the Union's military position. At this crucial moment, however, several Northern military victories, particularly the capture of Atlanta, Georgia, early in September, rejuvenated Northern morale and gave promise of Republican success in November.

The election was a smashing electoral triumph for Lincoln, who won 212 votes to McClellan's 21 and carried every state except Kentucky, New Jersey, and Delaware. Lincoln's popular majority, however, was uncomfortably small, 2,214,000 to 1,805,000, an advantage of only 400,000. A slight shift of popular votes in some of the more populous states would have changed the result. Had Union victories not occurred when they did, had Lincoln not made special arrangements to allow Union troops to vote (presumably for him), the Democrats might have won and the future course of the nation might have been altered considerably.

The Politics of Emancipation

Lincoln had faced a challenge in 1864 not only from the Democrats but from members of his own Republican party, who almost succeeded in blocking his renomination. For the Republicans, no less than the Democrats, were plagued with factional divisions: between two groups known as the Radicals and the Conservatives. On most questions, including economic matters, the two groups were in fundamental agreement. But they differed violently on slavery. Radicals wanted to seize the opportunity presented by the war to abolish slavery—immediately and decisively. They had the benefit of influential and articulate congressional leaders: Representative

Fugitives from Slavery
The photographer Timothy O'Sullivan took this picture of fugitive slaves fording the Rappahannock River in Virginia in August 1862. They were following the retreating Union army of General John Pope after the Second Battle of Bull Run. Southern blacks deserted the plantations in increasing numbers as the war dragged on, particularly in areas where Union troops were nearby to provide protection. By the end of the war, huge groups of blacks could be found trailing behind almost every Union army in the South.   (Library of Congress)

Thaddeus Stevens of Pennsylvania, master of the party machine in the House; Senator Charles Sumner of Massachusetts; and Senator Benjamin F. Wade of Ohio. The Conservatives opposed slavery too, but they wanted to eliminate it in what they thought would be a less disruptive way—slowly and gradually. And they had the support of the president. Lincoln feared that too rapid an effort to abolish slavery would divide Northern opinion and so antagonize the border states, whose allegiance to the Union was already precarious, that it would become impossible to prevent them from seceding.

Nevertheless, legal attacks on slavery had gathered steady momentum throughout the early years of the war. Lincoln had made several attempts to persuade the loyal slave states to agree to a program of compensated gradual emancipation, but without notable success. A Confiscation Act, passed in August 1861, declared free all slaves used for "insurrectionary" purposes. Subsequent laws in the spring of 1862 abolished slavery, with compensation to owners, in the District of Columbia and in the Western territories. In the summer of 1862, the Radicals decided that Northern opinion had reached a point where they could move still further. In July, they pushed through Congress the second Confiscation Act, a bold attempt to accomplish emancipation by legislative action. It declared free the slaves of persons aiding and supporting the insurrection, and authorized the president to employ blacks, including freed slaves, as soldiers.

As the war progressed, the country seemed slowly to accept emancipation as a central war aim; nothing less, many believed, would justify the enormous sacrifices of the prolonged and costly struggle. As a result, the Radicals gained increasing influence within the Republican party—a development that did not go unnoticed by the astute master of politics in the White House, who decided to seize the leadership of the rising antislavery sentiment himself.

On September 22, 1862, after the Union victory at the Battle of Antietam, the president issued a preliminary Emancipation Proclamation; and on the first day of 1863, he signed a final Emancipation Proclamation, which declared forever free the slaves in most areas of the Confederacy. He exempted from the edict those areas already under Union control: the state of Tennessee, western Virginia, and southern Louisiana. And the proclamation did not apply to the border slave states, which had never seceded from the Union. Since these areas were not enemy territory, the president reasoned that they were not subject to his war powers.

The proclamation freed immediately only a few slaves. But it clearly and irrevocably established that this was a war being fought not only to preserve the Union but also to eliminate slavery. Eventually, as federal armies occupied much of the South, the proclamation became a practical reality and led directly to the freeing of thousands of slaves. About 186,000 of these emancipated blacks served as soldiers, sailors, and laborers for the Union forces. And even in areas not directly affected by the proclamation, the antislavery impulse was gaining strength. By the end of the war, slavery had been abolished in two Union slave states, Maryland and Missouri, and in three "reconstructed" or occupied Confederate states, Tennessee, Arkansas, and Louisiana. The final step came early in 1865, when Congress approved the Thirteenth Amendment, which freed all slaves everywhere and abolished slavery as an institution. The required number of states ratified the amendment shortly after the end of the war. After more than two centuries, legalized slavery forever ceased to exist in the United States.

The War and Society

The Civil War did not, as many people once believed, transform the North from an agrarian to an industrial society. Industrialization was already far advanced when the war began; and in some respects, the war itself did not so much encourage as retard further growth—by diverting labor and resources to military purposes.

On the whole, however, the war served to advance the Northern industrial economy. That was in part a result of the new dominance of the Republican party and its promotion of nationalistic economic legislation. But it was also because the war itself required expansion in certain sectors. Coal production increased by nearly 20 percent during the war. Railroad facilities improved—mainly through the adoption of a standard gauge (track width). The loss of farm labor to the military forced many farmers to increase the mechanization of agriculture.

Not all the effects of the war were so progressive. Industrial workers experienced a substantial loss of purchasing power, as their wages failed to rise fast enough to keep pace with the substantial wartime inflation. Prices in the North rose by more than 70 percent during the war, while wages rose only about 40 percent. (Inflation was, however, a far less serious problem than in the South; see next section.) The liberalization of immigration laws began to introduce new competition into the labor market and helped keep wages low. The increasing mechanization of production threatened many skilled workers with the loss of their jobs. One result was a substantial increase in union membership in many industries and the creation of a group of national unions for coal miners, railroad engineers, and other workers. Employers reacted by establishing blacklists of union members and using brutal methods to prevent organization and suppress strikes.

Women found themselves, either by choice or by necessity, thrust into new and often unfamiliar roles. They took over positions vacated by men as teachers, retail sales clerks, office workers, and at times mill and factory hands. Above all, they became nurses. Nursing had previously been a primarily male occupation (although women had been entering the profession since the 1840s); in the course of the war, women became increasingly dominant within the field. In the process, they redefined the image of nursing. Gradually, society came to think of it as a profession less dependent on medical expertise than on a spirit of benevolence and self-sacrifice, a spirit that women were considered to possess in particular abundance. By the end of the century, nursing had become an almost entirely female profession.

The U.S. Sanitary Commission, an organization of civilian volunteers, mobilized large numbers of female nurses to serve in field hospitals. The federal government appointed the reformer Dorothea Dix to serve under the surgeon general and help mobilize a women's nursing corps. Female nurses not only cared for patients but performed other tasks considered particularly appropriate for women: cooking, cleaning, and laundering.

For many women, especially those who had become committed in the prewar years to feminist causes, the war seemed to be an enormously important and liberating experience. Clara Barton, who was active during the war in collecting and distributing medical supplies and who later became an important figure in the nursing professsion, said in 1888: "At the war's end, woman was at least fifty years in advance of the normal position which continued peace would have assigned her." That was a considerable exaggeration. But it captured the degree to which many women looked back on the war as a crucial moment in the redefinition of female roles and in the awakening of a sense of independence and new possibilities.

The Mobilization of the South

The first seven Southern states to secede left the Union as individual sovereignties. But they intended from the first to join together in a common confederation, which they hoped the states of the upper South would eventually join. Accordingly, representatives of the seceded states assembled at Montgomery, Alabama, early in February 1861, to create a Southern nation. When Virginia seceded, the government moved to Richmond—partly out of deference to Virginia, partly because Richmond was one of the few Southern cities large enough to house the government.

Southerners were acutely aware, and boastfully proud, of the differences between their new nation and the nation they had left. Those differences were real. But there were also important similarities between the Union and the Confederacy, which became particularly clear as they mobilized for war: similarities in their political systems, in the methods they used for financing the war and conscripting troops, and in the way they fought.

The Confederate Government

The Confederate constitution was in most respects identical to the Constitution of the United States, but it contained a number of provisions designed to satisfy particular Southern demands. It expressly recognized the sovereignty of the individual states (although it made no mention of the right of secession). It gave the president an "item veto"—the power to veto part of a bill without rejecting the whole thing. And it specifically sanctioned slavery and made its abolition (even by one of the states) practically impossible.

Besides framing a constitution and passing temporary laws, the Montgomery convention named a provisional president and a provisional vice president: Jefferson Davis of Mississippi and Alexander H. Stephens of Georgia. Later, in a general election, the same two men were chosen, without opposition, for regular six-year terms. Davis had been a firm but not extreme advocate of Southern rights in the former Union; he was a moderate but not an extreme secessionist. Stephens had been the chief among those who had contended that secession was unnecessary. Indeed the Confederate government, like the Union government, was dominated throughout the war by men of the center. Just as Radical Republicans never managed to dominate the Lincoln administration, so in the Confederacy the extremist fire-eaters found themselves generally excluded from power.

Jefferson Davis embodied the spirit of the nation he had been called to lead. His family, which was of Southern yeoman stock, had moved from Kentucky, where he was born, to the new lush cotton lands of Mississippi, where they became rich planters almost overnight. Davis was a first-generation aristocrat. So also were most of the members of his government. The Confederacy was run by the cotton nabobs of the newer lower (or "Western") South, not by the old aristocracy of the seaboard states.

Lincoln's task was to preserve a nation. Davis's was the far more difficult task of making one. Lincoln succeeded; Davis failed. He was a reasonably good administrator and served as his own secretary of war. And he dominated his administration completely, encountering little interference from the generally tame members of his unstable cabinet. But Davis rarely provided genuinely national leadership. He spent too much time on routine items, on what one observer called "little trash." Moreover, he demonstrated a punctiliousness about legal and constitutional niceties that was totally inappropriate to the task of ensuring the survival of a new nation. Lincoln, without clear constitutional sanction, suspended habeas corpus; Davis asked his Congress for permission to do so and received only part of what he asked. One shrewd Confederate official (R. G. H. Kean) wrote: "All the revolutionary vigor is with the enemy. . . . With us timidity—hair splitting."

Outside the administration—in the Confederate Congress and among the public at large—opposition and dissent were widespread. Just as in the North, disenchanted citizens throughout the South spoke openly and bitterly about the disappointing progress of the war effort, the incompetence of the president and the government, the problems of the economy. The Confederacy had been established on the ideal of the unity and homogeneity of the South; it was that ideal, in fact, that underlay the decision of the founders that there should be no party system in the new nation, that the public should form a single united group. (A similar impulse supported the effort to create the Union party in the North in 1864.) But the quest for unity was in many ways no more successful in the Confederacy than in the Union. And the absence of a party system meant that disagreements often became far more destructive than they did within the government of the United States.

Money and Manpower

In contrast to the burgeoning prosperity of the wartime North, the South in the war years experienced shortages, suffering, and sacrifice. The Southern economy, despite a frantic expansion of industrial facilities, was unable to supply the needs of its armies and civilian population.

The officials in charge of financing the Confederacy's war effort faced several hard facts. They had to create a national revenue system capable of supporting a major war effort; and they had to do so in a society whose people were unaccustomed to bearing large tax burdens. Southern banking houses, except in New Orleans, were fewer and smaller than those of the North. Because excess capital in the South was usually invested in slaves and land, liquid assets were in short supply. The Confederacy's only specie was that seized from the U.S. mints located in the South, and it amounted to only about $1 million.

The Confederate Congress, like its counterpart in the North, was reluctant to enact rigorous wartime taxes. At first, it attempted to requisition funds from the individual states—most of which were unwilling to impose taxes on their citizens and paid their shares by issuing bonds or their own notes. Moving more boldly in 1863, Congress passed a bill that included license levies and an income tax. A unique feature was the "tax in kind." Farmers and planters had to contribute one-tenth of their produce to the government. But taxation in the end provided the Confederacy with only modest revenue; it was the source of only about 1 percent of the government's total income.

The borrowing record of the Confederacy was little better than its tax program. Eventually, the government issued bonds in such large amounts that people doubted its ability to redeem them. The Confederacy also attempted to borrow money in Europe by pledging cotton stored in the South for future delivery. None of these efforts produced more than minimal results; and thus the Confederacy had to rely primarily on the least stable, most destructive form of financing: paper currency.

The Confederacy began issuing paper money and Treasury notes (the equivalent of the Northern greenbacks) in 1861. Once started, the process could not be stopped. By 1864, the staggering total of $1 billion had been issued, more than twice what the Northern government issued. And unlike the Union, the Confederacy did not establish a uniform currency system; thus states and cities issued their own notes. The result was a rapid depreciation of the value of Confederate money—inflation, of a kind far worse than anything the North experienced. Prices skyrocketed to astronomical heights, with predictable effects on the new nation's morale.

Like the United States, the Confederate States first raised armies by calling for volunteers. And as in the North, by the end of 1861 voluntary enlistments had begun to decline. By the beginning of 1862, the Confederacy was threatened by a manpower crisis. The government met the situation decisively. At Davis's recommendation, Congress in April enacted a Conscription Act, which declared that all able-bodied white males between the ages of eighteen and thirty-five were liable to military service for three years. A

Confederate Volunteers
Young Southern soldiers posed for this photograph in 1861, shortly before the first Battle of Bull Run. The Civil War was the first major military conflict in the age of photography, and it launched the careers of many of America's early photographers. (Cook Collection, Valentine Museum)

man who was drafted could escape his summons if he furnished a substitute. The prices for substitutes eventually went as high as $10,000 in Confederate currency. The purpose of the provision was to exempt men in charge of agricultural and industrial production. It aroused such bitter opposition from poorer whites, however, that it was repealed in 1863. But that was not the only feature of the draft that angered the common people of the region. A particular target of resentment was the provision exempting one white man on each plantation with twenty or more slaves. Angrily denounced as the "twenty-nigger law," it caused ordinary men to say: "It's a rich man's war but a poor man's fight."

Despite the opposition, conscription seemed for a time to work. At the end of 1862, an estimated 500,000 soldiers were in the Confederate armies. After that, however, conscription provided fewer and fewer men, and the armed forces steadily decreased in size. That was partly because federal armies seized large areas of the South and deprived the Confederacy of access to the manpower in the occupied regions. But it was also because of declining enthusiasm for the war within the areas the Confederacy continued to control. Military reverses in the summer of 1863 convinced many Southerners that the war was lost, causing a kind of passive resistance to the draft as men sought to avoid it by hiding in the hills and woods.

As 1864 opened, the government faced a critical manpower shortage. In a desperate move, Congress lowered the age limit for drafted men to seventeen and raised it to fifty, reaching out, it was said, toward the cradle and the grave. But the measure produced few new recruits in a nation now suffering from intense war weariness and becoming certain that defeat was inevitable. In 1864–1865, there were 100,000 desertions. An observant Confederate diarist, Mary Boykin Chesnut, wrote in her journal in March 1865: "I am sure our army is silently dispersing. Men are moving the wrong way, all the time. They slip by with no songs and no shouts now. They have given the thing up." In a frantic final attempt to raise men, Congress in 1865 authorized the drafting of 300,000 slaves. The war ended before this incongruous experiment could be attempted.

Both in financing the war and in raising men to fight it, the South used methods in many ways indistinguishable from those being used by the North. Only the results were different. As the war continued, the disparity between the resources—both economic and human—available to the two nations became increasingly clear. The North, despite many difficulties, managed to finance its war effort reasonably successfully and to raise enough men to fill its armies. The South suffered constantly, and increasingly, from shortages of both money and men.

States' Rights Versus Centralization

Many Southerners criticized the Davis administration's handling of the war. Many opposed the draft. But except for isolated pockets of Union sentiment in some of the mountain areas (see above, pp. 327–328), there was at first very little opposition in the Confederacy to the war itself. Southerners were, however, bitterly divided over how the war should be conducted.

The greatest dividing force was, ironically enough, the principle of states' rights—the foundation of Southern political philosophy, for whose conservation and consecration the South had left the Union. States' rights had become such a cult with many Southerners that they resisted virtually all efforts to exert national authority, even those necessary to win the war. The most adamant opponents of centralization were a group of quixotic men who counted Vice President Alexander Stephens as their leader. They supported the war, but they were unwilling to sacrifice one iota of state sovereignty to win it. If victory had to be gained at the expense of states' rights, they preferred defeat. As the pressures of centralization grew, Stephens and his followers became increasingly attracted to the idea of a negotiated peace with the North and even implied at times that Southern independence need not be a precondition of such a peace.

The states' righters obstructed the national government's conduct of the war at many points. They were particularly critical of Davis's efforts to impose martial law and suspend habeas corpus, and they placed crippling restrictions on his ability to use such powers. They obstructed conscription at many points. Recalcitrant governors such as Joseph Brown of Georgia and Zebulon M. Vance of North Carolina at times went so far as to attempt to keep their own states' troops separate from the Confederate forces. Brown at one point had a substantial surplus of uniforms, which were badly needed by undersupplied Southern soldiers; nevertheless, he refused to allow them to be used for any but Georgia troops.

Despite the opposition, however, the Confederate government did make substantial strides in centralizing power in the South. The Confederate bureaucracy grew rapidly and by war's end was even larger than the bureaucracy in Washington. Davis imposed not only a manpower draft but a food draft—soldiers of the Confederate armies were empowered to seize crops from farms in their path in order to feed themselves. The government impressed slaves, often over the objections of their owners, to work as laborers on military projects. The Confederacy seized control of the railroads and shipping; it imposed regulations on industry; it limited corporate profits. States' rights sentiment was a significant handicap; but the South nevertheless took dramatic steps in the direction of centralization—becoming in the process increasingly like the region whose institutions it was fighting to escape.

Social Effects of the War

The war worked to transform Southern society in many of the same ways that it was changing the society of the North. The forced expansion of industry caused a substantial swelling of the region's previously modest urban population. Atlanta, Mobile, Richmond, and other cities experienced major growth; the population of Richmond more than doubled during the war.

The wartime experience was particularly significant for Southern women. Because so many men left their farms and plantations to fight, the task of keeping families together and maintaining agricultural production fell increasingly to women. Slaveowners' wives often became responsible for managing large slave work forces; the wives of more modest farmers learned to plow fields and harvest crops. Many women, moreover, involved themselves in public activities that had previously been considered the province of men. Substantial numbers of females worked in government agencies in Richmond. Even larger numbers chose nursing, both in hospitals and in temporary facilities set up to care for wounded soldiers. Others became schoolteachers.

The long-range results of the war for Southern women are more difficult to measure but equally profound. The experience of the 1860s almost certainly forced many women to question the prevailing Southern assumption that females were unsuited for certain activities, that they were not fit to participate actively in the public sphere. A more concrete legacy was the decimation of the male population and the creation of a major sexual imbalance in the region. After the war, there were many thousands more women in the South than men. In Georgia, for example, women outnumbered men by 36,000 in 1870; in North Carolina by 25,000. The result, of course, was a large number of unmarried (or widowed) women who, both during and after the war, had no choice but to find employment—thus, by necessity rather than choice, expanding the number of acceptable roles for women in Southern society.

Perhaps the principal social effect of the war on the South, however, was widespread suffering and privation. Particularly once the effects of the Northern naval blockade began to be felt, the South experienced massive shortages of almost everything. The region was overwhelmingly agricultural; but since it had concentrated so single-mindedly for so long on producing cotton and other export crops, it did not grow enough food to meet its own needs. And despite the efforts of women to keep farms functioning, the departure of male workers seriously diminished the region's ability to keep up what food production there had been. Doctors were conscripted in large numbers to serve the needs of the military, leaving many communities without any medical care. Crafts-

men such as blacksmiths and carpenters were in short supply.

Many Southerners responded to the scarcity of crucial goods by hoarding them or by selling them at exorbitant prices on the black market. Such practices were encouraged further by the nation's disastrous inflation—prices rose more than 7,000 percent in the course of the war—which made many reluctant to exchange any goods for money that they had reason to believe would soon be worthless.

As the war continued, the shortages, the inflation, and the suffering created increasing instability in Southern society. There were major food riots in cities in Georgia, North Carolina, and Alabama in 1863, as well as a large demonstration in Richmond that soon turned violent. Resistance to conscription, food impressment, and taxation increased throughout the nation. And in the meantime, increasing numbers of Southerners were becoming aware that the privations of war were not equally shared by people of different classes. The traditional deference toward the great planters of the region was eroding.

Strategy and Diplomacy

In the realm of military planning, the objectives of the Union were positive and those of the Confederacy negative. To achieve a victory, the Union had to conquer the rebels and reduce them to subjection, to obedience to federal law. The Confederacy had only to stave off defeat.

In the realm of diplomacy, the situation was reversed. The objectives of the Confederacy in its dealings with European powers were positive, those of the Union negative. The Confederacy hoped to persuade foreign governments to step into the war and help make their independence a reality. The Union aimed only to preserve the status quo: to prevent foreign recognition and intervention.

The Commanders—North and South

It was the responsibility of the president as commander in chief of the army and navy—of Abraham Lincoln for the Union and Jefferson Davis for the Confederacy—to see to the making and carrying out of an overall strategy for winning the war. Lincoln, a civilian all his life, had had no military education and no military experience except for a brief militia interlude. Yet he became a great war president and a great commander in chief—superior to Davis, who was a trained soldier. Lincoln made himself a fine strategist, often showing keener insight than his generals. He recognized that numbers and resources were on his side, and he moved immediately to mobilize the maximum strength of Northern resources. He urged his generals to keep up a constant pressure on the whole defensive line of the Confederacy until a weak spot was found and a breakthrough could be made. At an early date, he realized that the proper objective of his armies was the destruction of the Confederate armies and not the occupation of Southern territory.

During the first three years of the war, Lincoln performed many functions that in a modern command system would be assumed by the chief of the general staff or the joint chiefs of staff. He formulated policy, devised strategic plans, and even directed tactical movements. Some of his decisions were wise, some wrong; but the general effect of his "interference" with the military machine was fortunate for the North.

At the beginning, Lincoln was inclined to take the advice of General Winfield Scott, the aging hero of the Mexican War who became the president's first chief of staff. The old general, however, was unable to adjust his thinking to the requirements of mass war. He retired from service on November 1, 1861, and Lincoln replaced him as general in chief with the young George B. McClellan, who was also the commander of the federal field army in the East, the Army of the Potomac. McClellan was a proud, even arrogant man who utterly lacked the abilities needed either to formulate strategy or to command an army. The one grand strategic design he submitted was defective because it envisioned operations in only one theater of the war, his own, and because it made places instead of enemy armies its objective. When McClellan took the field in March 1862, Lincoln removed him as general in chief and replaced him (four months later) with General Henry W. Halleck. The foremost American student of the art of war, Halleck had won an undeserved reputation as a successful general in the West. Now he cast himself in the role of an adviser instead of a decision maker. Again, Lincoln himself was forced to form and direct military strategy, a task that he performed until March 1864, when the nation finally achieved a modern command system.

In that system, Ulysses S. Grant, who had emerged as the North's greatest general, was named general in chief. Charged with directing the movements of all Union armies, Grant, because he disliked

Ulysses S. Grant
One observer said of Grant (seen here posing for a photograph during the Wilderness campaign of 1864): "He habitually wears an expression as if he had determined to drive his head through a brick wall, and was about to do it." It was an apt metaphor for Grant's military philosophy, which took little account of sophisticated theories of strategy and tactics but relied instead on constant, unrelenting assault. One result was that Grant was willing to fight when other Northern generals held back. Another was that Grant presided over some of the worst carnage of the Civil War.
(Library of Congress)

the political atmosphere of Washington, established his headquarters with the Army of the Potomac but did not technically become commander of that army. Grant proved to be the man for whom Lincoln had been searching. He possessed in superb degree the ability to think of the war in overall terms and to devise strategy for the war as a whole. Because Lincoln trusted Grant, he gave the general a relatively free hand. Grant, however, always submitted the broad outlines of his plans to the president for approval before putting them into action. By the new arrangement, Halleck became "chief of staff," acting as a channel of communication between Lincoln and Grant and between Grant and the departmental commanders.

Lincoln's active command role underlines one of the most important changes occurring with the advent of modern warfare: the emergence of the civilian in strategic planning. As war became larger and more technological, strategy became a problem of directing the whole resources of a nation. It was too vast a problem for any one set of leaders, especially for the military.

The most dramatic example of civilian intervention in military affairs was the Committee on the Conduct of the War, a joint investigative committee of both houses of Congress and the most powerful agency that the legislative branch has ever created to secure for itself a voice in formulating war policies. Established in December 1861, under the chairmanship of Senator Benjamin F. Wade of Ohio, it became the spearhead of the Radical attack on Lincoln's war program. The Radicals believed that many of the Northern generals were not animated by a sufficiently driving, ruthless desire for victory. In one sense, they were right. Many of the generals were for a time unable to abandon the eighteenth-century concept of war as a kind of game—as chessboard maneuvers conducted in leisurely fashion and without heavy casualties. But the Radicals ascribed the generals' hesitancy to a secret sympathy for slavery, which the professionals were supposed to have imbibed at West Point. The generals whom the committee favored—most of them incompetent amateurs—would have been no improvement; and the committee's efforts often seriously interfered with the conduct of the war. But the Radicals did help—even if not always in ways they had intended—to infuse a hard, relentless purpose into the conduct of the war.

Southern command arrangements centered on President Davis, and under his leadership the Confederacy failed to achieve a modern command system. Early in 1862, Davis assigned General Robert E. Lee to duty at Richmond, where, "under the direction of the President," he was "charged" with the conduct of the Confederate armies. Despite the fine words, Davis had no intention of sharing control of strategy with anyone. Thus Lee, who had a brilliant military mind, acted only as Davis's adviser, furnishing counsel when called on. After serving a few months, Lee went into the field, and Davis did not appoint another adviser until February 1864. Then he selected Braxton Bragg, whom he had been forced to remove from field command after Bragg was defeated in the West. Bragg had real strategic ability, but he understood the political weakness of his position and restricted his function to providing technical advice.

In February 1865, the Confederate Congress, in a move directed at Davis, created the position of general in chief, which was intended for Lee. Davis named Lee to the post but took care to announce that legally he himself was still commander in chief. Lee accepted the job on the basis offered by the president: as a loyal subordinate instead of the dictator some people wanted him to be. The war ended before the new command experiment could be fully tested.

Below the level of highest command, the war was conducted—in both North and South—by men of markedly similar backgrounds. Much of the professional military leadership on both sides was a product

Robert E. Lee

Lee provided a sharp contrast to his Northern counterpart, Ulysses S. Grant. Grant was slightly built, slouching, disheveled, and gruff. Lee was tall, dignified, and elegant in both dress and manner. He admired George Washington above all other men, and he attempted to emulate him in his conduct both of the war and of his life. Although he commanded a losing cause, he remained a national hero—in the South and in the North as well in later years. (Cook Collection, Valentine Museum)

of the national military academies of the United States—the army academy at West Point and the naval academy at Annapolis, Maryland. Union and Confederate officers, in other words, had been trained along similar lines; many were intimately acquainted, even friendly, with their counterparts on the other side. The amateurs who played an important role in both armies were also in many respects similar. These were the commanders of volunteer regiments—usually the acknowledged economic or social leaders of their communities, who appointed themselves officers and rounded up troops to lead. Although occasionally this system produced officers of real ability, it more often led to disorganization and frustration.

The Role of Sea Power

The Union had a particular advantage in the area of sea power, where it had an overwhelming preponderance of strength. Lincoln made the most of it. The Union navy had two principal functions. One was to enforce the blockade of the Southern coast that the president proclaimed at the beginning of the war, on April 19, 1861. The other was to assist the Union armies in combined land-and-water operations.

In the Western theater of war—the vast region between the Appalachian Mountains and the Mississippi River—the larger rivers were navigable by vessels of considerable size. The Union navy helped the armies to conquer this area by transporting supplies and troops for them and joining them in attacking Confederate strong points. In defending themselves against the Union gunboats on the rivers, the Confederates had to depend mainly on land fortifications because of their lack of naval power. These fixed defenses proved no match for the mobile land-and-water forces of the Union.

At first, the blockade of the South was too large a task for the Union navy; and even after the navy had grown to its maximum size, it was unable to seal off completely the long shoreline of the Confederacy. Although large ocean-going ships could generally be kept away, small blockade runners continued to carry goods into and out of some Southern ports. Gradually the federal forces tightened the blockade by occupying stretches of the coast and seizing one port after another. They seized the last remaining important port—Wilmington, North Carolina—early in 1865. Fewer and fewer blockade runners got through, and the blockade increasingly hurt the South's economy.

In bold and ingenious attempts to break the blockade, the Confederates introduced some new weapons, among them an ironclad warship. They constructed this ship by plating with iron a former United States frigate, the *Merrimac,* which the Yankees had scuttled in Norfolk harbor when Virginia seceded. On March 8, 1862, the *Merrimac* steamed out from Norfolk to attack the blockading squadron of wooden ships in nearby Hampton Roads. It destroyed two of the ships and scattered the rest—an event that caused jubilation in Richmond and consternation in Washington. But the federal government had already placed orders for the construction of several ironclads of its own (designed by Swedish immigrant engineer John Ericsson). One of these, the *Monitor,* arrived at Virginia on the night of March 8, shortly after the *Merrimac*'s dramatic foray. When the *Merrimac* emerged on the following day to hunt for more victims, it encountered the *Monitor,* and the first battle between ironclad ships ensued. Neither vessel was able to penetrate the other's armor, but the *Monitor* put an end to the raids of the *Merrimac.*

The Confederates later experimented with other new kinds of craft in the effort to pierce the blockade. One was a torpedo boat, which carried the torpedo on a long pole projecting in front. Another was a small, cigar-shaped, hand-powered submarine, the first ever to be used in war. In 1864, in Charleston harbor, such a submarine, pulling its mine behind it on a cable, dived under a blockading vessel, exploded the mine against the hull—and then was dragged to the bottom by the sinking ship. But such efforts, however ingenious, fell far short of breaking or even weakening the blockade.

After more than a year of these unsuccessful efforts, the South generally ceased trying to break the blockade and used its navy instead primarily to defend its ports. But the Confederacy never stopped hoping for a new way to challenge the blockade. The government tried, for example, to build or buy fast ships to prey on the Northern merchant marine on the high seas. The hope was that the Union would detach ships from the blockade to pursue the commerce raiders. The Confederates also hoped to purchase from abroad a specially built "ram" with which to smash the wooden blockading ships. As a result of these efforts, the naval war became an important element in the relations of both the Union and the Confederacy with the powers of Europe.

Europe and the Disunited States

Judah P. Benjamin, who occupied the Confederate foreign office for the greater part of the war, was a clever and intelligent man, but he lacked strong convictions and confined most of his energy to routine administrative tasks. William Seward, on the other hand, learned his job well after some initial blunders and went on to become one of the outstanding American secretaries of state. Of perhaps equal importance, the United States was represented in the key diplomatic post at London by a distinguished minister, Charles Francis Adams, who seemed to have inherited the diplomatic brilliance of his father, John Quincy Adams, and his grandfather, John Adams.

In the relationship of Europe to the Civil War, the key nations were Great Britain and France. They had acted together against Russia in the Crimean War and were united by an entente, one of the understandings of which was that questions concerning the United States fell within the sphere of British influence. Napoleon III, therefore, would not act in American affairs without the concurrence of Britain.

At the beginning of the war, the sympathies of the ruling classes of England and France lay largely with the Confederacy. But important English liberals such as John Bright and Richard Cobden saw the war as a struggle between free and slave labor, and they urged their followers to support the Union cause. The politically conscious but largely unenfranchised workers in Britain expressed their sympathy for the North frequently and unmistakably—in mass meetings, in resolutions, and, through the medium of Bright and other leaders, in Parliament itself. After Lincoln issued the Emancipation Proclamation, these groups intensified their activities on behalf of the Union cause.

In the minds of Southern leaders, cotton was their best diplomatic weapon. England and France needed Southern cotton to keep their textile industries functioning; they would intervene on behalf of the Confederacy so as not to lose their supply. But this King Cotton diplomacy never worked as its champions had envisioned. In 1861, English manufacturers had a surplus of both raw cotton and finished goods on hand; thus the immediate effect of the blockade was merely to enable textile manufacturers to dispose of their remaining goods at high prices. Thereafter, the supply became increasingly short, and many mills were forced to close. But even then, both England and France managed to avoid a complete shutdown of their textile industries by importing supplies from new sources, notably Egypt and India. Most important of all, the workers, the people most seriously affected by the shortage, did not clamor to have the blockade broken. Even the 500,000 English textile workers thrown out of jobs continued to support the North.

The result of all this was that no European nation extended diplomatic recognition to the Confederacy. Although several times England and France considered offering to mediate the conflict, they never moved to intervene in the war. Neither could afford to do so unless the Confederacy seemed on the point of winning; and the South never came close enough to victory to convince its potential allies to support it. Even so, several crises emerged during the war that almost produced hostilities between the United States and Great Britain.

Immediately after the outbreak of war, Great Britain issued a proclamation of neutrality, which implicitly gave the Confederacy the status of a belligerent. France and other nations followed suit. The Northern government, which officially insisted that the war was not a war but a domestic insurrection, bitterly resented England's action. But the British government had proceeded in conformity with accepted rules of neutrality and in accordance with the realities of the situation. The United States was fighting a *war*, a fact that Lincoln himself had recognized in his proclamation establishing a blockade. Thereafter three crises or near crises developed, any one of which could have resulted in war between the two countries.

The first crisis, and the most dangerous one—the so-called *Trent* affair—occurred late in 1861. The Confederate commissioners to England and France, James M. Mason and John Slidell, had slipped through the then ineffective blockade to Havana, Cuba, where they boarded an English steamer, the *Trent,* for England. Hovering in Cuban waters was an American frigate, the *San Jacinto,* commanded by Captain Charles Wilkes, an impetuous officer who knew that the Southern diplomats were on the *Trent.* Acting without authorization from his government, Wilkes stopped the British vessel, arrested the commissioners, and bore them off in triumph to Boston. The British government drafted a demand for the release of the prisoners, reparation, and an apology. Lincoln and Seward, well aware that war with England would be suicidal, spun out the negotiations until American opinion had cooled off, then returned the commissioners with an indirect apology.

The second issue—a case involving Confederate ships known as commerce destroyers—generated a long-lasting diplomatic problem. Lacking the resources to construct the vessels, the Confederacy contracted to have them built and equipped in British shipyards. British companies sold six ships to the Confederacy, of which the most famous were the *Alabama,* the *Florida,* and the *Shenandoah.* The British government liked to claim that these were private transactions of which they had no prior knowledge. In fact, they knew exactly what was going on; Charles Francis Adams was informing them of it constantly and indignantly. The United States protested that this sale of military equipment to a belligerent violated the laws of neutrality. The protests formed the basis, after the war, for damage claims that the United States served on Great Britain. (See below, pp. 453–454.)

The third incident—the affair of the Laird rams—could have developed into a crisis but did not because the British government suddenly decided to mend its ways. In 1863, the Confederacy placed an order with the Laird shipyards in England for two powerful ironclads with pointed prows for ramming and sinking Union vessels and thus breaking the blockade. Adams was instructed to inform the British that if the rams, or any other ships destined for the Confederacy, left port, there would be danger of war. Even before Adams delivered his message, the British government acted to detain the rams and to prevent the Confederacy from obtaining any other ships.

If Napoleon III had had his way, France and England would have intervened on behalf of the Confederacy at an early date. Unable to persuade Britain to act, he had to content himself with expressing sympathy for the Southern cause and permitting the Confederates to order commerce destroyers from French shipyards. The emperor's primary motive for desiring an independent South was his ambition to establish French colonial power in the Western Hemisphere. A divided America would be less able to block his plans. He seized the opportunity of the war to set up a French-dominated empire in Mexico.

Napoleon's Mexican venture was a clear violation of the Monroe Doctrine, perhaps the most serious one that had ever occurred. The United States viewed it in such a light, but for fear of provoking France into recognizing the Confederacy, it could do no more than register a protest. Only after the Civil War ended did the United States feel strong enough to put pressure on France to get out of Mexico. By then, the French venture was already in trouble in Mexico itself. In 1866, Napoleon withdrew his troops from Mexico; and the following year, the emperor he had installed there was captured and shot by insurrectionists led by a former (and future) Mexican president, Benito Juarez.

Campaigns and Battles

In the absence of direct intervention by the European powers, the two contestants in America were left to settle their conflict between themselves. They did so in four long years of bloody combat that produced more carnage than any war in American history, before or since. More than 600,000 Americans died in the course of the Civil War, far more than the 115,000 who perished in World War I or the 318,000 who died in World War II. And in proportion to the total population, the losses suffered in the 1860s were even higher. There were nearly 2,000 deaths for every 100,000 of population during the Civil War. In World War I, the comparable figure was only 109; in World War II, 241.

It was not only battle itself that produced the remarkable death toll. It was disease, to which the miserable conditions in which both armies had to live made soldiers highly vulnerable, and for which only the most primitive medical knowledge or facilities were available. Even minor battle injuries, moreover, could lead to death through infection or other com-

Family Life in Camp
Troops in the volunteer regiments that made up most of the Union army were not subjected to the same strict discipline as professional soldiers. Occasionally, wives would move into the camps to be with their husbands (at times bringing children as well)—as illustrated by this Matthew Brady photograph of the thirty-first Pennsylvania Regiment. (Library of Congress)

plications because of inadequate health care. Despite the efforts of such volunteer organizations as the American Sanitary Commission, military medicine on both sides remained primitive. Not until World War I would scientific knowledge reach the point where disease would claim fewer victims than battle.

And the combat itself in the Civil War was of frightful intensity. After the Battle of Antietam, according to observers, one could have walked all the way across the vast battlefield atop the bodies of the fallen soldiers; the ground was almost entirely covered with the dead. Nearly 5,000 soldiers had been killed in a single day's fighting.

Despite the gruesome cost, the Civil War has become perhaps the most romanticized, the most intently studied, of all American wars. In large part, that is because the conflict produced—in addition to hideous fatalities—a series of military campaigns of classic strategic interest and a series of military leaders who displayed unusual daring and charisma.

The Opening Clashes, 1861

The year 1861 witnessed several small battles that accomplished large results and one big battle that had no important outcome. The small engagements occurred in Missouri and in western Virginia, the mountainous region that shortly would become the state of West Virginia.

In Missouri, the contending forces were headed on the one hand by Governor Claiborne Jackson and other state officials, who wanted to take the state out of the Union, and on the other by Nathaniel Lyon, commanding a small regular army force at St. Louis. Lyon led his column into southern Missouri, where he was defeated and killed by a superior Confederate force at the Battle of Wilson's Creek (August 10). He had, however, seriously blunted the striking power of the Confederates, and Union forces were able to hold most of the state.

Crossing the Ohio River into western Virginia came a Union force that had been assembled in Ohio under the command of George B. McClellan. McClellan succeeded by the end of the year in "liberating" the mountain people, who created their own state government loyal to the Union. Although possession of the region placed the Union forces on the flank of Virginia, they could not, because of the transportation obstacles presented by the mountains, use it as a base from which to move eastward. The occupation of western Virginia was, however, an im-

portant propaganda victory for the North: A Union-sympathizing area in the Confederacy had been wrenched from Southern control.

The one big battle of the year was fought in Virginia in the area between the two capitals. Just south of Washington was a Union army of over 30,000 under the command of General Irvin McDowell. A Confederate army of over 20,000 under P. G. T. Beauregard was based at Manassas in northern Virginia, about thirty miles southwest of Washington. If McDowell's army could knock out Beauregard's, Union leaders believed, the war might be ended immediately. In mid-July, McDowell marched his inexperienced troops toward Manassas. His movement was well advertised to the Confederates by Northern newspapers and Southern spies.

Beauregard retired behind Bull Run, a small stream north of Manassas, and called for reinforcements. They reached him the day before the battle, making the two armies approximately equal in size. In the First Battle of Bull Run, or First Battle of Manassas (July 21), McDowell's attack almost succeeded. But the Confederates stopped a last strong Union assault, then began a counterattack. A sudden wave of panic struck the Union troops, wearied after hours of hot, hard fighting. They retreated across the Bull Run Creek in a rout. Unable to reorganize his troops north of the stream, McDowell had to order a retreat to Washington—a chaotic withdrawal complicated by the presence along the route of many civilians, who had ridden down from the capital, picnic baskets in hand, to watch the battle from nearby hills. The Confederates, as disorganized by victory as the Union forces were by defeat, and lacking supplies and transportation, were in no condition to undertake a forward movement.

Lincoln replaced McDowell with General McClellan, the victor of the fighting in western Virginia, and took measures to increase the army. Both sides girded themselves now for a real war.

The Western Theater

After the battle at Manassas, military operations in the East settled into a long and frustrating stalemate. The first decisive operations in 1862 occurred, therefore, in the Western theater. Here the Union forces were trying to secure control of the Mississippi River, which would enable them to divide the Confederacy and provide them with easy transportation into its heart. Most of their offensives were combined land-

The Virginia Theater, 1861–1863

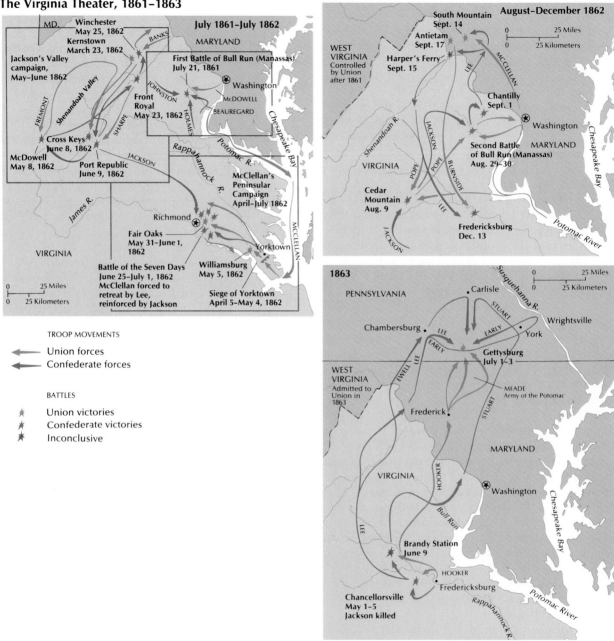

TROOP MOVEMENTS
← Union forces
← Confederate forces

BATTLES
✷ Union victories
✷ Confederate victories
✷ Inconclusive

and-water operations, as Union forces moved on the river itself or along its banks. Northern soldiers advanced on the southern Mississippi from both the north and south, moving down from Kentucky and up from the Gulf of Mexico toward New Orleans.

In April, a Union squadron of ironclads and wooden vessels commanded by David G. Farragut (destined to be the first American to be awarded the rank of admiral) appeared in the Gulf. Smashing past the weak Confederate forts near the mouth of the river, Farragut ran up to New Orleans, which had been left virtually defenseless because the Confederate high command had expected the attack to come from the north. Farragut forced the civil authorities to surrender the city on April 25—the first major Union victory (even if one that occurred virtually without bloodshed) and an important turning point in the war. Throughout the rest of the war, Union forces controlled New Orleans and southern Louisiana. They thus closed off the mouth of the great river to Confederate trade, grasped the South's largest city and greatest banking center, and secured a base for future operations.

All Confederate troops in the West were under the command of one general, Albert Sidney Johnston, who had permitted a fatal weakness to appear in his long line of defense. The center of that line lay in Tennessee, at Fort Henry on the Tennessee River and Fort Donelson on the Cumberland—and the forts were located well to the south of (and hence behind) the main Southern flanks. If the Union forces, with the aid of naval power, could capture these outposts, they would be between the two Confederate flanks and in a position to destroy either.

This was exactly what the Union forces did in February 1862. Ulysses S. Grant proceeded to attack Fort Henry, whose defenders, awed by the ironclad river boats accompanying the Union army, surrendered with almost no resistance (February 6). Grant then marched to Donelson, while his naval auxiliary moved to the Cumberland River. At Donelson, the Confederates put up a fight; but eventually the garrison of 20,000 had to capitulate (February 16). Grant, by the simple process of cracking the Confederate center and placing himself astride the river communications, had inflicted a near disaster on the Confederacy. As a result of his movement, the Confederates were forced out of Kentucky and had to yield half of Tennessee.

With about 40,000 men, Grant now advanced up the Tennessee River (southward) to seize control of railroad lines that were vital to the Confederacy. He landed his army at Pittsburg Landing, and marched to nearby Shiloh, where a force almost equal to his and commanded by Albert Sidney Johnston and P. G. T. Beauregard caught him with a surprise attack. In the ensuing Battle of Shiloh (April 6–7), the Southerners drove Grant back to the river in the first day's fighting (during which Johnston was killed). The next day, reinforced by 25,000 newly arrived troops, Grant took the offensive and recovered the lost ground. Beauregard then withdrew. After the narrow victory at Shiloh, Union forces managed to occupy Corinth, Mississippi, which was the hub of several important railroads, and established control of the banks of the Mississippi River as far south as Memphis.

The Confederate army in Mississippi, now under the command of Braxton Bragg, moved north to Chattanooga, to be in a position to launch an offensive and win back the lost territory. The Confederates still controlled the eastern half of Tennessee; Bragg's task was to recover the rest of the state and, if possible, to carry the war into Kentucky. Opposing him was a Union army under Don Carlos Buell, whose assignment was to capture Chattanooga. Bragg chose not to risk an engagement near there and decided instead to draw Buell away from Tennessee by going north. When the two armies met, in central Kentucky, they fought an indecisive battle at Perryville (October 8). Bragg then turned back to Tennessee, and Buell followed him slowly—so slowly that Lincoln finally removed him from command and replaced him with William S. Rosecrans. Bragg and Rosecrans met finally in the Battle of Murfreesboro, or Stone's River (December 31–January 2). Again Bragg withdrew to the south, his campaign a failure.

In the course of the year, the Union forces had made considerable progress toward the achievement of their objectives in the West. But the major conflict remained in the East; and they were having much less success with their land campaigns there.

The Virginia Front, 1862

In the Eastern theater in 1862, Union operations were directed by young George B. McClellan, commander of the Army of the Potomac and the most controversial general of the war. McClellan was a superb trainer of men, but he never seemed willing to commit his troops to decisive battle. Opportunities for important engagements came and went, and McClellan continually failed to take advantage of them—claiming always that his preparations were not yet complete or that the moment was not quite right.

During the winter of 1861–1862, McClellan had concentrated on training his army of 150,000 men near Washington. He finally settled on a plan of operations for the spring campaign designed to capture the Confederate capital at Richmond. Instead of heading overland directly toward Richmond, he decided on a roundabout route. He would have the navy transport his troops south down the Potomac to the peninsula between the York and the James rivers. Then he would move up the peninsula and approach Richmond from the east.

McClellan began his Peninsular campaign with

The War in the West, 1861-1863

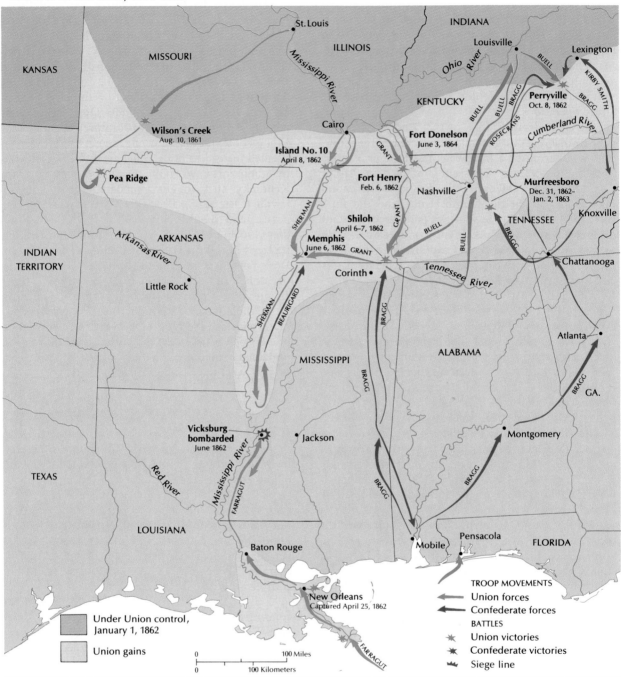

about 100,000 men. President Lincoln held back another 30,000—McDowell's corps—to protect the Union capital, although McClellan insisted that Washington would be safe as long as he was threatening Richmond. As he neared Richmond, he finally

persuaded Lincoln to send him the additional men. But before he could do so, the Confederates took steps to divert him. A Confederate army under Thomas J. ("Stonewall") Jackson marched rapidly northward in the Shenandoah Valley as if to cross the upper Potomac and attack Washington from above. Alarmed, Lincoln dispatched McDowell's corps to head off Jackson. In his brilliant Valley campaign (May 4–June 9), Jackson defeated two separate Union armies and slipped away before McDowell could catch him.

Meanwhile, just outside Richmond, Confederate troops under Joseph E. Johnston attacked McClellan's army, but in the two-day Battle of Fair Oaks, or Seven Pines (May 31–June 1), could not budge it. Johnston, badly wounded, was replaced by Robert E. Lee, who was to prove a masterly commander in leading the Army of Northern Virginia throughout the rest of the war. Lee recalled Jackson from the valley and, with a combined force of 85,000 (as compared with McClellan's 100,000), launched a new offensive, which resulted in a series of engagements known as the Battle of the Seven Days (June 25–July 1). Lee intended to cut McClellan off from his base on the York River and then to destroy McClellan's isolated army. Instead, McClellan managed to fight his way across the peninsula and set up a new base on the James. There, with naval support, the Army of the Potomac was safe. But so was Richmond.

Only twenty-five miles from Richmond, with a secure line of water communications, the Army of the Potomac was in a good position to renew the campaign. McClellan, however, time and again found reasons for delay. And Lincoln, instead of replacing McClellan with a more aggressive commander, decided to remove the army to northern Virginia and combine it with a smaller force under John Pope. Lincoln wished to start a new offensive on the direct Washington-to-Richmond overland route that he himself preferred.

As the Army of the Potomac left the peninsula by water, Lee moved the Army of Northern Virginia northward to strike Pope before McClellan could join him. Pope, who was as rash as McClellan was cautious, attacked the approaching Confederates without waiting for the arrival of all of McClellan's troops. In the ensuing Second Battle of Bull Run, or Second Battle of Manassas (August 29–30), Lee threw back the assault and routed Pope's army, which fled to Washington. Removing Pope from command, Lincoln put McClellan in charge of all the federal forces around the city.

Lee soon went on the offensive again, heading north through western Maryland. With some misgivings, Lincoln let McClellan move out to meet Lee. McClellan had the good luck to come into possession of a copy of Lee's orders, which revealed to him that the Confederate army was divided. A part of it, under Stonewall Jackson, had gone to capture Harpers Ferry. McClellan should have attacked quickly, before the Confederates could recombine. Instead, he gave Lee time to pull most of his forces together behind Antietam Creek, near the town of Sharpsburg. Here, in the bloodiest engagement of the war (September 17), McClellan with 87,000 men repeatedly assaulted Lee, who had 50,000. Late in the day—after appalling casualties on both sides—it seemed that the Confederate line might break, but the rest of Jackson's troops arrived from Harpers Ferry to fill the gap. Even then, McClellan might have broken through with one more effort. Instead, he allowed Lee to retreat into Virginia. Technically, Antietam was a Union victory; but in reality, it represented another opportunity squandered. In November, Lincoln finally removed McClellan from command, for good.

McClellan's replacement, Ambrose E. Burnside, was a short-lived mediocrity. He chose to drive at Richmond by crossing the Rappahannock at Fredericksburg, the strongest defensive point on the river. There (December 13) he flung his army at Lee's defenses in repeated attacks, all bloody, all hopeless. After losing a large part of his army, he withdrew to the north bank of the Rappahannock. He was relieved at his own request.

Year of Decision, 1863

As 1863 opened, Burnside's successor, Joseph Hooker (popularly known as "Fighting Joe"), was at the head of the Army of the Potomac, which, 120,000 strong, still lay north of the Rappahannock, opposite Fredericksburg. With part of the army, Hooker crossed the river upstream from Fredericksburg and threatened the town and Lee's army. But at the last minute, apparently, he lost his nerve and drew back to a defensive position in a desolate area of brush and scrub trees known as the Wilderness. Here, in the Battle of Chancellorsville (May 1–5), with only half as many men as Hooker had, Lee daringly divided the Confederate forces for a dual assault. He sent Jackson to hit the Union right while he himself charged the front. Hooker barely managed to extricate his army. Again Lee had frustrated Union objectives, but he had not won the decisive victory he was hoping for. And he had lost his ablest officer, Jackson, who was fatally wounded at the close of the battle.

While the Union forces were suffering repeated

Generals of the Confederacy

Charles Hoffbauer's painting *Summer* shows the principal Confederate commanders gathering at the beginning of the Battle of Chancellorsville in Virginia, on May 2, 1863. Robert E. Lee, seated on his horse Traveller, is in the foreground. On the far right, also on horseback, is Stonewall Jackson. That night, Jackson was shot and mortally wounded by his own sentries as he returned from a scouting mission.   (Virginia Historical Society)

frustrations in the East, they continued to do much better in the West. Ulysses S. Grant kept driving at Vicksburg, Mississippi, one of the Confederates' two remaining strongholds on the southern Mississippi River. Coming downriver with naval support, he struck several unsuccessful blows at the Confederate defenses. The terrain in front of Vicksburg was difficult, with rough country on the north and low, marshy ground on the west. Finally, in May, Grant had the navy run supply boats past the river batteries to a point below Vicksburg. He moved his army safely southward by land, down the Louisiana side of the river and out of range of Vicksburg's powerful guns. Then, once he was south of the city, he transported his troops back across the river. Here the terrain was much more suitable for maneuvering. Moving swiftly to the east, Grant twice defeated Confederates trying to stop him. Then he turned back to the west and approached Vicksburg from the rear. After attempting to take the town by storm, he settled into a prolonged siege. Six weeks later, on July 4, Vicksburg—whose residents were by then literally starving—surrendered. Almost immediately, the other Confederate strong point on the river, Port

Hudson, Louisiana, also surrendered—to a Union force that had moved north from New Orleans.

At last the Union had achieved one of its basic military aims: control of the whole length of the Mississippi. The Confederacy was split in two—Louisiana, Arkansas, and Texas were now cut off from the other seceded states. The victories on the Mississippi were one of the great turning points of the war.

The siege of Vicksburg had other effects on the Confederate war effort. Early in the siege, the Confederate government had begun considering various plans for relieving the town. Lee proposed an invasion of Pennsylvania, which would, he argued, serve to remove the pressure on Vicksburg. If he could win a sudden victory on Northern soil, he said, England and France would probably come to the Confederacy's aid, and the Union might even quit the war before Vicksburg fell.

Lee started the campaign into Pennsylvania in June. He moved west to the Shenandoah Valley and then north through Maryland and into Pennsylvania. Hooker moved his troops west, to keep parallel with the Confederates' movement and to remain between Lee and Washington. Then, in mid-campaign, he was replaced by George C. Meade, a solid if unimaginative soldier. Units of Lee's and Meade's armies finally encountered one another at the small town of Gettysburg. And there, from July 1–3, 1863, they fought the most celebrated battle of the war.

Meade's army established a strong, well-protected position on the hills south of the town. Lee, combative by nature and confident of his men, decided to attack even though his army was at a tactical disadvantage and was outnumbered 75,000 to 90,000. His first assault failed to reach the main line of the Union forces on Cemetery Ridge, so, a day later, he ordered a second and larger effort. In what is remembered as Pickett's Charge, a force of 15,000 advanced for almost a mile over open country that was swept by hostile fire. Only about 5,000 made it up the ridge, and this remnant finally had to surrender or retreat. Lee was compelled to withdraw from Gettysburg,

having lost nearly a third of his army. Meade failed to prevent the return of the Confederates to Virginia; but the Southern army had been so weakened that Lee never again attempted a serious invasion of the North. The Confederate retreat from Gettysburg, which began on the same day as the surrender at Vicksburg (July 4), was another great turning point in the war.

Before the end of the year, there was a third important turning point, this one in Tennessee. The Union army under Rosecrans occupied Chattanooga (September 9) after Bragg and the Confederates had evacuated the town. Rosecrans then went, unwisely, in pursuit of Bragg. Just across the Georgia line, Bragg, with reinforcements from Lee's army, was lying in wait. He fell upon Rosecrans in the Battle of Chickamauga (September 19–20), one of the few battles in which the Confederates enjoyed a numerical superiority (70,000 to 56,000). The Union right broke and ran, although the left, under George H. Thomas (who became known as "the Rock of Chickamauga"), continued to fight. Finally Thomas, along with the rest of the beaten army, sought refuge behind the Chattanooga defenses.

Soon the Union army in Chattanooga was under siege. Bragg held the heights nearby and controlled the roads and the Tennessee River, thus cutting off almost all fresh supplies. Finally Grant came to the rescue. In the Battle of Chattanooga (November 23–25), the reinforced Union army drove the Confederates back into Georgia. Northern troops then proceeded to occupy most of eastern Tennessee.

The Union forces had achieved a second important objective: control of the Tennessee River. At Chattanooga they were in a position to split the Confederacy again—what was left of it. No longer could the Southerners hope to gain their independence by some great military victory. They could hope to win only by holding on and exhausting the Northern will to fight.

The Last Stage, 1864–1865

Grant, who was now general in chief of all the Union armies, planned two grand offensives for 1864. In Virginia, the Army of the Potomac (which Meade continued to command but which Grant accompanied and actually directed) was to advance toward Richmond and force Lee into a decisive battle. In Georgia, the Western army, under William T. Sherman, was to advance east toward Atlanta and destroy

Assault on Vicksburg, May 1862–July 1863

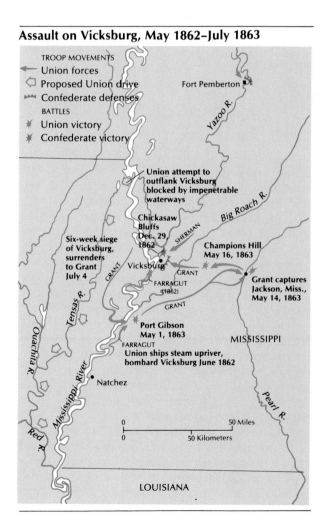

TROOP MOVEMENTS
Union forces
Proposed Union drive
Confederate defenses
BATTLES
Union victory
Confederate victory

Fort Pemberton

Yazoo R.

Union attempt to outflank Vicksburg blocked by impenetrable waterways

Big Roach R.

Chickasaw Bluffs Dec. 29, 1862

SHERMAN

Six-week siege of Vicksburg, surrenders to Grant July 4

Vicksburg

Champions Hill May 16, 1863

GRANT

FARRAGUT (1862)

Grant captures Jackson, Miss., May 14, 1863

GRANT

Tensas R.

Port Gibson May 1, 1863

FARRAGUT
Union ships steam upriver, bombard Vicksburg June 1862

MISSISSIPPI

Ouachita R.

Natchez

Mississippi River

Red R.

Pearl R.

0   50 Miles
0   50 Kilometers

LOUISIANA

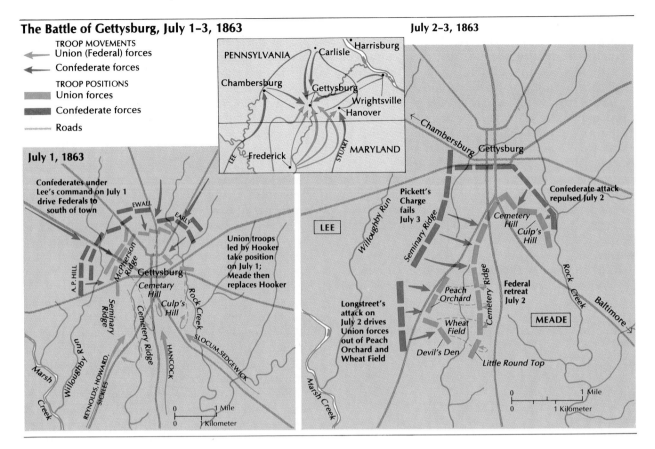

The Battle of Gettysburg, July 1–3, 1863

July 2–3, 1863

TROOP MOVEMENTS
Union (Federal) forces
Confederate forces

TROOP POSITIONS
Union forces
Confederate forces
Roads

July 1, 1863

Confederates under Lee's command on July 1 drive Federals to south of town

Union troops led by Hooker take position on July 1; Meade then replaces Hooker

Pickett's Charge fails July 3

Confederate attack repulsed July 2

Longstreet's attack on July 2 drives Union forces out of Peach Orchard and Wheat Field

Federal retreat July 2

the opposing Confederate force, now under the command of Joseph E. Johnston.

The twofold campaign began when the Army of the Potomac, 115,000 strong, crossed the Rappahannock and Rapidan rivers and plunged into the rough, wooded Wilderness area. Lee, with about 75,000 men, was determined to avoid a showdown unless he saw a chance to deal a decisive blow. In the Battle of the Wilderness (May 5–7), Lee stopped Grant, but only for the moment. Instead of withdrawing to rest and reorganize, as his predecessors had done after every battle, Grant resumed his march in the general direction of Richmond. Lee intercepted him a second time in the Battle of Spotsylvania Court House and engaged him in a bloody five-day struggle, which cost the Union armies 12,000 men; the heavy Confederate casualty figures were never released. Despite the enormous losses, Grant still refused to stop his advance. He moved now to the southeast, and Lee continued to keep between him and the Confederate capital. Just a few miles northeast of Richmond, at Cold Harbor (June 1–3), Grant made a desperate attack and was repulsed. In the whole month-long Wil-

derness campaign Grant had lost a total of 55,000 men (killed, wounded, and captured) to Lee's 31,000. And still, the decisive victory eluded him.

"I propose to fight it out on this line if it takes all summer," Grant had declared during the Battle of Spotsylvania; but he now tried a different tack. He slipped away with his army, bypassed Richmond, and headed for Petersburg, a railroad center directly south of the capital. If he could seize Petersburg, he could cut off the capital's communications and force Lee to fight for them. But Grant's initial assault on Petersburg failed. Both sides settled down to a siege, with trenches stretching for miles from Richmond to and around Petersburg. Grant kept trying to extend his left around Lee's right so as to get at the railroads that served as Lee's lifeline. But success was not to come until after nine months of struggle.

In Georgia, meanwhile, Sherman had been facing less resistance than Grant in Virginia. Sherman had 90,000 men and faced Confederate forces under Johnston of 60,000. Johnston was unwilling to risk the destruction of his army through a direct engagement with Sherman's superior force; and so, as

Virginia Campaigns, 1864–1865

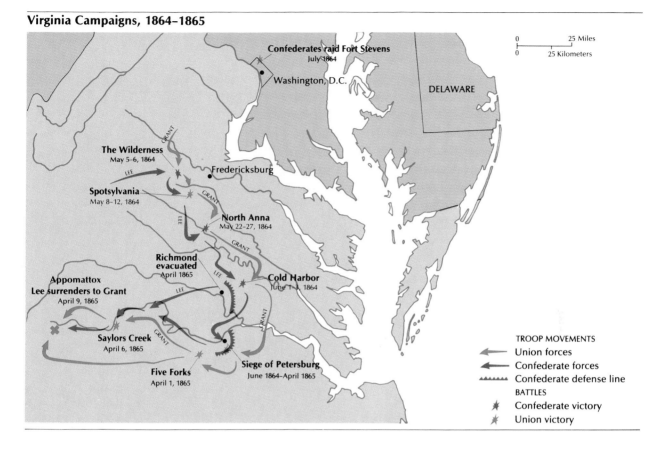

Sherman advanced, he tried to delay him by maneuvering. Johnston stopped long enough to fight only one real battle—Kennesaw Mountain, northwest of Atlanta (June 27). Despite an impressive victory there, Johnston was unable to stop the Union advance toward Atlanta. Realizing that Sherman would soon reach the city, President Davis replaced Johnston with the combative John B. Hood. Twice Hood daringly attacked; he accomplished nothing except seriously to weaken his own army. Sherman took Atlanta on September 2. (News of the victory electrified the North and helped unite the previously divided Republican party behind President Lincoln.)

Hood now schemed to draw Sherman out of Atlanta by moving back up through Tennessee and threatening an invasion of the North. Sherman refused to follow—he had other plans—but he sent reinforcements under George H. Thomas and John M. Schofield to help defend Nashville. Hood caught up with Schofield's force and, in the Battle of Franklin (November 30), further weakened his own army by ordering senseless charges against Schofield's well-protected positions. Then, in the Battle of Nashville

(December 15–16, 1864), Thomas not only put Hood's army to flight but practically disintegrated it.

Meanwhile Sherman had started on a march from Atlanta to the sea. Living off the land, destroying supplies it could not use, his army cut a sixty-mile-wide swath of desolation across Georgia. "War is hell," Sherman maintained. By that he meant not so much that war is terrible, and to be avoided, as that it should be made as horrible and costly as possible for the opponent. He sought not only to deprive the Confederate army of war materials and railroad communications but also to bring the war home to the Southern people and break their will to fight. By December 20, he had reached Savannah, which surrendered two days later and was offered to President Lincoln as a Christmas gift (and which, almost alone among the areas he conquered, he did not destroy; the city was, he claimed, too beautiful to burn). Early in 1865, Sherman turned northward and carried his destruction through South Carolina. On his entire march, he was virtually unopposed until he was well inside North Carolina, where a small force under Johnston could do no more than cause a brief delay.

Sherman's March to the Sea, 1863–1865

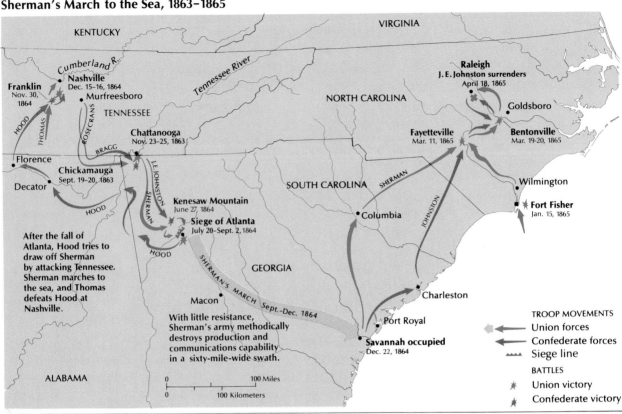

In April 1865, Grant's Army of the Potomac—still engaged in the prolonged siege at Petersburg—finally captured a vital railroad junction southwest of the town. Lee could no longer hope to defend Richmond. With the remnant of his army, now reduced to about 25,000, Lee began moving west in the forlorn hope of finding a way to avoid Union forces to his south so that he could move toward North Carolina and link up with Johnston. But the Union army pursued him and blocked his escape route. Realizing that further bloodshed was futile, Lee arranged to meet Grant at the courthouse at the small town of Appomattox, Virginia. There, on April 9, he surrendered what was left of his forces. Nine days later, near Durham, North Carolina, Johnston surrendered to Sherman.

In military terms, at least, the long war was now over. But Jefferson Davis remained defiant and refused to accept defeat. He fled south and was finally captured in Georgia. Only a few Southern diehards continued to fight; even their resistance collapsed before long. Well before the last shot was fired, the painful process of trying to reunite the shattered nation had begun.

SUGGESTED READINGS

General Studies   James M. McPherson, *Ordeal by Fire*, rev. ed. (1985), and James G. Randall and David Donald, *The Civil War and Reconstruction,* rev. ed. (1969), are two general studies that offer excellent overviews of the Civil War. Both have fine bibliographies, but McPherson's is more up-to-date. Allan Nevins, *The Ordeal of the Union*, 8 vols. (1947–1971), is the most thorough general history. Shelby Foote, *The Civil War: A Narrative*, 3 vols. (1958–1974), is a vivid military history. Bruce Catton, *This Hallowed Ground* (1956), is a one-volume military account.

The Secession Crisis   See Ralph A. Wooster, *The Secession Conventions of the South* (1962); David Potter, *Lincoln and His Party in the Secession Crisis* (1942); William L. Barney, *The Road to Secession* (1972) and *The Secessionist Impulse: Alabama and Mississippi in 1860* (1974); and Kenneth M.

SIGNIFICANT EVENTS

1860 South Carolina secedes from Union

1861 Ten more Southern states secede

Confederate States of America formed

Jefferson Davis named president of Confederacy

Conflict at Fort Sumter, South Carolina (April 12–14), begins Civil War

George B. McClellan appointed commander of Army of the Potomac

Union blockades Confederate coast

Trent affair imperils U.S. relations with Britain

First Battle of Bull Run (July 21)

1862 Battle of Shiloh (April 6–7)

Union forces capture New Orleans (May 1)

Second Battle of Bull Run (August 29–30)

Battle of Antietam (September 17)

Battle of Fredericksburg (December 13)

McClellan removed from command

Robert E. Lee named commander of Confederate armies

Homestead Act and Morrill Land Grant Act passed

Union Pacific Railroad chartered

Confederacy enacts military draft

1862 Republicans experience heavy losses in congressional elections

1863 Lincoln issues Emancipation Proclamation (January 1)

Battle of Chancellorsville (May 1–5)

Battle of Gettysburg (July 1–3)

Vicksburg surrenders (July 4)

Battle of Chattanooga (November 23–25)

Union enacts military draft

Antidraft riots break out in New York City

South experiences food riots

West Virginia admitted to Union

1864 Battle of the Wilderness (May 5–7)

Petersburg, Virginia, besieged

Sherman captures Atlanta (September 2)

Sherman's "march to the sea" begins

Lincoln reelected president

Central Pacific Railroad chartered

1865 Lee surrenders to Grant at Appomattox (April 9)

Thirteenth Amendment, abolishing slavery, ratified

Stampp, *And the War Came* (1950), which describes the crisis in the North. Richard N. Current, *Lincoln and the First Shot* (1963), examines the Sumter decision. See also Steven A. Channing, *Crisis of Fear* (1970). Michael P. Johnson, *Toward a Patriarchal Republic* (1977), and John M. McCardell, Jr., *The Idea of a Southern Nation* (1979), examine the origins of Southern nationhood.

Lincoln There is no end to the literature on Abraham Lincoln. Two excellent one-volume biographies are Benjamin Thomas, *Abraham Lincoln* (1952), and Stephen B. Oates, *With Malice Toward None* (1979). Classic multivolume works include James G. Randall, *Lincoln the President,* 4 vols. (1945–1955), the final volume completed by Richard N. Current; and Carl Sandburg, *Abraham Lincoln,* 6 vols. (1929–1939), notable more for its literary elegance and its emotional intensity than for its accuracy or balance. Specialized studies of Lincoln in the war years include T. Harry Williams, *Lincoln and the Radicals* (1941) and *Lincoln and His Generals* (1952); William B. Hesseltine, *Lincoln and the War Governors* (1948); Robert V. Bruce, *Lincoln and the Tools of War* (1956); and Harry J. Carman and Reinhard Luthin, *Lincoln and the Patronage* (1943). LaWanda Cox, *Lincoln and Black Freedom* (1981), examines the president's record on race.

Politics and Society in the North Several biographies of leading Union politicians also reveal the larger contours of Northern politics and society. David Donald, *Charles Sumner and the Rights of Man* (1970), is an excellent study of the leading Republican radical in the Senate. Benjamin P. Thomas and Harold M. Hyman, *Stanton* (1962), examines Lincoln's secretary of war; while Glyndon Van Deusen, *William Henry Seward* (1967), reveals the complex character of Lincoln's secretary of state. Martin Duberman, *Charles Francis Adams* (1961), is a fine portrait of the North's leading diplomat. James G. Randall, *Constitutional Problems Under Lincoln* (1926), is a classic study. Robert P. Sharkey, *Money, Class, and Party* (1959), examines the Union's economic problems. Wood Gray, *The Hidden Civil War* (1942), and Frank Klement, *The Copperheads in the Middle West* (1960), describe political dissent in the Northern states. George Fredrickson, *The Inner Civil War* (1965), is an important study of the attitudes of Northern intellectuals toward the conflict. Daniel Aaron, *The Unwritten War* (1973), considers reflections of the war in American literature, as does Edmund Wilson's *Patriotic Gore* (1962), a landmark in literary criticism.

Blacks and Emancipation The background of the Emancipation Proclamation is examined in many of the Lincoln biographies cited above. See also Benjamin Quarles, *Lincoln and the Negro* (1962) and *The Negro in the Civil War* (1953), for studies of the president's racial attitudes. James M. McPherson, *The Struggle for Equality* (1964), examines the role of abolitionists in pressing for emancipation during the war. McPherson is also the author of *The Negro's Civil War* (1965), which uses documents to depict the impact of the war on blacks. Peter Kolchin, *First Freedom* (1972), examines the immediate response of blacks in Alabama to emancipation; while John W. Blassingame, *Black New Orleans* (1973), does the same for that city. Dudley T. Cornish, *The Sable Arm* (1966), considers black soldiers in the Union army.

The Confederacy   The outstanding study of the South during the war is Emory Thomas, *The Confederate Nation* (1979), which supersedes Clement Eaton, *A History of the Southern Confederacy* (1954), long the standard work. Charles P. Roland, *The Confederacy* (1960), is a brief account. E. Merton Coulter, *The Confederate States of America* (1950), is a useful, if partisan, study. Clement Eaton, *Jefferson Davis* (1978), is the most recent biography of the Confederate president. A more detailed work is Hudson Strode, *Jefferson Davis,* 3 vols. (1955–1964). Thomas B. Alexander and Richard E. Beringer, *The Anatomy of the Confederate Congress* (1972), and W. Buck Yearns, *The Confederate Congress* (1960), consider the Southern legislature. Emory Thomas, *The Confederacy as a Revolutionary Experience* (1971), challenges the conventional view that states' rights survived virtually intact within the Confederacy, a view expressed in Frank L. Owsley, *State Rights in the Confederacy* (1952). Social histories of the Southern states during the war include the classic studies by Bell I. Wiley: *The Life of Johnny Reb* (1943)—companion volume to his study of the Northern soldier, *The Life of Billy Yank* (1952)—and *The Plain People of the Confederacy* (1943). See also Paul D. Escott, *After Secession* (1978), *Slavery Remembered* (1979), and *Many Excellent People* (1985); and James L. Roark, *Masters Without Slaves* (1977). Georgia Lee Tatum, *Disloyalty in the Confederacy* (1934), and Ella Lonn, *Desertion During the Civil War* (1928), examine dissent within the Confederacy. Emory Thomas, *The Confederate State of Richmond* (1971), is a local study of the Southern capital.

Diplomacy   David P. Crook is the author of two useful studies of Civil War diplomacy: *Diplomacy During the American Civil War* (1975) and *The North, the South, and the Powers, 1861–1865* (1974). Frank L. Owsley and Harriet Owsley, *King Cotton Diplomacy*, rev. ed. (1959), examines Southern efforts to win support from abroad. Gordon H. Warren, *Fountain of Discontent: The Trent Affair and Freedom of the Seas* (1981), and Stuart L. Bernath, *Squall Across the Atlantic: American Civil War Prize Cases and Diplomacy* (1970), examine some of the diplomatic controversies of the war years.

Military Histories   The classic biography of Robert E. Lee is Douglas Southall Freeman, *Robert E. Lee,* 4 vols. (1934–1935). Thomas L. Connelly, *The Marble Man* (1977), considers the popular image of Lee through the decades. John Carpenter, *Ulysses S. Grant* (1976), is a useful biography; but easily the finest work on the Union commander is William McFeely, *Grant* (1981). Military histories of the Civil War are so numerous as to defy adequate summary. See the bibliographies in the McPherson book and in the study by Randall and Donald, both cited above. Bruce Catton has produced a body of literature on the war that has long enjoyed popularity for its eloquence and vividness: *Mr. Lincoln's Army* (1951), *Glory Road* (1952), *A Stillness at Appomattox* (1954), *America Goes to War* (1958), *Banners at Shenandoah* (1965), *Grant Moves South* (1960). Kenneth P. Williams, *Lincoln Finds a General,* 4 vols. (1949–1952), is a lively study of the war from the Union point of view. Richard S. West, Jr., *Mr. Lincoln's Navy* (1957), and C. E. MacCartney, *Mr. Lincoln's Admirals* (1956), examine Union naval operations, as do several more specialized works, including John Niven, *Gideon Welles, Lincoln's Secretary of the Navy* (1973). On the Confederate navy, see two books by William N. Still, Jr.: *Iron Afloat: The Story of the Confederate Armorclads* (1971) and *Confederate Shipbuilding* (1969). T. Harry Williams, *McClellan, Sherman, and Grant* (1962), considers three Union generals; while his *P. G. T. Beauregard, Napoleon in Gray* (1955), examines a major Southern general. Burke Davis, *Sherman's March* (1980), depicts the last major offensive of the war. Thomas L. Livermore, *Numbers and Losses in the Civil War in America* (1957), reveals the appalling costs of the conflict. Herman Hattaway and Archer Jones, *How the North Won* (1983), and Archer Jones et al., *Why the South Lost the Civil War* (1986), examine the strengths and weaknesses of the contending forces.

A Reconstruction Era Tribute to the Election of Blacks to Congress
From left to right: Sen. Hiram R. Revels, Rep. Benjamin S. Turner, the Reverend Richard Allen, Frederick Douglass, Representative Josiah T. Walls, Representative Joseph H. Rainy, and writer William Wells Brown. (Library of Congress)

Chapter 15 Reconstructing the Nation

Few periods in the history of the United States have produced as much bitterness or created such enduring controversy as the era of Reconstruction—the years following the Civil War during which Americans attempted to reunite their shattered nation. Those who lived through the experience viewed it in sharply different ways. To white Southerners, Reconstruction was a vicious and destructive experience—a period of low, unscrupulous politics, a time when vindictive Northerners inflicted humiliation and revenge on the prostrate South and unnecessarily delayed a genuine reunion of the sections. Northern defenders of Reconstruction, in contrast, argued that their policies were the only way to prevent unrepentant Confederates from restoring Southern society as it had been before the war; without forceful federal intervention, there would be no way to forestall the reemergence of a backward aristocracy and the continued subjugation of blacks—no way, in other words, to prevent the same sectional problems that had produced the Civil War in the first place.

To most black Americans at the time, and to many people of all races since, Reconstruction was notable for other reasons. Not a vicious tyranny, as white Southerners charged, nor a drastic and necessary reform, as many Northerners claimed, it was, rather, an essentially moderate, even conservative program that fell far short of providing the newly freed slaves with the protection they needed. Reconstruction, in other words, was significant less for what it did than for what it failed to do. And when it came to an end, finally, in 1877—as a result of exhaustion and disillusionment among the white leaders of both sections, and of a series of complex bargains in the aftermath of the election of 1876—black Americans found themselves once again abandoned. Although they had, with the help of federal protection, won some important gains during Reconstruction, those gains were limited; and after 1877 nothing would save black people from being consigned to a system of economic peonage and legal subordination. The nation's racial problem, which had done so much to produce the Civil War, was left unresolved—to arise again and again in future generations.

The Problems of Peacemaking

In 1865, when the Confederacy finally surrendered to the North, no one knew quite what to do in response. Abraham Lincoln could not negotiate a treaty with the defeated government; he continued to insist that that government had no legal right to exist. Yet neither could he simply readmit the Southern states into the Union as if nothing had happened. The South had been devastated by the war—socially, economically, and politically. And there was now an enormous population of freed slaves, many of them wandering bewildered through the shattered land. Clearly the federal government had to act.

The Aftermath of War

In the North, the wartime prosperity continued into the postwar years; but Northerners who visited the South were appalled when they gazed on the desola-

tion left in the wake of the war—gutted towns, wrecked plantations, neglected fields, collapsed bridges, and ruined railroads. Much of the personal property of white Southerners had been lost with the lost cause. Confederate bonds and currency were now worthless, and capital that had been invested in them was gone forever. With the emancipation of the slaves, Southern whites were deprived of property worth an estimated $2 billion. Southern blacks were left with no property at all.

Matching the shattered economy of the South was the disorganization of its social system. In the months that followed the end of the war, thousands of soldiers drifted back to their homes; but 258,000 had died in the war, and additional thousands returned wounded or sick. Many families approached the difficult task of rebuilding, therefore, without the help of adult males. Many white Southerners faced the prospect of starvation and homelessness.

If conditions were bad for Southern whites, they were generally far worse for Southern blacks—the 4 million men and women now emerging from the bondage that had held them and their ancestors for up to two and a half centuries. Many of these people, too, had seen service of one kind or another during the war. Some had served as body servants for Confederate officers or as teamsters and laborers for the Confederate armies. Nearly 200,000 had fought as combat troops in the Union ranks, and more than 38,000 had given their lives for the Union cause. Countless other blacks, who had never worn a uniform or drawn army pay, had assisted the Union forces as spies or scouts. Still others had run off from the plantations and flocked to the Union lines in search of freedom and protection, often to be put to work for the Union armies. As soon as the war ended, many thousands more left the plantations in search of a new life in freedom. Old and young, many of them feeble and ill, they trudged to the nearest town or city or roamed the countryside, camping at night on the bare ground. Few had any possessions except the clothes they wore.

In 1865, in short, Southern society was in disarray. Blacks and whites, men and women faced a future of great uncertainty, in which traditional institutions and assumptions no longer seemed suitable. Nevertheless, people of both races had, even in 1865, distinct and very different ideas about how to respond to the new postwar world.

Many white Southerners hoped to restore their society to its antebellum form. Slavery, of course, had already been abolished in much of the South by the Emancipation Proclamation. The Thirteenth Amendment, which declared slavery unconstitutional, passed Congress on February 1, 1865; the amendment became law on December 18, 1865. But many white planters were determined to retain the essence of slavery even if its legal basis was now destroyed. Some planters continued to detain their black workers. In some instances, the former slaves simply did not learn that slavery had been abolished. But in other cases, they fell victim to efforts by white Southerners to re-create slavery in another form. Most planters agreed with a former Confederate leader who was saying (in June 1865) that slavery had been "the best system of labor that could be devised for the Negro race" and that the wise thing to do now would be to "provide a substitute for it."

Blacks, of course, had a very different vision of the postwar South. They wanted, above all, to know and feel their freedom and to be assured that they were not again to lose it. In the short run, they wanted protection from the threat of starvation. Beyond that, they wanted economic independence; and since the vast majority had always worked as farmers, that meant ownership of land. Blacks also longed for schooling—for their children if not for themselves. Finally, many blacks demanded political rights. "The only salvation for us besides the power of the Government is in the *possession of the ballot*," a convention of the black people of Virginia resolved in the summer of 1865. "All we ask is an *equal chance*."

In the immediate aftermath of the war, the federal government made modest efforts to help the emancipated slaves achieve their dreams of freedom. The government kept troops (many of them black) in the South to preserve order and protect the freedmen. In March 1865, Congress established the Bureau of Freedmen, Refugees, and Abandoned Lands (known as the Freedmen's Bureau) as an agency of the army. The bureau was empowered to provide former slaves with food, transportation, assistance in getting jobs and fair wages, and schools, and also to settle them on abandoned or confiscated lands. Under the able direction of General Oliver O. Howard, the bureau distributed 20 million rations. Missionaries and teachers, who had been sent to the South by Freedmen's Aid Societies and other private and church groups in the North, cooperated with the bureau in setting up schools for the former slaves. There were efforts as well to settle blacks on lands of their own. (The Freedmen's Bureau also offered considerable assistance to poor whites, many of whom were similarly destitute and homeless after the war.) But the Freedmen's Bureau was only a temporary expedient, not a permanent solution. Congress had given it authority to operate for only one year; and it was, in any case, far too small to deal by itself with the enormous problems facing Southern society. The real nature of Reconstruction, therefore, remained to be determined. It would be up to the federal government to determine whether the hopes of Southern whites or those of Southern blacks would prevail.

Issues of Reconstruction

At the time, it was by no means clear how the leaders of the North envisioned the future. The question of what kind of society should exist in the South and what kind of future blacks should enjoy there was tied to questions about the political and economic future of the North. The result was a prolonged debate about the proper course.

The terms by which the Southern states rejoined the Union had important implications for both major political parties. For the Democrats, a rapid readmission of the former Confederate states on easy terms was enormously appealing. To the Republicans, the prospect was alarming. The Republican victories in 1860 and 1864 had been a result, in large part, of the division of the Democratic party and the removal of the South from the electorate. The return of the South would, leaders of both parties believed, reunite the Democrats and reduce the Republicans to minority status—especially since the South's representation in Congress would, ironically, increase as a result of the abolition of slavery and with it the "three-fifths" clause of the Constitution, by which only three-fifths of the slave population had been counted in determining the number of members a state could send to the House of Representatives. The black population of the South would now be counted in full.

These political questions overlapped, of course, with important economic questions. The Republican party had taken advantage of the absence of the South from Congress to pass a program of nationalistic economic legislation—railroad subsidies, protective tariffs, and other measures of benefit to Northern business leaders and industrialists. Should the Democratic party regain power with heavy dependence on Southern support, these programs would be in jeopardy. Complicating these practical questions were emotional concerns of considerable importance: the widespread Northern belief that the South should in some way be punished for its rebellion and for the suffering and sacrifice that rebellion had cost; and the belief among many Northerners that the South should be transformed, made over in the North's image—its backward, feudal, undemocratic society civilized and modernized.

Even among the Republicans in Congress, there was considerable disagreement about the proper approach to Reconstruction—disagreements that reflected the same factional division (between the party's Conservatives and Radicals) that had created disputes during the war over emancipation. The Conservatives advocated a mild peace and the rapid restoration of the defeated states to the Union; they insisted that the South accept the abolition of slavery; but beyond that they did not propose to interfere with race relations or to alter the social system of the region. The Radicals, directed by such leaders as Thaddeus Stevens of Pennsylvania and Charles Sumner of Massachusetts, stood for a harder peace. Their most militant spokesmen urged that the civil and military chieftains of the late Confederacy be subjected to severe punishment, that large numbers of Southern whites be disfranchised, that the legal rights of blacks be protected, and that the property of rich Southerners who had aided the Confederacy be confiscated and distributed among the freedmen. Some Radicals favored granting suffrage to the former slaves, as a matter of right or as a means of creating a Republican electorate in the South. Other Radicals hesitated to state a position for fear of alienating public opinion—few Northern states permitted blacks to vote.

Between the Radicals and the Conservatives stood a faction of uncommitted Republicans, the Moderates. They rejected the punitive goals of the Radicals; but they supported measures to extract at least some concessions from the South on the matter of black rights. It would be this group, ultimately, that would determine the fate of the Reconstruction process.

Lincoln's Plan

Even before the war ended, President Lincoln formulated a Reconstruction plan that reflected his own sympathies for the Moderate and Conservative wings of his party. Lincoln believed there were a considerable number of actual or potential Unionists in the South—most of them former Whigs—who could be encouraged to join the Republican party and thus prevent the readmission of the South from strengthening the Democrats. More immediately, the Southern Unionists could serve as the nucleus for creating new, loyal state governments in the South. Lincoln was not uninterested in the fate of the freedmen; but he wanted to restore the Union as soon as possible and was willing, therefore, to defer considering questions about race relations.

Lincoln announced his plan in December 1863. It offered a general amnesty to all white Southerners—with the temporary exception of high civil and military officials of the Confederacy—who would take an oath pledging future loyalty to the government and acceptance of the wartime measures eliminating slavery. Whenever 10 percent of the number of voters in 1860 took the oath in any state, those loyal voters could proceed to set up a state government. Lincoln also hoped to extend the suffrage to at least a few blacks—to those who were educated, owned property, and had served in the Union army. In three Southern states—Louisiana, Arkansas, and Tennessee, all under Union occupation—loyal governments were reestablished under the Lincoln formula in 1864.

The Radical Republicans were angered and astonished at the mildness of Lincoln's program, and they persuaded Congress to repudiate the new governments. Congress refused to seat representatives from the three "reconstructed" states and refused to count the electoral vote of those states in the election of 1864. But the Radicals could not simply reject Lincoln's plan; they needed an alternative plan of their own. And for the moment, they were uncertain about what form that plan should take.

Their first effort to resolve that question was the Wade-Davis bill, passed by Congress in July 1864. By its provisions, the president would appoint for each conquered state a provisional governor who would take a census of all adult white males. If a majority of that group took an oath of allegiance to the Union, the governor was to call an election for a state constitutional convention. The privilege of voting for delegates to this meeting would be limited to those who would swear that they had never borne arms against the United States, the so-called ironclad oath. The state convention would be required to include provisions in the new constitution abolishing slavery, disfranchising Confederate civil and military leaders, and repudiating debts accumulated by the state governments during the war. After these conditions had been met, Congress would readmit the state to the Union.

The Wade-Davis bill was more drastic in almost every respect than the Lincoln plan. Instead of requiring 10 percent of prior voters to swear loyalty to the Union, the Radical plan called for a majority of all adult white males to do so. Instead of assuming, as Lincoln did, that the Southern states had never left the Union, it insisted that the states had in effect forfeited their rights as members of the republic and were thus subject to the dictates of Congress. Like the president's proposal, however, the Wade-Davis bill left up to the states the question of political rights for blacks.

Congress passed the bill a few days before it adjourned in 1864, and Lincoln disposed of it with a pocket veto. His action enraged the authors of the measure, Benjamin F. Wade and Henry Winter Davis, who issued a blistering denunciation of the veto, the Wade-Davis Manifesto, warning the president not to interfere with the powers of Congress to control Reconstruction. Lincoln could not ignore the bitterness and the strength of the Radical opposition. Practical as always, he realized that he would have to bow to at least some of the Radical demands; and so he began to move toward a new approach to Reconstruction.

The Death of Lincoln

What plan he might have produced no one can say. On the night of April 14, 1865, Lincoln and his wife attended a play at Ford's Theater in Washington. As they sat in the presidential box, John Wilkes Booth, an unsuccessful actor obsessed with aiding the Southern cause, entered the box from the rear and shot Lincoln in the head. Then he leaped to the stage (breaking his leg in the process), shouted "Sic, semper tyrannis!" ("Thus always to tyrants!"—the motto of the state of Virginia), and disappeared into the night. The president was carried unconscious to a house across the street, where early the next morning—surrounded by family, friends, and political associates (including a tearful Charles Sumner)—he died.

The circumstances of Lincoln's death—the heroic war leader, the Great Emancipator, struck down in the hour of victory—earned him immediate martyrdom. It also produced wild fears and antagonisms throughout the North. There were widespread accusations that Booth had acted as part of a great con-

Abraham Lincoln and His Son Tad
During the last difficult months of the Civil War, Lincoln often found relief from the strains of his office in the company of his young son, Thomas (known as "Tad"), shown here with his father in an 1864 photograph by Matthew Brady. Much has been written about Lincoln's turbulent family life. His wife, Mary Todd Lincoln, was apparently a moody and difficult woman; but the marriage seems generally to have been a happy one. The Lincolns did, however, experience a series of heartbreaking bereavements as three of their four sons died in childhood. Their second child, Edward, died in 1850 at the age of three; their third, "Willie," died of fever in 1862 at the age of eleven; Tad outlived his father by only a few years and died in 1871 at the age of eighteen. Robert Todd Lincoln, the president's eldest son, lived a long and successful life during which he served as secretary of war, American minister to England, and president of the Pullman Railroad Car Company. (Library of Congress)

spiracy—accusations that contained at least a grain of truth. Booth did indeed have associates, one of whom shot and wounded Secretary of State Seward the night of the assassination, another of whom set out to murder Vice President Johnson but abandoned the scheme at the last moment. Booth himself escaped on horseback into the Maryland countryside, where, on April 26, he was cornered by Union troops and shot to death in a blazing barn. Eight other conspirators were convicted by a military tribunal of participating in the conspiracy (at least two of them on the basis of virtually no evidence). Four were hanged.

To many Northerners, however, the murder of the president seemed evidence of an even greater conspiracy—one masterminded and directed by the unrepentant leaders of the defeated South. (There was never any conclusive evidence to support this—and many another—theory of the assassination; but questions continued to be raised about the event well into the twentieth century.) Militant Republicans exploited such suspicions relentlessly in the ensuing months, ensuring that Lincoln's death would doom his plans for a relatively generous peace.

Johnson and "Restoration"

The Conservative leadership in the controversy over Reconstruction fell to Lincoln's successor, Andrew Johnson. Of all the men who have accidentally inherited the presidency, Johnson was undoubtedly the most unfortunate. A Southerner and former slaveholder, he became president as a bloody war against the South was drawing to a close. A Democrat before he had been placed on the Union ticket with Lincoln in 1864, he became the head of a Republican administration at a time when partisan passions, held in some restraint during the war, were about to rule the government. As if these handicaps of background were not enough, Johnson himself was an intemperate and tactless man, filled with resentments and insecurities, and plagued by a serious drinking problem.

Johnson revealed his plan of Reconstruction—or "Restoration," as he preferred to call it—soon after he took office, and he proceeded to implement it during the summer of 1865 when Congress was not in session. In some ways Johnson's scheme resembled Lincoln's; in many other respects, it reflected the more drastic demands of the Radicals. Like his predecessor, Johnson assumed that the seceded states had never left the Union; and, also like Lincoln, he offered amnesty for past conduct to all who would take an oath of allegiance. High-ranking Confederate officials and any white Southerner with land worth $20,000 or more would have to apply to the president for individual pardons. (Himself a self-made man, Johnson harbored deep resentments toward the old Southern aristocracy and apparently relished the pros-

pect of these Confederate leaders humbling themselves before him to ask for amnesty.) For each state, the president appointed a provisional governor, who was to invite the qualified voters to elect delegates to a constitutional convention. Johnson did not specify that a minimum number of voters had to take the oath, as had the Lincoln and Wade-Davis proposals, but the implication was plain that he would require a majority. As conditions of readmittance, a state had to revoke the ordinance of secession, abolish slavery and ratify the Thirteenth Amendment, and repudiate the Confederate and state war debts—essentially the same stipulations that had been laid down in the Wade-Davis bill. The final procedure before restoration was for a state to elect a state government and send representatives to Congress.

By the end of 1865, all the states not previously reorganized under Lincoln's plan had complied with Johnson's requirements. All of the seceded states, therefore, had been reconstructed and were ready to resume their places in the Union—if Congress chose to recognize them when it met in December 1865. But the Radicals were determined not to recognize the Johnson governments, just as they had previously refused to recognize the Lincoln regimes. In that determination they had the support of much of the Northern public.

Many Northerners were disturbed by the seeming reluctance of some members of the Southern conventions to abolish slavery and by the refusal of all the conventions to grant suffrage to even a few blacks. They were astounded that states claiming to be "loyal" should elect as state officials and representatives to Congress prominent leaders of the recent Confederacy. Particularly hard to accept was Georgia's choice of Alexander H. Stephens, former vice president of the Confederacy, as a United States senator.

Radical Reconstruction

This initial phase of Reconstruction—often known as "presidential Reconstruction"—lasted only until Congress reconvened in December 1865. At that point, Republican leaders looked over Andrew Johnson's handiwork and expressed their displeasure. Congress immediately refused to seat the senators and representatives of the states the president had "restored." Instead, Radical leaders insisted, Congress needed to learn more about conditions in the postwar South. There must be assurances that the former Confederates had accepted their defeat and that emancipated blacks and loyal whites would be protected. Accordingly, Congress set up the new Joint Committee on Reconstruction to investigate conditions in the South and to advise Congress in laying down a Reconstruction policy of its own. The period of "congressional" or "Radical" Reconstruction had begun.

The Response to the Black Codes

During the next few months, the Radicals advanced toward a more severe program than their first plan—the Wade-Davis bill of 1864, which had left to the states the question of what rights the freed slaves should have. Johnson, unlike Lincoln, refused even to consider compromising; and his intransigence helped the Radicals gain the support of many Moderate Republicans. The president insisted that Congress had no right even to consider a policy for the South until his own plan had been accepted and the Southern congressmen and senators had been admitted.

In the meantime, Northerners were learning more about what was happening in the defeated South; and what they learned persuaded many of them—including most of the important leaders in Congress—that far more drastic measures were necessary than the president had contemplated. For throughout the South in 1865 and early 1866, state legislatures were enacting sets of laws known as the Black Codes. These measures were the white South's solution to the problem of the free black laborer, and they were modeled in many ways on the codes that had regulated free blacks in the prewar South. As such, they created a new set of devices to guarantee white supremacy. Economically, the codes were intended to regulate the labor of a race that, in the opinion of whites, would not work except under some kind of compulsion. Although there were variations from state to state, all codes authorized local officials to apprehend unemployed blacks, fine them for vagrancy, and hire them out to private employers to satisfy the fine. Some of the codes tried to force blacks to work on the plantations by forbidding them to own or lease farms or to take other jobs except as domestic servants. Socially, the codes were designed to invest blacks with a legal status outside slavery, but one that ensured that they would remain clearly subordinate to whites. To the white South, the Black Codes were a realistic approach to a great social problem. To the North, and to most blacks, they seemed to herald a return to slavery in all but name.

An appropriate agency for offsetting the Black Codes was the Freedmen's Bureau, but its scheduled year of existence was about to expire. In February 1866, Congress passed a bill to prolong the life of the bureau and to widen its powers. For settling labor disputes, it could now establish special courts, which could disallow work agreements forced on freedmen under the Black Codes. Johnson vetoed the bill, denouncing it as unconstitutional. Efforts to override him fell just short of the necessary two-thirds majority.

In April, Congress struck again at the Black Codes by passing the Civil Rights Act, which declared blacks to be U.S. citizens and empowered the federal government to intervene in state affairs when necessary to protect the rights of citizens. Johnson vetoed this bill, too. With Moderates and Radicals acting together, Congress promptly overrode the veto. Then Congress repassed the Freedmen's Bureau Act and overrode a second presidential veto of that law.

The Fourteenth Amendment

Emboldened by their evidently growing support in Congress, the Radicals now struck again. The Joint Committee on Reconstruction submitted to Congress, in April 1866, a proposed amendment to the Constitution, the Fourteenth, which constituted the second Radical plan of Reconstruction. The amendment was adopted by Congress and sent to the states for approval in the early summer. It consisted of three sections. Taken together, they constituted one of the most important additions to the Constitution in American history.

Section 1 of the amendment declared that all persons born or naturalized in the United States were citizens of the United States and of the state of their residence—the first official, national definition of citizenship. Next came a statement that no state could abridge the rights of citizens of the United States or deprive any person of life, liberty, or property without due process of law or deny to any person within its jurisdiction the equal protection of the laws. Section 2 provided that if a state denied the suffrage to any of its adult male inhabitants, its representation in the House of Representatives and the electoral college would suffer a proportionate reduction. Section 3 prohibited persons who had previously taken an oath to support the Constitution and later had aided the Confederacy (in other words, former Southern members of Congress and other former officials) from holding any state or federal office—until Congress by a two-thirds vote of each house should remove their disability.

The Southern legislatures knew that if they ratified the amendment their states would be readmitted and Reconstruction probably would end. But they could not bring themselves to approve the measure, mainly because of Section 3, which put a stigma on their late leaders. Johnson himself advised Southerners to defeat the amendment. Only Tennessee, of the former Confederate states, ratified it, thus winning readmittance. The other ten, joined by Kentucky and Delaware, voted it down. The amendment thus failed to receive the required approval of three-fourths of the states and was defeated—but only temporarily. When the time was more propitious, the Radicals would bring it up again. Meanwhile, its rejection by the South strengthened the Radical cause.

The Northern public gave striking evidence of its support for the Radical program in the elections of 1866. The Radicals could point to recent events in the South—bloody race riots in New Orleans and other Southern cities in which blacks were the victims—as further evidence of the inadequacy of Johnson's policy. Johnson attempted to derail the Radical cause by campaigning for Conservative candidates; but he did his own cause more harm than good by the intemperate, brawling (and, some believed, drunken) speeches he made on a stumping tour (a "swing around the circle," as it was called) from Washington to Chicago and back. The voters returned to Congress an overwhelming majority of Republicans, most of them Radicals. In the Senate, there were to be 42 Republicans to 11 Democrats; in the House, 143 Republicans to 49 Democrats. Now the Republicans could enact any kind of Reconstruction plan they could themselves agree on. Confidently they looked forward to the struggle with Johnson that would ensue when Congress assembled in December 1866—and to their final victory over the president.

The Congressional Plan

After compromising differences among themselves and with the Moderates, the Radicals formulated their third plan of Reconstruction in three bills that passed Congress in the early months of 1867. All three were vetoed by Johnson and repassed. Together, they constituted a single program. Finally, nearly two years after the end of the war, the federal government had established a consistent plan for Reconstruction.

That two-year delay had important effects on the way the South would react to the program. In 1865, with the South reeling from its defeat and nearly prostrate, the federal government could probably have imposed on the region an even more radical plan than it ultimately did, without provoking immediate resistance. But by 1867, the South had begun to recover from the humiliation of defeat and had begun to reconstruct itself under the reasonably generous terms Lincoln and Johnson had extended. By then, therefore, measures that might once have seemed moderate had come to seem radical; and the congressional reconstruction plan created deep resentments and continuing resistance.

The congressional plan was based squarely on the principle that the seceded states had forfeited their political identity. The Lincoln-Johnson governments were declared to have no legal standing, and the ten seceded states (Tennessee was now out of the Reconstruction process) were combined into five military districts. Each district was to have a military commander, supported by troops, who was to prepare his provinces for readmission as states. To this end, he was to institute a registration of voters, which was to include all adult black males and those white males who were not disqualified by participation in rebellion.

After the registration was completed in each province, the commanding general was to call the voters to elect a convention to prepare a new state constitution, which had to include provisions for black suffrage. If this document was ratified by the voters, elections for a state government could be held. Finally, if Congress approved the constitution, if the state legislature ratified the Fourteenth Amendment, and if this amendment was adopted by the required number of states and became a part of the Constitution—then the state was to be restored to the Union.

By 1868, seven of the former Confederate states (Arkansas, North Carolina, South Carolina, Louisiana, Alabama, Georgia, and Florida) had complied with the process of restoration outlined in the Reconstruction Acts—including ratification of the Fourteenth Amendment, which now became part of the Constitution. These states were readmitted to the Union. Delaying tactics by whites held up the return of Virginia and Texas until 1869 and Mississippi until 1870. And by then, Congress had added an additional

Political Reconstruction, 1866–1877

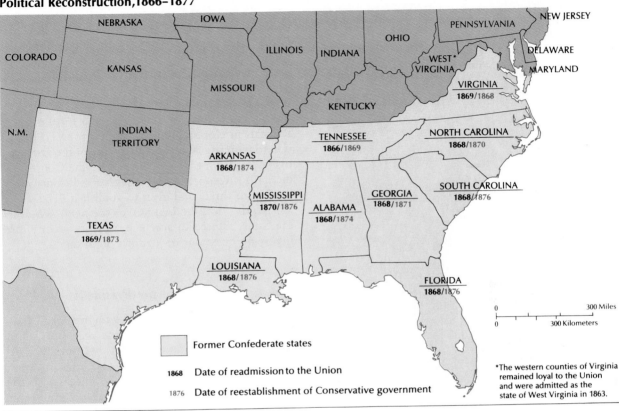

Former Confederate states

1868 Date of readmission to the Union

1876 Date of reestablishment of Conservative government

*The western counties of Virginia remained loyal to the Union and were admitted as the state of West Virginia in 1863.

requirement for readmission, which constituted the fourth and final congressional plan of Reconstruction. They had to ratify another constitutional amendment, the Fifteenth, which forbade the states and the federal government to deny the suffrage to any citizen on account of "race, color, or previous condition of servitude."

Sponsors of the Fifteenth Amendent were motivated by both idealistic and practical considerations. They wished to be consistent in extending to blacks in the North a right they had already given to them elsewhere. The great majority of the Northern states still denied the suffrage to blacks when the Reconstruction Acts granted it to blacks in the Southern states. At the same time the amendment would put into the Constitution, where it would be safe from congressional repeal, a provision that would serve as a basis of Republican strength in the South. Sponsors of the amendment also saw it as a vehicle for protecting the party's precarious future in the North. A warning of trouble ahead had appeared in the state elections of 1867 in Pennsylvania, Ohio, and Indiana,

all of which went Democratic that year. "We must establish the doctrine of national jurisdiction over all the states in state matters of the franchise," the Radical leader Thaddeus Stevens now concluded. "We must thus bridle Pennsylvania, Ohio, Indiana et cetera, or the South *being in*, we shall drift into Democracy." In several of the Northern states the black vote, although proportionally small, would be large enough to decide close elections in favor of the Republicans. A number of Northern and border states refused to approve the Fifteenth Amendment, and it was adopted only with the support of the four Southern states that had to ratify it in order to be readmitted to the Union.

The Radicals saw themselves as architects of a revolution, and they did not intend to let the executive or the judiciary get in their way. They were prepared, if necessary, to establish a kind of congressional dictatorship.

To stop the president from interfering with their designs, Congress in 1867 passed two remarkable laws. One, the Tenure of Office Act, forbade the

Thaddeus Stevens
Stern, uncompromising, and severe, Thaddeus Stevens of Pennsylvania was the incarnation of the North's vindictive designs in the eyes of many Southerners during (and long after) Reconstruction. Others admired him as one of the few white leaders who remained firmly committed to racial equality. He served in the House of Representatives from 1849 to 1853 and again, more prominently, from 1859 until his death in 1868. He spent much of the last year of his life organizing and managing the impeachment trial of Andrew Johnson. (Library of Congress)

The congressional Radicals also took action to curb the Supreme Court from interfering with their plans. The Court, under Chief Justice Salmon P. Chase, had in 1866 declared in *Ex parte Milligan* that military tribunals were unconstitutional in places where civil courts were functioning. Although the decision was applied to a case originating in the war, it seemed to threaten the system of military government that the Radicals were planning for the South. Radicals in Congress immediately proposed legislation to require a two-thirds majority of the justices to overrule a law of Congress, to deny the Court jurisdiction in Reconstruction cases, to reduce its membership to three, and even to abolish it. The judges apparently took the hint. Over the next two years, the Court refused to accept jurisdiction in any cases involving questions of jurisdiction in the South.

The Impeachment of the President

The most aggressive move of Congress against another branch of government was the effort of the Radicals to remove Andrew Johnson from office. Although the president had long since ceased to be a serious obstacle to the passage of Radical legislation, he was still the official charged with administering the Reconstruction programs; and as such, the Radicals believed, he was a serious impediment to their plans. Early in 1867, therefore, they began searching for evidence that Johnson had committed crimes or misdemeanors in office, the only legal grounds for impeachment; but they could find nothing on which to base charges. Then he gave them what was, in their view, a plausible reason for action by deliberately violating the Tenure of Office Act—in hopes of bringing a test case of the law before the courts. Johnson suspended Secretary of War Stanton, who had worked with the Radicals against the president, and named General Grant as his successor. When the state refused to concur in the suspension, Grant relinquished the office to Stanton. Johnson then dismissed Stanton.

In the House of Representatives the elated Radicals presented to the Senate eleven charges against the president. The first nine accusations dealt with the violation of the Tenure of Office Act. The tenth and eleventh charged Johnson with making speeches calculated to bring Congress into disrespect and with not faithfully enforcing the various Reconstruction Acts. The trial before the Senate lasted for two months—from March 25 to May 26, 1868. Johnson's lawyers maintained that he was justified in techni-

president to remove civil officials, including members of his cabinet, without the consent of the Senate. The principal purpose of the law was to protect the job of Secretary of War Edwin M. Stanton, who was cooperating with the Radicals. The other law, the Command of the Army Act, prohibited the president from issuing military orders except through the commanding general of the army (General Grant), whose headquarters were to be in Washington and who could not be relieved or assigned elsewhere without the consent of the Senate.

cally violating a law in order to force a test case. And they argued that the measure did not apply to Stanton anyway: It gave tenure to cabinet members for the term of the president by whom they had been appointed, and Stanton had been appointed by Lincoln. The House managers of the impeachment stressed the theme that Johnson had opposed the will of Congress and was thus guilty of high crimes and misdemeanors. They put heavy pressure on all the Republican senators, but seven Republicans joined the twelve Democrats to vote for acquittal. On three of the charges the vote was identical, 35 to 19, one short of the required two-thirds majority. After that, the Radicals dropped the impeachment campaign.

The South in Reconstruction

When white Southerners spoke bitterly in later years of the effects of Reconstruction, they referred most frequently to the governments Congress imposed on them—governments that were, they claimed, both incompetent and corrupt, that saddled the region with enormous debts, and that trampled on the rights of citizens. When black Southerners and their defenders condemned Reconstruction, in contrast, they spoke of its failure to guarantee to freedmen even the most elemental rights of citizenship—a failure that resulted in a new and cruel system of economic subordination. Controversy has raged for more than a century over which viewpoint is more nearly correct. (See "Where Historians Disagree," p. 446.) Most students of Reconstruction tend now to agree, however, that the complaints of Southern whites, although in some respects accurate, greatly exaggerated the real nature of the postwar governments; while the complaints of blacks, although occasionally overstated, were largely justified.

The Reconstruction Governments

In the ten states of the South that were reorganized under the congressional plan, approximately one-fourth of the white males were at first excluded from voting or holding office. The voter registration of 1867 enrolled a total of 703,000 black and 627,000 white voters. The black voters constituted a majority in half of the states—Alabama, Florida, South Carolina, Mississippi, and Louisiana—although only in the last three of these states did the blacks outnumber the whites in the population as a whole. But once new constitutions had been framed and new governments launched, most of them permitted nearly all whites to vote (although for several years the Fourteenth Amendment continued to keep the leading ex-Confederates from holding office). This meant that in most of the Southern states the Republicans could maintain control only with the support of a great many Southern whites.

These Southern white Republicans, whom their

"The First Vote"

This cover illustration from an 1867 issue of *Harper's Weekly* shows freedmen exercising the right recently guaranteed them by the Fifteenth Amendment. Before the development of the technology that permitted the printing of photographs, woodcuts such as this one—usually based on drawings made on the scene by an artist and then transferred to wood blocks by skilled engravers—brought a sense of immediacy to the reporting of the news. (New-York Historical Society)

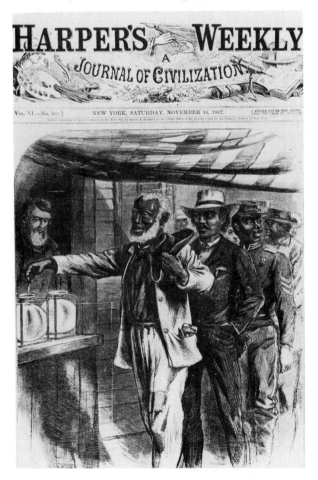

WHERE HISTORIANS DISAGREE

Reconstruction

Debate over the nature of Reconstruction—not only among historians, but among the public at large—has created so much controversy over the decades that one scholar, writing in 1959, described the issue as a "dark and bloody ground." Among historians, the passions of the debate have to some extent subsided since then; but in the popular mind, Reconstruction continues to raise "dark and bloody" images.

For many years, a relatively uniform and highly critical view of Reconstruction prevailed among historians, a reflection of broad currents in popular thought. By the late nineteenth century, most white Americans in both the North and the South had come to believe that few real differences any longer divided the sections, that the nation should strive for a genuine reconciliation. And most white Americans believed as well in the superiority of their race, in the inherent unfitness of blacks for political or social equality. In this spirit was born the first major historical interpretation of Reconstruction, through the work of William A. Dunning. In his *Reconstruction, Political and Economic* (1907), Dunning portrayed Reconstruction as a corrupt outrage perpetrated on the prostrate South by a vicious and vindictive cabal of Northern Republican Radicals. Reconstruction governments were based on "bayonet rule." Unscrupulous and self-aggrandizing carpetbaggers flooded the South to profit from the misery of the defeated region. Ignorant, illiterate blacks were thrust into positions of power for which they were entirely unfit. The Reconstruction experiment, a moral abomination from its first moments, survived only because of the determination of the Republican party to keep itself in power. (Some later writers, notably Howard K. Beale, added an economic motive—to protect Northern business interests.) Dunning and his many students (who together formed what became known as the "Dunning school") compiled evidence to show that the leg-acy of Reconstruction was corruption, ruinous taxation, and astronomical increases in the public debt.

The Dunning school not only shaped the views of several generations of historians. It also reflected and helped to shape the views of much of the public. Popular depictions of Reconstruction for years to come (as the book and movie *Gone with the Wind* suggested) portrayed the era as one of tragic exploitation of the South by the North. Even today, some white Southerners and many others continue to accept the basic premises of the Dunning interpretation. Among historians, however, the old view of Reconstruction has gradually lost all credibility.

W. E. B. Du Bois, the great black scholar, was among the first to challenge the Dunning view in a 1910 article and, later, in a 1935 book, *Black Reconstruction*. To him, Reconstruction politics in the Southern states had been an effort on the part of the masses, black and white, to create a truly democratic society. The misdeeds of the Reconstruction governments had, he claimed, been greatly exaggerated and their achievements overlooked. The governments had been expensive, he insisted, because they had tried to provide public education and other public services on a scale never before attempted in the South. But Du Bois's use of Marxist theory in his work caused many historians who did not share his philosophy to dismiss his argument; and it remained for a group of less radical white historians to shatter the Dunning image of Reconstruction for good.

In the 1940s, historians such as C. Vann Woodward, David Herbert Donald, Thomas B. Alexander, and others began to reexamine the history of the Reconstruction governments in the South and to suggest that their record was not nearly as bad as had previously been assumed. They looked, too, at the Radical Republicans in Congress and suggested that they had not been

opponents derisively called "scalawags," consisted in part of former Whigs who, after the breakup of the Whig organization in the 1850s, had acted with the Southern Democrats but had never felt completely at home with them. Some of the scalawag leaders were wealthy (or once wealthy) planters or businessmen. Many other Southern whites who supported the Republican party were farmers living in areas where slavery had been unimportant or nonexistent. These men, many of whom had been wartime Unionists,

WHERE HISTORIANS DISAGREE

motivated by vindictiveness and partisanship alone. By the early 1960s, a new view of Reconstruction had emerged from these efforts (and in response to the influence of the "second Reconstruction"—the civil-rights movement). This revisionist approach was summarized finally by John Hope Franklin in *Reconstruction After the Civil War* (1961) and Kenneth Stampp in *The Era of Reconstruction* (1965), which claimed that the postwar Republicans had been engaged in a genuine, if flawed, effort to solve the problem of race in the South by providing much-needed protection to the freedmen. The Reconstruction governments, for all their faults, had been bold experiments in interracial politics; and the congressional Radicals, while far from being saints, had displayed a genuine concern for the rights of former slaves. Andrew Johnson was not a martyred defender of the Constitution but an inept, racist politician who resisted reasonable compromise and brought the government to a crisis. There had been no such thing as "bayonet rule" or "Negro rule" in the South. Blacks had played only a small part in Reconstruction governments and had generally acquitted themselves well. The Reconstruction regimes had, in fact, brought important progress to the South, establishing the region's first public school system and other important social changes. Corruption in the South had been no worse than corruption in the North at that time. What was tragic about Reconstruction, the revisionist view claimed, was not what it did to Southern whites but what it did not do for Southern blacks. By stopping short of the reforms necessary to ensure blacks genuine equality, Reconstruction had consigned them to more than a century of injustice and discrimination.

By the 1970s, then, the Dunning view of Reconstruction had all but disappeared from serious scholarly discussion. Instead, historians seemed to agree that Reconstruction had, in fact, changed the South relatively little; and they began to debate why Reconstruction fell as short as it did of guaranteeing racial justice. Some scholars have claimed that conservative obstacles to change were so great that the Radicals, despite their good intentions, simply could not overcome them. Others have argued that the Radicals themselves were not sufficiently committed to the principle of racial justice, that they abandoned the cause quickly when it became clear to them that the battle would not easily be won.

In recent years, however, scholars have begun to question the revisionist view—not in an effort to revive the old Dunning interpretation but in an attempt to draw attention to those things Reconstruction in fact achieved. Leon Litwack's *Been in the Storm So Long* (1979) reveals that the former slaves used the relative latitude they enjoyed under Reconstruction to build a certain independence for themselves within Southern society. They strengthened their churches; they reunited their families; they refused to work in the "gang labor" system of the plantations and forced the creation of a new labor system in which they had more control over their own lives. Eric Foner, in *Nothing But Freedom* (1983), compares the aftermath of slavery in the United States to similar experiences in the Caribbean and concludes that what is striking about the American experience in this context is not how little was accomplished but how far the former slaves moved toward freedom and independence in a short time. Reconstruction permitted blacks a certain amount of legal and political power in the South. And even though some of that power did not survive, they used it for a time to strengthen their economic and social condition and win a position of limited but genuine independence that brought them, if not equality, something that emancipation alone had not guaranteed: freedom.

favored the Republican program of internal improvements, which would help them get their crops to market.

White men from the North also served as Republican leaders in the South. Opponents of Reconstruction referred to them as "carpetbaggers," thus giving the impression that they were penniless adventurers who had arrived with all their possessions in a carpetbag (then a common kind of suitcase covered with carpeting material) in order to take advantage of the black vote for their own power and profit. In fact, the majority of the so-called carpetbaggers were veterans of the Union army who had looked on the South as a new frontier, more promising than the West, and at the war's end had settled in it as hopeful planters or business or professional men.

The most numerous Republicans in the South were the freedmen, the vast majority of whom had no formal education and no previous experience in public affairs. Among the black leaders, however, were well-educated men, most of whom had never been slaves and many of whom had grown up in the North or abroad. The blacks quickly became politically self-conscious. In various states, they held their own conventions to chart their future course. One such "colored convention," as Southern whites called them, assembled in Alabama in 1867 and announced: "We claim exactly *the same rights, privileges and immunities as are enjoyed by white men*—we ask nothing more and will be content with nothing less." Blacks were also organized, often with the assistance of Freedmen's Bureau agents and other Northern whites, in chapters of the Union League, which had been founded originally as a Republican electioneering agency in the North during the war. In addition, black churches helped give unity and political self-confidence to the former slaves. After emancipation, blacks withdrew from the white churches and formed their own—institutions based on the elaborate religious practices they had developed (occasionally surreptitiously) under slavery. "The colored preachers are *the great power* in controlling and uniting the colored vote," a carpetbagger observed in 1868.

Blacks served as delegates to the conventions that, under the congressional plan, drew up new state constitutions in the South. Then, in the reconstructed states, blacks were elected to public offices of practically every kind. Altogether (between 1869 and 1901) twenty blacks were sent to the House of Representatives in Washington. Two went to the Senate, both of them from Mississippi. In 1870, Hiram R. Revels, an ordained minister and a former North Carolina free black who had been educated at Knox College in Illinois, took the Senate seat that Jefferson Davis once had occupied. In 1874, Blanche K. Bruce, who had escaped from slavery in Virginia and studied in the North, became a senator.

Yet while Southern whites complained loudly (both at the time and for generations to come) about "Negro rule" during Reconstruction, no such thing ever truly existed in any of the states. No black man was ever elected governor of a Southern state, al-

The Burdened South
This Reconstruction era cartoon expresses the South's sense of its oppression at the hands of Northern Republicans. President Grant (whose hat bears Abraham Lincoln's initials) rides in comfort in a giant carpetbag, guarded by bayonet-wielding soldiers, as the South staggers under the burden in chains. More evidence of destruction and military occupation is visible in the background.   (Culver Pictures)

though Lieutenant Governor P. B. S. Pinchback briefly occupied the governor's chair in Louisiana. Blacks never controlled any of the state legislatures, although for a time they held a majority in the lower house of South Carolina. In the South as a whole, the number of black officeholders was less than proportionate to the number of blacks in the population.

The record of the Reconstruction governments is many-sided. The financial programs they instituted were a compound of blatant corruption and well-designed, if sometimes impractical, social legislation. The corruption and extravagance are familiar aspects of the Reconstruction story. Officeholders in many states enriched themselves through graft and other illicit activities. State budgets expanded to hitherto unknown totals, and state debts soared to previously undreamed-of heights. In South Carolina, for example, the public debt increased from $7 million to $29 million in eight years.

But these facts are misleading when considered alone. In large measure, the corruption in the South was part of a national phenomenon, with the same social force—an expanding capitalism eager to secure quick results—acting as the corrupting agent in all sections of the country. Corruption did not decline in Southern state governments once Reconstruction came to an end; in many states, in fact, it increased.

And the state expenditures of the Reconstruction years seem huge only in comparison with the tight budgets of the conservative governments of the prewar era; they do not appear large when measured against the sums appropriated by later legislatures. The expenditures, moreover, represented an effort to provide the Southern states with services they desperately needed and that no governments had ever attempted to provide in the antebellum period: public education, public works programs, poor relief, and other costly new commitments. There was, to be sure, graft and extravagance in Reconstruction governments; there were also positive and permanent accomplishments.

Education

Perhaps the most important of those accomplishments was a dramatic improvement in Southern education—an improvement that benefited both whites and blacks. In the first years of Reconstruction, much of the impetus for educational reform in the South came from outside groups—from the Freedmen's Bureau and from Northern private philanthropic organizations—and from blacks themselves. Over the opposition of many Southern whites, who feared that education would give blacks "false notions of equality," these reformers established a large network of schools for former slaves—4,000 schools by 1870, staffed by 9,000 teachers (half of them black), and teaching 200,000 students (about 12 percent of the total school-age population of the freedmen). In the course of the 1870s, moreover, the Reconstruction governments of the states assumed the initiative and began to build a comprehensive public school system in the South. By 1876, more than half of all white

children and about 40 percent of all black children were being educated in Southern schools. Several black "academies" were also beginning to operate—institutions that were, perhaps, not yet genuine colleges but that were offering more advanced education to freedmen than the public schools provided. Gradually, these academies grew into an important network of black colleges and universities, which would form the basis of black higher education in the South for many decades. Among the early institutions, for example, were schools that later became Fisk and Atlanta universities and Morehouse College.

Already, however, Southern education was becoming divided into two separate systems—one black and one white. Early efforts to integrate the schools of the region were a dismal failure. The Freedmen's Bureau schools, for example, were open to students of all races, but almost no whites attended them. New Orleans set up an integrated school system under the Reconstruction government; again, whites almost universally stayed away. The one federal effort to mandate school integration—the Civil Rights Act of 1875—had its provisions for educational desegregation removed before it was passed. And as soon as the Republican governments of Reconstruction were replaced, the new Southern Democratic regimes quickly abandoned all efforts to promote integration.

Land Ownership

The most ambitious goal of the Freedmen's Bureau, and of some Republican Radicals in Congress, was to make Reconstruction the occasion for a fundamental reform of land ownership in the South. The effort failed. In the last years of the war and the first years of Reconstruction, the Freedmen's Bureau did oversee the redistribution of substantial amounts of land to freedmen in some areas—notably the Sea Islands off South Carolina and Georgia, and areas of Mississippi that had once belonged to the Davis family. By June 1865, the bureau had settled nearly 10,000 black families on their own land—most of it drawn from abandoned plantations. Blacks throughout the South were growing excited at the prospect of achieving a real economic stake in their region—the vision of "forty acres and a mule." By the end of that year, however, the experiment was already collapsing. Southern plantation owners were returning and demanding the restoration of their property. And Andrew Johnson was supporting their demands. Despite the resistance of General Oliver O. Howard and other officials of the Freedmen's Bureau, most of the confiscated land was eventually returned to the original white owners. Congress, moreover, never exhibited much stomach for the idea of land redistribution. Despite the pleas of such Radicals as Thaddeus Stevens, very few Northern Republicans believed that the federal government had the right to confiscate property. Land reform did not become a part of Reconstruction.

Nevertheless, there was a substantial change in the distribution of land ownership in the South in the postwar years—a result of many factors. Among whites, there was a striking decline in ownership of land. Whereas before the war more than 80 percent of Southern whites had lived on their own land, by the end of Reconstruction that proportion had dropped to about 67 percent. Some whites had fallen into debt and been forced to sell; some had fallen victim to increased taxes; some had chosen to leave the marginal lands they had owned to move to more fertile areas, where they rented. Among blacks, during the same period, the proportion who owned land rose from virtually none to more than 20 percent. Black landowners acquired their property through hard work, through luck, and at times through the assistance of such agencies as the Freedman's Bank, established in 1865 by antislavery whites in an effort to promote land ownership among blacks. (The bank failed in 1874, after a combination of internal corruption and a nationwide financial panic had destroyed its reserves.)

Despite these impressive achievements, however, the vast majority of blacks (and a growing minority of whites) did not own their own land during Reconstruction, and some of those who acquired land in the 1860s lost it in the 1890s. These nonlandowners worked for others, through a great variety of systems. Many black agricultural laborers—perhaps 25 percent of the total—simply worked for wages. Most, however, became tenants of white landowners—that is, they acquired control of their own plots of land, working them on their own and paying their landlord either a fixed rent or a share of their crop (hence the term "sharecropping"). The new system represented a breakdown of the traditional plantation system, in which blacks had lived together and worked together under the direction of a master. As tenants and sharecroppers, blacks enjoyed at least a physical independence from their landlords and had the sense of working their own land, even if in most cases they could never hope to buy it. (See Chapter 16 for a fuller discussion of the new Southern economy.)

Incomes and Credit

The economic effect of Reconstruction on the freedmen, to the extent that it can be gauged, was mixed. In some respects, the postwar years were a period of remarkable economic progress for blacks. If the food, clothing, shelter, and other material benefits they had received under slavery are considered as income, then prewar blacks had earned about a 22 percent share of the profits of the plantation system. By the end of Reconstruction, they were earning 56 percent of the return on investment in Southern agriculture. Measured another way, the per capita income of blacks rose 46 percent between 1857 and 1879, while the per capita income of whites declined 35 percent. This represented one of the most significant redistributions of income in American history.

Nevertheless, the economic status of blacks did not improve as much as these figures suggest. For one thing, while their share of the profits was increasing, the total profits of Southern agriculture were declining—a result of the dislocations of the war and of a reduction in the world market for cotton. For another thing, while blacks were earning a greater return on their labor than they had under slavery, they were working less. Women and children were less likely to labor in the fields than in the past. Adult men tended to work shorter days. In all, the black labor force worked about one-third fewer hours during Reconstruction than it had under slavery—a reduction that brought the working schedule of blacks roughly into accord with that of white farm laborers. The income redistribution of the postwar years raised both the absolute and the relative economic status of blacks in the South substantially. It did not, however, lift many blacks out of poverty. Black per capita income rose from about one quarter of white per capita income to about one-half in the first few years after the war. But after this initial increase, it rose virtually not at all.

For blacks and poor whites alike, whatever gains there might have been as a result of land and income redistribution were often overshadowed by the ravages of another economic burden: the crop lien system. In the postwar South, the traditional credit structure—based on "factors" (see pp. 322–325) and banks—was unable to reassert its former control. In its stead emerged a new system of credit, centered in large part on local country stores—some of them owned by planters, others owned by independent merchants. Blacks and whites, landowners and tenants: all depended on these stores for such necessities as food, clothing, seed, farm implements, and the like. And since the agricultural sector does not enjoy the same steady cash flow as other sectors of the economy, Southern farmers often had to rely on credit from these merchants in order to purchase what they needed. The credit came at high cost. Interest rates were, in effect, as high as 50 or 60 percent. Suppliers held liens (claims) on the crops of debtor farmers as collateral on the loans. If a farmer suffered a few bad years in a row, as often happened in the troubled agricultural markets of the 1870s, he could become trapped in a cycle of debt from which he could never escape.

This burdensome credit system had a number of effects on the South. One was that some blacks who had acquired land during the early years of Reconstruction gradually lost it as they fell into debt. (So, to a lesser extent, did white small landowners.) Another was that Southern farmers became utterly dependent on cash crops—and most of all on cotton—because only such marketable commodities seemed to offer any possibility of escape from debt. Thus Southern agriculture, never sufficiently diversified

even in the best of times, became more one-dimensional than ever. Before the war, the South had grown most of its own food. By the end of Reconstruction, the region was importing a large proportion—in some areas more than 50 percent—of what it needed to feed itself. The relentless planting of cotton, moreover, was contributing to an exhaustion of the soil. The crop lien system, in other words, was not only helping to impoverish small farmers; it was also contributing to a general decline in the Southern agricultural economy.

The Black Family in Freedom

One of the most striking features of the black response to Reconstruction was the concerted effort to build or rebuild family structures and to protect them from the interference they had experienced under slavery. A major reason for the rapid departure of so many blacks from the plantations on which they had spent their lives was the desire to find lost relatives

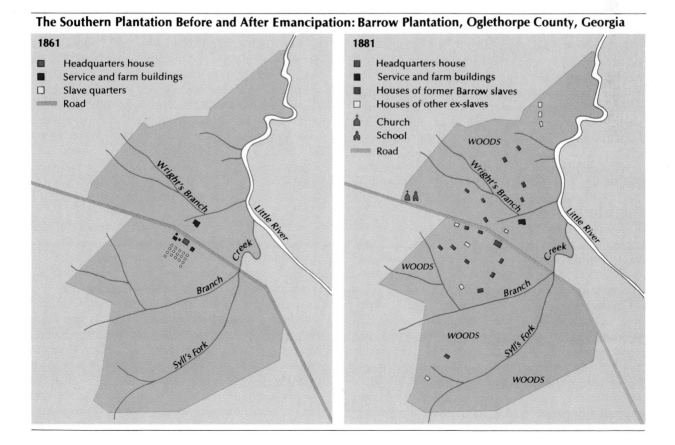

The Southern Plantation Before and After Emancipation: Barrow Plantation, Oglethorpe County, Georgia

1861

■ Headquarters house
■ Service and farm buildings
□ Slave quarters
░ Road

Wright's Branch   *Little River*   *Creek*   *Branch*   *Syll's Fork*

1881

■ Headquarters house
■ Service and farm buildings
■ Houses of former Barrow slaves
□ Houses of other ex-slaves
⛪ Church
🏫 School
░ Road

WOODS   *Wright's Branch*   *Little River*   WOODS   *Creek*   *Branch*   WOODS   *Syll's Fork*   WOODS and reunite families. Thousands of blacks wandered through the South looking for husbands, wives, children, or other relatives from whom they had been separated. Sometimes they found their loved ones, often by relying on an informal information network that quickly grew up in the black community or through advertising in newspapers. Sometimes, the search was in vain.

Former slaves were adamant in insisting that under the new economic system of the South they would acquire control over their own family lives. They rushed to have marriages, previously without legal standing, sanctified by church and law. At times, blacks held mass marriage ceremonies—sixty or seventy couples taking their vows simultaneously. Black families resisted living in the former slave quarters and moved instead to small cabins scattered widely across the countryside, where they could at least enjoy a modest level of privacy. It was often those blacks who had lived in closest proximity to whites—former house servants, for example—who were most determined to separate themselves from white society and create a home in which they would be able to control their own private lives.

Within the black family, the definition of male and female roles quickly came to resemble that within white families. Black men often forbade their wives and children to work in the fields. Such work, they believed, was a badge of slavery. Instead, women were to perform primarily domestic tasks—cooking, cleaning, gardening, raising children, attending to the needs of their husbands. Some black husbands refused to allow their wives to work as servants in white homes. "When I married my wife I married her to wait on me," one freedman told a former master who was attempting to hire his wife as a servant. "She got all she can do right here for me and the children."

But the effort to adapt the ideal of "domesticity" to the black family encountered at least some resistance. Not all black women wished to emulate the roles of their white counterparts—particularly those black women who, as former house servants, had observed the lives of white women closely. More important, however, economic necessity often required black women to engage in income-producing activities: working as domestic servants, taking in laundry, or helping their husbands in the field. By the end of Reconstruction, fully half of all black women over the age of sixteen were engaged in paid labor of some sort. And unlike among the whites, most black female income earners were married.

The Grant Administration

Exhausted by the political turmoil of the Johnson administration, American voters in 1868 yearned for a strong, stable figure to guide them through the troubled years of Reconstruction. They did not find one. Instead, they turned trustingly to General Ulysses S. Grant, the conquering hero of the war and, by 1868, a widely revered national idol. Grant had been an inspired general, but he was a disastrous president. During his two terms in office, he faced problems that would have taxed the abilities of a master of statecraft. Grant, whatever his qualities, was no such leader. He was, rather, a generally dull and unimaginative man with few political skills and little real vision.

The Soldier President

Grant could have had the nomination of either party in 1868. But as he watched the congressional Radicals triumph over President Johnson, he concluded that the Radical Reconstruction policy expressed the real wishes of the people; so he was receptive when the Radical leaders approached him with offers of the Republican nomination. Virtually without opposition, he received the endorsement of the party convention. The Democrats nominated former governor Horace Seymour of New York. The campaign was a bitter one, and Grant's triumph was by no means overwhelming. Grant carried twenty-six states and Seymour only eight. But Grant received only 3,013,000 popular votes to Seymour's 2,703,000, a scant majority of 310,000; and this majority was a result of black votes in the reconstructed states of the South.

Ulysses S. Grant entered the White House with no political experience of any kind. After graduating from West Point with no particular distinction, Grant had entered the regular army, from which after years of service he had resigned under something of a cloud. In civilian life he undertook several dismal ventures that barely yielded him a living. His career before 1861 could be characterized as forty years of failure. Then came the Civil War, and Grant found at last the one setting, the one vocation for which he was supremely equipped—combat.

In choosing his official family, Grant proceeded as if he were creating a military staff. He sent several appointments to the Senate for confirmation without asking the recipients if they would serve; they first heard the news in the papers. Hamilton Fish, whom Grant appointed secretary of state, had been out of politics for twenty years when he heard the news that his name had been submitted to the Senate. He wired Grant that he could not accept, but he ultimately agreed to serve. Fish proved to be one of Grant's few truly distinguished appointees. Most of his later appointments went to men who were at best average and at worst incompetent or corrupt or both. Increasingly, Grant came to rely on the machine leaders in the party—the group most ardently devoted to the spoils system.

Diplomatic Successes

The Grant administration and the Johnson administration achieved their greatest success in foreign affairs. These were the accomplishments not of the presidents themselves, who displayed little aptitude for diplomacy, but of two outstanding secretaries of state: William H. Seward, who had served Lincoln during the Civil War and remained in office until 1869; and Hamilton Fish, who served throughout the two terms of the Grant administration.

An ardent expansionist and advocate of a vigorous foreign policy, Seward acted with as much daring as the demands of Reconstruction politics and the Republican hatred of President Johnson would permit. When Russia let it be known that it would like to sell Alaska to the United States, Seward readily agreed to pay the asking price of $7.2 million. Only by strenuous efforts was he able to induce the Senate to ratify the treaty and the House to appropriate the money (1867-1868). Critics jeered that the secretary had bought a useless frozen wasteland—"Seward's Icebox" some critics called it. But Alaska was an important fishing center in the North Pacific, and it was potentially rich in such resources as gold (and, as the nation would discover much later, oil). Seward was not content with expansion in continental North America. In 1867, he engineered the annexation of the tiny Midway Islands west of Hawaii.

In contrast with its sometimes shambling course in domestic politics, the performance of the Grant administration in the area of foreign affairs was, under the direction of Hamilton Fish, generally decisive and firm. A number of delicate and potentially dangerous situations confronted Fish from the beginning, but the most serious one arose out of a burning American grievance against England that had origi-

"Seward's Folly"
The American purchase of Alaska from Russia (engineereed by Secretary of State William Seward) was ridiculed in this 1867 cartoon. The drawing suggests the widespread belief that Alaska was a useless frozen wasteland unfit for human habitation and populated only by polar bears. (Bettmann Archive)

nated during the Civil War. Many Americans believed that the British government had violated the laws of neutrality by permitting Confederate ships, the *Alabama* and others, to be built and armed in English shipyards and let loose to prey on Northern commerce. American demands that England pay for the damages committed by these vessels became known as the *"Alabama* claims."

Seward tried earnestly to settle the *Alabama* claims before leaving office, but to no avail. The one successful effort to negotiate a settlement—the Johnson-Clarendon Convention of 1869, which would have submitted claims on both sides to arbitration—was rejected by the Senate shortly after Johnson left office because it contained no British apology. The debate featured a speech by Charles Sumner, chairman of the Committee on Foreign Relations, arguing that Britain's conduct had prolonged the war by two years. Therefore, Sumner insisted, England owed the United States for "direct damages" committed by the ships and "indirect damages" for the cost of the war for two years—which would have reached the staggering total of some $2 billion.

England naturally would have nothing to do with any arrangement involving indirect claims, and settlement of the problem was temporarily stalled. Secretary Fish, however, continued to work for a solution, and finally, in 1871, the two countries agreed to the Treaty of Washington, providing for international arbitration of the issue and other pending controversies. In the treaty, Britain expressed regret for the escape of the *Alabama* and agreed to a set of rules governing neutral obligations that in effect conceded the case to the United States. This meant that the arbitrators would have only to fix the sum to be paid by Britain. They awarded $15.5 million to the United States.

The Defection of the Liberals

On both international and domestic matters, a wide breach soon developed between President Grant and a number of prominent Republicans, among them the famous Radical Charles Sumner. Sumner's extravagant demand for damages from Great Britain embarrassed Secretary Fish. Sumner also blocked a treaty for the annexation of Santo Domingo (now the Dominican Republic), a project in which Grant took a deep, even monomaniacal personal interest. The angry president got revenge by inducing his Senate friends to remove Sumner from the chairmanship of the Committee on Foreign Relations.

Among the principal political controversies of these years was the spoils system of presidential appointments, which Grant had used even more blatantly than most of his predecessors to reward party machine politicians. Sumner and other Republican leaders joined with reformers to agitate for a new civil service system to limit the president's appointive powers. Such scholarly journalists as E. L. Godkin of *The Nation* and George William Curtis of *Harper's Weekly* argued that the government should base its appointments not on services to the party but on fitness for office as determined by competitive examinations, as the British government already was doing. Grant reluctantly agreed to establish a civil service commission, which Congress authorized in 1871, to

devise a system of hiring based on merit. This agency, under the direction of Curtis, proposed a set of rules that seemed to meet with Grant's approval. But Grant was not really much interested in reform, and even if he had been he could not have persuaded his followers to accept a new system that would undermine the very basis of party loyalty—patronage. Congress declined to renew the commission's appropriation, and the commission disbanded.

Nevertheless, controversy over civil-service reform remained one of the leading political issues of the next three decades of American life. The debate involved more than simply an argument over patronage and corruption. It reflected, too, basic differences of opinion over who was fit to serve in public life. Middle-class reformers were saying, implicitly, that only educated, middle-class people (the "best men") should be permitted access to government office. Those opposing them—not simply party leaders but immigrant and labor groups, some farmers, and others—argued that the establishment of an elite corps of civil servants would exclude these groups from participation in government and restrict power to the upper classes.

Republican critics of the president also denounced him for his support of Radical Reconstruction. Grant continued to station federal troops in the South, and on many occasions he sent them to support Republican governments that were on the point of collapse. To growing numbers in the North this seemed like dangerous militarism, and they were more and more disgusted by the stories of governmental corruption and extravagance in the South. Some Republicans were beginning to suspect that there was corruption not only in the Southern state governments but also in the federal government. Still others criticized Grant because he had declined to speak out in favor of a reduction of the tariff.

Thus before the end of Grant's first term, members of his own party had begun to oppose him for a variety of reasons, all of which added up to what the critics called "Grantism." In 1872, hoping to prevent Grant's reelection, his opponents bolted the party. Referring to themselves as Liberal Republicans, they nominated their own presidential and vice-presidential candidates. Horace Greeley, veteran editor and publisher of the New York *Tribune*, headed their ticket. The Democratic convention, seeing in Greeley's candidacy (and in the alliance with the Liberals it would achieve) the only chance to unseat Grant and the Republicans, endorsed Greeley with no great enthusiasm. Despite Greeley's recent attacks on Radical Reconstruction, many Southerners, remembering his own Radical past, chose to stay home on election day. Grant polled 286 electoral votes and 3,597,000 popular votes to Greeley's 66 and 2,834,000. Greeley had carried only two Southern and four border states. Three weeks later, apparently crushed by his defeat, Greeley died.

The Grant Scandals

During the campaign, the first of a series of political scandals had come to light. It originated with the Crédit Mobilier construction company, which had helped build the Union Pacific Railroad. The Crédit Mobilier was, in fact, controlled by a few Union Pacific stockholders who had awarded huge and fraudulent contracts to the construction company, thus milking the Union Pacific, a company of which they owned only a minor share, of money that in part came from government subsidies. To avert a congressional inquiry into the deal, the directors in effect gave Crédit Mobilier stock to key members of Congress. A congressional investigation in 1872 revealed that some highly placed Republicans—including Schuyler Colfax, now Grant's vice president—had accepted stock.

One dreary episode followed another in Grant's second term. Benjamin H. Bristow, Grant's third Treasury secretary, discovered that some of his officials and a group of distillers operating as a "whiskey ring" were cheating the government out of taxes by means of false reports. Among those involved was the president's private secretary, Orville E. Babcock. Grant defended Babcock, appointed him to another office, and eased Bristow out of the cabinet. Then a House investigation revealed that William W. Belknap, secretary of war, had accepted bribes to retain an Indian-post trader in office. Belknap resigned with Grant's blessing before the Senate could act on impeachment charges brought by the House. Other, lesser scandals added to the growing impression that "Grantism" had brought rampant corruption to government.

The Greenback Question

Meanwhile, the Grant administration and the nation at large suffered another blow: the Panic of 1873. It began with the failure of a leading investment banking firm, Jay Cooke and Company, which had in-

The Grant Scandals
Grant's last years in office were plagued by revelations of scandals at various levels of the government. Although the president himself was never shown to have been involved, his reputation suffered nevertheless. This cartoon from *Puck* magazine shows Grant providing support for various corrupt members of his administration. (Historical Pictures Service)

vested too heavily in postwar railroad building. Depressions had come before with almost rhythmic regularity—in 1819, 1837, and 1857—but this was the worst one yet. It lasted four years.

Debtors pressured the government to follow an inflationary policy, which would have made it easier for them to pay their debts. But President Grant and most Republicans preferred what they called a "sound" currency—based solidly on gold reserves—

which was to the advantage of the banks, money-lenders, and other creditors. The money question had confronted Grant and the Republicans in Congress from the beginning of his administration. The question was twofold: How should the war bonds be paid? And what should be the permanent place of greenbacks in the national currency? Representatives of the debtor interests argued that the bonds should be redeemed in greenbacks, thus increasing the amount of currency in circulation. The president favored payment in gold, and the Republican Congress moved speedily to promise redemption in "coin or its equivalent"; but refunding of the debt was to stretch out over a number of years.

The question of what to do about the greenbacks, however, remained unresolved. When Grant entered the White House, approximately $356 million of greenbacks were circulating. And in 1873, when the Supreme Court reversed an earlier decision and, in *Knox* v. *Lee*, affirmed the legality of greenbacks, the Treasury moved to increase the amount in circulation in response to the panic. For the same reason Congress, in the following year, voted to raise the total further. Grant, responding to pressures from Eastern financial interests, vetoed the measure—over the loud objections of many members of his own party.

With the greenback issue becoming more and more heated and divisive, and with an election year approaching, Republican leaders in Congress began searching for some way to settle the controversy. Their solution—introduced initially by Senator John Sherman of Ohio—was the Specie Resumption Act of 1875. This law provided that after January 1, 1879, the government would redeem greenback dollars at par with gold; that is, the present greenbacks, whose value constantly fluctuated, could be exchanged for new paper currency, whose value would be firmly pegged to the price of gold. The law protected the interests of the creditor classes, who had worried that debts would be repaid in debased paper currency. In theory, the new law protected the interests of debtor groups as well, by calling for an increase in the amount of specie-backed currency in circulation. In fact, however, "resumption" did not satisfy those who had been clamoring for an increase in greenbacks, because the gold-based money supply was never able to expand as much as they believed was necessary.

Thus the greenback issue survived after 1875, and the question of the proper composition of the currency now emerged as one of the most controversial and enduring issues in American politics. Creditors and established financial interests continued to insist on a sound currency based on gold. Debtor groups—farmers, laborers, and some manufacturers—and debtor regions—the South and the West—continued to clamor for a currency based not on gold reserves but on the productive capacity of the nation. Otherwise, they claimed, they would continue to be strangled by an overvalued dollar circulating in insufficient quantities.

The question of greenbacks and the many other currency controversies that followed also became symbols of much deeper concerns. Agrarian dissidents and others came to see in the maintenance of the gold standard a conspiracy by entrenched financiers to keep farmers in economic bondage. Southerners and Westerners saw in the currency policies evidence of their subordination to the Northeast. Because in accepting the gold standard the United States was following the example of Great Britain and other European nations, many Americans came to view the policy as part of a dire international plot to enslave the American people. The greenbackers, as they were called, expressed their displeasure in 1875 by forming their own political organization: the National Greenback party. Active in the next three presidential elections, it failed to gain widespread support. But it did keep the money issue alive. And in the 1880s, the greenback forces began to merge with another, more powerful group of currency reformers—those who favored silver as the basis of currency—to help produce a political movement that would ultimately attain enormous strength.

The Abandonment of Reconstruction

As the North grew increasingly preoccupied with its own political and economic problems, interest in Reconstruction began to wane. The Grant administration continued to protect Republican governments in the South, but less because of any interest in ensuring the position of freedmen than because of a desire to prevent the reemergence of a strong Democratic party in the region. But even the presence of federal troops was not enough to prevent white Southerners from overturning many of the Republican governments that they believed had been so ruthlessly thrust upon them. In a few states, the Democrats (or Conservatives) returned to power almost as soon as civilian government was restored. In Virginia, North Carolina, and Georgia, Republican rule came to an end before or by 1871. In other states, the Democrats gradually regained control over several years. Texas was "redeemed"—as Southerners liked to call the restoration of Democratic rule—in 1873; Alabama and Arkansas in 1874; and Mississippi in 1876. For three other states—South Carolina, Louisiana, and Florida—the end of Reconstruction had to wait for the withdrawal of the last federal troops in 1876, a withdrawal that was the result of a long process of political bargaining and compromise at the national level.

The Southern States "Redeemed"

In the states where whites constituted a majority—the states of the upper South—overthrow of Republican control was a relatively simple matter. The whites had only to organize and win the elections. Restoration of suffrage to those whites who had been deprived of it helped them in their task. Presidential and congressional pardons returned the vote to numerous individuals; and in 1872, Congress passed the Amnesty Act, which restored political rights to 150,000 ex-Confederates and left only 500 excluded from political life.

In other states, where blacks were in the majority or the populations of the two races were almost equal, the whites resorted to intimidation and violence. Secret societies, complete with hooded robes and elaborate rituals, appeared in many parts of the South: the Ku Klux Klan, the Knights of the White Camellia, and others. They were frankly terroristic and attempted to frighten or physically prevent blacks from voting. Moving quickly to stamp out these societies, Congress passed two bills (1870 and 1871), which white Southerners called "force acts," and the Ku Klux Klan Act (also in 1871). These measures authorized the president to use military force and martial law in areas where the orders were active. Only rarely, however, did the laws have a significant impact.

More potent than the secret orders were open semimilitary organizations in the South that operated as rifle clubs under such names as Red Shirts and White Leagues. The first such society was founded in Mississippi, and the idea soon spread to other states; their tactics were called the Mississippi Plan. The plan called for whites in each community to organize and arm, and to be prepared, if necessary, to use force to win elections. But the heart of the scheme was in the phrase "drawing the color line." By one method or another, legal or illegal, every white man was to be

Klansmen

Two members of the Ku Klux Klan, dressed in their regalia, posed in a studio for this photograph. (The figure on the left has apparently been defaced through the addition of a beard and side whiskers.) Organized at first as a social club, the Klan became a powerful political organization in the early years of Reconstruction. Ex-Confederate General Nathan Bedford Forrest became "Grand Wizard" in 1867 and attempted to make the order a respectable, patriotic organization. But Klansmen increasingly resorted to violence and intimidation in their efforts to suppress their foes, and they suffered as well from crimes committed in their name by outsiders. In 1869 Forrest resigned as leader and ordered the organization to disband. Shortly thereafter, Congress passed legislation restricting Klan activities and ultimately declared the organization illegal. It maintained a covert life, however, until the late nineteenth century. The modern Ku Klux Klan, founded in 1915, has no direct link to the Reconstruction order.   (Rutherford B. Hayes Library) forced to join the Democratic party or leave the community. By similar methods, every black male was to be excluded from political activity. In a few states, blacks were to be permitted to vote—if they voted Democratic.

Perhaps an even stronger influence than the techniques practiced by the armed bands was the simple weapon of economic pressure. The war had freed the slaves, but they were still laborers—hired workers or tenants—dependent on whites for their livelihood. Whites quickly discovered ways to use this dependence to increase their power over blacks. Planters refused to rent land to Republican blacks; storekeepers refused to extend them credit; employers refused to give them work. Without a secure economic base of their own—something Reconstruction had done nothing to give them—blacks were powerless to resist these pressures.

Southern blacks were, in the meantime, losing the support of many of their former supporters in the North, even of many humanitarian reformers who had worked for emancipation and equal rights. After the adoption of the Fifteenth Amendment in 1870, most reformers convinced themselves that their long campaign in behalf of black people at last was over; that with the vote, blacks ought to be able to take care of themselves. The party split of 1872, in part a response to the perceived corruption in Southern Reconstruction governments, weakened the Republicans in the South still further. Former Radical leaders such as Charles Sumner and Horace Greeley now began calling themselves Liberals, cooperating with the Democrats and outdoing even the Democrats in denunciations of what they viewed as black-and-carpetbag misgovernment. Within the South itself, many white Republicans joined the Liberals and moved into the Democratic party. Friction between black Republicans and those whites who remained in the party grew because of a well-justified feeling on the part of the blacks that they were not receiving a fair share of the power and the jobs.

The depression that began in 1873 aggravated political discontent in both the North and the South. In the congressional elections of 1874, the Democrats gained a majority of the seats in the House of Representatives, thus denying the Republicans control of the whole Congress for the first time since 1861. And President Grant, in view of the changing temper of the North, no longer was willing to use military force to prop up the Republican regimes that were still standing in the South. In 1875, when the Mississippi governor, Adelbert Ames (originally from Maine),

appealed to Washington for troops to protect blacks from the terrorism of the Democrats, he received in reply a telegram that quoted Grant as saying: "The whole public are tired out with these annual autumnal outbreaks in the South, and the great majority are now ready to condemn any interference on the part of the government."

After the Democrats gained political control of Mississippi, only three states were left in the hands of the Republicans—South Carolina, Louisiana, and Florida. In the elections of 1876, again using terrorist tactics, the Democrats claimed victory in all three. But the Republicans claimed victory as well, and they were able to continue holding office because federal troops happened to be on the scene. If the troops were to be withdrawn, the last of the Republican regimes would fall. Resolution of the conflict would depend on the presidential election of 1876, which was itself in dispute because of the electoral controversies in the South.

The Compromise of 1877

Ulysses S. Grant was eager to run for another term in 1876, but the majority of the Republican leaders refused to consider him. Impressed by the recent upsurge of Democratic strength and fearful that a third-term campaign would create controversy, they searched for a candidate who was not associated with the scandals of the past eight years and could entice the Liberals back into the fold and unite the party until after the election. Senator James G. Blaine of Maine offered himself, but he had recently been involved in an allegedly crooked railroad deal. The Republican convention settled instead on Rutherford B. Hayes, a former Union army officer and congressman, three times governor of Ohio, and a champion of civil-service reform.

No personal rivalries divided the Democrats. Only one aspirant commanded serious attention: Governor Samuel J. Tilden of New York, whose name had become synonymous with governmental reform. A corporation lawyer and a millionaire, Tilden had long been a power in the Democratic organization of his state, but he had not hesitated to turn against the corrupt Tweed Ring of New York City's Tammany Hall and aid in its overthrow. His fight against Tweed brought him national fame and the governorship, in which position he increased his reputation for honest administration.

The campaign was an unusually bitter one, but there were in fact almost no differences of principle between the candidates. Hayes supported withdrawal of troops from the South and civil-service reform, and his record for probity was equal to Tilden's. Tilden vaguely supported a tariff reduction, but on other economic issues he was at least as conservative as his rival. He supported the gold standard—"sound money"—and he believed that government had no business interfering with economic interests. He looked on himself as a modern counterpart of Thomas Jefferson.

The November election produced an apparent Democratic victory. Tilden carried the South and several large Northern states, and his popular vote was 4,301,000 to 4,036,000 for Hayes. But the situation was complicated by the disputed returns from Louisiana, South Carolina, and Florida, whose total electoral vote was 19. Both parties claimed to have won these states, and double sets of returns were presented to Congress. Adding to the confusion was a contested vote in Oregon, where one of the three successful Republican electors was declared ineligible because he held a federal office. The Democrats contended that the place should go to the Democratic elector with the highest number of votes; but the Republicans insisted that according to state law, the remaining electors were to select someone to fill the vacancy. The disputed returns threw the outcome of the election into doubt. As tension and excitement gripped the country, two clear facts emerged from the welter of conflicting claims. Tilden had undisputed claim to 184 electoral votes, only one short of the majority. The 20 votes in controversy would determine who would be president, and Hayes needed all of them to secure the office.

With surprise and consternation, the nation now learned that no method existed to determine the validity of disputed returns. The Constitution stated: "The President of the Senate shall, in the presence of the Senate and House of Representatives, open all the certificates and the votes shall then be counted." The question was, how and by whom? The Senate was Republican and so, of course, was its president; the House was Democratic. Constitutional ambiguity and congressional division rendered a fair and satisfactory solution of the crisis impossible. If the president of the Senate counted the votes, Hayes would be the victor. If the Senate and House judged the returns separately, they would reach opposite decisions and checkmate each other. And if the houses voted jointly, the Democrats, with a numerical ma-

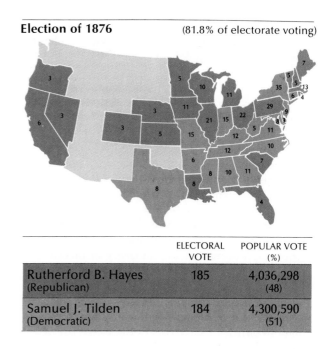

Election of 1876 (81.8% of electorate voting)

	ELECTORAL VOTE	POPULAR VOTE (%)
Rutherford B. Hayes (Republican)	185	4,036,298 (48)
Samuel J. Tilden (Democratic)	184	4,300,590 (51)

jority, would decide the result. Resort to any one of these lines of action promised to divide the country and possibly result in chaos.

Not until the last days of January 1877 did Congress act to break the deadlock by creating a special electoral commission to pass on all the disputed votes. The commission was to be composed of five senators, five representatives, and five justices of the Supreme Court. The congressional delegation would consist of five Republicans and five Democrats. The Court delegation, as established by the legislation creating the commission, would consist of two Republicans, two Democrats, and an independent. But before the commission could meet, the designated independent was elected to the Senate and resigned his seat on the Court. His place on the commission fell to a more partisan Republican. The commission sat throughout February and reached decisions by a straight party vote of 8 to 7, awarding every disputed vote to Hayes. Congress accepted the final verdict of the commission on March 2, only two days before the inauguration of the new president.

Ratification of the commission's findings, however, required a series of elaborate compromises among leaders of both parties. Behind the dealing, and partially directing it, were certain powerful economic forces with a stake in the outcome. Republican leaders, hoping to end a Democratic filibuster in the Senate, met secretly with Southern Democratic leaders to work out terms by which they would support the election of Hayes. According to the traditional account, certain Republicans and Southern Democrats met at Washington's Wormley Hotel, and the Republicans pledged that Hayes, after becoming president, would withdraw the troops from the South. Since withdrawal would mean the downfall of the last carpetbag governments, the Southerners, convinced they were getting as much from Hayes as they could get from Tilden, agreed to abandon the filibuster.

Actually, the story behind the "Compromise of 1877" is somewhat more complex. Hayes was on record before the election as favoring withdrawal of the troops, and in any event the Democrats in the House could have forced withdrawal simply by cutting out appropriations for the army in the Reconstruction process. The real agreement, the one that won the Southern Democrats over, was reached before the Wormley meeting. As the price of their cooperation, the Southern Democrats (among them some old Whigs) exacted from the Republicans the following pledges: the appointment of at least one Southerner to the Hayes cabinet, control of federal patronage in their areas, generous internal improvements, federal aid for the Texas and Pacific Railroad, and, finally, withdrawal of the troops. Many of the Conservatives who controlled the Democratic parties of the redeemed Southern states were interested in industrializing the South, and they believed that the Republican program of federal aid to business would be more beneficial for their region than the archaic states' rights policy of the Democrats.

In his inaugural address, Hayes spoke primarily about the Southern problem. While he was careful to say that the rights of blacks must be preserved, he announced that the most pressing need of the South was the restoration of "wise, honest, and peaceful local self-government"—a signal that he planned to withdraw the troops and let the whites take over control of the state governments. Hayes knew that this would lend weight to charges that he was paying off the South for acquiescing in his election and would strengthen those critics who referred to him as "his Fraudulency." But in fact, the political crisis surrounding the election had already created such bitterness there was probably nothing Hayes could have done to mollify his critics.

The president hoped to build up a "new Republican" party in the South composed of whatever conservative white groups could be weaned away from the Democrats and committed to some acceptance of black rights. But his efforts, which included a tour of Southern cities and even the decoration of a memorial to the Confederate war dead, failed. Although many Southern leaders sympathized with the economic credo of the Republicans, they could not advise their people to support the party that had imposed Reconstruction. Nor were Southerners pleased by Hayes's bestowal of federal offices on carpetbaggers or by his vetoes of Democratic attempts to repeal the force acts. The "solid South," although not yet fully formed, was beginning to take shape. Neither Hayes nor any other Republican could reverse the trend—particularly since no one was willing to use federal power to protect black voting rights, which alone held promise of giving the Republicans lasting strength in the region. The withdrawal of the troops was a signal that the national government was giving up its attempt to control Southern politics and to determine the place of blacks in Southern society.

The Tragedy of Reconstruction

The record of the Reconstruction years is not one of complete failure, as many have charged. That slavery would be abolished was clear well before the end of the war; but Reconstruction worked other changes upon Southern society as well. There was a significant redistribution of income, from which blacks benefited. There was a more limited but not unimportant redistribution of land ownership, which enabled some former slaves to acquire property for the first time. There was both a relative and an absolute improvement in the economic circumstances of most blacks.

Nor was Reconstruction as disastrous an experience for Southern whites as most believed at the time. The region had emerged from a prolonged and bloody war defeated and devastated; and yet within a decade, the South had regained control of its own institutions and, to a great extent, restored its traditional ruling class to power. No harsh punishments were meted out to former Confederate leaders. No drastic program of economic reform was imposed on the region. Few lasting political changes were forced on the South. Not many conquered nations fare as well.

Yet for all that, Americans of the twentieth century cannot help but look back on Reconstruction as a tragic era. For in those years the United States made its first serious effort to resolve its oldest and deepest social problem—the problem of race. And it failed in the effort. What was more, the experience so disap-

SIGNIFICANT EVENTS

1863 Lincoln announces preliminary Reconstruction plan

1864 Louisiana, Arkansas, Tennessee readmitted to Union under Lincoln plan

Wade-Davis bill passed

1865 Lincoln assassinated; Andrew Johnson becomes president (April 14)

Johnson readmits rest of Confederate states to Union under Lincoln plan

Black Codes enacted in South

Freedmen's Bureau established

Congress reconvenes (December) and refuses to admit Southern representatives; creates Joint Committee on Reconstruction

1866 Freedmen's Bureau renewed over Johnson's veto

Congress approves Fourteenth Amendment; most Southern states reject it

Republicans gain in congressional elections

Ex parte Milligan challenges Radicals' Reconstruction plans

Ku Klux Klan formed in South

1867 Military Reconstruction Act (and two supplementary acts) outlines congressional plan of Reconstruction

Tenure of Office Act and Command of the Army Act restrict presidential power

Southern states establish Reconstruction governments under congressional plan

Alaska purchased

1868 Most Southern states readmitted to Congress under congressional plan

Andrew Johnson impeached but not convicted

Fourteenth Amendment ratified

Ulysses S. Grant elected president

1869 Congress passes Fifteenth Amendment

First "redeemer" governments elected in South

1870 Last Southern states readmitted to Congress

Force Act passed

1871 *Alabama* claims settled

1872 Liberal Republicans defect

Grant reelected president

1873 Commercial and financial panic disrupts economy

1875 Civil Rights Act passed

Specie Resumption Act passed

"Whiskey ring" scandal discredits Grant administration

1877 Rutherford B. Hayes elected president after disputed election

Last federal troops withdrawn from South after Compromise of 1877

Last Southern states "redeemed"

---

pointed, disillusioned, and embittered the nation that it would be many years before an attempt would be made again.

Why did this great assault on racial injustice—an assault that had emerged over a period of more than fifty years—end so badly? In part, of course, it was because of the weaknesses and errors of the people who directed it. But in greater part, it was because the resolution of the racial problem required a far more fundamental reform of society than Americans of the time were willing to make. One after another, attempts to produce solutions ran up against conservative obstacles so deeply embedded in the nation's life that they could not be dislodged. Veneration of the Constitution sharply limited the willingness of

national leaders to infringe on the rights of states and individuals in creating social change. A profound respect for private property and free enterprise prevented any real assault on economic privilege in the South, ensuring that blacks would not win title to the land and wealth they believed they deserved. Above all, perhaps, a pervasive belief among even the most liberal whites that the black race was inherently inferior served as an obstacle to the full equality of the freedmen. Given the context within which Americans of the 1860s and 1870s were working, what is surprising, perhaps, is not that Reconstruction did so little, but that it did even as much as it did. The era was tragic not just because it was a failure—the failure may have been inevitable from the beginning—

but also because it revealed how great the barriers were to racial justice in the United States.

Given the odds confronting them, therefore, black Americans had reason for pride in the limited gains they were able to make during Reconstruction. And the nation at large had reason for gratitude that, if nothing else, the postwar era produced two great charters of freedom—the Fourteenth and Fifteenth amendments to the Constitution—which, although largely ignored at the time, would one day serve as the basis for a "Second Reconstruction," one that would renew the drive to bring freedom and equality to all Americans.

SUGGESTED READINGS

General Studies The studies by McPherson and by Randall and Donald cited in the readings for the previous two chapters are likewise valuable for the Reconstruction period, both for their narratives of the era and for their bibliographies. William A. Dunning, *Reconstruction, Political and Economic, 1865–1977* (1907), long the standard study of Reconstruction, is now widely conceded to be marred by deep prejudices. More recent overviews of the period, better in tune with contemporary values, are Kenneth Stampp, *The Era of Reconstruction* (1965), and John Hope Franklin, *Reconstruction After the Civil War* (1961). W. E. B. Du Bois, *Black Reconstruction* (1935), is an early challenge to the pro-Southern orthodoxy about the period; whereas E. Merton Coulter, *The South During Reconstruction* (1947), adheres strictly to traditional views of the period as a time of Northern vindictiveness and Southern suffering. Rembert Patrick, *The Reconstruction of the Nation* (1967), is a modern overview that provides more detail than the relatively brief studies by Stampp and Franklin.

Presidential Reconstruction Herman Belz, *Reconstructing the Union* (1969), examines the theoretical basis of the Reconstruction problem. William B. Hesseltine, *Lincoln's Plan of Reconstruction* (1960), considers the first presidential plan; and Willie Lee Rose, *Rehearsal for Reconstruction: The Port Royal Experiment* (1964), describes wartime reconstruction policies in an area of South Carolina captured early by the Union. Louis S. Gerteis, *From Contraband to Freedman* (1973), examines federal policy toward blacks during the war itself. Richard H. Abbott, *The First Southern Strategy* (1986), is a study of early Southern efforts to shape postwar politics and society.

Congressional Reconstruction There are several valuable studies of the political battles that accompanied the switch from presidential to congressional Reconstruction. William R. Brock, *An American Crisis* (1963), is a particularly judicious work. Howard K. Beale, *The Critical Year: A Study of Andrew Johnson and Reconstruction* (1930), is a traditional approach to the subject; Eric McKitrick, *Andrew Johnson and Reconstruction* (1960), is far more hostile toward Johnson. Two works by Michael Les Benedict, *A Compromise of Principle: Congressional Republicans and Reconstruction, 1863–1869* (1974) and *The Impeachment and Trial of Andrew Johnson* (1973), consider congressional politics and antagonisms toward the president. Hans L. Trefousse, *The Radical Republicans* (1963), and David Donald, *The Politics of Reconstruction* (1965), also examine congressional Radicals. Hans Trefousse is the author of another study of the impeachment proceedings, *The Impeachment of a President* (1975). La Wanda Cox and John H. Cox, *Politics, Principles, and Prejudice, 1865–1867* (1963), is an early work that was important in revising previous views of Reconstruction politics. Also useful for the politics of the era are biographies of leading Reconstruction figures. Richard N. Current, *Old Thad Stevens* (1942), is a hostile view; Fawn Brodie, *Thaddeus Stevens* (1959), is more sympathetic. David Donald, *Charles Sumner and the Rights of Man* (1970), is also important. Harold Hyman, *A More Perfect Union* (1973), and Stanley Kutler, *The Judicial Power and Reconstruction Politics* (1968), examine the constitutional problems that Reconstruction posed. Mark W. Summers, *Railroads, Reconstruction, and the Gospel of Prosperity* (1984), explores some of the economic factors shaping policy. Charles Fairman, *Reconstruction and Reunion* (1971), considers the Supreme Court in the postwar years. See also Herman Belz, *A New Birth of Freedom* (1976) and *Emancipation and Equal Rights* (1978). William Gillette, *The Right to Vote* (1965), is a study of the framing of the Fifteenth Amendment.

The South in Reconstruction Two works by Michael Perman, *Reunion Without Compromise* (1973) and *The Road to Redemption: Southern Politics, 1869–1879* (1984), examine white Southern resistance to Reconstruction. Valuable works on individual states include Joel G. Taylor, *Louisiana Reconstructed* (1974); Vernon Wharton, *The Negro in Mississippi, 1865–1890* (1965); Peyton McCrary, *Abraham Lincoln and Reconstruction* (1978), on policies toward Louisiana; Joel Williamson, *After Slavery: The Negro in South Carolina During Reconstruction* (1965); Thomas Holt, *Black over White* (1977), also on South Carolina; C. Peter Ripley, *Slaves and Freedmen in Civil War Louisiana* (1976); and Michael Wayne, *The Reshaping of Plantation Society: The Natchez District* (1983), on Mississippi. William Gillette, *Retreat from Reconstruction* (1980), examines the end of Reconstruction in the South. A valuable study of the economic impact of Reconstruction on the South is Roger Ransom and Richard Sutch, *One Kind of Freedom* (1977). Robert Higgs, *Competition and Coercion* (1977), is a controversial economic analysis of the period. Crandall A. Shifflett, *Patronage and Poverty in the Tobacco South: Louisa County, Virginia, 1860–1900* (1982), examines planters during Reconstruction. Leon Litwack, *Been in the Storm So Long* (1979), Eric Foner, *Nothing But Freedom: Emancipation and Its Legacy* (1983), and Peter

Kolchin, *First Freedom* (1972), examine the effects of Reconstruction on blacks. Allen Trelease, *White Terror* (1967), discusses the Ku Klux Klan. William S. McFeely, *Yankee Stepfather: General O. O. Howard and the Freedmen* (1968), portrays the head of the Freedmen's Bureau; and George Bentley, *A History of the Freedmen's Bureau* (1955), examines the institution itself. On carpetbaggers, see Otto Olsen, *Carpetbagger's Crusade: Albion Winegar Tourgée* (1965); L. N. Powell, *New Masters: Northern Planters During the Civil War and Reconstruction* (1980); William C. Harris, *The Day of the Carpetbagger: Republican Reconstruction in Mississippi, 1867–1975* (1979); and Elizabeth Jacoway, *Yankee Missionaries in the South* (1979). Sarah Wiggins, *The Scalawag in Alabama Politics, 1865–1881* (1977), examines Southern "collaborationists." Likewise valuable are Jacqueline Jones, *Soldiers of Light and Love* (1980), and James Sefton, *The United States Army and Reconstruction* (1967).

The Grant Administration   The best biography of the president is William McFeely, *Grant* (1981). Allan Nevins, *Hamilton Fish* (1936), is a biography of the secretary of state that provides a portrait of the administration as a whole. William B. Hesseltine, *U. S. Grant, Politician* (1935), is another study of the Grant presidency. On the scandals of the era, see David Loth, *Public Plunder* (1938). John G. Sproat, *The Best Men* (1968), examines the role of liberal reformers during the period. Specific political controversies of the time are considered in Ari Hoogenboom, *Outlawing the Spoils* (1961), on civil-service reform, and Irwin Unger, *The Greenback Era* (1964), on monetary controversies. Two views of the compromise of 1877 are C. Vann Woodward, *Reunion and Reaction* (1951), and K. I. Polakoff, *The Politics of Inertia* (1973). Edwin C. Rozwenc (ed.), *Reconstruction in the South*, rev. ed. (1952), is a valuable collection of essays on the subject.

Appendices

CANADA

WASHINGTON
Seattle
Tacoma
Olympia
Spokane

MONTANA
Helena
Billings

NORTH DAKOTA
Bismarck

OREGON
Portland
Salem
Eugene

IDAHO
Boise

SOUTH DAKOTA
Pierre
Rapid City

WYOMING
Casper

NEBRASKA

Reno
Sacramento
Berkeley
Oakland
San Francisco
Sunnyvale
San Jose
Stockton
Modesto
Carson City
NEVADA

UTAH
Salt Lake City
Provo

Laramie
Cheyenne

Lincoln

Fresno

CALIFORNIA
Bakersfield

Las Vegas

COLORADO
Boulder
Denver
Aurora
Lakewood
Colorado Springs
Pueblo

KANSAS

Wic

Oxnard
Glendale
Pasadena
Los Angeles
San Bernardino
Torrance
Riverside
Long Beach
Anaheim
Huntington Beach
Santa Ana

ARIZONA

Taos
Santa Fe
Albuquerque

OKLAHOM
Amarillo
Oklahoma City

San Diego

Phoenix
Tempe
Mesa

NEW MEXICO

Lubbock

Dallas
Gar
Irving
Fort Worth
Arlington

PACIFIC OCEAN

Tucson

El Paso

Wa

Kauai
HAWAII
Oahu
Honolulu
Ewa
Maui
Hawaii

U.S.S.R.

TEXAS
Austin

0   100 Miles
0   100 Kilometers

ALASKA
Fairbanks

San Antonio

0   300 Miles
0   300 Kilometers

Anchorage

CANADA

Juneau

MEXICO

Corp
Chri

CANADA

Lake Superior

MINNESOTA

Minneapolis ■ St. Paul

WISCONSIN

Milwaukee ■
Madison ○

IOWA

Cedar Rapids ○
Des Moines ○
Iowa City ○
Davenport ○
maha

Kansas City ○

MISSOURI
Independence ■ Kansas City
eka △
rence
Jefferson City ○ St. Louis ■

Springfield ○

ARKANSAS
Fayetteville △
Little Rock ○
lsa

Lake Michigan

MICHIGAN

Grand Rapids ○
Flint ○
Lansing ○ Warren ☆
Sterling Heights ○
Detroit ■
Livonia
Ann Arbor ○

Rockford ○
Chicago ▣
Gary ■ South Bend ○
Fort Wayne ○

Peoria ○

ILLINOIS
Springfield ○
Urbana ○

INDIANA
Indianapolis ■
Bloomington ○
Louisville ○
Evansville ○

Lake Huron

Toledo ○
Cleveland ■
Akron ▣

OHIO
Columbus ■
Dayton ▣
Cincinnati ■

Frankfort ☆
Lexington ○

KENTUCKY

Lake Erie
Lake Erie

Youngstown ○
Pittsburgh ■

Buffalo ■

Lake Ontario
Rochester ○

NEW YORK
Albany ▣
Syracuse ▣

PENNSYLVANIA
Allentown ▣
Harrisburg ○
Newark
Trenton

VERMONT
Burlington ○
Montpelier ☆

NEW HAMPSHIRE
Concord ☆

MAINE
Augusta ☆
Portland ○

Manchester ○

Worcester ▣ Boston ■
Springfield ▣ **MASSACHUSETTS**
Hartford ▣ Providence ■
CONNECTICUT **RHODE ISLAND**
New Haven ○
Bridgeport ○
Stamford ○
New York ▣
Jersey City ■

Baltimore ■
WASHINGTON D.C. ▣
Alexandria ○
MARYLAND

Philadelphia ■
NEW JERSEY
Dover ☆
DELAWARE
Annapolis ☆

WEST VIRGINIA
Charleston ○

VIRGINIA
Richmond ○
Hampton ☆
Newport News ○ Norfolk ■
Portsmouth ○ Virginia Beach ○
Roanoke ○ Chesapeake ○

Springfield ○

Memphis ▣

Huntsville ○
Oxford △
Birmingham ○
University ▣

MISSISSIPPI
ALABAMA
Montgomery ○

Knoxville ○
Nashville ▣
TENNESSEE
Chattanooga ○

Atlanta ■
Athens △
GEORGIA
Macon ○

Columbus ○

Greensboro ○ Durham ○
Winston-Salem ○ Raleigh ☆
Asheville ○ **NORTH CAROLINA**
Charlotte ○

Greenville ○

Columbia ○
SOUTH CAROLINA

Charleston ●

Savannah ○

ATLANTIC OCEAN

Shreveport ○

LOUISIANA
Beaumont
uston
Galveston ○

Baton Rouge ○ Biloxi ○
Jackson ○

Mobile ○ Pensacola ○
New Orleans ■

Gulf of Mexico

Tallahassee ☆
Jacksonville ▣
Gainesville △

Orlando ○

Tampa ■
St. Petersburg ○ **FLORIDA**

Hialeah ○
Hollywood ▣
Miami ■
Fort Lauderdale ○

URBAN POPULATION CENTERS

▣ Over 5,000,000

■ 1,000,000–5,000,000

▣ 500,000–1,000,000

○ 100,000–500,000

☆ State capitals

△ Major university centers

0 ⊢——⊢——⊢——⊢ 300 Miles
0 ⊢——⊢——⊢——⊢ 300 Kilometers

A3

Lake Superior

Lake Huron

Lake Michigan

Lake Ontario

Lake Erie

St. Croix R.

Mississippi R.

St. Croix R.

Iowa R.

Des Moines R.

Cedar R.

Rock R.

Fox R.

Kankakee

Illinois R.

Wabash R.

Scioto R.

Ohio R.

Allegheny R.

APPALACHIAN MOUNTAINS

Adirondack Mts.

Mohawk R.

Hudson R.

Delaware R.

Susquehanna R.

St. Lawrence R.

Kennebeck R.

Connecticut R.

CENTRAL PLAINS

Missouri R.

Osage R.

Ozark Plateau

White R.

S. Francis R.

Arkansas R.

Ouachita R.

Yazoo R.

Tombigbee R.

Red R.

Sabine R.

Mississippi R.

Pearl R.

Alabama R.

Chattahoochee R.

Ohio R.

Cumberland R.

Tennessee R.

Allegheny Mts.

Kanawha R.

APPALACHIAN MOUNTAINS

Blue Ridge Mountains

Saluda R.

Savannah R.

Altamaha R.

Roanoke R.

James R.

Shenandoah Valley

Potomac R.

Chesapeake Bay

ATLANTIC COASTAL PLAIN

COASTAL PLAIN

Galveston Bay

Gulf of Mexico

ATLANTIC OCEAN

50°

45°

40°

35°

30°

25°

65°

70°

75°

90°

85°

80°

A5

World Political Map

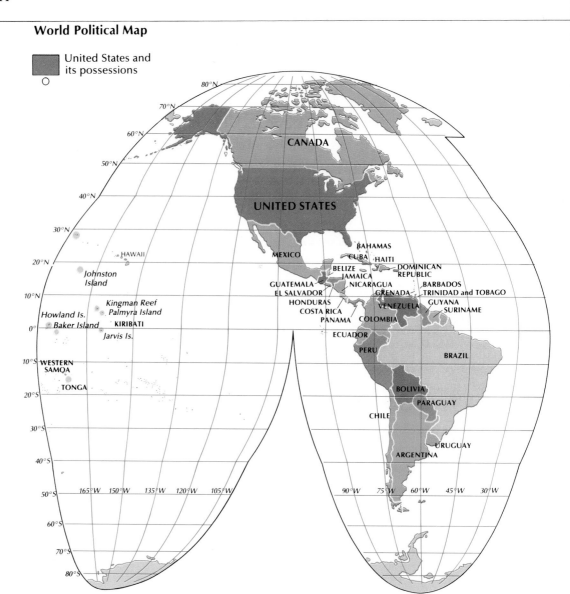

United States and
its possessions

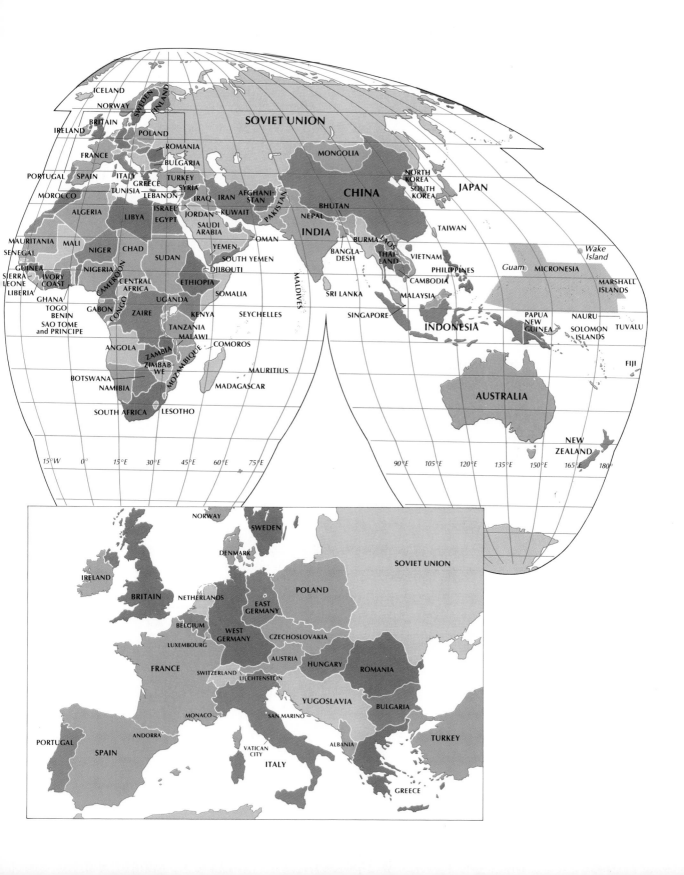

United States Territorial Expansion, 1783–1898

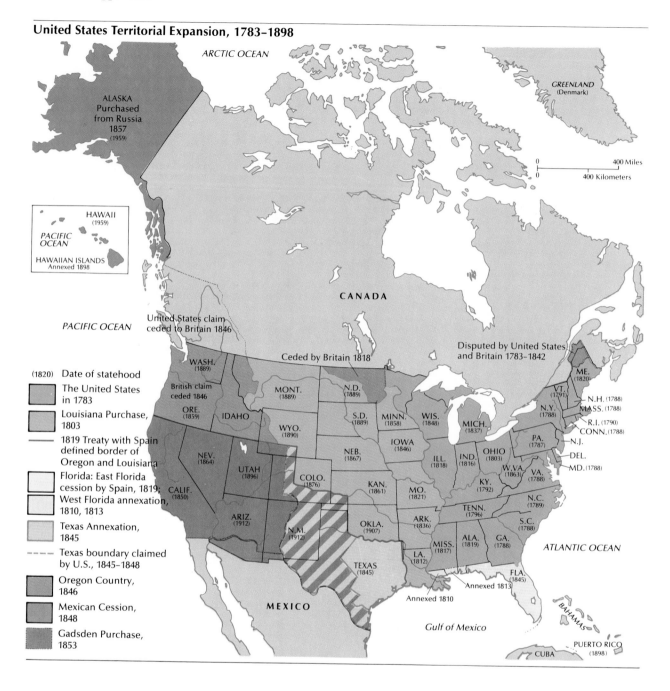

ARCTIC OCEAN

ALASKA
Purchased
from Russia
1857
(1959)

GREENLAND
(Denmark)

0 ————— 400 Miles
0 ————— 400 Kilometers

HAWAII
(1959)

PACIFIC
OCEAN

HAWAIIAN ISLANDS
Annexed 1898

CANADA

PACIFIC OCEAN

United States claim
ceded to Britain 1846

Ceded by Britain 1818

Disputed by United States
and Britain 1783–1842

(1820)   Date of statehood

The United States
in 1783

Louisiana Purchase,
1803

1819 Treaty with Spain
defined border of
Oregon and Louisiana

Florida: East Florida
cession by Spain, 1819;
West Florida annexation,
1810, 1813

Texas Annexation,
1845

- - - -   Texas boundary claimed
by U.S., 1845–1848

Oregon Country,
1846

Mexican Cession,
1848

Gadsden Purchase,
1853

WASH.
(1889)

British claim
ceded 1846

ORE.
(1859)

IDAHO

MONT.
(1889)

WYO.
(1890)

N.D.
(1889)

S.D.
(1889)

MINN.
(1858)

WIS.
(1848)

MICH.
(1837)

ME.
(1820)

VT.
(1791)

N.H. (1788)

MASS. (1788)

N.Y.
(1788)

R.I. (1790)

CONN. (1788)

N.J.

PA.
(1787)

NEV.
(1864)

UTAH
(1896)

COLO.
(1876)

NEB.
(1867)

IOWA
(1846)

ILL.
(1818)

IND.
(1816)

OHIO
(1803)

W.VA.
(1863)

VA.
(1788)

DEL.

MD. (1788)

CALIF.
(1850)

ARIZ.
(1912)

N.M.
(1912)

KAN.
(1861)

MO.
(1821)

KY.
(1792)

N.C.
(1789)

OKLA.
(1907)

ARK.
(1836)

TENN.
(1796)

S.C.
(1788)

MISS.
(1817)

ALA.
(1819)

GA.
(1788)

ATLANTIC OCEAN

TEXAS
(1845)

LA.
(1812)

FLA.
(1845)

Annexed 1813

Annexed 1810

MEXICO

Gulf of Mexico

BAHAMAS

CUBA

PUERTO RICO
(1898)

The Declaration of Independence

In Congress, July 4, 1776,

THE UNANIMOUS DECLARATION OF THE THIRTEEN UNITED STATES OF AMERICA

When, in the course of human events, it becomes necessary for one people to dissolve the political bands which have connected them with another, and to assume, among the powers of the earth, the separate and equal station to which the laws of nature and of nature's God entitle them, a decent respect to the opinions of mankind requires that they should declare the causes which impel them to the separation.

We hold these truths to be self-evident, that all men are created equal; that they are endowed by their Creator with certain unalienable rights; that among these, are life, liberty, and the pursuit of happiness. That, to secure these rights, governments are instituted among men, deriving their just powers from the consent of the governed; that, whenever any form of government becomes destructive of these ends, it is the right of the people to alter or to abolish it, and to institute a new government, laying its foundation on such principles, and organizing its powers in such form, as to them shall seem most likely to effect their safety and happiness. Prudence, indeed, will dictate that governments long established, should not be changed for light and transient causes; and, accordingly, all experience hath shown, that mankind are more disposed to suffer, while evils are sufferable, than to right themselves by abolishing the forms to which they are accustomed. But, when a long train of abuses and usurpations, pursuing invariably the same object, evinces a design to reduce them under absolute despotism, it is their right, it is their duty, to throw off such government and to provide new guards for their future security. Such has been the patient sufferance of these colonies, and such is now the necessity which constrains them to alter their former systems of government. The history of the present King of Great Britain is a history of repeated injuries and usurpations, all having, in direct object, the establishment of an absolute tyranny over these States. To prove this, let facts be submitted to a candid world:

He has refused his assent to laws the most wholesome and necessary for the public good.

He has forbidden his governors to pass laws of immediate and pressing importance, unless suspended in their operation till his assent should be obtained; and, when so suspended, he has utterly neglected to attend to them.

He has refused to pass other laws for the accommodation of large districts of people, unless those people would relinquish the right of representation in the legislature; a right inestimable to them, and formidable to tyrants only.

He has called together legislative bodies at places unusual, uncomfortable, and distant from the depository of their public records, for the sole purpose of fatiguing them into compliance with his measures.

He has dissolved representative houses repeatedly for opposing, with manly firmness, his invasions on the rights of the people.

He has refused, for a long time after such dissolutions, to cause others to be elected; whereby the legislative powers, incapable of annihilation, have returned to the people at large for their exercise; the state remaining, in the meantime, exposed to all the danger of invasion from without, and convulsions within.

He has endeavored to prevent the population of these States; for that purpose, obstructing the laws for naturalization of foreigners, refusing to pass others to encourage their migration hither, and raising the conditions of new appropriations of lands.

He had obstructed the administration of justice, by refusing his assent to laws for establishing judiciary powers.

He has made judges dependent on his will alone, for the tenure of their officers, and the amount and payment of their salaries.

He has erected a multitude of new offices, and sent hither swarms of officers to harass our people, and eat out their substance.

He has kept among us, in time of peace, standing armies, without the consent of our legislatures.

He has affected to render the military independent of, and superior to, the civil power.

He has combined, with others, to subject us to a jurisdiction foreign to our Constitution, and unacknowledged by our laws; giving his assent to their acts of pretended legislation:

For quartering large bodies of armed troops among us:

For protecting them by a mock trial, from punishment, for any murders which they should commit on the inhabitants of these States:

For cutting off our trade with all parts of the world:

For imposing taxes on us without our consent:

For depriving us, in many cases, of the benefit of trial by jury:

For transporting us beyond seas to be tried for pretended offences:

For abolishing the free system of English laws in a neighboring province, establishing therein an arbitrary government, and enlarging its boundaries, so as to render it at once an example and fit instrument for introducing the same absolute rule into these colonies:

For taking away our charters, abolishing our most valuable laws, and altering, fundamentally, the powers of our governments:

For suspending our own legislatures, and declaring themselves invested with power to legislate for us in all cases whatsoever.

He had abdicated government here, by declaring us out of his protection, and waging war against us.

He has plundered our seas, ravaged our coasts, burnt our towns, and destroyed the lives of our people.

He is, at this time, transporting large armies of foreign mercenaries to complete the works of death, desolation, and tyranny, already begun, with circumstances of cruelty and perfidy scarcely paralleled in the most barbarous ages, and totally unworthy the head of a civilized nation.

He has constrained our fellow citizens, taken captive on the high seas, to bear arms against their country, to become the executioners of their friends, and brethren, or to fall themselves by their hands.

He has excited domestic insurrections amongst us, and has endeavored to bring on the inhabitants of our frontiers, the merciless Indian savages, whose known rule of warfare is an undistinguished destruction of all ages, sexes, and conditions.

In every stage of these oppressions, we have petitioned for redress, in the most humble terms; our repeated petitions have been answered only by repeated injury. A prince, whose character is thus marked by every act which may define a tyrant, is unfit to be the ruler of a free people.

Nor have we been wanting in attention to our British brethren. We have warned them, from time to time, of attempts made by their legislature to extend an unwarrantable jurisdiction over us. We have reminded them of the circumstances of our emigration and settlement here. We have appealed to their native justice and magnanimity, and we have conjured them, by the ties of our common kindred, to disavow these usurpations, which would inevitably interrupt our connections and correspondence. They, too, have been deaf to the voice of justice and consanguinity. We must, therefore, acquiesce in the necessity which denounces our separation, and hold them as we hold the rest of mankind, enemies in war, in peace, friends.

We, therefore, the representatives of the United States of America, in general Congress assembled, appealing to the Supreme Judge of the world for the rectitude of our intentions, do, in the name, and by the authority of the good people of these colonies, solemnly publish and declare, that these united colonies are, and of right ought to be, free and independent states: that they are absolved from all allegiance to the British Crown, and that all political connection between them and the state of Great Britain is, and ought to be, totally dissolved; and that, as free and independent states, they have full power to levy war, conclude peace, contract alliances, establish commerce, and to do all other acts and things which independent states may of right do. And, for the support of this declaration, with a firm reliance on the protection of Divine Providence, we mutually pledge to each other our lives, our fortunes, and our sacred honor.

The foregoing Declaration was, by order of Congress, engrossed, and signed by the following members:

JOHN HANCOCK

New Hampshire
Josiah Bartlett
William Whipple
Matthew Thornton

New York
William Floyd
Philip Livingston
Francis Lewis
Lewis Morris

Delaware
Caesar Rodney
George Reed
Thomas M'Kean

North Carolina
William Hooper
Joseph Hewes
John Penn

Massachusetts Bay
Samuel Adams
John Adams
Robert Treat Paine
Elbridge Gerry

New Jersey
Richard Stockton
John Witherspoon
Francis Hopkinson
John Hart
Abraham Clark

Maryland
Samuel Chase
William Paca
Thomas Stone
Charles Carroll,
    of Carrollton

South Carolina
Edward Rutledge
Thomas Heyward, Jr.
Thomas Lynch, Jr.
Arthur Middleton

Rhode Island
Stephen Hopkins
William Ellery

Connecticut
Roger Sherman
Samuel Huntington
William Williams
Oliver Wolcott

Pennsylvania
Robert Morris
Benjamin Rush
Benjamin Franklin
John Morton
George Clymer
James Smith
George Taylor
James Wilson
George Ross

Virginia
George Wythe
Richard Henry Lee
Thomas Jefferson
Benjamin Harrison
Thomas Nelson, Jr.
Francis Lightfoot Lee
Carter Braxton

Georgia
Button Gwinnett
Lyman Hall
George Walton

Resolved, That copies of the Declaration be sent to the several assemblies, conventions, and committees, or councils of safety, and to the several commanding officers of the continental troops; that it be proclaimed in each of the United States, at the head of the army.

The Constitution of the United States of America[1]

We the People of the United States, in Order to form a more perfect Union, establish Justice, insure domestic Tranquility, provide for the common defence, promote the general Welfare, and secure the Blessings of Liberty to ourselves and our Posterity, do ordain and establish this CONSTITUTION for the United States of America.

Article 1

Section 1.

All legislative Powers herein granted shall be vested in a Congress of the United States, which shall consist of a Senate and House of Representatives.

Section 2.

The House of Representatives shall be composed of Members chosen every second Year by the People of the several States, and the Electors in each State shall have the Qualifications requisite for Electors of the most numerous Branch of the State Legislature.

No Person shall be a Representative who shall not have attained to the Age of twenty-five Years, and been seven Years a Citizen of the United States, and who shall not, when elected, be an Inhabitant of that State in which he shall be chosen.

[Representatives and direct Taxes[2] shall be apportioned among the several States which may be included within this Union, according to their respective Numbers, which shall be determined by adding to the whole Number of free Persons, including those bound to Service for a Term of Years, and excluding Indians not taxed, three fifths of all other Persons.][3] The actual Enumeration shall be made within three Years after the first Meeting of the Congress of the United States, and within every subsequent Term of ten Years, in such Manner as they shall by Law direct. The Number of Representatives shall not exceed one for every thirty Thousand, but each State shall have at Least one Representative; and until such enumeration shall be made, the State of New Hampshire shall be entitled to chuse three, Massachusetts eight, Rhode-Island and Providence Plantations one, Connecticut five, New York six, New Jersey four, Pennsylvania eight, Delaware one, Maryland six, Virginia ten, North Carolina five, South Carolina five, and Georgia three.

When vacancies happen in the Representation from any State, the Executive Authority thereof shall issue Writs of Election to fill such Vacancies.

The House of Representatives shall chuse their Speaker and other Officers; and shall have the sole Power of Impeachment.

Section 3.

The Senate of the United States shall be composed of two Senators from each State, chosen by the Legislature thereof, for six Years; and each Senator shall have one Vote.

Immediately after they shall be assembled in Consequence of the first Election, they shall be divided as equally as may be into three Classes. The Seats of the Senators of the first Class shall be vacated at the Expiration of the second Year, of the second Class at the Expiration of the fourth Year, and of the third Class at the Expiration of the sixth Year, so that one-third may be chosen every second Year; and if Vacancies happen by Resignation, or otherwise, during the Recess of the Legislature of any State, the Executive thereof may make temporary Appointments until the next Meeting of the Legislature, which shall then fill such Vacancies.

No Person shall be a Senator who shall not have attained to the Age of thirty Years, and been nine Years a Citizen of the United States, and who shall not, when elected, be an Inhabitant of that State for which he shall be chosen.

The Vice President of the United States shall be President of the Senate, but shall have no vote, unless they be equally divided.

The Senate shall chuse their other Officers, and also a President pro tempore, in the absence of the Vice President, or when he shall exercise the Office of President of the United States.

---

[1] This version, which follows the original Constitution in capitalization and spelling, was published by the United States Department of the Interior, Office of Education, in 1935.

[2] Altered by the Sixteenth Amendment.

[3] Negated by the Fourteenth Amendment.

The Senate shall have the sole Power to try all Impeachments. When sitting for that purpose they shall be on Oath or Affirmation. When the President of the United States is tried, the Chief Justice shall preside: And no person shall be convicted without the Concurrence of two thirds of the Members present.

Judgment in Cases of Impeachment shall not extend further than to removal from Office, and disqualification to hold and enjoy any Office of honor, Trust, or Profit under the United States: but the Party convicted shall nevertheless be liable and subject to Indictment, Trial, Judgment, and Punishment, according to Law.

Section 4.

The Times, Places and Manner of holding Elections for Senators and Representatives, shall be prescribed in each State by the Legislature thereof; but the Congress may at any time by Law make or alter such Regulations, except as to the Places of Chusing Senators.

The Congress shall assemble at least once in every Year, and such Meeting shall be on the first Monday in December, unless they shall by Law appoint a different Day.

Section 5.

Each House shall be the Judge of the Elections, Returns and Qualifications of its own Members, and a Majority of each shall constitute a Quorum to do Business; but a smaller number may adjourn from day to day, and may be authorized to compel the Attendance of absent Members, in such Manner, and under such Penalties, as each House may provide.

Each House may determine the Rules of its Proceedings, punish its Members for disorderly Behaviour, and, with the Concurrence of two thirds, expel a Member.

Each House shall keep a Journal of its Proceedings, and from time to time publish the same, excepting such Parts as may in their Judgment require Secrecy; and the Yeas and Nays of the Members of either House on any question shall, at the Desire of one fifth of those Present, be entered on the Journal.

Neither House, during the Session of Congress, shall, without the Consent of the other, adjourn for more than three days, nor to any other Place than that in which the two Houses shall be sitting.

Section 6.

The Senators and Representatives shall receive a Compensation for their Services, to be ascertained by Law, and paid out of the Treasury of the United States. They shall in all Cases, except Treason, Felony, and Breach of the Peace, be privileged from Arrest during their Attendance at the Session of their respective Houses, and in going to and returning from the same; and for any Speech or Debate in either House, they shall not be questioned in any other Place.

No Senator or Representative shall, during the Time for which he was elected, be appointed to any civil Office under the Authority of the United States, which shall have been created, or the Emoluments whereof shall have been increased, during such time; and no Person holding any Office under the United States shall be a Member of either House during his continuance in Office.

Section 7.

All Bills for raising Revenue shall originate in the House of Representatives; but the Senate may propose or concur with Amendments as on other bills.

Every Bill which shall have passed the House of Representatives and the Senate, shall, before it become a Law, be presented to the President of the United States; If he approve he shall sign it, but if not he shall return it, with his Objections, to that House in which it shall have originated, who shall enter the Objections at large on their Journal, and proceed to reconsider it. If after such Reconsideration two thirds of that House shall agree to pass the bill, it shall be sent, together with the objections, to the other House, by which it shall likewise be reconsidered, and if approved by two thirds of that House, it shall become a Law. But in all such Cases the Votes of both Houses shall be determined by Yeas and Nays, and the Names of the Persons voting for and against the Bill shall be entered on the Journal of each House respectively. If any Bill shall not be returned by the President within ten Days (Sundays excepted) after it shall have been presented to him, the Same shall be a Law, in like Manner as if he had signed it, unless the Congress by their Adjournment prevent its Return, in which Case it shall not be a Law.

Every Order, Resolution, or Vote to which the Concurrence of the Senate and House of Representatives may be necessary (except on a question of Adjournment) shall be presented to the President of the United States; and before the Same shall take

Effect, shall be approved by him, or being disapproved by him, shall be repassed by two thirds of the Senate and House of Representatives, according to the Rules and Limitations prescribed in the Case of a Bill.

Section 8.

The Congress shall have Power To lay and collect Taxes, Duties, Imposts and Excises, to pay the Debts and provide for the common Defence and general Welfare of the United States; but all Duties, Imposts and Excises shall be uniform throughout the United States;

To borrow money on the credit of the United States;

To regulate Commerce with foreign Nations, and among the several States, and with the Indian Tribes;

To establish an uniform rule of Naturalization, and uniform Laws on the subject of Bankruptcies throughout the United States;

To coin Money, regulate the Value thereof, and of foreign Coin, and fix the Standard of Weights and Measures;

To provide for the Punishment of counterfeiting the Securities and current Coin of the United States;

To establish Post Offices and post Roads;

To promote the Progress of Science and useful Arts, by securing for limited Times to Authors and Inventors the exclusive Right to their respective Writings and Discoveries;

To constitute Tribunals inferior to the Supreme Court;

To define and punish Piracies and Felonies committed on the high Seas, and Offenses against the Law of Nations;

To declare War, grant Letters of Marque and Reprisal, and make Rules concerning Captures on Land and Water;

To raise and support Armies, but no Appropriation of Money to that Use shall be for a longer Term than two Years;

To provide and maintain a Navy;

To make Rules for the Government and Regulation of the land and naval forces;

To provide for calling forth the Militia to execute the Laws of the Union, suppress Insurrections and repel Invasions;

To provide for organizing, arming, and disciplining the Militia, and for governing such Part of them as may be employed in the Service of the United States, reserving to the States respectively, the Appointment of the Officers, and the Authority of training the Militia according to the discipline prescribed by Congress;

To exercise exclusive Legislation in all Cases whatsoever, over such District (not exceeding ten Miles square) as may, by Cession of particular States, and the acceptance of Congress, become the Seat of the Government of the United States, and to exercise like Authority over all Places purchased by the Consent of the Legislature of the State in which the Same shall be, for the Erection of Forts, Magazines, Arsenals, Dock-yards, and other needful Buildings;—And

To make all Laws which shall be necessary and proper for carrying into Execution the foregoing Powers, and all other Powers vested by this Constitution in the Government of the United States, or in any Department or Officer thereof.

Section 9.

The Migration or Importation of such Persons as any of the States now existing shall think proper to admit, shall not be prohibited by the Congress prior to the Year one thousand eight hundred and eight, but a tax or duty may be imposed on such Importation, not exceeding ten dollars for each Person.

The privilege of the Writ of Habeas Corpus shall not be suspended, unless when in Cases of Rebellion or Invasion the public Safety may require it.

No bill of Attainder or ex post facto Law shall be passed.

No capitation, or other direct, Tax shall be laid unless in Proportion to the Census or Enumeration herein before directed to be taken.

No Tax or Duty shall be laid on Articles exported from any State.

No Preference shall be given by any Regulation of Commerce or Revenue to the Ports of one State over those of another: nor shall Vessels bound to, or from, one State, be obliged to enter, clear, or pay Duties in another.

No Money shall be drawn from the Treasury, but in Consequence of Appropriations made by Law; and a regular Statement and Account of the Receipts and Expenditures of all public Money shall be published from time to time.

No Title of Nobility shall be granted by the United States: And no Person holding any Office of Profit or Trust under them, shall, without the Consent of the Congress, accept of any present, Emolument, Office, or Title, of any kind whatever, from any King, Prince, or foreign State.

Section 10.

No State shall enter into any Treaty, Alliance, or Confederation; grant Letters of Marque and Reprisal; coin Money; emit Bills of Credit; make any Thing but gold and silver Coin a Tender in Payment of Debts; pass any Bill of Attainder, ex post facto Law, or Law impairing the Obligation of Contracts, or grant any Title of Nobility.

No State shall, without the Consent of the Congress, lay any Imposts or Duties on Imports or Exports, except what may be absolutely necessary for executing its inspection Laws; and the net Produce of all Duties and Imposts, laid by any State on Imports or Exports, shall be for the use of the Treasury of the United States; and all such Laws shall be subject to the Revision and Control of the Congress.

No state shall, without the Consent of Congress, lay any duty of Tonnage, keep Troops, or Ships of War in time of Peace, enter into any Agreement or Compact with another State, or with a foreign Power, or engage in War, unless actually invaded, or in such imminent Danger as will not admit of delay.

Article II

Section 1.

The executive Power shall be vested in a President of the United States of America. He shall hold his Office during the Term of four years, and, together with the Vice President, chosen for the same Term, be elected, as follows:

Each State shall appoint, in such Manner as the Legislature thereof may direct, a Number of Electors, equal to the whole Number of Senators and Representatives to which the State may be entitled in the Congress: but no Senator or Representative, or Person holding an Office of Trust or Profit under the United States, shall be appointed an Elector.

[The Electors shall meet in their respective States, and vote by Ballot for two persons, of whom one at least shall not be an Inhabitant of the same State with themselves. And they shall make a List of all the Persons voted for, and of the Number of Votes for each; which List they shall sign and certify, and transmit sealed to the Seat of the Government of the United States, directed to the President of the Senate. The President of the Senate shall, in the Presence of the Senate and House of Representatives, open all the Certificates, and the Votes shall then be counted. The Person having the greatest Number of Votes shall be the President, if such Number be a Majority of the whole Number of Electors appointed; and if there be more than one who have such Majority, and have an equal Number of Votes, then the House of Representatives shall immediately chuse by Ballot one of them for President; and if no Person have a Majority, then from the five highest on the List the said House shall in like Manner chuse the President. But in chusing the President, the Votes shall be taken by States, the Representation from each State having one Vote; a quorum for this Purpose shall consist of a Member or Members from two-thirds of the States, and a Majority of all the States shall be necessary to a Choice. In every Case, after the Choice of the President, the Person having the greatest Number of Votes of the Electors shall be the Vice President. But if there should remain two or more who have equal votes, the Senate shall chuse from them by Ballot the Vice President.][4]

The Congress may determine the Time of chusing the Electors, and the Day on which they shall give their Votes; which Day shall be the same throughout the United States.

No person except a natural-born Citizen, or a Citizen of the United States, at the time of the Adoption of this Constitution, shall be eligible to the Office of President; neither shall any Person be eligible to that Office who shall not have attained to the Age of thirty-five years, and been fourteen Years a Resident within the United States.

In Case of the Removal of the President from Office, or of his Death, Resignation, or Inability to discharge the Powers and Duties of the said Office, the same shall devolve on the Vice President, and the Congress may by Law provide for the Case of Removal, Death, Resignation, or Inability, both of the President and Vice President, declaring what Officer shall then act as President, and such Officer shall act accordingly, until the disability be removed, or a President shall be elected.

The President shall, at stated Times, receive for his Services a Compensation, which shall neither be increased nor diminished during the Period for which he shall have been elected, and he shall not receive within that Period any other Emolument from the United States, or any of them.

Before he enter on the execution of his Office, he shall take the following Oath or Affirmation:—"I do solemnly swear (or affirm) that I will faithfully execute the Office of President of the United States, and

---

[4] Revised by the Twelfth Amendment.

will, to the best of my Ability, preserve, protect, and defend the Constitution of the United States."

Section 2.

The President shall be Commander in Chief of the Army and Navy of the United States, and of the Militia of the several States, when called into the actual Service of the United States; he may require the Opinion, in writing, of the principal Officer in each of the executive Departments, upon any subject relating to the Duties of their respective Offices, and he shall have Power to Grant Reprieves and Pardons for Offenses against the United States, except in Cases of Impeachment.

He shall have Power, by and with the Advice and Consent of the Senate, to make Treaties, provided two-thirds of the Senators present concur; and he shall nominate, and by and with the Advice and Consent of the Senate, shall appoint Ambassadors, other public Ministers and Consuls, Judges of the supreme Court, and all other Officers of the United States, whose Appointments are not herein otherwise provided for, and which shall be established by Law: but the Congress may by Law vest the Appointment of such inferior Officers, as they think proper, in the President alone, in the Courts of Law, or in the Heads of Departments.

The President shall have Power to fill up all Vacancies that may happen during the Recess of the Senate, by granting Commissions which shall expire at the End of their next Session.

Section 3.

He shall from time to time give to the Congress Information of the State of the Union, and recommend to their Consideration such Measures as he shall judge necessary and expedient; he may, on extraordinary occasions, convene both Houses, or either of them, and in Case of Disagreement between them, with respect to the Time of Adjournment, he may adjourn them to such Time as he shall think proper; he shall receive Ambassadors and other public Ministers; he shall take care that the Laws be faithfully executed, and shall Commission all the Officers of the United States.

Section 4.

The President, Vice President and all civil Officers of the United States, shall be removed from Office on Impeachment for, and Conviction of, Treason, Bribery, or other high Crimes and Misdemeanors.

Article III

Section 1.

The judicial Power of the United States, shall be vested in one supreme Court, and in such inferior Courts as the Congress may from time to time ordain and establish. The Judges, both of the supreme and inferior Courts, shall hold their Offices during good Behaviour, and shall, at stated Times, receive for their Services, a Compensation, which shall not be diminished during their Continuance in Office.

Section 2.

The judicial Power shall extend to all Cases, in Law and Equity, arising under this Constitution, the Laws of the United States, and Treaties made, or which shall be made, under their Authority;—to all Cases affecting ambassadors, other public ministers and consuls;—to all cases of admiralty and maritime Jurisdiction;—to Controversies to which the United States shall be a Party;—to Controversies between two or more States;—between a State and Citizens of another State;[5]—between Citizens of different States—between Citizens of the same State claiming Lands under Grants of different States, and between a State, or the Citizens thereof, and foreign States, Citizens, or Subjects.

In all Cases affecting Ambassadors, other public Ministers and Consuls, and those in which a State shall be Party, the supreme Court shall have original Jurisdiction. In all the other Cases before mentioned, the supreme Court shall have appellate Jurisdiction, both as to Law and Fact, with such Exceptions, and under such Regulations as the Congress shall make.

The trial of all Crimes, except in Cases of Impeachment, shall be by Jury; and such Trial shall be held in the State where the said Crimes shall have been committed; but when not committed within any State, the Trial shall be at such Place or Places as the Congress may by Law have directed.

Section 3.

Treason against the United States, shall consist only in levying War against them, or in adhering to their

---

[5] Qualified by the Eleventh Amendment.

Enemies, giving them Aid and Comfort. No Person shall be convicted of Treason unless on the Testimony of two Witnesses to the same overt Act, or on Confession in open Court.

The Congress shall have power to declare the Punishment of Treason, but no Attainder of Treason shall work Corruption of Blood, or Forfeiture except during the Life of the Person attainted.

Article IV

Section 1.

Full Faith and Credit shall be given in each State to the public Acts, Records, and judicial Proceedings of every other State. And the Congress may by general Laws prescribe the Manner in which such Acts, Records and Proceedings shall be proved, and the Effect thereof.

Section 2.

The Citizens of each State shall be entitled to all Privileges and Immunities of Citizens in the several States.

A Person charged in any State with Treason, Felony, or other Crime, who shall flee from Justice, and be found in another State, shall on demand of the executive Authority of the State from which he fled, be delivered up, to be removed to the State having Jurisdiction of the crime.

No Person held to Service or Labour in one State, under the Laws thereof, escaping into another, shall, in Consequence of any Law or Regulation therein, be discharged from such Service or Labour, but shall be delivered up on Claim of the Party to whom such Service or Labour may be due.

Section 3.

New States may be admitted by the Congress into this Union; but no new State shall be formed or erected within the Jurisdiction of any other State; nor any State be formed by the Junction of two or more States, or parts of States, without the Consent of the Legislatures of the States concerned as well as of the Congress.

The Congress shall have Power to dispose of and make all needful Rules and Regulations respecting the Territory or other Property belonging to the United States; and nothing in this Constitution shall be so construed as to Prejudice any Claims of the United States, or of any particular State.

Section 4.

The United States shall guarantee to every State in this Union a Republican Form of Government, and shall protect each of them against Invasion; and on Application of the Legislature, or of the Executive (when the Legislature cannot be convened) against domestic Violence.

Article V

The Congress, whenever two-thirds of both Houses shall deem it necessary, shall propose Amendments to this Constitution, or, on the Application of the Legislatures of two-thirds of the several States, shall call a Convention for proposing Amendments, which, in either Case, shall be valid to all Intents and Purposes, as part of this Constitution, when ratified by the Legislatures of three-fourths of the several States, or by Conventions in three-fourths thereof, as the one or the other Mode of Ratification may be proposed by the Congress; Provided that no Amendment which may be made prior to the Year One thousand eight hundred and eight shall in any Manner affect the first and fourth Clauses in the Ninth Section of the first Article; and that no State, without its Consent, shall be deprived of its equal Suffrage in the Senate.

Article VI

All Debts contracted and Engagements entered into, before the Adoption of this Constitution, shall be as valid against the United States under this Constitution, as under the Confederation.

This Constitution, and the Laws of the United States which shall be made in Pursuance thereof; and all Treaties made, or which shall be made, under the Authority of the United States, shall be the supreme Law of the Land; and the Judges in every State shall be bound thereby, any Thing in the Constitution or Laws of any State to the Contrary notwithstanding.

The Senators and Representatives before mentioned, and the Members of the several State Legislatures, and all executive and judicial Officers, both of the United States and of the several States, shall be bound by Oath or Affirmation to support this Constitution; but no religious Tests shall ever be required as a qualification to any Office or public Trust under the United States.

Article VII

The Ratification of the Conventions of nine States shall be sufficient for the Establishment of this Constitution between the States so ratifying the same.

George Washington
President and deputy and deputy from Virginia

Done in Convention by the Unanimous Consent of the States present the Seventeenth Day of September in the Year of our Lord one thousand seven hundred and Eighty seven, and of the Independence of the United States of America the Twelfth. In Witness whereof We have hereunto subscribed our Names.[6]

New Hampshire
John Langdon
Nicholas Gilman

New Jersey
William Livingston
David Brearley
William Paterson
Jonathan Dayton

Delaware
George Read
Gunning Bedford, Jr.
John Dickinson
Richard Bassett
Jacob Broom

North Carolina
William Blount
Richard Dobbs
   Spaight
Hugh Williamson

Massachusetts
Nathaniel Gorham
Rufus King

Pennsylvania
Benjamin Franklin
Thomas Mifflin
Robert Morris
George Clymer
Thomas FitzSimons
Jared Ingersoll
James Wilson
Gouverneur Morris

Maryland
James McHenry
Daniel of
   St. Thomas Jenifer
Daniel Carroll

South Carolina
John Rutledge
Charles Cotesworth
   Pinckney
Charles Pinckney
Pierce Butler

Connecticut
William Samuel
   Johnson
Roger Sherman

New York
Alexander Hamilton

Virginia
John Blair
James Madison, Jr.

Georgia
William Few
Abraham Baldwin

Articles in Addition to, and Amendment of, the Constitution of the United States of America, Proposed by Congress, and Ratified by the Legislatures of the Several States, Pursuant to the Fifth Article of the Original Constitution[7]

[Article I]

Congress shall make no law respecting an establishment of religion, or prohibiting the free exercise thereof; or abridging the freedom of speech, or of the press; or the right of the people peaceably to assemble, and to petition the Government for a redress of grievances.

[Article II]

A well regulated Militia, being necessary to the security of a free State, the right of the people to keep and bear Arms shall not be infringed.

[Article III]

No Soldier shall, in time of peace, be quartered in any house, without the consent of the Owner, nor in time of war, but in a manner to be prescribed by law.

[Article IV]

The right of the people to be secure in their persons, houses, papers, and effects, against unreasonable searches and seizures, shall not be violated, and no

---

[6] These are the full names of the signers, which in some cases are not the signatures on the document.

[7] This heading appears only in the joint resolution submitting the first ten amendments.

Warrants shall issue, but upon probable cause, supported by Oath or affirmation, and particularly describing the place to be searched, and the persons or things to be seized.

[Article V]

No person shall be held to answer for a capital or otherwise infamous crime, unless on a presentment or indictment of a Grand Jury, except in cases arising in the land or naval forces, or in the Militia, when in actual service in time of War or public danger; nor shall any person be subject for the same offence to be twice put in jeopardy of life or limb; nor shall be compelled in any criminal case to be a witness against himself, nor be deprived of life, liberty, or property, without due process of law; nor shall private property be taken for public use, without just compensation.

[Article VI]

In all criminal prosecutions, the accused shall enjoy the right to a speedy and public trial, by an impartial jury of the State and district wherein the crime shall have been committed, which district shall have been previously ascertained by law, and to be informed of the nature and cause of the accusation; to be confronted with the witnesses against him; to have compulsory process for obtaining witnesses in his favour, and to have the Assistance of Counsel for his defence.

[Article VII]

In suits at common law, where the value in controversy shall exceed twenty dollars, the right of trial by jury shall be preserved, and no fact tried by a jury, shall be otherwise reexamined in any Court of the United States, than according to the rules of the common law.

[Article VIII]

Excessive bail shall not be required, nor excessive fines imposed, nor cruel and unusual punishments inflicted.

[Article IX]

The enumeration of the Constitution, of certain rights, shall not be construed to deny or disparage others retained by the people.

[Article X]

The powers not delegated to the United States by the Constitution, nor prohibited by it to the States, are reserved to the States respectively, or to the people.
  [Amendments I-X, in force 1791.]

[Article XI][8]

The Judicial power of the United States shall not be construed to extend to any suit in law or equity, commenced or prosecuted against one of the United States by Citizens of another State, or by Citizens or Subjects of any Foreign State.

[Article XII][9]

The Electors shall meet in their respective States and vote by ballot for President and Vice-President, one of whom, at least, shall not be an inhabitant of the same State with themselves; they shall name in their ballots the person voted for as President, and in distinct ballots the person voted for as Vice-President, and they shall make distinct lists of all persons voted for as President, and of all persons voted for as Vice-President, and of the number of votes for each, which lists they shall sign and certify, and transmit sealed to the seal of the government of the United States, directed to the President of the Senate;—The President of the Senate shall, in the presence of the Senate and House of Representatives, open all the certificates and the votes shall then be counted;—The person having the greatest number of votes for President, shall be the President, if such number be a majority of the whole number of Electors appointed; and if no person have such majority, then from the persons having the highest numbers not exceeding three on the list of those voted for as President, the House of Representatives shall choose immediately, by ballot, the President. But in choosing the President, the votes

---

[8] Adopted in 1798.

[9] Adopted in 1804.

shall be taken by states, the representation from each state having one vote; a quorum for this purpose shall consist of a member or members from two-thirds of the states, and a majority of all the states shall be necessary to a choice. And if the House of Representatives shall not choose a President whenever the right of choice shall devolve upon them, before the fourth day of March next following, then the Vice-President shall act as President, as in the case of the death or other constitutional disability of the President.—The person having the greatest number of votes as Vice-President, shall be the Vice-President, if such number be a majority of the whole number of Electors appointed, and if no person have a majority, then from the two highest numbers on the list, the Senate shall choose the Vice-President; a quorum for the purpose shall consist of two-thirds of the whole number of Senators, and a majority of the whole number shall be necessary to a choice. But no person constitutionally ineligible to the office of President shall be eligible to that of Vice-President of the United States.

[Article XIII][10]

Section 1.

Neither slavery nor involuntary servitude, except as a punishment for crime whereof the party shall have been duly convicted, shall exist within the United States, or any place subject to their jurisdiction.

Section 2.

Congress shall have power to enforce this article by appropriate legislation.

[Article XIV][11]

Section 1.

All persons born or naturalized in the United States, and subject to the jurisdiction thereof, are citizens of the United States and of the State wherein they reside. No State shall abridge the privileges or immunities of citizens of the United States; nor shall any State deprive any person of life, liberty, or property, without due process of law; nor deny to any person within its jurisdiction the equal protection of the laws.

Section 2.

Representatives shall be apportioned among the several States according to their respective numbers, counting the whole number of persons in each State, excluding Indians not taxed. But when the right to vote at any election for the choice of electors for President and Vice-President of the United States, Representatives in Congress, the Executive and Judicial officers of a State, or the members of the Legislature thereof, is denied to any of the male inhabitants of such State, being twenty-one years of age, and citizens of the United States, or in any way abridged, except for participation in rebellion, or other crime, the basis of representation therein shall be reduced in the proportion which the number of such male citizens shall bear to the whole number of male citizens twenty-one years of age in such State.

Section 3.

No person shall be a Senator or Representative in Congress, or elector of President and Vice-President, or hold any office, civil or military, under the United States, or under any State, who, having previously taken an oath, as a member of Congress, or as an officer of the United States, or as a member of any State legislature, or as an executive or judicial officer of any State, to support the Constitution of the United States, shall have engaged in insurrection or rebellion against the same, or given aid or comfort to the enemies thereof. But Congress may by a vote of two-thirds of each House, remove such disability.

Section 4.

The validity of the public debt of the United States, authorized by law, including debts incurred for payment of pensions and bounties for services in suppressing insurrection or rebellion, shall not be questioned. But neither the United States nor any State shall assume or pay any debts or obligation incurred in aid of insurrection or rebellion against the United States, or any claim for the loss or emancipation of any slave; but all such debts, obligations, and claims shall be held illegal and void.

Section 5.

The Congress shall have the power to enforce, by appropriate legislation, the provisions of this article.

---

[10] Adopted in 1865.
[11] Adoped in 1868.

[Article XV]¹²

Section 1.

The right of citizens of the United States to vote shall not be denied or abridged by the United States or by any State on account of race, color, or previous condition of servitude—

Section 2.

The Congress shall have power to enforce this article by appropriate legislation.

[Article XVI]¹³

The Congress shall have power to lay and collect taxes on incomes, from whatever source derived, without apportionment among the several States, and without regard to any census or enumeration.

[Article XVII]¹⁴

The Senate of the United States shall be composed of two Senators from each State, elected by the people thereof, for six years; and each Senator shall have one vote. The electors in each State shall have the qualifications requisite for electors of the most numerous branch of the State legislatures.

When vacancies happen in the representation of any State in the Senate, the executive authority of such State shall issue writs of election to fill such vacancies: *Provided,* That the legislature of any State may empower the executive thereof to make temporary appointments until the people fill the vacancies by election as the legislature may direct.

This amendment shall not be so construed as to affect the election or term of any Senator chosen before it becomes valid as part of the Constitution.

[Article XVIII]¹⁵

Section 1.

After one year from the ratification of this article the manufacture, sale, or transportation of intoxicating liquors within, the importation thereof into, or the exportation thereof from the United States and all territory subject to the jurisdiction thereof for beverage purposes is hereby prohibited.

Section 2.

The Congress and the several States shall have concurrent power to enforce this article by appropriate legislation.

Section 3.

This article shall be inoperative unless it shall have been ratified as an amendment to the Constitution by the legislatures of the several States, as provided in the Constitution, within seven years from the date of the submission hereof to the States by the Congress.

[Article XIX]¹⁶

The right of citizens of the United States to vote shall not be denied or abridged by the United States or by any State on account of sex.

Congress shall have power to enforce this article by appropriate legislation.

[Article XX]¹⁷

Section 1.

The terms of the President and Vice-President shall end at noon on the 20th day of January, and the terms of Senators and Representatives at noon on the 3d day of January, of the years in which such terms would have ended if this article had not been ratified; and the terms of their successors shall then begin.

Section 2.

The Congress shall assemble at least once in every year, and such meeting shall begin at noon on the 3d day of January, unless they shall by law appoint a different day.

Section 3.

If, at the time fixed for the beginning of the term of the President, the President elect shall have died, the

---

¹² Adopted in 1870.
¹³ Adopted in 1913.
¹⁴ Adopted in 1913.
¹⁵ Adopted in 1918.

---

¹⁶ Adopted in 1920.
¹⁷ Adopted in 1933.

Vice-President elect shall become President. If a President shall not have been chosen before the time fixed for the beginning of his term or if the President elect shall have failed to qualify, then the Vice-President elect shall act as President until a President shall have qualified; and the Congress may by law provide for the case wherein neither a President elect nor a Vice-President elect shall have qualified, declaring who shall then act as President, or the manner in which one who is to act shall be selected, and such person shall act accordingly until a President or Vice-President shall have qualified.

Section 4.

The Congress may by law provide for the case of the death of any of the persons from whom the House of Representatives may choose a President whenever the right of choice shall have devolved upon them, and for the case of the death of any of the persons from whom the Senate may choose a Vice-President whenever the right of choice shall have devolved upon them.

Section 5.

Sections 1 and 2 shall take effect on the 15th day of October following the ratification of this article.

Section 6.

This article shall be inoperative unless it shall have been ratified as an amendment to the Constitution by the legislatures of three-fourths of the several States within seven years from the date of its submission.

[Article XXI][18]

Section 1.

The eighteenth article of amendment to the Constitution of the United States is hereby repealed.

Section 2.

The transportation or importation into any State, Territory, or possession of the United States for delivery or use therein of intoxicating liquors, in violation of the laws thereof, is hereby prohibited.

Section 3.

This article shall be inoperative unless it shall have been ratified as an amendment to the Constitution by conventions in the several States, as provided in the Constitution, within seven years from the date of the submission hereof to the States by the Congress.

[Article XXII][19]

No person shall be elected to the office of the President more than twice, and no person who has held the office of President, or acted as President, for more than two years of a term to which some other person was elected President shall be elected to the office of the President more than once.

But this Article shall not apply to any person holding the office of President when this Article was proposed by the Congress, and shall not prevent any person who may be holding the office of President, or acting as President, during the term within which this Article becomes operative from holding the office of President or acting as President during the remainder of such term.

This article shall be inoperative unless it shall have been ratified as an amendment to the Constitution by the legislatures of three-fourths of the several states within seven years from the date of its submission to the states by the Congress.

[Article XXIII][20]

Section 1.

The District constituting the seat of Government of the United States shall appoint in such manner as the Congress may direct:

A number of electors of President and Vice-President equal to the whole number of Senators and Representatives in Congress to which the District would be entitled if it were a State, but in no event more than the least populous State; they shall be in addition to those appointed by the States, but they shall be considered, for the purposes of the election of President and Vice-President, to be electors appointed by a State; and they shall meet in the District and perform such duties as provided by the twelfth article of amendment.

---

[18] Adopted in 1933.

[19] Adopted in 1961.

[20] Adopted in 1961.

Section 2.

The Congress shall have power to enforce this article by appropriate legislation.

[Article XXIV][21]

Section 1.

The right of citizens of the United States to vote in any primary or other election for President or Vice President, for electors for President or Vice President, or for Senator or Representative in Congress, shall not be denied or abridged by the United States or any state by reason of failure to pay any poll tax or other tax.

Section 2.

The Congress shall have the power to enforce this article by appropriate legislation.

[Article XXV][22]

Section 1.

In case of the removal of the President from office or of his death or resignation, the Vice President shall become President.

Section 2.

Whenever there is a vacancy in the office of the Vice President, the President shall nominate a Vice President who shall take office upon confirmation by a majority vote of both Houses of Congress.

Section 3.

Whenever the President transmits to the President Pro Tempore of the Senate and the Speaker of the House of Representatives his written declaration that he is unable to discharge the powers and duties of his office, and until he transmits to them a written declaration to the contrary, such powers and duties shall be discharged by the Vice President as Acting President.

Section 4.

Whenever the Vice President and a majority of either the principal officers of the executive departments or of such other body as Congress may by law provide, transmit to the President Pro Tempore of the Senate and the Speaker of the House of Representatives their written declaration that the President is unable to discharge the powers and duties of his office, the Vice President shall immediately assume the powers and duties of the office as Acting President.

Thereafter, when the President transmits to the President Pro Tempore of the Senate and the Speaker of the House of Representatives his written declaration that no inability exists, he shall resume the powers and duties of his office unless the Vice President and a majority of either the principal officers of the executive departments or of such other body as Congress may by law provide, transmit within four days to the President Pro Tempore of the Senate and the Speaker of the House of Representatives their written declaration that the President is unable to discharge the powers and duties of his office. Thereupon Congress shall decide the issue, assembling within forty-eight hours for that purpose if not in session. If the Congress, within twenty-one days after receipt of the latter written declaration, or, if Congress is not in session, within twenty-one days after Congress is required to assemble, determines by two-thirds vote of both Houses that the President is unable to discharge the powers and duties of his office, the Vice President shall continue to discharge the same as Acting President; otherwise, the President shall resume the powers and duties of his office.

[Article XXVI][23]

Section 1.

The right of citizens of the United States, who are eighteen years of age or older, to vote shall not be denied or abridged by the United States or by any State on account of age.

Section 2.

The Congress shall have power to enforce this article by appropriate legislation.

---

[21] Adopted in 1964.
[22] Adopted in 1967.

---

[23] Adopted in 1971.

Presidential Elections

Year	Candidates	Parties	Popular Vote	Percentage of Popular Vote	Electoral Vote	Percentage of Voter Participation
1789	**GEORGE WASHINGTON (Va.)**★				69	
	John Adams				34	
	Others				35	
1792	**GEORGE WASHINGTON (Va.)**				132	
	John Adams				77	
	George Clinton				50	
	Others				5	
1796	**JOHN ADAMS (Mass.)**	Federalist			71	
	Thomas Jefferson	Democratic-Republican			68	
	Thomas Pinckney	Federalist			59	
	Aaron Burr	Dem.-Rep.			30	
	Others				48	
1800	**THOMAS JEFFERSON (Va.)**	Dem.-Rep.			73	
	Aaron Burr	Dem.-Rep.			73	
	John Adams	Federalist			65	
	C. C. Pinckney	Federalist			64	
	John Jay	Federalist			1	
1804	**THOMAS JEFFERSON (Va.)**	Dem.-Rep.			162	
	C. C. Pinckney	Federalist			14	
1808	**JAMES MADISON (Va.)**	Dem.-Rep.			122	
	C. C. Pinckney	Federalist			47	
	George Clinton	Dem.-Rep.			6	
1812	**JAMES MADISON (Va.)**	Dem.-Rep.			128	
	De Witt Clinton	Federalist			89	
1816	**JAMES MONROE (Va.)**	Dem.-Rep.			183	
	Rufus King	Federalist			34	
1820	**JAMES MONROE (Va.)**	Dem.-Rep.			231	
	John Quincy Adams	Dem.-Rep.			1	
1824	**JOHN Q. ADAMS (Mass.)**	Dem.-Rep.	108,740	30.5	84	26.9
	Andrew Jackson	Dem.-Rep.	153,544	43.1	99	
	William H. Crawford	Dem.-Rep.	46,618	13.1	41	
	Henry Clay	Dem.-Rep.	47,136	13.2	37	
1828	**ANDREW JACKSON (Tenn.)**	Democratic	647,286	56.0	178	57.6
	John Quincy Adams	National Republican	508,064	44.0	83	
1832	**ANDREW JACKSON (Tenn.)**	Democratic	687,502	55.0	219	55.4
	Henry Clay	National Republican	530,189	42.4	49	
	John Floyd	Independent			11	
	William Wirt	Anti-Mason	33, 108	2.6	7	

★ State of residence at time of election.

Year	Candidates	Parties	Popular Vote	Percentage of Popular Vote	Electoral Vote	Percentage of Voter Participation
1836	**MARTIN VAN BUREN (N.Y.)**	Democratic	765,483	50.9	170	57.8
	W. H. Harrison	Whig			73	
	Hugh L. White	Whig	739,795	49.1	26	
	Daniel Webster	Whig			14	
	W. P. Magnum	Independent			11	
1840	**WILLIAM H. HARRISON (Ohio)**	Whig	1,274,624	53.1	234	80.2
	Martin Van Buren	Democratic	1,127,781	46.9	60	
	J. G. Birney	Liberty	7,069		—	
1844	**JAMES K. POLK (Tenn.)**	Democratic	1,338,464	49.6	170	78.9
	Henry Clay	Whig	1,300,097	48.1	105	
	J. G. Birney	Liberty	62,300	2.3	—	
1848	**ZACHARY TAYLOR (La.)**	Whig	1,360,967	47.4	163	72.7
	Lewis Cass	Democratic	1,222,342	42.5	127	
	Martin Van Buren	Free-Soil	291,263	10.1	—	
1852	**FRANKLIN PIERCE (N.H.)**	Democratic	1,601,117	50.9	254	69.6
	Winfield Scott	Whig	1,385,453	44.1	42	
	John P. Hale	Free-Soil	155,825	5.0	—	
1856	**JAMES BUCHANAN (Pa.)**	Democratic	1,832,955	45.3	174	78.9
	John C. Frémont	Republican	1,339,932	33.1	114	
	Millard Fillmore	American	871,731	21.6	8	
1860	**ABRAHAM LINCOLN (Ill.)**	Republican	1,865,593	39.8	180	81.2
	Stephen A. Douglas	Democratic	1,382,713	29.5	12	
	John C. Breckinridge	Democratic	848,356	18.1	72	
	John Bell	Union	592,906	12.6	39	
1864	**ABRAHAM LINCOLN (Ill.)**	Republican	2,213,655	55.0	212	73.8
	George B. McClellan	Democratic	1,805,237	45.0	21	
1868	**ULYSSES S. GRANT (Ill.)**	Republican	3,012,833	52.7	214	78.1
	Horatio Seymour	Democratic	2,703,249	47.3	80	
1872	**ULYSSES S. GRANT (Ill.)**	Republican	3,597,132	55.6	286	71.3
	Horace Greeley	Democratic; Liberal Republican	2,834,125	43.9	66	
1876	**RUTHERFORD B. HAYES (Ohio)**	Republican	4,036,298	48.0	185	81.8
	Samuel J. Tilden	Democratic	4,300,590	51.0	184	
1880	**JAMES A. GARFIELD (Ohio)**	Republican	4,454,416	48.5	214	79.4
	Winfield S. Hancock	Democratic	4,444,952	48.1	155	
1884	**GROVER CLEVELAND (N.Y.)**	Democratic	4,874,986	48.5	219	77.5
	James G. Blaine	Republican	4,851,981	48.2	182	
1888	**BENJAMIN HARRISON (Ind.)**	Republican	5,439,853	47.9	233	79.3
	Grover Cleveland	Democratic	5,540,309	48.6	168	
1892	**GROVER CLEVELAND (N.Y.)**	Democratic	5,556,918	46.1	277	74.7
	Benjamin Harrison	Republican	5,176,108	43.0	145	
	James B. Weaver	People's	1,041,028	8.5	22	
1896	**WILLIAM McKINLEY (Ohio)**	Republican	7,104,779	51.1	271	79.3
	William J. Bryan	Democratic-People's	6,502,925	47.7	176	
1900	**WILLIAM McKINLEY (Ohio)**	Republican	7,207,923	51.7	292	73.2
	William J. Bryan	Dem.-Populist	6,358,133	45.5	155	
1904	**THEODORE ROOSEVELT (N.Y.)**	Republican	7,623,486	57.9	336	65.2
	Alton B. Parker	Democratic	5,077,911	37.6	140	
	Eugene V. Debs	Socialist	402,283	3.0	—	

Year	Candidates	Parties	Popular Vote	Percentage of Popular Vote	Electoral Vote	Percentage of Voter Participation
1908	**WILLIAM H. TAFT (Ohio)**	Republican	7,678,908	51.6	321	65.4
	William J. Bryan	Democratic	6,409,104	43.1	162	
	Eugene V. Debs	Socialist	420,793	2.8	—	
1912	**WOODROW WILSON (N.J.)**	Democratic	6,293,454	41.9	435	58.8
	Theodore Roosevelt	Progressive	4,119,538	27.4	88	
	William H. Taft	Republican	3,484,980	23.2	8	
	Eugene V. Debs	Socialist	900,672	6.0	—	
1916	**WOODROW WILSON (N.J.)**	Democratic	9,129,606	49.4	277	61.6
	Charles E. Hughes	Republican	8,538,221	46.2	254	
	A. L. Benson	Socialist	585,113	3.2	—	
1920	**WARREN G. HARDING (Ohio)**	Republican	16,152,200	60.4	404	49.2
	James M. Cox	Democratic	9,147,353	34.2	127	
	Eugene V. Debs	Socialist	919,799	3.4	—	
1924	**CALVIN COOLIDGE (Mass.)**	Republican	15,725,016	54.0	382	48.9
	John W. Davis	Democratic	8,386,503	28.8	136	
	Robert M. LaFollette	Progressive	4,822,856	16.6	13	
1928	**HERBERT HOOVER (Calif.)**	Republican	21,391,381	58.2	444	56.9
	Alfred E. Smith	Democratic	15,016,443	40.9	87	
	Norman Thomas	Socialist	267,835	0.7	—	
1932	**FRANKLIN D. ROOSEVELT (N.Y.)**	Democratic	22,821,857	57.4	472	56.9
	Herbert Hoover	Republican	15,761,841	39.7	59	
	Norman Thomas	Socialist	881,951	2.2	—	
1936	**FRANKLIN D. ROOSEVELT (N.Y.)**	Democratic	27,751,597	60.8	523	61.0
	Alfred M. Landon	Republican	16,679,583	36.5	8	
	William Lemke	Union	882,479	1.9	—	
1940	**FRANKLIN D. ROOSEVELT (N.Y.)**	Democratic	27,244,160	54.8	449	62.5
	Wendell L. Willkie	Republican	22,305,198	44.8	82	
1944	**FRANKLIN D. ROOSEVELT (N.Y.)**	Democratic	25,602,504	53.5	432	55.9
	Thomas E. Dewey	Republican	22,006,285	46.0	99	
1948	**HARRY S TRUMAN (Mo.)**	Democratic	24,105,695	49.5	304	53.0
	Thomas E. Dewey	Republican	21,969,170	45.1	189	
	J. Strom Thurmond	State-Rights Democratic	1,169,021	2.4	38	
	Henry A. Wallace	Progressive	1,156,103	2.4	—	
1952	**DWIGHT D. EISENHOWER (N.Y.)**	Republican	33,936,252	55.1	442	63.3
	Adlai E. Stevenson	Democratic	27,314,992	44.4	89	
1956	**DWIGHT D. EISENHOWER (N.Y.)**	Republican	35,575,420	57.6	457	60.6
	Adlai E. Stevenson	Democratic	26,033,066	42.1	73	
	Other	—	—	—	1	
1960	**JOHN F. KENNEDY (Mass.)**	Democratic	34,227,096	49.9	303	62.8
	Richard M. Nixon	Republican	34,108,546	49.6	219	
	Other	—	—	—	15	
1964	**LYNDON B. JOHNSON (Tex.)**	Democratic	43,126,506	61.1	486	61.7
	Barry M. Goldwater	Republican	27,176,799	38.5	52	

Year	Candidates	Parties	Popular Vote	Percentage of Popular Vote	Electoral Vote	Percentage of Voter Participation
1968	**RICHARD M. NIXON (N.Y.)**	Republican	31,770,237	43.4	301	60.6
	Hubert H. Humphrey	Democratic	31,270,533	42.7	191	
	George Wallace	American Indep.	9,906,141	13.5	46	
1972	**RICHARD M. NIXON (N.Y.)**	Republican	47,169,911	60.7	520	55.2
	George S. McGovern	Democratic	29,170,383	37.5	17	
	Other	—	—		1	
1976	**JIMMY CARTER (Ga.)**	Democratic	40,828,587	50.0	297	53.5
	Gerald R. Ford	Republican	39,147,613	47.9	241	
	Other	—	1,575,459	2.1	—	
1980	**RONALD REAGAN (Calif.)**	Republican	43,901,812	50.7	489	52.6
	Jimmy Carter	Democratic	35,483,820	41.0	49	
	John B. Anderson	Independent	5,719,722	6.6	—	
	Ed Clark	Libertarian	921,188	1.1	—	
1984	**RONALD REAGAN (Calif.)**	Republican	54,455,075	59.0	525	53.3
	Walter Mondale	Democratic	37,577,185	41.0	13	

Vice Presidents and Cabinet Members

The Washington Administration (1789–1797)

Vice President	John Adams	1789–1797
Secretary of State	Thomas Jefferson	1789–1793
	Edmund Randolph	1794–1795
	Timothy Pickering	1795–1797
Secretary of Treasury	Alexander Hamilton	1789–1795
	Oliver Wolcott	1795–1797
Secretary of War	Henry Knox	1789–1794
	Timothy Pickering	1795–1796
	James McHenry	1796–1797
Attorney General	Edmund Randolph	1789–1793
	William Bradford	1794–1795
	Charles Lee	1795–1797
Postmaster General	Samuel Osgood	1789–1791
	Timothy Pickering	1791–1794
	Joseph Habersham	1795–1797

The John Adams Administration (1797–1801)

Vice President	Thomas Jefferson	1797–1801
Secretary of State	Timothy Pickering	1797–1800
	John Marshall	1800–1801
Secretary of Treasury	Oliver Wolcott	1797–1800
	Samuel Dexter	1800–1801
Secretary of War	James McHenry	1797–1800
	Samuel Dexter	1800–1801
Attorney General	Charles Lee	1797–1801
Postmaster General	Joseph Habersham	1797–1801
Secretary of Navy	Benjamin Stoddert	1798–1801

The Jefferson Administration (1801–1809)

Vice President	Aaron Burr	1801–1805
	George Clinton	1805–1809
Secretary of State	James Madison	1801–1809
Secretary of Treasury	Samuel Dexter	1801
	Albert Gallatin	1801–1809
Secretary of War	Henry Dearborn	1801–1809
Attorney General	Levi Lincoln	1801–1805
	Robert Smith	1805
	John Breckinridge	1805–1806
	Caesar Rodney	1807–1809
Postmaster General	Joseph Habersham	1801
	Gideon Granger	1801–1809
Secretary of Navy	Robert Smith	1801–1809

The Madison Administration (1809–1817)

Vice President	George Clinton	1809–1813
	Elbridge Gerry	1813–1817
Secretary of State	Robert Smith	1809–1811
	James Monroe	1811–1817
Secretary of Treasury	Albert Gallatin	1809–1813
	George Campbell	1814
	Alexander Dallas	1814–1816
	William Crawford	1816–1817
Secretary of War	William Eustis	1809–1812
	John Armstrong	1813–1814
	James Monroe	1814–1815
	William Crawford	1815–1817
Attorney General	Caesar Rodney	1809–1811
	William Pinkney	1811–1814
	Richard Rush	1814–1817
Postmaster General	Gideon Granger	1809–1814
	Return Meigs	1814–1817
Secretary of Navy	Paul Hamilton	1809–1813
	William Jones	1813–1814
	Benjamin Crowninshield	1814–1817

The Monroe Administration (1817–1825)

Vice President	Daniel Tompkins	1817–1825
Secretary of State	John Quincy Adams	1817–1825
Secretary of Treasury	William Crawford	1817–1825
Secretary of War	George Graham	1817
	John C. Calhoun	1817–1825
Attorney General	Richard Rush	1817
	William Wirt	1817–1825
Postmaster General	Return Meigs	1817–1823
	John McLean	1823–1825
Secretary of Navy	Benjamin Crowninshield	1817–1818
	Smith Thompson	1818–1823
	Samuel Southard	1823–1825

The John Quincy Adams Administration (1825–1829)

Vice President	John C. Calhoun	1825–1829
Secretary of State	Henry Clay	1825–1829
Secretary of Treasury	Richard Rush	1825–1829
Secretary of War	James Barbour	1825–1828
	Peter Porter	1828–1829
Attorney General	William Wirt	1825–1829
Postmaster General	John McLean	1825–1829
Secretary of Navy	Samuel Southard	1825–1829

The Jackson Administration (1829–1837)

Vice President	John C. Calhoun	1829–1833
	Martin Van Buren	1833–1837
Secretary of State	Martin Van Buren	1829–1831
	Edward Livingston	1831–1833
	Louis McLane	1833–1834
	John Forsyth	1834–1837
Secretary of Treasury	Samuel Ingham	1829–1831
	Louis McLane	1831–1833
	William Duane	1833
	Roger B. Taney	1833–1834
	Levi Woodbury	1834–1837
Secretary of War	John H. Eaton	1829–1831
	Lewis Cass	1831–1837
	Benjamin Butler	1837
Attorney General	John M. Berrien	1829–1831
	Roger B. Taney	1831–1833
	Benjamin Butler	1833–1837
Postmaster General	William Barry	1829–1835
	Amos Kendall	1835–1837
Secretary of Navy	John Branch	1829–1831
	Levi Woodbury	1831–1834
	Mahlon Dickerson	1834–1837

The Van Buren Administration (1837–1841)

Vice President	Richard M. Johnson	1837–1841
Secretary of State	John Forsyth	1837–1841
Secretary of Treasury	Levi Woodbury	1837–1841
Secretary of War	Joel Poinsett	1837–1841
Attorney General	Benjamin Butler	1837–1838
	Felix Grundy	1838–1840
	Henry D. Gilpin	1840–1841
Postmaster General	Amos Kendall	1837–1840
	John M. Niles	1840–1841
Secretary of Navy	Mahlon Dickerson	1837–1838
	James Paulding	1838–1841

The William Harrison Administration (1841)

Vice President	John Tyler	1841
Secretary of State	Daniel Webster	1841
Secretary of Treasury	Thomas Ewing	1841
Secretary of War	John Bell	1841
Attorney General	John J. Crittenden	1841
Postmaster General	Francis Granger	1841
Secretary of Navy	George Badger	1841

The Tyler Administration (1841–1845)

Vice President	None	
Secretary of State	Daniel Webster	1841–1843
	Hugh S. Legaré	1843
	Abel P. Upshur	1843–1844
	John C. Calhoun	1844–1845
Secretary of Treasury	Thomas Ewing	1841
	Walter Forward	1841–1843
	John C. Spencer	1843–1844
	George Bibb	1844–1845
Secretary of War	John Bell	1841
	John C. Spencer	1841–1843
	James M. Porter	1843–1844
	William Wilkins	1844–1845
Attorney General	John J. Crittenden	1841
	Hugh S. Legaré	1841–1843
	John Nelson	1843–1845
Postmaster General	Francis Granger	1841
	Charles Wickliffe	1841
Secretary of Navy	George Badger	1841
	Abel P. Upshur	1841
	David Henshaw	1843–1844
	Thomas Gilmer	1844
	John Y. Mason	1844–1845

The Polk Administration (1845–1849)

Vice President	George M. Dallas	1845–1849
Secretary of State	James Buchanan	1845–1849
Secretary of Treasury	Robert J. Walker	1845–1849
Secretary of War	William L. Marcy	1845–1849
Attorney General	John Y. Mason	1845–1846
	Nathan Clifford	1846–1848
	Isaac Toucey	1848–1849
Postmaster General	Cave Johnson	1845–1849
Secretary of Navy	George Bancroft	1845–1846
	John Y. Mason	1846–1849

The Taylor Administration (1849–1850)

Vice President	Millard Fillmore	1849–1850
Secretary of State	John M. Clayton	1849–1850
Secretary of Treasury	William Meredith	1849–1850
Secretary of War	George Crawford	1849–1850
Attorney General	Reverdy Johnson	1849–1850
Postmaster General	Jacob Collamer	1849–1850
Secretary of Navy	William Preston	1849–1850
Secretary of Interior	Thomas Ewing	1849–1850

The Fillmore Administration (1850–1853)

Vice President	None	
Secretary of State	Daniel Webster	1850–1852
	Edward Everett	1852–1853
Secretary of Treasury	Thomas Corwin	1850–1853

The Fillmore Administration (1850–1853) *continued*

Secretary of War	Charles Conrad	1850–1853
Attorney General	John J. Crittenden	1850–1853
Postmaster General	Nathan Hall	1850–1852
	Sam D. Hubbard	1852–1853
Secretary of Navy	William A. Graham	1850–1852
	John P. Kennedy	1852–1853
Secretary of Interior	Thomas McKennan	1850
	Alexander Stuart	1850–1853

The Pierce Administration (1853–1857)

Vice President	William R. King	1853–1857
Secretary of State	William L. Marcy	1853–1857
Secretary of Treasury	James Guthrie	1853–1857
Secretary of War	Jefferson Davis	1853–1857
Attorney General	Caleb Cushing	1853–1857
Postmaster General	James Campbell	1853–1857
Secretary of Navy	James C. Dobbin	1853–1857
Secretary of Interior	Robert McClelland	1853–1857

The Buchanan Administration (1857–1861)

Vice President	John C. Breckinridge	1857–1861
Secretary of State	Lewis Cass	1857–1860
	Jeremiah S. Black	1860–1861
Secretary of Treasury	Howell Cobb	1857–1860
	Philip Thomas	1860–1861
	John A. Dix	1861
Secretary of War	John B. Floyd	1857–1861
	Joseph Holt	1861
Attorney General	Jeremiah S. Black	1857–1860
	Edwin M. Stanton	1860–1861
Postmaster General	Aaron V. Brown	1857–1859
	Joseph Holt	1859–1861
	Horatio King	1861
Secretary of Navy	Isaac Toucey	1857–1861
Secretary of Interior	Jacob Thompson	1857–1861

The Lincoln Administration (1861–1865)

Vice President	Hannibal Hamlin	1861–1865
	Andrew Johnson	1865
Secretary of State	William H. Seward	1861–1865
Secretary of Treasury	Samuel P. Chase	1861–1864
	William P. Fessenden	1864–1865
	Hugh McCulloch	1865
Secretary of War	Simon Cameron	1861–1862
	Edwin M. Stanton	1862–1865
Attorney General	Edward Bates	1861–1864
	James Speed	1864–1865

Postmaster General	Horatio King	1861
	Montgomery Blair	1861–1864
	William Dennison	1864–1865
Secretary of Navy	Gideon Welles	1861–1865
Secretary of Interior	Caleb B. Smith	1861–1863
	John P. Usher	1863–1865

The Andrew Johnson Administration (1865–1869)

Vice President	None	
Secretary of State	William H. Seward	1865–1869
Secretary of Treasury	Hugh McCulloch	1865–1869
Secretary of War	Edwin M. Stanton	1865–1867
	Ulysses S. Grant	1867–1868
	Lorenzo Thomas	1868
	John M. Schofield	1868–1869
Attorney General	James Speed	1865–1866
	Henry Stanbery	1866–1868
	William M. Evarts	1868–1869
Postmaster General	William Dennison	1865–1866
	Alexander Randall	1866–1869
Secretary of Navy	Gideon Welles	1865–1869
Secretary of Interior	John P. Usher	1865
	James Harlan	1865–1866
	Orville H. Browning	1866–1869

The Grant Administration (1869–1877)

Vice President	Schuyler Colfax	1869–1873
	Henry Wilson	1873–1877
Secretary of State	Elihu B. Washburne	1869
	Hamilton Fish	1869–1877
Secretary of Treasury	George S. Boutwell	1869–1873
	William Richardson	1873–1874
	Benjamin Bristow	1874–1876
	Lot M. Morrill	1876–1877
Secretary of War	John A. Rawlins	1869
	William T. Sherman	1869
	William W. Belknap	1869–1876
	Alphonso Taft	1876
	James D. Cameron	1876–1877
Attorney General	Ebenezer Hoar	1869–1870
	Amos T. Ackerman	1870–1871
	G. H. Williams	1871–1875
	Edwards Pierrepont	1875–1876
	Alphonso Taft	1876–1877
Postmaster General	John A. J. Creswell	1869–1874
	James W. Marshall	1874
	Marshall Jewell	1874–1876
	James N. Tyner	1876–1877
Secretary of Navy	Adolph E. Borie	1869
	George M. Robeson	1869–1877
Secretary of Interior	Jacob D. Cox	1969–1870
	Columbus Delano	1870–1875
	Zachariah Chandler	1875–1877

The Hayes Administration (1877–1881)

Vice President	William A. Wheeler	1877–1881
Secretary of State	William M. Evarts	1877–1881
Secretary of Treasury	John Sherman	1877–1881
Secretary of War	George W. McCrary	1877–1879
	Alex Ramsey	1879–1881
Attorney General	Charles Devens	1877–1881
Postmaster General	David M. Key	1877–1880
	Horace Maynard	1880–1881
Secretary of Navy	Richard W. Thompson	1877–1880
	Nathan Goff, Jr.	1881
Secretary of Interior	Carl Schurz	1877–1881

The Garfield Administration (1881)

Vice President	Chester A. Arthur	1881
Secretary of State	James G. Blaine	1881
Secretary of Treasury	William Windom	1881
Secretary of War	Robert T. Lincoln	1881
Attorney General	Wayne MacVeagh	1881
Postmaster General	Thomas L. James	1881
Secretary of Navy	William H. Hunt	1881
Secretary of Interior	Samuel J. Kirkwood	1881

The Arthur Administration (1881–1885)

Vice President	None	
Secretary of State	F. T. Frelinghuysen	1881–1885
Secretary of Treasury	Charles J. Folger	1881–1884
	Walter Q. Gresham	1884
	Hugh McCulloch	1884–1885
Secretary of War	Robert T. Lincoln	1881–1885
Attorney General	Benjamin H. Brewster	1881–1885
Postmaster General	Timothy O. Howe	1881–1883
	Walter Q. Gresham	1883–1884
	Frank Hatton	1884–1885
Secretary of Navy	William H. Hunt	1881–1882
	William E. Chandler	1882–1885
Secretary of Interior	Samuel J. Kirkwood	1881–1882
	Henry M. Teller	1882–1885

The Cleveland Administration (1885–1889)

Vice President	Thomas A. Hendricks	1885–1889
Secretary of State	Thomas F. Bayard	1885–1889
Secretary of Treasury	Daniel Manning	1885–1887
	Charles S. Fairchild	1887–1889
Secretary of War	William C. Endicott	1885–1889
Attorney General	Augustus H. Garland	1885–1889
Postmaster General	William F. Vilas	1885–1888
	Don M. Dickinson	1888–1889
Secretary of Navy	William C. Whitney	1885–1889
Secretary of Interior	Lucius Q. C. Lamar	1885–1888
	William F. Vilas	1888–1889
Secretary of Agriculture	Norman J. Colman	1889

The Benjamin Harrison Administration (1889–1893)

Vice President	Levi P. Morton	1889–1893
Secretary of State	James G. Blaine	1889–1892
	John W. Foster	1892–1893
Secretary of Treasury	William Windom	1889–1891
	Charles Foster	1891–1893
Secretary of War	Redfield Proctor	1889–1891
	Stephen B. Elkins	1891–1893
Attorney General	William H. H. Miller	1889–1891
Postmaster General	John Wanamaker	1889–1893
Secretary of Navy	Benjamin F. Tracy	1889–1893
Secretary of Interior	John W. Noble	1889–1893
Secretary of Agriculture	Jeremiah M. Rusk	1889–1893

The Cleveland Administration (1893–1897)

Vice President	Adlai E. Stevenson	1893–1897
Secretary of State	Walter Q. Gresham	1893–1895
	Richard Olney	1895–1897
Secretary of Treasury	John G. Carlisle	1893–1897
Secretary of War	Daniel S. Lamont	1893–1897
Attorney General	Richard Olney	1893–1895
	James Harmon	1895–1897
Postmaster General	Wilson S. Bissell	1893–1895
	William L. Wilson	1895–1897
Secretary of Navy	Hilary A. Herbert	1893–1897
Secretary of Interior	Hoke Smith	1893–1896
	David R. Francis	1896–1897
Secretary of Agriculture	Julius S. Morton	1893–1897

The McKinley Administration (1897–1901)

Vice President	Garret A. Hobart	1897–1901
	Theodore Roosevelt	1901
Secretary of State	John Sherman	1897–1898
	William R. Day	1898
	John Hay	1898–1901
Secretary of Treasury	Lyman J. Gage	1897–1901
Secretary of War	Russell A. Alger	1897–1899
	Elihu Root	1899–1901
Attorney General	Joseph McKenna	1897–1898
	John W. Griggs	1898–1901
	Philander C. Knox	1901

The McKinley Administration (1897–1901) *continued*

Postmaster General	James A. Gary	1897–1898
	Charles E. Smith	1898–1901
Secretary of Navy	John D. Long	1897–1901
Secretary of Interior	Cornelius N. Bliss	1897–1899
	Ethan A. Hitchcock	1899–1901
Secretary of Agriculture	James Wilson	1897–1901

The Theodore Roosevelt Administration (1901–1909)

Vice President	Charles Fairbanks	1905–1909
Secretary of State	John Hay	1901–1905
	Elihu Root	1905–1909
	Robert Bacon	1909
Secretary of Treasury	Lyman J. Gage	1901–1902
	Leslie M. Shaw	1902–1907
	George B. Cortelyou	1907–1909
Secretary of War	Elihu Root	1901–1904
	William H. Taft	1904–1908
	Luke E. Wright	1908–1909
Attorney General	Philander C. Knox	1901–1904
	William H. Moody	1904–1906
	Charles J. Bonaparte	1906–1909
Postmaster General	Charles E. Smith	1901–1902
	Henry C. Payne	1902–1904
	Robert J. Wynne	1904–1905
	George B. Cortelyou	1905–1907
	George von L. Meyer	1907–1909
Secretary of Navy	John D. Long	1901–1902
	William H. Moody	1902–1904
	Paul Morton	1904–1905
	Charles J. Bonaparte	1905–1906
	Victor H. Metcalf	1906–1908
	Truman H. Newberry	1908–1909
Secretary of Interior	Ethan A. Hitchcock	1901–1907
	James R. Garfield	1907–1909
Secretary of Agriculture	James Wilson	1901–1909
Secretary of Labor and Commerce	George B. Cortelyou	1903–1904
	Victor H. Metcalf	1904–1906
	Oscar S. Straus	1906–1909
	Charles Nagel	1909

The Taft Administration (1909–1913)

Vice President	James S. Sherman	1909–1913
Secretary of State	Philander C. Knox	1909–1913
Secretary of Treasury	Franklin MacVeagh	1909–1913
Secretary of War	Jacob M. Dickinson	1909–1911
	Henry L. Stimson	1911–1913
Attorney General	George W. Wickersham	1909–1913
Postmaster General	Frank H. Hitchcock	1909–1913
Secretary of Navy	George von L. Meyer	1909–1913
Secretary of Interior	Richard A. Ballinger	1909–1911
	Walter L. Fisher	1911–1913
Secretary of Agriculture	James Wilson	1909–1913
Secretary of Labor and Commerce	Charles Nagel	1909–1913

The Wilson Administration (1913–1921)

Vice President	Thomas R. Marshall	1913–1921
Secretary of State	William J. Bryan	1913–1915
	Robert Lansing	1915–1920
	Bainbridge Colby	1920–1921
Secretary of Treasury	William G. McAdoo	1913–1918
	Carter Glass	1918–1920
	David F. Houston	1920–1921
Secretary of War	Lindley M. Garrison	1913–1916
	Newton D. Baker	1916–1921
Attorney General	James C. McReyolds	1913–1914
	Thomas W. Gregory	1914–1919
	A. Mitchell Palmer	1919–1921
Postmaster General	Albert S. Burleson	1913–1921
Secretary of Navy	Josephus Daniels	1913–1921
Secretary of Interior	Franklin K. Lane	1913–1920
	John B. Payne	1920–1921
Secretary of Agriculture	David F. Houston	1913–1920
	Edwin T. Meredith	1920–1921
Secretary of Commerce	William C. Redfield	1913–1919
	Joshua W. Alexander	1919–1921
Secretary of Labor	William B. Wilson	1913–1921

The Harding Administration (1921–1923)

Vice President	Calvin Coolidge	1921–1923
Secretary of State	Charles E. Hughes	1921–1923
Secretary of Treasury	Andrew Mellon	1921–1923
Secretary of War	John W. Weeks	1921–1923
Attorney General	Harry M. Daugherty	1921–1923
Postmaster General	Will H. Hays	1921–1922
	Hubert Work	1922–1923
	Harry S. New	1923
Secretary of Navy	Edwin Denby	1921–1923
Secretary of Interior	Albert B. Fall	1921–1923
	Hubert Work	1923
Secretary of Agriculture	Henry C. Wallace	1921–1923
Secretary of Commerce	Herbert C. Hoover	1921–1923
Secretary of Labor	James J. Davis	1921–1923

The Coolidge Administration (1923–1929)

Vice President	Charles G. Dawes	1925–1929
Secretary of State	Charles E. Hughes	1923–1925
	Frank B. Kellogg	1925–1929

Secretary of Treasury	Andrew Mellon	1923–1929
Secretary of War	John W. Weeks	1923–1925
	Dwight F. Davis	1925–1929
Attorney General	Henry M. Daugherty	1923–1924
	Harlan F. Stone	1924–1925
	John G. Sargent	1925–1929
Postmaster General	Harry S. New	1923–1929
Secretary of Navy	Edwin Derby	1923–1924
	Curtis D. Wilbur	1924–1929
Secretary of Interior	Hubert Work	1923–1928
	Roy O. West	1928–1929
Secretary of Agriculture	Henry C. Wallace	1923–1924
	Howard M. Gore	1924–1925
	William M. Jardine	1925–1929
Secretary of Commerce	Herbert C. Hoover	1923–1928
	William F. Whiting	1928–1929
Secretary of Labor	James J. Davis	1923–1929

The Hoover Administration (1929–1933)

Vice President	Charles Curtis	1929–1933
Secretary of State	Henry L. Stimson	1929–1933
Secretary of Treasury	Andrew Mellon	1929–1932
	Ogden L. Mills	1932–1933
Secretary of War	James W. Good	1929
	Patrick J. Hurley	1929–1933
Attorney General	William D. Mitchell	1929–1933
Postmaster General	Walter F. Brown	1929–1933
Secretary of Navy	Charles F. Adams	1929–1933
Secretary of Interior	Ray L. Wilbur	1929–1933
Secretary of Agriculture	Arthur M. Hyde	1929–1933
Secretary of Commerce	Robert P. Lamont	1929–1932
	Roy D. Chapin	1932–1933
Secretary of Labor	James J. Davis	1929–1930
	William N. Doak	1930–1933

The Franklin D. Roosevelt Administration (1933–1945)

Vice President	John Nance Garner	1933–1941
	Henry A. Wallace	1941–1945
	Harry S. Truman	1945
Secretary of State	Cordell Hull	1933–1944
	Edward R. Stettinius, Jr.	1944–1945
Secretary of Treasury	William H. Woodin	1933–1934
	Henry Morgenthau, Jr.	1934–1945
Secretary of War	George H. Dern	1933–1936
	Henry A. Woodring	1936–1940
	Henry L. Stimson	1940–1945
Attorney General	Homer S. Cummings	1933–1939
	Frank Murphy	1939–1940
	Robert H. Jackson	1940–1941

Attorney General	Francis Biddle	1941–1945
Postmaster General	James A. Farley	1933–1940
	Frank C. Walker	1940–1945
Secretary of Navy	Claude A. Swanson	1933–1940
	Charles Edison	1940
	Frank Knox	1940–1944
	James V. Forrestal	1944–1945
Secretary Interior	Harold L. Ickes	1933–1945
Secretary of Agriculture	Henry A. Wallace	1933–1940
	Claude R. Wickard	1940–1945
Secretary of Commerce	Daniel C. Roper	1933–1939
	Harry L. Hopkins	1939–1940
	Jesse Jones	1940–1945
	Henry A. Wallace	1945
Secretary of Labor	Frances Perkins	1933–1945

The Truman Administration (1945–1953)

Vice President	Alben W. Barkley	1949–1953
Secretary of State	Edward R. Stettinius, Jr.	1945
	James F. Byrnes	1945–1947
	George C. Marshall	1947–1949
	Dean G. Acheson	1949–1953
Secretary of Treasury	Fred M. Vinson	1945–1946
	John W. Snyder	1946–1953
Secretary of War	Robert P. Patterson	1945–1947
	Kenneth C. Royall	1947
Attorney General	Tom C. Clark	1945–1949
	J. Howard McGrath	1949–1952
	James P. McGranery	1952–1953
Postmaster General	Frank C. Walker	1945
	Robert E. Hannegan	1945–1947
	Jesse M. Donaldson	1947–1953
Secretary of Navy	James V. Forrestal	1945–1947
Secretary of Interior	Harold L. Ickes	1945–1946
	Julius A. Krug	1946–1949
	Oscar L. Chapman	1949–1953
Secretary of Agriculture	Clinton P. Anderson	1945–1948
	Charles F. Brannan	1948–1953
Secretary of Commerce	Henry A. Wallace	1945–1946
	W. Averell Harriman	1946–1948
	Charles W. Sawyer	1948–1953
Secretary of Labor	Lewis B. Schwellenbach	1945–1948
	Maurice J. Tobin	1948–1953
Secretary of Defense	James V. Forrestal	1947–1949
	Louis A. Johnson	1949–1950
	George C. Marshall	1950–1951
	Robert A. Lovett	1951–1953

The Eisenhower Administration (1953–1961)

Vice President	Richard M. Nixon	1953–1961
Secretary of State	John Foster Dulles	1953–1959
	Christian A. Herter	1959–1961
Secretary of Treasury	George M. Humphrey	1953–1957
	Robert B. Anderson	1957–1961

The Eisenhower Administration (1953–1961)
continued

Attorney General	Herbert Brownell, Jr.	1953–1958
	William P. Rogers	1958–1961
Postmaster General	Arthur E. Summerfield	1953–1961
Secretary of Interior	Douglas McKay	1953–1956
	Fred A. Seaton	1956–1961
Secretary of Agriculture	Ezra T. Benson	1953–1961
Secretary of Commerce	Sinclair Weeks	1953–1958
	Lewis L. Strauss	1958–1959
	Frederick H. Mueller	1959–1961
Secretary of Labor	Martin P. Durkin	1953
	James P. Mitchell	1953–1961
Secretary of Defense	Charles E. Wilson	1953–1957
	Neil H. McElroy	1957–1959
	Thomas S. Gates Jr.	1959–1961
Secretary of Health, Education, and Welfare	Oveta Culp Hobby	1953–1955
	Marion B. Folsom	1955–1958
	Arthur S. Flemming	1958–1961

The Kennedy Administration (1961–1963)

Vice President	Lyndon B. Johnson	1961–1963
Secretary of State	Dean Rusk	1961–1963
Secretary of Treasury	C. Douglas Dillon	1961–1963
Attorney General	Robert F. Kennedy	1961–1963
Postmaster General	J. Edward Day	1961–1963
	John A. Gronouski	1963
Secretary of Interior	Stewart L. Udall	1961–1963
Secretary of Agriculture	Orville L. Freeman	1961–1963
Secretary of Commerce	Luther H. Hodges	1961–1963
Secretary of Labor	Arthur J. Goldberg	1961–1962
	W. Willard Wirtz	1962–1963
Secretary of Defense	Robert S. McNamara	1961–1963
Secretary of Health, Education, and Welfare	Abraham A. Ribicoff	1961–1962
	Anthony J. Celebrezze	1962–1963

The Lyndon Johnson Administration (1963–1969)

Vice President	Hubert H. Humphrey	1965–1969
Secretary of State	Dean Rusk	1963–1969
Secretary of Treasury	C. Douglas Dillon	1963–1965
	Henry H. Fowler	1965–1969
Attorney General	Robert F. Kennedy	1963–1964
	Nicholas Katzenbach	1965–1966
	Ramsey Clark	1967–1969
Postmaster General	John A. Gronouski	1963–1965
	Lawrence F. O'Brien	1965–1968
	Marvin Watson	1968–1969
Secretary of Interior	Stewart L. Udall	1963–1969
Secretary of Agriculture	Orville L. Freeman	1963–1969
Secretary of Commerce	Luther H. Hodges	1963–1964
	John T. Connor	1964–1967
	Alexander B. Trowbridge	1967–1968
	Cyrus R. Smith	1968–1969
Secretary of Labor	W. Willard Wirtz	1963–1969
Secretray of Defense	Robert F. McNamara	1963–1968
	Clark Clifford	1968–1969
Secretary of Health, Education, and Welfare	Anthony J. Celebrezze	1963–1965
	John W. Gardner	1965–1968
	Wilbur J. Cohen	1968–1969
Secretary of Housing and Urban Development	Robert C. Weaver	1966–1969
	Robert C. Wood	1969
Secretary of Transportation	Alan S. Boyd	1967–1969

The Nixon Administration (1969–1974)

Vice President	Spiro T. Agnew	1969–1973
	Gerald R. Ford	1973–1974
Secretary of State	William P. Rogers	1969–1973
	Henry A. Kissinger	1973–1974
Secretary of Treasury	David M. Kennedy	1969–1970
	John B. Connally	1971–1972
	George P. Shultz	1972–1974
	William E. Simon	1974
Attorney General	John N. Mitchell	1969–1972
	Richard G. Kleindienst	1972–1973
	Elliot L. Richardson	1973
	William B. Saxbe	1973–1974
Postmaster General	Winton M. Blount	1969–1971
Secretary of Interior	Walter J. Hickel	1969–1970
	Rogers Morton	1971–1974
Secretary of Agriculture	Clifford M. Hardin	1969–1971
	Earl L. Butz	1971–1974
Secretary of Commerce	Maurice H. Stans	1969–1972
	Peter G. Peterson	1972–1973
	Frederick B. Dent	1973–1974
Secretary of Labor	George P. Shultz	1969–1970
	James D. Hodgson	1970–1973
	Peter J. Brennan	1973–1974
Secretary of Defense	Melvin R. Laird	1969–1973
	Elliot L. Richardson	1973
	James R. Schlesinger	1973–1974
Secretary of Health, Education, and Welfare	Robert H. Finch	1969–1970
	Elliot L. Richardson	1970–1973
	Caspar W. Weinberger	1973–1974

Office	Name	Years
Secretary of Housing and Urban Development	George Romney James T. Lynn	1969–1973 1973–1974
Secretary of Transportation	John A. Volpe Claude S. Brinegar	1969–1973 1973–1974

The Ford Administration (1974–1977)

Office	Name	Years
Vice President	Nelson A. Rockefeller	1974–1977
Secretary of State	Henry A. Kissinger	1974–1977
Secretary of Treasury	William E. Simon	1974–1977
Attorney General	William Saxbe Edward Levi	1974–1975 1975–1977
Secretary of Interior	Rogers Morton Stanley K. Hathaway Thomas Kleppe	1974–1975 1975 1975–1977
Secretary of Agriculture	Earl L. Butz John A. Knebel	1974–1976 1976–1977
Secretary of Commerce	Frederick B. Dent Rogers Morton Elliot L. Richardson	1974–1975 1975–1976 1976–1977
Secretary of Labor	Peter J. Brennan John T. Dunlop W. J. Usery	1974–1975 1975–1976 1976–1977
Secretary of Defense	James R. Schlesinger Donald Rumsfeld	1974–1975 1975–1977
Secretary of Health, Education, and Welfare	Caspar Weinberger Forrest D. Mathews	1974–1975 1975–1977
Secretary of Housing and Urban Development	James T. Lynn Carla A. Hills	1974–1975 1975–1977
Secretary of Transportation	Claude Brinegar William T. Coleman	1974–1975 1975–1977

The Carter Administration (1977–1981)

Office	Name	Years
Vice President	Walter F. Mondale	1977–1981
Secretary of State	Cyrus R. Vance Edmund Muskie	1977–1980 1980–1981
Secretary of Treasury	W. Michael Blumenthal G. William Miller	1977–1979 1979–1981
Attorney General	Griffin Bell Benjamin R. Civiletti	1977–1979 1979–1981
Secretary of Interior	Cecil D. Andrus	1977–1981
Secretary of Agriculture	Robert Bergland	1977–1981
Secretary of Commerce	Juanita M. Kreps Philip M. Klutznick	1977–1979 1979–1981
Secretary of Labor	F. Ray Marshall	1977–1981
Secretary of Defense	Harold Brown	1977–1981
Secretary of Health, Education, and Welfare	Joseph A. Califano Patricia R. Harris	1977–1979 1979
Secretary of Health and Human Services	Patricia R. Harris	1979–1981
Secretary of Education	Shirley M. Hufstedler	1979–1981
Secretary of Housing and Urban Development	Patricia R. Harris Moon Landrieu	1977–1979 1979–1981
Secretary of Transportation	Brock Adams Neil E. Goldschmidt	1977–1979 1979–1981
Secretary of Energy	James R. Schlesinger Charles W. Duncan	1977–1979 1979–1981

The Reagan Administration (1981–   )

Office	Name	Years
Vice President	George Bush	1981–
Secretary of State	Alexander M. Haig George P. Shultz	1981–1982 1982–
Secretary of Treasury	Donald Regan James A. Baker, III	1981–1985 1985–
Attorney General	William F. Smith Edwin A. Meese, III	1981–1985 1985–
Secretary of Interior	James Watt William P. Clark, Jr. Donald P. Hodel	1981–1983 1983–1985 1985–
Secretary of Agriculture	John Block Richard E. Lyng	1981–1986 1986–
Secretary of Commerce	Malcolm Baldrige	1981–
Secretary of Labor	Raymond Donovan William E. Brock	1981–1985 1985–
Secretary of Defense	Caspar Weinberger	1981–
Secretary of Health and Human Services	Richard Schweiker Margaret Heckler Otis R. Bowen	1981–1983 1983–1985 1985–
Secretary of Education	Terrel H. Bell William J. Bennett	1981–1985 1985–
Secretary of Housing and Urban Development	Samuel Pierce	1981–
Secretary of Transportation	Drew Lewis Elizabeth Dole	1981–1983 1983–
Secretary of Energy	James Edwards Donald P. Hodel John S. Herrington	1981–1982 1982–1985 1985–

Population of the United States, 1790–1985

Year	Population	Percent Increase	Population Per Square Mile	Percent Urban/ Rural	Percent White/ Nonwhite	Median Age
1790	3,929,214		4.5	5.1/94.9	80.7/19.3	NA
1800	5,308,483	35.1	6.1	6.1/93.9	81.1/18.9	NA
1810	7,239,881	36.4	4.3	7.3/92.7	81.0/19.0	NA
1820	9,638,453	33.1	5.5	7.2/92.8	81.6/18.4	16.7
1830	12,866,020	33.5	7.4	8.8/91.2	81.9/18.1	17.2
1840	17,069,453	32.7	9.8	10.8/89.2	83.2/16.8	17.8
1850	23,191,876	35.9	7.9	15.3/84.7	84.3/15.7	18.9
1860	31,443,321	35.6	10.6	19.8/80.2	85.6/14.4	19.4
1870	39,818,449	26.6	13.4	25.7/74.3	86.2/13.8	20.2
1880	50,155,783	26.0	16.9	28.2/71.8	86.5/13.5	20.9
1890	62,947,714	25.5	21.2	35.1/64.9	87.5/12.5	22.0
1900	75,994,575	20.7	25.6	39.6/60.4	87.9/12.1	22.9
1910	91,972,266	21.0	31.0	45.6/54.4	88.9/11.1	24.1
1920	105,710,620	14.9	35.6	51.2/48.8	89.7/10.3	25.3
1930	122,775,046	16.1	41.2	56.1/43.9	89.8/10.2	26.4
1940	131,669,275	7.2	44.2	56.5/43.5	89.8/10.2	29.0
1950	150,697,361	14.5	50.7	64.0/36.0	89.5/10.5	30.2
1960	179,323,175	18.5	50.6	69.9/30.1	88.6/11.4	29.5
1970	203,302,031	13.4	57.4	73.5/26.5	87.6/12.4	28.0
1980	226,545,805	11.4	64.0	73.7/26.3	86.0/14.0	30.0
1985	237,839,000	5.0	64.0	NA/NA	85.0/15.0	31.3

NA = Not available.

Employment, 1870–1985

Year	Number of Workers (in Millions)	Male/Female Employment Ratio	Percentage of Workers in Unions
1870	12.5	85/15	—
1880	17.4	85/15	—
1890	23.3	83/17	—
1900	29.1	82/18	3
1910	38.2	79/21	6
1920	41.6	79/21	12
1930	48.8	78/22	7
1940	53.0	76/24	27
1950	59.6	72/28	25
1960	69.9	68/32	26
1970	82.1	63/37	25
1980	108.5	58/42	23
1985	108.9	57/43	19

Production, Trade, and Federal Spending / Debt, 1790–1985

Year	Gross National Product (GNP) (in billions $)	Balance of Trade (in millions $)	Federal Budget (in billions $)	Federal Surplus/Deficit (in billions $)	Federal Debt (in billions $)
1790	—	−3	.004	+0.00015	.076
1800	—	−20	.011	+0.0006	.083
1810	—	−18	.008	+0.0012	.053
1820	—	−4	.018	−0.0004	.091
1830	—	+3	.015	+0.100	.049
1840	—	+25	.024	−0.005	.004
1850	—	−26	.040	+0.004	.064
1860	—	−38	.063	−0.01	.065
1870	7.4	−11	.310	+0.10	2.4
1880	11.2	+92	.268	+0.07	2.1
1890	13.1	+87	.318	+0.09	1.2
1900	18.7	+569	.521	+0.05	1.2
1910	35.3	+273	.694	−0.02	1.1
1920	91.5	+2,880	6.357	+0.3	24.3
1930	90.7	+513	3.320	+0.7	16.3
1940	100.0	−3,403	9.6	−2.7	43.0
1950	286.5	+1,691	43.1	−2.2	257.4
1960	506.5	+4,556	92.2	+0.3	286.3
1970	992.7	+2,511	196.6	+2.8	371.0
1980	2,631.7	+24,088	579.6	−59.5	914.3
1985	4,087.7	−148,480	946.3	−212.3	1,827.5

Index

Note: Some page numbers are in *italics* and are preceded by letters. They refer to (*i*) illustrations, (*m*) maps, and (*c*) charts.

About the Authors

Richard N. Current is University Distinguished Professor of History Emeritus at the University of North Carolina at Greensboro. He is coauthor of the Bancroft Prize-winning *Lincoln the President*. His books include: *Three Carpetbag Governors; The Lincoln Nobody Knows; Daniel Webster and the Rise of National Conservatism;* and *Secretary Stimson*. Professor Current has lectured on United States history in Europe, Asia, South America, Australia, and Antarctica. He has been a Fulbright Lecturer at the University of Munich and the University of Chile at Santiago and has served as Harmsworth Professor of American History at Oxford. He is past president of the Southern Historical Association.

T. Harry Williams was Boyd Professor of History at Louisiana State University. He was awarded both the 1969 Pulitzer Prize and National Book Award for his biography of *Huey Long*. His books include: *Lincoln and His Generals; Lincoln and the Radicals; P. G. T. Beauregard; Americans at War; Romance and Realism in Southern Politics; Hayes of the Twenty-Third; McClellan, Sherman, and Grant; The Union Sundered;* and *The Union Restored*. Professor Williams was a Harmsworth Professor of American History at Oxford and President of both the Southern Historical Association and the Organization of American Historians.

Frank Freidel is Charles Warren Professor Emeritus of History at Harvard University and most recently was Bullitt Professor of American History at the University of Washington. He is writing an eight-volume biography of Franklin D. Roosevelt, four volumes of which have been published. Among his other books are: *Our Country's Presidents; F.D.R. and the South;* and *America in the Twentieth Century*. He is co-editor of the 1974 edition of the *Harvard Guide to American History* and past president of the Organization of American Historians. He is also a former president of the New England Historical Society.

Alan Brinkley is Dunwalke Associate Professor of American History at Harvard University. He has also taught at the Massachusetts Institute of Technology. He is a graduate of Princeton University, received his Ph.D. from Harvard, and has been awarded fellowships by the John Simon Guggenheim Foundation, the Woodrow Wilson Center for International Scholars, the American Council of Learned Societies, and the National Endowment for the Humanities. He is the author of *Voices of Protest: Huey Long, Father Coughlin, and the Great Depression*, for which he won the American Book Award in 1983. He is coauthor of *America in the Twentieth Century* and has published many articles, essays, and reviews.

A Note on the Type

The text of this book was set in a digitized version of Bembo, a well-known Monotype face. Named for Pietro Bembo, the celebrated Renaissance writer and humanist scholar who was made a cardinal and served as secretary to Pope Leo X, the original cutting of Bembo was made by Francesco Griffo of Bologna only a few years after Columbus discovered America.

Sturdy, well-balanced, and finely proportioned, Bembo is a face of rare beauty, extremely legible in all of its sizes.

BOOKS OF RELATED INTEREST

ALFRED A. KNOPF, INC.
201 East 50th Street
New York, New York   10022

394–34302–6